BACKCOUNTRY TRIPS IN CALIFORNIA'S SIERRA NEVADA

SIERRA NORTH

10TH Edition

BACKCOUNTRY TRIPS IN CALIFORNIA'S SIERRA NEVADA

SIERRA NORTH

10TH Edition

ELIZABETH WENK
and MIKE WHITE

 WILDERNESS PRESS . . . on the trail since 1967

Sierra North: Backcountry Trips in California's Sierra Nevada

1st edition, 1967; 2nd edition, 1971; 3rd edition, 1976; 4th edition, 1982; 5th edition, 1985; 6th edition, 1991; 7th edition, 1997; 8th edition, 2002; 9th edition, 2005; 10th edition, 2021
  2nd printing 2022

Cover design: Scott McGrew
Text design: Andreas Schüller, with updates by Annie Long
Cartography: Scott McGrew, Elizabeth Wenk, and Mike White
Cover photo: © aaronj9/Shutterstock
Frontispiece: A towering Jeffrey pine near Camp Lake in the Emigrant Wilderness *(Hike 20, page 103)*;
  © Elizabeth Wenk
Project editor: Holly Cross
Copy editor: Kerry Smith
Proofreader: Emily Beaumont
Indexer: Potomac Indexing LLC

Library of Congress Cataloging-in-Publication Data

Names: Wenk, Elizabeth, author. | White, Michael C., 1952– author.
Title: Sierra North : backcountry trips in California's Sierra Nevada /
  Elizabeth Wenk, Mike White.
Description: 10th edition. | Birmingham, AL : Wilderness Press, 2021. | Revised edition of:
  Sierra North : backcountry trips in California's Sierra Nevada / Kathy Morey [and others].
  9th edition. 2005
Identifiers: LCCN 2020040269 (print) | LCCN 2020040270 (ebook) |
  ISBN 9780899978864 (paperback) | ISBN 9780899978871 (ebook)
Subjects: LCSH: Hiking—Sierra Nevada (Calif. and Nev.)—Guidebooks. | Backpacking—Sierra
  Nevada (Calif. and Nev.)—Guidebooks. | Sierra Nevada (Calif. and Nev.)—Guidebooks.
Classification: LCC GV199.42.S55 S54 2020 (print) | LCC GV199.42.S55 (ebook) |
  DDC 796.5109794/4—dc23
LC record available at https://lccn.loc.gov/2020040269
LC ebook record available at https://lccn.loc.gov/2020040270

Published by: **WILDERNESS PRESS**
  An imprint of AdventureKEEN
  2204 First Ave. S., Ste. 102
  Birmingham, AL 35233
  800-678-7006, fax 877-374-9016

Manufactured in the United States of America
Distributed by Publishers Group West

Visit wildernesspress.com for a complete listing of our books and for ordering information. Contact us at our website, at facebook.com/wildernesspress1967, or at twitter.com/wilderness1967 with questions or comments. To find out more about who we are and what we're doing, visit blog.wildernesspress.com.

Safety Notice Although Wilderness Press and the authors have made every attempt to ensure that the information in this book is accurate at press time, they are not responsible for any loss, damage, injury, or inconvenience that may occur to anyone while using this book. You are responsible for your own safety and health while in the wilderness. The fact that a trail is described in this book does not mean that it will be safe for you. Be aware that trail conditions can change from day to day. Always check local conditions and know your own limitations.

WE DEDICATE THIS BOOK TO ROSLYN BULLAS (1961–2020),

former managing editor and associate publisher at Wilderness Press. We will forever remember the opportunities she gave us to share our explorations of the Sierra Nevada through guidebooks, and we know she enjoyed exploring wild places as much as we do.

—*The Authors*

Acknowledgments

I have thoroughly enjoyed the opportunity to be a part of the 10th edition of the original hiking guide by Wilderness Press. Hiking 59 trips for this book required a bit of a time commitment, and I always appreciate my family's enthusiasm for book-driven Sierra adventures, as well as my husband's willingness to be a single parent for a month each summer while I continue exploring the mountains on my own.

Thank you as well to the many friends who have joined me on trips, especially the Rengers, who are my companions each summer. A number of friends have read segments of this book, confirming that my writing matches their memory of trips: thank you, Inga Aksamit, John Ladd, Ethan Gallogy, and Peter Hirst.

As my coauthor, Mike White, will attest, updating this book did not go quite as smoothly as either of us had planned, with record snowpacks in 2017 and 2019 and fires in the region in 2017 and 2018 repeatedly interrupting hiking schedules; I felt unusually relieved when I finished mapping the trails.

I hope that you have the chance to experience many of the trips described—and that you consider the landscape as beguiling as I do.

—*Elizabeth Wenk*

I am always indebted to the ongoing support of my wife, Robin, for the opportunity to be in the wilderness and to write about its wonders. Companionship on the trail is usually desirable, and many have walked along with me on this project, including Dal and Candy Hunter, Keith Catlin, and Joe and Chris Tavares. The folks at Wilderness Press certainly deserve kudos for guiding this project to completion, especially with the delays caused by forest fires and a pandemic. Thank you to Tim Hauserman for revising the Wolf Creek Meadows trip. Thanks also to my coauthor, Lizzy Wenk, for all of her support and help in making this new edition a reality.

—*Mike White*

Finally, we jointly wish to acknowledge the Indigenous tribes who have been the custodians of the northern Sierra's lands for millennia and who continue to maintain a close cultural connection to these lands and waters.

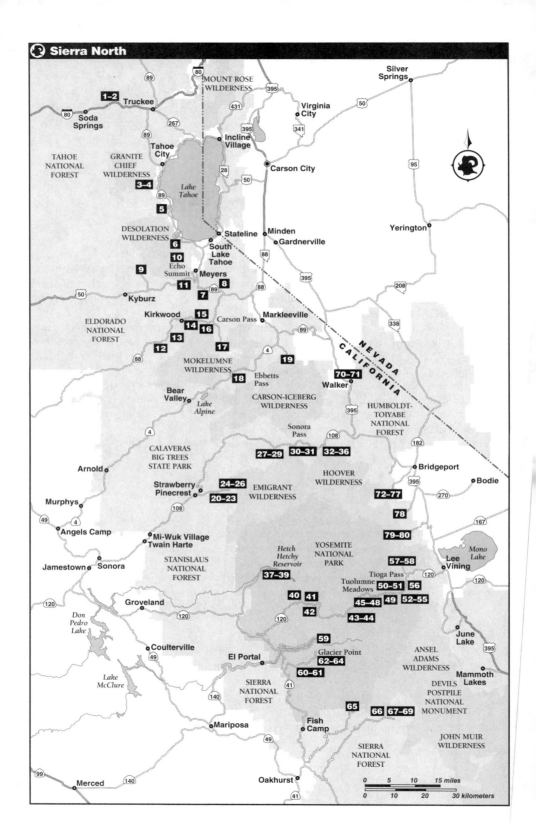

Contents

View toward Summit Lake as you descend from Virginia Lake's Burro Pass (Hike 79, page 376)
Photo by Elizabeth Wenk

Going High to Get High

Note for the 10th Edition

Sierra North was Wilderness Press's first book, providing California's outdoors enthusiasts with an in-depth guide to the northern Sierra's best trails. Over many subsequent editions, it has remained a prized tome on many backpackers' shelves, showcasing a sublime collection of on- and off-trail hikes between Tahoe and Yosemite. Sadly, I never had the privilege of meeting Tom Winnett, but I am delighted to have collaborated with Mike White on the latest update, reworking the selection of hikes included and updating the information to match the expectations and use patterns of today's hikers.

—E. W.

SIERRA NORTH

100 Back-country trips in California's Sierra

by Karl Schwenke and Thomas Winnett

Wilderness Press Trail Guide Series $2.95

By Thomas Winnett (1922–2011), Wilderness Press Founder

It was the summer of 1967, and to promote the first edition of *Sierra North*—a one-of-a-kind book that my friend Karl Schwenke and I had written to recommend 100 of the best backpacking trips into the northern Sierra—we celebrated in the backcountry with a high-altitude cocktail party. We invited everyone we thought would help get the word out about the book: people from the Sierra Club, outdoor writers, and friends.

We held the celebration in August, in Dusy Basin, in the eastern Sierra, 8 miles from the nearest car. The hike went over a 12,000-foot pass, so we were delighted when 15 people showed up. It was a real party. We used snow to make our martinis, ate hors d'oeuvres, and spent the night. In a mention of the event, *San Francisco Chronicle* columnist Herb Caen wondered, "How high can you get to get high?"

It was a spectacular occasion, not only because we were launching the book but also because we were starting a new company, Wilderness Press. Karl and I had been complaining about how hard it was to get accurate information about the out-of-doors. At the time, there were only one or two guidebooks to the Sierra—our favorite place—so we decided to write our own. We planned to create prepackaged trips that specified which trails to take and where to stop each night. We would do a series of small books, each covering a 15-minute quadrangle, and they would be called the Knapsacker/Packer Guide Series.

In the summer of 1966, we started doing the field research. Our approach was simple: we wanted to accurately describe where the trails led and what was there. On my scouting trips, I carried more than your average backpacker. In addition to all the standard gear, I packed two cameras, two natural history books to help me identify flowers and birds, and my Telmar tape recorder. The tape recorder ran about half the speed of the recording devices that are available today, and I'd walk along, dictating into the microphone everything I thought our customers would be interested in reading. So in addition to the basics—how to get to where you start walking, where to go, the best campsites—we also described what we saw: the animals, flowers, birds, and trees.

By the end of the summer, we had enough material to cover most of the trails in the northern Sierra, so we published a book of 100 trails and called it *Sierra North*. We decided orange would be the official color of Wilderness Press, so we used an orange cover with some illustrations of bighorn sheep and mountains sketched by my wife, Lu.

That first edition sold like the proverbial hotcakes; we sold out our entire print run of 3,000 books. Since then, this book has sold more than 150,000 copies.

As I think back to that high-altitude cocktail party in 1967, I wonder how many people have used this book to "go high to get high" in the Sierra. I have personally walked more than 2,000 miles in this most beautiful of mountain ranges, and although I can't do that anymore, I am still hooked on the experience—the splendid isolation, the scenery that really lights up your eyeballs, the strength you feel climbing with the weight of your pack on your back, the myriad trout. I hope this guidebook hooks you too.

A surreal boulder atop Rock Island Pass with Kettle Peak in the background (Hike 75, page 361)
Photo by Elizabeth Wenk

TRIP CROSS-REFERENCE TABLE

TRIP NO.	PAGE NO.	TRIP TYPE				BEST SEASON			HIKING DAYS	MILEAGE	GOOD FOR BEGINNERS
		OUT & BACK	LOOP	SEMILOOP	SHUTTLE	EARLY	MID	LATE			
1	23	•					•	•	2	17.8	
2	25		•				•	•	3	20	
3	31	•					•	•	2	13.5	
4	33		•		•		•	•	3	25/26.5	
5	37				•		•	•	4	30.2/27.5	
6	45			•			•	•	2	11.8	
7	49				•		•	•	2	10.9	
8	52	•					•	•	2	12.8	
9	57		•				•	•	2	8.0	
10	61	•					•	•	2	8.0	
11	63				•		•	•	2	13.4	
12	69	•					•		2	18.0	
13	73	•					•		2	13.0	•
14	77		•				•		2	5.2	•
15	81	•					•		2	10.2	•
16	83			•			•	•	2	14.0	
17	88	•					•	•	2	12.0	
18	92			•			•		3	10.0	
19	95				•		•	•	3	24.0/26.0	
20	103		•				•	•	4	14.9	
21	106	•				•	•	•	4	23.2	•
22	108			•			•	•	5	29.3	
23	112			•			•	•	6	43.1	
24	119	•					•	•	2	12.4	•
25	121	•					•	•	4	25.2	
26	123				•		•	•	4	27.2	
27	129	•				•	•	•	2	13.6	•
28	132			•			•	•	5	30.0	
29	136			•			•	•	5	37.7	
30	141				•		•	•	4	31.0	
31	148				•		•	•	8	73.9	
32	159			•		•	•		2	17.8	
33	163			•			•	•	4	30.0	
34	167			•			•	•	5	36.4	
35	172			•			•	•	5	35.1	
36	177				•		•	•	4	31.1	
37	185	•				•	•		2	13.0	•
38	187		•			•	•		4	27.7	
39	190		•				•		7	56.3	
40	197				•		•	•	4	30.1	
41	204				•		•	•	3	20.5	
42	209				•	•	•	•	2	12.1	•
43	215	•					•	•	2	10.4	•
44	216				•		•	•	2	16.3	
45	223	•					•	•	2	7.6	•

TRIP CROSS-REFERENCE TABLE

TRIP NO.	PAGE NO.	TRIP TYPE				BEST SEASON			HIKING DAYS	MILEAGE	GOOD FOR BEGINNERS
		OUT & BACK	LOOP	SEMILOOP	SHUTTLE	EARLY	MID	LATE			
46	225				•		•	•	5	31.4	
47	230				•		•	•	4	23.0	
48	233				•		•	•	3	20.8	
49	236	•					•	•	2	11.0	
50	240			•			•	•	2	14.1	•
51	245				•		•	•	3	16.8	
52	252	•					•	•	2	20.2	
53	254			•			•	•	3	19.3	•
54	258			•			•	•	4	27.5	
55	262			•			•	•	6	47.8	
56	268				•		•	•	3	20.1	
57	275			•			•	•	2	8.6	•
58	278				•		•	•	3	21.7	
59	285	•				•	•	•	4	26.8	
60	289			•		•	•		4	29.2	
61	294				•	•	•		4	29.8	
62	299				•	•	•	•	2	13.9	
63	305		•				•	•	6	50.1	
64	311				•		•	•	5	41.0	
65	319	•					•	•	2	11.2	•
66	322		•				•	•	3	12.2	•
67	327			•			•	•	3	17.1	
68	332		•				•	•	4	31.6	
69	337		•				•	•	3	23.5	
70	345			•			•	•	2	14.0	
71	349	•					•		2	14.0	
72	354	•					•	•	2	16.2	•
73	356				•		•	•	3	22.7	
74	358	•					•	•	4	27.0	
75	361			•			•	•	3	22.6	
76	363	•					•	•	5	39.2	
77	366			•			•	•	6	51.0	
78	372	•					•	•	2	8.8	•
79	376				•		•	•	2	11.8	
80	379				•		•	•	3	21.0	

Introduction

Welcome to what we think is just about the most spectacular mountain range in the contiguous 48 states. The Sierra Nevada is a hiker's paradise filled with huge wilderness areas; thousands of miles of trails; countless lakes, rugged peaks, and canyons; vast forests; giant sequoias; and terrain ranging from deep, forested river valleys to sublime, rugged alpine country.

Updates for the 10th Edition

Welcome, too, to the 10th edition of the inaugural book of Wilderness Press, *Sierra North*. As always, the authors involved in the update have rotated, and the updates this time have been led by Elizabeth Wenk and Mike White, with assistance from Tim Hauserman.

In the 15 years since the ninth edition was published, GPS units have become commonplace additions to hikers' gear lists, and the waypoints and trail distances included in this book have (nearly) all been verified by electronic devices. While most of the trips remain the same, there were regions where the hikes included had been unchanged for 52 years but trail networks and use patterns have greatly evolved. Hence, some hike routes have been altered, while a few have been removed and replaced with new hikes. We've strived to include the vast majority of the northern Sierra's trails, as we expect readers want to explore widely. In addition, all-new elevation profiles clearly show junctions and waypoints described in the text.

For this edition, coordinates for waypoints are given as latitude and longitude in decimal degrees, a relatively simple format to enter into digital devices. If you'd like to upload the waypoints embedded in the text directly to a GPS device, visit tinyurl.com/sierranorthgps to download a file that you can view online or on your device. *Note:* This file does not contain all trail junctions—just trailheads, notable campsites, and the occasional cryptic junction where having a coordinate is particularly useful.

The maps provided in the book are nearly identical to those in previous editions; that is, they are simple sketch maps of the hikes, including prominent nearby place-names. The only notable change is that, where relevant, we reference nearby or overlapping trips, by number, to make it easier for users to merge segments of different described hikes into a unique route of their choosing. Similarly, in the text, at junctions we reference how different trips link together.

As in the ninth edition, *Sierra North* spans existing and proposed wilderness areas from just north of I-80 south through CA 120 and on to the southern Yosemite National Park boundary, including trailheads to the west, east, and south of Yosemite's boundaries.

Middle Fork Stanislaus River (Hike 27, page 129)   Photo by Elizabeth Wenk

A handful of hikes accessed via Beasore Road and Sky Ranch Road out of Oakhurst have bounced between this book and its companion title, *Sierra South*. For this edition, the Quartz Mountain, Fernandez, Walton, and Isberg Trailheads (Ansel Adams Wilderness) are back in *Sierra North*. (*Sierra South* then covers the Sierra from a little south of Yosemite to the Kern Plateau, including the rest of Ansel Adams Wilderness, John Muir Wilderness, Kings Canyon National Park, Sequoia National Park, and the Golden Trout Wilderness.)

Measuring distances in the backcountry used to be more art than science, but modern GPS units make it possible to accurately determine trail distances. Your authors each have their own methods to measure trail distance, but Lizzy Wenk measures all tracks she walks with a pair of GPS units, verifies the tracks in Google Earth, and generally trusts the resultant distances to within 2%. With a few exceptions, trail distances are still rounded to the closest 0.1 mile.

It's our hope that this new edition will help you enjoy our magnificent northern Sierra as well as give you an incentive to work to preserve it.

We appreciate hearing from our readers. Many of the changes and updates for this edition are a direct result of readers' requests and comments. Please let us know what did and didn't work for you in this new edition, and about any errors you find. You can email us at info@wildernesspress.com or leave comments at our website: go to wildernesspress.com and click "Contact Us" at the top of the page.

Care and Enjoyment of the Mountains

Be a Good Guest: Wilderness and Leave No Trace

The Sierra is home—the only home—to a spectacular array of plants and animals. We humans are merely guests—uninvited ones at that. Be a careful, considerate guest in this grandest of nature's homes. Indeed, the vast majority of hikes included in this guide lie within one of the Sierra's many wilderness areas, lands designated by the 1964 Wilderness Act to remain *untrammeled,* defined in the *Oxford English Dictionary* as "not deprived of freedom of action or expression; not restricted or hampered." Moreover, *wilderness* is defined as areas where humans and their works do not dominate the landscape and indeed where humans are visitors who do not remain.

About 200,000 people camp in the northern Sierra's wilderness areas each year. The vast majority care about the wilderness and try to protect it, but it is threatened by those who still need to learn the art of living lightly on the land. The solution depends on each of us. We can minimize our impact. The saying "Take only memories (or photos), leave only footprints" sums it up. Hikers or equestrians entering the Sierra's many wilderness areas must accept that, in order to preserve the wilderness in its natural form, perhaps they cannot enter the trailhead they want because the quota is filled or they might be slightly inconvenienced by packing out toilet paper or not lighting a campfire.

Following the seven Leave No Trace principles is an easy way to ensure you are minimizing your impact when camping in (and out of) wilderness areas. Indeed, if you look carefully at the regulations on your backpacking permit, you will realize that the specific requirements—from human-waste management to campfire regulations to campsite selection and food storage—are all necessary if visitors are going to "leave no trace," as embodied by these principles:

- Plan ahead and prepare.
- Travel and camp on durable surfaces.
- Dispose of waste properly.

- Leave what you find.
- Minimize campfire impacts.
- Respect wildlife.
- Be considerate of other visitors.

© *1999 by the Leave No Trace Center for Outdoor Ethics: lnt.org.*

The information below applies Leave No Trace principles to on-the-ground guidelines for hikers. More than anything else, learn to go light. John Muir, traveling along the crest of the Sierra in the 1870s with little more that his overcoat and his pockets full of biscuits, was the archetype. Muir's example may be too extreme for many (and he did stay warm by building campfires in locations now deemed unacceptable), but the concept that you should strive to get by with less, not more, is a powerful starting point. A lot of the stuff people take into the mountains is burdensome, harmful to the wilderness, or just plain annoying to other people seeking peace and solitude.

Carry Out Your Trash

- Pack out all trash—do not attempt to burn plastic, foil packaging, or toilet paper. The remnants of foil-lined hot-chocolate packets linger indefinitely in fire pits to the ire of rangers and backpackers alike.
- Anglers, take all your lures, bait, and monofilament out with you. Don't leave fishing line tangled over trees, shrubs, or logs or floating in the lake.
- Prepare only as much food as you think you will eat in a sitting. Discarded leftovers are likely to attract bears and other wildlife (see page 5).

Protect the Water

Keeping the Sierra's water sources pristine is as important for wilderness users as for nature itself. Humans (and stock) can damage Sierra water sources by introducing disease agents through poor sanitation practices, by adding nutrients to the Sierra's naturally low-nutrient waters, or by increasing streambank erosion. Notably, augmenting nutrient concentrations in the water leads to algal blooms that, in turn, provide habitat for waterborne parasites such as *Giardia* (see page 7).

- Wash and rinse dishes, clothes, and yourself a minimum of 100 feet away from water sources; never wash in lakes or streams. Even though a soap may be marketed as biodegradable, it still isn't OK to put it in the water. A good, lightweight solution is to carry a large zip-top bag for washing clothes and then carry the water away from the creek or lake.
- Do not put any soap in water—even biodegradable soap.
- Follow the sanitation practices described in the next section.

Practice Good Sanitation

- Bury waste 6 inches deep, a minimum of 100 feet from trails, and 200 feet from water sources. Intestinal bacteria can survive for years in feces when they're buried, but burial reduces the chances that critters will come in contact with them and carry pathogens into the water, or that these pathogens will wash into the water following snowmelt or a thunderstorm.
- Pack out toilet paper. This is now a requirement throughout the Sierra, but one that is poorly complied with by many hikers. Burying your toilet paper does not work—animals

rapidly dig it up, and tissue "flowers" are a blossoming problem in popular areas. Also pack out facial tissues, wet wipes, tampons, and sanitary pads.

Place used toilet paper and sanitary products in a heavy-duty zip-top bag. Add a little baking soda to the bag to minimize odors, and/or place the plastic bag in an opaque ditty bag to keep it out of sight.

- Consider using a bidet instead of toilet paper. A growing contingent of Sierra hikers has ditched (or mostly ditched) toilet paper in favor of portable bidets. In addition, many women now carry a "pee cloth" to greatly reduce their backcountry use of toilet paper. You can use a standard cotton bandanna or purchase a dedicated cloth.

Practice Good Campsite Selection

- Whenever possible, camp in an established campsite.
- Otherwise, pick a campsite on a durable surface, such as sand, a polished granite slab, or the forest floor.
- Camp at least 100 feet from water (in some wilderness areas you can camp closer than 100 feet *if* you are using an established site).
- Never camp in meadows, on lakeshores, or on streamsides. The fragile sod is easily compacted and, once the soil is hardened, meadow grasses are replaced by shrubs and trees.
- Don't make campsite "improvements" like rock walls or tent ditches. These are illegal.
- For your safety, don't camp beneath a dead tree or large dead branch. So-called widow-makers are a particular danger in forests hard hit by recent droughts and bark-beetle and leaf-miner infestations.
- Also take care with the vegetation beside your tent—walking back and forth to a water source can also damage riparian vegetation, and moving rocks exposes the roots of nearby plants, possibly killing them.

Avoid Campfires

- Use a modern, lightweight backpacking stove. Campfires waste a precious resource: wood that would otherwise shelter animals and, upon decaying, return vital nutrients to the soil. Campfires can also start—and have started—forest fires. As detailed on your wilderness permit, campfires are prohibited in many areas, especially at high elevations and at lower elevations during the hot midsummer months.
- Each year, campfires are prohibited in ever more popular areas—because some wilderness visitors use the available wood resources irresponsibly. If having a *small* campfire is an important part of your backcountry experience, take care to build only legal and responsible fires, so that you will have this option on future trips.
- Build a small fire.
- Only build a fire in an existing campfire ring.
- Never leave the fire unattended.
- Make sure your fire is out and cold before leaving your campsite (or retiring to your tent).
- *Always* obey campfire bans when they are in effect.
- Likewise, *do not* build a campfire in areas where they are prohibited. This increasingly includes popular subalpine lake basins where previous campers have scoured the landscape for every piece of dead wood, leaving nothing to decompose or as shelter for the animal residents.

- Make sure to pick up a California Campfire Permit at a ranger station (or online) if you don't need a wilderness permit or if your wilderness permit doesn't double as a campfire permit.

Protect Your Food from Wildlife

Remember, the wilderness is wildlife's home, not yours, and you must always respect the wildlife. Avoid trampling on nests, burrows, or other homes of animals. Observe all fishing limits. If you come across an animal, just quietly observe it. Don't go near any nesting animals and their young. Get "close" with binoculars or telephoto lenses. And most importantly, make sure only you eat your food—letting animals eat your food not only cuts short your trip, but is bad for the animals. They may become too aggressive toward humans, dependent on human food, or sick from eating processed food (and wrappers).

Bears are the animals most likely to attempt to eat your food, but marmots, ravens, and even deer will grab a snack if your food is accessible to them. While most animals can easily be thwarted by hanging your food sloppily in a tree or off a rock, bears are very clever and innovative: mothers give their cubs a piggyback to reach a low-lying bag. Mothers encourage their cubs to climb out on the branch, too flimsy to hold an adult bear's weight, but perfect for a cub. And even a perfectly hung pair of counterbalanced food bags can be foiled if a bear shakes a tree until one bag drops down.

Bear canisters—plastic, carbon fiber, or metal containers, generally in a cylindrical shape—first appeared on the market in the early 1990s and are now considered the *only* acceptable way to store your food in some of the Sierra's wilderness areas (including Hoover and Yosemite). Other wilderness areas (including Carson-Iceberg, Emigrant, Mokelumne, and Desolation) still allow hikers to hang their food using the counterbalance method but strongly recommend the use of canisters. Another alternative, prohibited in Yosemite but currently allowed in all national-forest wilderness areas described in this book, is the Ursack, a Kevlar bag in which you can store your food. Most ranger stations rent bear canisters for a modest fee, so if you don't own one, you can pick one up together with your wilderness permit.

Marmots love people food, so take precautions to make sure they don't steal yours.

Photo by Walt Lehmann

In addition, a few established camping areas have food-storage lockers—colloquially known as bear boxes. In Yosemite they are located at the five High Sierra Camps (Glen Aulin, May Lake, Sunrise, Merced Lake, and Vogelsang), in Little Yosemite Valley, and at Lake Eleanor. Food-storage lockers are also located at many Sierra trailheads to store your extra food before a trip. Everyone shares the bear box; you may not put your own locks on one. Never leave a bear box unlatched or open, even when people are around.

Overall:

- Store all food in your bear canister (or hung or in an Ursack, where legal) anytime you leave it unattended.
- All toiletries and fragrant items from your first aid kit must be stored with your food.
- After cooking, clean up food residue and leave your pots out.
- Don't leave any food in your backpack when you aren't wearing it.
- Don't store any food in your tent.
- Do not leave any food in your car at the trailhead. Many trailheads have animal-proof food storage lockers in which to store your extra supplies.
- Never use a backcountry bear box as a food drop; its capacity is needed for people actually camping in its vicinity.

Safety and Well-Being

Hiking in the high country is far safer than driving to the mountains, and a few precautions can shield you from the discomforts and dangers that do threaten you in the backcountry.

Health Hazards

ALTITUDE SICKNESS If you normally live at sea level and you come to the Sierra Nevada to hike, it will take your body several days to adjust. Headaches and a sense of nausea are the most common symptoms of acute mountain sickness (AMS), the least severe and by far most common type of altitude sickness at the northern Sierra's mostly moderate elevations. Though most cases of altitude sickness occur above 10,000 feet in elevation, 20%–25% of people experience some degree of altitude sickness already at 8,200 feet (2,500 meters). For unknown reasons, some people are much more prone to altitude sickness than others—if you hike often at higher elevations, you will know how susceptible you are and how hard you can plan to push yourself at altitude. While going slowly, staying hydrated, and regularly eating some food are important to reduce the chance you will experience nausea or headache, they aren't explicitly reducing your AMS symptoms—the only way you can actually reduce the likelihood of altitude sickness is to acclimate. Afterall, acclimation refers to the multiday physiological adjustments to altitude that your body can make only through exposure to high elevation. One of the best things you can do is to stay in a trailhead campground the night before your trip to begin the acclimization process, especially one above 6,000 feet. If you are particularly susceptible to altitude sickness, either avoid the hikes in this guide that suggest a campsite above 9,000 feet for the first night, or spend several nights car camping and day hiking before you begin your backpacking trip.

An Unofficial Acclimatization Guideline: Your High-Altitude Guideline for the John Muir Trail is a handy, inexpensive reference you can read in advance and load onto your mobile device to read on the trail. It covers the symptoms associated with different types of altitude sickness, prophylactic medications, and treatment options. Free copies of this guide are also available in the archives of the Altitude Acclimatization Facebook group: facebook.com /groups/altitudeacclimatization.

WATERBORNE ILLNESS For many decades, hikers in the Sierra Nevada have been advised to filter their water due to the risk of contamination by *Giardia lamblia,* a waterborne protozoan, and other waterborne pests that cause severe diarrhea and abdominal pain. Aside from areas with cattle grazing and very high stock use, the risk of waterborne illness is actually quite low, but most hikers treat all their drinking water as a precaution. *Giardia* populations are generally only high in water bodies where algae provide habitat for the cysts. In the Sierra, algal blooms are generally associated with cattle grazing and high stock use, but in the future poor human sanitation or camp practices (see pages 3–4) or warming water temperatures could increase algal prevalence and in turn *Giardia* risk.

Some hikers are likely asymptomatic *Giardia* carriers, and their sloppiness in burying waste or cooking for a group can contaminate water sources and infect others, so always assume you're contagious and sanitize your hands before sharing food. Note that with *Giardia,* symptoms appear two to three weeks after exposure.

There are additional disease agents that could be present in Sierran lakes and rivers. *Cryptosporidium* is another, smaller, very hardy pest that causes a disease similar to giardiasis. It's been found in the streams of the San Gabriel Mountains of Los Angeles and is spreading throughout Southern California; probably it will eventually infest Sierran waters. A recent study has found the feces of the resident yellow-bellied marmots contains strains of *Cryptosporidium* that could infect humans, although no one has collected evidence that it regularly contaminates water sources.

Viruses do not survive long in the cold, harsh conditions of the alpine environment and are unlikely to infect water in the Sierra. *E. coli* is uncommon but could be present in lower-elevation Sierra water bodies.

Hikers have myriad water-treatment options. Keep in mind that different treatments kill or remove different microbes:

This may look cool and refreshing, but it's advisable to chemically treat, filter, or boil water before drinking it.

Photo by J. Brian Anderson

- **Chemical purification** *(for example, iodine or chlorine)*: This is the easiest method of treating water—simply add drops or a tablet—but you have to wait about 20 minutes to drink your water. Some chemical purification methods leave a distinct chemical flavor, while others do not. In addition, chemical purification might not kill *Cryptosporidium,* so if this microbe becomes more common in the Sierra, this method will no longer be practical.
- **Water filters:** Water filters should remove all bacteria and protozoa, but the pores of many filters are too large to remove viruses. The advantages of filtering are removal of all microorganisms of concern (in the Sierra Nevada) and not leaving a flavor in your water. There are both pump filter and gravity filter setups. The prior requires you to actively pump your water through the filter, while with the latter, filtering is a passive process; you fill a bag with water and return 5 minutes later to find a gallon of freshly filtered water. Another variant of water filters are squeeze filters (for example, Sawyer Mini) that screw straight onto your water bottle. You effectively purify the water as you drink. They are lightweight and allow each person to easily carry his or her own filter, but some brands clog easily and have quite low flow.
- **Ultraviolet light purifier** *(such as SteriPen)*: Ultraviolet light damages the DNA of all microorganisms, rendering them harmless. Water must be clear for the ultraviolet light to function, so water with silt must settle or be filtered through a cloth or equivalent. And make sure you have spare batteries with you. (As an aside, a clear, still alpine lake, devoid of algae, is the best place from which to drink if you aren't purifying your water. The top 6 inches of an alpine lake have been irradiated by the sun to a similar extent as a UV purifier performs.)
- Boiling: This kills all microorganisms but is very time-consuming and uses considerable fuel.

HYPOTHERMIA Hypothermia refers to subnormal body temperature. Caused by exposure to cold, often intensified by wet, wind, and weariness, the first symptoms of hypothermia are uncontrollable shivering and imperfect motor coordination. These are rapidly followed by loss of judgment, so that you yourself cannot make the decisions to protect your own life. "Death by exposure" is death by hypothermia.

To prevent hypothermia, stay warm: carry wind- and rain-protective clothing, and put it on as soon as you feel chilly. Stay dry: carry or wear wool or a suitable synthetic (not cotton), and bring raingear even for a hike with an apparently sunny forecast.

Treat shivering at once: get the victim out of the wind and wet, replace all wet clothes with dry ones, put him or her in a prewarmed sleeping bag with hot water bottles, and give him or her warm drinks.

LIGHTNING Although the odds of being struck are small, almost everyone who goes to the mountains thinks about it. If a thunderstorm comes upon you, avoid exposed places—mountain peaks, passes, open fields, a boat on a lake—and avoid small caves and rock overhangs. The safest place is an area where you are less than 50 feet from, but not directly next to, a much taller object such as a tree.

If you are stuck in flattish terrain above treeline, crouch on top of a rock (but not the highest one, of course) that is somewhat elevated or otherwise detached from the rocks underneath it to protect yourself from any current flowing through the ground. Make sure to get all metal—such as frame packs, hiking poles, tent poles, and so on—away from you. The best body stance is one that minimizes the area where your body touches the ground. The National Outdoor Leadership School recommends squatting on the balls of your feet as low as possible and wrapping your arms around your legs. This position minimizes your body's surface area, so there's less chance for a ground current to flow through you, reducing the seriousness of injuries should you be struck. Close your eyes, cover your ears, hold your breath, and keep your feet together to prevent the current from flowing in one foot and out the other. Once a storm is upon you, getting in this position is more important than trying to seek more sheltered ground.

If you get struck by lightning, hope that someone in your party is adept at CPR—or at least artificial respiration if your breathing has stopped but not your heart. Eighty percent of lightning victims are not killed, but it can take hours for a victim to resume breathing on his or her own. As soon as possible, a victim should be evacuated to a hospital; other problems often develop in lightning victims.

SUNBURN Sunburns can be particularly bad at high elevations, where the ultraviolet radiation is greater. You can even get burned on cloudy days because the radiation penetrates clouds. Therefore, always wear a wide-brimmed hat and apply strong sunscreen to all exposed skin. The best sun protection is, of course, long sleeves and long pants—even if you've been resistant to long clothing in the past, try some of the new fabrics on the market. Some of them are—finally—true to their advertisement of keeping you pleasantly cool on a hot day.

Wildlife Hazards

RATTLESNAKES Rattlesnakes mainly occur below 7,000 feet but have been seen up to 9,000 feet. They live in a range of habitats but most commonly along canyon bottoms. Watch where you place your hands and feet; listen for the rattle. If you hear a snake rattle, stand still long enough to determine where it is, then leave in the opposite direction. They are frequently curled up alongside a rock or beneath a fallen log—look carefully before stepping across a fallen log or sitting atop a log or rock for a break.

Rattlesnake bites are rarely fatal to an adult, but a bite that carries venom may still cause extensive tissue damage. If you are bitten, get to a hospital as soon as possible. There is no substitute for proper medical treatment.

MOSQUITOES Mosquitoes in the Sierra fall more in the nuisance category than the danger category, but as they may (at lower elevations) carry diseases, it is best to avoid being bitten. That is easier said than done, for mosquitoes are common near stagnant water sources (including many Sierra lakes and slow-flowing rivers) and in moist forest terrain until mid-July. In some years they are only pesky near dusk and other years are an all-day nuisance. Camping in windier, drier, higher-elevation locations is one good way to avoid them—but such campsites don't appeal to everyone.

The best way to avoid being bitten by mosquitoes is to cover your skin by wearing long sleeves, long pants, and a wide-brim hat, possibly topped by a head net. There are a number of topical solutions hikers carry to thwart mosquitoes on exposed skin. N,N-diethyl-meta-toluamide, known commercially as DEET, is the most common, and products with at least 20% DEET do a very good job of keeping mosquitoes off of you, but also can etch plastics and must be kept far from your mouth, eyes, and so on. You must also never wash yourself in streams or lakes with DEET on your skin—it is toxic to many animals, including frogs. Other products, such as picaridin and lemon eucalyptus, do as well as DEET in trials (commercial trials and your authors') but must be reapplied more frequently. An alternative (or additional) approach is to, before your hike, spray or soak your clothes in permethrin. Permethrin can be purchased in ready-to-spray formulations or as a concentrate. There are also companies that commercially apply permethrin—and a growing contingent of outdoor clothing retailers that sell pretreated clothing.

Of course, the best method of mosquito prevention is to plan your trips from late July to September.

BLACK BEARS The bears of the Sierra are American black bears; their coats range from black to light brown. American black bears are fast, immensely strong, and very intelligent. They're not usually aggressive, however, unless they're provoked, and their normal diet consists largely of plants. In California's mountains they pose no danger to you, just to your food; some of the black bears in Canada and Alaska are more aggressive. Long ago black bears learned to associate humans with easy sources of food, leading to incessant human–bear conflicts, especially broken-into cars and stolen food. Over past decades steady progress has been made in outsmarting the bears—or, more specifically, educating humans about the need to store food in bear canisters and not leave food in unattended cars (see pages 5–6). Sadly, a food-habituated bear is usually soon a dead bear.

Don't let the possibility of meeting a bear keep you out of the Sierra. Respect these magnificent creatures. Just remember, if a bear does get your food, it now belongs to the bear, not you; don't attempt to get it back, but do realize it is your responsibility to pick up the wrappers that get scattered around.

Terrain Hazards

SNOW BRIDGES AND CORNICES Stay off of these.

STREAMS Stream flows can be dangerous during peak snowmelt or following a severe thunderstorm. When stream flows are high, drowning is the greatest danger facing a backpacker. Peak snowmelt usually occurs in June, but it can extend into July in high snow years. Stream flows can also rise (and drop) rapidly following a summer thunderstorm. If a river is running high, you should not cross it solo, and you should spend considerable effort looking for an alternative (for example, a log or a broader, shallower, less turbulent ford) before starting across. And if a stream is dauntingly high or swift, forget it; the best option is to retreat or wait until the water level subsides. Snowmelt flows are much higher in the evening than the following morning, and thunderstorm flows usually subside within 12 hours.

Here are some suggestions for stream crossing:

- Wear closed-toe shoes, which will protect your feet from injury and give them more secure placement. If you don't have good water shoes—not flip-flops—wear your hiking boots or shoes.
- Cross in a stance in which you're angled upstream. If you face downstream, the water pushing against the back of your knees could cause them to buckle. Or, following the other school of thought, face slightly downstream, where you're not battling against the current.
- Move one foot only when the other is firmly placed.
- Keep your legs apart for a more stable stance. You'll find a cross-footed stance unstable even in your own living room, much less in a Sierra torrent.
- One or two hiking sticks will help keep you stable while crossing. You can also use a stick to probe ahead for holes and other obstacles that may be difficult to see and judge under running water.
- One piece of advice used to be that you should unfasten your pack's hip belt in case you fell in and had to jettison the pack. However, modern quick-release buckles probably make this precaution unnecessary. Keeping the hip belt fastened will keep the pack more stable, and this will in turn help *your* stability. You may wish, however, to unfasten the sternum strap so that you have only one buckle to worry about.

Maps and Profiles

Today's Sierra traveler is confronted by a bewildering array of maps, and it doesn't take much experience to learn that no single map fulfills all needs. Three main categories of maps are described below: government-issued topographic maps, trail maps, and online maps. While the book includes grayscale maps for each hike (see page 18 for an example), these do not suffice for on-the-trail navigation; they are included only to provide an overview of the regions through which the trip wanders.

USGS Topographic Maps

Topographic maps of various scales exist for all areas covered in this guidebook. The most detailed maps are those produced by the U.S. Geological Survey (USGS), generally referred to as the 7.5-minute (abbreviated henceforth as 7.5′) topo series. These have become increasingly hard to purchase except directly from the USGS, but if you plan to explore off-trail, they are still the gold standard. The data from these maps is available to the public, and you can download the maps to print yourself directly from the USGS: visit the **National Map Viewer** at usgs.gov/core-science-systems/national-geospatial-program/national-map. The trail locations depicted on the National Map Viewer are more current than those on the print maps.

While some visitor centers still stock USGS 7.5′ (1:24,000-scale) maps for the local area, they are increasingly difficult to find in outdoor-equipment stores. For an off-trail trip when you truly need the detail only provided by USGS maps, plan ahead and order them directly through the USGS website.

Since USGS maps are public domain, they are also used as the base maps by other online services, such as the free **CalTopo.com,** where you can easily print the pieces of map required for your trip. The USGS maps required for each hike are indicated in the introductory material for that hike. If the hike traverses more than one USGS map, they are listed in the order they are encountered on the walk.

Trail Maps

While USGS topo maps provide the best detail for landscape features, they do not include trail distances, trail names, or similar annotations. The U.S. Forest Service publishes a series of "inch to the mile"–scale (1:63,360-scale) maps for many wilderness areas and national forests. These are excellent resources for driving to trailheads because they include all U.S. Forest Service road names (and numbers) and provide a good overview of the local trail network. However, they lack trail distances, often fail to acknowledge which trails haven't been maintained in a generation, and are a bit bulky for backpacking. These maps are generally available at ranger stations or can be ordered through store.usgs.gov. (In this book, Granite Chief Wilderness is the only wilderness that lacks such a map.) The content from these maps can also be purchased as georeferenced PDFs from **Avenza** (avenza.com) for use on digital devices.

In addition, a number of other cartography companies produce topo maps annotated with trail distances. These vary in accuracy, but the two brands most commonly used for Sierra trails are **Tom Harrison Maps** and **National Geographic Trails Illustrated maps,** which cover nearly every hike in this book.

Map Apps

The past decade has brought a change in how people navigate in the wilderness. A growing number of people no longer carry paper maps, instead using an app to preload topo maps onto their phones, GPS units, or other digital devices. Of these, the **Gaia GPS** app is the most widely used and allows you to upload both waypoints (that is, those provided in this book) and USGS 7.5′ topo maps. CalTopo.com offers a similar service.

The benefits of these apps are obvious:

- You're already carrying a phone, so you now have maps at no additional weight.
- You always know where you are; your location is identified by a little dot on your screen.
- These apps are an easy way to plot waypoints onto a map.

The downsides of these apps *should* also be obvious—and scare your authors into *always* carrying a paper map as well:

- Digital devices eventually run out of battery power—and map apps are notorious battery sinks.
- Digital devices can break, get wet, and so on.
- You have a very limited understanding of the broader landscape because you see only a tiny piece of the map at once.
- It is very easy to have the maps for some segment of your trip not download properly—and you won't realize it until you're on your trip.

One of your authors (Lizzy) has, over the past five years, transitioned to doing a fair bit of navigating using Gaia GPS. She finds it incredibly convenient for trying to follow a trail across snow and making sure she is aiming for the correct cross-country location. However, she also still carries USGS 7.5′ topo maps when hiking off-trail and either a trail or topo map when hiking on trail because she has (1) had her phone's battery run out faster than expected, (2) been frustrated with herself for forgetting to look at the big picture and made poor big-picture navigation decisions off-trail, and (3) realized the maps downloaded at the wrong scale and were useless for cross-country navigation.

But really, the biggest problem is that people no longer have that wonderful sense of connectedness to the entire landscape that you have if you stare at your entire trip on a giant mosaic of maps.

How to Use This Book

Terms This Book Uses

DESTINATION/COORDINATES In this edition, coordinates are provided in latitude and longitude, in decimal degrees. If you prefer UTM coordinates (which are easier to plot on a paper map), download a copy in that format from tinyurl.com/sierranorthgps or use a GPS coordinate conversion program (many are available online). All the coordinates provided by your authors have been field-checked or checked on a mapping program like Google Earth. The coordinates use the WGS 84 horizontal datum (equivalent to the NAD83 for UTM coordinates).

TRIP TYPE This book classifies a trip as one of four types. An **out-and-back** trip goes out to a destination and returns the way it came. A **loop** trip goes out by one route and returns by another with relatively little or no retracing of the same trail. A **semiloop** trip has an out-and-back part and a loop part; the loop part may occur anywhere along the way. A **shuttle** trip starts at one trailhead and ends at another; usually, the trailheads are too far apart for you to walk between them, so you will need to leave a car at the ending trailhead, have someone pick you up there, or rely on public transportation to get back to your starting trailhead. The shuttle information indicates whenever public transportation is an option.

BEST SEASON Deciding when in the year is the best time for a particular trip is a difficult task because of California's enormous year-to-year variation in snowpack and melt-off times. In one year the subalpine and alpine lands are mostly snow free by Memorial Day (late May) and another year you must wait until mid-July to cross the higher passes—and even then you will encounter considerable snow, which may require the use of an ice axe and crampons. On the other end of the season, some years receive their first winter storm in mid-September, and in others you can traverse the high country until late October. Therefore, describing hiking season by month is problematic; if you aren't sure how the current year tracks the long-term average, visit cdec.water.ca.gov/snowapp/swcchart.action to get a sense.

Hence, instead of describing hikes by month or descriptors like "early summer," this book uses the terms **early, mid,** and **late season.** In an average year, early season is mid-May–June, midseason is July and August, and late season is September–mid-October. Low-country hikes, which are almost always listed as early season, are perfect as warm-up excursions for the itchy hiker who may be stiff from a winter's inactivity.

And if a hike lists a variety of hiking seasons, in addition to snow pack consider the following to help you decide when to go:

- Mosquitoes can be bad through mid-July; mosquitoes are especially infamous in northern Yosemite and Emigrant Wilderness during these months.
- June–mid-July is the peak wildflower bloom.
- Day length starts to shorten noticeably starting in August, with days becoming quite short by September.
- Temperatures are warmest in mid- to late July.
- Thunderstorms can occur anytime but are most prevalent in July and August, corresponding with monsoon moisture coming north from the Gulf of Mexico and Gulf of California.
- Wildfires become increasingly likely as the summer progresses; these rarely pose a danger to hikers, but they can ruin the views with hazy air or make the air unhealthy to breathe.

PACE For each trip, we give a suggested number of days to spend completing the trip as well as the number of layover days (see below) you might want to take. Galen Clark, Yosemite's beloved "Old Man of the Valley," was once asked how he "got about" the park. Clark scratched his beard and then replied, "Slowly!" And that is the philosophy we have adopted in this book. Most trips are divided across enough days to be either **leisurely** or **moderate** in pace, depending on where the best overnight camping places are along the route. We also call a few trips **strenuous,** usually because the terrain requires significant elevation gain on one or more days. In today's era of lightweight backpacking gear and short vacations, hiking longer days is in vogue—your authors are also guilty of this—but, with extra time, a leisurely pace lets hikers absorb more of the sights, smells, and "feel" of the country they have come to see. If you do choose to hike two of the described days in a single day or come up with your own itinerary, make use of some of the other campsites described in the text. Pace may not be everything, but Old Man Clark lived to the ripe old age of 96, and it behooves us to follow in his footsteps.

LAYOVER DAYS Also called "zero days" by long-distance thru-hikers, these are days when you'll remain camped at a particular site. You can spend your layover day on a day hike to see other beautiful places around the area, enjoy some adventures like peak bagging, or spend a quiet day fishing or reading in camp. The number of layover days you take will most likely be dictated by how many days you have off work and how much food you can fit in your bear canister. In the text, we often provide suggestions for activities on your layover day, usually an easy peak to ascend or a spur trail that is good to explore.

TOTAL MILEAGE The trips in this book range in length between 7.6 miles and 73.9 miles, and many trips can be shortened or extended, based on your interest and time.

CAMPSITES The trips are divided to spend each night in a location with a decent camp-site and, whenever possible, one that can accommodate several groups and that is eco-logically robust enough to host campers most nights throughout the summer. Scattered throughout the daily hike descriptions are mentions of other established campsites if you wish to make your day shorter or longer. If you establish your own campsite, make sure you follow both the regulations detailed on your wilderness permit and follow good campsite-selection practices, outlined on page 4. Occasionally we reference "packer campsites"; these are generally larger, long-established sites favored by large stock groups, often with log furniture. Some are, to many backpackers, objectionably overused, dusty, and accompanied with piles of dung, but others are very pleasant stopping points and are usually in ecologically appropriate areas. Using this descriptor is not meant to be an explicit slight—it's simply a description.

FISHING Angling, for many, is a prime consideration when planning a trip. Many of the lakes in the Sierra were historically stocked and still hold healthy fish populations. Within the scope of Sierra North, all fish in Emigrant Wilderness and Yosemite National Park above the lowest westside valleys were stocked; there were no native fish populations in these lakes. Parts of Hoover Wilderness have native populations of cutthroat trout, but the majority of its lakes were also once fishless.

Today, to protect native frog populations—and to simply comply with wilderness desig-nations—fish are no longer stocked within the Sierra's wilderness areas. Most lakes that were once stocked still have self-sustaining fish populations, but fish have vanished from some lakes (usually at high elevations, without good spawning habitat), and fish have been explic-itly removed from a few other lakes to provide frog habitat (almost always off-trail). While we note the most recent information on which lakes have which fish species, accept that this is a bit of a moving target. For the eastern Sierra south of Sonora Pass, visit fs.usda.gov /activity/inyo/recreation/fishing to download a pamphlet detailing which fish are currently in each water body. And, of course, that indefinable something known as "fisherman's luck"

Photo by Walt Lehmann

Photo by Bryan Rodgers

Be careful to observe all camping and fishing regulations.

plays a big role in what you'll catch. Generally speaking, the old "early and late" adage holds: fishing is better early and late in the day, and early and late in the season.

STREAM CROSSINGS We mention man-made bridges and other means of crossing streams. We also include descriptions of currently available naturally fallen logs, as these may last for decades or—like some bridges—be washed out during high flows. Asking the rangers about stream-crossing conditions when you pick up your permit is always a good idea. (See page 10 for stream-crossing tips.)

TRAIL TYPE AND SURFACE Most of the trails described here are well maintained (the exceptions are noted) and are properly signed. If the trail becomes indistinct, look for blazes (peeled bark at eye level on trees) or cairns (two or more rocks piled one atop another; also called *ducks*). Trails may fade out in wet areas like meadows, and you may have to scout around to find where they resume. Continuing in the direction you were going when the trail faded out is often, but not always, a good bet.

Two other significant trail conditions are also described in the text: the degree of openness (type and degree of forest cover, if any, or else *meadow, brush,* or whatever) and underfooting (talus, scree, pumice, sand, duff—a deep ground cover of humus, or rotting vegetation—or other material).

A *use trail* is an unmaintained, unofficial trail that is more or less easy to follow because it is well worn by use. For example, nearly every Sierra lakeshore has a use trail worn around it by anglers in search of their catch.

LANDMARKS The text contains occasional references to points, peaks, and other landmarks. These places are shown on the appropriate topographic maps cited at the beginning of the trip. For example, "Point 9,426" in the text would refer to a point designated as simply "9426" on the map itself. The actual numbers are an eclectic mix of feet and meters because USGS topo maps vary in the units they use.

FIRE DAMAGE Fire creates a mosaic of habitats throughout the Sierra Nevada. Historically, ground fires were common throughout the Sierra's montane forests and an essential ecological disturbance. In the process of clearing the ground and understory of thick brush, fire significantly altered the populations of ground-dwelling plants and animals. These fires would rarely have killed most of the canopy trees, allowing the landscape to rapidly recover from the fire. Then, from the late 1800s until 1971 (in Yosemite) or later (for the national forests), fire suppression was a general policy; every fire was extinguished immediately. This led to the accumulation of thick litter, dense brush, and overmature trees—all prime fuel for a hot, destructive blaze when a fire inevitably sparked to life. Foresters now know that natural fires should not be prevented but only regulated.

In recent decades, a combination of controlled burns (mostly alongside road corridors) and large wildfires (started by a combination of lightning strikes, careless campers, and arson) have passed through many of the Sierra's low- and midelevation forests. The years of fuel accumulation mean many of these fires become behemoths, often decimating the entire forest and killing the vast majority of trees, a very different process to what ecologists hypothesize occurred previously. If most of the trees in a region are killed, there is no longer a seed source, and it can be decades before seedlings establish, dependent on the rare seeds that arrive from afar. A second problem is that the hottest fires burn organic material within the soil and sterilize it, such that even wildflowers and shrubs struggle to establish.

Nonetheless, you should not consider fire as a negative force. Without fires, a plant community evolves toward a climax, an end stage, of plant succession, and only the plant and animal species that thrive in this climax community remain common. The mosaic of burned and unburned patches allows such a diversity of plant and animal species to thrive in the Sierra. For instance, species of the genus *Ceanothus* rapidly colonize the burned landscape, only to be shaded out by young lodgepoles and Jeffrey pines a few decades later. They are in turn replaced by red and white firs, the main species in the characteristic climax communities of the Sierra's midelevations.

From a practical hiker's standpoint, fire-ravished landscapes offer less shade but an abundance of spring wildflowers. Less-traveled trails often become yet more difficult to navigate as mountain whitethorn, a particularly fast-growing, dense, prickly shrub, consumes the trail. We have substituted a few hikes that have become much less traveled after fires but mostly simply note when fire more recently passed across patches of landscape and how much forest remains. We recommend visiting charred landscapes in spring and early summer, for vibrant blooms make up for the lack of shade.

How This Book Is Organized

With one exception, the trips are organized according to the highways that you must take to get to the trailheads in this book: I-80, CA 89, US 50, CA 88, CA 4, CA 108, CA 120, CA 41, and US 395. (The Western Yosemite Trips are not organized around a highway.) Within these major book sections are trailheads.

TRAILHEAD AND TRIP ORGANIZATION As previously noted, each trip is located within trailhead sections in the book. These sections begin with a summary table, such as the example below, that uses the trailhead's name, elevation, and latitude–longitude coordinates as its title. If relevant, the table also includes the names of shuttle trips that start at a different trailhead but end at this trailhead; these are included should you want to walk a described trip in reverse—for example, because you are unable to obtain a permit for the direction as described.

Sunrise Lakes Trailhead					8,166'; 37.82573°N, 119.46996°W	
Destination/ GPS Coordinates	**Trip Type**	**Best Season**	**Pace & Hiking/ Layover Days**	**Total Mileage**	**Permit Required**	
43 Sunrise Lakes and Sunrise High Sierra Camp 37.79404°N, 119.43412°W	Out-and-back	Mid to late	Moderate 2/1	10.4	Sunrise Lakes	
44 Clouds Rest Traverse to Yosemite Valley 37.76784°N, 119.48923°W (Clouds Rest)	Shuttle	Mid to late	Moderate 2/1	16.3	Sunrise Lakes *(Happy Isles to Sunrise Pass Thru if reversed)*	
47 Cathedral Lakes, Echo Creek and Sunrise Lakes *(in reverse of description; see page 230)*	Shuttle	Mid to late	Moderate 4/1	23.0	Sunrise Lakes	
51 High Sierra Camp Loop, northwest section *(in reverse of description; alternate start point; see page 245)*	Shuttle	Mid to late	Moderate 3/0	16.75	May Lake	

Following the table are details about information and permits, along with driving directions to the trailhead.

Next comes the first trip from this trailhead. The trip data—GPS coordinates, total mileage, and hiking/layover days—is included with each trip entry. All trips include an elevation profile, a list of maps, and highlights. Some include Heads Up!, or special considerations for that trip; shuttle trips include directions to the ending trailhead.

trip 43　Sunrise Lakes and Sunrise High Sierra Camp

Trip Data:　37.79404°N, 119.43412°W; 10.4 miles; 2/1 days
Topos:　*Tenaya Lake*

HIGHLIGHTS: This trip follows very popular trails, but the breathtaking scenery you enjoy along the route more than makes up for the lack of solitude. The terrain passed on this quite short hike is varied and scenic, with two superb camping possibilities, the upper Sunrise Lake and Sunrise High Sierra Camp. The former offers sheltered camping beside a scenic subalpine lake, while those at the latter are rewarded with a beautiful sunrise.

DAY 1 (Sunrise Lakes Trailhead to Sunrise High Sierra Camp, 5.2 miles): From the trailhead parking area, follow the eastbound trail, after a few steps passing a small spur trail that departs to the right (south) toward May Lake and Olmsted Point, then crossing the usually flowing outlet of Tenaya Lake on large rock blocks (an early-season wade). Just beyond this crossing you reach a trail junction, where left (northeast) leads to Tenaya Lake's southeastern shore, while you go right (south-southwest) toward Sunrise High Sierra Camp. . . . Just a few steps beyond the backpackers' camp you intersect the John Muir Trail (JMT) at the edge of Long Meadow.

DAY 2 (Sunrise High Sierra Camp to Tenaya Lake Trailhead, 5.2 miles): Retrace your steps.

After this comes the next trip, if any, from this same trailhead. Trips in the same general area, especially multiple trips from the same trailhead, often share the same first day's hiking. For example, the first trip from a trailhead is usually the shortest—one day out to a destination, the next day back to the trailhead. The second trip will build on—extend—the first trip by following the first trip's first day and then continuing on a second and subsequent days to more-distant destinations. Rather than repeat the full, detailed description for the first trip's first day, we simply reference the first day's description from the first hike.

TRAILHEAD MAPS A simple sketch map is included for each trailhead (see the following page for an example). It shows the location of roads, trailheads, and trails. It shows the route of each described trail and the names of key landmarks, but it is not meant to be a comprehensive hiking map of the area. The goal of these maps is for you to easily be able to find the described route on a larger topographic map or trail map. Gray numbers indicate trips departing from other trailheads that share a trail segment or traverse adjacent trail segments, should you wish to piece together your own route, combining pieces of multiple trail descriptions. Nearby trailheads are also marked and named, again in gray, so you can easily find adjacent trailhead maps.

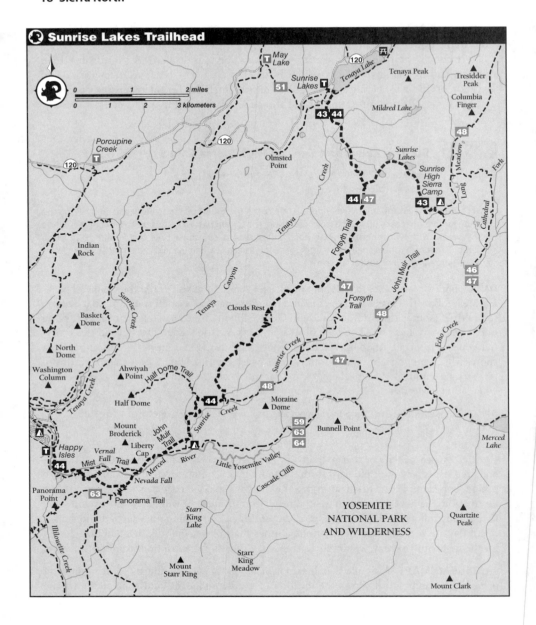

Sunrise Lakes Trailhead

Map Legend

- - - - - - - - - - Main trail	28 56 Trip Number/linked
- - - - - - - - - Other trail	T T Trailhead/linked
• • • • • • • • • • • Cross-country route	P P Parking/linked
- - - - - - - - - - - - - Use-trail	⌂ Ranger station
- - - - - - - - - - - 4WD road	? Information
══════════ Freeway	▲ Campground
══════════ Major road	⊞ Picnic area
══════════ Minor road	⌐ Dam
= = = = = = = Unpaved road	▲ Peak/summit
	■ General point of interest

National Park	Glacier
National Forest Wilderness	Lake
National Forest	River/creek
■ ■ ■ ■ ■ ■ ■ Adjacent boundary	

I-80 TRIPS

The terrain around Donner Summit is a popular recreational playground for a host of northern Californian residents and visitors to the greater Lake Tahoe area. Despite this popularity, backpackers can find serenity at a trio of backcountry lakes cupped into granite cirques, part of the once-proposed Castle Peak Wilderness Area. The northbound Pacific Crest Trail (PCT) takes you from I-80 into this lovely backcountry. All trips from I-80 start from that northbound PCT trailhead.

Trailhead: Castle Peak

Flower-lined stream from the Warren Lake Trail (see Hike 2, page 25)   Photo by Mike White

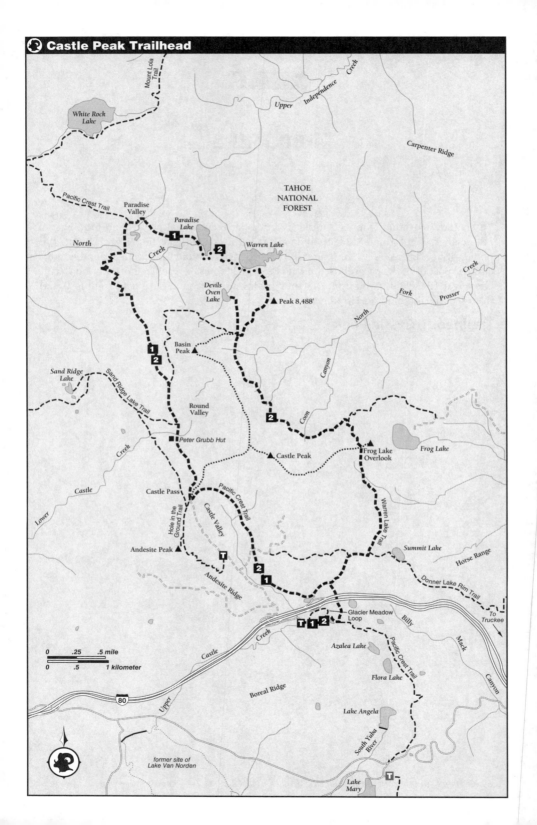

Mount Lola Trail

Upper Independence Creek

White Rock Lake

Carpenter Ridge

TAHOE NATIONAL FOREST

Pacific Crest Trail

Paradise Valley

Paradise Lake

1

2

Warren Lake

North Creek

Devils Oven Lake

Peak 8,488′

Fork Prosser Creek

Basin Peak ▲

North Canyon

1
2

Sand Ridge Lake

Sand Ridge Lake Trail

Round Valley

Cony Canyon

2

Creek

■ Peter Grubb Hut

▲ Castle Peak

Frog Lake Overlook ▲

Frog Lake

Castle

Castle Pass

Pacific Crest Trail

Hole in the Ground Trail

Castle Valley

Warren Lake Trail

Lower

Andesite Peak ▲

T

Summit Lake

Horse Range

Andesite Ridge

2
1

Donner Lake Rim Trail

To Truckee

T **1** **2**

Glacier Meadow Loop

Billy

Mack Canyon

Azalea Lake

Pacific Crest Trail

Castle Creek

Flora Lake

0   .25   .5 mile
0   .5   1 kilometer

Upper

Boreal Ridge

Lake Angela

80

South Yuba River

former site of Lake Van Norden

Lake Mary **T**

Castle Peak Trailhead				7,213'; 39.33959°N, 120.34285°W			
Destination/ GPS Coordinates	Trip Type	Best Season	Pace & Hiking/ Layover Days	Total Mileage	Permit Required		
1 Paradise Lake 39.39969°N 120.36382°W	Out-and-back	Mid to late	Moderate 2/0	17.8	None for backpacking		
2 Castle Peak Wilderness Loop 39.38950°N 120.35646°W	Loop	Mid to late	Moderate, part cross-country 3/1	20.0	None for backpacking		

INFORMATION AND PERMITS: The Castle Peak area is in Tahoe National Forest: 631 Coyote St., Nevada City, CA 95959; 530-265-4531, fs.usda.gov/tahoe. For now, you don't need a wilderness permit, but you do need a California Campfire Permit for campfires and stoves.

DRIVING DIRECTIONS: West of Donner Summit, take the Castle Peak/Boreal Ridge Road Exit 176 from I-80, drive to the frontage road on the south side of the freeway, and then proceed east 0.3 mile to the PCT parking area. The large parking lot has trailer parking, pit toilets, and running water in season.

trip 1   Paradise Lake

> **Trip Data:** 39.39969°N, 120.36382°W; 17.8 miles; 2/0 days
> **Topos:** *Norden, Independence Lake*

HIGHLIGHTS: The PCT combined with a 1-mile stretch of abandoned jeep road provides a well-graded route to island-dotted Paradise Lake, one of the most picturesque subalpine lakes in the greater Tahoe area. For those who aren't up to the more difficult trek of the full loop past Warren Lake, with a side trip to Devils Oven Lake on the way (Trip 2), an out-and-back trip to Paradise Lake is a great way to spend a couple of days or more.

DAY 1 (Castle Peak Trailhead to Paradise Lake, 7.7 miles): From the parking lot, follow a well-signed gravel path to a stone bridge over a seasonal stream and continue on dirt track through lodgepole pines, western white pines, and white firs. Soon you encounter a junction with the Glacier Meadow Loop and proceed ahead (east) toward the PCT. After a short distance you pass by a second junction with the Glacier Meadow Loop and continue ahead (east) toward the PCT. Head past a shallow pond, where mountain hemlocks join the

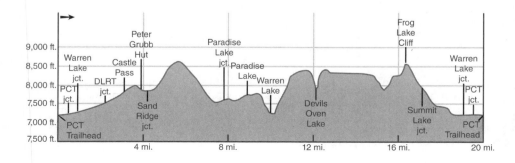

Peter Grubb Hut   Photo by Mike White

mixed forest, and then make a short descent to the well-signed PCT junction near the edge of a grass-and-willow-filled meadow.

Turn left and head north on the PCT around the fringe of the meadow to a pair of large pedestrian culverts underneath the eastbound and westbound lanes of I-80. Pass under the freeway and beyond the culverts, make a moderate climb to the crossing of a seasonal creek, and then come to a well-signed junction, 1 mile from the trailhead.

At the junction, turn left (southwest) on the PCT, following signed directions to Castle Pass. The PCT rises and then drops to the north shore of a small pond and an unsigned path to the westbound Donner Summit Rest Area. Stay on the PCT here.

Beyond the unmarked junction, follow the gently graded PCT through mixed forest toward Castle Valley. The trail nears Castle Creek for a brief time and then travels just east of the verdant meadows of Castle Valley, where two use trails branch away toward the creek and meadows. At 2.3 miles from the trailhead, reach a junction with the Donner Lake Rim Trail on the right, and then continue generally north upstream through Castle Valley, hopping over a number of lushly lined tributaries along the way. Nearing the head of the valley, the PCT bends west, then south-southwest on an ascending traverse to a signed junction with a connecting trail from the Castle Valley Road. From there, make a short but stiff climb to Castle Pass and a junction with a trio of paths: northeast to the summit of Castle Peak, southeast to a connection with the trail to Andesite Peak, and north on the PCT toward Round Valley.

Take the middle fork north from Castle Pass, remaining on the PCT, on a traverse across a lightly forested slope. After about a half mile, begin a moderate, switchbacking descent toward Round Valley below. Nearing the floor of the valley, pass a very short use trail on the left that leads to Peter Grubb Hut.

PETER GRUBB HUT

Following a ski trip to the Swiss Alps, Harold T. Bradley, university professor and former president of the Sierra Club, proposed a string of six alpine huts between Donner and Echo Passes, similar to the ones he'd experienced in the Alps. Although only four of the six were eventually completed, the huts have provided warm shelter for many visitors since the late 1930s. Peter Grubb Hut is complete with a wood-burning stove and firewood, a gas stove and cooking utensils, a table and chairs, a loft with sleeping platforms, solar lights, and a detached outhouse. Interesting old photos and memorabilia cover the walls and provide a sample of the area's history. Except for emergency shelter, overnight use of Peter Grubb Hut is by reservation only. Contact the Sierra Club at Clair Tappaan Lodge, PO Box 36, Norden, CA 95724; 530-426-3632, sierraclub.org/outings/lodges/ctl.

The PCT crosses Lower Castle Creek just north of the hut and then soon comes to a Y-junction with the Sand Ridge Trail, where you continue ahead, northbound.

Skirt the western fringe of Round Valley through light forest and then follow a moderate climb with occasional filtered views of the terrain to the west. Break out of the trees to sweeping views farther up the southwest shoulder of Basin Peak and ascend open slopes carpeted with willows and wildflowers.

BASIN PEAK

Peak baggers can leave the trail anywhere near the high point and make a straightforward climb of flower-covered, volcanic slopes to the top of 9,017-foot Basin Peak, which affords a wide-ranging vista of the northern Tahoe Sierra. A use trail along the crest of the ridge connecting the summits of Basin and Castle Peaks offers climbers with some extra time the opportunity to double summit.

After cresting the shoulder of Basin Peak, the PCT follows a mellow descending traverse across flower-laden slopes before returning to light forest, where an extended, switchbacking descent heads toward the floor of Paradise Valley. At the bottom of the descent, stroll amid pines and firs with a lush understory of plants and flowers to a bridged crossing of lazy North Creek meandering through the tall grass. A gentle, winding climb from the bridge leads past a pond surrounded by the meadows of Paradise Valley to a signed junction with the track of an old jeep road traveling east toward Paradise Lake, 7.8 miles from the parking lot. Early-season visitors to Paradise Valley will be alternately rewarded with a fine display of wildflowers and cursed with hordes of pesky mosquitoes.

Leaving the PCT, turn right (east) at the junction and follow the easy grade of the jeep road around the northern perimeter of Paradise Valley, a verdant clearing carpeted with a dense swath of plants and flowers. Leaving the clearing behind, the jeep road makes a moderate climb through scattered conifers and granite boulders. Eventually, the track of the old road falters, but a ducked route continues the climb toward the obvious location of the lake at the head of the cirque.

Several campsites are clustered around the west side of the picturesque lake (7,729'; 39.39969°N, 120.36382°W) in sandy pockets between the numerous granite slabs scattered around the shoreline. More secluded camping is available along the southwest shore and the saddle above the east shore, where the view down to Warren Lake is quite impressive.

DAY 2 (Paradise Lake to Castle Peak Trailhead, 7.7 miles): Retrace your steps to return.

| trip 2 | **Castle Peak Wilderness Loop** |

see map on p. 22

> **Trip Data:** 39.38950°N, 120.35646°W; 20.0 miles; 3/1 days
> **Topos:** *Norden, Independence Lake*

HIGHLIGHTS: While the elevation gain and loss experienced along this route requires hikers to be in very good physical condition, the rewards of incomparable views, picturesque lakes, vibrant wildflowers, and exquisite scenery more than make up for the extra effort. Additional cross-country routes to the summits of Basin or Castle Peaks and plenty of connecting trails provide tantalizing ways to extend your visit to these lands.

HEADS UP! *Because of the potentially dangerous cross-country route between Paradise and Warren Lakes and the indistinct trail to Devils Oven Lake, this trip is appropriate for experienced hikers only.*

DAY 1 (Castle Peak Trailhead to Paradise Lake, 8.9 miles): From the Castle Peak Trailhead, take the gravel path over the stone bridge, and then follow the dirt track eastward, going ahead (east) at both junctions with the Glacier Meadow Loop. Where you meet the Pacific Crest Trail (PCT), turn left (north) and pass under I-80 to a seasonal stream and a signed junction where you turn left (southwest) to stay on the PCT, heading for Castle Pass. The trail presently curves northwest to an unsigned junction where you go ahead (north) to stay on the PCT along Castle Valley, passing by use trails into the valley. Pass by a junction with the Donner Lake Rim Trail and continue on the PCT as it bends west and then southwest to a junction with a trail to Castle Valley Road. Stay on the PCT here, climbing southwest to Castle Pass and a junction with three trails. Take the middle fork, the PCT, north toward Round Valley, passing the use trail to the Peter Grubb Hut. Skirt Round Valley, ascend the shoulder of Basin Peak, and descend into Paradise Valley. At the junction with the old road to Paradise Lake, turn right (east) to leave the PCT and follow first the road and then ducks to the lake (7,729'; 39.39969°N, 120.36382°W).

DAY 2 (Paradise Lake to Devils Oven Lake, 2.2 miles, part cross-country): A short climb up and over some bedrock cliffs at the south end of Paradise Lake is necessary in order to reach the saddle and the continuation of the loop trip via the cross-country route down to Warren Lake.

From the saddle above the east shore of Paradise Lake, look for a large cairn at the head of a rock slot that signifies the beginning of the ducked cross-country route down to Warren Lake. Head south from the saddle on an angling descent across the headwall of Warren Lake's cirque to a slightly rising traverse below the base of some steep cliffs. Drop down some steep rocks and then follow a rocky swale through shrubs to easier terrain below, where the route bends left to avoid some talus. Continue the descent over rock slabs interspersed with sandy patches through waist-high shrubs toward the tree-lined southwest shore. Nearing the lake, very briefly follow an alder-lined stream to a secluded campsite and proceed a very short distance to the use trail that hugs the shoreline. Head right (east) on the use trail and stroll past several campsites and over a couple of tiny streams to the

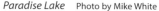

Paradise Lake   Photo by Mike White

midpoint of Warren Lake's south shore (7,259'; 39.39500°N, 120.35103°W), where a maintained trail resumes in an attack of the steep, 1,000-foot slope above.

Leaving the south shore of Warren Lake, one of the steepest miles of trail in the greater Lake Tahoe region winds tightly up a bedrock gully toward a high saddle in the ridge directly southwest of Peak 8,488. Complicating matters somewhat, the trail is quite rocky in places, providing laboring hikers with poor footing for a steep ascent. By getting an early start, at least the seemingly interminable climb can be done under shade and the relatively cool temperatures of morning. After cresting the lip of the basin, a more moderate climb over the last 150 vertical feet leads across drier slopes with widely scattered mountain hemlocks and western white pines. Persistence is finally rewarded at the saddle with an impressive view to the south of North Fork Prosser Creek's sweeping basin arcing past Basin Peak and the impressive battlements of Castle Peak to Frog Lake Overlook, and also westward down the creek's verdant canyon to Carpenter Valley. At the saddle a use trail veers left, petering out before reaching an exposed overlook of the canyon below, including an inviting-looking pond surrounded by lush greenery.

Turn right (west) at the saddle and follow a more reasonably graded trail to the crest of a ridge and across an open, flower-filled slope to a junction with the trail to Devils Oven Lake. A sign at the junction provides this ominous warning for those bound for the lake: ROUGH TRAIL.

To reach Devils Oven Lake, turn sharply right (north), away from the Warren Lake Trail, and follow the Devils Oven Lake Trail on a climb to a level area on the crest of a ridge. Close attention must be paid here, as the more obvious route on the ground leads not to the lake but on an arcing traverse on abandoned roads around the north and east sides of Basin Peak to a connection with the PCT southwest of the summit (a route that seems to be increasingly popular with the equestrian crowd). The deteriorating route to Devils Oven Lake heads north from the level area on a curving descent that bends northwest before arriving at the southeast shore (7,918'; 39.38950°N, 120.35646°W). Campsites appear to be more limited here than at the neighboring lakes, a testament to the fact that most backpackers are unwilling to make the steep climbs out of both Devils Oven and Warren Lakes.

DAY 3 (Devils Oven Lake to Castle Peak Trailhead, 8.9 miles): Return to the junction between the Devils Oven Lake and Warren Lake trails. From the junction, turn right (south) to begin an undulating 2.5-mile traverse of the head of North Fork Prosser Creek's upper basin, across flower-filled slopes and several willow-and-flower-lined streams. Over the course of this traverse between the junction and the saddle below Frog Lake Overlook, the trail gradually curves east as it gains and loses a considerable amount of elevation due to the uneven terrain of the upper basin. After crossing the last stream in Coon Canyon, the trail begins a final, stiff climb toward the saddle. You reach a junction at a small flat on top of a ridge midway through this climb, where an old, lesser-used trail heads left (east) to the formerly privately owned environs around Frog Lake (the area was recently acquired by the Truckee Donner Land Trust). You go right (south). After the brief respite, the gently rising trail leads across a stream before a steep, winding climb to a junction on the saddle below Frog Lake Overlook. The short path on the left (east) to the overlook shouldn't be missed, as the view straight down Frog Lake Cliff to the lake is a dramatic sight.

Return to the main trail and turn left (south) back onto the Warren Lake Trail. After the previous undulating route across North Fork Prosser Creek's basin, you're grateful to find that the trail from the saddle is all downhill back to the parking lot. Initially, the trail follows a gentle-to-moderate descent across a slope covered with acres and acres of mule ears—

Warren Lake Photo by Mike White

a beautiful sight at peak bloom—before a steeper descent leads back into the cover of mixed forest. Amid the trees, the trail crosses several trickling, flower-lined little streams on the way to an extensive clearing covered with wildflowers and shrubs that grants one last expansive vista—this one of the Carson Range to the east and the Donner Pass peaks to the south. Returning to a shady forest, the trail makes a winding descent down to a junction with the Donner Lake Rim Trail. On the left, the short lateral heads eastward to tree-rimmed Summit Lake, while the right-hand trail provides a connection to the PCT. Backpackers reluctant to end their journey may find reasonable campsites at this popular lake.

Go right (west) from the Summit Lake junction and continue through the forest cover, broken momentarily by a substantial, open meadow thick with flowers and willows. The forest thins for a while again where the trail passes through an area sprinkled with granite boulders and slabs as the trail makes its way to closing the loop at the junction with the PCT. From there, turn right (south-southeast) to retrace your steps 1 mile to the parking lot.

CA 89 TRIPS

Trips in this section start from five trailheads (from north to south): the Powderhorn Trailhead into Granite Chief Wilderness, Lake Tahoe's Meeks Bay Trailhead into Desolation Wilderness, Lake Tahoe's Bayview Trailhead, the Big Meadow Trailhead into Meiss Country, and the Armstrong Pass Trailhead to Star Lake and Freel Peak.

Although set within the popular Tahoe Basin, Granite Chief Wilderness is extremely lightly used in comparison to other areas around the lake, particularly the ever-popular Desolation Wilderness. Instead of permits and quotas, backpackers will experience deep forests, rushing streams, seasonal wildflowers, excellent views, and fewer people.

Above the southwest shore of Lake Tahoe, Desolation Wilderness encompasses 63,690 acres of federally protected backcountry. The terrain resembles a miniature High Sierra, albeit at a lower elevation, with deep blue lakes, craggy summits, and granite peaks and basins showing extensive signs of glaciation from the last ice age. (The Meeks Bay Trailhead also features the beginning of the unofficial Tahoe-Yosemite Trail [TYT], which stretches almost 186 miles from Lake Tahoe's Meeks Bay to Yosemite's Tuolumne Meadows and traverses some of the northern Sierra's loveliest territory. A fine complement to the John Muir Trail [JMT], the TYT is even more of an adventure.)

South of Lake Tahoe, bounded on the east by CA 89, and in between US 50 and CA 88 lies Meiss Country, an area of deep forests, scenic lakes, and expansive meadows that saw far fewer visitors before the construction of the Tahoe Rim Trail. Despite this increased popularity, the area still affords backpackers a reasonable dose of serenity along with the stunning scenery.

Farther south still, the Freel Peak area offers a chance to climb to the top of the Tahoe Basin's highest summit and enjoy the shore of one of its highest lakes.

Trailheads: Powderhorn
Meeks Bay
Bayview
Big Meadow
Armstrong Pass

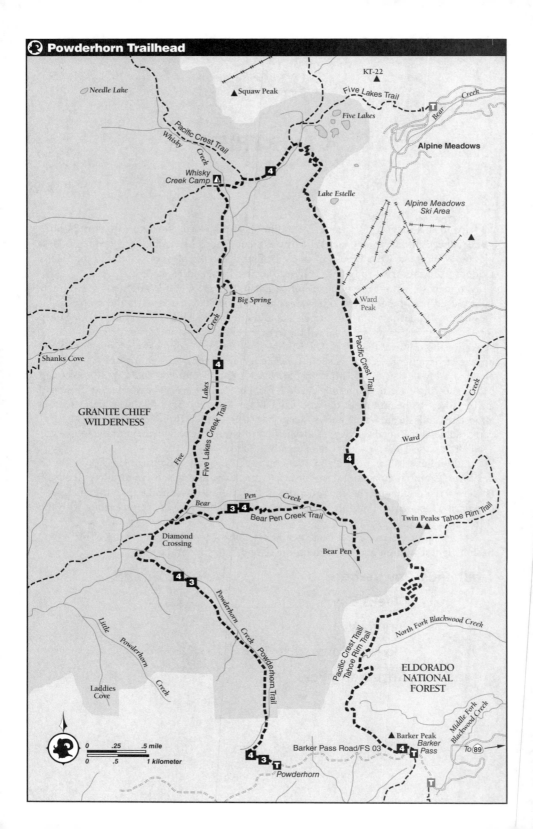

Needle Lake

▲ Squaw Peak

KT-22 ▲

Five Lakes Trail

Five Lakes

Bear Creek

Pacific Crest Trail

Whisky Creek

Whisky Creek Camp ▲

4

Lake Estelle

Alpine Meadows

Alpine Meadows Ski Area

▲

Big Spring

Creek

Pacific Crest Trail

▲ Ward Peak

Shanks Cove

Creek

Ward

Creek

GRANITE CHIEF WILDERNESS

Five

Lakes

Five Lakes Creek Trail

4

4

Pen   Creek

Bear

3 **4**

Bear Pen Creek Trail

Diamond Crossing

Bear Pen

Twin Peaks ▲▲ Tahoe Rim Trail

4 **3**

Powderhorn   Creek   Powderhorn Trail

North Fork Blackwood Creek

Little

Powderhorn

Creek

Pacific Crest Trail / Tahoe Rim Trail

ELDORADO NATIONAL FOREST

Laddies Cove

Middle Fork Blackwood Creek

▲ Barker Peak

4 **3** T

Barker Pass Road/FS 03

Powderhorn

Barker Pass

4 T

To (89) →

T

0   .25   .5 mile

0   .5   1 kilometer

Powderhorn Trailhead			7,654'; 39.07467°N, 120.26134°W		
Destination/ GPS Coordinates	Trip Type	Best Season	Pace & Hiking/ Layover Days	Total Mileage	Permit Required
3 Bear Pen 39.11187°N 120.24570°W	Out-and-back	Mid to late	Moderate 2/1	13.5	None for backpacking
4 Barker Pass 39.16627°N 120.27192°W (Whiskey Camp Creek)	Shuttle or loop	Mid to late	Strenuous 3/1	25.0 (shuttle) or 26.5 (loop)	None for backpacking

INFORMATION AND PERMITS: Granite Chief Wilderness is in the Tahoe National Forest: 631 Coyote St., Nevada City, CA 95959; 530-265-4531, fs.usda.gov/tahoe. You don't need a wilderness permit for overnight travel, but you do need a California Campfire Permit for campfires and stoves. Currently, dogs are banned from fawning areas from May 15 to July 15; check with Tahoe National Forest for details.

DRIVING DIRECTIONS: From CA 89, about 4 miles south of its junction with CA 28 in Tahoe City, turn west onto Barker Pass Road (Forest Service Road 03), marked SNO-PARK and KASPIAN CAMPGROUND. Follow FS 03 along the north side of the valley, bend left to cross Blackwood Creek near the 2-mile mark, and then continue up the south side of Blackwood Canyon to the PCT trailhead parking area near Barker Pass (7,673'; 39.07698°N, 120.23509°W), 7 miles from CA 89. To get to the Powderhorn Trailhead, continue downhill from Barker Pass another 1.5 miles to the signed Powderhorn Trailhead (7,654'; 39.07467°N, 120.26134°W), where limited parking is available for two or three vehicles.

trip 3   **Bear Pen**

> **Trip Data:** 39.11187°N, 120.24570°W; 13.5 miles; 2/1 days
> **Topos:** *Wentworth Springs*

HIGHLIGHTS: Follow a pair of delightful streams to a secluded basin rimmed by granite cliffs on the eastern fringe of Granite Chief Wilderness.

DAY 1 (Powderhorn Trailhead to Bear Pen, 6.75 miles): From the trailhead, make a short climb through selectively logged fir forest to a switchback and continue to where the route merges with a dirt road on the way to the top of a hill. As the road bends left, proceed ahead toward a cairn, where the singletrack trail begins a protracted drop into the canyon of Powderhorn Creek. Follow this steep, winding descent into the trees, soon crossing the nascent, flower-lined stream and proceeding downstream.

Continue the descent past the signed Granite Chief Wilderness boundary down Powderhorn Creek's canyon. Along the descent, avalanche swaths have thinned the forest enough in spots to allow a profusion of wildflowers, plants, and shrubs to flourish. Amid a thickening forest, cross a narrow stream flowing through a tangle of alders and colorful wildflowers and proceed on a gentle-to-moderate descent down the canyon. The grade eventually eases where the trail crosses a wildflower-carpeted meadow and then encounters

Lovely Bear Pen in the Granite Chief Wilderness   Photo by Mike White

a boulder-hop ford of Powderhorn Creek (may be difficult in early season). There's a marginal campsite near the crossing.

Heading northeast, the trail proceeds through the trees for about 300 yards to the open meadow known as Diamond Crossing. Pass by a marked junction in this meadow, where a very faint trail (the old Hell Hole Trail) heads southwest toward a trailhead near Hell Hole Reservoir. Bear right (northwest) at this junction to continue through the meadow, and then reenter forest on the way to a second junction, this one with a slightly more distinct trail heading up the canyon of Bear Pen Creek.

Turn right and head east on the Bear Pen Creek Trail on a moderate climb up a canyon filled with thick forest. The trail to Bear Pen is infrequently used, and the tread tends to falter crossing a small meadow. After 2.75 miles from the last junction of the mostly forested trail, reach a willow-and-grass-filled meadow known as Bear Pen (7,424′; 39.11187°N, 120.24570°W), an opening in the thick forest backdropped by a dramatic amphitheater of cliffs. Little-used, hemlock-shaded campsites around the meadow's perimeter offer secluded camping to solitude seekers. With a little luck, visitors may also see a namesake critter or two.

DAY 2 (Bear Pen to Powderhorn Trailhead, 6.75 miles): Retrace your steps.

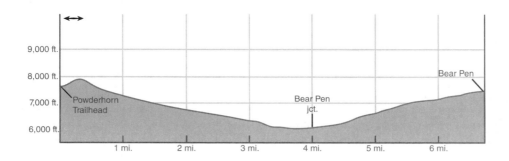

see
map on
p. 30

trip 4   **Barker Pass**

> **Trip Data:**   39.16627°N, 120.27192°W (Whiskey Camp Creek);
> 25.0 miles (shuttle) or 26.5 miles (loop); 3/1 days
> **Topos:**   *Wentworth Springs, Granite Chief, Tahoe City, Homewood*

HIGHLIGHTS: On the first part of this journey, backpackers are treated to a shady, old-growth forest that escaped the axes of the lumbermen who denuded the Tahoe Basin of most of its timber during the Comstock Lode frenzy in the 19th century. Secluded camping, colorful wildflowers, and dancing streams are delightful attractions. The second part of the trip follows a section of the Pacific Crest Trail (PCT) on a ridge route that offers sweeping vistas. To do this trip as a loop, see the directions at the bottom of page 35.

HEADS UP! *The heart of Granite Chief Wilderness is a lonely parcel of land where little-used trails can disappear in grassy meadows—make sure you carry a map and compass.*

SHUTTLE DIRECTIONS: If taking the shuttle trip between the Powderhorn Trailhead and the Barker Pass Trailhead, leave your first car at the Barker Pass Trailhead (7,673'; 39.07698°N, 120.23509°W) and your second at the Powderhorn Trailhead (7,654'; 39.07467°N, 120.26134°W), 1.5 miles farther west down Barker Pass Road.

DAY 1 (Powderhorn Trailhead to Bear Pen, 6.75 miles): From the Powderhorn Trailhead, climb on the trail to a dirt road and follow that road to a bend where the marked route continues ahead. Descend the old roadbed to a sharp curve, where a trail marker directs hikers to veer left (generally north) onto singletrack trail. Make a steep, winding descent to another dirt road, which you briefly follow until the singletrack trail resumes. Continue on this trail to the wilderness boundary and then down Powderhorn Creek's canyon to the junction with the Bear Pen Creek Trail. Turn right and take this trail 2.75 miles to Bear Pen (7,424'; 39.11187°N, 120.24570°W).

DAY 2 (Bear Pen to Whisky Creek Camp, 7.0 miles): Retrace your steps 2.75 miles to the junction of the Bear Pen Creek and Five Lakes Creek trails. From the junction, turn right and head north on the Five Lakes Creek Trail, immediately encountering the crossing of Bear Pen Creek. Beyond the crossing, briefly follow alongside the alder-lined course of Bear Pen Creek until it bends eastward, and then proceed up the trail in forested Five Lakes Creek's canyon. Cross the rocky channel of the seasonal outlet from Grouse Canyon and then continue another quarter mile to a rivulet.

Another half mile from the rivulet leads to a signed junction just before a good-size meadow. The signed trail to Whisky Creek Camp is virtually impossible to follow. Therefore, continue straight ahead (north), following signed directions for Big Spring.

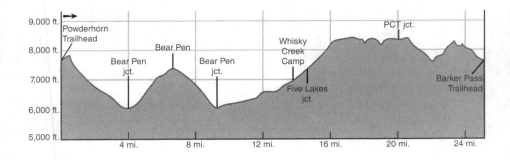

Crossing the meadow north of the junction, the tread may be difficult to follow through the tall grasses, but a distinct path reappears where the trail reenters the forest. From the meadow, an easy half mile leads to Big Spring at the south end of a large meadow; nearby conifers harbor campsites. Although the defined trail disappears in the meadow grass beyond the spring and the campsites, the trail resumes at the west edge of the meadow, about midway through the clearing and shortly to a ford of Five Lakes Creek and then to a junction (39.14986°N, 120.27241°W).

Turn right (north) at the junction and follow the west side of alder-lined Five Lakes Creek for 0.3 mile and then cross a side stream. Beyond this stream, climb moderately to the forested flat that harbors Whisky Creek Camp (6,927'; 39.16627°N, 120.27192°W). Observe posted regulations here.

DAY 3 (Whisky Creek Camp to Barker Pass, 11.25 miles, or to Powderhorn Trailhead, 12.75 miles): From Whisky Creek Camp, head east a short distance to the crossing of Five Lakes Creek, and then make a 0.3-mile switchbacking climb through the trees to a T-junction with the PCT. Turn right at the junction, following signed directions for the Alpine Meadows Trailhead, and proceed on the PCT on a moderate climb through a gradually lightening forest, where shrubs and wildflowers become more and more prominent. Follow occasional switchbacks up the left-hand side of Five Lakes Creek canyon across initially dry slopes, followed by a hillside of flourishing wildflowers and willows. Beyond this incredibly verdant hillside, where conifers start to reappear, is a signed junction with a lateral to Five Lakes. (Backpackers seeking campsites must find one at least 600 feet away from any of the lakes in the Five Lakes basin.)

From the junction with the Five Lakes lateral, veer right (east), remaining on the PCT, and follow the gently graded trail across a meadow sprinkled with lodgepole pines and firs to a boulder hop of Five Lakes Creek. From the crossing, climb an open hillside carpeted with patches of alder and willows and interspersed with a fine assortment of wildflowers, including delphinium, yarrow, paintbrush, aster, corn lily, and daisy. Beyond this colorful area, many long switchbacks zigzag up a forested hillside toward the crest of the ridge above. Before the end of these switchbacks, thinning trees allow the first of many sweeping views to come: Squaw Peak is the prominent mountain to the northwest, and below to the

Granite Chief   Photo by Mike White

west is the heart of Granite Chief Wilderness; farther on, where the switchbacks end and the trail approaches the crest, views expand to the south of peaks in Desolation Wilderness, along with a varied assortment of communications equipment and ski lift machinery littering the summit of Ward Peak directly ahead. When the trail reaches a small saddle, the views include Lake Tahoe and Alpine Meadows to the east.

With the stiff climbing behind you, traverse around Peak 8,474 to a second saddle, pass by a snow fence built to minimize cornices overhanging the ski slopes of Alpine Meadows, and continue through low-growing flowers and shrubs across the west side of Ward Peak, enjoying continuous views of the surrounding terrain along the way. Beyond Ward Peak, the PCT reaches two more saddles before dipping below impressive-looking volcanic cliffs on the west side of Peak 8,522.

Briefly enter a grove of western white pines, firs, and hemlocks, the first significant pocket of forest since the switchbacks above the crossing of Five Lakes Creek. Leave the trees for a while to regain the crest and enjoy fine views of Ward Canyon and Lake Tahoe to the east and ahead to Twin Peaks. Then head back into the trees, where a subsidiary ridge abuts the main crest, and follow a pair of short switchbacks on a brief climb back to the top of the shrub-covered ridge.

Continue along the ridge, where waist-high tobacco brush threatens to overgrow the path in places and where proclaiming the expansive views along this part of the journey becomes redundant. Eventually, the views diminish as the trail follows a gentle grade through mixed forest to a junction with the Tahoe Rim Trail (TRT) just southwest of Twin Peaks.

From the junction, the PCT and TRT share a similar course for many miles, almost to Carson Pass. Initially the trail continues through the trees, but eventually it emerges into the open again with excellent views of Twin Peaks and Blackwood Canyon. In order to avoid a knife-edge ridge, the trail next makes several long switchbacks down into the canyon of North Fork Blackwood Creek. The switchbacking trail loses 600 feet of elevation before ultimately climbing back out of the canyon. The trail crosses a few lushly lined streams and seeps along the way, all tributaries of North Fork Blackwood Creek, where a limited number of nearby campsites serve overnighters.

CLIMBING TWIN PEAKS

Peak baggers can easily add a notch to their belts by heading east from the junction on the TRT to a use trail that ascends the east ridge of the easternmost of Twin Peaks' summits. The route climbs steeply up the ridge, offering excellent views of Lake Tahoe, the summits of Desolation Wilderness, and the surrounding canyons along the way, culminating in an even more impressive 360-degree view from the top.

A short but stiff climb from the campsites leads to the top of a ridge directly west of Peak 8,355. An extremely short use trail leads to a scramble of this volcanic pinnacle, where hikers can enjoy fine views of the surrounding terrain.

Away from the ridge, the trail traverses the head of a canyon of a subsidiary stream of Middle Fork Blackwood Creek, passing in and out of a light fir forest. Good views of Lake Tahoe, Barker Peak, and Ellis Peak are available along the way through gaps in the forest. A final, moderate descent across the south slopes of Barker Peak leads to the Barker Pass Trailhead (7,673'; 39.07698°N, 120.23509°W), where your shuttle ride should be waiting.

If you are doing the loop option, add 1.5 miles to your day and close the loop by turning right and descending generally west on Barker Pass Road to the Powderhorn Trailhead (7,654'; 39.07467°N, 120.26134°W).

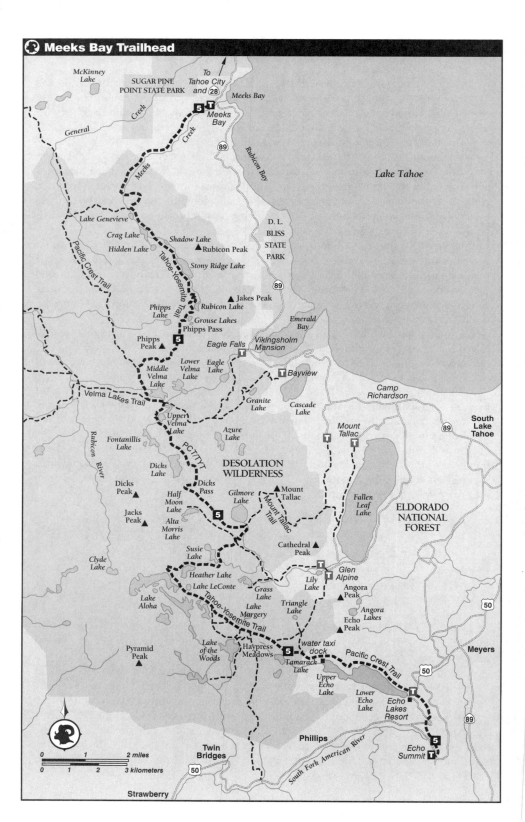

McKinney
Lake

SUGAR PINE
POINT STATE PARK

To
Tahoe City
and 28

Meeks Bay

General

Creek

Meeks Bay

5 T

Meeks
Bay

89

Rubicon Bay

Lake Tahoe

Meeks

Creek

Lake Genevieve

Crag Lake

Hidden Lake

Shadow Lake

▲ Rubicon Peak

Stony Ridge Lake

D. L.
BLISS
STATE
PARK

89

Pacific Crest Trail

Tahoe-Yosemite Trail

Phipps
Lake

Rubicon Lake

▲ Jakes Peak

Grouse Lakes

Phipps Pass

Phipps
Peak ▲

5

Eagle Falls

T

Emerald
Bay

Vikingsholm
Mansion

Lower
Velma
Lake

Eagle
Lake

Middle
Velma
Lake

T Bayview

Camp
Richardson

Velma Lakes Trail

Upper
Velma
Lake

Granite
Lake

Cascade
Lake

Mount
Tallac

T

South
Lake
Tahoe

89

Fontanillis
Lake

Rubicon River

PCT/TYT

Azure
Lake

DESOLATION
WILDERNESS

Dicks
Lake

Dicks
Peak ▲

Dicks
Pass

Gilmore
Lake

▲ Mount
Tallac

Fallen
Leaf
Lake

ELDORADO
NATIONAL
FOREST

Half
Moon
Lake

5

Mount Tallac
Trail

Jacks
Peak ▲

Alta
Morris
Lake

Cathedral ▲
Peak

Clyde
Lake

Susie
Lake

Heather Lake

Lake LeConte

Grass
Lake

T

Glen
Alpine

Lily Lake

Angora
Peak ▲

Lake
Aloha

Lake
Margery

Triangle
Lake

Angora
Lakes

Tahoe-Yosemite Trail

Echo
Peak ▲

50

Meyers

Pyramid
Peak ▲

Lake
of the
Woods

Haypress
Meadows

5

water taxi
dock

Pacific Crest Trail

Tamarack
Lake

Upper
Echo
Lake

Lower
Echo
Lake

Echo
Lakes
Resort

T

50

Phillips

South Fork American River

Twin
Bridges

50

Echo
Summit

5

T

89

Strawberry

0   1   2 miles

0   1   2   3 kilometers

Meeks Bay Trailhead					6,244'; 39.03737°N, 120.12645°W	
Destination/ GPS Coordinates	Trip Type	Best Season	Pace & Hiking/ Layover Days	Total Mileage	Permit Required	
5 Meeks Bay Trailhead to Echo Summit Trailhead 38.81487°N 120.03408°W	Shuttle	Mid to late	Moderate 4/1	30.2 or 27.5	Desolation Wilderness: Stony Ridge Zone	

INFORMATION AND PERMITS: All backpackers must secure and pay for a wilderness permit for entry into Desolation Wilderness. The region is heavily used, and strict zone quotas are in place for the number of overnighters departing from every trailhead that enters the wilderness. A majority of permits are available by reservation, with the remainder handed out on a first-come, first-served basis. Reserved permits can be obtained online at recreation .gov. During business hours, walk-in permits may be picked up at the Taylor Creek Visitor Center, Pacific Ranger Station, Lake Tahoe Basin Management Unit (LTBMU) Supervisor's Office, and LTBMU North Shore Office.

DRIVING DIRECTIONS: Follow CA 89 on the west shore of Lake Tahoe to Meeks Bay and locate the trailhead near a closed gate on the west side of the highway, 0.1 mile north of the entrance into Meeks Bay Campground. The trailhead is approximately 16.5 miles north of the junction of CA 89 and US 50 in South Lake Tahoe or 11 miles south of the junction of CA 89 and CA 28 in Tahoe City.

trip 5 Meeks Bay Trailhead to Echo Summit Trailhead

Trip Data: 38.81487°N, 120.03408°W; 30.2 or 27.5 miles; 4/1 days
Topos: *Homewood, Rockbound Valley, Pyramid Peak, Echo Lake*

HIGHLIGHTS: This first section of the unofficial Tahoe-Yosemite Trail (TYT), from Meeks Bay to Adventure Mountain Lake Tahoe, a winter recreation area just west and south of US 50's Echo Summit, lies almost entirely within one of California's best-known wilderness areas, Desolation. The section is never far from a road, and frequent glimpses of Lake Tahoe may call forth images of noisy casinos and crowded beaches. Yet near the trail you may find many campsites that feel utterly remote.

HEADS UP! *Extensive sections of the trail are strewn with sharp, angular rock—be sure to wear sturdy footwear. Wood fires are banned within the wilderness, so plan on using a stove for cooking. Bear canisters are strongly recommended.*

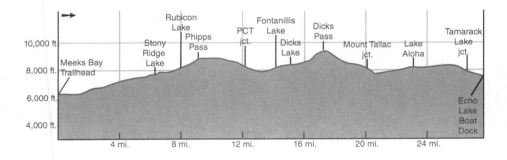

SHUTTLE DIRECTIONS: Follow US 50 to Echo Summit, and from there go west to a paved access road on the south side of the highway, 0.2 mile west of Echo Summit. A sign for Adventure Mountain Lake Tahoe resort marks the turnoff. Proceed 0.2 mile to the large Pacific Crest Trail (PCT) parking lot just before the resort.

DAY 1 (Meeks Bay Trailhead to Rubicon Lake, 8.0 miles): The "trail" begins as a dirt road beyond a locked gate near CA 89. The gate bars access to the general public, but vehicles may still be infrequently encountered along the road. Beyond the gate, head generally southwest through mixed forest of incense cedars, white firs, lodgepole pines, and sugar pines on the right, and verdant meadows along Meeks Creek on the left. Continue along the dusty road to a junction about 1.5 miles from the trailhead.

Obeying signed directions for the Tahoe-Yosemite Trail, turn right (southwest) and leave the road behind to follow a climbing singletrack trail past luxuriant foliage bordering a seeping spring to the signed Desolation Wilderness boundary, 2.5 miles from the trailhead.

A moderate ascent on rocky trail continues and leads past a spring surrounded by thriving currant bushes and corn lilies. Above the spring, purple lupine and red paintbrush carpet the slope. Beyond the spring, the grade eases, and mountain junipers start to line the path.

MOUNTAIN JUNIPERS

These rugged trees with thick, sienna-barked trunks are members of the cypress family, very unlike the more common needle-bearing conifers of the High Sierra. Botanists consider junipers to be more closely related to incense cedars, also members of the cypress family. The twigs of junipers, incense cedars, and giant sequoias (not in the cypress family) are covered with overlapping scalelike leaves rather than needlelike leaves that extend from the twig as do the pines, firs, and spruces.

Nearing Meeks Creek, the sound of the gurgling stream delights passersby. Along the banks of a seep beside the creek, paintbrush, monkeyflower, columbine, and tiger lily blossom in early summer. Veering away from the stream, the sandy, now-level tread passes through a meadow and then a forested meadow glade of ferns before encountering another meadow holding a forest of drowned trees, bare and silvery in death. The large yellow flowers from a garden of mule ears soften the bleak ambiance created by the dead trees. A gentle-to-moderate ascent under sparse, mixed forest cover gives way to a short, moderate-to-steep climb on rocky trail, where red fir joins the other conifers.

RED FIRS

Sometimes referred to as silvertips, red firs are found between 5,000 and 9,000 feet in California, although they are most common around 7,000 and 8,000 feet. In fully developed stands, very little groundcover is found due to the lack of sunlight reaching the forest floor. Saprophytes—plants that don't perform photosynthesis, such as snow plant and pine drops—may be found randomly thrusting out of the shady soil.

Near a sturdy log-and-timber bridge over Meeks Creek is an attractive campsite—unfortunately, its close proximity to the creek makes the site illegal for camping. However, across the bridge and 80 yards upstream is a shady campsite that's suitable for overnight stays. Nearby, pan-size brook and brown trout lie in small holes shaded by thickets of dogwood, alder, willow, and mountain ash.

The sandy trail steadily ascends the east wall of the canyon, looping away from the creek to gain the height of a steep cascade, as the gracefully curved tips of mountain hemlocks

Scenic Crag Lake in Desolation Wilderness   Photo by Mike White

herald your arrival in the higher elevations. Just beyond a waterfall, the trail leads to a junction with the seldom-used Lake Genevieve Trail and then soon reaches the shore of Lake Genevieve, a shallow, warm, pine-rimmed, green lake. A few fair campsites at the north end and along the east side provide views across the water of photogenic Peak 9,054, a beautiful sight in early morning with sunrise light crowning a mantle of blue shadows. Campsites at Genevieve and the upcoming lakes are limited and are generally fair to poor in quality. With the canyon's floor shoehorned between steep ridges, the campsites are sandwiched tightly between the trail and the shorelines.

From Lake Genevieve the trail makes a short, gentle ascent under red fir, western white pine, and Jeffrey pine to Crag Lake, where fair campsites on the glacial moraine forming the east side of the lake's basin may tempt overnighters.

DAMS
The flow-maintenance dam across Crag Lake's outlet is one of many such dams in the high country built by the state's Department of Fish and Game (DF&G), U.S. Forest Service, or private sportsmen's groups. DF&G biologists and wardens making adjustments of the outlet valve during the summer ensure adequate flow continues into Meeks Creek.

The route now ascends moderately on rocky tread to a ford of Meeks Creek. Just beyond the ford is a junction with a path right (south) and down to Hidden Lake, which appears through gaps in the forest a short distance farther up the trail. Despite increasing use and subsequent fishing pressure, Hidden Lake seems to maintain a healthy population of brook trout.

Go ahead (southeast) here, veering away from the creek, to make a gentle ascent through dense pine forest that passes above meadow-bordered and lily-dotted Shadow Lake. Make a steady diagonal ascent up a curving moraine, beside rapids and cataracts, to Stony Ridge Lake, the largest of the six Tallant Lakes occupying this valley, 6.3 miles from the trailhead.

Backpackers will find fair campsites near the outlet, as well as a few along the west shore. Anglers can test their skills on both rainbow and brown trout. A forest primarily of lodge-pole pines rims the lake except along the eastern shore. A short distance up the rocky western slope, gray-green sagebrush calls into question the notion that sagebrush defines desert.

At the head of Stony Ridge Lake, make a slight ascent overlooking a pond and a green, marshy meadow above the lake. For the next half mile, the trail is mostly level across a wet hillside carpeted by the best flower gardens seen so far on the TYT. After a 300-foot elevation gain via a series of switchbacks, the trail turns south, paralleling the east side of a small, north-facing glacial cirque. Black, lichen-streaked cliffs stand 200 feet high above a talus-block fan. In early season, the wide, sweeping snowbank in this cirque, stained red by millions of minute algae, is a small reminder of the glacier that sculpted the curving headwall.

Eight miles from the trailhead you find Rubicon Lake (8,277'; 38.96675°N, 120.13523°W), the crown jewel of the Tallant Lakes. Encircled by lodgepole pines and mountain hemlocks, the green-tinted lake offers a number of fair-to-good campsites scattered around its shoreline.

DAY 2 (Rubicon Lake to Dicks Lake, 7.1 miles): About 100 yards up the cool, shaded trail from Rubicon Lake is a lateral on the left to Grouse Lakes. The TYT goes right (ahead, south) here, and, after a couple of switchbacks, the snow-covered north slope of Mount Tallac springs into view above the gray-green valley of Eagle Creek.

On rocky trail, ascend moderately until the grade eases on a traverse of the far side of a ridge overlooking Grouse Lakes and the Eagle Creek drainage, along which Cascade and Fallen Leaf Lakes are visible to the southeast. Where the route to Phipps Lake departs to the right (west), the TYT continues ahead (south-southwest) as the traverse is interrupted by a set of steps of milled lumber held in place by steel pegs. For some unclear reason, the next section of trail contours around the south side of Phipps Peak until it heads almost due north, at which point hikers might begin to worry, knowing that they should be heading south toward the Velma Lakes. Ultimately, they will.

Dicks Peak comes into view near Phipps Pass, and some of the mountains of the Crystal Range appear over its right shoulder. You've been traveling through gray granite country since the beginning of the journey; now, the reddish-brown metasedimentary rocks of Dicks Peak and outliers are quite striking. Leaving the pass, the trail descends briefly but over the next half mile seems to climb more often than drop.

Soon, all three Velma Lakes come into view at once. Named for a daughter of Nevada mining king Harry Comstock, the lakes lie close together in a single basin—but Upper and Lower Velma Lakes drain into Lake Tahoe and ultimately Nevada's Pyramid Lake, while Middle Velma Lake drains into the Rubicon River and ultimately the Pacific Ocean. From this vantage point, experienced cross-country enthusiasts may elect to head straight for Middle Velma Lake, as the TYT route is quite indirect.

Veering west onto Phipps Peak's dry and exposed west flank, the TYT provides excellent views of the north part of the Crystal Range, including Rockbound Pass—the deepest notch visible—and the basins of Lakes Lois and Schmidell, landmarks that remain visible for a mile or more as the trail arcs around Phipps Peak. Finally, at a hairpin turn, the trail heads back toward Velma Lakes. A few yards northwest of this turn, a viewpoint overlooks much of Rockbound Valley, including the namesake lake, which sits near the wilderness's northwest corner. Beyond this vista point, a steady, sandy descent incorporating three long switchbacks passes through moderate-to-dense forest cover to a junction with the 2,600-mile PCT, 4 miles from Rubicon Lake.

Turn left (south-southeast) onto the southbound PCT. From the PCT junction to Middle Velma Lake, the route wanders more than seems necessary, eventually crossing a sluggish creek to reach the first of two junctions with the Velma Lakes Trail, which here heads right (generally west) to Camper Flat on the Rubicon River. The PCT/TYT, briefly joined by the Velma Lakes Trail, goes left (generally east) at this junction. At the southwest end of forested Middle Velma Lake, the PCT/TYT skirts a cove and rises above the lake into red fir forest.

The shady duff tread of the PCT/TYT soon leads to the second junction with the Velma Lakes Trail, which here goes left (east) while the PCT/TYT goes right (generally south). (To visit Upper Velma Lake, make a 200-yard stroll up this trail to a junction marked by a post and turn south, reaching the southwest shore of the lake after another half a mile. Backpackers will find fair campsites near the inlet.)

POCKET GOPHER TUNNELS

In a meadow of sedge and corn lilies, where the trail first nears Upper Velma Lake, "ropes" of soil are the telltale signs of the pocket gopher. During the winter, the rodent tunnels in the snow to eat the aboveground parts of plants. Later, the gopher tunnels in the earth, filling the snow tunnels with the extracted dirt. Following snowmelt, these casts of dirt that once filled snow tunnels descend to the ground, where you see them.

From the second Velma Lakes Trail junction, the PCT/TYT ascends south on a moderate grade while overlooking Upper Velma Lake. As the slope eases to gentle, Dicks Pass, Lake Tahoe, and then Fontanillis Lake come into view. After a short, gentle descent, cross the outlet and reach Fontanillis Lake, cradled in a rocky basin and towered over by Dicks Peak. Fair campsites are shaded by stands of lodgepole pines and mountain hemlocks. On the east shore, a lavish display of red and sienna rocks complements the familiar gray granite—scramble up the slope to find them.

Leaving Fontanillis Lake, the sandy trail ascends a boulder-covered granite hillside with several meltwater tarns that could offer a refreshing swim at just the right time of the season. At the top of this rise, there's a junction where a short lateral heads right (south) to Dicks Lake (8,429'; 38.91616°N, 120.14561°W). This cirque lake below Dicks Peak offers several fair campsites and one good one on the timbered east shore. Anglers will appreciate a self-sustaining population of brook trout.

DAY 3 (Dicks Lake to Tarn Above Heather Lake, 7.4 miles): At the junction of the PCT/TYT and the Dicks Lake lateral, the PCT/TYT turns north (left if you've not gone down to Dicks Lake, right if you are coming from the lake) and proceeds a short distance to another junction in a saddle overlooking the drainage of Eagle Creek to the east. Turn right (southeast) here as the rocky trail ascends steadily on a granite slope sparsely dotted with lodgepole pines. Far below, a large area of downed timber on the southwest slope of the Dicks Lake cirque provides graphic evidence of a former avalanche.

The grade increases as more than a dozen switchbacks assault the northwest slope of Peak 9,579, which often remains snow covered into July. The ascent concludes at Dicks Pass (9,380'), which is somewhat east of the actual low point of the divide. Standing at the pass with pack off and shoulders recuperating, the backpacker surveys a considerable part of California, from Sierra Buttes beyond Yuba Pass in the north to Round Top beyond Carson Pass in the south. Nearer to the south, Pyramid Peak rises majestically above island-dotted Lake Aloha, and from just beyond the pass, Susie and Grass Lakes are clearly seen in the wooded basin of Glen Alpine Creek. The trail sign at the pass stands at the center of several almost flat acres, strewn with the rocky products of erosion. The surrounding trees are all whitebark pines, the highest-dwelling conifer encountered along the TYT. When snowmelt provides a reliable source of water, good campsites provide an overnight haven east of the pass.

Descending from the pass to the actual saddle, Susie, Gilmore, and Half Moon Lakes and Lake Aloha can be seen ahead, while Fontanillis and Dicks Lakes are visible to the rear. The trail descends the warm, south-facing slope, and when there is still much snow on the north side, the south side offers a springtime display of vibrant wildflowers, including paintbrush, sulfur flower, white heather, western wallflower, white and lavender phlox, and elderberry. At the saddle on this divide, a use trail provides access westward to the summit of Dicks Peak.

Go left (southeast) here to stay on the PCT/TYT as it traverses gently down the side of a ridge toward Gilmore Lake. Along this traverse, the variety of wildflowers seems to multiply with each step. At the peak of the blossoming season, delphinium, deer brush, spiraea, creamberry, red heather, buckwheat, groundsel, serviceberry, corn lily, penstemon, white heather, pussypaws, and buttercups will delight passersby. Near the first sign of red firs, a lateral heads left (northeast) a short way to Gilmore Lake, where backpackers will find good campsites and anglers can test their skill on three species of trout. For peak baggers, the trail to Gilmore Lake continues toward the 9,735-foot, view-packed summit of Mount Tallac.

The PCT/TYT goes right (ahead, east) at the junction to begin a switchbacking descent through mixed forest to a junction where a trail on the right heads north to Half Moon Lake and a trail to the left goes east-southeast to Glen Alpine. You go ahead (southwest) on the PCT/TYT down rocky trail toward Susie Lake for a half mile to a swampy, flower-filled meadow and a junction with another trail left (south) to Glen Alpine and Fallen Leaf Lake. Go right (west-southwest) and make a short, moderate, winding ascent that culminates at a rise overlooking Susie Lake, one of the most popular lakes in Desolation Wilderness, despite the poor-to-fair campsites. After crossing the outlet, a difficult ford in early season, the PCT/TYT meets a use trail heading down the canyon to large, forested campsites.

Staying on the PCT/TYT, curve right (southwest) to continue around the shore of Susie Lake and then climb steadily up to the V at the outlet of the Heather Lake basin, formed by the slopes of Jacks Peak on the north and Cracked Crag on the south. (In early season there is always snow here.) Notice the clear line of division on Jacks Peak that separates the metasedimentary rock of the "Mount Tallac pendant" and the gray granite to the south. Follow a rocky

Aloha Lake   Photo by Mike White

course well above Heather Lake over a small ridge and then just above a placid tarn. Although Heather Lake offers no decent, legal places to camp, good campsites can be found beside a tarn (8,022'; 38.87756°N, 120.14490°W) that lies just below the headwall of the lake's cirque. This is the better place to stop, as upcoming Lake Aloha is extremely windy and has almost no decent, legal campsites. Heather Lake has rainbow, brook, and brown trout.

DAY 4 (Tarn Above Heather Lake to Echo Summit, 7.7 miles or 5.0 miles via water taxi): A short, rocky climb leads to the crest of the divide that separates the Heather Lake basin and Desolation Valley. This high point offers a magnificent, close-up view of the Crystal Range.

CRYSTAL RANGE

Rising above the far shore of shallow, island-dotted Lake Aloha, this classic range is a superb glacial ridge left standing high after moving ice on both sides plucked immense quantities of rock from its flanks and carried them downslope. Parts of the ridge are knife edged—which geologists call an *arête*—and snowfields at the base of the knife blade look like little glaciers.

Foregrounding Mount Price, Pyramid Peak, and the peaks between is a blue sheet of water, Lake Aloha, which is more than 2 miles long and dotted with a thousand tiny granite islands, some of which harbor a single weather-beaten lodgepole snag. Campsites at Lake Aloha are very few, very poor, and very windy. However, some will find camping near the lake worthwhile for the sight of the morning sun turning the Crystal Range from blue-gray to gold.

Nearing the northeast edge of Lake Aloha, the trail to Mosquito Pass and Rockbound Valley heads right (west), but the PCT/TYT veers left (southeast) to follow the shore of the lake, composed of glacier-polished, barren granite. After 0.5 mile the trail turns and immediately comes to a flat, where an unsigned and little-used spur darts left (north) to Lake Le Conte. This lake has several small, fair campsites on the east side. The PCT/TYT goes right and continues southeast around Lake Aloha's shore.

DESOLATION VALLEY

Even in this "desolation valley," formerly called Devils Basin, life is plentiful. Coyotes are often heard and sometimes seen, and yellow-bellied marmots virtually infest the talus slopes of Cracked Crag. Water snakes and skinks fill their ecological niches. Lake Aloha itself has thousands of brook and rainbow trout. Wildflowers abound, and besides lodgepole pine, conifers include mountain hemlock, western white pine, red fir, and junipers.

Approaching sparse forest cover, as stands of lodgepole pine alternate with meadows, the PCT/TYT goes left (southeast) at a junction with a trail straight ahead (south) to Lake of the Woods. After a short ascent, the trail enters a highly scenic area, where, in early to midseason, numerous tarns reflect the green pines and hemlocks and the house-size gray boulders dumped here by the glacier. Near the westernmost tarn, a trail to Lakes Margery and Lucille leads off left (east) to good campsites around both lakes and to bearably warm swimming. The PCT/TYT goes right (southeast).

In a short quarter mile, a well-used spur trail from Lake Aloha merges with the TYT from the right, and 0.3 mile farther, the southern trail to Lake Lucille goes left (north). The excavated, level patch of ground next to the junction once held a log cabin used by trail crews and others needing emergency shelter. Go right (east-southeast) here to stay on the PCT/TYT.

The PCT/TYT next meets a pair of laterals that go right to Lake of the Woods, one in about 200 yards from the last junction and the other 350 yards farther on. Continue ahead (east-southeast) on the PCT/TYT at both junctions as the wide, sandy trail skirts above

Haypress Meadows, site of one of the largest expanses of grass on the TYT. The grass was once harvested for sale to wagon trains crossing Echo Summit. Raised walkways help protect the fragile meadows from being trampled. As the PCT/TYT passes an abandoned trail, Echo Lakes come into view down the valley of Echo Creek, and the trail becomes steep and rocky. Where a trail veers left (east) up the hill toward Lily and Fallen Leaf Lakes, the PCT/TYT continues ahead (east-southeast) toward Echo Lakes. At the last switchback in a series, rocks to sit on, water, and shade provide a fine place for a rest stop.

Watch your footing on the next section, a long traverse down a moderately graded tread filled with loose granite rocks. Even though many day hikers and equestrians routinely travel this far from Echo Lakes, it's hard to justify the extensive blasting and grading of this section of trail that many refer to as a freeway.

Go left (briefly northeast) at a junction with a lateral right (southwest) to Tamarack Lake (camping prohibited) and reenter forest: a heavy cover of lodgepole, later thinning somewhat and showing inclusions of Jeffrey pine. Beyond the forest, another unsigned trail to the Fallen Leaf Lake area goes left (north) up the hill as the PCT/TYT continues ahead (generally southeast). Exit Desolation Wilderness in 300 more yards and soon encounter the signed lateral going right to the water taxi landing at the north shore of Upper Echo Lake.

> **WATER TAXI**
> The Echo Lake Chalet offers water taxi service from the resort's upper dock at the south end of Lower Echo Lake to the public dock at the far end of Upper Echo Lake, reducing the hiking distance by 2.5 miles. The normal season runs from the Fourth of July through Labor Day weekend, although service is usually extended through September, depending on weather conditions and lake levels. The fee in 2019 was $15 per person one-way with a three-person minimum for service. A direct-line phone to the Chalet at the upper dock can be used to arrange for pickup. (Visit their website, echochalet.net, or call 530-659-7207, 8 a.m.–6 p.m. during summer, for more information.)

Beyond the water taxi lateral, the trail skirts the north side of Upper and Lower Echo Lakes. The 2.5-mile walk is unremarkable on a wide and well-trod trail that travels discouragingly high above the lakes. The final section is on a dusty, exposed, south-facing slope, making the trip uncomfortably warm in the afternoon sun.

After a milkshake or other morale-booster at Echo Lake Resort, take a very steep trail from the back of the public restrooms next to the resort up to the large parking lot (an alternate end point if you want to skip the last 1.75 miles between the Echo Lake and Echo Summit Trailheads), and on the west edge of the paved lot, find a segment of PCT/TYT built in 1978. This segment first makes a long switchback leg west before turning east to climb gently through red firs above the many summer-home cabins. The trail veers south and then southwest and, just past a rusty tank on the left, meets a junction: Ahead is a 4WD road; turn left (southeast) to continue on the signed PCT. Immediately dip across a small seasonal stream and follow the trail on a gradual curve through white fir and lodgepole pine to meet paved Johnson Pass Road at a ditch so abrupt you may wish to cut left, almost to a driveway, to avoid it.

From the ditch intersection, angle right across the road toward PCT signs and continue gently winding down to meet US 50 about 100 yards east (uphill) of the defunct Little Norway Resort. Cross the highway and on the south side find the next section of trail, which crosses another ditch and turns left (south-southeast) to climb as it parallels the highway toward Echo Summit. After a mile, this section meets a paved road coming south from US 50. Turn right (south) onto the paved road and end your trip at a paved PCT trailhead parking lot (7,385'; 38.81487°N, 120.03408°W), south of which is an area that operates as Adventure Mountain Lake Tahoe resort in winter.

Bayview Trailhead					6,889'; 38.94354°N, 120.10004°W	
Destination/ GPS Coordinates	Trip Type	Best Season	Pace & Hiking/ Layover Days	Total Mileage	Permit Required	
6 Velma, Fontanillis, and Dicks Lakes 38.92595°N 120.15068°W (Upper Velma Lake)	Semiloop	Mid to late	Moderate 2/1	11.8	Desolation Wilderness: Lower Velma Zone	

INFORMATION AND PERMITS: All backpackers must secure and pay for a wilderness permit for entry into Desolation Wilderness. The region is heavily used, and strict quotas are in place for the number of overnighters departing from every trailhead that enters the wilderness. A majority of permits are available by reservation, with the remainder handed out on a first-come, first-served basis. Reserved permits may be obtained online at recreation.gov. During business hours, walk-in permits may be picked up at the Taylor Creek Visitor Center, Pacific Ranger Station, LTBMU Supervisor's Office, and LTBMU North Shore Office.

DRIVING DIRECTIONS: Follow CA 89 to Emerald Bay and find the turnoff for the Bayview Campground and Trailhead on the south side of the highway, approximately 7.5 miles from the junction of US 50 in South Lake Tahoe, or 19.5 miles south from the junction of CA 28 in Tahoe City. The trailhead is at the south end of Bayview Campground.

trip 6   **Velma, Fontanillis, and Dicks Lakes**

see map on p. 46

> **Trip Data:** 38.92595°N, 120.15068°W (Upper Velma Lake); 11.8 miles; 2/1 days
> **Topos:** *Emerald Bay, Rockbound Valley*

HIGHLIGHTS: This hike through the heart of Desolation Wilderness visits several cirque-bound lakes surrounded by the characteristic granite terrain for which the area is renowned.

DAY 1 (Bayview Trailhead to Upper Velma Lake, 4.7 miles): Soon after leaving the trailhead, turn right to go generally southwest at a junction with the trail on the left to Cascade Lake. Follow a steep, switchbacking climb through mixed forest. After crossing the Desolation Wilderness boundary, follow the crest of a ridge, from where good views of Emerald Bay and Lake Tahoe appear through gaps in the forest. Leave the ridge and follow the alder-lined outlet of Granite Lake on a gentle ascent through lush foliage, reaching the hillside above Granite Lake. To visit the lake, drop down to the shoreline via one of the use trails on the northwest side.

Well above the far end of the lake, the Bayview Trail begins a steep, switchbacking climb across the south-facing slope below Maggies Peaks. Exiting Granite Lake's basin, the grade mercifully eases to a gentle stroll along the back side of South Maggies Peak, followed by a gentle descent along the forested southwest ridge. You reach a junction with the Eagle Lake Trail at a saddle, 2.7 miles from the trailhead (8,179'; 38.92833°N, 120.12703°W).

Turn right (generally west) at the junction and follow sandy tread on a gently undulating route through scattered conifers and around granite boulders and slabs for 0.6 mile to a junction with the Velma Lakes Trail (8,228'; 38.92644°N, 120.13714°W).

Bear right (north-northwest) here and descend, with occasional glimpses through scattered pines of the unnamed pond directly north of Upper Velma Lake. Reach the floor of

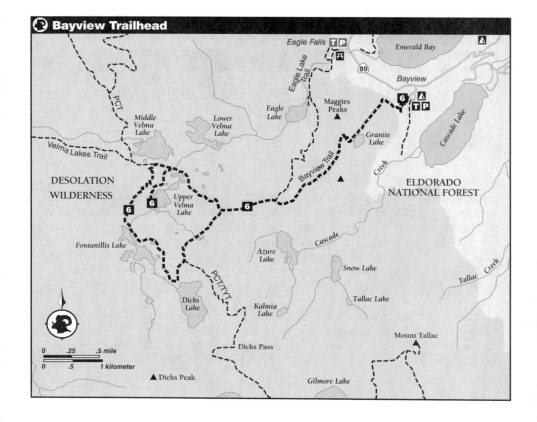

the basin and follow the north shore of the pond to a ford of the outlet and to a junction just beyond, 4.1 miles from the trailhead. Turn left (south) and proceed 0.6 mile to campsites near the inlet on the southwest shore of Upper Velma Lake (7,966'; 38.92595°N, 120.15068°W).

DAY 2 (Upper Velma Lake to Bayview Trailhead, 7.1 miles): Retrace your steps 0.6 mile to the last junction and turn left (west) to make a short climb to a junction with the Pacific Crest Trail (PCT) (7,958'; 38.93346°N, 120.14898°W). (To see Middle Velma Lake, continue west on the PCT a short distance to a fine viewpoint. A number of pleasant and popular campsites on the south shore are easily reached cross-country from the PCT.)

To continue the loop part of this trip, follow the PCT south-southwest on a moderate, winding climb along a forested ridge above the west shore of Upper Velma Lake.

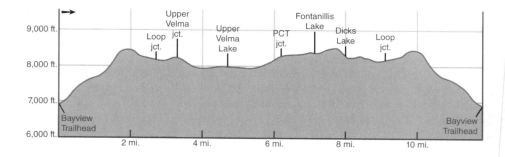

Eventually, Dicks Pass and Fontanillis Lake pop into view as the trees thin and the grade eases. A short drop leads to the crossing of Fontanillis Lake's outlet, followed by a traverse across the east side of the lake's multihued rock basin, which lies in the shadow of towering Dicks Peak. Legal campsites are absent on the trailside of the lake, but open benches above the west shore provide a number of excellent opportunities for overnight accommodations.

Leaving Fontanillis Lake, a brief ascent across boulder-covered slopes leads to the top of a rise and a junction with a 100-yard lateral right (south) to Dicks Lake. Backpackers will find excellent, although popular, campsites on the north shore and east peninsula of Dicks Lake.

Assuming you don't take the lateral, the PCT heads left (generally north), away from Dicks Lake, on an easy ascent to a junction where the PCT and the Tahoe-Yosemite Trail (TYT) turn right (southeast) toward Dicks Pass. You go ahead here (north) to descend moderate switchbacks to the floor of a pond-dotted basin, and then traverse the basin northeastward to the junction of the Eagle Lake and Velma Lakes Trails, closing the loop part of this trip.

From there, turn right (east) and retrace your steps 2.7 miles past Granite Lake to the Bayview Trailhead.

A glorious view of Lake Tahoe and Emerald Bay from the trail to Velma Lakes   Photo by Mike White

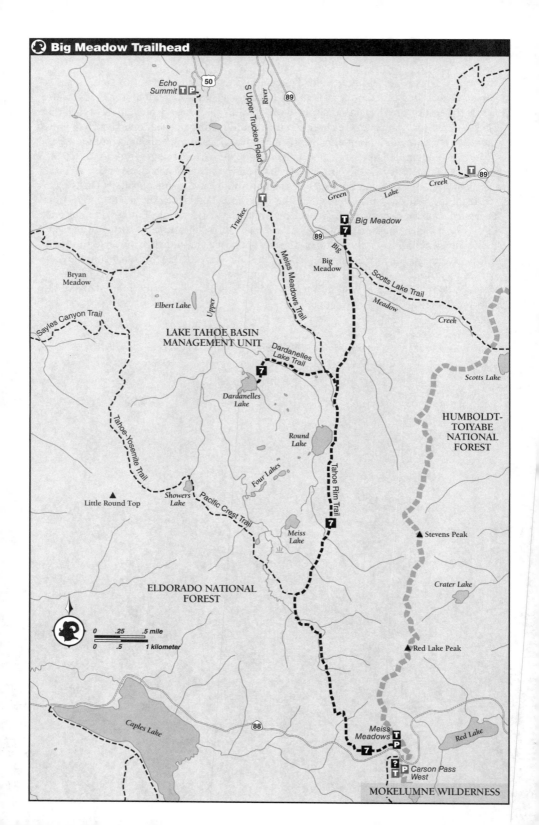

Big Meadow Trailhead			7,257'; 38.78867°N, 120.00077°W		
Destination/ GPS Coordinates	Trip Type	Best Season	Pace & Hiking/ Layover Days	Total Mileage	Permit Required
7 Meiss Meadows 38.69672°N 119.99189°W	Shuttle	Mid to late	Moderate 2/0	10.9	None for backpacking

INFORMATION AND PERMITS: Meiss Country is administered by the Lake Tahoe Basin Management Unit: USDA Forest Service, Lake Tahoe Basin Management Unit, 35 College Dr., South Lake Tahoe, CA 96150; 530-543-2600, fs.usda.gov/ltbmu. No wilderness permits are required, but you must have a California Campfire Permit to have a campfire or use a stove. Day-use parking fee at the Meiss Meadows Trailhead parking lot is $5.

DRIVING DIRECTIONS: Drive on CA 89 to the well-signed Big Meadow/Tahoe Rim Trail parking lot, 6 miles from the CA 88 junction in Hope Valley, and 5 miles from the US 50 junction near Meyers.

trip 7 **Meiss Meadows**

> **Trip Data:** 38.69672°N, 119.99189°W; 10.9 miles; 2/0 days
> **Topos:** *Caples Lake, Carson Pass*

HIGHLIGHTS: This trip travels through the heart of the Meiss Meadows area. Following sections of the Tahoe Rim Trail (TRT), the unofficial Tahoe-Yosemite Trail (TYT), and the Pacific Crest Trail (PCT), recreationists can travel from CA 89 to CA 88, visiting Big Meadow, Dardanelles Lake, Round Lake, and Meiss Meadows along the way.

SHUTTLE DIRECTIONS: To get to the Meiss Meadows Trailhead, follow CA 88 0.3 mile west of Carson Pass. There's a daily fee of $5 to park, and the drive between the trailheads is approximately 16 miles.

DAY 1 (Big Meadow Trailhead to Dardanelles Lake, 4.0 miles): Leave the southwest side of the parking area and follow the singletrack TRT a short distance to a crossing of CA 89. Once across the highway, pick up the TRT and start a winding, moderate, southward climb through a forest of Jeffrey pines, lodgepole pines, and red firs. At a switchback, you have a fine view of the aspen-lined, rocky channel of Big Meadow Creek, which is vibrantly alive with snowmelt in early July and golden color in autumn. Following more switchbacks, the grade eases just before reaching a junction a half mile from the trailhead, where a trail to Scotts Lake branches left (southeast).

Go right (south) at the junction and quickly leave the trees behind, emerging into grassy, flower-covered Big Meadow. Follow the trail through the meadow to a wood-plank bridge that spans the gurgling creek and proceed to the far edge, where a lightly forested ascent resumes. Sagebrush, currant, and drought-tolerant wildflowers, principally mule ears, line the path. Farther up the trail, wood-beam-reinforced steps help you over the steeper sections of trail that follows a diminishing tributary of Big Meadow Creek, a sprightly watercourse lined with luxuriant foliage.

Continue climbing to a densely forested saddle and then follow a switchbacking descent into the next canyon, through which flows an Upper Truckee River tributary. Reach the floor of the canyon and proceed to a junction marked by a post, where you meet the Dardanelles Lake Trail.

Turn right (west) and make a very brief descent to a junction with the Meiss Meadows Trail. Immediately past the junction, ford an Upper Truckee River tributary, and soon ford a wider stretch of the stream. Early in the season, search for logs upstream in order to avoid getting your feet wet. Away from the streams, stroll across a bench holding a small meadow and seasonal ponds.

Descend from the bench through a dense forest of western white pines, red firs, and lodgepole pines and follow an alder-and-willow-lined stream down a canyon. The grade eases as the trail passes through meadowlike vegetation of grasses, wildflowers, and willows on the way to a boulder hop of Round Lake's outlet. A short climb amid boulders and granite slabs leads to the east shore of Dardanelles Lake (7,762'; 38.76036°N, 120.02030°W), 1.3 miles from the TRT. Far enough off the thoroughfare of the TRT, you may be able to enjoy the relative seclusion of this lake. The lakeshore is shaded by light forest and dotted with boulders and slabs, and the picturesque cliffs of the Dardanelles loom above the south shore.

DAY 2 (Dardanelles Lake to Meiss Meadows Trailhead, 6.9 miles): Retrace your steps 1.3 miles back to the Meiss Meadows Trail junction, going right (southeast) at the last junction you passed and continuing to the next junction, where you turn right (south) onto the TRT.

From this junction, the TRT follows a steady climb through dense forest. After 0.6 mile, you crest the lip of Round Lake's basin above the northeast shore and reach an informal junction. From the junction, a use trail wraps around the lake's west shore, which is lined with rock outcrops and scattered forest, and then follows a cross-country route to Meiss Lake. You continue south on the TRT, skirting the east shore of Round Lake below the ziggurat-like formation that towers above and passing through thick forest, staying away from the lush meadows and thick willows bordering the inlet at the south end.

Beyond the lake, the climb resumes, soon reaching an extensive sloping meadow carpeted with willows, wildflowers, and other lush foliage, well watered by a thin, rock-lined rivulet spilling across the trail. Past the meadow, you reenter forest cover and hop across a pair of trickling rivulets. Eventually the grade eases to a mellow stroll where the trail breaks out into an open forest sprinkled with stands of aspen and swaths of drier groundcover, including sagebrush, currant, grasses, and drought-tolerant wildflowers.

Part of extensive Meiss Meadows soon appears through scattered lodgepole pines to the right of the trail, with out-of-sight Meiss Lake lying just a third of a mile to the west (an optional out-and-back detour). Leaving the meadow behind, hop across Round Lake's inlet and proceed to cross a creek that runs through a rocky channel 0.4 mile farther, where open terrain allows views of the rugged slopes leading up to 10,059-foot Stevens Peak. Continue

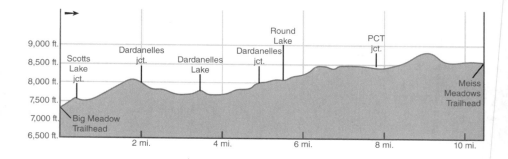

on gently graded trail through lodgepole pines to the heart of Meiss Meadows and a well-signed junction with the PCT/TYT.

> **BYGONE DAYS**
>
> Near the junction, an old cabin harkens back to the days, not so long ago, when cattle were allowed to graze the lush grasses of picturesque and pastoral Meiss Meadows. This was once Meiss Cow Camp. Fortunately, the cows are gone, the trampling of the meadows is over, the cow pies have decomposed, and the trails have been left to wildlife and humans.

Leaving the TRT, you turn left (south) on the PCT/TYT at the junction and stroll across the pleasant meadowlands, making several crossings of the nascent Upper Truckee River along the way. Eventually the terrain gets steeper as the trail begins a moderate climb of the narrowing gorge toward a saddle at the head of the canyon. Wildflowers grace the slopes on the way, and just past a lovely pond you reach the saddle, from where there's a fine view north to Lake Tahoe and south to the jagged peaks of the Carson Pass area, including Elephants Back, Round Top, Sisters, Fourth of July Peak, and Thimble Peak. Red Lake Peak towers immediately to your left.

Leaving the saddle, the trail descends steeply across open hillsides and seasonal streams; these slopes are famed for their seasonal wildflower displays. The final leg of the journey is through a light forest on a long traverse across the hillside above CA 88. Early-season wildflowers are prevalent along this final stretch of trail, although intermittent highway noise may disrupt the ambiance a bit. Soon you reach the parking lot at the Meiss Meadows Trailhead (8,560'; 38.69672°N, 119.99189°W) just off noisy CA 88.

Hikers enjoy a view of Round Top and neighboring peaks on the way toward Meiss Meadows Trailhead. Photo by Mike White

Armstrong Pass Trailhead				8,289'; 38.83020°N, 119.90072°W	
Destination/ GPS Coordinates	Trip Type	Best Season	Pace & Hiking/ Layover Days	Total Mileage	Permit Required
8 Star Lake 38.87742°N 119.88954°W	Out-and-back	Mid to late	Moderate 2/1	11.6	None for backpacking

INFORMATION AND PERMITS: The area around Star Lake is administered by the Lake Tahoe Basin Management Unit: U.S. Forest Service, Lake Tahoe Basin Management Unit, 35 College Drive, South Lake Tahoe, CA 96150; 530-543-2600; fs.usda.gov/ltbmu. No wilderness permits are required, but you must have a California Campfire Permit to have a campfire or use a stove.

DRIVING DIRECTIONS: Take CA 89, south from the junction of US 50 in Meyers or north from Picketts Junction with CA 88, to Forest Service Road 051, which is 1.8 miles below Luther Pass. Follow the sometimes-rough dirt tread northwest for nearly 3.5 miles to an intersection with FS 051F on your left, which is blocked to traffic by large boulders (this intersection is immediately after the second bridge over Willow Creek). Park your vehicle along the roadside as space allows.

trip 8   Star Lake

> **Trip Data:** 38.87742°N, 119.88954°W; 11.6 miles; 2/1 days
> **Topos:** *Freel Peak* (trail not shown on map)

HIGHLIGHTS: Follow a section of the Tahoe Rim Trail (TRT) to Star Lake, the Tahoe Basin's highest lake, if not for the much-less-impressive-looking Mud Lake on the northeast shore. Backdropped by volcanic slopes of rugged Jobs Sister, the lake is one of the area's most beautiful. A layover day offers the opportunity to hike to the summit of Freel Peak, the highest peak in the basin at 10,881 feet.

DAY 1 (Armstrong Pass Trailhead to Star Lake, 5.8 miles): From the parking area, head west on the dirt road for 0.5 mile to a wide turnaround, where a TRT sign designates the beginning of singletrack trail. Climb moderately steeply, soon crossing a diminutive tributary of Willow Creek. Beyond the creek, switchbacks zigzag up a hillside covered with sagebrush, currant, and tobacco brush below widely scattered western white pines and junipers. The stiff climb abates a mile from the trailhead at the saddle of Armstrong Pass amid a light forest of red firs, where you reach a four-way junction with the Tahoe Rim and Trout Creek Trails.

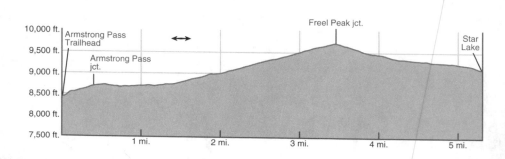

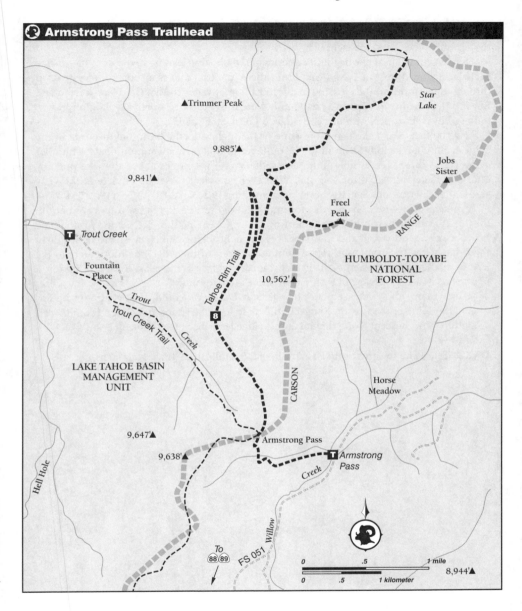

Armstrong Pass Trailhead

▲Trimmer Peak

9,885'▲

9,841'▲

Star Lake

Jobs Sister ▲

T *Trout Creek*

Fountain Place

Freel Peak ▲

RANGE

HUMBOLDT-TOIYABE NATIONAL FOREST

Tahoe Rim Trail

Trout

Trout Creek Trail

Creek

8

10,562'▲

LAKE TAHOE BASIN MANAGEMENT UNIT

CARSON

Horse Meadow

9,647'▲

9,638'▲

Armstrong Pass

T *Armstrong Pass*

Creek

Hell Hole

To (88)(89)

FS 051

Willow

| 0 | | .5 | | 1 mile |
| 0 | .5 | | 1 kilometer | |

8,944'▲

Turn right and follow the pleasantly graded TRT on a rising traverse below the west side of the Carson Range crest. You soon emerge from the forest onto mostly open slopes, dotted occasionally by a western white pine or juniper. Past the rock cliff known as Fountain Face, you have fine views of the Trout Creek drainage and the meadows below in Hell Hole and Fountain Place, as well as across the shimmering surface of Lake Tahoe to the Crystal Range towering over Desolation Wilderness. Continue the steadily rising traverse, hopping over a few tiny rivulets along the way. Just shy of 3.5 miles, the trail angles across the slope via the first of a pair of long-legged switchbacks. About 1.25 miles farther, the climb reaches a crescendo at 9,730 feet at the base of the northwest ridge of Freel Peak. Here, the trail to the summit veers off to the right.

The descent to Star Lake begins on a series of switchbacks leading to the floor of a cirque basin north-northwest of Freel Peak. From there, the trail makes a short, moderate drop through open forest to the crossing of a thin ribbon of water from a Cold Creek tributary. Beyond the stream, you follow a nearly mile-long traverse to the north ridge of Jobs Sister, followed by a short decline along the ridge to lovely Star Lake.

At 9,100 feet, Star Lake is not only one of the highest in the basin but also one of the coldest, although a chilly swim might be quite refreshing on a hot summer day. A number of overused campsites can be found along the shore, with ones above the lake possibly offering greater potential for solitude. Wherever you elect to set up your tent, the view across the water of Jobs Sister is never disappointing (9,155'; 38.87742°N, 119.88954°W).

If you choose to use a layover day for the ascent of Freel Peak, retrace your steps back to the junction at the base of the peak's northwest ridge. Leaving the TRT behind for the time being, ascend sandy tread and rock steps on a switchbacking climb across the right side of the ridge below rock outcrops. After gaining the crest of the ridge, the route veers to the left on an angling ascent across the gravelly northwest face of the peak. Reaching the top, a marvelous 360-degree view of the greater Tahoe area unfolds.

Rather than simply retrace your steps to Star Lake, you could double summit by following the spine of the Carson Range a mile or so to 10,823-foot Jobs Sister. From there a straightforward descent along the northwest ridge leads back to the lake.

DAY 2 (Star Lake to Armstrong Pass Trailhead, 5.8 miles): Retrace your steps.

US 50 TRIPS

Merely driving US 50 can be a visual treat; for hikers, there's even more: the beauty of Desolation Wilderness north of the highway and of Meiss Country to the south. We offer a trip from each of these trailheads (from west to east): Wrights Lake's Twin Lakes Trailhead north of the highway and into Desolation Wilderness, Echo Lakes Trailhead also into Desolation, and the Echo Summit Trailhead south of the highway into Meiss Country.

The scenic Wrights Lake area is a favorite gateway to western Desolation Wilderness. Despite this popularity, backpackers willing to step off the trail can still find peace and quiet amid the extraordinary scenery.

Meiss Country is the headwaters of the Truckee River and a beautiful region of wildflowers, streams, lakes, meadows, and peaks.

Note that this book has two Twin Lakes Trailheads: this one, starting from US 50, and another from US 395.

Trailheads: Twin Lakes

Echo Lakes

Echo Summit

Twin Lakes Trailhead					6,962'; 38.85011°N, 120.22624°W
Destination/ GPS Coordinates	Trip Type	Best Season	Pace & Hiking/ Layover Days	Total Mileage	Permit Required
9 Island, Tyler, and Gertrude Lakes Loop 38.87565°N 120.19080°W (Island Lake)	Loop	Mid to late	Moderate, part cross-country 2/0	8.0	Desolation Wilderness: Twin Zone

INFORMATION AND PERMITS: All backpackers must secure and pay for a wilderness permit for entry into Desolation Wilderness. The region is heavily used, and strict zone quotas are in place for the number of overnighters departing from every trailhead that enters the wilderness. A majority of permits are available by reservation, with the remainder handed out on a first-come, first-served basis. Reserved permits may be obtained online at recreation .gov. During business hours, walk-in permits may be picked up at the Taylor Creek Visitor Center, Pacific Ranger Station, LTBMU Supervisor's Office, and LTBMU North Shore Office.

DRIVING DIRECTIONS: Approximately 4 miles west of Strawberry, turn north from US 50 onto Forest Service Road 4 and, following signs for Wrights Lake, drive 8 miles on FS 4 past the Lyons Creek Trailhead and a junction with FS 32 to the vicinity of Wrights

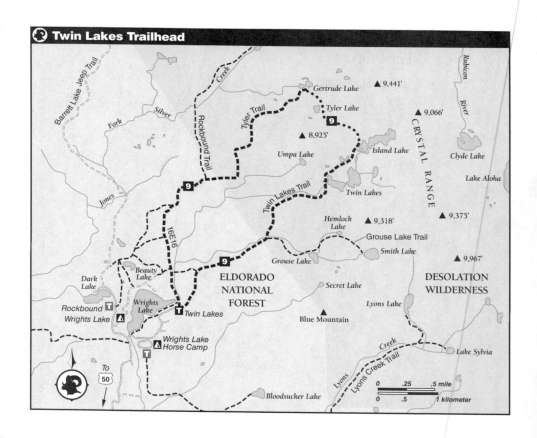

Lake. At a stop sign near the Wrights Lake Visitor Information Center, 0.1 mile past the entrance to the Equestrian Camp and Bloodsucker Lake Trailhead, turn right and proceed on a narrow, paved road 0.8 mile to the end of the pavement at the Twin Lakes Trailhead parking area. The trailhead, near the east end of Wrights Lake, is equipped with a pit toilet and bear-proof dumpster.

trip 9 Island, Tyler, and Gertrude Lakes Loop

> **Trip Data:** 38.87565°N, 120.19080°W (Island Lake); 8.0 miles; 2/0 days
> **Topos:** *Pyramid Peak, Rockbound Valley*

HIGHLIGHTS: Classic Desolation Wilderness scenery, including craggy granite peaks and glacier-scoured cirques harboring crystal-blue lakes, abounds on this trip into two tributary canyons of Silver Creek. While the maintained trails up both canyons are relatively short and accessible for scads of hikers and backpackers, the mile-long cross-country route over the ridge between is difficult enough to dissuade all but the hardy few from attempting this loop.

HEADS UP! *The cross-country leg on Day 2 is only for experienced backpackers with navigational and Class 2–3 climbing skills. Novice backpackers should return the way they came. Note that some maps are misleading: there is no trail directly to Tyler Lake; the maintained trail goes to Gertrude Lake.*

DAY 1 (Twin Lakes Trailhead to Island Lake, 3.25 miles): From the parking lot, walk down a very short section of paved road past a black steel gate and a bridge over Wrights Lake's lazy inlet (don't cross the bridge) to the start of the Twin Lakes Trail, marked by a Desolation Wilderness signboard. Proceed on a wide, gently graded dirt path through a mixed-forest canopy shading a lush understory of plants and flowers to a Y-junction with Trail 16E17 (signed LOOP). Turn right (northeast) and begin a stiff climb through alternating sections of open granite terrain and stands of mixed forest, crossing a trickling stream and the wilderness boundary on the way to a junction with the Grouse Lake Trail, marked by a post.

Following the directions for Twin Lakes, turn left (east) at the junction, immediately step across the seasonal outlet of Grouse Lake, and continue the ducked climb over granite slabs interspersed with scattered lodgepole pines. The stiff ascent is momentarily interrupted by an easy stretch of trail that leads near Twin Lakes' outlet creek. Following another section of steep, rocky climbing alongside the creek, the trail makes a brief descent past a small pond, followed by a slightly rising ascent to the sparsely treed west shore of Lower Twin Lake,

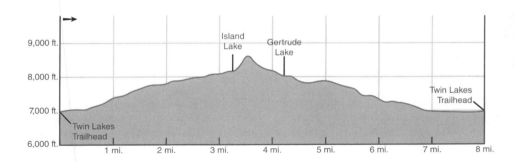

Wildflowers and pond near Twin Lakes   Photo by Mike White

where the deep blue water picturesquely reflects the towering granite walls of the basin's cirque. Decent campsites can be found amid the glacier-polished terrain between the two Twin Lakes. Anglers can ply the waters in search of rainbow and brook trout.

Cross the outlet of Lower Twin Lake on the stone remains of an old dam, follow the trail around the west shore, and then make a short, rocky climb to skirt Boomerang Lake's south shore. Beyond the lake, proceed through a lush pocket meadow and past a cigar-shaped pond. A short, steep, rocky, and winding climb leads to austere Island Lake (8,156'; 38.87565°N, 120.19080°W). As most parties seem content with either of the Twin Lakes as their destination, the open shoreline of rock-island-dotted Island Lake should offer campers a bit of peace and quiet (e.g., 8,149'; 38.87349°N, 120.190498°W). Because the fishing pressure is lower at Island Lake, anglers should do better here than at Twin Lakes. Mountaineers with a layover day could challenge themselves with a climb of 9,975-foot Mount Price.

DAY 2 (Island Lake to Twin Lakes Trailhead, 4.75 miles, part cross-country): From the west shore of Island Lake, leave the maintained trail and start climbing cross-country northwest up the steep slope above the lake, selecting a path that avoids the most brush en route to the crest of the ridge—aim for the low spot (8,596'; 38.87834°N, 120.19321°W) directly northeast of a tan-colored rock outcrop. A short section of Class 2–3 climbing just below the crest may be necessary in order to gain the ridge. Once at the top, views of both canyons are excellent.

The hardest part of the cross-country route is now over, as the climb from the crest down to Tyler Lake is less steep than the climb up from Island Lake. Initially, the way down travels roughly north over talus- and grass-covered slopes before an angling descent over granite slabs leads to the northeast shore of Tyler Lake (8,232'; 38.88083°N, 120.19808°W). Shaded by a smattering of droopy-tipped hemlocks and upright pines, rimmed with low granite humps and angled slabs, and occupying a cirque with less severe walls, the shoreline of Tyler Lake offers visitors more of a pastoral, subalpine ambiance than that of the alpine-looking lakes in the previous canyon. Despite the less dramatic scenery, the lake does offer a reasonable opportunity for solitude because, contrary to what you'll see on some maps, there exists no maintained trail or boot-beaten path from Tyler Lake to Gertrude Lake, where most visitors prefer to stop.

Go around Tyler's northeast shore to begin the short and straightforward descent to Gertrude Lake. A light forest canopy obscures your view of Gertrude Lake for much of the trip, so pay close attention to where you're going as you descend northwest and then north to Gertrude's south side (7,996'; 38.88400°N, 120.20093°W). Gertrude Lake is a shallow, irregularly shaped body of water encircled by a mixture of grasses, slabs, and stands of conifers, offering limited campsites.

Finding the maintained trail from the vicinity of Gertrude Lake may be a bit of a challenge—look for a large cairn or a series of ducks on the granite bench south of the lake. Having located the ducks or cairn, follow a ducked course southwest on a moderate descent over granite slabs and through boulder- and conifer-sprinkled terrain. Where the trail passes through groves of light forest, the tread becomes easier to follow. The heather-lined path crosses several seasonal meltwater streams before a gentle ascent leads past a small pond. Then a short, steep climb leads to the apex of the ridge dividing the drainage of Jones Fork Silver Creek from the drainage of South Fork Silver Creek.

Breaking out of the trees to open views of Wrights Lake, the trail descends steeply before briefly moderating through a stretch of light forest, where lush vegetation carpets the forest floor. A moderately steep descent resumes down open, shrub-covered terrain that offers excellent views of the canyon holding Twin Lakes. Cross the signed Desolation Wilderness boundary and follow a gently graded path to a post marking a junction with the Rockbound Trail.

Turn left and head southwest on the Rockbound Trail, climb over a low hill, and proceed on the gradually descending trail to another junction, a half mile from the previous one. Here, turn left (south), leaving the Rockbound Trail to follow Trail 16E16 (follow signs to Wrights Lake at all junctions).

From the junction, follow the gently graded, sandy trail through open terrain until a steeper descent on rocky trail leads back into the forest. Pass by an unmarked junction with a short connector southwest to the Rockbound Trail and proceed to a major junction, where two side trails enter, the first from the right and the second from the left several yards farther on. Continuing straight ahead at both side-trail junctions, you soon see a large meadow through the trees to the left, where Wrights Lake's inlet follows a lazy, serpentine course toward the reservoir. An easy stroll eventually leads alongside this stream and shortly to the well-constructed bridge over the inlet, where you close the loop. From there, follow the paved access road a very short distance back to the trailhead parking lot (6,962'; 38.85011°N, 120.22624°W).

Echo Lakes Trailhead

7,407'; 38.83501°N, 120.04416°W

Destination/ GPS Coordinates	Trip Type	Best Season	Pace & Hiking/ Layover Days	Total Mileage	Permit Required
10 Ropi Lake 38.83501°N 120.04416°W	Out-and-back	Mid to late	Moderate 2/1	8.8 (14.0 without water taxi)	Desolation Wilderness: Avalanche Zone

INFORMATION AND PERMITS: All backpackers must secure and pay for a wilderness permit for entry into Desolation Wilderness. The region is heavily used, and strict quotas are in place for the number of overnighters departing from every trailhead that enters the wilderness. A majority of permits are available by reservation, with the remainder handed out on a first-come, first-served basis. Reserved permits may be obtained online at recreation.gov. During business hours, walk-in permits may be picked up at the Taylor Creek Visitor Center, Pacific Ranger Station, LTBMU Supervisor's Office, and LTBMU North Shore Office.

DRIVING DIRECTIONS: Follow US 50 toward Echo Summit. Turn east onto Johnson Pass Road, 1.25 miles westbound of the summit and 1.8 miles eastbound of the Sierra-at-Tahoe ski resort, and proceed 0.5 mile to a left turn onto Echo Lakes Road. Continue up this road another 0.9 mile to the large trailhead parking lot above the south shore of Lower Echo Lake.

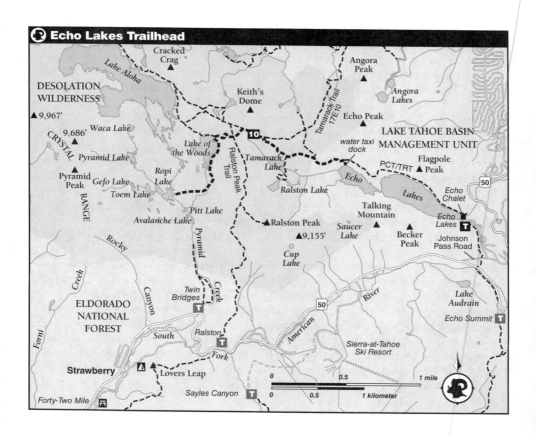

trip 10   **Ropi Lake**

> **Trip Data:** 38.83501°N, 120.04416°W; 8.8 miles (14.0 without water taxi); 2/1 days
> **Topos:** *Echo Lake*

HIGHLIGHTS: Numerous coves, islands, and campsites make Lake of the Woods a popular destination. The rest of Desolation Valley beyond is one of the most picturesque corners of Desolation
Wilderness, where a sparkling granite, glacier-scoured basin holds a plethora of picturesque lakes
and tarns, many of which are not accessible by developed and maintained trails, making the area
a cross-country enthusiast's dream. The beauty of the area is further highlighted by the majestic
profile of Pyramid Peak towering over the basin.

HEADS UP! *Taking the water taxi service from Echo Lake Chalet cuts off 2.5 miles of
uninteresting hiking along the shoreline of Echo Lakes. The service typically runs from the
Fourth of July through sometime in September, depending on weather conditions and
suitable water levels. Check out the resort's website for pricing and more information at
echochalet.com.*

DAY 1 (Echo Lakes Trailhead to Ropi Lake, 4.4 miles): *Note:* Without water taxi service,
you will have to walk the extra 2.6 miles around the north shore of Echo Lakes and add
that distance to the following mileages. From the water taxi pier at the north shore of Upper
Echo Lake, climb up the trail to the junction with the Pacific Crest Trail (PCT)/Tahoe
Rim Trail (TRT). Turn left and proceed on rocky tread across open slopes on a westbound
course away from the lake. Near the Desolation Wilderness boundary, 0.7 mile from the
pier, reach a junction with a lightly used trail heading north toward Triangle Lake. Travel
another 0.4 mile to another junction, this one with a short lateral on the left to Tamarack,
Ralston, and Cagwin Lakes. These pretty lakes are definitely worth a visit if you have the
extra time and energy.

Beyond the junction, the PCT/TRT follows a moderate climb to a crossing of a diminutive
rivulet coursing through a ravine. Then the trail continues up a pair of switchbacks to an
open bench and a junction with Tamarack Trail 17E10 heading east, 1.1 miles from the pier.

Gently ascending trail leads along the northern fringe of the broad expanse of grassy
Haypress Meadows, where early- to midsummer wildflowers put on a fine floral display.
Near the far end of the meadows, at 2 miles, you reach your junction with the trail to Lake
of the Woods.

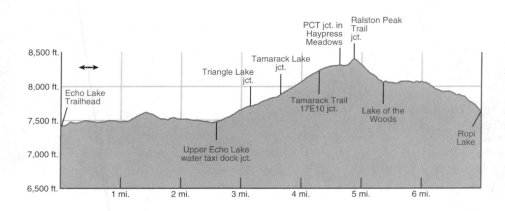

Leave the PCT/TRT and head southwest, skirting the edge of Haypress Meadows and climbing to the crest of a low ridge, where you intersect the Ralston Peak Trail.

Continue ahead, following a moderately steep switchbacking descent to a junction near the northwest shore of Lake of the Woods, 2.6 miles from the Upper Echo Lake pier. The aptly named, forest-rimmed lake offers visitors a peaceful feeling belying its popularity.

To reach Ropi Lake, head south along the east shore of Lake of the Woods and then make a brief ascent over the lip of the lake's basin. On descending tread, head down the canyon of the outlet to a crossing of the stream at 3.5 miles. From there, follow the trail as it bends west and descends around a knob to the east shore of Ropi Lake (7,636'; 38.83945°N, 120.12797°W). The sparse smattering of conifers around the lake afford excellent views of Pyramid Peak and the classic granite terrain for which Desolation Wilderness is famous. Since the lake lies at the end of a maintained trail, fewer visitors seem to travel this far than the stunning scenery would otherwise demand. Layover days offer the opportunity to travel off-trail to the named lakes and scads of smaller tarns sprinkled throughout the Pyramid Creek drainage. The stiff scramble to the summit of 9,983-foot Pyramid Peak can be quite rewarding as well.

DAY 2 (Ropi Lake to Echo Lakes Trailhead, 4.4 miles): Retrace your steps.

The classic granite terrain of Desolation Valley sprawls across the basin.   Photo by Mike White

Echo Summit Trailhead				7,400'; 38.81243°N, 120.03405°W	
Destination/ GPS Coordinates	Trip Type	Best Season	Pace & Hiking/ Layover Days	Total Mileage	Permit Required
11 Echo Summit Trailhead to Meiss Meadows Trailhead 38.69672°N 119.99189°W	Shuttle	Mid to late	Moderate 2/0	13.4	None for backpacking

INFORMATION AND PERMITS: "Meiss Country" is the current term for this area in the Lake Tahoe Basin Management Unit. For information: USDA Forest Service, Lake Tahoe Basin Management Unit; 35 College Dr., South Lake Tahoe, CA 96150; 530-543-2600, fs.usda.gov/ltbmu. No wilderness permits are required at this time, but you must have a California Campfire Permit to have a campfire or use a stove.

DRIVING DIRECTIONS: Follow US 50 to Echo Summit. From there go west to a paved access road on the south side of the highway, 0.2 mile west of Echo Summit. A sign for Adventure Mountain Lake Tahoe resort marks the turnoff. Proceed 0.2 mile to the large Pacific Crest Trail (PCT) parking lot.

trip 11

Echo Summit Trailhead to Meiss Meadows Trailhead

see map on p. 64

Trip Data: 38.69672°N, 119.99189°W; 13.4 miles; 2/0 days
Topos: *Echo Lake, Caples Lake, Carson Pass*

HIGHLIGHTS: This second leg of the unofficial Tahoe-Yosemite Trail (TYT) begins with an unpromising walk through a summer-dusty winter recreation area just south and west of Echo Summit (on US 50). But soon you leave this behind for the remarkable scenery of Meiss Country, where seasonal wildflowers from here to Carson Pass can be amazing at peak bloom. This section coincides with the Pacific Crest Trail (PCT).

HEADS UP! *Hunters also favor this area: when hiking during deer season, wear bright clothing and stay near major trails.*

SHUTTLE DIRECTIONS: To get to Meiss Meadows Trailhead, take CA 88 to Carson Pass and go 0.3 mile west to a large parking lot on the highway's north side that serves this trailhead. There is a daily fee of $5 to park here.

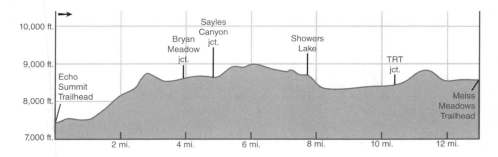

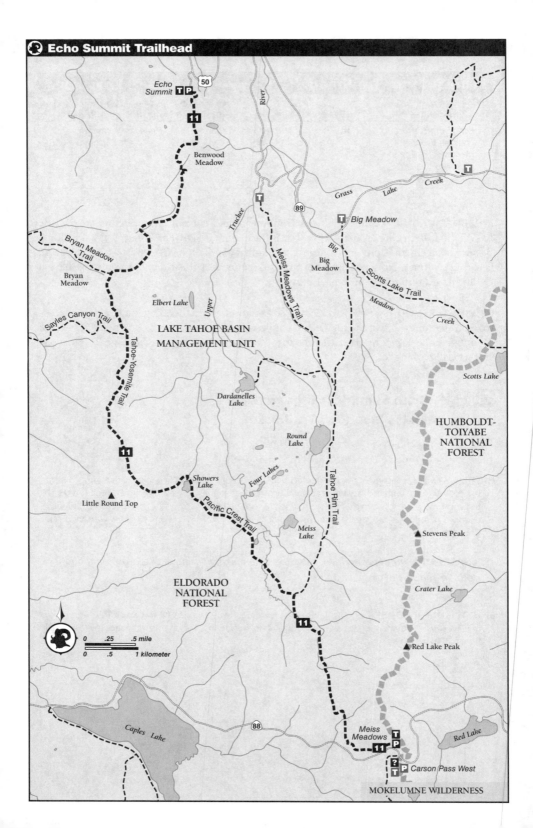

DAY 1 (Echo Summit Trailhead to Showers Lake, 8.3 miles): First, walk a short way down the paved road (south) from the parking lot and then through the ski area to pick up the trail on the snow park's south edge. You've just passed through an old ski area, now Adventure Mountain Lake Tahoe resort. The former ski lodge now houses a unit of the California Conservation Corps.

Start hiking through shrubs and low pines, immediately crossing a section of old paved roadway, and then making a moderate climb of the old ski hill. The route, well signed, levels, merges with an old road for a short distance, and then veers right (south) on well-marked, singletrack trail. Follow the rocky trail up a shrub-covered slope to intersect a sandy road, and then turn right and climb up the road about 100 yards to the resumption of singletrack trail at a Tahoe Rim Trail sign.

Swinging south, stroll along granite-dotted slopes sparsely covered by white firs and lodgepole and Jeffrey pines, with a generous understory of huckleberry oak bushes. Approximately 1 mile from the parking lot, a momentary descent leads past a lateral heading northeast to an unnamed pond; go right (west) here to Benwood Meadow, which can dry up by late season.

Proceed through the forest around the edge of the usually boggy meadow and across a pair of seasonal streams to a wood-plank bridge over an alder-lined creek. After a moderate, winding climb from the bridge, the trail switchbacks and ascends into thinning forest, which allows periodic glimpses of Lake Tahoe over the next mile or so. Continue the moderate climb to the south past large granitic boulders.

Reach a saddle about 1.5 miles from Benwood Meadow, where an excellent view to the southeast includes the Upper Truckee River basin and surrounding peaks as well as Elephants Back and Round Top. Past the viewpoint, continue climbing for another 0.3 mile, staying at the foot of a row of nearly vertical cliffs, and reach a tiny creek. Half a dozen people could camp on the flat above the creek's southeast bank. From the vicinity of this campsite, the trail switchbacks and climbs quite steeply to a hillside meadow with water and a campsite on a rise near the creek.

The grade soon eases upon entering a dense-to-moderate lodgepole forest as the trail crosses a ridge and descends gently to a shallow pass. Just beyond the pass, reach a junction with the Bryan Meadow Trail near the east end of the picturesque clearing. Nearby are several campsites with water plentiful in early season. Go left (ahead, south) here, staying on the PCT/TYT.

From Bryan Meadow, the trail leads south on sandy footing, undulating and then ascending gently to a minor summit, followed by a brief descent to a saddle and a junction with the Sayles Canyon Trail. Again, go left (ahead, south) here on the PCT/TYT.

A mile of gradually increasing ascent leads over the east ridge of Peak 9,020, which separates the two branches of the headwaters of Sayles Canyon Creek. At the upper lobes of a hillside meadow, there may be water into late season and campsites on a sandy rise nearby. At the first saddle beyond the ridge, a use trail crosses the PCT/TYT at right angles, and a short distance farther on is a junction with an infrequently maintained trail to Schneider's cow camp. Once more, go left (ahead, south) here on the PCT/TYT.

The trail next curves through a willow-covered meadow and crosses its larger, flower-covered neighbor; both may provide late-season water. Keen eyes will begin to notice how the character of the rocks begins to change from granitic to volcanic and the sandy tread turns pinkish.

A descent leads into a large bowl whose southwest rim may be draped with snow cornices for much of the summer. The slopes of this bowl are very open and laced with runoff streams, which support lavish gardens of shrubs and flowers, including blue elderberry, rangers buttons (also called swamp whiteheads), mountain bluebells, green gentian, aster, wallflower, penstemon, cinquefoil, spiraea, corn lily, and columbine. This highly colorful bowl, harboring as-yet-unseen Showers Lake, offers photographers a great choice of hues, subjects, and compositions.

Make a gentle descent through the bowl, passing beneath a palisade-like outcropping below the cornice-laden rim. The trail, which here differs from the route shown on the topo, veers northeast and eventually drops below Showers Lake to cross the lake's outlet. Beyond the ford, zigzag steeply uphill south-southwest a short distance to Showers Lake (8,658'; 38.74251°N, 120.03419°W).

DAY 2 (Showers Lake to Meiss Meadows Trailhead, 5.1 miles): Heading toward CA 88, the trail climbs as it curves around the lake's east side to a junction at a small saddle above Showers Lake. Take the left fork southeast and away from the lake (the right fork is a seldom-used lateral to Schneider's cow camp). Descend a switchback and drop down a slope with vegetation and colors much like the previous bowl. This trail segment offers panoramic views of the large meadows around the headwaters of the Truckee River. The best views occur when there's just a bit of snow left on the west side of the Crystal Range.

Make a steady descent to traverse another meadow and reenter forest on the west slope of the Upper Truckee River valley. The trail begins to resemble an old four-wheel-drive road, which it once was, on the way past a large pond. Just north of your first ford of the Truckee River, a use trail heads roughly north-northeast across Meiss Meadows a half mile to Meiss Lake. Reaching the lake in early season may be a bit of a challenge, as parts of the trail are quite mucky and the ford of the creek on the way to the lake will most likely be a wet one. You, however, stay on the main PCT/TYT and ford the young Upper Truckee River.

> **MEISS MEADOWS**
>
> During the last ice age, a lake occupied all these meadows, which subsequently were filled with sediment—except for the small remnant of Meiss Lake. The meadows offer many attractions for the birder and also for those who wish to see Belding's ground squirrels. The house and barn are the remains of a former cow camp—thank goodness, grazing here was banned several years ago.

Near the buildings is a defunct stock gate and a well-signed junction with the Tahoe Rim Trail heading left (northeast) to Round Lake. Go ahead (south) to stay on the PCT/TYT. Beyond this junction, the PCT/TYT fords the river again and begins a final, moderate ascent to a saddle dividing the Truckee River and American River drainages. On the climb, increasingly fine views culminate at the saddle, with the Round Top complex dominating the scene immediately to the south, Lake Tahoe capturing the eye in the distance to the north, and Red Lake Peak towering immediately to the east (you're on its western slope).

From the saddle, the route descends steeply on the rocky-dusty tread of a former jeep road. After several hundred yards, the trail veers left (east) and follows a few switchbacks down sagebrush-covered slopes dotted with mule ears and a variety of other flowers. Follow the trail across a runoff stream and then around the nose of a ridge through a moderate forest cover of fir and pine.

Soon the sound of cars on CA 88 below heralds the approach to Meiss Meadow Trailhead. The final leg takes longer than you'd expect because the trail curves well to the east before exiting at the trailhead parking lot (8,560'; 38.69672°N, 119.99189°W) just off the noisy road.

CA 88 TRIPS

We feature five trailheads along scenic CA 88. Four of them lead south into Mokelumne Wilderness; one leads north into Meiss Country.

South of CA 88 lies 105,165-acre Mokelumne Wilderness, a wonderland of colorful volcanic peaks, contrasting granitic terrain, amazing wildflower displays, stunning canyons, and picturesque lakes. We visit Mokelumne Wilderness and neighboring areas from four trailheads along or just off of CA 88 (from west to east): Silver Lake–Granite Lake Trailhead, Thunder Mountain Trailhead, Carson Pass Trailhead, and Upper Blue Lake–Grouse Lake Trailhead.

Superb scenery, mixing volcanic and granitic rocks, is the hallmark of the region around Silver Lake and Thunder Mountain, particularly in Mokelumne Wilderness. During peak season, backpackers will experience some of the best flower displays in the entire Sierra. The trips from the Woods Lake Trailhead and the Carson Pass Trailhead head into the extremely popular Carson Pass Management Area, famed for rugged peaks, shimmering lakes, and colorful wildflowers. The beauty of the area is your reward for putting up with the designated campsites you're forced to use.

Off Blue Lakes Road, this highway section features a series of out-of-the-way reservoirs that lure campers, boaters, and anglers. The area beyond these reservoirs presents some equally attractive and less-used backcountry sure to please even the most discriminating of backpackers.

North of CA 88 in the Carson Pass area lies wonderful Meiss Country, once proposed for wilderness status. Wide-ranging vistas, expansive meadows, and splendid wildflowers are just a few of the area's pleasures. From CA 88, the Meiss Meadows Trailhead, located in the west-to-east order between the Thunder Mountain and Carson Pass Trailheads, is your gateway to Meiss Country.

Trailheads: **Silver Lake–Granite Lake**

Thunder Mountain

Woods Lake

Meiss Meadows

Carson Pass

Upper Blue Lake–Granite Lake

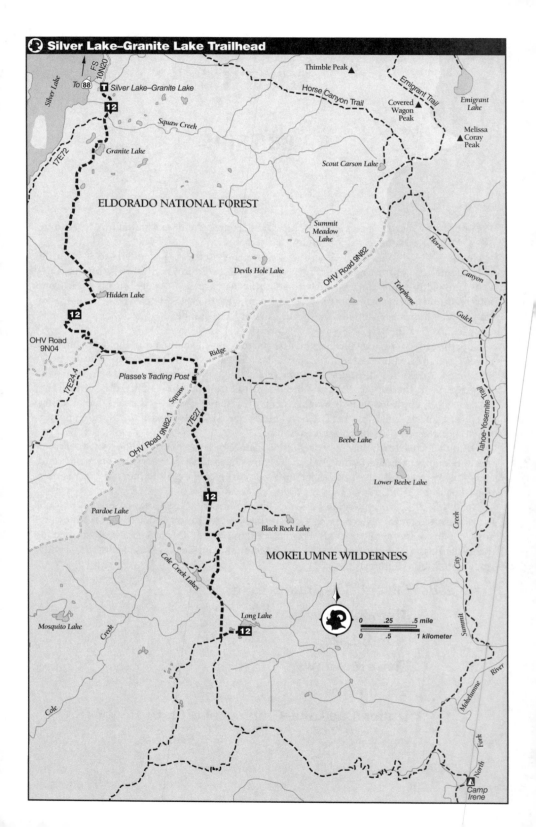

Silver Lake–Granite Lake Trailhead

Thimble Peak ▲

Emigrant Trail

Emigrant Lake

To 88

FS 10N20

T Silver Lake–Granite Lake

12

Silver Lake

Horse Canyon Trail

Covered Wagon Peak ▲

Melissa Coray Peak ▲

Squaw Creek

Granite Lake

Scout Carson Lake

17E72

ELDORADO NATIONAL FOREST

Summit Meadow Lake

Horse

Devils Hole Lake

OHV Road 9N82

Canyon

Hidden Lake

12

Telephone

OHV Road 9N04

Ridge

17E24.4

Plasse's Trading Post

OHV Road 9N82.1

Squaw

17E27

Beebe Lake

Lower Beebe Lake

Pardoe Lake

12

Tahoe-Yosemite Trail

Black Rock Lake

MOKELUMNE WILDERNESS

Cole Creek Lakes

Mosquito Lake

Creek

Long Lake

12

City

Creek

Summit

0   .25   .5 mile

0   .5   1 kilometer

Cole

Mokelumne River

North

Fork

Camp Irene

Silver Lake–Granite Lake Trailhead			7,303'; 38.65997°N, 120.10958°W		
Destination/ GPS Coordinates	**Trip Type**	**Best Season**	**Pace & Hiking/ Layover Days**	**Total Mileage**	**Permit Required**
12 Long Lake 38.57401°N 120.08186°W	Out-and-back	Mid	Moderate 2/1	18.0 (round-trip)	Mokelumne Wilderness

INFORMATION AND PERMITS: This trailhead is in Eldorado National Forest: 100 Forni Rd., Placerville, CA 95667; 530-622-5061, fs.usda.gov/eldorado. You must have a permit to camp overnight in Mokelumne Wilderness; download your permit at fs.usda.gov/Internet /FSE_DOCUMENTS/fseprd754168.pdf.

DRIVING DIRECTIONS: From CA 88 near the north end of Silver Lake, leave the highway following signs east along the lake's north end for Kit Carson Resort. Continue past the resort to the east side of the lake and the small trailhead parking area, 1.4 miles from CA 88.

trip 12 Long Lake

> **Trip Data:** 38.57401°N, 120.08186°W; 18.0 miles; 2/1 days
> **Topos:** *Caples Lake, Mokelumne Peak*

HIGHLIGHTS: A hike full of wonderful views leads to one of the area's loveliest lakes, above which travelers will find campsites on granite benches that command spectacular views of the surrounding peaks.

DAY 1 (Silver Lake–Granite Lake Trailhead to Long Lake, 9.0 miles): Locate the trailhead on the left-hand side of the road marked by a sign reading MANKALO TRAIL 17E72, GRANITE LAKE 1, PLASSES 3. Trail 17E23 begins on a gentle-to-moderate climb through a scattered forest of Jeffrey pines, lodgepole pines, and white firs. Proceed through granitic terrain dotted with aspens and manzanita past a seasonal pond/meadow and across a bridge over Squaw Creek. Beyond the bridge, reach a junction and turn left (south), following signed directions for Granite Lake. A steep climb leads up open terrain of granite slabs and shrubs to well-named Granite Lake, occupying a shallow basin of granite on a bench 550 feet above Silver Lake. Although the lake offers a few Spartan campsites sheltered by scattered conifers, the 1-mile distance from the trailhead ensures these sites are heavily used and therefore not recommended.

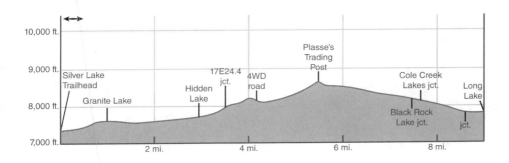

Granite Lake   Photo by Mike White

Pass around the west shore of the lake and proceed through mixed forest past a stagnant pond and a flower-filled meadow. Continue straight ahead (south) at a T-junction, where the faint tread of Trail 17E72 heads right, providing an infrequently used connector to Plasse's Resort. Beyond the junction, a mostly gentle ascent leads through the forest to the crossing of a seasonal stream, followed by a short but steeper climb to Hidden Lake. Conifers shade the near lakeshore, while the far shore is composed of meadows and clumps of willow backdropped nicely by granite cliffs. Good campsites will lure overnighters.

Climb out of Hidden Lake's basin around pockets of willow-and-flower-carpeted meadows to a signed junction on top of a low ridge. Veer left (south) at the junction to pass by a verdant meadow and then a spring on a hemlock-shaded climb to a divide between the American River and Bear River drainages. Descending from this view-packed ridge, cross a drift fence and in less than 100 yards turn left (east-southeast) onto a four-wheel-drive road.

Traveling along the road, the grade is level past the Allen Ranch and then across the seasonal headwaters of Bear River. Now ascending, cross some perennial trickles and then veer to the right, leaving the road just before a small creek. Rejoin the road on the crest of Squaw Ridge, where a sign indicates the former site of Plasse's Trading Post.

RAYMOND PLASSE

While traveling the Carson Emigrant Route, French immigrant Raymond Plasse fell in love with the area around Silver Lake. He established a trading post on Squaw Ridge in 1853 and ran it for many years before moving his family to the south end of the lake to raise cattle and operate a resort. No sign of the trading post exists today, but Plasse's Resort, which includes a campground, boat rentals, restaurant and bar, and a general store, is in full operation each summer (plassesresort.com).

About 130 yards down from the ridge, leave the road by turning left (southeast) onto Trail 17E27 and soon entering Mokelumne Wilderness. In 1984, motorized vehicles were banned when the Mokelumne Wilderness was enlarged from 50,165 acres to the current 105,165 acres. The former roadbed began a process of rehabilitation. Just past the wilderness boundary the route passes above Horse Thief Spring, which usually flows all year. Sadly, due to intense cattle grazing, the springs are mere remnants of their former glory, but fill up here anyway, as this may be the last water before Cole Creek Lakes.

Continuing south, the nearly level trail passes some long meadows and then joins a broad volcanic ridge where views extend south all the way into the Carson-Iceberg Wilderness. As the trail descends the ridge, continue ahead (south) at a junction with the faint, old, unmapped trail to Cole Creek Lakes. At the next junction, with the trail heading left (northeast) to Black Rock Lake, you go right (south).

Now on granite terrain, cross another view-blessed ridge, which includes a closer look at Mokelumne Peak. Descending the rocky ridge, you meet a signed trail right (southwest) to Cole Creek Lakes. A level half-mile stroll through the forest is followed by a brief descent to the southernmost Cole Creek Lake. From the lake's seasonal outlet, the trail makes a gentle descent southeast and then south for most of a mile before gradually ascending to the signed junction with the lateral to Long Lake.

Turn left (east-northeast) onto Trail 17E66 toward Long Lake, and in a short half mile, arrive at the south shore of many-bayed Long Lake (7,829'; 38.57401°N, 120.08186°W). People seemingly overuse the immediate lakeshore, but nice camping is available by skirting the south shore, crossing one of the tiny dams that enlarge this lake, and then heading east, away from the lake, onto open granite benches (e.g., 7,803'; 38.57523°N, 120.07810°W). Within several hundred yards of the lake are level, dry, cow- and mosquito-free campsites with fabulous views to the southeast over Wester Park to the headwaters of the Mokelumne River and the peaks around Ebbetts Pass.

DAY 2 (Long Lake to Silver Lake–Granite Lake Trailhead, 9.0 miles): Retrace your steps.

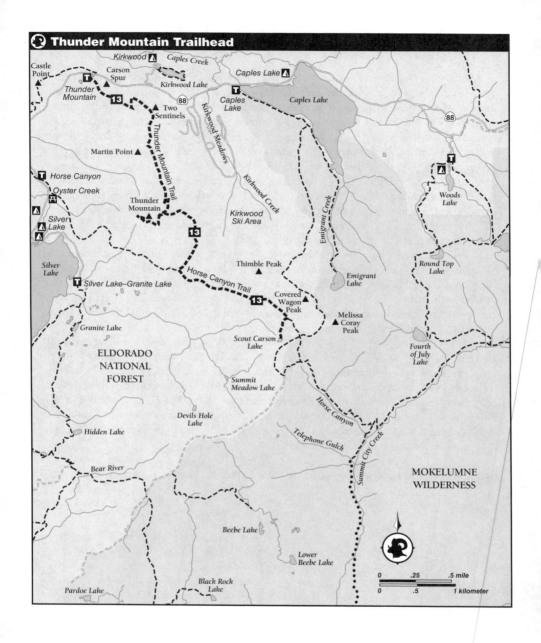

Castle
Point

Kirkwood
Carson
Spur

*Thunder
Mountain*

13

Caples Creek

Kirkwood Lake

Caples Lake

Two
Sentinels

Caples
Lake

(88)

Caples Lake

(88)

Martin Point ▲

Kirkwood Meadows

Woods
Lake

Horse Canyon

Oyster Creek

*Thunder
Mountain*
Thunder
Mountain Trail

Kirkwood Creek

Kirkwood
Ski Area

Emigrant Creek

Round Top
Lake

Silver
Lake

Silver
Lake

13

Thimble Peak ▲

Emigrant
Lake

Silver Lake–Granite Lake

Horse Canyon Trail

Covered
Wagon
Peak ▲

Melissa
Coray Peak ▲

Fourth
of July
Lake

Granite Lake

13

Scout Carson
Lake

ELDORADO
NATIONAL
FOREST

Summit
Meadow Lake

Horse Canyon

Devils Hole
Lake

Telephone Gulch

Hidden Lake

Summit City Creek

Bear River

MOKELUMNE
WILDERNESS

Beebe Lake

Lower
Beebe Lake

Pardoe Lake

Black Rock
Lake

| 0 | | .25 | | .5 mile |
| 0 | | .5 | | 1 kilometer |

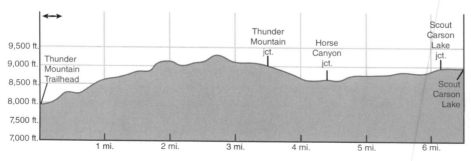

Thunder Mountain Trailhead			7,942'; 38.70553°N, 120.10741°W		
Destination/ GPS Coordinates	Trip Type	Best Season	Pace & Hiking/ Layover Days	Total Mileage	Permit Required
13 Scout Carson Lake 38.64808°N 120.05375°W	Out-and-back	Mid	Leisurely 2/1	13.0 (round-trip)	None for backpacking

INFORMATION AND PERMITS: This trailhead is on Eldorado National Forest: 100 Forni Rd., Placerville, CA 95667; 530-622-5061, fs.usda.gov/eldorado. For visitor information, call 530-644-6048. Because this trip lies just outside of Mokelumne Wilderness, no permits are required at this time, but you must have a California Campfire Permit to have a campfire or use a stove.

Note: The Thunder Mountain Trailhead and the trail segment from there to the Horse Canyon Trail appear on the *Mokelumne Wilderness* map but not on the 1992 *Caples Lake* 7.5' topo.

DRIVING DIRECTIONS: Follow CA 88 to the roadside trailhead for the Thunder Mountain Loop near Carson Spur, 3.25 miles east of Silver Lake and 1.75 miles west of the Kirkwood Meadows junction, on the south side of the highway.

trip 13   **Scout Carson Lake**

> **Trip Data:**   38.64808°N, 120.05375°W; 13.0 miles; 2/1 days
> **Topos:**   *Caples Lake*

HIGHLIGHTS: A lovely, small, near-timberline lake is the goal of this trip, which passes through interesting geologic scenery along the way. An optional 1-mile round-trip detour to the 9,408-foot summit of Thunder Mountain offers an expansive 360-degree vista of the Carson Pass region. The route continues with fine views of the surrounding volcanic battlements on the way to Scout Carson Lake.

HEADS UP! *A 1.7-mile section of the Horse Canyon Trail between the junction with the Thunder Mountain Trail and the spur to Scout Carson Lake is open to motorcycles. However, they seldom travel that far up the trail from Silver Lake.*

DAY 1 (Thunder Mountain Trailhead to Scout Carson Lake, 6.5 miles): Pass through a deteriorating cattle gate in a wire fence and proceed through a mixed forest of red firs, lodgepole pines, and western white pines, soon encountering a T-junction with a lightly used path that heads east to cross CA 88 and then travels west to Castle Point. Continue straight ahead (southeast) on the main trail on a moderate climb, breaking out of the trees on a climb across a sagebrush-and-wildflower-covered hillside below Carson Spur, where the rocky crags of Two Sentinels spring into view. Briefly gain the crest at a saddle before a climb across the west side of the ridge leads into thickening forest. Following a pair of switchbacks, traverse below the pinnacles of Two Sentinels to an open saddle, where the peaks of the Carson Pass area burst into view, along with Kirkwood Meadows and Caples Lake below.

Head south along the ridge toward Martin Point, with additional eastward views along the way. A couple of switchbacks lead to an upward traverse around the east side of Martin Point, revealing the impressive profile of Thunder Mountain's north face, where the dark volcanic rock, punctuated with numerous clefts, gashes, pinnacles, and arêtes, creates a dramatic alpine scene. Continue the ascent along the ridgecrest toward Thunder Mountain. As you approach the northeast ridge of the peak, you make two more switchbacks and then follow a gentle traverse around the back of the ridge to the Thunder Mountain junction marked by a post, 3.5 miles from the trailhead.

THUNDER MOUNTAIN

Those who would like to bag a peak before continuing to Scout Carson Lake should turn right (southwest) at the junction and follow an ascending, westward traverse through scattered lodgepole pines, western white pines, mountain hemlocks, and whitebark pines. The trees diminish near the crest as the trail angles sharply to the east to follow the ridge to the summit. The top offers an incredible view in all directions, from the mountains of northern Yosemite in the south to the peaks of Desolation Wilderness in the north. Nearby landmarks include Silver and Caples Lakes and Round Top. After thoroughly enjoying the views, retrace your steps back to the junction.

Whether you're skipping the side trip to the summit or returning from the top of Thunder Mountain, head east from the junction, traveling downhill across dry slopes through scattered to light timber to a junction with a faint path branching left (northeast) toward Kirkwood Meadows. Veer right and continue the descent into thickening forest until breaking out of the trees onto open, flower-filled slopes with excellent views of Silver Lake and Horse Canyon. Reach a junction at the bottom of the descent with the Horse Canyon Trail (17E21).

Turn left (southeast) at the junction and climb an open hillside, drop briefly to cross an unnamed, year-round creek, and then climb a sagebrush-dotted slope. Now at 8,800 feet, the trail follows a mile-long traverse across an open, flower-sprinkled bench on the south side of Thimble Peak. To the east of the peak are the tops of some of the ski lifts servicing Kirkwood Meadows in the next valley to the north. After passing an abandoned, overgrown path to Kirkwood Meadows, marked by an old post with a missing sign, ascend moderately through granite boulders to a signed junction in a sandy meadow with Trail 17E24.

Turn right (southwest) and stroll an easy half mile on a winding ascent through stands of mixed forest and pocket meadows to Scout Carson Lake (8,964'; 38.64808°N, 120.05375°W) on the edge of, but not in, Mokelumne Wilderness. Perched on a small bench, ringed by meadow, and surrounded by a forest of lodgepole pine, western white pine, and mountain hemlock, diminutive Scout Carson Lake is a sweet example of Sierra Nevada charm. Perhaps not so charming are the numerous mosquitoes buzzing through the air until late season. You can reduce if not eliminate this annoyance by camping away from the meadow-fringed lakeshore in favor of drier and rockier terrain to the west. The lake supports a small but fat population of brook trout, which gratefully eat the mosquitoes. Emigrant Peak to the east is a straightforward climb offering a superb view from the summit of much of Mokelumne Wilderness.

DAY 2 (Scout Carson Lake to Thunder Mountain Trailhead, 6.5 miles): Retrace your steps.

Stream in Horse Creek Canyon   Photo by Mike White

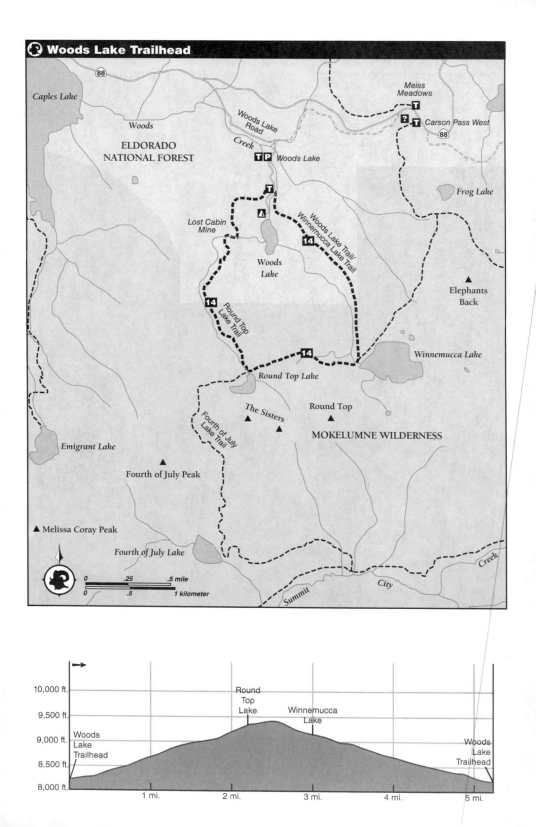

Woods Lake Trailhead

Caples Lake

88

Meiss Meadows

T

Carson Pass West

?

T

88

Woods

Woods Lake Road

ELDORADO NATIONAL FOREST

Creek

T P Woods Lake

T

Frog Lake

Lost Cabin Mine

Woods Lake

14

Woods Lake Trail/ Winnemucca Lake Trail

Elephants Back

14

Round Top Lake Trail

14

Winnemucca Lake

Round Top Lake

Fourth of July Lake Trail

The Sisters

Round Top

MOKELUMNE WILDERNESS

Emigrant Lake

Fourth of July Peak

Melissa Coray Peak

Fourth of July Lake

Fourth of July Lake

Creek

Summit City

0   .25   .5 mile
0   .5   1 kilometer

10,000 ft.

Round Top Lake

9,500 ft.

Winnemucca Lake

9,000 ft.

Woods Lake Trailhead

Woods Lake Trailhead

8,500 ft.

8,000 ft.

1 mi.   2 mi.   3 mi.   4 mi.   5 mi.

Woods Lake Trailhead				8,199'; 38.69124°N, 120.00916°W		
Destination/ GPS Coordinates	Trip Type	Best Season	Pace & Hiking/ Layover Days	Total Mileage	Permit Required	
14 Round Top and Winnemucca Lakes 38.66881°N 120.01173°W (Round Top Lake)	Loop	Mid	Leisurely 2/0	5.2	Carson Pass Management Area	

INFORMATION AND PERMITS: Camping in the Carson Pass Management Area (CPMA) is allowed only in designated sites at Winnemucca, Round Top, and Fourth of July Lakes. Permits for camping in these sites are only issued on a first-come, first-served basis at the Carson Pass Information Station, which is open seven days a week in the summer. The Carson Pass Information Station is located at the top of Carson Pass on CA 88, 6 miles east of the Kirkwood Mountain Resort. See the Eldorado National Forest website for details. Campfires are prohibited within the CPMA at all times. There's a fee to park at the trailhead, which is in the Eldorado National Forest: 100 Forni Rd., Placerville, CA 95667; 530-622-5061, fs.usda .gov/eldorado. For visitor information, call 530-644-6048.

DRIVING DIRECTIONS: Turn off CA 88 at the signed Woods Lake access road, 1.7 miles west of Carson Pass. Follow the paved road 0.8 mile to a junction and turn right, proceeding another 0.1 mile to the Woods Lake Trailhead, where motorists must cough up a nominal fee for parking. Toilets and water are available.

trip 14   **Round Top and Winnemucca Lakes**

> **Trip Data:** 38.66881°N, 120.01173°W (Round Top Lake); 5.2 miles; 2/0 days
> **Topos:** *Caples Lake, Carson Pass*

HIGHLIGHTS: Two picturesque lakes backdropped by craggy volcanic summits provide the main highlights on this very popular loop trip through Mokelumne Wilderness. Midsummer visitors will have the added bonus of a number of wildflower-laden meadows. Ambitious peak baggers can make a side trip to the summit of Round Top.

DAY 1 (Woods Lake Trailhead to Round Top Lake, 2.2 miles): From the trailhead parking lot, walk a short distance on the access road toward Woods Lake Campground and find the official start of the Round Top Lake Trail just past a bridge (don't cross the bridge). Stroll along on a dirt trail through mixed forest, soon rising above Woods Lake Campground, where singletrack trail merges with an old roadbed. Follow the road on a stiff, winding climb to the signed Lost Cabin Mine Trailhead, a half mile from the parking lot.

Now on singletrack again, make a moderate climb with filtered views of Round Top and Woods Lake through the trees. Hop across boulder- and willow-lined Woods Creek and follow a switchbacking climb above the old structures of the Lost Cabin Mine, which produced gold, silver, copper, and lead before shutting down in the early 1960s. The mine is still considered private property, so resist the urge to trespass. Continue the steady ascent, roughly following the west branch of Woods Creek. The grade eventually eases near the signed Mokelumne Wilderness boundary as the volcanic summits of Round Top and the Sisters come into view. The canyon broadens farther upstream amid more open vegetation of willow, heather, and wildflowers, which allows even better views. Reach a junction with

Carson Pass Information Station   Photo by Mike White

the Fourth of July Lake Trail near the north shore of Round Top Lake (9,350'; 38.66881°N, 120.01173°W), 2.2 miles from the parking lot.

Round Top is a stunningly scenic lake rimmed with stands of whitebark pines and backdropped by the broodingly dark slopes of Round Top and the Sisters. To promote revegetation of the shoreline, overnighters are limited to six designated, mostly hard-to-find campsites on the northwest side of the lake, available by reservation only.

CLIMBING ROUND TOP

Competent peak baggers can climb nearby Round Top (10,381'). From Round Top Lake, leave the trail and travel southeast on a well-defined use trail up the prominent gully located between the east Sister and Round Top. Initially, the route heads toward the saddle between the two peaks, but higher up the slope, it veers left of the saddle to a prominent notch in Round Top's northwest ridge. Follow the backside of the ridge to a false summit that should satisfy most nonclimbers as their ultimate destination. The true summit is only a few feet higher and is separated from the false summit by a steep cleft of loose rock that should be negotiated only by skilled mountaineers, as the exposure is quite significant. Both summits offer spectacularly expansive views of the northern Sierra.

OPTIONAL HIKES

Emigrant Lake: From the junction near the north shore of Round Top Lake, turn onto the Fourth of July Lake Trail and follow an arcing traverse around the west shoulder of the Sisters to the crest of a divide. From there, experienced cross-country travelers can access Emigrant Lake by traversing west to a notch directly southeast of Point 9,020, as shown on the *Caples Lake* quadrangle, and then dropping steeply to the lake's outlet.

Fourth of July Lake: From the crest mentioned above, continue on the Fourth of July Lake Trail on a switchbacking descent that loses 1,000 feet of elevation on the way to Fourth of July Lake. Colorful wildflowers should cheer midsummer hikers along the descent. Fourth of July Lake is quite scenic, cradled in a rocky amphitheater between Fourth of July Peak and Peaks 9,795 and 9,607. A mixture of open meadows, pockets of willow, and stands of white fir and western white pine ring the shoreline. Six designated campsites are scattered around the lake, one near the outlet, two on a forested rise above the northeast shore, and three near the edge of the meadow on the northwest side.

DAY 2 (Round Top Lake to Woods Lake Trailhead, 3 miles): Return to the junction with the trail (on your right) that you took to get up to Round Top Lake. Here, go ahead (east toward Winnemucca Lake) on a gradually rising ascent over a granite ridge peppered with wind-battered whitebark pines and ground-hugging shrubs. Once across the crest, follow the trail downslope through open terrain and across the outlet of Winnemucca Lake to its west shore and a junction.

Windswept Winnemucca Lake sits majestically at the base of Round Top Peak's north face, with the rounded hump of Elephants Back a mile to the northeast. The mostly open terrain is broken by scattered clumps of whitebark pine that shelter three designated campsites above the north shore.

At a junction at Winnemucca's west end, turn left (north) toward Woods Lake and follow the trail along the course of the east branch of Woods Creek through sagebrush, willows, and a fine assortment of wildflowers in season. Exit Mokelumne Wilderness about a half mile from the lake and continue the steady descent into mixed forest. Nearing the trailhead, pass a lateral on the left to Woods Lake, stroll across a wood bridge, walk across the paved access road, and walk a short distance to the parking area.

Round Top   Photo by Mike White

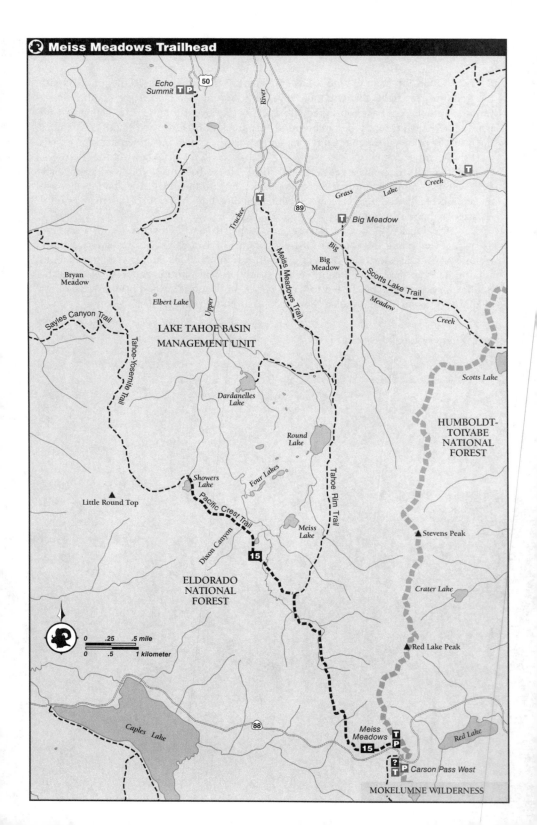

Echo
Summit 🅣🅟 50

Truckee River

89 Grass Lake Creek 🅣

🅣 Big Meadow

Bryan
Meadow

Elbert Lake

Sayles Canyon Trail

Tahoe-Yosemite Trail

Upper

Meiss Meadow Trail

Big

Big
Meadow

Scotts Lake Trail

Meadow Creek

LAKE TAHOE BASIN
MANAGEMENT UNIT

Scotts Lake

Dardanelles
Lake

Round
Lake

HUMBOLDT-
TOIYABE
NATIONAL
FOREST

Showers
Lake

Four Lakes

Little Round Top ▲

Pacific Crest Trail

Tahoe Rim Trail

Meiss
Lake

Stevens Peak ▲

Dixon Canyon

15

Crater Lake

ELDORADO
NATIONAL
FOREST

Red Lake Peak ▲

0   .25   .5 mile
0   .5   1 kilometer

Caples Lake

88

Meiss
Meadows 🅣🅟

15

❓🅟 Carson Pass West
🅣

Red Lake

MOKELUMNE WILDERNESS

Meiss Meadows Trailhead			8,560'; 38.69672°N, 119.99189°W		
Destination/ GPS Coordinates	Trip Type	Best Season	Pace & Hiking/ Layover Days	Total Mileage	Permit Required
15 Showers Lake 38.74251°N 120.03419°W	Out-and-back	Mid	Moderate 2/1	10.2	None for backpacking

INFORMATION AND PERMITS: Wilderness permits aren't required in Meiss Country, but you must have a California Campfire Permit to have a campfire or use a stove. There's a fee of $5 to park at the trailhead, which is in the Eldorado National Forest: 100 Forni Road, Placerville, CA 95667; 530-622-5061, fs.usda.gov/eldorado. For visitor information, call 530-644-6048.

DRIVING DIRECTIONS: From Carson Pass on CA 88, drive 0.3 mile west to the Meiss Meadows Trailhead and the parking lot on the north side of the road.

trip 15   Showers Lake

> **Trip Data:** 38.74251°N, 120.03419°W; 10.2 miles; 2/1 days
> **Topos:** *Caples Lake*

HIGHLIGHTS: Showers Lake is one of the best camping areas between US 50 and CA 88, with numerous campsites and good angling for brook trout. En route, the trail passes through the Upper Truckee River drainage, offering panoramic views of immense volcanic formations.

HEADS UP! *There is a daily fee to park at the Meiss Meadows Trailhead.*

DAY 1 (Meiss Meadows Trailhead to Showers Lake, 5.1 miles): Leave the parking lot and follow singletrack tread on an undulating traverse across the hillside above the highway. Continue through a light, mixed forest sprinkled with boulders and scattered wildflowers. Soon the trail veers north and exits the forest on a steep ascent across an open slope carpeted with sagebrush and flowers, crossing over a pair of seasonal rivulets on the way to a prominent saddle. Here, at 1.25 miles from the parking lot, you're blessed with an extensive view to the south of peaks in the Mokolumne Wilderness and north of the Upper Truckee River basin.

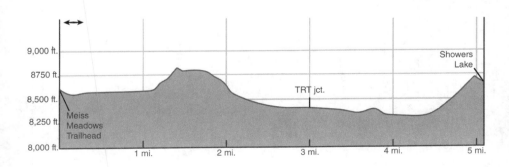

The gently graded trail leads past a lushly lined pond nestled into the saddle before descending tread drops you to the headwaters of the Upper Truckee River, crossing the nascent watercourse a few times on the way to the floor of the canyon. An easy stroll crosses flower-filled meadows and over the river once more prior to reaching the vicinity of some rustic cabins from the old days of the Meiss Meadows Cow Camp. Just past the cabins is a signed junction between the Tahoe Rim and Pacific Crest Trails.

Bear left (northwest) from the junction and follow the Pacific Crest Trail (PCT) to another crossing of the river, which might necessitate an ankle-deep ford in early season. Gentle trail leads away from the river crossing, traveling through alternating sections of open meadow and stands of forest. Just past a shallow pond and a tributary draining Dixon Canyon, the trail begins a stiff climb to the crest of a hill and an unmarked X-junction. The faint path to the southwest heads to Schneider's cow camp, and the old route of the PCT travels around the south side of Showers Lake basin. Turn right at the junction and follow the realigned section of the PCT descending northeast to granite-bound Showers Lake, where several shady campsites may be found near the outlet. (8,658'; 38.74251°N, 120.03419°W).

DAY 2 (Showers Lake to Meiss Meadows Trailhead, 5.1 miles): Retrace your steps.

Showers Lake   Photo by Mike White

Carson Pass Trailhead   8,588'; 38.69476°N, 119.98936°W

Destination/ GPS Coordinates	Trip Type	Best Season	Pace & Hiking/ Layover Days	Total Mileage	Permit Required
16 Fourth of July Lake 38.65045°N 120.01550°W	Semiloop	Mid to late	Moderate 2/1	14.0	Carson Pass Management Area

INFORMATION AND PERMITS: Camping in the Carson Pass Management Area (CPMA) is allowed only in the designated sites at Winnemucca, Round Top, and Fourth of July Lakes. Permits for camping in these sites are only issued on a first-come, first-served basis at the Carson Pass Information Station, which is open seven days a week in the summer. The Carson Pass Information Station is located at the top of Carson Pass on CA 88, 6 miles east of the Kirkwood Mountain Resort. See the Eldorado National Forest website for more information. Campfires are prohibited within the CPMA at all times. There's a fee to park at the trailhead, which is in the Eldorado National Forest: 100 Forni Road, Placerville, CA 95667; 530-622-5061; fs.usda.gov/eldorado. For visitor information, call 530-644-6048.

DRIVING DIRECTIONS: The trailhead is right at Carson Pass on CA 88, on the highway's south side, where you'll also find the Carson Pass Information Station. The trailhead is on the station's west side. As trails emanating from Carson Pass are extremely popular, the main parking lot usually fills up by midmorning. Secondary parking may be available a very short distance eastbound from the pass on the shoulders of an old road (you'll still have to pay a fee to park there).

trip 16   Fourth of July Lake

    Trip Data: 38.65045°N, 120.01550°W; 14.0 miles; 2/1 days
        Topos: *Caples Lake, Carson Pass*

HIGHLIGHTS: Backpackers who don't mind regaining lost elevation will appreciate this semiloop trip through the northeast section of Mokelumne Wilderness, which includes several ponds and lakes, wildflower-covered slopes, sweeping vistas, and a deep canyon.

DAY 1 (Carson Pass Trailhead to Fourth of July Lake, 5.5 miles): Find this section of the Pacific Crest Trail (PCT)/Tahoe-Yosemite Trail (TYT) on the west side of the Carson Pass Information Station, and head south on the wide, well-traveled path through a mixed forest of lodgepole pines, mountain hemlocks, and western white pines. The gradually descending

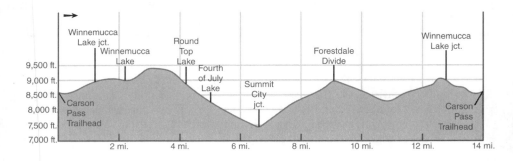

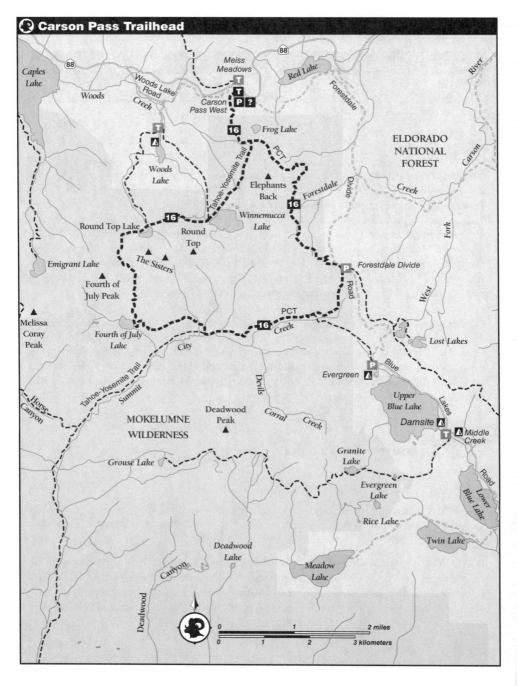

trail leads past a small pond surrounded by willows before making a gentle-to-moderate ascent as the trail crosses the Mokelumne Wilderness and CPMA boundary and switch-backs toward the Sierra Crest. The forest thins on the approach to a ridge, allowing glimpses of the volcanic summits of Round Top and the Sisters. On a plateau, reach a junction with a short trail left (northeast) to Frog Lake (no camping), which fills a shallow depression in an open bowl dotted with widely scattered pines. The 10-minute walk to the far end of the lake is a worthy diversion for views straight down the edge of a cliff to Red Lake and out toward Hope Valley and peaks of the southern Carson Range. Just as impressive is the view across the lake of the dark ramparts of Round Top. Early-season visitors will be treated to a fine display of wildflowers as well.

JOHN C. FRÉMONT

With Kit Carson as his scout, John C. Frémont made the first winter crossing of the Sierra somewhere on this plateau in February of 1844. From an encampment in Faith Valley a few miles to the east, Frémont, along with his chief cartographer, Charles Preuss, climbed Red Lake Peak, just north of Carson Pass. From the summit, they were the first Europeans to see the great mountain lake we now know as Tahoe. The climb of Red Lake Peak was the first recorded ascent by Europeans of an identifiable Sierra mountain.

From the unmarked junction to Frog Lake, go ahead (south) a short way to a junction and turn right (south-southwest), leaving the PCT behind to follow the TYT on a descent across open slopes on the west side of Elephants Back. Continue the mile-long descent toward Winnemucca Lake through shrub-covered slopes dotted with small groves of whitebark and lodgepole pines, enjoying excellent views of hulking Round Top along the way. Seasonally, a meadow near Winnemucca Lake offers an unbelievable wildflower display. Cruise picturesque Winnemucca's west shore beneath Round Top to a junction, marked by a post, with a trail to Woods Lake.

Winnemucca Lake   Photo by Mike White

Hikers descend through Summit City Canyon.   Photo by Mike White

WHITEBARK PINES
Stands of high-altitude-loving whitebark pines provide nesting places for hundreds of Clark's nutcrackers, which swoop back and forth over the heads of hikers. These birds eat lots of whitebark pine nuts. The Clark's nutcracker's fondness for these nuts is probably one of the main reasons whitebarks expand their territory. These large, noisy, crowlike, gray-and-white birds are messy eaters, dropping seeds to the ground while picking the cones apart, thus helping to propagate new pines.

Go ahead (south-southwest) from the junction, ford the lake's outlet, and begin a moderate climb up a gully covered with pockets of willow, heather, and grasses to the crossing of a stream. Continue the ascent to a saddle and then descend shortly to a junction near the north shore of Round Top Lake, with another trail to Woods Lake.

Go left (southwest) from the junction and follow an arcing traverse around the west shoulder of the Sisters to the crest of a divide. On the far side of Round Top Lake, the steep cliff is a mélange of grays, greens, and browns, and the surrounding talus slopes vary in color according to which bedrock yielded up which talus blocks. All the rock outcroppings in this region are dark colored. Volcanic rocks are normally dark, but even the granite here is much darker than the shining granites found in Desolation Valley. Along this stretch of trail, views are excellent (scanning from east to north to west) of Markleeville Peak, Hawkins Peak, the Crystal Range, the slopes above Caples Creek, and Caples Lake.

Soon the TYT descends to a saddle, leaving the basin of the American River and entering the Mokelumne River drainage. From the crest, avoid a faint use trail to Fourth of July Peak and follow the main trail as it descends almost 1,000 feet on gradual-to-moderate switchbacks through a handsome bowl toward Fourth of July Lake. Colorful wildflowers should cheer midsummer hikers along the descent.

At a junction abreast of Fourth of July Lake, turn right (west) to the lake (8,201';38.65045°N, 120.01550°W), which is quite scenic, cradled in a rocky amphitheater between Fourth of July Peak and Peaks 9,795 and 9,607. A mixture of open meadows, pockets of willow, and stands of white fir and western white pine ring the shoreline. Your campsite is one of the six designated sites at this pretty lake.

DAY 2 (Fourth of July Lake to Carson Pass Trailhead, 8.5 miles): From Fourth of July Lake, the trail heads south to follow a switchbacking course through mixed forest out of the Carson Pass Management Area before veering northeast and emerging onto open, brush-covered slopes allowing expansive views of Summit City Canyon. A long, descending traverse across these slopes leads down toward the floor of the canyon and into lodgepole pine forest on the way to a junction with the trail on the canyon's floor. Here, the Tahoe-Yosemite Trail turns right (west, then southwest), but your trip turns left (east) to head through the trees, passing a campsite and soon reaching a second junction, marked by a post.

Take the left fork, following signed directions generally east to the PCT on a 3-mile climb, initially through a lodgepole pine forest with a lush understory of plants and flowers. A steady ascent on the sometimes-rocky trail leads away from the floor of Summit City Canyon, where the groundcover soon disappears beneath a dense forest of red firs and western white pines. After a few long switchbacks, the trail emerges from the forest and onto brush-covered slopes with fine views of the canyon rimmed by impressive-looking mountains to the south. The shrubs are quite thick, threatening to overgrow the trail in spots and at times reaching over-the-head heights. Well-watered slopes farther upslope harbor ferns, willows, alders, young aspens, and an assortment of wildflowers, including tall alpine knotweeds. Sagebrush heralds the final approach to Forestdale Divide and a junction with the PCT.

Turn left (west) onto the PCT at the junction and make a short climb over the crest of Forestdale Divide, exiting the Mokelumne Wilderness and beginning a winding descent to a verdant bench harboring a group of subalpine ponds near the head of Forestdale Creek's canyon. Although the ponds are never more than knee deep, the sweeping views extending from Elephants Back to Hope Valley create a picturesque setting quite suitable for a lingering break.

Continue the descent away from the bench to cross a branch of Forestdale Creek. Past the creek, a stiff, winding climb begins across flower-covered slopes on the east side of Elephants Back, where amateur botanists will see a diverse assortment of wildflower species during the height of the season. The 900-foot ascent leads to the crest of Elephants Back's north ridge and back into Mokelumne Wilderness and Carson Pass Management Area, topping out south of Frog Lake. A short descent leads to the junction with the TYT on its way from Carson Pass (right) to Winnemucca Lake (left). You close the loop here, turn right (ahead, first west and then north), and retrace your steps along the PCT/TYT to the Carson Pass Trailhead.

Upper Blue Lake– Granite Lake Trailhead
8,134'; 38.62790°N, 119.94065°W

Destination/ GPS Coordinates	Trip Type	Best Season	Pace & Hiking/ Layover Days	Total Mileage	Permit Required
17 Granite and Grouse Lakes 38.62231°N 120.00766°W (Grouse Lake)	Out-and-back	Mid to late	Leisurely 2/1	12.0	Mokelumne Wilderness

INFORMATION AND PERMITS: As with other Mokelumne Wilderness destinations off CA 88, this trailhead is in the Eldorado National Forest: 100 Forni Rd., Placerville, CA 95667; 530-622-5061, fs.usda.gov/eldorado. For visitor information, call 530-644-6048.

You must have a permit to camp overnight in Mokelumne Wilderness; download your permit at fs.usda.gov/Internet/FSE_DOCUMENTS/fseprd754168.pdf.

DRIVING DIRECTIONS: Leave CA 88 at 6.3 miles east of Carson Pass and head south on Blue Lakes Road through Hope Valley and over Forestdale Divide to a junction with the road to Lower Blue Lake, 10.3 miles from the highway. Continue straight ahead for another mile and turn right at the Mokelumne Hydro Project. Proceed past Middle Blue Lake to a small parking area on the left, just below the spillway of Upper Blue Lake, 13 miles from CA 88.

trip 17 Granite and Grouse Lakes

Trip Data: 38.62231°N, 120.00766°W (Grouse Lake); 12.0 miles; 2/1 days
Topos: Carson Pass, Pacific Valley, Mokelumne Peak

HIGHLIGHTS: Nestled into a little-traveled corner of Mokelumne Wilderness, Grouse Lake sits high above Summit City Canyon. Requiring only modest effort, this hike offers both the spectacular scenery of sweeping vistas and the intriguing beauty of geologic diversity.

DAY 1 (Upper Blue Lake–Granite Lake Trailhead to Grouse Lake, 6.0 miles): Grouse Lake Trail begins just south of Middle Creek Campground. From the parking area, cross the

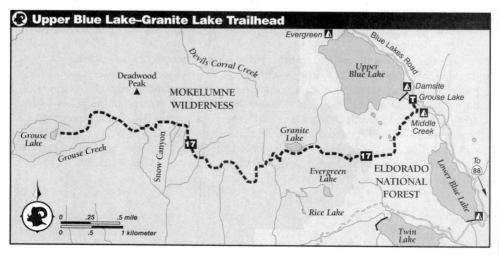

Upper Blue Lake–Granite Lake Trailhead

seasonal channel of the spillway overflow on a steel pedestrian bridge and immediately turn left (south) into lodgepole pine forest and head briefly downstream alongside the overflow channel until the trail veers away and reaches a log crossing of the perennial outflow from Upper Blue Lake. The nearly level trail leads past an unsigned lateral to the campground (ignore it) before your trail swings west on a gentle ascent with tree-shrouded views of the surrounding peaks, including Round Top. The grade eases momentarily at the signed crossing of the Mokelumne Wilderness boundary. Continuing west, skirt a small pond to the crossing of the outlet, climb steeply northwest to a shoulder, and go west through small meadows and past a tarn. Ascend a small ridge and then descend to swing west-southwest next to the flower-lined, seasonal outlet from Granite Lake. Soon the lake springs into view, cradled in a small basin surrounded by weathered granite outcrops.

Skirt the south shore of the lake past campsite laterals and veer left over a low ridge. Beyond the lake, you leave most day hikers behind, as the trail winds west for most of a mile through the weathered granite landscape, passing pockets of mixed forest and a small, flower-lined creek. Farther on, a very steep climb on deteriorating tread leads to a stunning vista: Clockwise from the east is the Carson Range (mostly in Nevada); dark, volcanic Raymond Peak; metamorphic Highland, Stanislaus, and Leavitt Peaks; and the polished, light granite of the deep cleft of North Fork Mokelumne River Canyon.

Continue through open terrain past an old gravesite, followed by a gradual descent across a verdant, flower-dotted meadow. Beyond the meadow, a lengthy ascent leads across several gullies to a sloping bench bisected by several spring-fed rills.

GEOLOGY LESSON

On the sloping bench, notice how light granite overlies dark volcanic bedrock. A slope change typically occurs at such a contact zone, as the overlying volcanic rock is softer and more easily eroded than granite. The numerous spring-fed rills indicate that the volcanic rock above holds more water than the granite below.

Descend west to a small creek, remaining on the north side, and climb through willows a short distance past the source of the creek. Continue climbing as the trail fades on an open slope. A ducked route levels off and contours northwest for 0.25 mile, until multiple paths descend a flower-filled gully dotted with boulders, where Grouse Lake appears several hundred feet below. Eventually the paths merge into a single trail that continues the descent into thickening forest to the shore of the secluded lake (8,563'; 38.62231°N, 120.00766°W). On a hot day, Grouse Lake provides a wonderful wilderness swimming pool. Nearby viewpoints offer glimpses of Summit City Canyon below to the west. Golden eagles, which traditionally nest in the canyon, may occasionally be seen riding thermals to dizzying heights above.

DAY 2 (Grouse Lake to Upper Blue Lake–Granite Lake Trailhead, 6.0 miles): Retrace your steps to the trailhead.

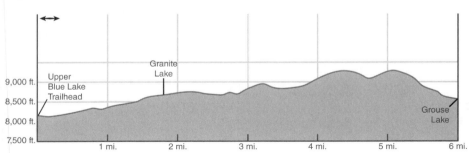

CA 4 TRIPS

CA 4 over Ebbetts Pass is something of an anomaly. It's a fine, two-lane mountain highway from the town of Arnold on the west to Lake Alpine. Beyond, the pavement shrinks to a narrow, winding, one-lane road with steep drops and climbs, and demanding hairpin turns on a climb over Ebbetts Pass and a descent eastward to a junction with CA 89.

You're rewarded with spectacular scenery in the Carson-Iceberg Wilderness, such a lightly used area that you may begin to wonder if anyone but you knows it's there. From CA 4, we offer trips from two major trailheads, from west to east: the Mosquito Lakes Trailhead on the west side of Ebbetts Pass, and the High Trailhead on the east side. Note that for trail information, the USDA/USGS *Carson-Iceberg Wilderness* map is usually more accurate than the topos.

While Lake Alpine and hiking trails nearby attract a majority of the visitors to this general area, far fewer visitors press on from the west or come up from the east to see the beautiful backcountry around Mosquito Lakes and Wolf Creek (the High Trail).

Trailheads: Mosquito Lakes
High

Mosquito Lakes Trailhead			8,068'; 38.51526°N, 119.91485°W		
Destination/ GPS Coordinates	Trip Type	Best Season	Pace & Hiking/ Layover Days	Total Mileage	Permit Required
18 Heiser and Bull Run Lakes 38.50557°N 119.93871°W (Stanislaus Meadow Trailhead)	Balloon	Mid	Leisurely 3/0	10.0	Carson-Iceberg Wilderness: Heiser Lake

INFORMATION AND PERMITS: You must have a wilderness permit for overnight visits to this part of Carson-Iceberg Wilderness. This trip is in the Stanislaus National Forest: Calaveras Ranger District, PO Box 500, Hathaway Pines, CA 95233; 209-795-1381, fs.usda .gov/stanislaus.

DRIVING DIRECTIONS: From the east end of Lake Alpine, travel 6 miles northeast up CA 4, or, from Ebbetts Pass, drive 8.4 winding miles west (just west of Pacific Grade Summit), to the west end of Mosquito Lakes (a single lovely pond at high water, or a pair of attractive ponds at low water) and the signed trailhead. There's a vault toilet in the Mosquito Lakes Campground across the highway.

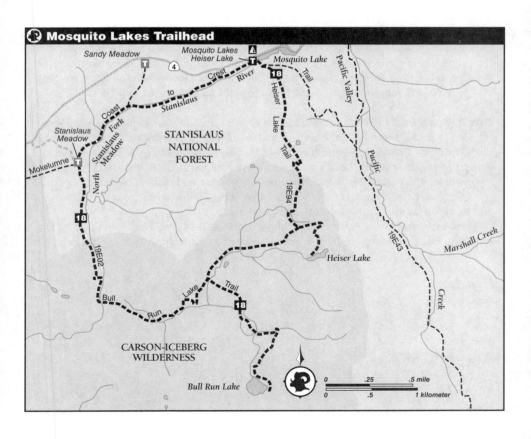

trip 18   **Heiser and Bull Run Lakes**

see
map on
p. 91

Trip Data: 38.50557°N, 119.93871°W (Stanislaus Meadow Trailhead);
10.0 miles; 3/0 days

Topos: *Pacific Valley, Spicer Meadow Reservoir*

HIGHLIGHTS: You'll visit two of the better, scenic, trout-stocked lakes off CA 4 on this easy hike. Day hikers and anglers may choose to hike only to Heiser Lake via the Heiser Lake Trail (Mosquito Lakes Trailhead), or only to larger Bull Run Lake via the Bull Run Trail (Stanislaus Meadow Trailhead).

DAY 1 (Mosquito Lakes Trailhead to Heiser Lake, 2.0 miles): Head briefly south on the Heiser Lake Trail, almost immediately meeting a junction with the Emigrant and Mokelumne Coast to Crest Trails on the right heading west to Lake Alpine (not shown on the topo). Step across the Emigrant Trail and continue ahead (south), remaining on the Heiser Lake Trail and curving around the western Mosquito Lake to a junction marked by a post with the recently designated Mokelumne Coast to Crest Trail on the left. Veering to the right, your trail makes a steep climb up a moraine south of the lake through moderate-to-sparse forest. Gaining the ridge at last, descend the sandy trail and enter Carson-Iceberg Wilderness near the half-mile mark. Continue generally southeast through forest interrupted by a pair of small meadows and then, at 0.75 mile, climb up the next moraine.

On fresh-looking, glacially scoured rock, descend the moraine and follow a winding route that takes the path of least resistance down rock slabs. After leveling off in deep forest, climb 0.3 mile to a small flat and a junction where tomorrow's route will turn right (southwest) down a creekside trail. For today, you turn left (east) at the junction and make a quarter-mile ascent to a switchback and then climb south over the low granitic ridge that hides shallow Heiser Lake (8,365'; 38.49481°N, 119.90675°W). Dotted with several small granite islands, the conifer-fringed lake presents anglers with a picturesque distraction while they contemplate a meal of fresh trout. Campsites lie on the north and south shores under a pleasant canopy of red firs, lodgepole pines, western white pines, and mountain hemlocks.

DAY 2 (Heiser Lake to Bull Run Lake, 2.5 miles): First, retrace your steps a quarter mile to the trail junction. From here, the route, usually well-blazed and ducked, leads southwest to the brink of a rocky slope and then down the slope on very steep switchbacks. Paralleling Heiser Lake's outlet, head west across a flat basin shaded by mountain hemlocks. Approaching the basin's west edge, cross four closely spaced branches of a tributary that joins the outlet creek just south of the trail. After a brief climb west, the trail turns south and leads to a signed junction with the Bull Run Trail.

Turn left (east) at the junction and almost immediately ford Heiser Lake's outlet, a ford that could present a problem in early season when the creek is a small torrent of

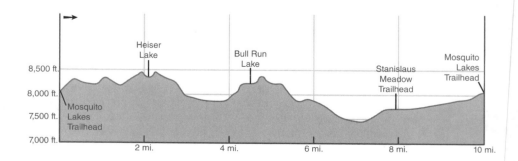

whitewater. After following a nearly level granite bench for 0.3 mile, the route angles south to cross the first of many small rivulets. The winding route climbs and gyrates up toward Bull Run Lake from one granite slab to another. Broken into two distinct ascents, the first climb trends southeast up and around a secondary ridge; the second trends southwest past a trailside pond before approaching the outlet and then ascending alongside to the lake's bedrock dam (8,348'; 38.48193°N, 119.91489°W).

Although not large by Sierra standards, this popular lake can accommodate a large number of campers, particularly on the spacious flats shaded by large red firs. Swimming in the lake is comfortable by early August, and fishing is reported to be good for brook trout.

DAY 3 (Bull Run Lake to Mosquito Lakes Trailhead, 5.5 miles): Backtrack to the trail junction west of Heiser Lake's outlet and turn left (southwest) onto the Bull Run Trail. Descend, steeply at times, 350 vertical feet down rock slabs covered with lodgepole and western white pines, red firs, and mountain junipers, staying well above the outlet creek from both lakes before the grade eases in a shady flat. A short, forested traverse leads to a crossing of this creek, which may entail a cold, wide, knee-deep ford in early season. Beyond the ford, follow the course of the creek on a shady, long 0.3 mile to a ford of the twin-branched outlet, which may also present early-season challenges. Beyond the ford the trail maintains a westbound course for 100 yards to an even wider ford of the headwaters of North Fork Stanislaus River. A search for logs across this stream may result in a quicker and drier crossing.

Bull Run Lake   Photo by Kathy Morey

Immediately beyond the North Fork, cross a seasonally dry wash before turning north and roughly paralleling the river upstream. A wide path leads up a moderate grade to Stanislaus Meadow, where a chorus of cowbells may herald the presence of cattle munching away on the verdant grasses. A fence helps to keep the cattle in the meadow while the trail follows an easy route through the trees near the west edge for 0.3 mile to the signed Stanislaus Meadow Trailhead (7,776'; 38.50557°N, 119.93871°W).

Away from the trailhead, follow the dirt access road to the left of a barbed wire fence enclosing expansive Stanislaus Meadows to a 3-way junction marked by a post. Turn right onto the combined singletrack of the Emigrant and Mokelumne Coast to Crest Trails and continue along the fenced meadow on gently graded tread, crossing some usually dry seasonal streams on the way through the fringe of a lodgepole pine forest. Beyond the end of the fence, ignore an unmarked dirt trail angling across your path and proceed to a signed three-way junction with a lateral on the left to the Sandy Meadows Trailhead. Continue ahead shortly to a lobe of the meadows and a usually easy crossing of the trickling, nascent North Fork Stanislaus River. Soon the trail begins a moderate climb through a light forest of lodgepole pines, western white pines, and mountain hemlocks. Make another usually easy crossing of the river and continue the ascent. Eventually, the grade becomes steeper and the tread turns rocky just before a level stretch delivers you to the final junction with the Heiser Lake Trail near the highway. From there, turn left and retrace your steps a very short distance to the trailhead.

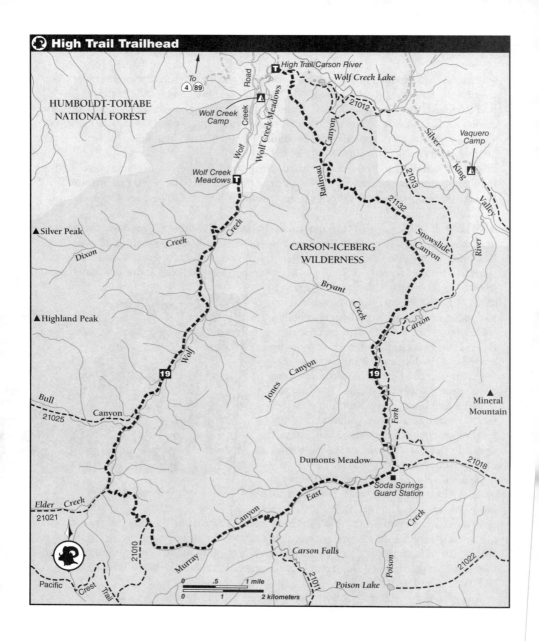

HUMBOLDT-TOIYABE
NATIONAL FOREST

To
4 89

High Trail/Carson River
Wolf Creek Lake

21012

Wolf Creek
Camp

Wolf Creek Meadows

Vaquero
Camp

Wolf Creek
Meadows

Road

Wolf Creek

21013

Silver King

▲Silver Peak

Dixon   Creek   Creek

CARSON-ICEBERG
WILDERNESS

Railroad Canyon

21132

Snowslide Canyon

Valley

▲Highland Peak

Bryant Creek

Carson

River

19

Wolf

Jones Canyon

19

Bull
21025   Canyon

Fork

▲
Mineral
Mountain

Elder Creek
21021

Dumonts Meadow

21018

Soda Springs
Guard Station

East   Canyon   Creek

Poison

21010

Murray

Carson Falls

Pacific   Crest   Trail

21011

Poison Lake

21022

0   .5   1 mile
0   1   2 kilometers

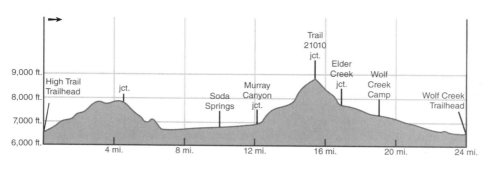

9,000 ft.
8,000 ft.
7,000 ft.
6,000 ft.

High Trail
Trailhead

jct.

Soda
Springs

Murray
Canyon
jct.

Trail
21010
jct.

Elder
Creek
jct.

Wolf
Creek
Camp

Wolf Creek
Trailhead

4 mi.   8 mi.   12 mi.   16 mi.   20 mi.   24 mi.

High Trailhead				6,481'; 38.60111°N, 119.68468°W		
Destination/ GPS Coordinates	Trip Type	Best Season	Pace & Hiking/ Layover Days	Total Mileage	Permit Required	
19 Wolf Creek Meadows 38.57595°N 119.69774°W (Wolf Creek Trailhead)	Shuttle (or point-to- point)	Mid to late	Strenuous 3/0	24.0/26.0	Humboldt- Toiyabe National Forest, Carson Ranger District	

INFORMATION AND PERMITS: Wilderness permits are required here, but there are no quotas, so you can get one at the trailhead. This High Trailhead trip is in the Humboldt-Toiyabe National Forest: Carson Ranger District, 1536 S. Carson St., Carson City, NV 89701; 775-331-6444, fs.usda.gov/htnf.

DRIVING DIRECTIONS: From the junction of CA 4 and CA 89 south of Markleeville and east of Ebbetts Pass, drive about 2.5 miles south on CA 4 and then turn southeast on the signed Wolf Creek Road. Proceed 3.3 miles to a fork, turn left following signed directions for the High Trail and Carson River Trailhead, and descend northeast around the north end of Wolf Creek Meadows. Past the meadows, the road climbs through the trees and, at 0.6 mile from Wolf Creek Road, reaches a spur road heading southeast a short distance to the trailhead.

SHUTTLE DIRECTIONS: Driving to the endpoint at the Wolf Creek Meadows Trailhead begins the same as driving to the High Trailhead: From the junction of CA 89 and CA 4 south of Markleeville and east of Ebbetts Pass, drive about 2.5 miles south on CA 4 and then turn southeast onto Wolf Creek Road. Proceed 3.3 miles to a fork. Avoiding the left fork (which leads to the High Trailhead), continue ahead (south) on Wolf Creek Road 1.5 miles to where the road bends sharply left. The signed Wolf Creek Meadows Trail is on the right immediately after the bend.

Note: This hike can be done as either a two-day or three-day trip. In the past it was described as two 12-mile days, but given the strenuous character of the climb up Murray Canyon it might suit many hikers better as a three-day hike, hiking 10 miles to Soda Springs the first day, then 9 tough miles to camp along Wolf Creek, followed by a shorter 5-mile-out day, which would be especially appreciated if you only brought one car and would need to do a 2-mile walk back to your car from the Wolf Creek Trailhead.

trip 19 **Wolf Creek Meadows**

Trip Data: 38.57595°N, 119.69774°W (Wolf Creek Trailhead); 24.0 miles; 3/0 days
Topos: *Wolf Creek, Disaster Peak*

HIGHLIGHTS: This lightly traveled trail provides access to true wilderness; don't be surprised if you see more bears than people. Enjoy excellent views of deep valleys from the High Trail ridge and stunning vistas of surrounding peaks from the top of Murray Canyon.

HEADS UP! *Much of this route is not shown, or is shown incorrectly, on maps and in previous guidebooks, as the trail network has changed significantly over the years. These trails are lightly used and maintenance has been spotty, so they can be indistinct and a real challenge to follow. Bring a friend, a compass, and a good sense of direction to make good decisions.*

DAY 1 (High Trailhead to Soda Springs, 10.0 miles): At the edge of a volcanic slope covered with sagebrush, bitterbrush, and mule ears, the High Trail climbs upward into an open forest of Jeffrey pine and white fir to the Carson-Iceberg Wilderness boundary and shortly after a junction of the High Trail and the faint East Fork Carson River Trail.

Turn right (south) at the junction onto the High Trail, experiencing brief views of Wolf Creek Meadows. Leaving the views of the meadows behind, you climb steeply through a shady forest. At 1.2 miles you reach a large split boulder and a large mountain mahogany as the trail parallels the ridge up to a level crest and then climbs steeply to a small, grassy flat at about 2 miles from the trailhead. Past the flat, the trail makes an uphill traverse across a grassy, gentle slope containing a curious combination of water-loving aspens and drought-resistant junipers. Jeffrey pines, white firs, willows, sagebrush, and mule ears complete the cast of unlikely plant combos.

Climb shady slopes for about 0.75 mile beyond the meadow until the steep grade of the trail eases across a level area. Here, you get your first views into the expansive Silver Valley, as well as a brief view of the Vaquero Camp cabins to the east.

You now begin a lengthy jaunt along the volcanic ridgeline with frequent views of Silver Valley. The jaunt begins with a short journey through a thick forest, then goes back and forth between open views north into Bagley Valley and distant Freel Peak (beyond whose summit lies Lake Tahoe), and to the east of Silver Valley.

AUTOBRECCIATED LAVA FLOW

Along this short, open traverse is a good exposure of a blocky volcanic rock common to this "land of fire and ice" and known as an autobrecciated (self-broken) lava flow. Geologists speculate that from the middle Miocene epoch through the late Pliocene epoch, thick andesitic lava flows poured from summits that were perhaps similar to the Oregon Cascades of our time. These lava flows covered an area of the Sierra Nevada from Sonora Pass north to Lassen Park and from east of the present Sierra Crest westward to the Central Valley. Flowing along their downward paths, the thick lava flows cooled and became less and less able to move, particularly on the rapidly cooling edges that eventually solidified. Pressure from the still-flowing internal areas fractured the edges, creating the broken-up texture seen today.

"Autobrecciated lava flow" is a mouthful. The Hawaiians, who live intimately with volcanoes, call such flows *aa*, pronounced "Ah! Ah!" and equivalent to "Ow! Ow!," which is what you might say if you walked on *aa* in bare feet. We'll use *aa* instead of "autobrecciated lava flow."

With most of your climbing done, you are now traversing the steep volcanic slope, and in places the trail is narrow, eroded, and requires concentration on your footing to avoid a slip. At about 4.5 miles you reach a junction. The main trail goes straight and a trail loop leads in about 50 yards to a view at the top of a knoll. Here you get the best views of the day—a good place for lunch. The wide expansive view of the valley below makes you feel alone in the world.

Back on the trail, pass through a forest of Jeffrey pine and firs, then descend steeply south through the open slope above Snowslide Canyon. Volcanic rocks give way to granitic ones as you leave the brushy canyon on a descent through forest. Near the bottom of the descent you can look up at interesting granite rock pilings.

The descent briefly ends with a short uphill, before the first views of East Fork Carson River Canyon and the river itself foretell a series of short, steep switchbacks through the rocky granitic terrain. Then the trail diagonals less steeply across the slope southwest to a junction with the East Fork Carson River Trail. Your trail goes straight and parallels the river, soon fording a creek.

Soda Springs   Photo by Tim Hauserman

Older maps and previous guidebooks describe crossing the river here, but there is no longer a crossing. Now you follow a lovely trail that parallels the river without crossing for the next 2 miles. It is mostly level, through an open forest of Jeffrey pines, and gives frequent glimpses of the river. While there are no obvious campsites, you could certainly camp here.

FISH IN THE EAST FORK CARSON RIVER

A likely catch for anglers is the mountain whitefish, which resembles a cross between a trout and a sucker. A small mouth on the lower part of its head is the sucker characteristic, but the presence of an adipose fin on the lower back identifies it as a close relative of trout and salmon. As with those two fish, the whitefish is good to eat. The river also is home to the Tahoe sucker, whose protractile mouth on the bottom of its head is ideally suited for scavenging the river bottom. Although bony, the Tahoe sucker is quite tasty.

Near the end of this easy romp along the river, you cross a grassy meadow and then reach a ford of the river. While by late summer the water is fairly low, you still have to walk about 20 feet across the water. Bring your water sandals because there is a more difficult ford ahead. Across the river, it can be a challenge to find the trail, but it wanders through more grassy meadow to the south, and then into the forest again, where you meet the Poison Flat Trail to the left.

Straight ahead you shortly cross Poison Creek, which is not poisonous. Just after the creek you note a fenced-in meadow to your right and continue ahead a short distance to the Soda Springs Administrative Site.

SODA SPRINGS ADMINISTRATIVE SITE

The buildings and corral complex that compose the Soda Springs Administrative Site were constructed as a guard station during World War II by a group of conscientious objectors. It was staffed by U.S. Forest Service personnel until it became part of the Carson-Iceberg Wilderness, and it was placed on the National Register of Historic Places in 1994. After bear break-ins an electric bear fence was constructed around the buildings.

Backpacker campsites are available by Poison Creek (6,776'; 38.50960N°, 119.65245°W), or near a small creek 0.3 mile along the trail west of the guard station, or farther down the trail at a ford of the East Fork Carson River. Camping is prohibited in the administrative site's immediate vicinity; read and follow all posted regulations.

DAY 2 (Soda Springs to Wolf Creek, 9.0 miles): From the administrative site, the trail continues west through an open forest just a short distance upslope of the meandering creek, which is often obscured by brush. In about a mile the trail bends to the north and crosses a meadow and heads to a challenging ford of the river. Here, just before the crossing, lies a campsite in the grass.

This ford is shorter than the first one, but deeper. Across the river, the trail may be challenging to find, but your goal is to follow the river upstream. Once you locate the trail, it winds along a level, sandy, open forest with a gentle ascent. Keep your eyes peeled because overgrowth and lack of trail maintenance will most likely cause you trouble with keeping on the trail. You cross several small streams before reaching a junction just after crossing Murray Canyon Creek. Here the Murray Canyon Trail and Golden Canyon Trail meet, and several campsites can be found near here if you decide this is where you want to camp to do the trail in two days.

At the signed trail junction, take the right fork generally westward, and climb, steeply at times, up more than a dozen switchback legs that lead high up a brushy, open-forested slope and into Murray Canyon. Nice views of Falls Meadows open up quickly.

MURRAY CANYON GLACIER

Like virtually every tributary of East Fork Carson River upstream of Soda Springs, Murray Canyon held a glacier at the same time as a glacier occupied the East Fork Carson River's canyon. However, being much smaller, the Murray Canyon glacier was unable to keep pace with the tremendous excavating power of East Fork Carson River's glacier, which was estimated to be as thick as 800 feet in this area. As a result, the glacier cut deeper, leaving Murray Canyon as a hanging valley—the same valley hikers enter at the top of the upcoming switchbacks.

From the top of the switchbacks, travel 200 yards to a crossing of lushly lined and crystal-clear Murray Canyon Creek, and then continue steeply up to a trail fork, go right, and keep climbing. About a quarter mile past the junction you cross a creek lined with willows and alders, then ford another stream a quarter mile farther. Here you pass through a lovely area of grass and ancient aspens.

The route becomes steeper past the stream. The trail builders didn't mess around too much with switchbacks, they just headed straight up the slope. Talus from volcanic formations above has buried much of the granite bedrock, becoming very widespread where the grade eases and the trail enters a small gully flowered with mule ears. A rocky viewpoint off to your right might be worth a look. Beyond this gully, climb steadily north for a half mile to a crest saddle and come to a junction a few hundred yards northwest of the actual crest.

From the junction, the left fork eventually connects with the PCT, but you go right on switchbacking trail that heads northwest down open volcanic slopes toward Wolf Creek, descending through thick, horizontal lava flows with a huge talus slope below. But first, stop at the top because the views here are the best of the whole trip. You gaze out at a good portion of the Carson-Iceberg Wilderness, including Highland Peak at 10,935 feet to the northwest, and Arnot Peak to the southwest. And the break is good as well because the descent is a challenging one: a series of long switchbacks heading northwest down the steep slope.

One difficulty of note is a steep drop into a gully where the trail has eroded away. Catch your breath by enjoying some beautiful juniper trees, as well as mini groves of aspens. Sometimes the trail is hard to follow on the thin, rocky slopes. After a descent of about 1,400 feet you reach a cattle fence at the floor of the canyon. Go through the fence and then slightly left into the meadow. Look for a signpost for the trail to Elder Creek; your trail then goes right and soon fords Wolf Creek. In late summer you might be able to rock-hop across; in early season you will get wet.

Find the trail on the other side of the creek. Apparently the trail from here on out was a jeep road at one time, but that has mostly eroded away. The trail parallels the creek through a meadow but may be tough to locate because the meadow holds cattle who have created a number of trails of their own. The trail continues to parallel above the creek, staying above the small gorge that the creek has cut through the volcanic rock. Small, tempting pools appear in the creek, particularly just before a gate on a low, descending ridge. Beyond this gate, the route descends very steeply to a crossing of Bull Canyon Creek, a wet ford except in late season. Past the creek crossing you see sandy aspen groves along Wolf Creek with several campsites (7,350'; 38.52002°N, 119.72672°W). Three-day hikers may camp here; those doing it all in two, keep on hiking.

DAY 3 (Wolf Creek to Wolf Creek Trailhead, 5.0 miles): Past the aspen campsites you soon meet the Bull Canyon Trail, which climbs 2,000 feet in just 3 miles to the Pacific Crest Trail. Past it, the trail journeys on a gentle descent, approaching and veering away from Wolf Creek several times. In places the trail is right next to a steep drop to the river, and in others the creekbed and the valley around it are wide. Keep your eyes open for places to dip your feet in the sparkling pools, and enjoy views of fascinating rock formations lifting straight up from the river's edge. Continue to Dixon Creek, which usually runs too high to ford without getting wet feet—the last such ford en route to the trailhead. Beyond the ford, the trail first parallels and then veers northwest away from the creek. Skirt a grove of aspens and cottonwoods, and then curve east around a well-weathered granite knob. From here, an easy 1-mile stroll leads to the Wolf Creek Meadows Trailhead (6,567'; 38.57595°N, 119.69774°W) just outside the wilderness boundary.

From trail's end, if you only have one car you have a 2-mile walk back to it on the dirt road. It's a pleasant gentle ascent through lush fields dotted with cows for 1.5 miles to a junction. From there a quick descent leads past a ranch house, then you cross a meadow and do a quick steep ascent to the High Trailhead, at 0.6 mile from the junction.

CA 108 TRIPS

Southward toward northern Yosemite National Park. To the southeast of Sonora Pass, lake-filled Emigrant Wilderness unfolds southward toward northern Yosemite National Park. To the southeast of Sonora Pass is Hoover Wilderness, which lies in Humboldt-Toiyabe National Forest. Except for Emigrant Wilderness's lack of high granite peaks, the scenery is hard to beat anywhere in the Sierra. We explore these wilderness areas from trailheads that are, from west to east, Crabtree, Gianelli Cabin, Kennedy Meadows, Sonora Pass, and Leavitt Meadows. From the Crabtree Trailhead on the western edge of Emigrant Wilderness, we offer four journeys to some of the wilderness's more delightful spots. The Gianelli Cabin Trailhead, also on Emigrant Wilderness's west side, is a gateway to many of the wilderness's most beautiful and dramatic destinations, and we present three exciting trips from there. From the Kennedy Meadows Trailhead, major trails lead into Emigrant Wilderness, as well as into northern Yosemite National Park. Two trips depart south from the summit of Sonora Pass, both initially following the Pacific Crest Trail (PCT) southbound, following the boundary between the Emigrant and Hoover Wilderness areas. Finally, once east of Sonora Pass, five trips depart south from the Leavitt Meadows Trailhead, a gateway to a string of subalpine lakes set like jewels in a long bracelet of handsome peaks.

Trailheads: Crabtree

Gianelli Cabin

Kennedy Meadows

Sonora Pass

Leavitt Meadows

Crabtree Trailhead				7,164'; 38.17868°N, 119.90675°W	
Destination/ GPS Coordinates	Trip Type	Best Season	Pace & Hiking/ Layover Days	Total Mileage	Permit Required
20 Bear, Y Meadow, and Chewing Gum Lakes 38.19510°N 119.85126°W (Chewing Gum Lake)	Loop	Mid to late	Leisurely, part cross-country 4/0	14.9	Emigrant Wilderness: Crabtree
21 Deer Lake 38.16635°N 119.76606°W	Out-and-back	Early to late	Leisurely 4/2	23.2	Emigrant Wilderness: Crabtree
22 Pingree Lake 38.13412°N 119.80026°W	Semiloop	Mid to late	Moderate 5/2	29.3	Emigrant Wilderness: Crabtree
23 Huckleberry Lake 38.13503°N 119.70242°W	Semiloop	Mid to late	Moderate 6/1	43.1	Emigrant Wilderness: Crabtree
26 Crabtree Trailhead (in reverse of description; see page 123)	Shuttle	Mid to late	Leisurely 4/1	27.2	Emigrant Wilderness: Crabtree

INFORMATION AND PERMITS: This trailhead is in Stanislaus National Forest, accessing Emigrant Wilderness. Permits are required for overnight stays, but there are no quotas. Permits for this trailhead are most conveniently picked up at the Summit District Ranger Station, located at 1 Pinecrest Road, in Pinecrest, California. If you will be arriving outside of office hours, call 209-965-3434; you can request a permit up to two days in advance and it will be left in a dropbox for you. No campfires above 9,000 feet and no campfires within a half mile of Emigrant Lake. One-night camping limit per trip at the following lakes: Bear, Camp, Grouse, Powell, and Waterhouse. If you will be entering Yosemite National Park or Hoover Wilderness, bear canisters are required, and pets are prohibited in Yosemite.

DRIVING DIRECTIONS: There are two possible routes departing off CA 108; here the more northerly option is described because it departs from the CA 108–Pinecrest Road junction, immediately adjacent to the Summit Ranger Station in Pinecrest, where you must pick up your Wilderness Permit. Along CA 108, drive 36.5 miles east of the CA 108–CA 120 junction (or 36.2 miles west of Sonora Pass), turning east onto Pinecrest Road. After 0.3 mile, turn right (south) onto Dodge Ridge Road. Follow Dodge Ridge Road for a windy 3.0 miles to the entrance to the Dodge Ridge Ski Area, then turn right (south) onto the Dodge Ridge Loop Road, signposted for Crabtree and Gianelli Trailheads. After 0.5 mile turn left (east) onto Crabtree Road and follow it 4.3 miles, past the Aspen Meadow Pack Station to a Y-junction; shortly before the pack station the trail becomes gravel. At the Y-junction, stay right on Crabtree Road descending a now-rougher road. After 0.4 mile stay left at a minor junction, and 0.25 mile later reach a large parking area with toilets and a few trailhead campsites (1-night stay only). *Note:* The minor junction 0.25 mile from the trailhead is labeled as OVERFLOW PARKING but does not lead to any defined lot; the road verges simply provide additional parking spaces if the roadsides closer to the parking lot are full—a common weekend occurrence. Also, if you do not need to pick up a Wilderness Permit, you can turn from CA 108 directly onto Crabtree Road in Cold Springs, located 2.0 miles before Pinecrest.

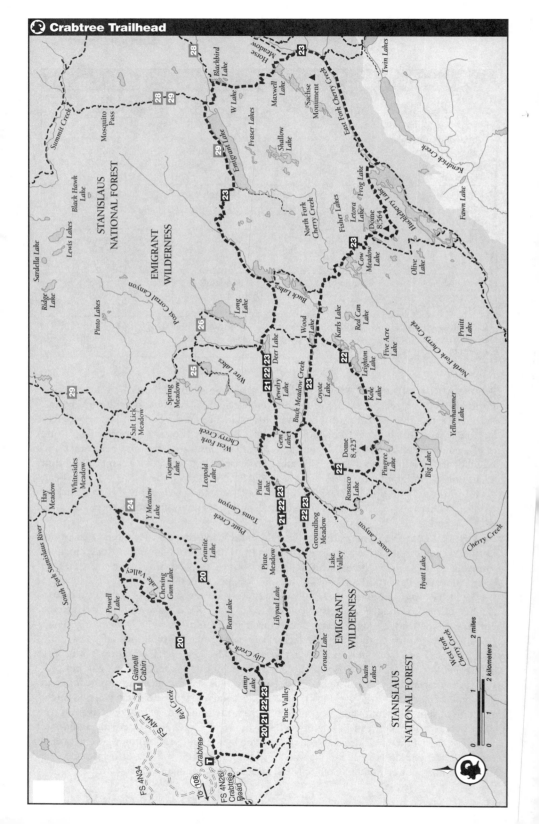

trip 20   **Bear, Y Meadow, and Chewing Gum Lakes**

> **Trip Data:**   38.19510°N, 119.85126°W
> (Chewing Gum Lake); 14.9 miles; 4/0 days
> **Topos:**   *Pinecrest, Cooper Peak*

HIGHLIGHTS: This partially off-trail loop links four stunning granite-basin lakes. Distances are short, even on the entirely on-trail days, leaving plenty of time for fishing, exploring, and relaxing at each lake. This hike can easily be completed in a weekend—or even a day by an ambitious hiker—but if you have the time, spread the hike over four days, as described.

DAY 1 (Crabtree Trailhead to Bear Lake, 3.8 miles): Leaving the Crabtree Trailhead, the trail crosses Bell Creek on a bridge, turns south, and quickly comes to a junction with a left-bearing (east) lateral to Chewing Gum Lake (shown on the *Emigrant Wilderness* map, but not on the USGS 7.5' topo map). Your route continues ahead (south), the usually dusty trail undulating across bouldery-scrubby slopes and through dry white fir forest, before curving east to climb steeply up a narrow, seasonally flower-filled draw. You soon attain a broad white fir–shaded saddle with a junction, where right (south) leads to Pine Valley, while you head straight ahead (east) toward Camp Lake following a south-facing shelf high above Pine Valley.

Alternating between mixed-conifer shade and scrubbier slopes with huckleberry oak and greenleaf manzanita, the trail is funneled into a draw between a pair of granite ribs, the upslope bluffs tall and impressive. This leads past the Emigrant Wilderness boundary and to the west end of shallow Camp Lake (invigorating swimming). Campsites here are limited to a selection atop the granite ridge to the south. At a saddle just past Camp Lake, you turn left (north) onto the trail to popular Bear Lake, while right (east) leads to Piute Meadow (Trips 21–23).

Skirting the edge of a tannin-rich tarn rimmed by bracken fern and mixed conifers, the trail climbs briefly onto open, slabbier, scrubbier terrain, but soon drops into a pocket meadow colored by corn lilies, shooting stars, tall asters, larkspur, and dusty horkelia. Slowly the expanses of wildflowers yield to a short stretch of granite slab, and then the trail leads back to a flat of flowers and willows beside Lily Creek. After a final, brief creekside ascent you emerge on glacier-polished, white granite slabs near Bear Lake's outlet. There are campsites to the right (south) toward the outlet and others all along the northwestern and northern shores (for example, 7,720'; 38.17530°N, 119.86666°W); all the campsites close to the lake are sandy patches among slabs, while there are sites among scattered trees set back from the northern shore. *Note:* There is a one-night stay limit at Bear Lake, so don't plan a layover day here!

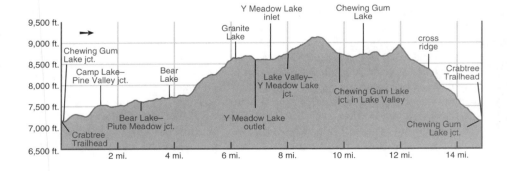

DAY 2 (Bear Lake to Y Meadow Lake, 3.6 miles): Continuing around the left (north) side of Bear Lake, you walk alternately on granite slabs and sandy trail segments. About 0.6 mile into the day and just as you're passing a small tarn (7,761'; 38.17811°N, 119.85935°W), the use trail becomes less clear; you're now staring up the Lily Creek drainage at endless granite slab. From here to Granite Lake and on to Y Meadow Lake, where you reunite with a built trail, there are countless possible routes, some staying along Lily Creek the entire way (and bypassing Granite Lake) and others veering farther southeast, aiming for Granite Lake. Whatever route you take you'll encounter cairns; these rock piles indicate that someone has been here before you, rather than that you're on a perfect route—one of the reasons you shouldn't add to these distractions (their violation of Leave No Trace principles is another reason).

The key is to walk upslope, crossing to the southeast side of Lily Creek sometime soon; heading from the tarn directly across the creek is a good option. Beyond, aim to ascend sandy or forested corridors between slabs, or climb up unbroken expanses of rock. Avoid staying too close to the creek, where the landscape is more incised and rougher. Also avoid sections with scrub, for the brush often grows alongside broken rock that is more cumbersome to ascend. One pleasant option is to cross Lily Creek and then aim for a broad granite slab rib about 0.25 mile southeast of the creek and parallel it up, ultimately turning due east around 8,530 feet (38.18330°N, 119.83959°W) and following a shelf beneath bluffs straight to Granite Lake; for the final 0.25 mile you are back on a use trail.

Granite Lake is ringed by steep granite slabs and cliffs broken by just occasional shoreline pockets of hemlock or lodgepole pine. Small—and only small—campsites are nestled on all sides, the lake's intricate shoreline and alcoves ensuring you have a private nook even when other groups are present.

Continuing to Y Meadow Lake, the going is easiest heading from Granite Lake's northwestern corner straight (northwest trending) toward Y Meadow Lake's dam. You climb broken slab, then weave across a nearly flat granite ridge where every depression is a snowmelt pond in early summer and a few tarns persist all summer. A gentle descent leads toward Y Meadow Lake's outlet, where you'll find a 25-foot-tall dam. This is one of 18 small dams built across lake and meadow outlets in Emigrant Wilderness and is the only one that created a lake where none previous existed. Like all of Emigrant's backcountry dams, it is no longer being maintained and will eventually breach. You now follow the lake's southeastern slab shore, passing countless campsites, including some large ones near the inlet (for example, 8,624'; 38.19565°N, 119.82490°W).

DAY 3 (Y Meadow Lake to Chewing Gum Lake, 3.3 miles): You'll pick up a trail near Y Meadow Lake's inlet. Follow it upstream, initially alongside the drainage, then onto slab, and soon back beside the early-drying creeklet, crossing it several times and admiring expanses of shaggy lupine and corn lilies in pocket meadows. This easy walking leads to a junction, where you turn left (southwest), signposted for Lake Valley, while right (northeast) leads on to Whitesides Meadow (Trips 25 and 26).

The trail climbs up broken slab, broad views emerging as you climb. Soon you're looking southeast into Yosemite; Tower Peak is the most obvious summit, but you can see all the way to the Clark Range, sitting southeast of Yosemite Valley. The ascent ends atop a nearly flat ridge, where you suddenly transition to volcanic scree—a small remnant of the 20-million-year-old volcanic deposits that created the intriguingly shaped summits on the ridge to the north (Cooper Peak, Castle Rock, and the Three Chimneys) and the massive volcanic peaks to the northeast, of which Relief Peak and Molo Mountain are most obvious. After crossing the sagebrush top and ogling at the phenomenal views, you descend just over 400 feet, transitioning back onto granite bedrock as you enter lodgepole pine forest

Granite Lake   Photo by Elizabeth Wenk

and reach a junction. Here, you turn left (south) toward Chewing Gum Lake, while right (west) leads to the Gianelli Cabin Trailhead (Trips 24–26).

The trail begins descending Lake Valley, principally filled with marshy meadows and a few small lakelets; Chewing Gum Lake is the only noteworthy water body here. But the meadows are lovely—Sierra ragwort, shaggy lupine, and buttercups all add color—and you quickly walk the length of two parallel meadow tentacles to reach slab-encrusted Chewing Gum Lake. This lake feels larger than its modest footprint belies, for it has a splendidly convoluted shoreline comprised predominately of low-angle, polished slab, broken by just enough forest pockets to ensure endless small, scenic campsites. There is also a larger forested site along the lake's northwest shore (8,719'; 38.19510°N, 119.85126°W).

DAY 4 (Chewing Gum Lake to Crabtree Trailhead, 4.2 miles): The final day's hike begins by skirting Chewing Gum Lake's western shore, passing a selection of amoeboid tarns, then climbing gently up sandy corridors between slabs to a broad slab saddle from which you look across the Lily Creek watershed to line upon line of distant summits. It then follows a series of Bell Creek tributaries downward. You descend through pleasant lodgepole pine forest, cross a minor saddle, and continue more steeply down an open red fir slope to the top of a striking meadow—a giant expanse of corn lilies and willows, with just a small, robust creek flowing through the center.

Following the creek's southern bank downslope, the trail ultimately trends due west, while the tributary turns north to meet Bell Creek. Without an uphill step, the trail traverses around a spur into another Bell Creek tributary, this one drying early. With continued descent, white fir replace the higher-elevation red fir. Soon the trail crosses onto rockier, scrubbier slopes, where the tread is harder on the feet and boulders and other moraine debris are scattered across the hillside, with huckleberry oak and pinemat manzanita growing alongside them. This leads back to the junction just steps from the Crabtree Trailhead; turn right (north), cross Bell Creek on a bridge, and quickly reach the trailhead.

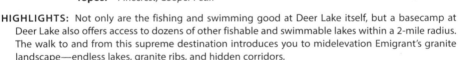

trip 21 **Deer Lake**

see map on p. 102

Trip Data: 38.16635°N, 119.76606°W; 23.2 miles; 4/2 days
Topos: *Pinecrest, Cooper Peak*

HIGHLIGHTS: Not only are the fishing and swimming good at Deer Lake itself, but a basecamp at Deer Lake also offers access to dozens of other fishable and swimmable lakes within a 2-mile radius. The walk to and from this supreme destination introduces you to midelevation Emigrant's granite landscape—endless lakes, granite ribs, and hidden corridors.

DAY 1 (Crabtree Trailhead to Lilypad Lake, 5.1 miles): Leaving the Crabtree Trailhead, the trail crosses a bridge over Bell Creek, turns south, and quickly comes to a junction with a left-bearing (east) lateral to Chewing Gum Lake (shown on the *Emigrant Wilderness* map but not on the USGS 7.5' topo map). Your route continues ahead (south), the usually dusty trail undulating across bouldery-scrubby slopes and through dry white fir forest, before curving east to climb steeply up a narrow, seasonally flower-filled draw. You soon attain a broad white fir-shaded saddle with a junction, where right (south) leads to Pine Valley, while you stay straight ahead (east) toward Camp Lake along a south-facing shelf high above Pine Valley.

Alternating between mixed-conifer shade and scrubbier slopes with huckleberry oak and greenleaf manzanita, the trail is funneled into a draw between a pair of granite ribs, the upslope bluffs tall and impressive. This leads past the Emigrant Wilderness boundary and to the west end of shallow Camp Lake (invigorating swimming). Campsites here are limited to a selection atop the granite ridge to the south. At a saddle just past Camp Lake, you go right (east), while the trail to popular Bear Lake leads left (north; Trip 20). (The 1.1-mile lateral to Bear Lake leads to a fine selection of slab-ringed campsites; there is a 1-night stay limit at Bear Lake.)

Passing a U-shaped tarn, the trail turns south, switchbacking down a steep, exposed scrubby slope parallel to Lily Creek's bedrock base, to reach a marshy lodgepole pine flat where you must ford Lily Creek; a log is available in the early season and later the stream may dry. There are little-used campsites just west of the stream.

Beyond the ford, switchbacks carry you up a rocky slope, where the conifer cover was mostly burned in the 2003 Mountain Fire, to a pleasantly graded draw that is alight with flower color until midseason. The shooting stars, larkspur, and stickseed bloom first, followed by Sierra tiger lilies, ragwort, lupine, and cow parsnip a few weeks later. Continuing along meadow corridors south of black-streaked granite outcrops, you transition onto granite slab and sandier passageways to reach Lilypad Lake, offering good campsites among slabs south of the trail (7,868'; 38.15923°N, 119.85228°W). Lilypad Lake, its surface covered with yellow pond lilies, is not named on the USGS 7.5' topo map or on trail maps of Emigrant Wilderness.

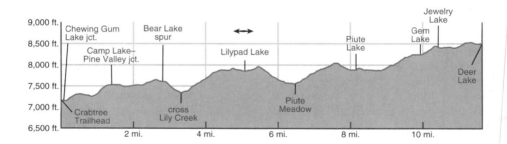

DAY 2 (Lilypad Lake to Deer Lake, 6.5 miles): A short climb east of Lilypad Lake leads up a narrow corridor to a saddle. Beyond, the trail descends briefly to a point overlooking large Piute Meadow (east), dome-guarded Toms Canyon (northeast), Groundhog Meadow (southeast), and, on the far eastern horizon, Bigelow Peak and the jutting prominence of Tower Peak. Rocky switchbacks carry you down 400 feet to Piute Meadow. You loop through lodgepole pine forest fringing the southern then western edges of meadow lobes (there are acceptable campsites under lodgepole pine cover at the meadow's edge). Stepping across Piute Creek, you reach a signed junction, where your route continues left (east) toward Piute Lake, while right (south) leads to Groundhog Meadow (and onto Buck Meadow Creek; Trip 23).

Almost immediately you must climb again; the granite here is endlessly crisscrossed by major landscape-wide joints, leading to the numerous, closely spaced near-parallel valleys you must cut across—or expressed more bluntly, must climb in and out of. The 500-foot ascent up dark-colored diorite slabs is exposed, hot, and dry with little vegetation cover. The slabs have just a shallow veneer of soil and, most years, the flowers will be parched by mid-July. The switchbacks lead to a rib, from which you admire a distant ridge of rolling domes to the south. Descending again, you quickly reach tiny, 2-acre Piute Lake (7,865') and the good shady campsites on its northeastern and northwestern sides. To the north is a dome decorated with an impressive swarm of near-parallel dikes, lines of lighter-colored rock.

A few steps up, a few more down, and you reach a meadow strip that quickly leads to the West Fork Cherry Creek, a sandy wade at higher flows, but often dry by late season.

Looking east toward Piute Meadow   Photo by Elizabeth Wenk

Once across, you climb another 400 feet, beginning with zigzags up broken slab outcrops where spreading phlox, pennyroyal, Sierra stonecrop, and prettyfaces provide dots of color. Higher you ascend an open red fir ramp that leads pleasantly to a minor saddle and, just beyond, to warm little Gem Lake (8,224'), where you'll find larger partially shaded campsites to the northwest and smaller, view-rich sites on slabs south of the lake. Passing a lateral that leads right (south) to the Buck Meadow Creek Trail, you continue left (east), climbing a little under 200 feet up slab and along a gully to reach Jewelry Lake (8,399'). Here there are more trailside campsites and fishing for rainbow trout in the lake and the lagoons around the inlet.

The final mile to Deer Lake begins alongside expanses of willows, then the trail ascends an awkward corridor to reach a lovely little shelf and soon Deer Lake's outlet. Deer Lake is a splendid destination, sitting in an open slab-ringed basin, with islands big and small, water that can be pleasantly warm for swimming by midsummer, shallow bays and deep drop-offs. There is a healthy population of nice-size rainbow trout, with good fishing in both the lake and inlet streams. The most popular campsites are about halfway along the north shore (8,482'; 38.16635°N, 119.76606°W), just before you reach a junction with the trails that lead left (north) toward Salt Lick Meadow (and Long Lakes and the Wire Lakes; Trips 25 and 26) and right (east) to the Buck Lakes (Trip 23), but there are also choices near the outlet, south of the outlet, and on slabs along the northeastern side of the lake. Deer Lake is an excellent location to take several layover days and explore this corner of Emigrant Wilderness; the Wire Lakes, Long Lake, the Buck Lakes, and Wood Lake all lie within about 2 trail miles, while Karls Lake (Trip 22), Cow Meadow Lake (Trip 23), and Emigrant Lake (Trip 23) are also all accessible on a day hike from this base camp.

DAYS 3 AND 4 (Deer Lake to Crabtree Trailhead, 11.6 miles): Retrace your steps.

trip 22 **Pingree Lake**

see map on p. 102

Trip Data: 38.13412°N, 119.80026°W; 29.3 miles; 5/2 days
Topos: *Pinecrest, Cooper Peak*

HIGHLIGHTS: This partially off-trail trip visits some of Emigrant Wilderness's most beautiful lakes, hidden not far from the main trail network. The cross-country walking is straightforward and the slab expanses are impressive, even by Emigrant's lofty standards. All the off-trail lakes you pass are ringed by granite slab, but they differ in character from dramatic, isolated Kole Lake, nestled just below a saddle, to Pingree Lake, set in a larger basin and ringed by both slabs and lodgepole pine flats. Incomparable beauty is found at every step.

HEADS UP! *The cross-country route between Wood Lake and Pingree Lakes is not difficult but requires navigational skills and is not recommended for beginners.*

DAY 1 (Crabtree Trailhead to Lilypad Lake, 5.1 miles): Follow Trip 21, Day 1 to Lilypad Lake (7,868'; 38.15923°N, 119.85228°W).

DAY 2 (Lilypad Lake to Deer Lake, 6.5 miles): Follow Trip 21, Day 2 to Deer Lake (8,482'; 38.16635°N, 119.76606°W).

DAY 3 (Deer Lake to Pingree Lake, 5.2 miles, part cross-country): From the junction on Deer Lake's north shore, go right (east) toward the Buck Lakes for 0.6 mile to reach another junction, where you turn right (south) toward Wood Lake; left (east) continues to the Buck Lakes (Trip 23). After walking past a small tarn and through seasonally boggy meadows, the descent slowly gathers momentum, first transitioning to bouldery lodgepole pine forest, then broken slab where ocean spray and mountain pride penstemon decorate the rock verges. Ultimately following a lodgepole pine corridor you reach the northern edge of Wood Lake (8,265') near a good campsite. Here you bear right (west) along a sandy shelf toward Wood Lake's outlet.

At 0.2 mile later you'll be forgiven for being confused. The USGS 7.5' topo map (and other maps) shows three different trails crossing Buck Meadow Creek near the Wood Lake outlet—and trails in all three locations exist and serve unique purposes; from upstream (east) to downstream (west), they are a ford that can be waist deep at high flows but dry by late season; a log balance that is a good choice for hikers at high flows; and a broad stock crossing that hikers will find quite deep at high flows. If you trend left (south) toward Wood Lake's outlet on the first spur departing south from the high shelf, you will reach the easternmost ford and be unable to reach the log due to cliff bands—so if you suspect you'll want to cross on the log, stay on the shelf to the second spur before dropping to creek level. All three routes converge at a signed junction on the south side of Buck Meadow Creek (8,286'; 38.15247°N, 119.76490°W), with good camping nearby. At this junction, turn left (east) and continue 0.35 mile right along Wood Lake's shore to where the trail diverges just slightly from the lake, curving south into a hemlock-shaded draw. Here you'll find the unsigned, faint "trail" to Karls Lake (8,298'; 38.15096°N, 119.76027°W).

Turn right (southwest) onto this once-upon-a-time trail and ascend the sheltered draw to a drier saddle between two small domes. Long unmaintained, the 0.5 mile to Karls Lake that is ostensibly trail is actually some of the roughest going to Pingree Lake, for you must hurdle many downed logs; once past Leighton Lake it is almost all slab walking. You drop down a dry gully to Karls Lake (8,292'), reaching the lakeshore in a thicket of corn lilies; there are campsites a little away from the water's edge where you first reach it and even better options where the lake narrows halfway along its northwest side. Karls Lake is a lovely big lake, edged almost entirely by lodgepole pine stands (contrary to the topo), with slab peninsulas and islands adding intrigue.

From here to Pingree Lake there is no visible trail. The easiest route forward follows Karls Lake's northwestern shore, cuts west past a pair of tarns, then turns southwest to follow a corridor to Leighton Lake (8,279'). While just about any route leads to Leighton's shores—and the temptation is always to head straight for the next lake—the walking is easier if you stay inland a little longer and aim to reach the lake just 0.2 mile from its western end. Alternatively, in mid to late season, when the water level is low, a good route around Leighton Lake (8,280') is along its north shore right at the water's edge, but you will have to leapfrog many a dead tree. Leighton Lake's shore is an eerily beautiful wasteland of dead trees, because, like so many of Emigrant's lakes, it has a small check dam at its outlet that

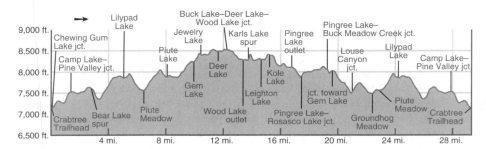

Pingree Lake Photo by Elizabeth Wenk

flooded the low-lying lodgepole pine flats ringing the lake. As a result, there is also little appealing camping around Leighton Lake.

From the lake's western end, you want to head up slabs and across a minor saddle to Kole Lake. Loop briefly around a lodgepole pine stand and start up at 38.14150°N, 119.77322°W for the easiest walking—here you are far enough south that you can follow a route that is parallel to small fissures in the slab, so you don't have to try and cut across any fractures. Be sure to look back into the lake basin during the climb to observe the cracks in these slabs that are slowly breaking up the mountainside. About 0.25 mile later you are atop a broad sand-and-slab saddle with stunning views east and northeast: Granite Dome, Black Hawk Mountain, and Molo Mountain to the northeast; Forsyth and Tower Peaks to the east; and Haystack, Schofield, and Richardson Peaks are the most prominent in the southeast. You could happily camp right here—it is just 0.1 mile to fetch water from Kole Lake.

Continuing west, you drop just slightly and reach Kole Lake (8,384'), positioned beneath a steep dome at the head of its watershed. There are ample campsites all along its shores, some on open sandy patches and others beneath lodgepole pine cover. From the lake's southwestern corner, you drop more steeply down broken slabs, aiming west until the terrain flattens, then southwest across sand and slab and sand and slab, laced with creeklets. You won't encounter many cairns here—nor should you leave any; there is no "right" or "wrong" way across this landscape. Instead, just savor the experience! About 0.25 mile before you reach Pingree Lake you must traverse two shallow forested notches. You then descend a final length of slab to the lake's forested eastern shore, where a thicket of bracken fern bisected by a quite decent trail greets you. There are forested campsites along the eastern and northern lake lobes, and more open, sandier choices to the west (8,093'; 38.13412°N, 119.80026°W). The trail loops around the northern shore and once at the outlet, you can easily continue south to the westside sites. Pingree Lake's elongate islands and peninsulas are particularly striking—linear ribs of granite that emerge above the water—and tempt photographers and sunbathers alike.

BIG LAKE

One or more layover days are required at Pingree Lake. Perhaps you will choose to enjoy the intricate shoreline and relax at your campsite; maybe you wish to enjoy the view from one of the surrounding domes; or, most likely, you'd also add a visit to Big Lake and the Yellowhammer cabin complex. The fastest route there is up and over the ridge southeast of Pingree Lake—aiming to reach the saddle a tad east of its low point makes for the easiest walking down the south side: excepting a few junipers at the top of the slope, you'll be staring down a completely unbroken expanse of glacier-polished slab extending all the way to Big Lake! Alternatively, you can retrace your steps about one-third of the way to Kole Lake before descending a shallow seasonal drainage. Big Lake's size is further aggrandized by the open, bedrock basin surrounding it—the view from the ridge is phenomenal in early morning or evening light. From the northeastern corner of Big Lake you'll hopefully pick up cairns that mark the trail southeast, east, then northeast to the cabins north of Yellowhammer Lake, built by the same Fred Leighton who envisioned the many small dams as a way to maintain stream flows all summer and develop self-sustaining trout populations.

On the USGS 7.5' topo maps (but not on most trail maps), you'll also see a trail that loops from Pingree Lake to Big Lake—this alternative, while longer, should be your return route. But do not expect a trail; there is a faint pad around Big Lake and up to the first saddle, then a fainter trail southwest to cross a second rib. Ahead there is no trail and barely a cairn, for there can't be: you traverse an even longer, more grandiose expanse of perfectly polished granite. Where the slab ends, you'll again pick up a faint trail that leads briefly north on a sand-and-slab shelf to cross a small creek, follows the west bank of the creek north until you are due west of Pingree Lake, and ascends broken granite and diorite slabs back to Pingree Lake. Expect to lose the trail from time to time and be prepared to use map-and-compass skills to follow the route.

DAY 4 (Pingree Lake to Lilypad Lake, 7.4 miles): From Pingree Lake you could retrace your steps to the trailhead via Wood Lake and Deer Lake, but this is a shorter, also very pleasant alternative. Reposition yourself at the northwestern corner of Pingree Lake, along the trail you followed around the lake's northern bay (8,108'; 38.13608°N, 119.80052°W). From here a trail continues west at the base of Dome 8,425, descending sandy corridors through the pervasive granite and diorite slabs. After 0.15 mile (38.13569°N, 119.80306°W), your route will diverge from the route to Rosasco Lake depicted on the USGS 7.5' topo maps, instead trending to the northwest; the trail due west toward Rosasco Lake has vanished here. Instead, a newer trail established for stock use bears northwest and after 0.5 mile merges with a trail shown on USGS 7.5' maps (but not all trail maps) that leads north and then northeast to Buck Meadow Creek. The trail is mostly in good condition, first trending down broken, barren slabs to an unnamed drainage and then turning north. A short uphill segment leads to flat walking alongside a seasonal stream. At 1.25 mile after leaving Pingree Lake the trail steps across a second seasonal creek and makes a sharp right, now trending northeast. Following a sheltered lodgepole pine corridor just beneath steep granite bluffs, the route leads to a pair of pocket meadows on a saddle and then descends briefly to the Buck Meadow Creek Trail.

You turn left (west), while right (east) leads back to Wood Lake. After a quick zigzag down a hemlock-shaded slope you must ford Buck Meadow Creek—although it is broad and not too deep, the current is stronger than you expect; take care at high flows. You then climb briefly up slabs to a junction, where you continue left (southwest) alongside Buck Meadow Creek, while right (north) leads to Gem Lake. For the coming 1.2 miles you are back on slab, a mix of light-colored granite and darker gray diorite, with lines of shrubs filling fractures. Buck Meadow Creek flows down a deeply incised course to your south; you are far above the water. As you approach the confluence with the West Fork Cherry Creek, take a few moments to imbibe your environs: In early summer the West Fork bounces down a series of cascades, punctuated by swirling pools, while by late season just drying swimming holes remain; there are lovely places to camp near the trail and along the west bank of the West Fork Cherry Creek.

Shortly you reach a ford of the West Fork, easier than you expect, for the river is braided and the many channels are shallow and dispersed. Across the creek you pass an unsigned trail left (south) down Louse Canyon (good campsites a short ways along; this is where the route from Rosasco Lake merges) and begin a steep, rocky climb out of the canyon. Switchbacks up the scrubby slope lead to a lush corridor positioned beneath steep bluffs—aspen, willows, and endless flowers fill the verges of a mucky tarn. A tiny Piute Creek tributary soon emerges, and the trail descends alongside it under white fir shade, the walls still looming to either side. The gradient eases as the trail approaches Groundhog Meadow, a densely vegetated reedy, marshy meadow that offers no campsites. Here you meet a junction where you turn right (north) toward Piute Meadow, while left (west) leads to Pine Valley. (*Note:* Continuing west past Grouse Lake and through Pine Valley before turning back north to the Crabtree Trailhead is 0.8 mile shorter than the described route but is a hotter, dustier alternative. There are lovely campsites at Grouse Lake if you take this option.) Turning toward Piute Meadow, you climb gently up, then across open slabs and through landscape lightly charred by the 2008 Groundhog Fire. In just 0.45 mile you reach the junction you passed on Day 2, where left leads to Lilypad Lake and Camp Lake: turn left (west) and retrace the first 1.4 mile of Day 2 to Lilypad Lake to spend the night. Or continue to Bear Lake (requires an extra 1.1 miles up a spur) or Camp Lake for variety.

DAY 5 (Lilypad Lake to Crabtree Trailhead, 5.1 miles): Retrace your steps from Day 1.

trip 23 Huckleberry Lake

see map on p. 102

Trip Data: 38.13503°N, 119.70242°W
(Huckleberry Lake); 43.1 miles; 6/1 days
Topos: *Pinecrest, Cooper Peak, Emigrant Lake*

HIGHLIGHTS: This trail follows a narrow east–west slice across Emigrant Wilderness, visiting lake upon lake en route. Not only are the camping, fishing, wildflower viewing, and scenery excellent, but you will finish this trip with a newfound appreciation of Emigrant's landscape. Regional joints break the granite along parallel fractures, creating corridors between bluffs, sandy shelves, and basins filled with elongate lakes.

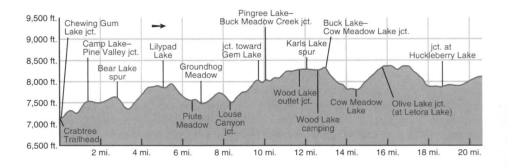

HEADS UP! *Notations in the text indicate where this trip connects with other routes described, in particular those out of the nearby Gianelli Cabin Trailhead or Kennedy Meadows Trailhead, in case you want to extend this loop.*

DAY 1 (Crabtree Trailhead to Lilypad Lake, 5.1 miles): Follow Trip 21, Day 1 to Lilypad Lake (7,868'; 38.15923°N, 119.85228°W).

DAY 2 (Lilypad Lake to Wood Lake via Buck Meadow Creek, 7.5 miles): A short climb east of Lilypad Lake leads up a narrow corridor to a saddle. Beyond, the trail descends briefly to a point overlooking large Piute Meadow (east), dome-guarded Toms Canyon (northeast), Groundhog Meadow (southeast), and, on the far eastern horizon, Bigelow Peak and the jutting prominence of Tower Peak. Rocky switchbacks carry you down 400 feet to Piute Meadow. You loop through lodgepole pine forest fringing the southern then western edges of meadow lobes (there are acceptable campsites under lodgepole pine cover at the meadow's edge). Stepping across Piute Creek, you reach a signed junction, where you turn right (south) toward Groundhog Meadow, while left (east) leads to Piute, Gem, and Wood Lakes (Trips 21 and 22) and is your return route. You cross open slabs—mostly dark-gray-colored diorite ones—the hot dry landscape leading gently downhill to reach Groundhog Meadow after just 0.45 mile. This densely vegetated, reedy, marshy meadow offers no campsites. Here you meet a junction, where you turn left (east) toward Wood Lake, while right (west) leads to Pine Valley and Grouse Lake. Slowly the meadow segues to a white fir–shaded passageway set beneath tall walls. You climb pleasantly beside a Piute Creek tributary, early-season flowers providing endless distraction. The ascent moderates beside a mucky tarn edged by aspens and willows. The bluffs continue to loom to either side until the corridor abruptly ends and you're staring down a steep, rocky slope to the confluence of the West Fork Cherry Creek and Buck Meadow Creek.

Switchbacks lead 200 feet to the broad valley floor. Passing the unsigned trail down Louse Canyon, the trail loops briefly through the valley-bottom forest; you could trend north here, alongside the West Fork, to pleasant slab campsites at the base of impressive early-summer cascades (and late-season swimming holes). The ford of West Fork Cherry Creek is easier than you expect, for the river is braided and the many channels are shallow and dispersed.

The trail proceeds up open slab separating Buck Meadow Creek from the West Fork. You hear, but barely see, Buck Meadow Creek, which follows a deeply incised channel to your south, while the West Fork commands your attention in early summer as it bounces down the granite slope. This climb is hot and open, with only the occasional Jeffrey pine providing a dot of shade. Continued ascent leads up the slabs, across a shrubbier slope, and

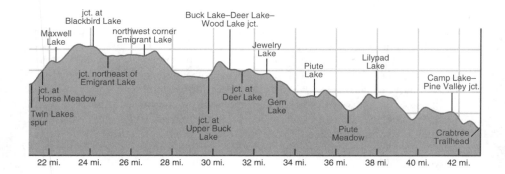

over more slabs, to reach a lateral trending left (north) up a steep slope to Gem Lake, while you stay right (east). A short descent leads to a ford of Buck Meadow Creek—although it is broad and not too deep, the current is stronger than you expect; take care at high flows. A quick zigzag up a hemlock-shaded slope takes you to an unsigned, unobvious junction that is actually a quite decent trail to Pingree Lake (Trip 22).

The contrast between the barren slab climb you just completed and the coming 1.5 miles is surreal; you are now on a cool north-facing slope under dense hemlock cover, following Buck Meadow Creek's narrow drainage beneath imposing domes. Slowly the walls to the north are set farther back, and then the trail descends to ford Buck Meadow Creek; a log is currently available, but otherwise it is a broad wade at high flows. After bypassing a north-bank cliff, the trail descends back to another ford, well suited to stock users. Here there is no log, and in early summer the flow is quite deep—but there is currently a massive log about 250 feet upstream that you can detour to, located where a more-easterly trail is shown on the USGS 7.5' topo maps.

The hiker and stock trails coalesce at a signed junction (near a few good campsites), and you begin a long walk along the southern shore of lovely Wood Lake. Wood Lake has bulbous eastern and western ends, linked by a deep, narrow channel that extends for 0.5 mile. After arcing around the lake's western lobe, the trail loops into a sheltered draw where you pass the unsigned, abandoned trail leading right (south) to Karls Lake (and onto Pingree Lake; Trip 22), while you stay left (east), sauntering just steps from Wood Lake through pleasant heath cover—red mountain heather, dwarf bilberry, and the delightful white mountain heather. As the corridor opens onto Wood Lake's eastern end you'll see one of two scenes: in late summer, a trail continuing across a narrow meadow strip separating two "lakes"; in early summer, a single lake, with the trail departing straight through the center on a raised rock causeway that can be nearly waist deep underwater. If this is what lies before you, in the morning you'll have to choose between wading and looping around to the south, but for now, turn south, off the main trail and soon find a delightful campsite beneath lodgepole pine cover (8,268'; 38.15022°N, 119.75231°W).

DAY 3 (Wood Lake to Huckleberry Lake, 5.9 miles): Once across the Wood Lake causeway, the trail climbs gently, passes an oval-shaped tarn full of yellow pond lilies, and drops to a junction, where you turn right (southeast) to Cow Meadow Lake, while left (north) leads to the Buck Lakes. Passing a stock drift fence, you begin switchbacking steeply through lodgepole pine forest, the trees regularly yielding to shrubs: pinemat manzanita, chokecherry, and oceanspray are all common. After a 600-foot drop, the mostly rocky trail transitions back to forest duff, and you reach a ford of the North Fork Cherry Creek. On the west bank—that is just before the ford—is a junction with two abandoned trails, one ascending the North Fork Cherry Creek to Emigrant Lake and one descending the North Fork alongside Cow Meadow Lake; both are now just faint use trails. After crossing the North Fork on either a log or rocks, the trail sidles around a series of tarns to Cow Meadow Lake. A broad, unexpectedly deep lake separated from the North Fork Cherry Creek by broad meadows and offering lots of lakeside slab, Cow Meadow Lake sadly doesn't afford many campsites, for there is almost nowhere flat that isn't within 100 feet of water. The best sites are along the creek, but far from the lake, with just a single tiny trailside site at the lake's northeastern tip.

Looping around Cow Meadow Lake's northeast shore, you switchback up broken slab and past big boulders, admiring some giant, beautiful western white pine and equally lovely hemlock. As you climb, ponder how most of the ascents and descents on this route are 300–600 feet, but appear bigger: the landscape-wide joints that dictate the location of the valleys (and lakes) mean the granite erodes into steep-sided walls and narrow valleys, visually exaggerating the relief. The 560-foot climb from Cow Meadow Lake leads to a junction, marked by a signless post, where you trend left (east, then south) to Letora Lake and Huckleberry Lake's inlet, while right (southwest) heads to Olive Lake and Huckleberry Lake's outlet. Perched high on the divide between Cherry Creek's north and east forks, Letora Lake (8,351') offers endless swimming coves, enticing islands, angling for brook and rainbow trout, slabs for sunbathing, and plenty of unseen campsites for one to two tents; look in the direction of the giant southwestern peninsula. And notice how the glacier-polished slabs and islands are elongate, matching the widespread fracture patterns.

Passing some of Letora's satellite tarns, the sandy forest trail winds between slabs, then drops more steeply to an unnamed lake. The trail now curves around Dome 8,564, trending south, east, and ultimately northeast onto a shelf high above Huckleberry Lake. The rough, rocky tread meanders along the base of vertical, fractured bluffs, working across dry scrubby slopes and through more lushly vegetated corridors, losing elevation only sporadically as the terrain allows. Throughout the traverse, you have views southeast to Bigelow, Kendrick and Michie Peaks. You welcome the sight of lodgepole pine stands marking Huckleberry Lake's north shore (brook and rainbow trout), finally approaching the lakeshore among extensive willow-and-bracken flats. The trail loops around the northern and eastern sides of the lake, avoiding marshlands and the many peninsulas, to reach a huge, dispersed camping area under lodgepole pine cover (before the East Fork Cherry Creek ford). Continuing across the East Fork—hopefully you'll find a log to avoid the deep ford—you find additional campsites south of the creek with easier lake access (7,870'; 38.13503°N, 119.70242°W).

DAY 4 (Huckleberry Lake to Emigrant Lake, 6.8 miles): From your campsite, be sure to return to the trail where you left it, or it would be easy to miss the upcoming junction (7,880'; 38.13491°N, 119.70168°W). Here you turn left (northeast) toward Horse Meadow, while right (southwest) leads down the East Fork Cherry Creek to Lord Meadow and into Yosemite National Park via Styx Pass. The trail stays south of the creek's broad, marshy riparian meadows, ascending gently through mixed-conifer forest and passing sporadic campsites. Passing a drift fence as the meadow pinches closed, the trail is routed onto the dry, rocky hillside above the now-narrow creek corridor. Impressive Sachse Monument rises to the north, its dark diorite and gabbro walls dotted with hardy junipers and cut by white dikes.

A tarn between Letora and Huckleberry Lakes   Photo by Elizabeth Wenk

Underfoot, you also cross from Huckleberry Lake's white granite onto gabbro, the oldest batholith rocks in the area (those that cooled underground), and next to ancient metasedimentary rocks. Near the contact are tungsten deposits, extracted from the nearby Cherry Creek mine until the early 1960s; today just scattered rusty mining equipment remains to mark the location (just west of the trail). Once you pass the mine access spur, you're on a 1943 vintage road, extending to Leavitt Lake, east of Sonora Pass and constructed to transport the mine's ore. A few steps later, you ford the East Fork Cherry Creek, requiring big jumps between rocks or a wade at high flows, and 0.15 mile later pass the unsigned spur leading right (south) to Twin Lakes; you continue straight (north), ascending the old road for another 0.5 mile to a signed junction. Here you turn left (northwest), while the road trends right (north) to Horse Meadow and onto Emigrant Pass and Bond Pass (Trips 29 and 34).

Your trail ascends above Horse Meadow through lodgepole and western white pines, transitioning onto slab as it crosses a rib and drops just slightly to Maxwell Lake, a mostly shallow lake cupped high in an open slab catchment. The lake's astonishingly intricate shoreline includes several peninsulas along which you could camp, or there are closer-to-trail options along the eastern and northeastern sides, with views of both the lake and Sachse Monument. (Sachse Monument can be ascended from the rib you cross, staying on the northwest side of the ridgeline and working your way along sandy shelves.)

Ahead the trail climbs an additional 400 feet, switchbacking generally northward through moderate lodgepole pine cover to an even higher perched basin. Here it winds through a long, rock-lined meadow past several beautiful lakelets to shallow Blackbird Lake (9,402'; excellent camping along trail corridor). At Blackbird Lake's northwestern corner, the trail reaches a junction, where you turn left (west) toward Emigrant Lake, while right (northeast) leads to Middle Emigrant Lake (Trip 28). The trail follows a vegetated corridor set between a pair of granite ribs, then switchbacks down a hemlock-shaded slope to emerge in a broad meadow flanking Emigrant Lake's inlet, the North Fork Cherry Creek. A spur just before the ford leads east to lovely creekside campsites. Once across the sandy-bottomed ford (often a wade), you come to a junction, where you turn left (west) to follow Emigrant Lake's northern shore, while right (northeast) leads over Mosquito Pass to Lunch Meadow and on to Kennedy Meadows (Trip 28). Most of Emigrant Lake's campsites are along the coming 0.4 mile (there are a few near the outlet), for along most of the lake, the granite slabs slope straight up from the shore. Look for good options north of the trail under lodgepole pine cover (for example, 8,840'; 38.18020°N, 119.68739°W; rainbow trout).

DAY 5 (Emigrant Lake to Piute Lake, 9.7 miles): Today is a long but relatively easy day, with lengthy flat sections. If you have spare days, you could easily split the day in half with a night at Upper Buck Lake or Deer Lake. Begin by skirting Emigrant Lake's northern shore west for nearly 1.5 miles. Broken slabs and bluffs rise to the north, while you stare south to a more intact, steep face. Consider how Emigrant Lake's length, like Huckleberry Lake's, reflects the landscape-wide joints—the rock preferentially erodes in this direction (and along a second set of often-perpendicular joints), so many of the region's lakes are remarkably elongate.

At the west end of Emigrant Lake, the trail turns right (north); a faint pad continuing along the lake's shore is an old abandoned trail descending the North Fork Cherry Creek toward Cow Meadow Lake, the "indistinct trail" mentioned there. You continue on the main trail, winding away from Emigrant Lake through meadow strips, across slabs, and between bluffs to a minor pass, most notable for the big dark inclusions (blobs of a different rock) in the granite slab. Switchbacks lead down through hemlock, lodgepole pine, and western white pine forest, the trail tread becoming softer as you approach the valley floor. Tall, striking walls frame Buck Meadow Creek's headwaters. The trail fords the creek—

a sandy wade or easy hop—and heads along the northern edges of a long meadow, passing a few small campsites in lodgepole pine stands (and you spy others across the creek).

Soon you reach Upper Buck Lake, its deep waters broken by parallel slab-rib islands and peninsulas, marking the orientation of the secondary joints. Just beyond the inlet you pass a lovely campsite between the trail and the lake, with lodgepole pine duff for your tent and lakeside slabs for relaxing. There are many additional campsites around the Buck Lakes, including off-trail options west of the creek between the two largest lakes.

Walking along Upper Buck Lake's western shore, you reach a junction, where you turn right (southwest) toward Deer Lake, while left (south) heads to the lower Buck Lakes and back to Cow Meadow Lake and Wood Lake. A rocky climb ensues, carrying you up an exposed, scrubby slope to a tarn-dotted corridor 400 feet higher. The passageway segues to a gentle drop through lodgepole pine leading to a junction where left (south) is a lateral back to Wood Lake, while you stay right (west), continuing beneath forest cover and then across a polished slab rib to Deer Lake's steep-edged, deep eastern end. Looping north of the lake through seasonally marshy flats and fording two inlet streams, you reach a junction, where you stay left (southwest) toward Jewelry Lake, while right (north) leads toward Salt Lick Meadow (Trip 26). Soon after the junction you'll spy a selection of good lodgepole pine–shaded campsites north of the trail. Note, however, that along the western half of Deer Lake's northern shore, camping is explicitly prohibited between the trail and lake because the requisite 100 feet from the water is not available. Although this trip directs you onward for the night, hopefully you have a spare hour to dawdle at Deer Lake—with splendid islands big and small, this lake is perfect for a midday swim, with ample smooth slabs to dry off on afterward.

At Deer Lake's western end, the trail assumes a due-west trajectory, following a joint-defined route, first along a lovely shelf above the drainage, hemmed to the north by bluffs, then dropping down an awkward corridor to a lodgepole pine flat. This quickly leads to meadow-and-willow expanses that presage Jewelry Lake (lodgepole pine–shaded campsite at northeastern end and sandy sites at western end). Continuing west, the trail is squeezed between a pair of domes and then drops down a slab face to reach warm little Gem Lake (8,224'), sitting on a shelf above Buck Meadow Creek. Gem Lake has a selection of splendid campsites—view-rich options on slabs south of the lake and larger, partially lodgepole pine–shaded options to the northwest.

At Gem Lake's northeastern corner is a junction, where left (south) leads to Buck Meadow Creek, while you stay right (west), signposted for Piute Meadow. Crossing a minor saddle, a 400-foot descent ensues, first down an open red fir ramp and later zigzagging down broken slab outcrops. Gradually the slope eases and then the slabs abruptly yield to riparian vegetation fringing West Fork Cherry Creek (a sandy wade at higher flows but can be dry by late season). After a brief walk alongside a meadow strip, the trail climbs again, reaching a sandy shelf beneath a dome decorated with an impressive swarm of near-parallel dikes. To the south, you admire a distant ridge of rolling domes, while Buck Meadow Creek itself and the trail you followed on Day 2 is hidden from view. Soon you pass tiny Piute Lake, with campsites on its northeastern (7,985'; 38.16269°N, 119.81022°W) and northwestern sides.

DAY 6 (Piute Lake to Crabtree Trailhead, 8.1 miles): From Piute Lake, you climb up dry diorite slabs, cross a flat saddle, and descend again. Now at much lower elevations and on slabs with just a shallow veneer of soil, the flowers will be parched by mid-July most years. Piute Meadow is a patch of green far below, as you follow switchbacks past chinquapin and huckleberry oak. After a nearly 500-foot descent the slope flattens and you reach a junction where left (south) leads to Groundhog Meadow, while you turn right (west) toward Camp Lake and retrace your steps from Day 1 to the Crabtree Trailhead.

Gianelli Cabin Trailhead

8,593'; 38.19841°N, 119.88424°W

Destination/ GPS Coordinates	Trip Type	Best Season	Pace & Hiking/ Layover Days	Total Mileage	Permit Required
24 Y Meadow Lake 38.19565°N 119.82490°W	Out-and-back	Mid to late	Leisurely 2/0	12.4	Gianelli Cabin
25 Wire Lakes 38.18004°N 119.77447°W	Out-and-back	Mid to late	Leisurely 4/1	25.2	Gianelli Cabin
26 Crabtree Trailhead 38.17883°N 119.75398°W (Long Lake)	Shuttle	Mid to late	Leisurely 4/1	27.2	Gianelli Cabin (or Crabtree in reverse)

INFORMATION AND PERMITS: This trailhead is in Stanislaus National Forest, accessing Emigrant Wilderness. Permits are required for overnight stays, but there are no quotas. Permits for this trailhead are most conveniently picked up at the Summit District Ranger Station, located at 1 Pinecrest Road, in Pinecrest, California. If you will be arriving outside of office hours, call 209-965-3434; you can request a permit up to two days in advance and it will be left in a dropbox for you. No campfires above 9,000 feet and no campfires within

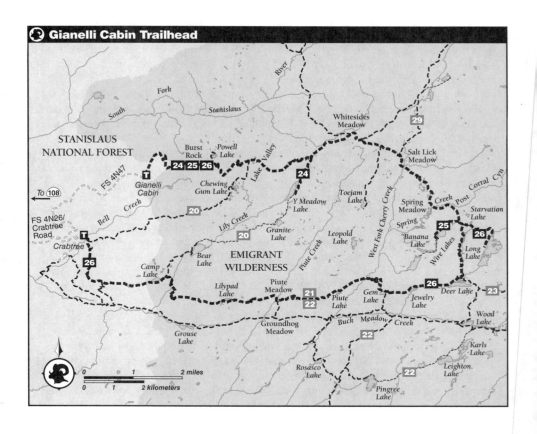

a half mile of Emigrant Lake. One-night camping limit per trip at the following lakes: Bear, Camp, Grouse, Powell, and Waterhouse. If you will be entering Yosemite National Park or Hoover Wilderness, bear canisters are required, and pets are prohibited in Yosemite.

DRIVING DIRECTIONS: There are two possible routes departing off CA 108; here the more northerly option is described, since it departs from the CA 108–Pinecrest Road junction, immediately adjacent to the Summit Ranger Station in Pinecrest where you must pick up your Wilderness Permit. Along CA 108, drive 36.5 miles east of the CA 108–CA 120 junction (or 36.2 miles west of Sonora Pass), turning east onto Pinecrest Road. After 0.3 mile, turn right (south) onto Dodge Ridge Road. Follow Dodge Ridge Road a windy 3.0 miles to the entrance to the Dodge Ridge Ski Area, then turn right (south) onto the Dodge Ridge Loop Road, signposted for Crabtree and Gianelli Trailheads. After 0.5 mile turn left (east) onto Crabtree Road and follow it 4.3 miles, past the Aspen Meadow Pack Station to a Y-junction; shortly before the pack station the trail becomes gravel. At the Y-junction, turn left onto FS 4N47 and follow it 4.0 miles to the road-end parking area. Minor spur roads branch off en route, but all are minor compared with this wide, well-built gravel road. (*Note:* If you do not need to pick up a Wilderness Permit, you can turn from CA 108 directly onto Crabtree Road in Cold Springs, located 2.0 miles before Pinecrest.)

trip 24 Y Meadow Lake

Trip Data: 38.19565°N, 119.82490°W; 12.4 miles; 2/0 days
Topos: *Pinecrest, Cooper Peak*

HIGHLIGHTS: This beautiful route parallels a segment of a historic emigrant trail. Early-trip views from Burst Rock are panoramic. Y Meadow Lake sits in a splendid, broad slab basin with endless campsite choices.

HEADS UP! *Y Meadow Lake as such doesn't appear on the topo or the wilderness map; look for the lake above the label "Y Meadow Dam."*

DAY 1 (Gianelli Cabin Trailhead to Y Meadow Lake, 6.2 miles): The signed trailhead sits at the northern corner of the parking area; it is northwest of the old trailhead and Gianelli Cabin site. Until you are close to Burst Rock the trail's route does not even slightly resemble that depicted on USGS 7.5' topo maps.

Paralleling a Bell Creek tributary, the trail heads due north through open red fir forest, reaching a ridge overlooking the South Fork Stanislaus River after 0.4 mile. Now

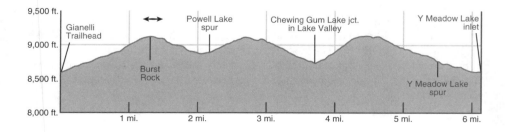

Y Meadow Lake   Photo by Elizabeth Wenk

approximately following the sandy ridge, the trail slowly bends east, climbing beside an impressive drop-off. It eventually switchbacks south, continuing up a west-facing slope of hemlock and western white pine. Zigging back to the north, you again reach the escarpment at a splendid vantage point that offers views to the north of Liberty Hill, Elephant Rock, the Dardanelles, Castle Rock, and the Three Chimneys, all lying across the South Fork Stanislaus River. After trending back to the south, the trail turns northeast and rolls onto a sandy ridge top. Here you'll find a plaque commemorating the Clark-Skidmore Party of 1852 who pioneered this short-lived emigrant route across the Sierra. (A brief detour north would take you to Burst Rock proper.) Amid spectacular western white pine and hemlock you cross into Emigrant Wilderness, enjoy expansive views south into the Tuolumne River watershed, and soon drop more steeply southeast, reaching a small tarn. Proceeding along one of the joint-defined passageways that break the granite slabs, you reach a denser lodgepole pine and hemlock glade. Just beyond is the unsigned junction to splendid Powell Lake, an attractive spot for a lunch break or fishing for brook trout. Offering a variety of sublime campsites, this is a perfect spot for a night if you're in search of a truly short hike; the sites toward the north end are more sheltered, while those along the southwestern side are higher above the lake on slab and offer views to the Three Chimneys.

Staying right (east) at the Powell Lake junction, your route switchbacks up, crosses a small ridge, and follows a sandy corridor northeast; views to the south are again outstanding—you can see to Mount Lyell in far southeastern Yosemite. Soon switchbacks carry you down through a forest of lodgepole pine, red fir, and mountain hemlock, arriving at a signed junction at the northern tip of Lake Valley. You stay left (east), signposted for Whitesides Meadow, while right (south) leads to Chewing Gum Lake (0.7 mile; another splendid slab-ringed lake with ample camping; Trip 20). The trail quickly climbs again, your third ascent since the trailhead; there are no long ascents, but this route certainly roller-coasters, repeatedly climbing 300–500 feet and then losing some of this hard-earned elevation as it works around and over successive ridges.

Climbing, you transition onto volcanic scree—a small remnant of the 20-million-year-old volcanic deposits that are responsible for the intriguingly shaped Three Chimneys and the massive volcanic peaks near Kennedy Meadows. After crossing the sagebrush top and ogling the unbroken views, you cross back onto the underlying granite and descend again, once again enjoying views southeast into Yosemite. Winding down broken slab, you reach a junction at the edge of a sandy meadow, a nearly imperceptible saddle that is the Stanislaus River–Cherry Creek watershed divide.

Turning south, the trail follows the corridor of the Y Meadow Lake inlet creek, criss-crossing the early-drying drainage several times. In the pocket meadows you admire expanses of shaggy lupine and corn lilies, while you must follow cairns where the trail detours onto slab. Before long, the trail arrives at Y Meadow Lake, a long skinny lake almost completely surrounded by glacial-polished granite slabs. There are flat, sandy perches that make view-rich campsites around much of the north and east sides of the lake (for example, 8,624'; 38.19565°N, 119.82490°W). The lake doesn't support fish due to fluctuating water levels. Hikers comfortable with cross-country walking can head southwest 0.7 mile from Y Meadow Lake to Granite Lake (Trip 20; smaller campsites, surrounded by steep granite bluffs; good fishing for brook trout).

A FRED LEIGHTON DAM

Like 14 other lakes in Emigrant Wilderness, Y Meadow Lake has a check dam at its outlet. This one was engineered by Fred Leighton and constructed by the Civilian Conservation Corps in the 1930s to ensure year-round stream flow for introduced fisheries. Y Meadow Lake's dam is 25 feet high—by far the tallest of Emigrant's backcountry dams—creating a lake where none existed before. Y Meadow "Reservoir" is the only completely artificial lake in Emigrant Wilderness. Following a 2006 lawsuit these dams are no longer being maintained and will slowly breach with the passage of time. Fortunately for anglers, it has been established that many of Emigrant's lakes will still have self-sustaining fisheries.

DAY 2 (Y Meadow Lake to Gianelli Cabin Trailhead, 6.2 miles): Retrace your steps.

trip 25 **Wire Lakes**

see map on p. 118

Trip Data: 38.18004°N, 119.77447°W; 25.2 miles; 4/1 days
Topos: *Pinecrest, Cooper Peak*

HIGHLIGHTS: The Wire Lakes are a stepladder set of three memorable mountain lakes offering excellent angling and opportunities for secluded camping. Their location in the heart of the Emigrant Wilderness means you have easy access to many other lakes on a layover day.

DAY 1 (Gianelli Cabin Trailhead to Y Meadow Lake, 6.2 miles): Follow Trip 24, Day 1 to Y Meadow Lake (8,624'; 38.19565°N, 119.82490°W).

ABOUT GIANELLI CABIN

Gianelli Cabin is a hunting cabin dating back to 1905, according to Peter Browning's *Place Names of the Sierra Nevada*. Now, only part of the log cabin's base remains. As an Italian name, Gianelli is pronounced "jah-NEL-lee." Since the current trail does not pass it, detour briefly east from the trailhead to have a look before starting your hike.

DAY 2 (Y Meadow Lake to Upper Wire Lake, 6.4 miles): First, retrace your steps from Y Meadow Lake to the last trail junction. Here you turn right (northeast) toward Whitesides Meadow, cross the top of a long meadow finger, and continue across rolling, low-angle granite slabs alongside a creek corridor. Quite quickly you reach massive Whitesides Meadows, verdant along the creek corridor with a mix of granitic and volcanic outcrops lapping at the meadow's edge. After crossing a short stretch of granite and diorite slabs (camping here; and excellent camping across the outlet, easily crossed on a dam), the trail launches straight across the meadow to reach a junction, where you turn right (east, then south) signposted for Upper Relief Valley, while left (west, then northwest) leads back across Whitesides Meadow and onto Cooper Meadow and Eagle Pass. A short 0.4-mile trail segment leads above the meadow, winding up corridors through steeper granite outcrops to reach a forest flat and another junction. Your route leads right (southeast) toward Salt Lick Meadow, while left (northeast) leads down Relief Valley and on to Kennedy Meadows (Trip 29).

Your trail briefly follows a forested flat south, then, as directed by the convoluted topography of slab ribs and passageways, turns southeast to drop down a narrow corridor to an elongate pocket meadow. Another length in sandy lodgepole pine forest, another heath-bound meadow, and you reach the spur that leads right (south) to Toejam Lake (1.4 miles; gorgeous lake with excellent campsites). You stay left (southeast), dropping more steeply through open lodgepole pine forest to your next junction, where you stay right (south), while left (northeast) is an alternate route toward Relief Valley (Trip 29). Within a few minutes you enter Salt Lick Meadow (8,505') and cross the nascent West Fork Cherry Creek (a sandy wade at higher flows, but drying in late season). Pleasantly rounded granite outcrops pepper the meadow, and behind those at the meadow's southeastern edge you'll find campsites.

Leaving Salt Lick Meadow, the trail continues southeast, climbing steeply up a joint-delineated corridor—always the best route across Emigrant's tortuous landscape of fractured granite slab—to reach an extensive lodgepole pine flat scattered with about a dozen tarns and carpeted with dwarf bilberry and red mountain heather. The trail next drops to Spring Meadow, harboring a shallow lake and very marshy meadows in early summer; the mosquitoes and buttercup displays can both be quite intense as you wade sandy-bottomed Spring Creek (brook trout) in July, while later you can enjoy displays of lupine and paintbrush in peace. Ascending out of Spring Meadow, you are staring straight up Post Corral Canyon at a collection of steep, polished granite domes, the extension of ridges off Granite Dome.

Turning back to the south, you leave the Spring Creek corridor and soon meet a junction where you turn right (west) toward the Wire Lakes, while the main trail continues left (south) to Deer Lake. The Wire Lakes Trail is much fainter and narrower than your route so far. It initially trends due west past a clutch of tarns, then, 0.25 mile from the junction, bends nearly due south, passing a final tarn and descending down a narrow gully to the shores of Upper Wire Lake (Lake 8,839). The main trail trends around Upper Wire Lake's northwestern shore, while a minor spur south leads to additional small campsites.

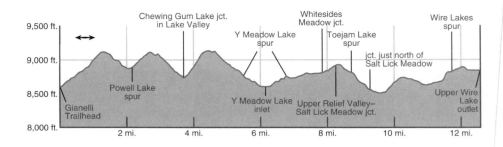

Red mountain heather grows thickly along the shores of Upper Wire Lake.   Photo by Elizabeth Wenk

Continuing southwest on the main trail, you'll pass numerous signs reminding you not to camp between the lake and trail—for there is nowhere you can camp 100 feet from water, as Leave No Trace principles compel (and wilderness regulations demand). However, as you approach the south end of the lake you'll pass big, legal lodgepole-pine-and-hemlock-forested sites just north of the trail (8,870'; 38.18004°N, 119.77447°W). Turning south around the lake's southwestern tip you'll come to additional 1–2 tent sites in slabs just west of the lake's outlet that offer splendid views the length of the lake.

All three of the Wire Lakes harbor brook trout, although your chances of catching dinner are higher in the less visited lower two lakes. Cross-country travel to these lakes is easy, first following the outlet south, then skirting west around the southern side of Middle Wire Lake, also known as Banana Lake (8,734'). Banana Lake offers few campsites, but Lower Wire Lake (also 8,734', per USGS topos), broad, open and island-dotted, has some good sites at its northern end. The Wire Lakes make idyllic basecamps for exploring the many lakes nearby. From the inlet of Middle Wire Lake you can head south toward Deer Lake's outlet or you can return to the main trail and visit Long Lake (see also Trip 26).

Days 3 and 4 (Wire Lakes to Gianelli Cabin Trailhead, 12.6 miles): Retrace your steps. For variety, consider camping at Whitesides Meadow or Chewing Gum Lake.

trip 26   Crabtree Trailhead

see map on p. 118

Trip Data: 38.17883°N, 119.75398°W (Long Lake); 27.2 miles; 4/1 days
Topos: *Pinecrest, Cooper Peak*

HIGHLIGHTS: This route is popular with all hikers: anglers, naturalists, photographers, and those just out to experience the trails. High, cold-water lakes and streams vie with deep pine and fir forests and alpine meadows for visitors' attention, and the shortness of the shuttle for this trip almost makes it a loop.

SHUTTLE DIRECTIONS: The roads to the Crabtree versus Gianelli Cabin Trailheads split at the Y-junction described in the driving directions (see page 119). Instead of turning left (more north) toward the Gianelli Trailhead, you take the right-hand (more south) road toward the Crabtree Trailhead. After 0.4 mile stay left at a minor junction, and 0.25 mile after reach a large parking area with toilets and a few trailhead campsites (1-night stay only). *Note:* The minor junction 0.25 mile from the trailhead is labeled as OVERFLOW PARKING but does not lead to any defined lot; the road verges simply provide additional parking spaces if the roadsides closer to the parking lot are full—a common weekend occurrence.

HEADS UP! *There are endless lakes that make enticing campsites along this route. Y Meadow Lake, Long Lake, and Piute Lake were chosen because they split the trip into fairly even-length days. Some alternative destinations to consider include Chewing Gum Lake (described in Trip 20), Toejam Lake, Upper Relief Valley Lakes (Trip 29), Wire Lakes (Trip 25), Deer Lake (Trip 21), and Gem Lakes (Trip 21).*

DAY 1 (Gianelli Cabin Trailhead to Y Meadow Lake, 6.2 miles): Follow Trip 24, Day 1 to Y Meadow Lake (8,624'; 38.19565°N, 119.82490°W).

DAY 2 (Y Meadow Lake to Long Lake, 6.7 miles): Follow Trip 25, Day 2 for the 5.6 miles from Y Meadow Lake to the Wire Lakes junction and then continue an additional 1.1 miles as described here. At the Wire Lakes junction, you stay left (south), while right (west) leads to the Wire Lakes. After just 0.1 mile, you reach another junction where left (east) is your route toward Long Lake, while the main trail to Deer Lake continues right (south).

Long Lake fills a basin southeast of, and parallel to, the Deer Creek drainage you're at the head of. Striking east through mixed-conifer forest, you soon cross the ephemeral Deer Lake inlet stream and climb across a shallow granite ridge, the trail passing through a narrow bluff-bounded corridor. To avoid outcropping slab, the descending trail then follows a circuitous route to Long Lake, staying in a dense mix of lodgepole pine, hemlock, and western white pine. Wandering fleabane (a daisy) and dwarf bilberry carpet the more shaded areas, while diminutive Brewer's lupine is common in open sandy stretches.

Turning to the south, you are suddenly beside Long Lake's northern bay and in a few more steps enjoy an excellent view of the gorgeous big basin ahead. Long Lake is island dotted and sports a wonderfully intricate shoreline—there is many a slab rib jutting into the lake on which you can sit and admire the environs, with views stretching northeast to the summits of Granite Dome and Black Hawk Mountain. You pass pleasant forested campsites as soon as you reach Long Lake (8,737'; 38.17883°N, 119.75398°W), and thereafter the trail fizzles.

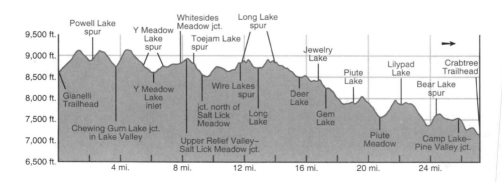

However, there are many additional campsites scattered along the western and southern shores, with some particularly splendid open slab sites about halfway along the lake; the farther you walk from the "trail end," the more solitude you can expect. As with many other Emigrant Wilderness lakes, the dead trees in the lake are the result of small check dams built between the 1920s and 1950s to raise lake levels; they were built to ensure ongoing stream flow all summer to support introduced fisheries.

DAY 3 (Long Lake to Piute Lake, 6.2 miles): Retrace your steps to the junction with the main trail and turn left (south) toward the main trail. The coming 1.6-mile segment follows one of Deer Lake's inlets steadily downward. The first miles are through lush conifer forest, mostly a mix of lodgepole pine and hemlocks, often with an understory of dwarf bilberry and occasional swaths of tall white-flowered corn lilies. The trail leads past a chain of unnamed lakelets, mostly meadow-rimmed with just sporadic tongues of bedrock extending to their shores. By midseason, drier pocket meadows are brightly decorated with the purple flowers of shaggy lupine. Soon after the fourth lakelet, the gradient increases and the trail switchbacks down slab, crossing the outlet twice in close succession. These crossings are for the benefit of stock—if water levels are high, you may want to stay on the west side of the creek for this closely spaced pair of crossings to avoid wading. Enjoying the bright pink blooms of the rock spiraea, the gradient eventually eases and you cross the creek twice more; rock hops are usually possible. Ahead you approach a junction just north of Deer Lake, where you turn right (southwest), signposted for Jewelry Lake, while left (east) leads to the Buck Lakes (Trip 23).

Long Lake   Photo by Elizabeth Wenk

Soon after the junction you'll spy a selection of good lodgepole pine–shaded campsites north of the trail. Note, however, that along the western half of Deer Lake's northern shore, camping is explicitly prohibited between the trail and lake because the requisite 100 feet from the water is not available. Although this trip directs you onward for the night, hopefully you have a spare hour to dawdle at Deer Lake—with splendid islands big and small, this lake is perfect for a midday swim, with ample smooth slabs to dry off on afterward.

At Deer Lake's western end, the trail assumes a due-west trajectory, following a joint-defined route, first along a lovely shelf above the drainage, hemmed to the north by bluffs, then dropping down an awkward corridor to a lodgepole pine flat. This quickly leads to meadow-and-willow expanses that presage Jewelry Lake (lodgepole pine–shaded campsite at northeastern end and sandy sites at western end). Continuing west, the trail is squeezed between a pair of domes and then drops down a slab face to reach warm little Gem Lake (8,224'), sitting on a shelf above Buck Meadow Creek. Gem Lake has a selection of splendid campsites—view-rich options on slabs south of the lake and larger, partially lodgepole pine–shaded options to the northwest.

At Gem Lake's northeastern corner is a junction, where left (south) leads to Buck Meadow Creek, while you stay right (west), signposted for Piute Meadow. Crossing a minor saddle, a 400-foot descent ensues, first down an open red fir ramp and later zigzagging down broken slab outcrops where spreading phlox, pennyroyal, Sierra stonecrop, and prettyfaces provide dots of color. Gradually the slope eases and then the slabs abruptly yield to riparian vegetation fringing the West Fork Cherry Creek (sandy wade at higher flows but can be dry by late season). After a brief walk alongside a meadow strip, the trail climbs again, reaching a sandy shelf beneath a dome decorated with an impressive swarm of near-parallel dikes. To the south, you admire a distant ridge of rolling domes, while Buck Meadow Creek itself and the trail you followed on Day 2 is hidden from view. Soon you pass tiny Piute Lake, with campsites on its northeastern (7,985'; 38.16269°N, 119.81022°W) and northwestern sides.

DAY 4 (Piute Lake to Crabtree Trailhead, 8.1 miles): From Piute Lake, you climb up dry diorite slabs, cross a flat saddle, and descend again. Now at much lower elevations and on slabs with just a shallow veneer of soil, the flowers will be parched by mid-July most years. Piute Meadow is a patch of green far below, as you switchback past chinquapin and huckleberry oak. After a nearly 500-foot descent the slope flattens, and you reach a junction where you turn right (west) toward Camp Lake, while left (south) leads to Groundhog Meadow.

In just a few steps, ford early-drying Piute Creek and loop around the southern and western edges of Piute Meadow. Then you almost immediately climb again; the granite here is endlessly crisscrossed by major landscape-wide joints, leading to the numerous, closely spaced valleys you must cut across—or rather climb in and out of. This ascent leads to a nice viewpoint, then into a corridor that carries you to Lilypad Lake, offering good campsites in slabs south of the trail (7,868'; 38.15923°N, 119.85228°W). If you need to walk the 4.7 miles from the Crabtree Trailhead to your car at the Gianelli Cabin Trailhead, you may decide to camp here (or ahead at Bear Lake or Camp Lake) and walk to the Crabtree Trailhead early in the morning, then retrieve your car.

Continue past scattered tarns and down a pleasantly graded draw that is alight with flower color until midseason—the shooting stars, larkspur, and stickseed bloom first, followed by Sierra tiger lilies, ragwort, lupine, and cow parsnip a few weeks later. Switchbacks carry you down a slope partially burned in the 2003 Mountain Fire to a lodgepole pine flat and ford of Lily Creek; a log is available in the early season, and later the stream may dry. Back up

Salt Lick Meadow   Photo by Elizabeth Wenk

again, a few short but rocky and exposed switchbacks lead up a slope of huckleberry oak and pinemat manzanita to a junction where you stay left (west), while right (northeast) leads to Bear Lake (1.1 mile away; Trip 20). You almost immediately reach little Camp Lake, which offers only overused campsites on the ridge to the south, for the lake is in a sloping basin.

The trail follows Camp Lake's ephemeral outlet and you enjoy lush flower-filled flats as long as water is available to irrigate them. Pleasant walking beneath a blocky escarpment leads to a junction with a lateral left (south) to Pine Valley, while you stay right (west), crossing a minor saddle under white fir shade. Ahead the trail drops steeply down a draw, then turns due north undulating through dry white fir forest and across bouldery-scrubby slopes of moraine debris. You reach a junction where you continue straight (north), while right (east) leads to Chewing Gum Lake (Trip 20), and just beyond cross Bell Creek on a good bridge. A few more steps lead to the Crabtree Trailhead (7,164'; 38.17868°N, 119.90675°W) and an extensive parking area and trailhead one-night campsites. Hopefully your group has shuttled a car here—otherwise it is another 4.7 miles back to the Gianelli Cabin Trailhead.

OPTION: CLOSING THE LOOP BY WALKING THE ROAD

If your group has only a single car, consider making this a five-day trip, camping at either Lilypad Lake or Camp Lake on the final night. You'll then reach the Crabtree Trailhead early on the final day and can walk back to your car. From the trailhead sign it is 0.7 mile west to a junction. From there you turn right (northeast) onto Forest Service Road 4N47 and walk almost exactly 4 miles to the Gianelli Cabin Trailhead.

Kennedy Meadows Trailhead   6,315'; 38.31075°N, 119.74515°W

Destination/ GPS Coordinates	Trip Type	Best Season	Pace & Hiking/ Layover Days	Total Mileage	Permit Required
27 Summit Creek 38.23433°N 119.72074°W	Out-and-back	Early to late	Leisurely 2/1	13.6	Kennedy Meadows
28 Emigrant Lake and Emigrant Meadow Lake 38.18020°N 119.68739°W (Emigrant Lake)	Semiloop	Mid to late	Leisurely 5/2	30.0	Kennedy Meadows
29 Emigrant Lake, Buck Lakes, and Relief Valley 38.16595°N 119.74106°W (Upper Buck Lake)	Semiloop	Mid to late	Moderate 5/2	37.7	Kennedy Meadows
30 Big Sam and Grizzly Meadow (in reverse of description; see page 141)	Shuttle	Mid to late	Moderate 4/1	31.0	Kennedy Meadows (Sonora Pass as described)

INFORMATION AND PERMITS: This trailhead is in Stanislaus National Forest, accessing Emigrant Wilderness. Permits are required for overnight stays, but there are no quotas. Permits for this trailhead are most conveniently picked up at the Summit District Ranger Station, located at 1 Pinecrest Road, in Pinecrest, California. If you will be arriving outside of office hours, call 209-965-3434; you can request a permit up to two days in advance and it will be left in a dropbox for you. No campfires above 9,000 feet and no campfires within a half mile of Emigrant Lake. One-night camping limit per trip at the following lakes: Bear, Camp, Grouse, Powell, and Waterhouse. If you will be entering Yosemite National Park or Hoover Wilderness, bear canisters are required, and pets are prohibited in Yosemite.

DRIVING DIRECTIONS: The turnoff to Kennedy Meadows from CA 108 is 63.6 miles east of the CA 108–CA 120 junction and 9.1 miles west of Sonora Pass. Turn south onto the signed spur road to Kennedy Meadows. At 0.5 mile down the road, turn left (east) into a large U.S. Forest Service trailhead parking area with toilets and hiker campsites, requiring a wilderness permit and limited to a 1-night stay. The actual trailhead is an additional 0.5 mile down the road at the Kennedy Meadows Resort (lodgings, café, saloon, store, pack station). You can drive here to drop off packs and passengers but need to leave your car at the aforementioned Forest Service parking lot.

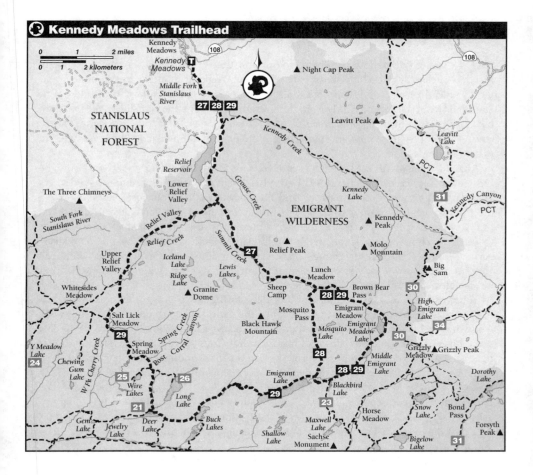

---

trip 27 ## Summit Creek

Trip Data: 38.23433°N, 119.72074°W; 13.6 miles; 2/1 days
Topos: *Sonora Pass, Emigrant Lake*

HIGHLIGHTS: This weekend walk has three distinct highlights. The first is the river, initially the meandering course of the Middle Fork Stanislaus River, followed by tumbling cascades along two of its principal tributaries, Summit Creek and Kennedy Creek. Later, it is the expansive waters of Relief Reservoir that dominate your hike. Finally, scenery along the way is an absorbing study in the contrast between glacial-polished granitic and volcanic terrain.

HEADS UP! *The trailhead is marked as a locked gate at the Kennedy Meadows Resort. However, backpackers must park their car in a lot 0.5 mile to the north. You can drop most group members and gear at this gate so that just one person parks the car and walks the road.*

HEADS UP! *The trip officially describes a route to campsites along Summit Creek, but a shorter alternative is to camp along Relief Reservoir (there are some sites 3.8 miles from the trailhead), while a more distant destination is Sheep Camp, an additional 1.7 miles upstream, described in the text for Trip 28.*

DAY 1 (Kennedy Meadows Trailhead to Summit Creek, 6.8 miles): From the Kennedy Meadows Resort, strike south on the gated dirt road. Walking among scattered juniper and Jeffrey pine, the trail crosses a minor saddle and drops back to the banks of the Middle Fork Stanislaus River. Diverging a little from the river, the trail skirts the east side of the meadow, passing a pair of out-of-place sequoias planted long ago. The road is sometimes under forest cover—a mix of Jeffrey pine, incense cedar, white fir, and juniper—and elsewhere you are at the meadow's edge.

After 1.0 mile, just as the trail bends east, you pass a sign indicating you are at the official U.S. Forest Service trailhead and just beyond is a sign marking the Emigrant Wilderness boundary. The valley rapidly narrows and the trail now climbs purposefully, soon crossing the turbulent river on a stout bridge. Just across the bridge you'll spy an unmarked trail turning sharply right (west), a longer route that is used by pack stock. You stay left (southeast), climbing along the river's southwestern bank, passing beneath impressively vertical—indeed, slightly overhung—black-stained walls. To the east you spy Kennedy Creek tumbling down its steep boulder-and-bedrock-lined course, while you follow Summit Creek's blocky, incised gorge south.

You cross Summit Creek on a second bridge, staring down at the impressively cascading river. Just across the bridge the trail splits; the main trail continues right (southwest), while the left-hand (more southerly) alternative is a steeper, 400-foot-shorter route used by some hikers. Your route now diverges from Summit Creek, continuing past brushy slopes beneath a granite dome and passing rusting equipment abandoned after the construction of the 145-foot-tall Relief Reservoir dam between 1906 and 1910. A few more steps lead to a junction where your route remains right (south), while left (east) leads to Kennedy Lake. Numerous use trails depart right (west), first anglers' (and view seekers') trails leading to a selection of splendid Summit Creek views (and fishing holes) and, once you've climbed 0.4 mile past the Kennedy Lake junction, a right-bearing use trail leads to a reservoir overlook and toward the Relief Reservoir dam.

Onward, the trail contours high above the reservoir on hot sandy, brushy slopes with just the occasional Jeffrey pine or juniper providing dots of shade. About two-thirds of the way south along the reservoir you reach a shallow ford of Grouse Creek; it can usually be crossed on an assortment of logs. To either side of the crossing, spur trails head right (west) toward the reservoir's shore, leading to good lakeside camping options; there are a few more choices an additional 0.4 mile south.

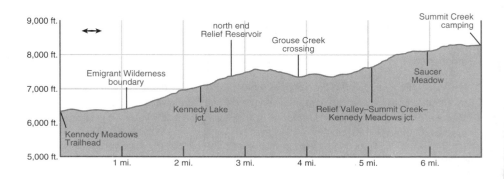

Bridge high above Summit Creek   Photo by Elizabeth Wenk

Leaving the reservoir behind, the trail now ascends a forested corridor east of Summit Creek's drainage. Passing the junction with the trail right (west, then southwest) to Relief Valley (Trip 29), you continue left (southeast) and ascend ever steeper, rockier slopes; shrubs and junipers soon replace the cool white fir stands. Views to East Flange Rock, the volcanic pinnacle due west, and Granite Dome, the steep granite ridge to the southwest, dominate the view. The contrast between the younger, dark-colored volcanic rocks and older, polished, light-colored granite is unmissable. The volcanics sit atop the granite, and while they've been eroded from the river valleys and are mostly gone from the Granite Dome ridge, the ridge to your left is still entirely cloaked in volcanic rock. As you ascend, you increasingly cross volcanic rubble that has spilled down endless gullies on the steep slope. Dropping across a saddle into tiny Saucer Meadow you are back in granite—a vertical, but flat-topped granite bluff guards this little flower-filled marsh from the debris, and so the meadowed flat persists.

The trail remains well above Summit Creek, following a sandy corridor at the granite-volcanics boundary, before finally uniting with Summit Creek. Here, around 8,300 feet, you'll find a cluster of campsites. First you pass one under red fir and lodgepole pine cover and a short distance later a small selection of sandy sites on a slab knob east of the trail (8,283'; 38.23433°N, 119.72074°W). The forested flats in the direction of the creek are clearly marked as NO CAMPING, for they are less than 100 feet from water. These are the last campsites until you reach Sheep Camp, another 1.7 miles up the trail.

While Summit Creek itself is not an enticing location for a layover day—especially because the fishing is reported to be poor—this is a good departure point to climb up the steep granite slabs west toward either Iceland Lake or the Lewis Lakes, launching you quickly into a subalpine landscape of near-endless slab. Or, from a base camp here, you can continue up to Sheep Camp and Lunch Meadow without a pack on your back.

DAY 2 (Summit Creek to Kennedy Meadows Trailhead, 6.8 miles): Retrace your steps.

see
map on
p. 129

trip 28 **Emigrant Lake and**
Emigrant Meadow Lake

Trip Data: 38.18020°N, 119.68739°W (Emigrant Lake);
30.0 miles; 5/2 days
Topos: Sonora Pass, Emigrant Lake

HIGHLIGHTS: Scenically, this route splits the terrain into two distinctly different parts. To the north, the colorful reds and black volcanic slopes vividly disclose the violent eruptions that occurred (mainly) about 9.5 million years ago. To the south, in contrast, glaciers have polished the 85-million-year-old granite into shining mirror slabs. This hike leads you across both. One premier destination is Emigrant Lake, a longtime favorite with anglers, especially since so many additional lakes lie close by. The second standout locale is Emigrant Meadow Lake, a broad, shallow lake in a sublime open basin that offers surreal views of the surrounding ridges and was a stopping point for early emigrant groups along the West Walker Route.

HEADS UP! *If you're searching for a slightly shorter trip, consider an out-and-back to either Emigrant Lake or Emigrant Meadow Lake—or maybe just to Mosquito Pass along the trail to Emigrant Lake. For a longer trip, consider Trips 23 or 29, yet grander tours of Emigrant Wilderness's high elevation lakes.*

DAY 1 (Kennedy Meadows Trailhead to Summit Creek, 6.8 miles): Follow Trip 27, Day 1 to the Summit Creek campsites (8,283'; 38.23433°N, 119.72074°W).

DAY 2 (Summit Creek to Emigrant Lake, 6.8 miles): Continuing southeast, the trail rapidly leaves granite slab behind, crossing back onto volcanic rubble. For nearly a mile you cross an endless progression of long-ago debris flows, interspersed with a few more-recent, deeply incised flood channels. Look east at the pinnacled volcanic visage and imagine how an immense summer thunderstorm would send rocks and water tumbling down the myriad tiny passageways, the material slowing as it approaches the stream corridor. Red fir thrive in the fine, nutrient-rich material and form a near monoculture. As the valley narrows and steepens, you are back on fractured granite outcrops, winding upward beneath the steep cliffs. A 400-foot rocky ascent leads to a little saddle and just beyond the massive camping area called Sheep Camp; in part it is open and sandy and elsewhere under lodgepole pine shade.

Curving around Sheep Camp among eroded granite ribs, the trail continues close to the creek (and passes additional campsites), before diverging back onto volcanic scree. Climbing upward, the walls slowly shrink in height and you reach the beginning of massive Lunch

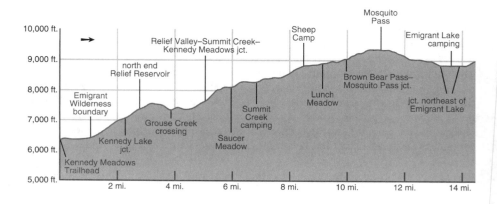

Meadow. There are two major lobes, pinched in the middle by granite outcrops. You'll find campsites at the northwestern end of the western lobe, the northeastern side of the eastern lobe, and more choices if you cross the creek. As you traverse above the meadow, alternatively on volcanic rock and granite slab, you can't help but think about how the two rock types erode into such different profiles, creating the disparate landscapes to either side of the trail.

At Lunch Meadow's east end, you reach a junction where the loop part of this trip begins: today's route leads right (south) across the creek to Mosquito Pass and onto Emigrant Lake, while left (ahead, east) to Emigrant Meadow Lake is your return route. Go right, ford Summit Creek (a shallow wade, transitioning to a rock hop by midsummer), and immediately begin winding up broken granite slab. Approaching Mosquito Pass, the 9,370-foot pass unlabeled on most maps, you cross some magnificently polished slabs. Take a breather to look north to the volcanic ridge: Relief Peak on the left (west), whose base you've followed for many miles, and Molo Pinnacle and Molo Peak to the right. To the west is Black Hawk Mountain, granitic at its core with an icing of volcanic sediments draped across the summit ridge. To the southwest you can just see to the Yosemite border. Mosquito Pass itself offers glorious sandy, albeit exposed, campsites, with nearby water as long as snowmelt trickles persist. Cairns mark an off-trail route east to Mosquito Lake (good camping).

The broad pass slowly transitions to concave terrain, and the trail begins descending south into a fracture-defined valley, with steep, elegant granite domes rising to the west; despite its fractures, the granite here has enough integrity to form vertical walls. Staying well east of and above the broad, grassy valley bottom, the trail is pleasantly dry and partly shaded, at first, by whitebark pine and later by lodgepole pine, hemlock, and western white pine. Slowly the trail reaches a ford of the unnamed creeklet—a broad leap or easy wade—and descends a final stretch to a junction. Here, right (west) leads to the shores of Emigrant Lake and tonight's campsite suggestion, while left (south) is tomorrow's route to Blackbird Lake and onto Middle Emigrant Lake.

Turning right (west), you quickly reach the northeastern corner of elongate Emigrant Lake and, to the north of (above) the trail, find several lodgepole pine–shaded campsites (8,840'; 38.18020°N, 119.68739°W; rainbow trout). Note that camping is prohibited between the trail and lake, so you won't find lakeside camping again until you've traveled another 1.5 miles west, nearly to Emigrant Lake's outlet. An alternative place to find campsites is to turn left at the aforementioned junction (the beginning of Day 3's route), ford North Fork Cherry Creek, and immediately follow spur trails east to creekside campsites. Make sure you have spare hours in your day—or a layover day—to walk the length of Emigrant Lake!

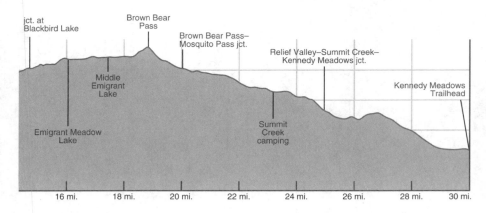

DAY 3 (Emigrant Lake to Emigrant Meadow Lake, 4.3 miles): Today is short in miles but passes three spectacular lakes—you'll happily wile away the hours. From the aforementioned junction at the northeastern corner of Emigrant Lake, now turn right (south), signposted for Middle Emigrant Lake. You ford the North Fork Cherry Creek, a broad sandy wade, that can be reasonably deep, but is never dangerous, and switchback up through cool hemlock forest to a slab-confined corridor that opens to reveal Blackbird Lake. Quite shallow Blackbird Lake sits in an open slab basin and has a mostly sand-and-slab perimeter, therefore offering endless campsites congruent with Leave No Trace principles (in contrast to most nearby lakes, which are meadow ringed). Look along the western or eastern shores for good options.

At Blackbird Lake you reach a signed junction; you turn left (east) toward Middle Emigrant Lake, while right (south) leads to Horse Meadow (Trip 23). The coming 2.7-mile trail segment is not one of the major routes used by pack animals and is rarely maintained; pay attention to your map to make sure you stay on route, which generally follows what is depicted on the USGS 7.5' topo maps. For the first 0.75 mile, the trail winds up the southern bank of the North Fork Cherry Creek, in places on broken slab and intervening sandy corridors, and elsewhere at the edge of pocket meadows, generally under partial lodgepole pine shade. The creek initially cascades hurriedly down its block channel, its gradient subsiding by the time you need to ford it (lovely campsites nearby). The crossing, located where the creek jogs south, is usually a wade, although rock-hop options emerge at lower flows.

Once on the north bank, you diverge from the creek, trending northwest of a shallow granite rib. The now-incised trail ascends first along the southern edge of one small meadow, then across an early-drying creeklet, up a sandy-rocky slope, and around the northern edge of a large willow-choked meadow. This leads easily to the southwestern tip of Middle Emigrant Lake (9,335'; rainbow trout) and an excellent campsite on a whitebark pine–dotted knob. Mostly, however, Middle Emigrant Lake lacks camping—it is surrounded by wet meadows and slopes that rise immediately beyond the lakeshore.

Heading from Mosquito Pass to Emigrant Lake   Photo by Elizabeth Wenk

The trail skirts the lake's west side and continues north at the edge of the marshy willow-cloaked turf fringing its meandering inlet, still the North Fork Cherry Creek. About 0.15 mile north of the lake, where the meadow pinches closed, you must ford the North Fork. The location is indistinct, the trail disguised by the willows—you simply have to push your way through them, wade the sandy channel (or step across in late season), and relocate the trail. The trail then trends northeast, parting ways with the north-trending creek. A short ascent beside Dome 9,667 leads to a low, rocky saddle overlooking Emigrant Meadow Lake's windy basin (9,407'; rainbow trout). There are excellent campsites in sandy nooks right atop this saddle (9,453'; 38.19725°N, 119.64838°W).

The mileage is marked to the lake's northern side, so you continue down to the southern tip of Emigrant Meadow Lake and make your way north along the lake's eastern shore, a marshy expanse of meadow. In early summer, if you follow the trail, you will (hopefully) cringe with each step, knowing you are damaging the delicate meadow turf and decide to skirt farther east to drier, sandier, more ecologically robust terrain. At the northeastern edge of the lake is a junction, where right (southeast) leads to Grizzly Meadow (Trip 30), while you turn left (northwest), signposted for Kennedy Meadows. Walking along the northeastern side of the lake, the terrain here a tad drier, you reach extensive sandy flats and low-lying granite slabs near the northwestern tip of the lake (9,449'; 38.20833°N, 119.65140°W).

DAY 4 (Emigrant Meadow Lake to Summit Creek, 5.3 miles): The first emigrants to cross the Sierra via the West Walker River route stopped at Emigrant Meadow Lake and adjoining Emigrant Meadow; this landscape would have been welcome after the trials of working their wagons from Fremont Lake to Emigrant Pass. You've camped on an ever-so-slight rise in the broad basin and begin by dropping a token 10 feet to marshier Emigrant Meadow, where you cross the North Fork Cherry Creek a final time. It will again be a sandy wade until midsummer.

Bound for Brown Bear Pass, the trail's gradient now increases and almost immediately crosses onto volcanic rock. The nutrient-rich volcanics host a different and more diverse collection of plant species—the early-summer hiker will be treated to the periwinkle-flowered western blue flax and white-flowered Drummond's anemone, the latter's shoots emerging just hours after the snow melts. To the south of the trail are granite slabs, distinctly pink-hued due to mineral alterations that occurred as the volcanic rock flowed across it. Once atop Brown Bear Pass (9,763'), be sure to turn around and stare across the broad Emigrant Meadow basin and beyond to Saurian Crest, looking very much like the spiny back of a monstrous lizard, and Tower Peak. Looking west and northwest, the volcanic ridge extending from Relief Peak to Molo Peak and the summits of Black Hawk Mountain and Granite Dome are in view again.

Your descent to the headwaters of Summit Creek is steep and rocky for the first 0.4 mile, then moderating as you approach Summit Creek and small campsites, some on whitebark pine–sheltered knobs and others in sandy flats. In stretches you walk through wetter vegetation alongside the creek, elsewhere on broken granite slabs, and yet other sections across broad sagebrush flats, decorated in season with wavyleaf paintbrush, spreading phlox, and low-growing Brewer's lupine. Soon you reach the junction from Day 2, where left (south) leads to Emigrant Lake, while you continue right (straight ahead, west), toward Kennedy Meadows, closing the loop portion of the trip. You now retrace your steps to the trailhead; for variety, I recommend you stay in a different campsite than you did on the ascent, possibly in nearby Lunch Meadow, at Sheep Camp, or at Relief Reservoir.

DAY 5 (Summit Creek to Kennedy Meadows Trailhead, 6.8 miles): Retrace your steps.

see map on p. 129

trip 29 Emigrant Lake, Buck Lakes, and Relief Valley

Trip Data: 38.16595°N, 119.74106°W (Upper Buck Lake);
37.7 miles; 5/2 days

Topos: Sonora Pass, Emigrant Lake, Cooper Peak

HIGHLIGHTS: This trip journeys through a cross-section of Emigrant Wilderness, touching some justly popular base-camping lakes and less-visited Relief Valley. From every campsite you have access to the unusual and exciting surrounding country.

DAY 1 (Kennedy Meadows Trailhead to Summit Creek, 6.8 miles): Follow Trip 27, Day 1 to the Summit Creek campsites (8,283'; 38.23433°N, 119.72074°W).

DAY 2 (Summit Creek to Emigrant Meadow Lake, 6.3 miles): Continuing southeast, the trail rapidly leaves granite slab behind, crossing back onto volcanic rubble. For nearly a mile you cross an endless progression of long-ago debris flows, interspersed with a few more-recent, deeply incised flood channels. Look east at the pinnacled volcanic visage and imagine how an immense summer thunderstorm would send rocks and water tumbling down the myriad tiny passageways, the material slowing as it approaches the stream corridor. Red fir thrive in the fine, nutrient-rich material and form a near monoculture. As the valley narrows and steepens, you are back on fractured granite outcrops, winding upward beneath the steep cliffs. A 400-foot rocky ascent leads to a little saddle and just beyond the massive camping area called Sheep Camp; in part it is open and sandy and elsewhere under lodgepole pine shade.

Curving around Sheep Camp among eroded granite ribs, the trail continues close to the creek (and passes additional campsites), before diverging back onto volcanic scree. Climbing upward, the walls slowly shrink in height and you reach the beginning of massive Lunch Meadow. There are two major lobes, pinched in the middle by granite outcrops. You'll find campsites at the northwestern end of the western lobe, the northeastern side of the eastern lobe, and more choices if you cross the creek. As you traverse above the meadow, alternatively on volcanic rock and granite slab, you can't help but think about how the two rock types erode into such different profiles, creating the disparate landscapes to either side of the trail.

At Lunch Meadow's east end, you reach a junction where you stay left (east) toward Brown Bear Pass, while the Trip 28 description trends right (south) toward Emigrant Lake. In stretches you walk through wetter vegetation alongside the creek, elsewhere on broken granite slabs, and other sections across broad sagebrush flats, decorated in season with

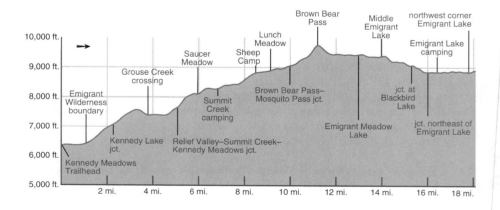

wavyleaf paintbrush, spreading phlox, and low-growing Brewer's lupine. Near where now-tiny Summit Creek diverges north, you pass a couple of pleasant campsites on whitebark pine–covered knobs north of the trail.

Slowly the trail curves south and the gradient increases; the final 0.4 mile to Brown Bear Pass (9,763') is hard work, climbing steeply up a rocky tread. Taking a well-earned break, you revel in the views from the pass. Stare east across the broad Emigrant Meadow basin and beyond to Saurian Crest, looking very much like the spiny back of a monstrous lizard, and Tower Peak. The view northwest to the volcanic ridge extending from Molo Peak to Relief Peak and west to the summits of Black Hawk Mountain and Granite Dome is now unbroken. The line dividing volcanic and granitic rocks is drawn obviously across the landscape, extending right to your pass: south of the trail are granite slabs, distinctly pink-hued due to mineral alterations that occurred as volcanic rock once flowed across it. Notice how Black Hawk Mountain is mostly granitic, with a thin icing of volcanic rock draped across its summit.

The trail descends through the nutrient-rich volcanics, hosting a wildflower garden that includes a diverse collection of plant species—the early-summer hiker will be treated to the periwinkle-flowered western blue flax and white-flowered Drummond's anemone, the latter's shoots emerging just hours after the snow melts. You cross back onto granite sand as you reach Emigrant Meadow. You soon ford the North Fork Cherry Creek, a sandy wade until midsummer, and traverse just north of marshy Emigrant Meadow. Between 1852 and 1854, emigrant wagons following the West Walker River route made a welcome stop here. The trail climbs an imperceptible 10 feet, crosses a sandy divide (plenty of campsites south of the trail), and drops toward even marshier Emigrant Meadow Lake (9,407'; rainbow trout). Looping around its northern end, you reach a junction where you turn right (south) to Middle Emigrant Lake, while left (east) continues to Grizzly Meadow (Trip 30). The trail immediately dives into the marshy expanse of meadow on Emigrant Meadow Lake's eastern shore. In early summer, environmentally conscious hikers cringe with each wet step, knowing they are damaging the delicate meadow turf by compacting the soil; instead skirt farther east to drier, sandier terrain. At the lake's end you climb slightly to a sand-and-slab saddle south of the lake. You'll find excellent campsites in sandy nooks right atop this saddle (9,453'; 38.19725°N, 119.64838°W).

DAY 3 (Emigrant Meadow Lake to Upper Buck Lake, 7.8 miles): As you continue southwest, Middle Emigrant Lake quickly comes into view. The trail leads to an often-boggy meadow-and-willow expanse north of the lake and soon dives cryptically into the willow

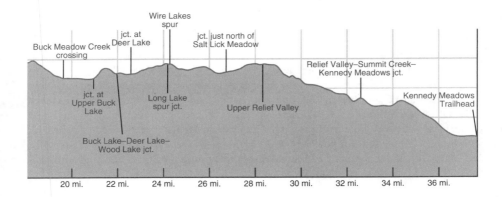

thickets fringing the North Fork Cherry Creek. Don't walk toward the meadow, but instead simply follow the disappearing trail through the willows, wade the sandy channel (or step across it in late season), and relocate the trail. The route now continues easily south, skirting Middle Emigrant Lake's (9,335'; rainbow trout) western shore at the base of a steep slope. The only camping here is at the lake's southwestern tip where there is an excellent campsite on a whitebark pine–dotted knob.

Continuing downstream, the tread is, in places, obscure, but the route is easy. Heading southwest, follow around the northern edge of a large willow-choked meadow, down a sandy-rocky slope where the trail is incised, across an early-drying creeklet, along the southern edge of a smaller meadow, and back to the banks of the North Fork Cherry Creek. The crossing, located where the creek jogs north, is usually a wade, although rock-hop options emerge at lower flows. (Ignore the misleading trails continuing along the creek's north shore; you need to cross sometime in the next 0.2 mile before the creek's gradient increases.) There are lovely campsites once across the creek. For the next 0.75 mile, the trail winds down the southern bank of the North Fork Cherry Creek, in places on broken slab and intervening sandy corridors, and elsewhere at the edge of pocket meadows, generally under partial lodgepole pine shade. Diverging a little south of the tumbling (or dry) river, you reach the northern tip of Blackbird Lake, which offers splendid campsites on both its eastern and western sides, for unlike most nearby lakes, its shores are sand, not grass. In a few steps you're at a junction, where you turn right (east) toward Emigrant Lake, while left (south) leads to Maxwell Lake and Horse Meadow (Trip 23).

The trail first proceeds along a vegetated corridor set between a pair of granite ribs, then switchbacks down a hemlock-shaded slope to emerge in a broad meadow flanking the North Fork Cherry Creek; you see Emigrant Lake just beyond. Before fording the creek, a spur leads east to pleasant creekside campsites. Once across the sandy-bottomed ford (often a wade), you come to a junction, where you turn left (west) to follow Emigrant Lake's northern shore (rainbow trout), while right (northeast) leads over Mosquito Pass and back to Lunch Meadow (Trip 28). There are good lodgepole-shaded campsites north of the trail for the coming 0.4 mile, but along the rest of Emigrant Lake's north shore the granite slabs slope straight up from the trail, making camping impractical. Broken slabs and bluffs rise to the north, while you stare south to a more intact, steep face. Consider how Emigrant Lake's length reflects the landscape-wide joints along which the rock preferentially erodes (and along a second set of often-perpendicular joints), so many of the region's lakes are remarkably elongate, but often with notably perpendicular bays and protruding granite ribs from the secondary fractures.

At the west end of Emigrant Lake, the trail turns right (north); an old trail descending the North Fork Cherry Creek to Cow Meadow Lake is shown on USGS 7.5' topo maps, but the trail is, in places, indistinct and the junction unmarked. Passing some small campsites, you stay on the main trail, winding away from Emigrant Lake through meadow strips, across slabs, and between bluffs to a minor pass, most notable for the big dark inclusions (blobs of a different rock) in the granite slab. Switchbacks lead down through hemlock, lodgepole pine, and western white pine forest, the trail tread becoming softer as the valley floor is approached. Tall, striking walls frame Buck Meadow Creek's headwaters. The trail fords the creek—a sandy wade or easy hop—and continues along the northern edge of a long meadow, passing a few small campsites in lodgepole pine stands (and you spy others across the creek).

Soon you reach Upper Buck Lake, its deep waters broken by parallel slab-rib islands and peninsulas. Just beyond the inlet you pass a lovely campsite between the trail and the lake, with lodgepole pine duff for your tent and lakeside slabs for relaxing (8,362'; 38.16595°N, 119.74106°W). There are many additional campsites around the Buck Lakes, including off-trail options to the west, along the creek between the two largest lakes.

DAY 4 (Upper Buck Lake to Upper Relief Valley, 7.5 miles): Continuing along Upper Buck Lake's western shore, you promptly reach a junction, where you turn right (southwest) toward Deer Lake, while left (south) leads to the lower Buck Lakes and onto Cow Meadow Lake and Wood Lake (toward Trip 23). A rocky climb ensues, leading you up an exposed, scrubby slope to a tarn-dotted corridor 400 feet higher. The passageway segues to a gentle drop through lodgepole pine, leading to a junction where left (south) is a lateral to Wood Lake (Trip 22), while you stay right (west), continuing beneath forest cover and then across a slab rib to Deer Lake's steep-edged, deep eastern end. Looping north of the lake through seasonally marshy flats and fording two inlet streams, you reach a junction, where you turn right (north) to Salt Lick Meadow, while left (southwest) leads toward Jewelry Lake. There are good campsites along Deer Lake's northern shore, just west of this junction. If you have time for a break, Deer Lake's warm water and bedrock islands make it an enticing swimming stop; detour toward the shoreline a little west of the junction.

Back on route, the coming 1.6-mile segment follows one of Deer Lake's inlets steadily upward. Crossing the unnamed creek twice, the trail soon begins climbing a broken-slab slope, reaching another pair of closely spaced creek crossings; you can stay on the west bank and avoid this pair of crossings if water levels are high and the crossings cumbersome. Beyond, the gradient decreases and you enter a lodgepole pine and hemlock–clad valley of unnamed lakelets, mostly meadow rimmed with just sporadic tongues of bedrock extending to their shores. By midseason, drier pocket meadows are brightly decorated with the purple flowers of shaggy lupine. Soon after the fourth lake, you reach a junction, where you stay left (north), while right (east) leads to Long Lake (described in Trip 26; wonderful campsites). Just 0.1 mile later, you reach a second junction, where left (west) leads to the Wire Lakes (described in Trip 25; also good campsites).

You continue right (north) through lush lodgepole pine forest to the Spring Creek corridor. Curving northwest, then west, the trail follows Spring Creek down to Spring Meadow; on the descent, look up Post Corral Canyon at a collection of steep, polished granite domes, the extension of ridges off Granite Dome. Spring Meadow harbors a shallow lake and very marshy meadows in early summer; the mosquitoes and buttercup displays here can both be quite intense as you wade sandy-bottomed Spring Creek (brook trout). Later you can enjoy displays of lupine and paintbrush in peace. Climbing again, the trail leads through an extensive lodgepole pine flat scattered with about a dozen tarns and carpeted with dwarf bilberry and red mountain heather. The route then drops steeply down a joint-delineated corridor to reach Salt Lick Meadow (8,505'). A drier meadow peppered with pleasantly rounded granite outcrops, you'll find campsites at the meadow's southeastern edge (although no late-season water). Here you ford the nascent West Fork Cherry Creek (a sandy wade at higher flows, but drying in the late season) and just beyond the meadow reach a junction where you turn right (northeast) toward Upper Relief Valley, while left (northwest) leads to Whitesides Meadow (Trips 25 and 26).

The coming 1.6 miles are mostly through seasonally boggy lodgepole pine forest carpeted with dwarf bilberry, with scattered boulders to the sides. You climb gently, occasionally on a rockier tread, but generally through pocket meadows or on forest duff. The final length cuts across an early-drying lobe of Upper Relief Valley meadow, reaching a junction at the north side of the meadow; you continue right (east) to descend back to Summit Creek and Kennedy Meadows, while left (west) leads toward Whitesides Meadow. There are a number of campsite options in Upper Relief Valley, all splendidly situated in this broad open grassland, with Granite Dome rising to the southeast. The closest options are atop the shallow granite slab-and-sand lump you pass after 0.1 mile (8,790'; 38.22272°N, 119.78008°W; mileage to here), followed by a selection of choices north of the trail under lodgepole pine cover. Then 0.2 mile beyond the junction an unsigned use trail departs across the meadow, passing between the pair of Upper Relief Valley lakes. Once across the meadow, you are back on shallow slabs and in fringing lodgepole pine forest and will find a selection of sites, including lovely ones at the northeastern end of the northeastern lake, that would add 0.7 mile to your distance (8,785'; 38.22873°N, 119.76853°W). On the main trail, there is also a good campsite 0.5 mile east of the junction in a large stand of lodgepole pine and hemlock just as you reach the end of the Upper Relief Valley meadow (8,797'; 38.22774°N, 119.77640°W).

DAY 5 (Upper Relief Valley to Kennedy Meadows Trailhead, 9.3 miles): This day is longer in miles, but (almost) all downhill. If you want to split this day, there are campsites just past the Summit Creek ford (3.9 miles from Night 4) and at Relief Reservoir near where Grouse Creek flows into the lake (5.4 miles from Night 4).

You regain the trail in Upper Relief Valley and proceed northeast, then north along the meadow's edge, passing the aforementioned forest campsites and dropping down a gravelly, eroded gorge with rounded granite bluffs to the east and volcanic cliffs to the west and north. Rocky, awkward walking leads you down the gully and across the creek, becoming an easier tread as you cross onto volcanic soils beneath impressive East Flange Rock. Junipers dot the hillside, while shrubs and flowers grow densely underfoot.

GEOLOGY LESSON WITH BREWER

Contrasts between the dark volcanic rock and the white granite underlayment of this part of the Sierra are nowhere more marked than in this valley, and the viewer is assailed with dark battlements of multihued basalt and sheer escarpments of glacially smoothed batholithic granite. William H. Brewer, head of the Brewer Survey party that passed near here in July 1863, took note of the volcanic surroundings, saying, "In the higher Sierra, along our line of travel, all our highest points were capped with lava, often worn into strange and fantastic forms: rounded hills of granite, capped by rugged masses of lava, sometimes looking like old castles with their towers and buttresses and walls, sometimes like old churches with their pinnacles, all on a gigantic scale, and then again shooting up in curious forms that defy description."

As you approach Relief Valley, you pass a pleasant campsite beneath red fir shade. The same emigrant wagon trains that earlier passed by Emigrant Meadow Lake descended Summit Creek then climbed to here, feeling understandably relieved to reach some flatter terrain. For you, it is a pleasant walk through sagebrush and wildflowers (Leichtlin's mariposa lily, orange sneezeweed, and wavyleaf paintbrush are all common), your thoughts wandering to impressive Granite Dome, East Flange Rock, and the general inaccessibility of Relief Creek due to willow thickets, but fortunately not how to navigate your wagon through cliff bands. Rounding a knob, the trail departs through a saddle well north of Relief Creek's course and drops through white fir forest. Now down at lower elevations, the granite bluffs beside the trail are lichen-covered and have weathered gray surfaces—such a contrast to the bright pink and white exposures on the higher slopes.

Shortly you reunite with Relief Creek on an exposed, steep, scrubby slope and wind down in tandem with the creek. Soon after the confluence of Relief Creek into Summit Creek, the creek drops deep into a granite gorge—you're still beside it, but the banks are no longer accessible. The trail switchbacks down the dry slope, flattening only as it approaches the Summit Creek ford. The ford is a mix of boulders with sand between, a difficult wade during peak flows. Across the creek, you pass a pleasant campsite and switchback across a bedrock rib to reach the Summit Creek Trail. Now retrace your steps the final 5.1 miles to the trailhead.

Sonora Pass Trailhead
9,654'; 38.32800°N, 119.63730°W

Destination/ GPS Coordinates	Trip Type	Best Season	Pace & Hiking/ Layover Days	Total Mileage	Permit Required
30 Big Sam and Grizzly Meadow 38.19300°N 119.62799°W (Grizzly Meadow)	Shuttle	Mid to late	Moderate 4/1	31.0	Sonora Pass *(or Kennedy Meadows in reverse)*
31 Pacific Crest Trail to Tuolumne Meadows 37.87889°N 119.35854°W (Glen Aulin Trailhead)	Shuttle	Mid to late	Strenuous 8/1	73.9	Sonora Pass *(or Yosemite: Glen Aulin in reverse)*

INFORMATION AND PERMITS: This trailhead lies on the boundary of Stanislaus and Humboldt-Toiyabe National Forests, accessing Emigrant and Hoover Wilderness Areas, and is administered by Stanislaus National Forest. Permits are required for overnight stays, but there are no quotas. Permits for this trailhead are most conveniently picked up at the Summit District Ranger Station, located at 1 Pinecrest Road, in Pinecrest, California. If you will be arriving outside of office hours, call 209-965-3434; you can request a permit up to two days in advance and it will be left in a dropbox for you. Campfires are prohibited above 9,000 feet, as are campfires within a half mile of Emigrant Lake. Bear canisters are required if you camp in Hoover Wilderness or Yosemite National Park. Trip 31 enters Yosemite National Park, and once in the park, pets and firearms are prohibited.

DRIVING DIRECTIONS: This trailhead is located exactly atop Sonora Pass along CA 108. This is 72.6 miles east of the CA 108–CA 120 junction and 14.7 miles west of the CA 108–US 395 junction. There is a small parking area directly across from the trailhead and additional parking spaces and toilets along a spur road 0.2 mile to the west. The closest water is, to the east, at the Leavitt Meadows Campground (adjacent to the trailhead) or, to the west, at the Kennedy Meadows Trailhead (and adjacent campgrounds).

trip 30   **Big Sam and Grizzly Meadow**

see map on p. 142

Trip Data: 38.19436°N, 119.63009°W (Grizzly Meadow); 31.0 miles; 4/1 days

Topos: *Sonora Pass, Pickel Meadow* (just briefly), *Tower Peak, Emigrant Meadow*

HIGHLIGHTS: With splendid views, geological and botanical intrigue, and the opportunity to follow two historically important routes, much of this walk is a "highlight." The diverse terrain includes lakes, meadows, creeks, granite slabs, volcanic bluffs, and a peak that lies just 150 feet off the trail.

HEADS UP! *Kennedy Meadows Resort runs a regular shuttle service to Sonora Pass, facilitating the trailhead logistics for this shuttle hike. Check out their website at kennedymeadows.com to determine the current schedule; click on the "PCT Hikers" link.*

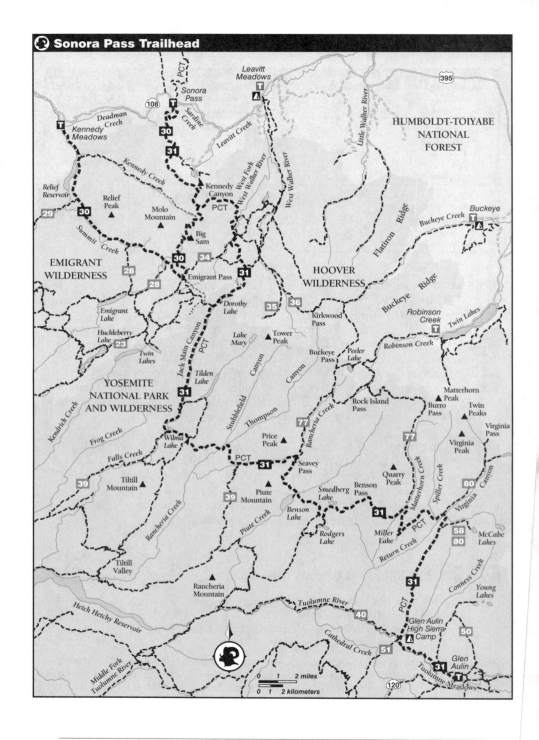

HEADS UP! *This first day is long in distance but has relatively little elevation gain. Since the springs at the headwaters of Kennedy Creek are the first reliable on-trail water source, only start on this walk if you are confident you can complete the distance in a day.*

SHUTTLE DIRECTIONS: From the Sonora Pass Trailhead, continue 9.1 miles west along CA 108. Turn south onto the signed spur road to Kennedy Meadows. At 0.5 mile down the road, turn left (east) into a large U.S. Forest Service trailhead parking area with toilets and hiker campsites, requiring a wilderness permit and limited to a 1-night stay. The actual trailhead is an additional 0.5 mile down the road at the Kennedy Meadows Resort (lodgings, café, saloon, store, pack station). You can drive here to pick up packs and passengers, but leave your car at the aforementioned Forest Service parking lot.

DAY 1 (Sonora Pass Trailhead to Kennedy Creek headwaters, 10.2 miles): Departing south from Sonora Pass, the famous Pacific Crest Trail (PCT) winds briefly through multistemmed whitebark pine clusters, then traverses onto an open volcanic slope that is one of the Sierra's best wildflower gardens. Late-lasting snowfields and the nutrient-rich volcanic rocks nurture dense expanses of flowers: the mule ears, western blue flax, scarlet gilia, California valerian, and mountain monardella are among the most colorful, although several dozen species grow here. The trail crosses two drainages, the first unnamed and the second Sardine Creek, before traversing south, then west, and finally north across a broad bowl beneath volcanic cliffs. Parts of this slope hold long-lasting snow—take care if you're hiking in June (or into August in a high snow year).

About 2 miles from the trailhead, the trail is back on the actual crest of the Sierra, passing through different phenomenal wildflower displays—now they are mainly cushion plants, some rising less than an inch above the soil, and include silky raillardella, showy penstemon, hoary groundsel, Pursh's milk vetch, and woolly sunflower. Looking far down to CA 108, the trail traipses across a west-facing slope high above Blue Canyon; the white-bark pine and currants have been wind-pruned into smooth, flat mounds. Eventually the trail crosses back to the east side of the crest, passes a small tarn, and climbs briefly but steeply to a saddle, from which you look 400 feet down upon Latopie Lake.

VOLCANIC ROCK

The volcanic rubble you're walking across is part of the Relief Peak Formation. It includes lava flows of various chemical compositions, lahars (mudflows triggered by volcanic eruptions), and what is termed "autobreccia." Autobreccia forms when the erupting magma causes either previously deposited volcanic rock or the underlying bedrock (in this case granite) to fracture and this fractured rock is engulfed in the magma. All the places you see chunks of one rock enveloped in a volcanic matrix are "autobreccia of volcanic origin."

Continuing to traverse with little elevation gain or loss, the trail cuts across the front of rugged, multicolored volcanic bluffs; this is one of the rockier trail sections underfoot. A broad arc leads to an east-trending spur (with a late-lasting snowbank) and then across another broad bowl, now with Koenig Lake far below.

LEAVITT PEAK

From the base of the aforementioned snowbank, it is just 0.7 mile up a ridge to the summit of Leavitt Peak. If you have spare time, it is a straightforward, albeit rock-and-talus covered, ridge walk with 750 feet of elevation gain to the summit. Once you're on the ridge, there are vestiges of a use trail. For reference, you've completed just over 5 miles and have 5.2 to reach tonight's camp. Leave the trail at 10,648'; 38.27906°N, 119.64363°W.

Back on a west-facing slope, you now look down upon the Kennedy Creek canyon to triangular Kennedy Lake and across to Molo, Kennedy, and Relief Peaks, the trio of volcanic summits to the southwest. Granitic Tower Peak surges into view to the southeast. You saunter across the volcanic rocks, admiring sky pilot (the northern variety, *Polemonium pulcherrimum*), narrow leaved fleabane, and Eaton's daisy (both rare species in most of the Sierra). Ahead, you reach a junction with a mining road climbing steeply from Leavitt Lake (left, east); you head right (south), now on the old road.

A short distance later the road cuts back onto the east side of the ridge and begins a long switchbacking descent into Kennedy Canyon. In line with Leave No Trace principles, you are encouraged to ignore shortcut trails down the slope and stick to the mining road. The coming 1.6 miles offer few botanical or geologic distractions, but the road tread is innocuous and of a sufficiently low gradient to be easy on the knees. Where the terrain levels, you reach a junction where you continue right (south) on the mining road, while the PCT turns left (east) to descend Kennedy Canyon (Trip 31). There are a few campsites a short distance along the PCT, near clusters of trees.

After so many barren miles, the upright whitebark pine clusters and grassy ground cover with a dense speckling of Leichtlin's mariposa lilies are most welcome—and unexpected, for you are still on the ridgetop. About 0.4 mile from the junction you'll notice sandy patches between whitebark pine to the right (west) that are ideal campsites, some even offering open views toward Kennedy Peak (9,655'; 38.23994°N, 119.61190°W). In the gully just 0.1 mile farther is a delightfully reliable robust spring, the headwaters of Kennedy Creek.

DAY 2 (Kennedy Creek headwaters to Grizzly Meadow, 7.0 miles): In the morning, regain the old mining road and begin a long but moderately graded uphill to the summit of Big Sam (labeled only as Peak 10,825 on the USGS 7.5' topo maps). The trail first trends west beneath Peak 10,827 and its western satellite, then turns south to curve into a high basin. (*Note:* There is one steep, late-lasting snowfield on this section. If present, you'll be able to see it from your campsite and will probably wish to avoid it—the best option is to walk about 0.2 mile down Kennedy Creek. You'll then see a rough trail, the old Kennedy Creek Trail, climbing up a rib and cutting beneath the snowfield to reunite with the mining road higher up.)

The trail winds up through the high bowl, hopscotching from color to color as you move between volcanic rock types. Looping across a band of krummholz whitebark pine, the trail ascends across dry west-facing slopes where singlehead goldenbrush and woolly sunflower are common, across a north-facing slope where Eschscholtz's buttercups emerge as the snow melts, and up six switchbacks to the summit of Big Sam (10,825'). The few-step detour from the trail to the summit is well worth it—the view from Big Sam is astounding. Standing high

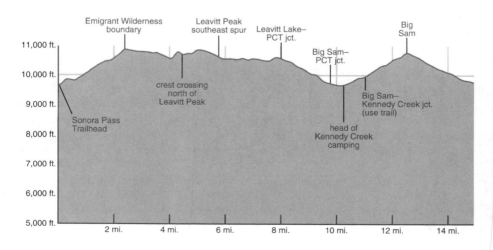

above the surrounding landscape, you look south upon the Emigrant Lakes Basin with its broad, shallow, grass-ringed lakes surrounded by granite ribs. In the distance you look toward Yosemite's highest summit, Mount Lyell, and neighboring Mount Maclure and to the Clark Range. Closer are the peaks on the northern Yosemite boundary, crowned by Tower Peak.

Continuing toward Emigrant Pass, think about the rich human history of the area as you plod downward—see the sidebar. First are more than a dozen switchbacks and then a long descent along the headwaters of the North Fork Cherry Creek to broad High Emigrant Lake. Mostly meadow ringed, the best campsites are on sandy flats on the lake's south side. In case you're wondering, the leaking dam across the lake's outlet is one of 15 engineered by Fred Leighton, a cattleman, who wanted to ensure streamflow was maintained all summer to increase the spawning success of introduced trout.

HUMAN HISTORY NEAR EMIGRANT PASS

The road you are following was constructed in 1943 to reach a profitable tungsten mine along the East Fork Cherry Creek, about a mile below Horse Meadow. During World War II the United States needed tungsten, used to harden steel, and the approximately 16.25-mile road from Leavitt Lake was built to reach the prospects. Ore was hauled out for more than a decade, but of course the road was soon in disrepair from winter avalanches and mining was discontinued by the 1960s. Meanwhile, one of the first emigrant groups to cross the Sierra, some members of the Clark-Skidmore Party of 1852, crossed broad Emigrant Pass below you. They ascended the West Walker River, then the West Fork West Walker River to Emigrant Pass, descending to Emigrant Meadow Lake. While you've followed the mining road for much of the first two days of your journey, you will be following the emigrant route for the next day and a half.

Beyond High Emigrant Lake, the trail climbs gently to Emigrant Pass, the pass crossed by the emigrant wagons, and on down to the actual low point in the divide. Here is a junction with the trail ascending the West Fork West Walker River (Trip 34; left, east). You continue right (south), signposted for Grizzly Meadow and, walking beside an increasingly marshy meadow corridor beneath imposing Grizzly Peak, reach another junction after 0.35 mile, where you turn right (northwest) signposted for Brown Bear Pass, while left (south) leads to Bond Pass (Trip 34).

You cut across the notably marshy meadow corridor to an unmarked junction, where you trend right (west), while left (south) is a cutoff route to Horse Meadow. Near this junction,

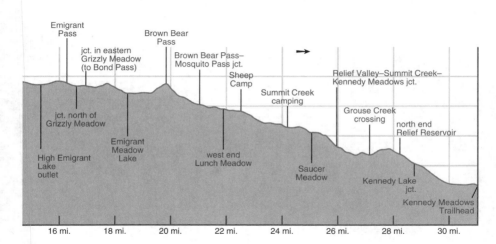

search for splendid—but usually small—campsites in sandy flats on the glacial-polished granite ribs surrounding lower Grizzly Meadow Lake (9,681'; 38.19300°N, 119.62799°W at junction). All sites have idyllic views of Grizzly Peak. There are also flat sandy areas farther west near upper Grizzly Meadow Lake, a little farther off the trail.

DAY 3 (Grizzly Meadow to Summit Creek, 7.0 miles): Today's route begins by cutting back into the North Fork Cherry Creek drainage, by sidling out of the Grizzly Meadow Lakes bowl and dropping down to Emigrant Meadow Lake. The trail generally follows joint-defined sandy passageways and minor drainages, forcing it to jog north, then west, and north and west a second time as it drops to the giant broad basin holding Emigrant Meadow Lake and adjacent Emigrant Meadow. At the northeast corner of Emigrant Meadow Lake is a junction, where you stay right (northwest), signposted for Kennedy Meadows, while left (south) leads to Middle Emigrant Lake (Trips 28 and 29). You continue along the northeastern side of the lake, first through marshy meadows and then to extensive sandy flats and low-lying granite slabs near the northwestern tip of the lake (nearby camping). Crossing an ever-so-slight rise in the broad basin, the trail drops a token 10 feet to marshier Emigrant Meadow, where you cross the North Fork Cherry Creek again, a sandy wade until midsummer.

Bound for Brown Bear Pass, the trail's gradient now increases and almost immediately crosses onto volcanic rock, although there are granite slabs just south of the trail. These are distinctly pink-hued due to mineral alterations that occurred as the volcanic rock flowed across it. Once atop Brown Bear Pass (9,763'), be sure to turn back and stare across the broad Emigrant Meadow basin and beyond to Saurian Crest, looking very much like the spiny back of a monstrous lizard, and Tower Peak. Looking west and northwest, the volcanic ridge extending from Molo Peak to Relief Peak and the summits of Black Hawk Mountain and Granite Dome are now in view.

Your descent to the headwaters of Summit Creek is steep and rocky for the first 0.4 mile, then moderates as you approach Summit Creek and small campsites, some on whitebark pine–sheltered knobs and others in sandy flats. In stretches you walk through wetter vegetation alongside the creek, elsewhere on broken granite slabs, and yet other sections across sagebrush flats, decorated in season with wavyleaf paintbrush, spreading phlox, and Brewer's lupine.

Emigrant Meadow Lake   Photo by Elizabeth Wenk

You reach a junction where you stay right (northwest), signposted for Kennedy Meadows, while left (south) leads across Summit Creek and over Mosquito Pass to Emigrant Lake (Trip 28). After a few more steps you reach the eastern lobe of Lunch Meadow (and a campsite). The trail traverses above the meadow, alternating between volcanic rubble and granite slab; you can't help but think about how the two rock types erode into such different profiles, creating the disparate landscapes to either side of the trail. At the west end of the western Lunch Meadow lobe is another excellent campsite, with additional options were you to cross the creek. Continuing west, the trail remains close to Summit Creek, passing through small meadow strips and along sandy corridors between eroded granite ribs. A broad sandy flat and adjacent lodgepole pine stand is Sheep Camp, your last plausible camp until the suggested campsites another 1.7 miles ahead. Sheep Camp accommodates a larger group and if 8.5 miles isn't too long for your final day, you may wish to stay here.

Ahead, the trail parts with Summit Creek and curves north, crossing a shallow sandy saddle and dropping steeply into a rocky valley. A 400-foot descent ensues, the trail working its way around outcrops and minor drop-offs; this is much slower walking than any of this trip's previous downhill miles. Admire the fractured granite, rising ever higher above you: steep walls adorned with vertical fractures that dictate where erosion preferentially occurs. Slowly the valley opens a little, the gradient lessens, and to the east the slopes are volcanic again—as is the rock underfoot. For nearly a mile you then cross an endless progression of long-ago debris flows, interspersed with a few more-recent deeply incised flood channels. Look east at the pinnacled volcanic visage and imagine an immense summer thunderstorm that sends rocks and water tumbling down the myriad tiny passageways, the debris slowing as it approaches the stream corridor. Red fir thrive in the fine, nutrient-rich material and form a near monoculture. Continuing south, the trail crosses back onto granite slab and the terrain flattens enough to entertain camping. First you pass a slab knob east of the trail with a small selection of sandy sites (8,283'; 38.23433°N, 119.72074°W) and a short distance later a large site under red fir and lodgepole pine cover, also to your right (east). The forested flats in the direction of the creek are clearly marked as NO CAMPING, for they are fewer than 100 feet from water.

DAY 4 (Summit Creek to Kennedy Meadows Trailhead, 6.8 miles): Just past the campsites, the trail again diverges from Summit Creek, following a sandy corridor at the granite-volcanics boundary that leads to tiny Saucer Meadow, a little flower-filled marsh. Climbing over a minor saddle, you again cross fans of volcanic scree. East Flange Rock, the volcanic pinnacle due west, and Granite Dome dominate the view. To the north, you catch your first glimpses of giant Relief Reservoir. The slope steepens and the tread becomes rockier as you descend a scrubby, open slope with just the occasional juniper. Beyond, the trail is channeled into a cooler draw where dense white firs provide shade and seasonal trickles irrigate wildflower pockets. At its base is a junction, where you continue right (north), while left (west and south) leads into the Relief Creek drainage (Trip 29).

The route follows an easy-to-navigate corridor, separated from Summit Creek's drainage by a blocky granite rib, initially through a lovely forest of aspen and white fir, then into more open terrain where towering Jeffrey pine and stringy-barked junipers predominate. You soon sense you're walking just east of Relief Reservoir; indeed, if you were to head west, you'd find camping in sandy flats set back from the shore. Then, about one-third of the way north along the reservoir, you reach a shallow ford of Grouse Creek that can usually be crossed on an assortment of logs. To either side of the crossing, spur trails head west toward the reservoir's shore and the best lakeside camping options. Climbing and dropping continually, the trail contours high above the reservoir on hot, sandy, brushy slopes with just the occasional Jeffrey pine or juniper providing dots of shade.

Toward the reservoir's north end, you reach a series of overlooks, culminating in the best one; a distinct spur trail leads first to the vista point and then toward the Relief Reservoir dam itself. Dropping past rusting equipment used in the dam's construction, numerous use trails depart left (west) to Summit Creek. Ahead is a signed junction, where your route continues left (north), while right (east) leads to Kennedy Lake. Crossing brushy slopes beneath a granite dome, the trail splits; the main trail switchbacks to the left (northwest), while the right-hand (more northerly) alternative is a steeper, 400-foot-shorter route used by some hikers. Just after the two routes merge you reunite with Summit Creek and cross a trestle bridge high above the tumultuous river, enjoying views to cascades upstream. Continuing north along the blocky, incised gorge, you soon spy Kennedy Creek to the east, tumbling down its steep boulder-and-bedrock-lined course. The trail descends the creek's western bank, passing beneath impressively vertical—even overhung—black-stained walls. At the confluence with Kennedy Creek, the flow becomes the Middle Fork Stanislaus River—a mighty torrent of water in early summer that you admire as you cross a second bridge.

The valley now quickly broadens and the trail turns first west, then north at the start of Kennedy Meadows. You leave Emigrant Wilderness and pass a U.S. Forest Service trailhead sign. The final 1.0 mile to the trailhead is along a dirt road, sometimes under forest cover—a mix of Jeffrey pine, incense cedar, white fir, and juniper—and elsewhere at the meadow's edge or just above the river's banks. Where the meadow pinches closed, the road crosses a minor saddle. Dropping again, you quickly reach a gate and Kennedy Meadows Resort, the effective "trailhead," although at least one person in your group will have to walk an additional 0.5 mile to the overnight parking area.

trip 31 Pacific Crest Trail to Tuolumne Meadows

see map on p. 142

Trip Data: 37.87889°N, 119.35854°W (Glen Aulin Trailhead);
73.9 miles; 8/1 days

Topos: Sonora Pass, Emigrant Lake, Tower Peak, Piute Mountain, Tiltill
Mountain, Matterhorn Peak, Falls Ridge, Dunderberg Peak, Tioga Pass

HIGHLIGHTS: The varied and incomparable scenery along this leg of the Pacific Crest Trail (PCT) from Sonora Pass to Tuolumne Meadows offers emerald meadows, granitic and metamorphic peaks, jewellike lakes, bubbling creeks, panoramic views from ridges, and visits to deep canyons. These rewards more than justify the trip's length and sometimes taxing ups and downs.

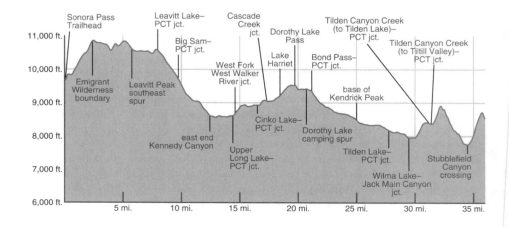

View to Kennedy Lake on the long traverse past Leavitt Peak   Photo by Elizabeth Wenk

---

HEADS UP! *Most people won't want to carry more than 8–10 days of food (and can't fit more in a bear canister), so the trip is divided into 8 days plus a layover day to have a midtrip rest. This translates into 10–11 miles on many days, making it one of the more strenuous trips in the book.*

SHUTTLE DIRECTIONS: The trip ends at the Glen Aulin Trailhead in Tuolumne Meadows in Yosemite. This is just off Tioga Road (CA 120) in Tuolumne Meadows, along the Tuolumne Meadows Stables Road at the base of Lembert Dome. The junction is located just 0.17 miles east of the Tuolumne Meadows Campground entrance, right after you cross the Tuolumne River, or 6.95 miles west of Tioga Pass. The "parking lot" is the dirt shoulder along the Tuolumne Meadows Stables Road with overflow parking available at the stables. Your trip ends at a gate at the west end of the road.

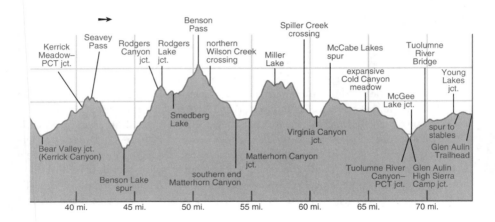

DAY 1 (Sonora Pass Trailhead to upper Kennedy Canyon, 10.1 miles): Follow Trip 30, Day 1 for 9.8 miles. At the PCT–Big Sam junction, you turn left (east) to continue along the PCT. After just 0.3 mile you'll see a selection of small campsites to the north of the trail beneath multistemmed whitebark pine clumps (9,477'; 38.24739°N, 119.60987°W). There are permanent springs nearby.

DAY 2 (Upper Kennedy Canyon to Dorothy Lake, 10.6 miles): The well-built PCT tread leads easily down Kennedy Canyon, first through meadows with abundant wildflower color and shortly into bare lodgepole pine forest. You cross through a repeat avalanche corridor—the logs littering the ground all face the same direction, and many surviving trees are missing lower branches. The trail then crosses a robust creek and heads down through lusher lodgepole pine forest, regularly crossing spring-fed rills where meadow rue, California valerian, and monkshood all grow robustly. Ever deeper into Kennedy Canyon, the trail traverses a drier slope and drops to cross the main drainage, often necessitating a shallow wade, and just beyond passes small campsites. Ahead, the valley bottom is flatter, the trail alternately passing through pleasant lodgepole pine forest and across small grassy benches above the gurgling creek. The route is on volcanic substrate until you come to the mouth of Kennedy Canyon; here the trail jogs briefly north, then turns decidedly southeast and you step onto granite slab. Nearby are some splendid campsites perched high above the river.

As the Kennedy Canyon creek drops more steeply to merge with the West Fork West Walker River, the PCT turns south, beginning a long traverse parallel to (and above) the West Fork West Walker River. Hawksbeak Peak on the Yosemite boundary is exceptionally impressive from here, a steep, angular fin shooting skyward. In 0.5 mile you pass a small waterfall dropping down a volcanic gorge (worth a look) and continue just at the forest-talus slope boundary, first passing beneath soaring volcanic ridges, then transitioning back to granite slab and winding your way along the fringe of Walker Meadows. Passing a large campsite to the right (south), you reach the West Fork West Walker River, crossed on a stout bridge. Just beyond is a junction, where you stay right (southwest) on the PCT toward Dorothy Lake Pass, while left (southeast) leads to the Long Lakes and Fremont Lake (Trips 32–36).

Ascending the West Fork West Walker River, in just 0.2 mile you reach a second junction (and more excellent campsites), where the PCT trends left (nearly due south; again signposted for Dorothy Lake Pass), while a trail toward Cinko Lake (Trip 33) and Emigrant Pass (Trip 34) diverges right (southwest), continuing along the river's southeast bank. The PCT ramps up slabs colored by bursts of Leichtlin's mariposa lily, mountain pride pentemon, and Brewer's aster, slowly diverging from the river. After 0.5 mile the trail turns east, winding along forested corridors between granite slabs and past early-drying tarns. Turning south again, the trail leaves the conifer cover for bare slab and you'll discover you've left the granite for a mosaic of older metavolcanic and metasedimentary rocks, including bands of marble and a wall sparkling with garnets.

Ducking briefly back into a cool, sheltered draw shaded by hemlock and lodgepole pine, you reach another junction where the PCT turns left (east, then southeast), while right (west) is another route to Cinko Lake (Trip 33); there are campsites at the junction. Just beyond you cross a small creek on rocks or logs. Still on metavolcanic rock, a 0.8-mile segment takes you across a broad saddle cradling a series of tarns (and more possible campsites) to a junction with a trail ascending Cascade Creek from Lower Piute Meadow (to the northeast; Trip 34). The PCT continues right (south), passing a pair of heath-bound tarns, looking down upon an often-flooded meadow, and reaching the banks of Cascade Creek in a pocket of lodgepole pine. The river must be crossed, requiring either a delicate log-and-rock hop or a broad wade; an old footbridge is long gone. The trail then follows up the creek's eastern bank, winding up bare, broken slabs between scattered lodgepole pine. The creek to your side is forever spilling down little falls, for the rock erodes in a blocky fashion. In a small patch of willows, just below 9,200 feet (38.18915°N, 119.56930°W), the PCT inconspicuously crosses Cascade Creek. At high flows, stay on the more obvious eastside trail, which leads to an easier crossing on logs and rocks at Lake Harriet's outlet; the eastbank use trail also leads to a fine selection of camps along Lake Harriet's east shore.

Across Harriet's outlet, the use trail and PCT reunite, continuing around Lake Harriet's western shore, then resuming a steady ascent up broken slab and completing six tight switchbacks to a tarn-filled flat. Here an unmarked spur trail leads west to Bonnie Lake (limited campsites). A short distance later the trail crosses into the drainage where Stella and Bonnie Lakes lie, converging with Stella Lake's outlet as the trail approaches the lake. Stella is a gorgeous lake with an intricate shoreline but offers very few campsites. The trail winds across gray diorite slab north of the lake, then barely rises to reach the summit of Dorothy Lake Pass, an elongate notch that marks your entrance into Yosemite National Park.

Looking forward, giant Dorothy Lake fills the valley ahead, with light-colored Tower Peak peering out to the southeast and the dark granite grenadiers of Forsyth Peak to the south. A slight descent leads to Dorothy's northern shore. You pass a few acceptable campsites early in your traverse but should continue to Dorothy's southwestern end for the night. Until late in the summer, water seeps from the base of upslope slabs, and endless rills irrigate the slopes, nurturing splashes of color (shooting star, elephant heads, goldenrod, paintbrush, whorled penstemon, pussypaws, and false Solomon's seal) and expanses of corn lilies and willows. The trail can be quite muddy—take care to walk on the wet tread or balance on rocks, instead of damaging the surrounding subalpine turf. At the lake's southwest end you'll see a sign pointing stock parties southeast around the lake; hikers should follow this use trail as well. They needn't walk the full 0.4 mile to the big stock campsites, but just a few hundred feet to some excellent campsites beside clusters of lodgepole pine (9,429'; 38.17422°N, 119.59511°W).

DAY 3 (Dorothy Lake to Wilma Lake, 8.7 miles): Beyond Dorothy Lake, the trail passes a satellite lakelet and meadows overgrown with straggly, crowded lodgepole pine, likely a legacy of meadow-trampling by sheep, cattle, or humans long ago. A brief descent brings you to, in quick succession, two trails that unite to climb northwest to nearby Bond Pass, the park's boundary; you stay left (south) at each. A 600-foot descent follows, carrying you into the upper end of lush, damp, and stunning Jack Main Canyon, where the trail roughly parallels Falls Creek. This next stretch of trail is an idyllic series of tiny meadows interspersed with dense forest, all alongside the murmuring creek. To the east, somber Forsyth Peak and black-and-white Keyes Peak cap the canyon walls. Throughout the coming miles, endless trickles descend from the west, making for wet, muddy feet in early season; take care not to trample the surrounding vegetation in an attempt to keep your feet dry. The largest meadow stretch is verdant Grace Meadow, Falls Creek meandering lazily along its western side. In Grace Meadow—and the meadows you'll pass to the south—you'll find tiny campsites in the fringing lodgepole, but no large sites, for most of the ground is vegetated or sloping.

Chittenden Peak and its northern satellite serve as impressive reference points for gauging your southward progress; about where you pass them the canyon's gradient steepens a little, ultimately leading to your first junction in 6.6 miles. You stay right (south) on the PCT, white left (east) leads to Tilden Lake. (*Note:* As described in Trip 39, Days 4–5, you could detour to Tilden Lake and rejoin the PCT tomorrow. Tilden Lake doesn't lie on the PCT but is one of northern Yosemite's absolute highlights.) There are good campsites near this junction.

For the 1.7 miles to your next junction, the meandering creek is mostly hidden from view by a veil of lodgepole pine. The trail crosses intermittently onto slabs, then back into lush forest with a near continuous groundcover of dwarf bilberry. At the north end of an expansive lodgepole flat, you pass a sometimes-staffed ranger cabin on the right, and soon thereafter a junction where the PCT turns left (southeast) toward Wilma Lake, while the route down Jack Main Canyon stays right (south; Trip 39). Near this junction is a selection of excellent campsites alongside broad, generally lazily flowing Falls Creek (7,959'; 38.07386°N, 119.64678°W). There is also a small camping area tucked among trees at Wilma Lake's southeastern end and in the flat due north of the lake, a little farther off-trail. Today will have been much easier than the previous two days, but if you're thinking of continuing, note that it is just a hair under 5 miles to Stubblefield Canyon, where you'll next have good camping and water in the same location.

DAY 4 (Wilma Lake to Rancheria Creek, 7.7 miles): You begin the day by fording Falls Creek (almost always wet feet) to reach a narrow isthmus separating Falls Creek from Wilma Lake. You then walk close to Wilma's shore on elegantly constructed trail. Climbing above Wilma Lake, you wind moderately up a canyon, mostly through lush heath-carpeted lodgepole forest, pass two pleasant tarns, and reach a junction with the trail that has descended Tilden Canyon Creek from Tilden Lake (left; north). Here you turn right (south) to follow the PCT. In just 0.1 mile, you reach a second junction, where you stay left (southeast) on the PCT, while right (south) leads down Tilden Canyon Creek and ultimately to Tiltill Valley and Hetch Hetchy Reservoir. Now begins a nearly 30-mile stretch of trail accurately referred to as *crossing the Washboard* (see sidebar); first up is a 550-foot ascent over 0.65 mile to reach a gap in Macomb Ridge.

CROSSING THE WASHBOARD

Macomb Ridge is the first ridge in a series of northeast-southwest ridge-and-canyon systems you will tackle as the PCT pushes its way generally southeastward against the "grain" of what's often called "northern Yosemite's washboard country." Northern Yosemite is comprised of a series of shallow near-parallel canyons—Jack Main Canyon is the first of these. As you experienced yesterday, walking up or down the canyons is easy going, but cutting across the steep granite ridges that separate them is not. Ascend a ridge, drop into the next canyon, and almost immediately ascend the next ridge, drop into the next canyon . . . until the mind reels and feet ache. Even so, the magnificent scenery of northern Yosemite is adequate reward for all your effort.

The descent into Stubblefield Canyon is slow and rocky. Near the top you pass through pleasant corn lily glades and token forest stands, but you soon transition to scrubby slopes—vast expanses of huckleberry oak and broken slab. Slowly you reach Stubblefield Canyon's shady floor and turn northeast to follow the creek briefly upstream to a ford. With no logs spanning the wide creek, it is always a wade, but with a slow current it isn't dangerous. There are campsites on both sides of the ford.

After traversing the lovely valley-floor red fir forest, the 0.4-mile hiatus from the washboards ends and you resume climbing, initially alongside Thompson Canyon's creek. A mostly rocky tread leads up nearly 1,000 feet to the unnamed ridge between Stubblefield and Kerrick Canyons, crossing the outlet creek from Lake 8,896 twice en route.

Surmounting the final short, steep, cobbly switchbacks you reach a shallow gap near the west end of a small lakelet (with small campsites).

Immediately descending again, the PCT drops down broken slabs and across brushy slopes, losing 700 feet to reach Rancheria Creek and Kerrick Canyon. Admire the dramatic cross-canyon views of Piute Mountain and Bear Valley Peak (Peak 9,800+, the steep granitic pyramid) to its west. The trail parallels Rancheria Creek briefly upstream, giving you a chance to absorb its often-turbulent flow. Voluminous and bouldery, during high runoff periods, the upcoming ford is generally considered the most dangerous of northern Yosemite's many tricky crossings. There are campsites to either side of the ford. In early summer, water levels can drop more than a foot overnight, so if the creek looks frightening to cross, camp in the north bank sites (7,980'; 38.04554°N, 119.57287°W) and proceed across in the morning. (If you want to hike farther, there are additional sites in about 2 miles, along Rancheria Creek, and between 3.5 and 4.5 miles at tarns near Seavey Pass.)

DAY 5 (Rancheria Creek to Smedberg Lake, 11.3 miles): Today is a long day, but your pack should be feeling lighter and your legs stronger. If you have a layover day, you could split today over two days, hiking the 7.0 miles to Benson Lake and having a restful afternoon and morning before continuing to Smedberg Lake.

Just across Rancheria Creek, you meet a junction where the PCT continues left (south, then east), while right (west, then south) leads to Bear Valley (Trip 39). The trail follows the rushing creek upstream along the base of bluffs, the foot of Piute Mountain; north of the river equally steep cliffs rise toward Price Peak. Major joints cut across this area's canyons, and this creek has eroded along them, resulting in an angular, joint-controlled course. Stretches of trail are in lush river bottom lodgepole and red fir forest (with a few small campsites) and elsewhere you cross dry flats displaying seasonal wildflower color. The narrow river canyon harbors evidence of past floods and avalanches, river cobble–strewn flats well above the creek's banks and toppled trees. As the canyon narrows further,

Looking back toward Volunteer Peak as you approach Benson Pass   Photo by Elizabeth Wenk

the trail makes a few unwelcome descents to bypass bluffs, followed in turn by additional ascents, eventually entering denser hemlock forest and climbing a steep slope to a junction, where you turn right (southwest) toward Seavey Pass, while left (northeast) leads to Kerrick Meadow and Buckeye Pass (Trips 75–77).

You switchback up a steep slope bedecked with mountain hemlocks to a little passageway nestled between two domes, the actual drainage divide between Rancheria and Piute Creeks, and past a cluster of small tarns (and accompanyingly small campsites, including one at the larger lake a little west of the trail). Winding along past wildflower patches, between slabs, and through two beautiful unnamed gaps, you finally cross Seavey Pass, one of the few geographic points in the Sierra named a "pass" that doesn't correspond with a drainage divide, but instead is just a passageway through the landscape. Your descent is gradual at first, continuing along a high shelf cradling additional lakes, all with slabs extending to their shores and some with worthwhile campsites. Scooting past the last in the series of lakes, the trail begins to drop more seriously; short switchbacks descend a steep, sheltered draw with lodgepoles and hemlocks.

The grade abruptly ends at a meadow at the imposing eastern base of Piute Mountain as the trail bends south to follow a tributary toward Piute Creek. Excepting brief forested glades, the trail diligently descends a dry slope where pinemat manzanita and huckleberry oak grow atop a mixture of light-colored granite and darker metamorphic rocks. This is a tough, slow descent for the track is steep, often gravelly, and you're forever stepping over embedded rocks, continually breaking your stride. Rounding a corner, you see Benson Lake ahead. Your trail eventually reaches the valley bottom, and after a short, flat stretch through lush forest, you reach a junction with a spur trail that leads right (southwest) to the lake's shore.

BENSON LAKE

Benson Lake lies 0.4 mile off the PCT. Hopefully you have time in your schedule to detour to its broad sandy beach, nicknamed northern Yosemite's Riviera. The spur trail leads through nearly flat forest of white fir, lodgepole pine, and the occasional aspen. To your side is Piute Creek, a gushing torrent in early summer, transforming to a lazy trickle with big sandbars by early fall. Just beyond, you reach the famous Benson Lake beach, growing ever wider as the lake's water level drops in late summer. Being at a relatively low elevation, Benson Lake is remarkably warm for swimming, or you can simply bury your feet in the warm sand while staring across the expanse of water and the dark cliffs descending from Piute Mountain. There are campsites at the back of the beach or in the forest at the far northeastern tip of the lake (7,591'; 38.02028°N, 119.52428°W). Fishing is good.

Continuing left (southeast) along the PCT, you must ford Piute Creek just where a substantial tributary merges; you cross both creeks independently, hopefully finding fallen logs. Should logs be missing, this is a dangerous crossing in early summer. Beyond, ascend a rocky knob and descend to the banks of the Smedberg Lake outlet creek—more of a raging stream in early summer when it is also a difficult ford.

Now begins an 1,800-foot climb as you head up a dry slope with occasional junipers decorating exposed knobs and small clusters of lodgepoles or hemlock growing on flatter creekside benches. Crossing the Smedberg Lake outlet creek again, you briefly enter a wet glade with possible campsites, then revert to dry, rocky terrain and gravelly corridors beside the cascading river. As you approach a headwall down which tumbles a small waterfall, you must again cross the creek, almost always a wade and a difficult one at high flow; head a little upstream of the trail for the best options.

Diverging from the creek, the trail's gradient now increases and you quite rapidly climb 700 feet via steep, tight switchbacks; thankfully the walking is on soft forest duff beneath cool hemlock cover. Soon after the ascent eases, you reach a trail junction where the PCT turns left (east), toward Smedberg Lake, while right (south) leads past Murdock Lake (good campsites just south of the lake) and down Rodgers Canyon toward Pate Valley. Your route leads across a lovely lodgepole pine and hemlock shelf, dwarf bilberry carpeting the forest floor, and quite soon reaches another junction, where the PCT stays left (north), while a right (south) turn heads over a pass to Rodgers Lake.

Continuing toward Smedberg Lake, you wind along forested shelves and between narrow passageways in the pervading slabs and bluffs, all the while circumnavigating the base of near-vertical Volunteer Peak. Climbing again, admire the views west to massive Piute Mountain, Benson Lake visible at its foot. Stripes of trees across the landscape indicate where landscape-wide joints in the rock have allowed deeper soils to accumulate. Soon you crest a small ridge and begin your final descent to Smedberg Lake. Small single-tent sites present themselves in sandy patches among the slabs as you descend, or as soon as you reach the lake, turn left (north) to find abundant, and justifiably popular, campsites along the lake's western edge (9,230'; 38.01270°N, 119.48802°W). Note this lake—like others nearby—is a mosquito haven until late July.

DAY 6 (Smedberg Lake to Spiller Canyon, 11.1 miles): Beyond the oasis of Smedberg Lake, you climb gradually alongside meadows, then more steeply as you trend toward Benson Pass and mount a series of sand-and-slab benches. The granite here decomposes to a coarse-grained sand that creates a decidedly slippery walking surface atop underlying slabs. Admire the giant rectangular feldspar crystals present in some of the outcrops. The gradient eases as you pass through a broad meadow that dries early and is covered with lupines in late summer. It segues to a narrow, sandy gully that, although unmarked on maps, is a good water source late into the summer. At its head the trail sidles south across a steep, gravelly, heavily eroded slope, leading to the flat summit of Benson Pass (10,125'). The pass boasts excellent views to the northeast.

Continuing east, the trail descends past knobs with multistemmed whitebark pine clusters, through more slippery decomposing granite, and then skirts north above a broad, often-dry meadow landscape (a few campsites at the perimeter). The topography again steepens, and while the trail descends steep switchbacks, the creek pours down a narrow slot in rocks. Below you reach a small meadow opening ringed by lodgepole pines (with campsites) and the banks of splashing Wilson Creek.

After crossing Wilson Creek atop logs or rocks, the trail turns southeast to begin a 2-mile descent to Matterhorn Canyon. There are massive avalanche scars down both canyon walls, a testament to the tremendous slides that sporadically tear down these slopes. The trees lay flattened, all pointing away from the flow of snow, meaning uphill directed trees were knocked down by slides that crossed the creek and flowed up the other side. Only beneath steep cliffs, where deep snow never accumulates, do mature forests persist. The beautiful slabs lining the creek also demand your attention—and perhaps a break. On this descent, camping is limited to a few small forested shelves overlooking the stream. Toward the bottom of the straightaway, topography dictates that the trail twice crosses the creek. Soon after the second crossing, the trail sidles away from Wilson Creek, leading you onto steep bluffs, where gnarled juniper trees clasp at small soil pockets, and your rocky route switchbacks steeply down among them. You are now staring at the lower reaches of Matterhorn Canyon and soon arrive at the relative flat of the canyon floor.

Here Matterhorn Creek is a meandering stream flowing alternately beside willowed meadows and mixed stands of lodgepole and western white pine. You are initially traipsing well west of the creek, slowly trending closer to the riparian corridor as you continue north. You will find an acceptable tent site just about anywhere you wish along the first mile, up to where the trail strikes east into the meadow and fords the creek. The crossing of Matterhorn Creek is a wade over rounded boulders in all but the lowest of flows and requires caution at peak runoff. Just beyond the ford, you reach a junction where the PCT turns right (south), while left (north) leads up Matterhorn Canyon (Trip 77).

Almost immediately you begin executing more than two dozen often steep switchbacks up a forested slope, gaining more than 1,100 feet by the time you attain a saddle 1.5 miles later. At the gap, there is a worthwhile vista point just north of the trail with views of Matterhorn Canyon and north to the Sawtooth Ridge. Continuing south, you follow a linear passageway, formed along a weakness in the rock. Modest descent leads to shallow Miller Lake (9,446') with tiny campsites along its forested west and north shores. Sitting in a broad, open bowl and ringed by sandy beaches, it is a lovely destination.

PEAK IDENTIFICATION

On the left of gaping Matterhorn Canyon are Doghead and Quarry Peaks and, farther away, some of the peaks of noted Sawtooth Ridge. The great white hulk just to the right of the canyon is multisummited Whorl Mountain, and to its right are the dark gray Twin Peaks, pointy and rusty-colored Virginia Peak, and light gray Stanton Peak.

At Miller Lake, the route makes a hairpin turn and climbs gently to pass a pair of tarns (small campsites), then cuts through a series of gaps between slab ribs. After climbing between a pair of slightly larger domes (good views to the Cathedral Range from the low dome to the southeast), the trail drops to the edge of a broad, early-drying meadow, providing decent campsites, with water always available from a narrow, slab-entrenched lake 0.3 mile to the south. Soon, the trail transports you to a landscape of unusually narrow eroded channels in coarse-crystalled decomposed granite (termed *grus*) and climbs, yet again, to a forested pass.

HISTORICAL NOTE

This pass was the original route between Spiller Creek and Matterhorn canyons, discovered by Lt. Nathaniel McClure of the Fourth U.S. Cavalry in 1894, during the time when the cavalry were the guardians of the new national park. Most of northern Yosemite's trail network was laid out during the cavalry years. McClure, Major Harry C. Benson, and others became expert trailblazers, establishing trails to evict shepherds and their sheep from the park. The cavalry patrolled the backcountry until the National Park Service was formed in 1916, and their efforts are today attributed to the survival of the national parks during these first decades.

Eventually you transition to forested switchbacks that carry you to the floor of Spiller Canyon, an 800-foot descent. Once alongside the river, you could head briefly north to off-trail campsites or continue to a large beautiful camping area nestled in a grove of hemlocks just northeast of Spiller Creek's high-volume crossing (8,772'; 38.00691°N, 119.39036°W).

DAY 7 (Spiller Canyon to Glen Aulin High Sierra Camp, 9.0 miles): Continuing downstream, the trail slowly diverges from the Spiller Creek drainage and is soon high above the cascading creek on a sandy slope with occasional junipers and expanses of pinemat manzanita. The trail rounds the blunt ridge into the Virginia Canyon drainage and descends a

A view west down the Grand Canyon of the Tuolumne as you pass Glen Aulin High Sierra Camp
Photo by Elizabeth Wenk

rocky-sandy slope above the valley to meet the trail descending Virginia Canyon (Trip 80); left (northeast) leads up Virginia Canyon, while the PCT, your route, turns right (south).

Within steps you must ford Return Creek, a broad, cobble-and-boulder-bottomed channel that requires extreme caution in early season and may be difficult throughout the summer. If the ford is too intimidating, walk about a quarter mile upstream to find a wider but easier ford—where campsites are nearby in the rocks above—and follow a use trail back downstream to the trail, passing good campsites along Return Creek's southeastern bank. The trail now hooks south and fords smaller McCabe Creek, a possibly frightening wade itself, for cascades churn just below the crossing. Fill up on water here, for the creeks from here to Glen Aulin dry early.

Once across, the trail begins a steady 600-foot climb up a cool, predominately hemlock-clad slope. The ground is uncharacteristically vegetated, with abundant flowers and even some moss cover. The forest thins near the top of the climb, where slabs again break to the surface and lodgepole pines dominate. A few switchbacks lead to a junction, where left (east) leads to Lower McCabe Lake (Trips 58 and 80), while right (south) is your route to Glen Aulin.

You have now completed the Washboard traverse and begun a long, gentle descent down Cold Canyon—you drop just 400 feet over the next 3.5 miles. In patches of moderate-to-dense forest, enjoy the abounding birdlife (chickadees, juncos, warblers, woodpeckers, robins, and evening grosbeaks). Elsewhere are meadows, where bluebirds and flycatchers flit about, and occasional drier stretches with broken slabs. When there's water, you can camp in the occasional forest opening or at a meadow edge, but the streams here can be dry by the middle of summer. You enter a particularly beautiful meadow after 3 miles, with some giant boulders along its western edge; like others, it is slowly being encroached on by young lodgepoles.

At the meadow's southern tip, you climb just briefly, drop steeply back to the river corridor, and continue onward, still mostly through lush lodgepole forest. Wandering fleabane spreads across the forest floor, joined by larkspurs, dwarf bilberry, and one-sided wintergreen. The trail trundles along—this is about as easy as walking gets in Yosemite, with a soft forest floor, gentle grade, and well-maintained trail. About 1.5 miles north of Glen Aulin you emerge from forest cover, crossing more open expanses and descending a bit more steeply. Here are a few possible campsites if there is water in the creek. On the final, rocky downhill to the river, you catch glimpses of Tuolumne Falls and the White Cascade, and their roar carries all the way across the canyon.

Within sight of Glen Aulin High Sierra Camp, you reach a junction with the trail that descends the Grand Canyon of the Tuolumne (Trip 40) and continuing straight ahead, after 50 feet, you come to a spur trail that goes left to Glen Aulin High Sierra Camp, crossing Conness Creek on a footbridge. To reach the backpacker's campground, loop north through the camp, passing the tiny store with its meager supplies, and onward to an open area with many tent sites (7,930'; 37.91051°N, 119.41699°W); there is potable water (when the camp is open), a pit toilet, and animal-proof food-storage boxes. This is the last legal camping before Tuolumne Meadows, so you must camp here or complete the entire Day 8 hike description.

DAY 8 (Glen Aulin High Sierra Camp to Tuolumne Meadows, 5.4 miles): Return to the PCT and cross the Tuolumne River on a bridge just below the roar and foam of stunning White Cascade. During high runoff, you may have to wade on the far side of this bridge—note the expanse of rounded river cobble and boulders strewn across the trail. A brief climb brings you to a trail junction, where you stay left (southeast), signposted to Tuolumne Meadows, while right (southwest) leads to McGee and May Lakes (Trip 51). Returning to the river's edge, you pass a fine viewpoint of crashing Tuolumne Falls. Beyond, you ascend past wide sheets of clear water spread out on slightly inclined granite slabs and a series of sparkling rapids separated by large pools, the views interrupted by a detour into a moist glen west of the river corridor.

At 1.3 miles above the High Sierra Camp, the trail crosses the river for the last time, again on a footbridge, and climbs a little way above the river gorge. The trail shortly descends to expansive, polished, riverside slabs. For the coming mile, the trail repeatedly dives into a lodgepole glade before emerging back on splendid slabs. Beyond, you come right to the river's bank at an extremely scenic, wide bend at the edge of a meadow—not yet Tuolumne Meadows—far across which rise granite domes and the peaks of the Cathedral Range. Just ahead, you cross the three branches of Dingley Creek (may be dry by late season). The trail now leaves the river behind for more than two miles, taking a rambling traverse across the landscape along a series of shallow, lodgepole pine–forested depressions, making for easier walking than cutting up and down slab ribs. Soon you meet the trail to Young Lakes (Trip 50; left, north), while you go ahead (right; still southeast) on the PCT, coming close to the northernmost lobe of Tuolumne Meadows before crossing Delaney Creek, a potentially difficult crossing at peak flows.

Just beyond that ford, a spur trail takes off left (east) for Tuolumne Stables, while you veer right (south) to ascend a long, dry, sandy ridge. From the tiny, reed-filled ponds atop this ridge, the trail drops gently to pass near Parsons Memorial Lodge and Soda Springs. After these historic landmarks—both worth a detour if time allows—the PCT picks up a closed dirt road bearing east above the north edge of Tuolumne Meadows and turns left to follow it past interpretive displays to a locked gate (8,590'; 37.87889°N, 119.35854°W). You may have parked a car along the stretch of road between here and Lembert Dome, 0.3 mile ahead.

Leavitt Meadows Trailhead				7,123'; 38.33229°N, 119.55358°W	
Destination/ GPS Coordinates	Trip Type	Best Season	Pace & Hiking/ Layover Days	Total Mileage	Permit Required
32 Fremont Lake 38.25047°N 119.54984°W	Semiloop	Early to late	Moderate 2/1	17.8	Leavitt Meadows
33 Cinko Lake 38.20568°N 119.58780°W	Semiloop	Mid to late	Moderate 4/0	30.0	Leavitt Meadows
34 Dorothy Lake 38.17422°N 119.59511°W	Semiloop	Mid to late	Moderate 5/1	36.4	Leavitt Meadows
35 Tower Lake 38.16084°N 119.54971°W	Semiloop	Mid to late	Moderate, part cross-country 5/1	35.1	Leavitt Meadows
36 Kirkwood Pass and Buckeye Forks 38.16656°N 119.50230°W (Kirkwood Pass)	Shuttle	Mid to late	Moderate 4/1	31.1	Leavitt Meadows (or Buckeye Creek in reverse)

INFORMATION AND PERMITS: This trailhead is in Humboldt-Toiyabe National Forest, accessing Hoover Wilderness. Wilderness permits are required for overnight stays and quotas apply from the last Friday in June through September 15. Fifty percent of permits can be reserved in advance through recreation.gov (search for "Humboldt-Toiyabe National Forest Wilderness Permits"), and 50% are available on a first-come, first-served basis at the Bridgeport Ranger District office beginning at 1 p.m. the day before your trip starts. Both reserved and first-come, first-served permits are picked up at the Bridgeport Ranger Station, located at 75694 US 395 at the south end of Bridgeport. If you want the ranger station to leave a reserved permit in their dropbox for you to pick up outside of office hours, call 760-932-7070. Bear canisters are required. Visit tinyurl.com/hoover wildernesspermits for more information on reserving permits. Trip 34 enters Yosemite National Park, and once in the park, pets and firearms are prohibited.

DRIVING DIRECTIONS: This trailhead is located along CA 108, 7.0 miles west of the CA 108–US 395 junction and 7.7 miles east of Sonora Pass. The dirt lot is on the east side of the road, just 400 feet west of the campground. There are toilets in the parking area and water faucets in the campground.

trip 32   Fremont Lake

see map on p. 160

Trip Data: 38.25047°N, 119.54984°W; 17.8 miles; 2/1 days
Topos: *Pickel Meadow, Tower Peak*

HIGHLIGHTS: This trip offers splendid upcanyon views as you skirt Leavitt Meadows, leads to four destination-worthy lakes, and follows some beautiful stretches of the West Walker River, making it an ideal weekender. For longer excursions from this trailhead see Trips 33–36.

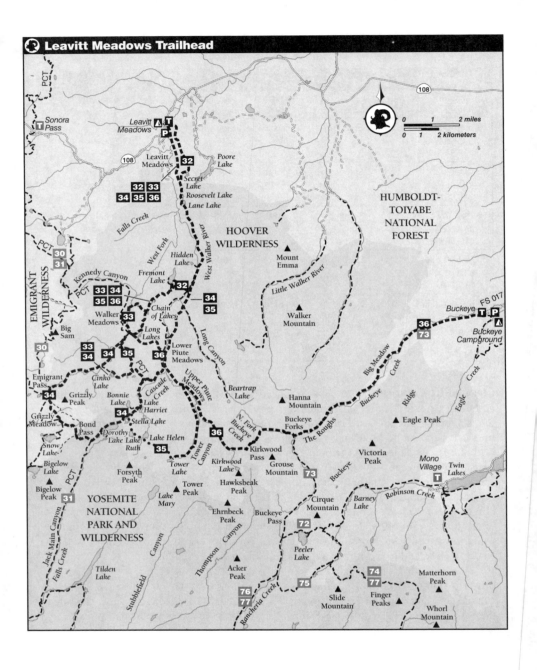

DAY 1 (Leavitt Meadows Trailhead to Fremont Lake, 8.6 miles): From the hiker parking lot, a trail leads north to the adjacent campground, then trends right (northeast) through the campground to a recently replaced bridge over the West Walker River. The trail turns east and soon south, following the edge of an outcrop, walking along the west side of a minor draw, and at 0.4 mile (from the trailhead parking) reaching a junction where left (east) leads to Secret Lake, the suggested return route, while you stay straight ahead (south), signposted for Roosevelt Lake and Lane Lake. Here you leave the route depicted on the old 7.5' topo maps and skirt the eastern edge of Leavitt Meadows.

TRAIL CHANGES

Contemporary online USGS maps, available on the National Map Viewer (see page 11), and trail maps, such as Tom Harrison's, show the correct trail locations, but the trail network depicted on the printed USGS maps bears little resemblance to today's trail locations.

After a brief walk across a sagebrush flat, the trail descends toward the West Walker River, traversing a slope just above its meandering flow decorated by the bright blooms of prickly poppy, wavyleaf paintbrush, and scarlet gilia. Far upcanyon, Tower Peak stands majestically on the Yosemite border. A succession of trails depart right (west) toward the riverbank and huge meadow, a collation of anglers' trails, unsigned trails to the pack station, and discontinued dead-end routes; in each case, remain straight ahead (south), even where a misrotated sign directs hikers downward. The trail soon climbs up a rocky slope, follows a corridor past a small tarn, and reaches the southern junction with the Secret Lake Trail (left, east) that you may choose to take on your return. You stay straight ahead (right, south) and in a few steps reach the Hoover Wilderness boundary, where a placard relays the trials of early emigrant voyages.

MOUNTAIN MAHOGANY

Close beside the trail, you may observe tall specimens of curl-leaf mountain mahogany, an almost tree-size shrub. Despite the leaves' dry, tough appearance, the local mule deer love to eat them. The plant is particularly striking from midsummer through early fall, when the styles, the part of the flower extending above the fruit, elongate. They are covered in very long white hairs; when the hundreds of plumes on each bush catch the sun, the entire shrub glows.

Continuing south, in 0.4 mile you reach Roosevelt Lake, ringed with a sparse fringe of Jeffrey and lodgepole pines. While Roosevelt Lake offers only small campsites, including one on a saddle west of the lake, Lane Lake, to the south, offers excellent choices on both its northern and southern shores. Brook trout and Lahontan cutthroat trout can both be caught in these lakes, although bag limits are lower than the standard regulations; check specific California Department of Fish and Wildlife restrictions.

From Roosevelt Lake, the trail leads over a granite shoulder to Lane Lake's inlet and over a second ridge to its often-dry outlet. Just beyond, spurs lead to lakeside campsites. Ahead, at the eastern corner of a large tarn, a well-used spur leads right (west) toward the West Walker River; this is the long-ago trail routing and leads to riverside campsites and after 0.8 mile to a 40-foot-tall roaring waterfall.

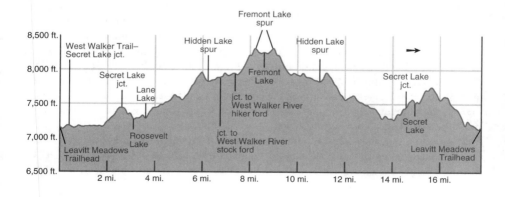

Secret Lake   Photo by Elizabeth Wenk

Continuing southeast on the main route, the rocky-dusty trail ascends briefly through volcanic deposits, then levels off as it passes several lovely aspen groves, some carpeted with lush grass even in late season. Following this corridor perched high above the West Walker River, you walk 1.25 miles before dropping back to the river's edge in a cool flat shaded by aspen, cottonwoods, water birch, and white fir. Beyond, the trail again trends away from the river, climbing a draw beside another tributary to a saddle with fine views north toward Leavitt Meadows and south up the West Walker Valley to Forsyth Peak on the Sierra Crest. Descending among picturesque Jeffrey pine and junipers, the trail again leads to the West Walker River's banks and soon reaches a signed turnoff right (west; requiring a ford across the river) to Hidden and Red Top Lakes; there is a large campsite at the junction. Continuing south, you ascend along the east bank of a narrow section of the West Walker River.

ALONG A GEOLOGIC CONTACT

This rocky stretch of trail alongside the river gives access to many pleasant, granite-bottomed potholes. Here the river tumbles along in a series of small falls and cascades through the narrows. The gorge was easily eroded in the fractured white granite that typifies the middle of the West Walker River Valley. To either side, walls are comprised of younger volcanic rock that ranges the color spectrum from black to reds and yellows.

Soon after the gorge opens and the river calms and widens, the trail splits. At a wide spot, signs direct stock users to go right (west, then south) and cross the river here, while hikers should continue south an additional 0.6 mile before fording. At high flows, the southern crossing is slightly easier, but either crossing works and the northern one saves you 0.3 mile off the listed distance. Assuming you stay on the east bank, you walk pleasantly through nearly flat valley-bottom lodgepole pine forest, the broad, deep West Walker River meandering to your right and bluffs rising to the left. Quickly, you reach a junction (7,935'; 38.24508°N, 119.53879°W), where right (west) leads to the hiker ford and onto Fremont Lake. After just 0.1 mile you ford the river (very dangerous in early season; a serious wade at any time) and 300 feet later reach a junction where you merge with the west-bank stock-users' trail and trend left (northwest) toward Fremont Lake.

Briefly crossing sandy slabs, the trail soon enters a corridor shaded by lodgepole pine and aspens, then begins a steeper climb, zigzagging up a broad slot between bluffs. After pausing to admire views to Tower and Forsyth Peaks, you continue beneath Jeffrey pine, lodgepole pine, and junipers leveling out at a junction where the spur to Fremont Lake trends right (northwest), while left (south) is signposted for Chain of Lakes and Walker Meadows. A 0.1-mile descent leads to Fremont Lake's shore, which the trail follows clockwise beneath a cover of lodgepole pine, white fir, and juniper. The eastern shore is mostly closed to camping, but there are abundant forested campsites along the southern and western shores (for example, 8,260'; 38.25047°N, 119.54984°W); rainbow trout occur here. If you have a layover day, good destinations to explore include Walker Meadows, Chain of Lakes, and the pair of Long Lakes (also with rainbow trout). On your explorations, you can return to the main trail junction east of Fremont Lake or, from Fremont Lake's southern end, follow a use trail south, which reconnects with the main trail closer to Chain of Lakes (at 8,389'; 38.24758°N, 119.55033°W).

DAY 2 (Fremont Lake to Leavitt Meadows Trailhead, 9.2): Retrace your steps of Day 1 for the 6.0 miles to the signed junction with the southern end of the trail to Secret Lake. This alternate route is 0.6 mile longer and, more notably, includes 570 feet more elevation gain (and loss) than retracing Day 1 for an out-and-back trip. However, on the shorter route you'll miss Secret Lake and some fine scenery.

To begin the loop part of this trip, turn right (north-northeast) toward Secret Lake. Various unsigned, puzzling spur trails lead right (east), generally leading to Secret Lake by other routes and onto Poore Lake; you stay left (north, then east) and curve across a saddle, dropping to Secret Lake's northern shore. Lovely, but no secret, Secret Lake, ringed by sparse Jeffrey pine and slabs, has several well-used campsites. Beyond the lake, the rocky trail ascends out of Secret Lake's basin and follows the crest, now on volcanic rock. Expansive views in all directions invite you to linger, especially atop two knobs that offer superb vistas (7,602'; 38.32078°, 119.54358°). The prevailing aroma from junipers and sagebrush leaves you feeling like you're walking through Nevada's Basin and Range Desert. Beyond a flat covered with sagebrush and mountain mahogany, the trail drops steeply through a wooded pocket, across a little meadow with a tarn, down sagebrush slopes, and past a line of aspens. After the aspens, the trail hooks sharply west across a meadow, in the middle of which you may notice faint use trails right (north) to Millie Lake (definitely not worth your trouble). Continue west across the seasonally iris-dotted meadow, bob over a low ridge, and reach a use trail on your left (south), a route used by horse riders to Secret Lake. Ignore it and proceed right (northwest), shortly reaching the junction with the main West Walker River Trail where you close the loop part of this trip.

From here, turn right (north) and retrace your steps to the bridge, campground, and, finally, the backpackers' parking lot.

trip 33 Cinko Lake

see map on p. 160

Trip Data: 38.20568°N, 119.58780°W; 30.0 miles; 4/0 days
Topos: *Pickel Meadow, Tower Peak*

HIGHLIGHTS: This interesting route traces the West Fork West Walker River to a headwater cirque beneath the Sierra Crest, passing through three life zones as it goes. Of the several trips in this drainage, this offers one of the best exposures to the geological, topographical, and biological features of this country across a short distance.

DAY 1 (Leavitt Meadows Trailhead to Fremont Lake, 8.6 miles): Follow Trip 32, Day 1 to Fremont Lake (8,260'; 38.25047°N, 119.54984°W).

DAY 2 (Fremont Lake to Cinko Lake, 6.1 miles): Return to the junction with the Fremont Lake spur trail and turn right (south-southwest) toward Chain of Lakes on an ascent that steepens as it winds across open, granite-sand slopes with little shade. At 0.5 mile past the junction, you enjoy a splendid view south to Tower Peak and just beyond reach a broad saddle where the use trail from the southern end of Fremont Lake merges (an alternate, steeper start to your day). Continuing southwest, then west, the trail drops onto a dry joint-delineated slope and skirts around the first of three large granite domes that separate the Chain of Lakes from the West Walker River. The gently descending path leads through dry-site shrubs and past scattered trees—the wind-shaped junipers and stately western white pine most alluring. The trail reaches the northernmost of the Chain of Lakes, with yellow pond lilies and often a duck family floating on the surface, then juts slightly west to encircle the lakes. An old trail toward Walker Meadows that once departed west from here has been restored; the newer alternative is 0.5 mile to the south.

> **A LANDSCAPE OF FRACTURES**
>
> The Fremont Lake granodiorite has extensive landscape-scale joints creating endless near-parallel corridors that trend south-southwest, paired with cross-cutting corridors angled to the northwest-southeast. The Chain of Lakes and Long Lakes sit in one of the most prominent of these fractures (and the West Walker River flows down a parallel, deeper valley), although the Long Lakes' "length" spills along the cross-fractured direction. You may have noticed how the trails here climb (usually steeply), then are suddenly flatter as they follow a line of tarns or a densely forested flat between granite ribs or domes; these easier stretches are along a joint. The trails then again climb or drop abruptly where one corridor ends and they jog to the next one, crossing the more rugged landscape between the fractured-defined passageways. A glimpse of the area on Google Earth before your trip gives immediate insight to the trail wanderings.

The trail continues approximately south, following the Chain of Lakes, but regularly bobbing across small granite outcrops and in between passing a selection of campsites in lodgepole pine–shaded flats. As you begin winding above the southernmost (and largest) lake in the chain, a signed lateral departs right (west) for Walker Meadows (the described return route). Staying left (south), you climb over another knob, the trail veneered with slippery sand and gravel; skirt a small, elongate lake; and veer around the north side of Lower Long Lake (lovely campsites with splendid views north to the Yosemite border; rainbow trout).

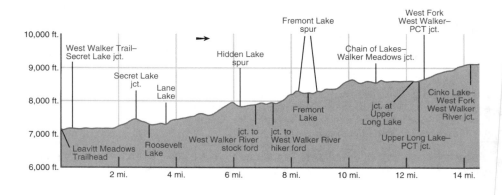

SANDPIPERS

The rocks at the edge of the lake are a favorite midday resting place for the sandpipers that live here, plying the banks for insects. The only shorebird to regularly nest in the upper montane and subalpine vegetation zones, it is hard to miss the sandpiper's persistent calls or low, skimming flight.

The trail then jogs around Upper Long Lake's northwest end, fords its intermittent outlet stream, and meets a lateral going left (southeast) to the West Walker River and Lower Piute Meadow (Trip 36). Your route turns right (northwest), passes a picturesque tarn, a signed junction with the little-used trail to Walker Meadows (the suggested return route), and just 100 feet later reaches a junction with the Pacific Crest Trail (PCT) on the east bank of the West Fork West Walker River. There is a selection of campsites on either side of the river.

You turn left (southwest) onto the PCT, following the famous trail for just 0.2 mile to another junction. The PCT now diverges left (due south; signed for Dorothy Lake Pass; your return route), while you stay right (southwest) toward Cinko Lake, continuing along the West Fork West Walker River's southeast bank (good campsites here).

The dry, sandy, rocky landscape of broken slab with scattered lodgepole pine slowly transitions to a wetter, streamside lodgepole-pine-and-hemlock forest carpeted with heath species. Leichtlin's mariposa lily, sanddune wallflower, mountain mule ears, rock spiraea, and mountain pride penstemon vie for your attention on the rock, while dwarf bilberry, western Labrador tea, red mountain heather, wandering fleabane, and crimson columbine are common in the shade. This gentle-to-moderate climb continues along the southeast side of the stream to the foot of a large, white granite dome. Here, the trail fords to the northwest side of the creek; there is currently a large log to balance on, but the sandy wade is not dangerous.

Your steady ascent leads around the dome's southeastern end to a dry meadow with a signed junction; right (southwest) is the route to Grizzly Meadow (Trip 34), while left (southeast) is your route to Cinko Lake. You ford the West Fork West Walker River (a sandy-bottom wade at higher flows) and pass a charming meadow with a tiny tarn. Then the trail makes a brief, moderate ascent to Cinko Lake, with meandering shorelines, several bays, and two bedrock peninsulas. The trail emerges at the lake's edge (9,212′; 38.20568°N, 119.58780°W), where, across the northern, intermittent outlet, there are several good campsites; additional campsites are found at the southeastern corner of the lake. Both rainbow and eastern brook trout are found in the lake.

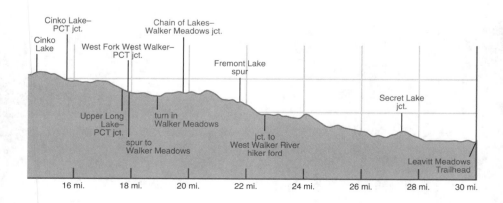

DAY 3 (Cinko Lake to West Walker River at the Fremont Lake Trail Junction, 7.8 miles): From Cinko Lake you could retrace your route to the trailhead, but I encourage a few alternative trails that only slightly increase the distance. Leaving your campsite, continue along Cinko Lake's north shore. From the southeast side of Cinko Lake, the trail climbs slightly to exit the Cinko Lake basin. It then winds first through lodgepole-and-hemlock forest and next onto broken slabs and past granite ribs and bluffs as it descends past a sequence of tarns and two beautifully round grass-rimmed lakelets. Snowmelt ponds fill every depression and can take many weeks—or longer—to drain or evaporate. Eventually curving around another broad knob, the trail descends to meet the PCT beside a small creek (and campsite). Here, right (east) leads to Dorothy Lake Pass (Trips 34 and 35), while you turn left (north), marked as the West Walker Trail (and PCT).

Heading north through a cool draw shaded by hemlock and lodgepole pine, the trail then abruptly leaves forest cover and traverses across bedrock. The rock is a mosaic of older metavolcanic and metasedimentary rocks, including a wall sparkling with garnets and bands of marble. Beyond, the trail turns west, again winding along forested corridors between granite slabs and past early-drying tarns. After 0.5 mile the trail turns north, paralleling the West Fork West Walker River on a sandy ramp high above the drainage. Over the coming 0.5 mile your passageway, colored by bursts of Leichtlin's mariposa lily, mountain pride penstemon, and Brewer's aster, slowly descends to meet the West Fork West Walker Trail at a junction you passed on Day 2; trend right (north) and in 0.2 mile reach the footbridge where the PCT continues left (west) toward Kennedy Canyon, while you turn right (east).

You could again retrace your steps from here, but you are encouraged to detour to Walker Meadows first. *Note:* This requires you to wade the West Fork West Walker River twice, once in 0.3 mile and again after an additional 0.7 mile; if the water flow is dangerous or this sounds unappealing, retrace your steps from Day 2 via the Long Lakes and Chain of Lakes. If you wish to visit Walker Meadows, after 100 feet turn left (north) and take the faint signposted trail along a lodgepole pine–shaded shelf above the West Fork West Walker River's eastern bank. After 0.3 mile the trail descends to ford the river, landing in a lush lodgepole pine forest

View to Tower Peak from near Fremont Lake   Photo by Elizabeth Wenk

with exquisitely dense patches of arrowleaf ragwort. A short distance later you emerge into Walker Meadows, where you're treated to views of the volcanic ridge to the west and endless flowers—iris, arnica, yampah, orange sneezeweed, and monkeyflowers. The trail may vanish in the meadows, but if you cross in a straight line, the trail reappears in the next lodgepole pine stand. After crossing an often-dry creeklet, you again trade forest cover for splendid meadow grasses until you reach a stand of lodgepole pine with a large campsite.

Here the trail makes a sharp right turn (east) and drops back to the banks of the West Fork West Walker River, a cobbly wade. Just across the creek is an additional campsite, this one on pink-hued granite with perfect views to the west. The Walker Meadows campsites are enticing, but stopping now would make Day 4 much longer, making this a better location for a lunch break. Beyond, the trail climbs briefly, passes a small tarn, then a larger lake, and meanders through open lodgepole pine forest to the Chain of Lakes, where it reunites with the trail to Fremont Lake; turn left (north) and retrace your steps 2.0 miles from Day 2 to the Fremont Lake junction. You can spend another night at undeniably pleasant Fremont Lake or, for an alternative experience, you could drop to campsites along the West Walker River. Following your route from Day 1, you reach the river at the junction with the hiker ford (right; south) versus stock ford (left; north). Turn right and cross at the hiker ford. Once across the river, head right (south) off-trail, and after approximately 0.1 mile you'll reach open flats with extensive tent sites (7,938'; 38.24540°N, 119.54061°W) and some fine swimming holes just a bit upstream. Fishing in the deeper holes of this section of the river is good for rainbow trout.

DAY 4 (West Walker River at the Fremont Lake Trail Junction to Leavitt Meadows, 7.5 miles): From the Fremont Lake Trail junction on the east side of the West Walker River, retrace the rest of Day 1 of this trip. If you want to follow a slightly different route, consider detouring to Secret Lake, described in Day 2 of Trip 32.

trip 34 # Dorothy Lake

see map on p. 160

Trip Data: 38.17422°N, 119.59511°W; 36.4 miles; 5/1 days
Topos: *Pickel Meadow, Tower Peak*

HIGHLIGHTS: Dorothy Lake, filling a broad subalpine basin on the Yosemite border, is "highlight" enough for a trip, but instead of simply walking the 15.25-mile out-and-back along the shortest route (Days 4 and 5), this semiloop entices you to visit some of the area's other treasures, especially Cinko Lake, Grizzly Meadows, and Bond Pass. For those accustomed to the Sierra's standard rock, gray-colored granite, an extra treat along this trip is the geologic diversity: multihued volcanic cliffs and twisted metamorphic rock are mixed with light- and dark-colored granitoid rocks.

DAY 1 (Leavitt Meadows Trailhead to Fremont Lake, 8.6 miles): Follow Trip 32, Day 1 to Fremont Lake (8,260'; 38.25047°N, 119.54984°W).

DAY 2 (Fremont Lake to Cinko Lake, 6.1 miles): Follow Trip 33, Day 2 to Cinko Lake (9,212'; 38.20568°N, 119.58780°W).

DAY 3 (Cinko Lake to Dorothy Lake, 6.5 miles): There are two routes from Cinko Lake to Dorothy Lake, the described one via Grizzly Meadow and a trail that cuts east from Cinko Lake to the Pacific Crest Trail (PCT), an alternative that is nearly a mile shorter. The described route passes by sublime Grizzly Meadows and avoids retracing a 3.3-mile length of the PCT you'll follow on Day 4.

You start by retracing the 0.5 mile from Cinko Lake to the West Fork West Walker River corridor, fording the creek again, and at the junction you'll recognize from yesterday, now turn left (southwest), signposted for Grizzly Meadow and Emigrant Pass. Parting ways with the river, a steep ascent immediately ensues, leading you through open lodgepole pine stands interspersed with slab outcrops. This trail is less maintained than those in the lower canyon and there are usually a handful of downed logs to navigate over or around. The ascent eases in a sagebrush flat—you're now walking on the volcanic rock that caps the granite.

Crossing a minor West Fork West Walker tributary chortling down from a high basin, you cross back onto granite, following a joint-defined sandy shelf southwest. Pay attention to the crossing, for 0.2 mile later (6–8 minutes for most hikers; at 9,379'; 38.20557°N, 119.60389°W), the trail bends 90 degrees to the right (northwest), gaining a rapid 130 feet up a sandy slope; this is well before the creek makes a similar turn. This is important to remember, for there are many stray use trails and cairns that encourage you to stay close to the river—a tempting alternative to the steep ascent the trail makes—but the terrain is rougher along the river corridor and the elevation must be gained either way. Ignoring your reticence to ascend, head uphill, wiggling a little right (east), then a little left (west) before resuming a west-trending traverse at 9,510 feet. Quite soon the trail is again obvious, following a sandy passage on granite before stepping back onto the volcanic scree and its accompanying sagebrush cover. As you look down onto the boggy willow-flats along the creek, you'll be glad you're higher.

A pleasant, low angle traverse continues, ultimately alongside granular granite outcrops, eroded into splendid ribs. Then suddenly you're perched above an enormous marshy meadow with an unforgettable view of Grizzly Peak, the steep volcanic tower to the southwest. The trail disappears here and the best choice is to immediately cross the flow (a shallow, sandy wade during high runoff), and follow the slightly more elevated, much drier southeastern side of the meadow, staying 150–200 feet (distance) above the river. Only at the far western end of the meadow does a good trail tread reappear, leading you up beside the strikingly eroded headwaters of the creek. Near the volcanic contact the minerals in the granite have been somewhat recrystallized, forming big-granuled, very friable rock that easily erodes, creating both the incised stream channels and the fantastically steep, rounded outcrops. A short distance later you flatten out in a dry meadow and meet a junction with an old mining road.

Turn left (south), signposted for Grizzly Meadow, while right (north) leads to Emigrant Pass (Trip 30). Just 0.35 mile later, now at the edge of Grizzly Meadow, you reach a second junction, where right (west) leads to the Grizzly Meadow lakes (unnamed on maps; offering some beautiful campsites on the surrounding knobs; Trip 30), and left (south) to Bond Pass. (*Note:* At this junction, old 7.5' USGS topo maps also show a higher left-trending high trail to Bond Pass, a long-abandoned route. The start of this old route has been disguised,

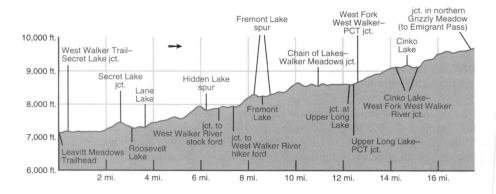

Forsyth Peak's gendarmes are visible behind Dorothy Lake.   Photo by Elizabeth Wenk

and the trail is quite hard to follow in places. It is a splendid route for the view seeker and adventurer and quite accurately follows the line drawn on the 7.5' topo map, but make sure you have good navigation skills if you follow it. It is about 0.3 mile shorter, but will likely take much longer in time.)

Continuing south, you are on the old Horse Meadow mining road, built in 1943 to service a tungsten mine beneath the Twin Lakes along the East Fork Cherry Creek. Needed to harden steel, tungsten was in short supply in the United States during World War II, and the effort to construct this road from Leavitt Lake was deemed worthwhile. You follow the road for just over a mile, initially on an open, flower-dotted shelf beneath Grizzly Peak that offers wide-reaching views down the East Fork Cherry Creek to Huckleberry Lake. At a junction where the road continues right (west) to Horse Meadow, you turn left (southeast) toward Bond Pass, dropping to Summit Meadow on a fork of the mining road that led to the Montezuma Mine at Snow Lake. Skirting the northern boundary of Summit Meadow through sagebrush scrub (and lovely flowers), you stay left (southeast) toward Bond Pass where a fork branches right (south) to Snow Lake and climb steeply to Bond Pass up the rutted road. Just a short distance before Bond Pass, you finally part ways with the road, which trends right (southwest) and ascends to unsuccessful prospects beneath Peak 10,414. Here you reach a collection of signs that announce your entry to Yosemite National

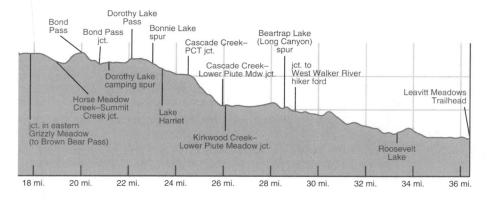

Park. The view seeker with spare time might choose to follow the mining road up to the prospects or yet farther to Peak 10,414 (also called Quartzite Peak) to enjoy the colorful, banded metamorphic rocks and, more importantly, the extensive views across Emigrant Wilderness and northwestern Yosemite.

From Bond Pass, the narrow, in places steep, trail descends 0.75 mile through lush lodgepole pine and hemlock forest. Slowly the grade lessens as the trail approaches the PCT at the head of Jack Main Canyon. Here you turn left (northeast) toward Dorothy Lake Pass, while right (south) leads down Jack Main Canyon (Trip 31). Alternating between drier and wetter forest patches, you soon reach a once-upon-a-time meadow that is now crowded with snow-twisted lodgepole pines that effectively block the view. Only as you reach the tarn south of Dorothy Lake does steep-fronted Forsyth Peak come into view, and soon you see Dorothy Lake itself.

Before you reach the lake's shores you pass a sign pointing stock parties southeast around the lake to legal campsites. Hikers should follow this use trail as well (9,420'; 38.17422°N, 119.59511°W); Dorothy Lake may be 0.7 mile long but offers few campsites along its northern shore, for either the terrain is sloping or the ground is marshy and vegetation-covered. Hikers needn't continue the full 0.4 mile to the big stock campsite, but just a few hundred feet to some excellent campsites beside clusters of lodgepole pine. From your campsite, take note of the massive rock glacier spilling down the valley north of Forsyth Peak—or in early summer the massive snow field covering it. Fishing is decent for rainbow and occasional eastern brook trout.

ROCK GLACIER

The rock glacier spilling down the canyon north of Forsyth Peak is best viewed from the unnamed lake south of Dorothy Lake. Seen from here, it is a prominent "river" of rock flowing in a long, northwest-curving arc. This arc begins on the northeast face of Forsyth Peak, then curves down the easternmost ravine, and points its moving head toward Dorothy Lake. The surface is composed of coarse rock that tumbled from Forsyth Peak's fractured face, hiding ice in its core. This ice, filling holes between boulders, allows a rock glacier to slowly creep downhill, just like a standard ice glacier.

DAY 4 (Dorothy Lake to Fremont Lake Trail Junction, 7.8 miles): Returning to the PCT, you head right (northeast) around Dorothy Lake. Until late in the summer, water seeps from the base of upslope slabs and the endless rills irrigate the slopes, nurturing splashes of color (shooting star, elephant heads, goldenrod, paintbrush, whorled penstemon, pussypaws, and false Solomon's seal) and expanses of corn lilies and willows. The trail can also be quite muddy—take care to walk on the wet tread or balance on rocks, instead of damaging the surrounding subalpine turf. Continuing to enjoy the view and, passing a few small campsites, you soon ascend a steeper 100 feet to reach Dorothy Lake Pass, a narrow notch between outcrops, where you again leave Yosemite National Park and reenter Hoover Wilderness. Before continuing, turn southeast and admire the V-notched views of light-colored Tower Peak and, to the south, the dark granite grenadiers of Forsyth Peak.

HISTORY LESSON

The meadows around Dorothy Lake were badly degraded by the time Yosemite became a national park. Lt. N. F. McClure, of the Fourth Cavalry, came this way in 1894, noting, "Grazing here was poor, and there had evidently been thousands of sheep about." It is plausible lodgepole pine are increasingly able to invade Yosemite's subalpine meadow because they were so trampled and compacted by sheep's hooves more than a century ago.

Just ahead is Stella Lake, offering only a few one-tent campsites because the dark-gray granodiorite slabs here do not erode to form those sought-after sandy patches common on lighter-colored granites. Continuing to enjoy backward views to Forsyth Peak and forward views to Bonnie Lake, the trail wiggles around Stella Lake (the departure point for Trip 35 to Tower Lake), drops to a small tarn (beside which is an unmarked spur to Bonnie Lake; limited campsites), and proceeds down six tight switchbacks through broken slab to Lake Harriet's western shore. You pass small campsites, but there are better, larger choices along Lake Harriet's eastern side.

The PCT brushes quickly past Lake Harriet's outlet and continues down, but if you are taking this trip under moderate to high water conditions, note that the PCT crosses the Lake Harriet outlet, Cascade Creek, just 0.1 mile downstream and this is often a wade. Meanwhile, you can easily rock-and-log hop across Lake Harriet's inlet and then pick up a good use trail on the east side that quickly leads back to the PCT. This option also treats you to a better view of Tower Peak and provides access to the east-shore campsites.

The trail winds down the creek's eastern bank, alternating between bare, broken slabs and clusters of lodgepole pine. The creek to your side is forever spilling down little falls, for the rock erodes in a blocky fashion. At 0.6 mile below Lake Harriet the trail fords Cascade Creek in a pocket of lodgepole pine (no camping), requiring either a delicate log-and-rock hop or a broad wade; a footbridge is long gone. Continuing briefly across dark slabs, the PCT looks down upon an often-flooded meadow, passes a pair of heath-bound tarns, and soon reaches a junction. Here the PCT trends left (north), while, for variety, you're directed right (northeast) to descend the Cascade Creek corridor to Lower Piute Meadow, although you could remain along the PCT if you want to revisit the Long Lakes and Fremont Lake.

After a brief traverse, your route drops down a draw shaded by fine hemlock stands and then transitions onto dry metamorphic outcrops—look how the rock upslope of the trail is layered and tipped on end. A few splendid junipers together with big western white pine grace the slopes above, but mostly the slope is scrubby—wax currant, tobacco brush, and pinemat manzanita. A long series of rocky switchbacks leads back to the stream corridor and welcome red fir shade. Here, Cascade Creek flows down a gorge incised in the metamorphic rock, tumbling down rough bedrock and dropping down small steps, the biggest drop named Cascade Falls. On the valley floor, the trail wanders through white fir and lodgepole pine beside a boggy meadow. About where the meadow pinches closed, the trail fords the West Walker River, always a reasonably deep, sandy wade. At high flows, it is best to walk slightly upstream, where you're likely to find a selection of logs to cross on. Across the creek, on a big cobble bar, you pick up the trail and follow it a quick 300 feet to a junction (38.20846°N, 119.55392°W, in case you lost the trail in the creekside thicket). Here, you turn left (north) toward Lower Piute Meadow and the Leavitt Meadows Trailhead, while right (southeast) leads up Kirkwood Creek to Upper Piute Meadow and Kirkwood Pass (Trip 36).

Walking through lodgepole pine forest, the trail passes just east of Lower Piute Meadow. Although there are few established campsites along the trail corridor (the large stock camps are mostly across the creek along the western edge of the meadow), you'll find ample places to pitch a tent.

Beyond Lower Piute Meadow the trail diverges from the West Walker River, trending northeast around a series of granite knobs before following a corridor that parallels the river north; camping options are limited to small sites near two tarns you pass. The route leads to a ford of Long Canyon's creek (usually logs present) and beyond to a junction with the trail that leads right (southeast) up Long Canyon to Beartrap Lake. You stay straight ahead (left; northeast), cross another minor saddle, and descend a narrow corridor to a broad valley-bottom lodgepole pine forest where you encounter the junction where, on

Day 1, you turned west, toward Fremont Lake (if you crossed the West Walker River at the official hiker crossing).

The route to Leavitt Meadows stays right (north), but the best nearby campsites are along the banks of the West Walker River. Walk straight toward the river from the junction and you'll reach open flats with extensive tent sites (7,938'; 38.24540°N, 119.54061°W) and some fine swimming holes just a bit upstream. Fishing in the deeper holes of this section of the river is good for rainbow trout. (Alternatively, you could continue to campsites near the Hidden Lake junction or at Lane or Roosevelt Lakes, described in Day 1.)

DAY 5 (Fremont Lake Trail Junction to Leavitt Meadows Trailhead, 7.4 miles): From the Fremont Lake Trail junction on the east side of the West Walker River, retrace the rest of Day 1 of this trip.

trip 35 **Tower Lake**

see map on p. 160

Trip Data: 38.16084°N, 119.54971°W; 35.1 miles; 5/1 days
Topos: *Pickel Meadow, Tower Peak*

HIGHLIGHTS: Tower Lake, nestled beneath splendid granite cliffs, is a magical location. The off-trail segment past Stella Lake, Lake Ruth, and Lake Helen takes you through little-visited country. Indeed, the strenuousness of all routes to Tower Lake usually ensures solitude. From Tower Lake, off-trail adventurers and peak baggers can easily access Yosemite's Tilden Lake or scramble to the summit of Tower Peak.

HEADS UP! *The cross-country segment makes this a trip for experienced backpackers only.*

DAY 1 (Leavitt Meadows Trailhead to Fremont Lake, 8.6 miles): Follow Trip 32, Day 1 to Fremont Lake (8,260'; 38.25047°N, 119.54984°W).

DAY 2 (Fremont Lake to Lake Harriet, 7.9 miles): Return to the junction with the Fremont Lake spur trail and turn right (south-southwest) toward Chain of Lakes on an ascent that steepens as it winds across open, granite-sand slopes with little shade. At 0.5 mile past the junction, you enjoy a splendid view south to Tower Peak and just beyond reach a broad saddle where the use trail from the southern end of Fremont Lake merges (an alternate,

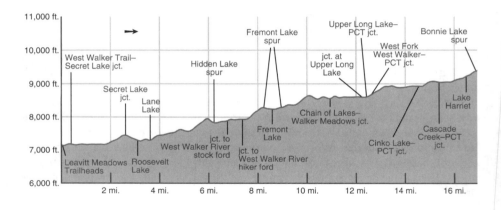

The Watchtower and Tower Peak rise above Tower Lake.   Photo by Elizabeth Wenk

steeper start to your day). Continuing southwest, then west, the trail drops onto a dry joint-delineated slope and skirts around the first of three large granite domes that separate the Chain of Lakes from the West Walker River. The gently descending path leads through dry-site shrubs, passing just scattered trees—the wind-shaped junipers and stately western white pine most alluring. The trail reaches the northernmost of the Chain of Lakes, with yellow pond lilies and often a duck family floating on the surface, then juts slightly west to encircle the lakes. An old trail toward Walker Meadows that once departed west from here has been restored; the newer alternative is 0.5 mile to the south.

The trail trends approximately south, following the Chain of Lakes, but regularly bobbing across small granite outcrops and in between passing a selection of campsites in lodgepole pine–shaded flats. As you begin winding above the southernmost, largest of the lakes in the chain, a signed lateral departs right (west) for Walker Meadows (Trip 33). You then climb over another knob, the trail veneered with slippery sand and gravel; skirt a small, elongate lake; and veer around the north side of Lower Long Lake (lovely campsites with splendid views north to the Yosemite border; rainbow trout). The trail then jogs around Upper Long Lake's northwest end, fords its intermittent outlet stream, and meets a lateral going left (southeast) to the West Walker River and Lower Piute Meadow. Your route turns right (northwest), passes a picturesque tarn, a signed junction with the little-used trail to Walker Meadows (Trip 33), and just 100 feet later reaches a junction with the Pacific Crest Trail (PCT) on the east bank of the West Fork West Walker River. There are a selection of

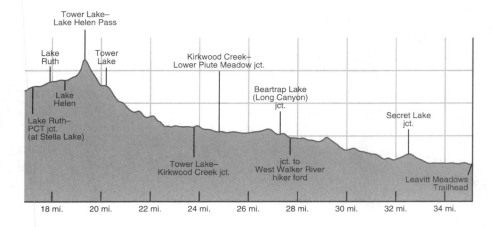

campsites clustered nearby, including one a short distance down the trail to Walker Meadows and one across a bridge on the river's western bank.

For your continued route, turn left (southwest) on the PCT, following the famous trail for 0.2 mile to a second junction, where the PCT, your route, stays left (due south), while a trail toward Cinko Lake (Trip 33) and Emigrant Pass (Trips 34) diverges right, continuing along West Fork West Walker River's southeast side. The PCT ramps up slabs colored by bursts of Leichtlin's mariposa lily, mountain pride penstemon, and Brewer's aster, slowly diverging from the river. After 0.5 mile the trail turns east, winding along forested corridors between granite slabs and past early-drying tarns. Turning south again, the trail leaves the conifer cover for bare slab and you'll discover you've left the granite for a mosaic of older metavolcanic and metasedimentary rocks, including bands of marble and a wall sparkling with garnets.

Ducking briefly back into a cool, sheltered draw shaded by hemlock and lodgepole pine, you reach another junction where your route, the PCT, turns left (east, then southeast), while right (west) is another route to Cinko Lake (Trip 33); there are campsites at the junction. Just beyond you cross a small creek on rocks or logs. Still on metavolcanic rock, a 0.8-mile segment takes you across a broad saddle cradling a series of tarns (and more possible campsites) to a junction with a trail ascending Cascade Creek from Lower Piute Meadow (to the northeast; Trip 34). The PCT trends right (south), passing a pair of heath-bound tarns, looking down upon an often-flooded meadow, and reaching the banks of Cascade Creek in a pocket of lodgepole pine. The river must be crossed, requiring either a delicate log-and-rock hop or a broad wade; an old footbridge is long gone. The trail follows up the creek's eastern bank, winding up bare, broken slabs between scattered lodgepole pine. The creek to your side is forever spilling down little falls. In a small patch of willows, just below 9,200 feet (38.18915°N, 119.56930°W), the PCT inconspicuously crosses Cascade Creek; however, stay on the more obvious eastside trail, for it leads to Lake Harriet's best campsites. In just 0.1 mile you reach Lake Harriet's outlet and will discover the use trail continues around its eastern side, leading to a fine selection of lakeshore camps (for example, 9,240'; 38.18591°N, 119.56851°W).

DAY 3 (Lake Harriet to Tower Lake, 3.7 miles): In the morning, return to Lake Harriet's outlet. You could return to the official PCT crossing point downstream, but crossing right at the lake's outlet is actually easier, with a selection of stable rocks and logs on offer, and you reunite with the PCT directly across the creek. Continuing around Lake Harriet's western shore, the trail soon resumes its steady ascent up broken slab, completing six tight switchbacks to a tarn-filled flat; here an unmarked spur trail leads west to Bonnie Lake (limited campsites). A short distance later the trail crosses into the drainage where Stella and Bonnie Lakes lie, converging with the Stella Lake outlet as the trail approaches the lake. Just before you cross the outlet creek is a good place to begin your off-trail route toward Tower Lake (9,512'; 38.18381°N, 119.57533°W). The distance from here to Tower Lake is just 3.0 miles, but the terrain between Lake Helen and Tower Lake is steep and slow—you'll probably walk about a third the speed you would on trails.

DOROTHY LAKE

If you've never seen Dorothy Lake, a detour is required. You have a few options. You can leave your pack at Stella Lake's outlet and walk to Dorothy Lake Pass unencumbered, but I recommend carrying your pack to Dorothy Lake Pass, just 0.6 mile southwest, then following Stella Lake's western shore toward Lake Ruth. If you want to add an extra day to camp at Dorothy Lake, see Trip 34; most of Dorothy Lake's campsites are at its southern end, nearly a mile from Dorothy Lake Pass.

A sometimes-ducked cross-country route to Lake Ruth follows the north arm of Stella Lake along grass-and-sand shelves and corridors not far from the water's edge. During high runoff Stella is a single lake, as the water fills a collection of depressions on a broad shelf, but by late summer Stella fractures into two large lakes and a smattering of shallow tarns. Your grass-and-slab route touches the east side of the southern lake and bears south, intersecting the intermittent inlet stream as you approach a clutch of tarns near Lake Ruth's outlet. Skirting the lake's eastern side, you soon pass excellent campsites beside whitebark pine–clad knobs.

The route continues around the east side of Lake Ruth for a short distance, then briefly ascends a gentle swale southeast. Several small tarns mark the crossover point to the Lake Helen drainage (good campsites between these and Lake Helen and at Lake Helen's north side). Once at the tarns, your route aims for the south side of Lake Helen, fords the tiny but noisy southwest inlet, and follows vegetated ramps cutting southeast from the lake. These lead to Lake Helen's southeast inlet, which you proceed up alongside to a lovely grass bench where you cross to the inlet's northern side.

The remaining ascent to the obvious saddle in the southeast is steeper. The best route first ascends a talus field; the rocks are quite stable if you track a band of vegetation that emerges between the rocks. Where the vegetation peters out, slowly cut south to a line of whitebark pine krumholz and continue up left (north) of the center of the cirque wall until you are just 50–100 feet from the pass. For the final ascent, trend farther right (south), to intersect the ridge at (or just barely north of) its low point. This steep pitch brings you to a saddle offering incomparable views (11,352'; 38.16577°N, 119.55846°W).

THE VIEWS FROM THE LAKE HELEN–TOWER LAKE SADDLE
The view from the pass is dominated by Tower Peak and the arête to its north, the Watchtower. The tallest peak along this stretch of Yosemite's boundary, Tower Peak has served as a landmark for over a century and is visible from just about every major Yosemite summit. To its east, from left (north) to right (south), you also see Walker Mountain, Flatiron Butte, and Hanna Mountain, sitting behind Buckeye Ridge, Eagle Peak, Victoria Peak, Grouse Mountain, and Hunewill Peak (far in the distance); stunning Hawksbeak Peak, Center Mountain, the Sawtooth Range (including Matterhorn Peak); and far in the corner, the red tip of Virginia Peak. The Kirkwood Creek drainage sits below these. To the west, the view is more staid, a rolling sea of granite with a few volcanic summits poking through—you can see from Black Hawk Mountain in the west to Sonora Peak and White Mountain nearly due north. If you often find yourself wanting to know the names of surrounding peaks, consider downloading the PeakFinder app before your trip.

Descending the southeast side of the saddle, you zigzag down sand-and-slab shelves, cross a rocky bench, and continue down a grass-and-ledge system to a lakelet just north of Tower Lake. For this descent, the terrain is easier if you stay on the northern side of the slope; farther south you'll encounter first steep scree and talus and then a willow-choked meadow. Skirting the lakelet, the route rounds the south nose of a granite ridge to Tower Lake's willowed outlet and fords the creek to reach small, but picturesque campsites in a cluster of whitebark pine on the east side of the outlet (9,540'; 38.16084°N, 119.54971°W). If the only campsites are occupied, you need to walk nearly a mile down-canyon to other options or search for small options near the lakelet you passed to the west. Note that Tower Lake has reverted to its natural fishless state—don't come here for remote fishing opportunities!

TOWER LAKE SIDE TRIPS

While Tower Lake is in a stunning location, you're unlikely to spend a full layover day sitting at the campsite—there is no fishing, and you'll have circled the lake within an hour. In low-snow periods (that is, late season or in dry summers) a fantastic excursion is the hike to Mary Lake or Tilden Lake, the latter about 4.5 miles to the south. You climb south up scree, talus, and slabs to the Tower Lake–Mary Lake pass and continue south down delightfully meadowed slopes to Mary Lake. Pleasant hiking, first through alpine meadows, then into lodgepole pine forest, leads to long, skinny Tilden Lake. (*Note:* The slope from Tower Lake to the pass holds late, steep, sometimes corniced snow.) Another option is to climb Tower Peak—it does require a little scrambling to ascend a chute up its southwestern face but is remarkably accessible for such an imposing summit. From the pass you walk east up slabs along the national park boundary, turning south in sync with the ridge. As the peak's towers rise above the ridge, cut south across its western face to a broad chute that you follow up to the summit.

DAY 4 (Tower Lake to West Walker River at the Fremont Lake Trail Junction, 7.5 miles): On the south side of Tower Lake's outlet, you find an eastbound trail. Initially faint, it briefly winds through willows on the southern bank, then crosses to the north bank. Now easier to follow, it descends a rocky slope close to the the outlet stream. The Watchtower, Tower Peak's northern satellite, dominates the upward view; Tower Lake's outlet, cascading down a deep chasm, is equally captivating.

The rocky descent soon reaches flatter landscape, where repeated avalanches obliterate tree cover—the enduring trees are small and often missing limbs or have sheared-off tops. You ford the river again where it meets the tiny stream draining the glacier to the south; avalanche-downed trees usually conveniently span the flow. (*Note:* On older USGS maps, Tower Lake's outlet is considered the headwaters of the West Walker River, but the Survey's maps now confer this honor to a longer, slightly higher creek that emanates from a cirque beneath Ehrnbeck and Hawksbeak Peaks.)

From here, the trail and the stream bear generally north, and you drop into a splendid hemlock forest cloaking a rib just east of the creek. Soon you'll find additional campsites, one on slab atop the rib (near where the trail distinctly switchbacks left) and others a short distance north in creekside flats. Easy, pleasant walking, still through a dense forest of lodgepole pine and hemlock, carries you deeper into Tower Canyon, across an unnamed tributary, and soon to another ford of the main creek, this time beside a marshy meadow; there is currently a handy log to balance across. Beyond, the creek, now in metavolcanic rock, has etched a deeply incised channel. The trail traverses a rocky slope high above the narrows and from it you stare across at the white granite walls that bracket the river to the east and down to the stream, a plummeting ribbon of water in a blocky gorge.

Ahead, you can see Upper Piute Meadow through the trees, marking the triple-confluence of Tower Canyon's creek, Kirkwood Creek, and the nascent West Walker River. A short, easy descent on duff trail brings you to a tangle of downed trees—the aftermath of a 2011 windstorm—and onward to beautiful Upper Piute Meadow. Skirt the huge meadow on its west side, a delightful stroll alongside the meandering river once the mosquitoes have moderated in late summer. Its north end is marshier, with a mosaic of arc-shaped oxbow lakes, formed as the river's meanders have been relocated during floods. As the meadow pinches closed, you pass the Piute Cabin complex, once a U.S. Forest Service trail-maintenance station, but now little used. At the meadow's edge, you drop to ford the river, either a broad, deep sandy wade in the meadow or a log balance where the river narrows. Across the river you meet the trail that follows Kirkwood Creek's canyon and find well-used campsites nearby. You turn left (northwest) to amble downstream, while right (southeast) leads to Kirkwood Pass (Trip 36).

The trail initially veers away from the river on a gentle descent that skirts another wet meadow, brushing against the river again after about a mile. Flat walking through lush lodgepole pine forest (think mosquitoes!), leads to a junction where you turn right (north), signposted for Leavitt Meadows, while left (southwest) is a trail that ascends Cascade Creek back toward the PCT. Walking through lodgepole pine forest, your trail continues just east of Lower Piute Meadow. Although there are few established campsites along the trail corridor (the large stock camps are mostly across the creek along the western edge of the meadow), you'll find ample places to pitch a tent.

Beyond Lower Piute Meadow the trail diverges from the West Walker River, trending northeast around a series of granite knobs before following a corridor that parallels the river north; camping options are limited to small sites near two tarns you pass. The route leads to a ford of Long Canyon's creek (usually logs present) and beyond to a junction with the trail that leads right (southeast) up Long Canyon to Beartrap Lake. You stay straight ahead (left; northeast), cross another minor saddle and descend a narrow corridor to a broad valley-bottom lodgepole pine forest where you encounter the junction where, on Day 1, you turned west, toward Fremont Lake (if you crossed the West Walker River at the official hiker crossing).

The route to Leavitt Meadows stays right (north), but the best nearby campsites are left (northwest), along the banks of the West Walker River. Walk straight toward the river from the junction and you'll reach open flats with extensive tent sites (7,938'; 38.24540°N, 119.54061°W) and some fine swimming holes just a bit upstream. Fishing in the deeper holes of this section of the river is good for rainbow trout. (Alternatively, you could continue to campsites near the Hidden Lake junction or at Lane or Roosevelt Lakes, described in Day 1.)

DAY 5 (Fremont Lake Trail Junction to Leavitt Meadows Trailhead, 7.4 miles): From the Fremont Lake Trail junction on the east side of West Walker River, retrace the rest of Day 1 of this trip. If you want to follow a slightly different route, consider detouring to Secret Lake, described in Day 2 of Trip 32.

trip 36   # Kirkwood Pass and Buckeye Forks

see map on p. 160

Trip Data: 38.16656°N, 119.50230°W (Kirkwood Pass);
31.1 miles; 4/1 days

Topos: *Pickel Meadow, Tower Peak, Buckeye Ridge*

HIGHLIGHTS: Following two major eastside drainages, this trip circumnavigates Walker Mountain and Flatiron Ridge, mostly along quiet trails. You traverse long flower-filled meadows and stare up at intricate volcanic summits and blocky, fractured granite ridges. The evolving views of Tower, Hawksbeak, and Ehrnbeck Peaks are particularly splendid.

SHUTTLE DIRECTIONS: To access the endpoint, the Buckeye Trailhead (in the Buckeye Campground), from US 395 near the northwest side of Bridgeport, take paved Twin Lakes Road southwest 7.2 miles. Turn right (north) onto dirt Buckeye Road and immediately pass Doc and Al's Resort. Continue 2.8 miles to a T-junction with Forest Service Road 017, soon after you cross Buckeye Creek. Turn left (west) here and go 1.3 miles, passing through a U.S. Forest Service campground, to a parking lot on the left (south) just before the end of the road.

DAY 1 (Leavitt Meadows Trailhead to Fremont Lake, 8.6 miles): Follow Trip 32, Day 1 to Fremont Lake (8,260'; 38.25047°N, 119.54984°W).

DAY 2 (Fremont Lake to Upper Piute Meadow, 7.0 miles): Return to the junction with the Fremont Lake spur trail and turn right (south-southwest) toward Chain of Lakes on an ascent that steepens as it winds across open, granite-sand slopes with little shade. At 0.5 mile past the junction, you enjoy a splendid view south to Tower Peak and just beyond reach a broad saddle where the use trail from the southern end of Fremont Lake merges (an alternate, steeper start to your day). Continuing southwest, then west, the trail drops onto a dry joint-delineated slope and skirts around the first of three large granite domes that separate the Chain of Lakes from the West Walker River. The gently descending path leads through dry-site shrubs and past scattered trees—the wind-shaped junipers and stately western white pine more alluring. The trail reaches the northernmost of the Chain of Lakes, with yellow pond lilies and often a duck family floating on the surface, then juts slightly west to encircle the lakes. An old trail toward Walker Meadows that once departed west from here has been restored; the newer alternative is 0.5 mile to the south.

The trail continues approximately south, following the Chain of Lakes, but regularly bobbing across small granite outcrops and in between passing a selection of campsites in lodgepole pine–shaded flats. As you begin winding above the southernmost (and largest) lake in the chain, a signed lateral departs right (west) for Walker Meadows. Staying left (south), you climb over another knob, the trail veneered with slippery sand and gravel; skirt a small, elongate lake; and veer around the north side of Lower Long Lake (lovely campsites with splendid views north to the Yosemite border; rainbow trout).

The trail then jogs around Upper Long Lake's northwest end, fords its intermittent outlet stream, and meets a lateral at a T-junction. You turn left (southeast) to descend back to the West Walker River at Lower Piute Meadow, while right (northwest) leads to Walker Meadows and the Pacific Crest Trail corridor (Trips 33–35). After traipsing the length of Upper Long Lake (with fringing campsites), you cross a shallow saddle and begin a gradual descent beside a side creek, some sections lusher, elsewhere dry and sandy. The trail trends southeast, then east, and ultimately southeast again, its route delineated by joint-defined corridors in the granite.

Soon after passing a pair of tarns the gradient increases and you drop steeply toward the West Walker River, reaching a four-way junction as the slope eases. This junction is confusing, for there are clearly four trails meeting, but only two directions signed, the way you came from, signed for Long Lakes and Kennedy Canyon and right (south), signed for Piute Meadow. Left (north) leads along the western edge of Lower Piute Meadow to popular

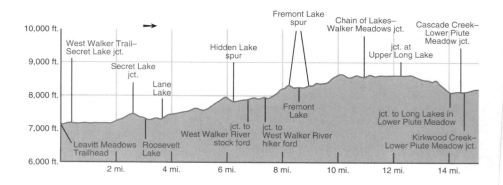

stock camps and an abandoned trail. Straight ahead (east) leads across the West Walker River (deep but calm-water ford) to the major trail on the east side of Lower Piute Meadow. Right (south), as signed, is the preferred route to Lower Piute Meadow, so turn onto it and continue 0.4 mile along the river until a meadow emerges upriver; here is an indistinct, unsigned junction. Straight ahead (south) leads up Cascade Creek toward Dorothy Lake Pass (Trip 34), while you need to ford the West Walker River (left; east). There are often logs present nearby, but otherwise it is a wade. Once on the east bank you'll pick up the trail near the center of a broad gravel bar and dive back into lodgepole pine forest. Just 300 feet later is a junction (38.20846°N, 119.55392°W, in case you lost the trail in the creekside thicket), where right (southeast), your route, is signposted for Upper Piute Meadow, while left (north) leads back to Leavitt Meadows.

You traipse through lush lodgepole pine forest where the base of nearly every tree trunk is decorated with a ring of alpine prickly currant and swaths of arnica fill the openings. The trail stays well north of the river as it skirts yet another marshy meadow, climbs just slightly, and passes a dilapidated drift fence that marks the beginning of Upper Piute Meadow. Just beyond are some large lodgepole pine–shaded campsites on riverside terraces (8,292'; 38.19841°N, 119.54249°W) and a junction with the Tower Lake Trail (Trip 35). Looking across the river you will see the Piute Cabin, a U.S. Forest Service cabin.

DAY 3 (Kirkwood Creek to Buckeye Forks, 6.4 miles): Onward, the trail skirts the edge of Upper Piute Meadow, remaining just east of the lodgepole pine fringe. Stepping into the expanse of grass proffers brilliant views upcanyon to Hawksbeak, Ehrnbeck, and Tower Peaks. The trail crosses one small rocky outcrop and drops back to a meadow lobe brimming with flowers—arrowleaf ragwort, Richardson's geranium, rein orchid, Coulter's fleabane, Sierra tiger lily, common yellow monkeyflower, and alpine shooting star to name just a few. The lack of trees upslope bespeaks to avalanches that regularly tear down the canyon walls.

The ascent steepens as the trail jogs east, then southeast along cascading Kirkwood Creek, which soon offers some inviting pools. Flower-lined side trickles spill endlessly across the trail; the granite ridge overhead is remarkably fractured, and the snowmelt on the peaks vanishes underground, reappearing as springs lower on the slopes. Around the 9,000-foot mark, the gradient lessens a little, and you'll find some alternative campsites if the mosquitoes in Upper Piute Meadow scared you upward. Beyond, the trail's gradient increases steeply, matching the terrain. While the creek spills over minor cascades and tumbles down its bouldery channel, the creekside trail ramps upward. Just below 9,400 feet the trail zags onto a drier slope of western white pine and lodgepole pine, with whitebark pine joining the mix as the trail approaches Kirkwood Pass (9,903'), unnamed on the topo maps. The view

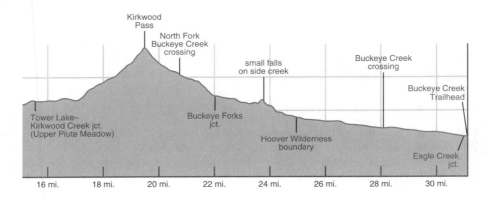

along both the ascent and at the pass are disappointing, but this can be rectified with a quick detour to the slabs just northwest of the pass; Tower and Forsyth Peaks dominate the view west. Just a tad farther north on the ridge sits a tarn where you could camp.

As you descend eroded gravelly slopes into the Buckeye Creek catchment, turn back and stare at the pass's blocky façade, so different than its forested western side. Dropping 400 feet in the first 0.4 mile, the sinuous route weaves across snowmelt trickles as you brush against the low-growing boughs of stunted hemlocks. The descent pauses briefly on a shelf, a plausible campsite, then resumes, the trail soon beside a meadowed creek corridor. Beneath increasing lodgepole pine cover, the trail reaches a broad flat (excellent camping) and the North Fork Buckeye Creek.

NORTH FORK BUCKEYE CREEK
If you have some spare hours, consider ascending the North Fork Buckeye Creek 1.5 miles to its headwaters, a saddle separating it from Beartrap Lake's Long Canyon. Indeed, for cross-country enthusiasts, this would be a way to loop back to the West Walker River and the Leavitt Meadows Trailhead, avoiding the need for a car shuttle. Cross to the east side of the creek and ascend steeply through lodgepole pine forest, staying well east of the willow-choked creek corridor. Only at about 9,600 feet, after a 500-foot ascent, should you cut closer to the creek. The second 500 feet of climbing is more gradual, first through lodgepole pine forest and then alongside the creek through subalpine meadows. Ultimately you reach expansive spring-fed meadows with a truly memorable view southeast to Matterhorn Peak and the Sawtooth Range; indeed, the landscape is so unexpectedly green right to the saddle you might imagine you've just traveled to the Swiss Alps and are staring at the genuine Matterhorn. If you wish to continue back to the West Walker River, from the pass, easy cross-country travel leads to Beartrap Lake, where you pick up a trail that you can follow 4.25 miles to the West Walker River Trail. *Note:* This trail is rarely maintained, but downed trees are cleared *just* often enough that you can still follow it reliably.

The trail drops beside the creek, fords it, passes more good campsites in a long lodgepole pine flat, and again drops steeply, the pinnacled valley walls rising ever higher. As the gradient eases, to your left (north) are the foundations of an old cabin and just beyond some good campsites to either side of the trail (8,460'; 38.17283°N, 119.47316°W). In a few more steps, near a second old cabin, this one still *just* standing, you meet the trail descending from Buckeye Pass to the south (Trip 73). There aren't many openings in the forest near the cabin, but there are other campsite choices once you are 0.1 mile east (for example, 8,445'; 38.17291°N, 119.47140°W). Fishing in Buckeye Creek is good for rainbow and eastern brook trout.

BUCKEYE FORKS CABIN
The old snow-survey cabin here—possibly the oldest U.S. Snow Survey shelter—is of log-tenon construction and is believed to have been built in 1928. When built, the cabin was surrounded by open meadow; the ubiquitous lodgepole and willow have since overgrown the meadow. This dense growth is undoubtedly because of a colony of beavers that were very active along Buckeye Creek many decades back. Their dams repeatedly flooded the valley floor between Buckeye Forks and the Roughs and the consequent buildup of sediments supported forest growth.

DAY 4 (Buckeye Forks to Buckeye Creek Trailhead, 9.1 miles): At the junction you turn left (east) heading down Buckeye Creek, while right (south) leads to Buckeye Pass. Your route for today begins with a gentle descent downriver, alternating between dry lodgepole forest and open slabs, passing a selection of small campsites en route. After about 0.75 mile, where the creek's gradient steepens, glades of trees become rarer, and glacial-polished slabs predominant, you enter a canyon segment named the Roughs. Here, the sometimes-swampy trail winds along the left bank of Buckeye Creek, overshadowed by sheer, rounded granite to the north and polished spires to the south.

Beyond, you make a steep ascent onto black metasedimentary shale that leads to a juniper-topped knob and then to a delightful little waterfall on a tributary descending from Ink Rocks. The views down Buckeye Canyon are spectacular: The lush grasslands of Big Meadow provide a soft counterpoint to the ruggedness of Flatiron and Buckeye Ridges.

Switchbacks drop you onto a brushy slope across which you make a mile-long descending traverse to the valley floor. Two talus lobes, alluvial fans dissected by debris flow channels, slow your downward progress. Then quite suddenly the terrain flattens, and you leave Hoover Wilderness. The remaining 6.2 miles are remarkably gentle—you lose just 600 feet from here to the trailhead as you walk through open sagebrush, aspen glades, and meadows. The trail is lightly used by humans, and for the first 2 flat miles it is often hard to discern the correct route. For the maze of trails in the meadows, you can thank the abundant cows that make this valley their summer home. The true trail stays at the base of ancient talus fans, the boundary demarcated by the transition from riparian meadow (below the trail) to aspen and willow stands (above); the landscape is much wetter and less hospitable for walking closer to the creek corridor. Eventually, you reach Big Meadow, a charming 2-mile-long grassland full of Belding's ground squirrels and morning-feeding deer.

Buckeye Ridge rises steeply to the south beyond Big Meadow.   Photo by Elizabeth Wenk

> **BACK IN 1870...**
> At one time, around 1870, this meadow rang with the sounds of axes and the whirring of a sawmill blade. Here, the Upper Hunewill mill operated to provide mining timber. Near the fence at the bottom of the meadow, the observant passerby can make out the signs of an abortive effort to construct a flume to carry water from Buckeye Creek to Bodie.

You pass one stock fence (7,556'; 38.21419°N, 119.41184°W) where the original trail crossed Buckeye Creek. This route is still easy to follow, but in recent decades most foot traffic has followed a parallel trail on the north bank for another 0.7 mile and is the route described here. You continue downslope, looping almost imperceptibly around the base of another talus fan, before reaching a point where Buckeye Creek's channel splits. This is a good place to cross because the flow is divided. You ford the first (seasonal) fork (7,474'; 38.22066°N, 119.40385°W) and 0.16 mile later the main channel (difficult in early season; 7,461'; 38.22205°N, 119.40234°W). Continuing across the meadow, you intersect the route of the alterative trail, and head east, now on an abandoned, two-track road. Stroll through a sagebrush field squeezed between the lodgepole pines that border the creek and a large stand of aspen trees on the nose of a ridge to the south. Arnicas, iris, and shooting stars all provide early-summer color in the meadows, while mule ears, scarlet gilia, and desert paintbrush color the expanses of sagebrush. Be sure to turn around and look at the view upcanyon—the broad, flat, green valley with rugged peaks rising to the west.

At the end of another fairly large meadow, you come to a fence with both a hikers' gate and a stock gate and begin the last mile of your journey under Jeffrey and ponderosa pines, red firs, and quaking aspens. The gentle downhill stroll passes a trail to Eagle Creek (right; south) and quickly arrives at a locked gate, the official trailhead, although not where you may leave your car (7,215'; 38.23458°N, 119.35158°W). A short walk along the road leads to a parking lot at Buckeye Campground's west end.

CA 120 TRIPS

No trans-Sierra highway offers as many delightful trailheads as does CA 120, which cuts across Yosemite National Park. It should be no surprise, then, that the scenery along the trips from CA 120 is simply spectacular—and quite varied, as it forms an east–west transect and offers trailheads starting at very different elevations. From west to east, we present trips from these trailheads: Hetch Hetchy, White Wolf, Ten Lakes, Yosemite Creek, Sunrise Lakes, Cathedral Lakes, Elizabeth Lake, Glen Aulin, Lyell Canyon, Mono Pass, and Saddlebag Lake. All are in Yosemite except for the last. Two additional Yosemite trailheads, May Lake and Murphy Creek, are included in the list because described hikes end at these.

Each trailhead is unique: Hetch Hetchy, the lowest, is best in late spring and early summer when its waterfalls are at their fullest. White Wolf, the westernmost of the high trailheads along CA 120, is a gateway to the Grand Canyon of the Tuolumne River. The Ten Lakes Trailhead, meanwhile, provides access to a stunning traverse high above the Tuolumne River Canyon. From the Yosemite Creek Trailhead, you can travel south to Yosemite Valley. The Sunrise Lakes Trailhead at Tenaya Lake offers quick access to the scenic backcountry around Sunrise Mountain. Cathedral Lakes is a very popular way to pick up the John Muir Trail (JMT) segment that leads to the Cathedral Lakes and beyond to enjoy some lovely creek corridors, meadows, and forest scenery between Tuolumne Meadows and Yosemite Valley. Elizabeth Lake leads to that lake and, better yet, to a beautiful cross-country jaunt to a lake in the heart of the Cathedral Range. The Glen Aulin Trailhead provides the easiest access to northern Yosemite and also, along a spur, to the quite secluded Young Lakes. The Lyell Canyon Trailhead marks the southbound continuation of the bustling JMT and Pacific Crest Trail route, and also provides access to what many consider Yosemite's most spectacular and wild backcountry around Vogelsang High Sierra Camp. From Mono Pass, backpackers can exit Yosemite via a lightly used route into a splendid lakes basin in Ansel Adams Wilderness. Saddlebag Lake, lying just east of Yosemite, offers easy access to a charming little lakes basin as well as a starting (or ending) point for cross-country adventures from that basin into Yosemite.

It's no wonder that aspiring backpackers from all over the world flock to CA 120!

Trailheads:	Hetch Hetchy	Cathedral Lakes
	White Wolf	Elizabeth Lake
	Ten Lakes	Glen Aulin
	Yosemite Creek	Lyell Canyon (JMT/PCT)
	May Lake	Mono Pass
	Sunrise Lakes	Saddlebag Lake
	Murphy Creek	

Hetch Hetchy Trailhead — 3,813'; 37.94645°N, 119.78752°W

Destination/ GPS Coordinates	Trip Type	Best Season	Pace & Hiking/ Layover Days	Total Mileage	Permit Required
37 Wapama Falls and Rancheria Falls 37.95633°N 119.71521°W (Rancheria Falls)	Out-and-back	Early to late	Leisurely 2/0	13.0	Rancheria Falls
38 Tiltill Valley– Lake Vernon Loop 38.01129°N 119.73251°W (Lake Vernon)	Loop	Early to late	Leisurely 4/0	27.7	Rancheria Falls (Beehive Meadows if reversed)
39 Grand Tour of North-western Yosemite 38.09391°N 119.61972°W (Tilden Lake outlet)	Loop	Mid to late	Strenuous 7/1	56.3	Rancheria Falls (Beehive Meadows if reversed)

INFORMATION AND PERMITS: These trips are in Yosemite National Park: wilderness permits and bear canisters are required; pets and firearms are prohibited. Quotas apply, with 60% of permits reservable online up to 24 weeks in advance and 40% available first-come, first-served starting at 11 a.m. the day before your trip's start date. Permits for Hetch Hetchy are best picked up at the Hetch Hetchy Entrance Station/Mather Ranger Station where you enter the park. Fires are prohibited above 9,600 feet. See nps.gov/yose/planyourvisit/wildpermits.htm for more details.

DRIVING DIRECTIONS: From CA 120 (Tioga Road), turn left onto Evergreen Road, located just 0.6 mile west of Yosemite National Park's Big Oak Flat Entrance Station. Drive 7.4 miles north on Evergreen Road to its junction with Hetch Hetchy Road, an intersection located in the middle of the small community of Camp Mather. Turn right, drive beneath an archway, and continue 1.3 miles to the Hetch Hetchy Entrance Station/Mather Ranger Station.

Road use is restricted beyond this point. In midsummer the road is open 7 a.m.–8 p.m., but open hours decrease with dwindling daylight hours. The current hours are posted where you turn onto Evergreen Road or on the Yosemite National Park website; just search for "Hetch Hetchy open hours." At the entrance, your license plate is registered, and you are given a placard to display on your dash. Once past this bottleneck, drive 7.1 miles to a junction branching left for the Hetch Hetchy Backpackers' Campground. Backpackers must park in the obvious parking area by the road's start, then walk 0.5 mile on the road to O'Shaughnessy Dam. Backpackers can stay at the trailhead backpackers' campground for a night before and/or after their trip.

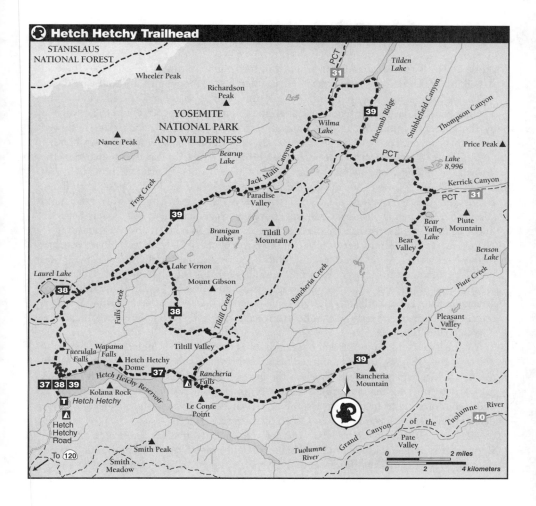

STANISLAUS
NATIONAL FOREST

Wheeler Peak

Richardson
Peak

YOSEMITE
NATIONAL PARK
AND WILDERNESS

Nance Peak

Bearup
Lake

Frog Creek

Jack Main Canyon

Paradise
Valley

Branigan
Lakes

Tiltill
Mountain

Laurel Lake

38

Falls Creek

Lake Vernon

Mount Gibson

38

Tiltill Creek

Tueeulala
Falls

Wapama
Falls

Hetch Hetchy
Dome

37

Hetch Hetchy Reservoir

37 **38** **39**

Kolana Rock

Hetch Hetchy

Hetch
Hetchy
Road

To **120**

Smith Peak

Smith
Meadow

Tiltill Valley

Rancheria
Falls

Le Conte
Point

Tuolumne
River

Tilden
Lake

PCT

31

39

Wilma
Lake

Macomb Ridge

Stubblefield Canyon

Thompson Canyon

PCT

Price Peak ▲

Lake
8,996

Kerrick Canyon

PCT **31**

Bear
Valley
Lake

Piute
Mountain

Bear
Valley

Rancheria Creek

Benson
Lake

Piute Creek

Pleasant
Valley

39

Rancheria
Mountain

Grand Canyon of the Tuolumne River

40

Pate
Valley

0   1   2 miles

0   2   4 kilometers

Wapama Falls and Rancheria Falls

Trip Data: 37.95633°N, 119.71521°W; 13.0 miles; 2/0 days
Topos: *Hetch Hetchy Reservoir, Lake Eleanor*

HIGHLIGHTS: This walk is the perfect choice for an early- or late-season ramble, accessible *most* times the road isn't snowed in. Wapama Falls is stupendous in spring, and beautiful 25-foot Rancheria Falls tumbles into large, inviting pools—a wonderful destination. *Note:* the park closes the Wapama Falls bridge under extreme run-off conditions.

DAY 1 (Hetch Hetchy Trailhead to Rancheria Creek, 6.5 miles): From the trailhead, cross 600-foot-long O'Shaughnessy Dam (3,813'), enjoying views across the water to, from the left (north), seasonal Tueeulala (twee-LAH-lah) Falls, Wapama Falls, Hetch Hetchy Dome, and Kolana Rock. Beyond, you immediately plunge into a quarter-mile-long tunnel.

Exiting, your trail is a badly deteriorated service road that once led to Lake Eleanor. The road winds along the hillside just above Hetch Hetchy's high-water mark through scattered canyon live oak, incense cedar, Douglas-fir, California bay, and big leaf maple, some sections burned in the 2013 Rim Fire. Watch out for poison oak here. Soon after the road begins a gentle ascent it reaches a junction, where you turn right (south, then east) onto the trail signed to Rancheria Creek, while the left (east, then north) fork climbs toward Laurel Lake.

The occasional airy gray pine and live oak provide little shade, as the trail winds along a sunny bench. Glacial polish and glacial erratics, boulders transported and then dropped by the glacier, remind you that at times during the Pleistocene Epoch glaciers flowed down this canyon. You descend the slabs gently, first south, then east, across an exfoliating granitic nose, then switchback once down to a broad sloping ledge, sparingly shaded by the grayish-green foliage of gray pine. From April to June this area is often decorated with an assortment of wildflowers, for the granite slabs are impervious and water pools atop them, creating miniature vernal wetlands. Follow these ledges 0.5 mile to a minor stream that, until about early summer, spills down the wall above you as ephemeral Hetch Hetchy Falls (an informal name, and incorrectly marked as Tueeulala Falls on many maps—keep reading).

Beyond it you continue across slabs on the north shore of Hetch Hetchy Reservoir to a bridge over a steep, generally dry cleft, followed almost immediately by a seasonally wet boulder crossing over the outflow from the waterfall that is actually Tueeulala Falls; it lies 0.2 mile east of where it is marked on most maps. Depending on the time of year, seasonal Tueeulala Falls either spills forcefully down a near-vertical wall or is absent because it is created by a seasonal overflow channel from Falls Creek, the creek whose main channel is Wapama Falls' source.

You next descend some 100 feet of granite stairs through a field of huge talus blocks. If you're passing this way in early summer, flecks of spray dampen your path as you approach the five bridges spanning Falls Creek at the base of Wapama Falls. Check with the park service before hiking here; in spring and early summer, vast, crashing, tumultuous Wapama Falls will cover these bridges with spray and even flowing water and at times they are deemed sufficiently hazardous to be closed by the park service.

Just past Falls Creek, the trail exits the dense fly-infested live oak forest onto a boulder slope—here a large rockslide in the spring of 2014 decimated the forest and trail. Beyond, the trail winds in and out of forest cover as it traverses the base of Hetch Hetchy Dome on a series of benches, eventually emerging onto a meadowy ledge system where you have an airy view of the water below. In spring, wildflowers such as monkeyflower, paintbrush, and Sierra onion color the ground.

Past the ledges, the trail makes a long descent, crossing Tiltill Creek on a bridge, from which you gaze upon the creek tumbling down its gorge 60 feet below you. The trail next climbs onto the low ridge separating Tiltill Creek and Rancheria Creek, traversing it to reach a shaded flat 0.8 mile beyond the bridge. Here is an unmarked junction with a spur trail leading right (south) to the Rancheria Falls streamside camp (4,515'; 37.95633°N, 119.71521°W; 6.0 miles from trailhead; elevation profile to here). Rancheria Falls, some

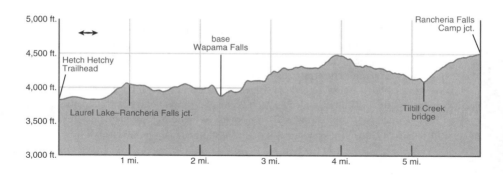

Wapama Falls   Photo by Elizabeth Wenk

quarter mile upstream, drops 25 feet into deep, swirling pools. Fishing in Rancheria Creek can be good for rainbow trout.

You'll note the trip's mileage indicates you have another 0.5 mile to hike, and indeed, after depositing your belongings at camp, I urge you to continue up to a bridge spanning Rancheria Creek: in spring, watching the water plummet past it is mesmerizing and, at low flows, descending below the bridge yields additional swimming holes. To reach it, continue up the main trail, turning right (south) toward Rancheria Mountain at a junction, where the left (north) fork leads to Tiltill Valley, and soon thereafter reaching the bridge spanning Rancheria Creek.

DAY 2 (Rancheria Creek to Hetch Hetchy Trailhead, 6.5 miles): Retrace your steps.

trip 38   Tiltill Valley–Lake Vernon Loop

see map on p. 185

Trip Data: 38.01129°N, 119.73251°W (Lake Vernon);
27.7 miles; 4/0 days

Topos: *Lake Eleanor, Hetch Hetchy Reservoir, Tiltill Mountain, Kibbie Lake*

HIGHLIGHTS: This loop hike is a perfect spring conditioner when higher elevations are still snow covered. It tours the majestic waterfalls and granite cliffs defining Hetch Hetchy Reservoir and visits two nearby low-elevation lakes, Lake Vernon and Laurel Lake.

DAY 1 (Hetch Hetchy Trailhead to Rancheria Creek, 6.0 miles): Follow Trip 37, Day 1 to the Rancheria Falls streamside camp (4,515'; 37.95633°N, 119.71521°W).

DAY 2 (Rancheria Creek to Lake Vernon, 9.8 miles): Return to the junction with the main trail, turn right (north) and begin climbing, soon reaching the next junction, where you follow the left-hand trail west to Tiltill Valley, while right (east) leads up Rancheria Mountain and to distant destinations, including Bear Valley (Trip 39). The trail to Tiltill Valley switchbacks 1,200 feet up a burned, dry, exposed slope well loved by rattlesnakes, to reach a timber-bottomed saddle and a small tarn brimming with yellow water lilies in spring. As the trail descends north off the saddle, it traverses a pine forest with a sprinkling of incense cedar and black oak.

This duff trail emerges toward the east end of Tiltill Valley, a long meadow that, in spring and early summer, is usually quite wet and boggy. The trail dives due north across it—either through water or tall grass. Despite a series of levies elevating the trail tread, your feet may well be wet before you reach a deeper ford of a Tiltill Creek tributary. Just beyond the tributary ford is a junction where continuing straight north across the meadow leads to Lake Vernon (your route), while a right-hand turn (east) traverses the rest of the meadow, then ascends the ridge radiating off Tiltill Mountain, ultimately leading to the Pacific Crest Trail.

Once on the north side of Tiltill Meadow, curve left (west) and traipse beneath lodgepole pine cover, winding between some massive boulders and finding excellent campsites to either side of the Tiltill Creek ford (5,595'; 37.97611°N, 119.69778°W). These camping places, located in isolated stands of lodgepole and sugar pines, afford campers uninterrupted vantage points from which to watch wildlife in the meadow. Fishing for rainbow trout in Tiltill Creek is excellent in early season.

While some hikers will split Day 2 in half, completing just the 3.4 miles to Tiltill Creek for the day, most will continue onto Lake Vernon, next ascending 1,400 feet up well-built switchbacks that climb northwest out of the Tiltill Creek drainage. Spring flowers are showy, as the trail alternates between tree-covered and brushier slopes, transitioning entirely to shrubs by the time the trail assumes a more westward trajectory, skirting around a ridge emanating from Mount Gibson. Here the whitethorn, together with companion shrubs like chokecherry and huckleberry oak, rapidly choke the trail between prunings—the aftermath of fires in 1960 and 2004—and can make for a scratchy walk. If the trail crew has been through recently, you barely notice the shrubs and delight in the views and the colorful wildflower displays; especially noteworthy here are the forget-me-nots.

The trail now arcs northeast to the crest of a lateral moraine, which, from our vantage point, is only a low ridge, though it stands a full 4,000 feet above the inundated floor of the Grand Canyon of the Tuolumne River. The glacier that left this moraine was therefore at least that thick. At 3.3 trail miles beyond Tiltill Valley, the gradient eases, and you begin a long,

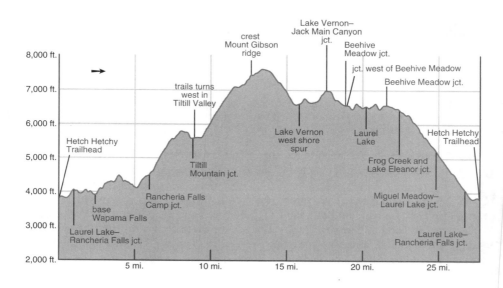

more forested traverse across the massive west flank of Mount Gibson, passing some delightful meadows and aspen glades and crossing minor ridges that are additional moraines. Another prominent moraine crest marks the start of the switchbacking descent, and after a drop of about 350 feet you suddenly transition from rubbly glacial deposits to smooth expanses of granite—indeed there are now granite slabs for as far as you can see. You follow three dozen switchbacks diligently down to the south shore of Lake Vernon, where the trail curves west toward the lake's outlet.

Camping options around the lake are varied. Those in search of a sandy home among slabs should search the lands south and west of the lake, while those wishing for lodgepole pine cover best continue along the trail, crossing Falls Creek on a sturdy footbridge. At the highest spring flows, it can be a thigh-deep wade to approach the bridge—take care!

Common yellow monkeyflower in a small pool on slabs Photo by Elizabeth Wenk

Soon you reach a junction (6,600'; 38.01129°N, 119.73251°W; mileage measured to here) with a trail that leads to tree-sheltered campsites along Lake Vernon's northwest shore. Most lakeside campsites are small, and almost all are well hidden from the trail; the largest one is about one-third of the way north along the western shore in a large stand of lodgepole pines. There is also a large campsite beyond the north end of the lake close to where the creek angles from northeast to north. The lake, mostly shallow and lying at about 6,564 feet, is one of the warmer park lakes for swimming.

DAY 3 (Lake Vernon to Laurel Lake, 4.4 miles): From the aforementioned junction, the main trail climbs left (southwest) to mount a shallow ridge, loops a little north, then resumes a southwest bearing following a route marked by cairns across smooth glacier-polished granite rimming the Falls Creek canyon. Climbing again, you reenter forest cover, and after 1.8 miles reach a moraine-crest junction with the trail leading right (northeast) to Jack Main Canyon. Your route is left (southwest), toward Laurel Lake and Hetch Hetchy. Ahead your trail winds down through a landscape burned repeatedly over the years and therefore mostly lacking shade but sporting a plethora of wildflower gardens due to abundant moisture and sunlight. An easy 1.25 miles brings you to a junction at the east edge of the Beehive, a meadow that is the site of an 1880s cattlemen's camp (and campsites). You turn right (west) toward Laurel Lake, while continuing ahead (left; southwest) leads to Hetch Hetchy Reservoir, tomorrow's route.

Walk along the northern edge of the meadow, reaching another trail split within 200 steps, where you strike left (west) toward Laurel Lake's south shore and outlet; right (north) is a sparsely used trail that loops to the lake's north shore. You drop easily down into a gully, then cross broad Frog Creek, often a wet, bouldery ford in late spring and early summer. Climb steeply west up the creek's north bank to a heavily forested ridge before gently dropping to good camps near Laurel Lake's outlet. A brief lakeshore stint brings you to a junction (6,490'; 37.99432°N, 119.79651°W) with the north-shore trail—branching right (northwest) from here leads to more secluded campsites. Western azalea grows thickly just beyond the grassy lakeshore, a fragrant accompaniment to edible huckleberry and thimbleberry. Fishing is fair for rainbow trout, and swimming, especially in July and early August, can be wonderful.

DAY 4 (Laurel Lake to Hetch Hetchy Reservoir, 7.5 miles): The final day is almost entirely downhill and on well-traveled trails. You begin by retracing your steps 1.4 miles to the northeast corner of the Beehive, now turning right (south) and skirting the long, narrow southeast lobe of the meadow. Traipsing through white fir and lodgepole forest and passing additional small meadows and seasonal rivulets, the 0.8 mile to your next junction is generally pleasantly shaded and low-angled as you traverse the slope above Frog Creek. At the upcoming junction, you continue straight ahead (left; south), while right (west) leads to Frog Creek and Lake Eleanor. All too quickly the conifer cover cedes to whitethorn on a slope that's been repeatedly scorched by fires, most recently the devastating 2013 Rim Fire. In places there is barely a mature, seed-producing tree still standing, much less any with sufficient foliage to provide decent shade. A gradual descent brings you to a seasonal linear lakelet, nestled on the inside slope of a broad lateral moraine. Mounting the moraine, a long descent ensues, 1,000 feet down a narrow, winding trail that fluctuates between notably steep, pleasantly shallow, and occasionally annoyingly uphill. Note that camping is not permitted once you're within 4 miles of the trailhead. Eventually, the slope pauses at a junction. Stay left (south), descending along a now-broad road tread, while the right-hand (westbound) trail was once a service road and leads to Miguel Meadow and Lake Eleanor.

The continued downhill walking is pleasant and the views rejuvenating, as you stare down to Hetch Hetchy Reservoir and its southern sentinel, Kolana Rock. This slope was mostly burned in 2013, but the live oaks rapidly resprouted, providing welcome shade. 1.9 miles of well-graded switchbacks brings you to the junction you passed on Day 1 near the shore of Hetchy Hetchy Reservoir. Here left (east) leads to Rancheria Falls, while you turn right (west) and retrace your steps the final mile around the reservoir, through the tunnel and across the dam to the trailhead.

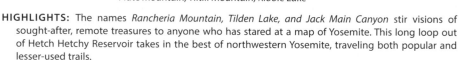

trip 39	**Grand Tour of Northwestern Yosemite**	see map on p. 185

> **Trip Data:** 38.09391°N, 119.61972°W (Tilden Lake outlet);
> 56.3 miles; 7/1 days
> **Topos:** *Lake Eleanor, Hetch Hetchy Reservoir, Ten Lakes,*
> *Piute Mountain, Tiltill Mountain, Kibbie Lake*

HIGHLIGHTS: The names *Rancheria Mountain, Tilden Lake,* and *Jack Main Canyon* stir visions of sought-after, remote treasures to anyone who has stared at a map of Yosemite. This long loop out of Hetch Hetchy Reservoir takes in the best of northwestern Yosemite, traveling both popular and lesser-used trails.

DAY 1 (Hetch Hetchy Trailhead to Rancheria Creek, 6.0 miles): Follow Trip 37, Day 1 to the Rancheria Falls streamside camp (4,515'; 37.95633°N, 119.71521°W).

DAY 2 (Rancheria Creek camping area to Rancheria Mountain, 5.9 miles): The next morning, return to the main trail, turn right, and ascend 0.3 mile moderately uphill to a junction where left (northeast) leads to Tiltill Valley (Trip 38), while you turn right (southeast), crossing Rancheria Creek on a bridge after 0.15 mile. The powerful frothing water is hypnotizing in spring, while well-worn potholes and slabs invite swimmers in late summer. Fill up on water at this creek, for your next source is at tonight's campsite 3,000 feet higher on the slopes of Rancheria Mountain. Your trail commences a 1,500-foot switchbacking ascent up generally open slopes, since most tree cover was removed by a 1999 fire and the regrowing black oaks currently provide little shade. At 2.2 miles past Rancheria Creek, the trail tops a 6,200-foot nose, littered with gravel and boulders, all glacial deposits. Detouring a mile west from here leads to the summit of Le Conte Point, an easily climbed, spectacular viewpoint.

Onward, your trail traverses a half mile east along sandy slopes, most places charred by fires at least once during the past two decades, to the head of a minor hanging canyon. Here you encounter the first white firs of your journey. The ascent resumes on dusty switchbacks up past some fire-cleared forest openings, showy during the June wildflower bloom and later dry and parched, when you'll step across one dry gully after another. At 6,750 feet, you swing onto a south-facing chaparral slope and can look south across the Grand Canyon of the Tuolumne River to the rolling upland region across it; take the time to enjoy these views, for they will be hidden later. Beyond, the trail leaves the benches and broken granite slabs and progresses up a slope shrouded with thickets of manzanita and whitethorn, a species of ceanothus that is the bane of hikers traveling the park's lesser-used midelevation trails for years following fire. Where more moisture irrigates the soils, willows dominate and water-loving flowers like crimson columbine decorate the trail verges. The trail first ramps upward, then begins to zigzag more tediously, finally leaving the burned areas and re-entering forested cover at around 7,600 feet. Not long afterward, the trail approaches a reliable stream. Above its eastern bank are campsites on a mostly open, gentle, gravelly slope with scattered red fir cover (7,711'; 37.95199°N, 119.65208°W). Additional camping options exist over the next 2.5 miles as you follow the creek up Rancheria Mountain. Because tomorrow is a longer day, you may wish to continue a little farther.

Bear Valley Lake   Photo by Elizabeth Wenk

DAY 3 (Rancheria Mountain to Bear Valley Lake, 9.8 miles): Onward, your trail ascends beneath lodgepoles and red firs, soon entering the shallow drainage of a second, smaller creek. You briefly parallel the creek upward, then angle northeast away from it, ascending up over a morainal divide back to the creek along which you camped, 1.7 miles beyond where you first crossed it. Now at an elevation of about 8,250 feet, in peak flowering season, you are standing in almost head-high stalks of larkspur, lupine, fireweed, umbrella-leaved cow parsnip, and four-petaled monument plant, and, of course, many shorter species, including lacy meadow rue, purple aster, white yarrow, yellow ragwort, aromatic pennyroyal (a mint), and leather-leaved mule ears. Under all these, at times, can be a mat of Jacob's ladder. There are additional campsites in this vicinity. From this flower garden, your path turns east-northeast up a broad, shallow swale and soon leaves the lush surroundings behind as it climbs gently along dry volcanic slopes of a broad, low ridge emanating west from the northeast summit of Rancheria Mountain.

RANCHERIA MOUNTAIN
The view from the summit of Rancheria Mountain to the bottom of Pate Valley, more than 5,000 feet below, is well worth the half mile detour south. The easiest route is to leave the trail shortly after you surmount the ridge, just under 8,600 feet (37.96630°N, 119.60842°W). Head slightly southeast toward a broad saddle, then turn southwest and follow the ridge a little under 400 feet up to the summit. Abundant flowers greet you throughout the walk.

A mile past the second creek crossing, your way becomes a ridgetop amble, bringing you to the trail's high point on Rancheria Mountain, at 8,680 feet. Ahead, you have a 1.2-mile-long, two-stage descent of about 600 feet, first to cross one minor saddle, then to reach a second, larger one. Five switchbacks spare your knees on the descent, and, where the trees disperse momentarily, you look northeast to distant Sawtooth Ridge and closer Volunteer Peak. A short distance later, atop an 8,060-foot saddle, you reach a junction where you trend left (north) toward Bear Valley, while right (east) leads to Pleasant Valley and beyond to Rodgers Canyon and Pate Valley.

The trail to Bear Valley gradually ascends a conifer-clad slope that is the divide between Piute Creek to the east and Rancheria and Breeze Creeks to the west. After crossing a

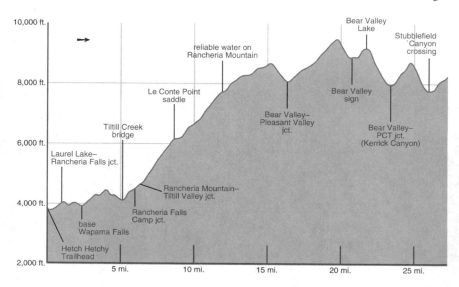

timbered saddle, climb north up a steep, shaded pitch to a small, grassy pond fringed with poisonous Labrador tea (and campsites)—detouring east from here leads to an astounding view of Pleasant Valley, far below. Continuing a half mile north along a sandy ridge leads to the willowy east bank of an unnamed creek. Then, after another half mile, the trail crosses the creek and climbs northwest through a grassy meadow to top a lateral moraine.

Soon you find yourself in the open, perched drainage of another unnamed creek that you ascend through a broad flower-filled meadow, reminiscent of less rugged Sierra landscapes farther north. In places the trail is faint, but walking upslope you cannot miss your goal: a 9,490-foot saddle flanked by huddled whitebark pines and hemlocks. Below is pastoral Bear Valley, overshadowed by knife-edge Bear Valley Peak. Bear Valley is reached by winding 500 feet down a steep hemlock-bedecked slope, lush with flowers. As the gradient lessens, the trail turns northwest to reach the south side of meadowed Bear Valley. Here the path can be lost for some 500 feet across the hummocky, frequently soggy grassland—traipse straight (due north) across the meadow, not left (west) in the direction of use trails leading to campsites, and you'll soon reach a handy metal sign proclaiming you're in Bear Valley.

On the meadow's north side, the trail is immediately obvious again, climbing easily over a forested moraine, then dropping to the east end of a small, hospitable lakelet circled by lodgepoles and western white pines. Just a minute north of it, you hop across Breeze Creek and ascend northeast along it over open, slabby terrain. After about 300 feet of elevation gain, the trail levels off, enters a delightful open stand of pines and hemlocks, and quickly arrives at the outlet of long-awaited Bear Valley Lake (9,154'; 38.03438°N, 119.57920°W; unnamed on maps). With picturesque islets and a slab-ringed shoreline, this shallow gem provides a stunning foreground for soaring, photogenic Bear Valley Peak (Peak 9,800+; also unnamed on maps). Excellent camps lie among conifers back from the north shore.

DAY 4 (Bear Valley Lake to Tilden Lake, 10.9 miles): From Bear Valley Lake's outlet the trail leads a short distance northwest to a small gap between two low domes and begins a 1,200-foot descent north into Kerrick Canyon. For the first 400 feet, the descent is shaded by hemlocks and western white pines, yielding to a denser lodgepole pine and hemlock forest lower down. Finally reaching morainal till rearranged by the sometimes raging Rancheria Creek, your descent abates and you turn east through dry lodgepole flats to arrive at a

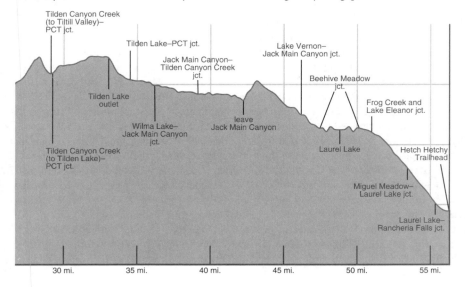

junction with the Pacific Crest Trail (PCT), 1.6 miles beyond last night's campsite. You take the left-hand (north) option toward Rancheria Creek, while right (east) leads to locations to the east, including Buckeye Pass and Seavey Pass (Trip 31).

Immediately, you cross voluminous Kerrick Canyon's bouldery Rancheria Creek, often a rough ford through mid-July—indeed generally considered the most dangerous of the northern Yosemite crossings and best crossed by mid-morning. After crossing the creek, the PCT passes a north-bank spur to popular campsites and follows Rancheria Creek briefly downstream. It then begins a steep rocky climb out of the drainage. Necessary breathers allow time to admire the dramatic cross-canyon views of Bear Valley Peak and Piute Mountain. Ascending first a brushy slope and later crossing broken slabs, the trail eventually gains 700 feet in elevation to reach a shallow gap near the west end of a small lakelet (with small campsites).

PARALLEL CANYONS

Northern Yosemite is famous for its series of near-parallel, glacial smoothed canyons: Jack Main, Tilden, Stubblefield, Kerrick, Matterhorn, and Virginia to name a few. The upper reaches of these gems are lush and pleasantly graded, making for fast, easy walking. Your route, following the PCT for a stretch, instead cuts across these canyons. This is an anything but gentle endeavor because tall rugged ridges separate them, earning this section of trail the name "The Washboard." Since this is the route on which most people experience northern Yosemite, the complaints about the knee-shocking descents and lung-searing ascents have become infamous. On your next trip to northern Yosemite, pick a route that emphasizes the length of a canyon, such as Trip 77 or 80 in this book, or drop your pack and walk up Stubblefield Canyon, for a very different adventure.

Proceeding north from the gap, a multitude of short, steep, cobbly switchbacks lead north. Crossing the diffuse outlet of Lake 8,896, which spills across the trail, you continue rockily downward, dropping almost 1,000 feet to the mouth of Thompson Canyon, then turning west and making a shady, short descent as you slowly converge with the canyon's stream. You step across the outlet creek from Lake 8,896 once more, then enter a lush red fir forest near the confluence of the Thompson Canyon and Stubblefield Canyon flows. Now 2.6 miles beyond the Kerrick Canyon junction, you cross the combined flow; with no logs spanning the wide creek, it is always a wade, but with a slow current it isn't dangerous. There are campsites on both sides of the ford.

Continuing downcanyon on the opposite bank, after a quarter mile, you leave the shady floor for slabs and brushy slopes, beginning a sometimes-steep climb toward a gap in Macomb Ridge. The walking is slow and rocky, with false passes repeatedly dashing your hopes that you are "almost on top." After crossing a corn lily meadow, the trail turns northwest, leading to the true highpoint, then descends 550 feet into Tilden Canyon. As the trail levels out you reach a junction, 3.1 miles past the Stubblefield crossing, where you turn right (north), still following the PCT, while left (south) leads to Tiltill Valley. Just 0.1 mile later is a second junction, where the PCT trends left (northwest) to Wilma (not Wilmer, as appears on some signs) Lake, while you leave this thoroughfare, taking the right-hand (northeast) option to Tilden Lake. *Note:* If you want to shorten your loop, you could at this point turn toward Wilma Lake, with campsites in 1.2 miles at the lake's eastern shore, and the next day continue straight ahead (west) 0.6 mile to rejoin the main circuit at a junction in Jack Main Canyon. This saves a total distance of 5.2 miles, but you miss Tilden Lake.

Continuing toward Tilden Lake, the now smaller trail tracks Tilden Canyon Creek north in a narrow drainage flanked by Macomb and Bailey Ridges. You stroll through a dense lodgepole forest with a lush understory of dwarf bilberry. Skirting first the western edge of a shallow pond, then a larger, equally shallow lake, you reach the headwaters of the Tilden Canyon Creek drainage and descend just slightly to Tilden Lake—and the Tilden Creek drainage. More than 2 miles in length, Tilden Lake is Yosemite's longest lake, but it pinches to less than 0.1 mile in width in places. Your route skirts the southern shore of the lake; soon after the trail turns decidedly westward, you can head north from the trail to find sandy campsites nestled among slabs with stunning views upcanyon to Saurian Crest. If you seek more sheltered campsites, continue west on the trail until you reach Tilden Lake's outlet (8,890'; 38.09391°N, 119.61972°W), cross to the north side, and follow the north shore, encountering a selection of campsites as you walk the first 0.75 mile of shoreline.

DAY 5 (Tilden Lake to Jack Main Canyon, 6.7 miles): Tilden Creek spills steeply from Tilden Lake's outlet, dashing toward Jack Main Canyon through a delightful hemlock forest. Your trail switchbacks beside it, with views across the canyon, up Chittenden Peak's steep black-streaked walls, and to the tumbling creek beside you. After a nearly 600-foot drop, the gradient eases, and you descend more gradually through lodgepole forest, passing a small tarn en route to a ford of Falls Creek. Beyond, you pass some small campsites and arrive shortly at a junction with the PCT. Here you turn left (south), while right (north) leads to the headwaters of Falls Creek and into Emigrant Wilderness at Dorothy Lake, the route of Trip 31.

Your route now descends alongside Falls Creek for nearly 8 miles. For the 1.7 miles to your next junction, the meandering creek is mostly hidden from view by a veil of lodgepole pine, as the trail crosses intermittently onto slabs, then back into forest. At the north end of an expansive lodgepole flat, you pass a ranger cabin on the right, and soon thereafter a junction where you continue straight down Falls Creek, while the PCT is the left (east) branch that almost immediately fords Falls Creek and reaches Wilma Lake.

Continuing through the lodgepole glade, you pass a selection of large campsites, then trending east to round a small knob, you pass a stock fence. This marks the start of the Jack Main Canyon Yosemite lovers come to see—Falls Creek tumbling, dashing, falling across granite slabs, punctuated by swimming pools (at low flows) and, where the gradient eases, a deep, aqua-colored meandering channel with steep domes behind. The next mile or so is probably the showiest section—first broad granite slabs with a thin veneer of water, then a narrower gorge with cascades and potholes. The trail skirts to the northwest across polished slabs, blasted in places for easier passage. Then quite suddenly, the river pours into a broad, flat meadow, 0.75 mile in length, and the trail turns to follow the meadow-slab boundary.

The meandering river channel is now broad and deep—and mostly hidden behind dense willows. Next, passing through a granite gap, while the river detours south, you skirt a picturesque lake backdropped by a lichen-covered cliff. A short distance later you reach a junction with a cutoff trail heading left (southeast), leading to the trail descending to Tiltill Meadow.

Continuing right (straight ahead; southwest), another 0.1 mile of hiking brings you to the northeastern end of a long meadow known informally as "Paradise Valley." Along its fringes you will find a selection of campsites. Lodgepole pine groves house the biggest sites, including a large stock camp, while smaller tent sites can be found among slabs ringing the meadow (7,670'; 38.04672°N, 119.67132°W).

DAY 6 (Jack Main Canyon to Laurel Lake, 9.5 miles): You begin this day walking to the western end of Paradise Valley, where Andrews Peak, an impressive dome, commands the view south, and Mahan Peak lies to the north. Their ridges come together, pinching the meadow closed, and the trail detours north across slabs. As it descends back to river level, you sneak along a narrow isthmus between the stream and an aspen-bordered pond that lies just north of the trail, fed by groundwater not the stream. Winding northward, you pass another beautiful lakelet. It is striking how these lakes and the adjacent river, separated by only 30 feet in places, are not linked by channels. Continuing down, the never-fast trail undulates moderately, alternately visiting sunny benches of glaciated granite dotted with huckleberry oak thickets and precariously rooted western junipers, as well as pocket stands of lodgepoles and stately red firs, underlain by a thicket of ferns. Campsites are sparse and tiny, but swimming holes abound.

Descending a long run of stone steps, you reach the point where the trail parts ways with Falls Creek, the creek descending steeply toward Lake Vernon, while you begin a 600-foot, 0.9-mile climb to the crest of Moraine Ridge. Midway, you transition from granite slab to deeper soil with stands of trees, indicating you've just crossed onto the morainal deposits for which the ridge is named. From the high point you have just over a 3-mile descent along Moraine Ridge, a generally gradual, easy, sandy walk—it would be perfect were it not for the lack of shade, the aftermath of fires in the past decades. The route stays mostly west of the edge, but detour east to its crest at least once to gaze out across the granite slab country about Lake Vernon.

Eventually you reach a junction, where your route is right (southwest), toward Laurel Lake and Hetch Hetchy Reservoir, while the lateral to Lake Vernon heads left (northeast; Trip 38). Ahead your trail winds down through a landscape burned repeatedly over the years and therefore generally lacking shade but sporting a plethora of wildflower gardens due to abundant moisture and sunlight. An easy 1.25 miles brings you to a junction at the east edge of the Beehive, the site of an 1880s cattlemen's camp (and campsites), where you turn right (west) toward Laurel Lake, while straight ahead (left; southwest) leads to Hetch Hetchy Reservoir, tomorrow's route.

Walk along the northern edge of the Beehive to reach another trail split within 200 steps, where you strike left (west) toward Laurel Lake's south shores and outlet, while right is a sparsely used trail that loops to the lake's northern shore. You drop easily down into a gully, then cross broad Frog Creek, often a wet, bouldery ford in late spring and early summer. Climb steeply west up the creek's north bank to a heavily forested ridge before dropping gently to good campsites near Laurel Lake's outlet. A brief shoreline stint brings you to a junction (6,490'; 37.99432°N, 119.79651°W) with the north-shore trail—branching right (northwest) from here leads to more secluded campsites. Western azalea grows thickly just back of the locally grassy lakeshore, a fragrant accompaniment to tasty huckleberry and thimbleberry. Fishing is fair for rainbow trout, but swimming, especially in July and early August, can be wonderful.

DAY 7 (Laurel Lake to Hetch Hetchy Reservoir, 7.5 miles): Follow Trip 38, Day 4 to the Hetch Hetchy Trailhead.

White Wolf Trailhead			7,866'; 37.86992°N, 119.64884°W		
Destination/ GPS Coordinates	**Trip Type**	**Best Season**	**Pace & Hiking/ Layover Days**	**Total Mileage**	**Permit Required**
40 Grand Canyon of the Tuolumne 37.93424°N 119.50032°W (Cathedral Creek confluence)	Shuttle	Mid to late	Moderate 4/0	30.1	White Wolf to Pate Valley *(Glen Aulin if reversed)*

INFORMATION AND PERMITS: This trip is in Yosemite National Park: wilderness permits and bear canisters are required; pets and firearms are prohibited. Quotas apply, with 60% of permits reservable online up to 24 weeks in advance and 40% available first-come, first-served starting at 11 a.m. the day before your trip's start date. Fires are prohibited above 9,600 feet. See nps.gov/yose/planyourvisit/wildpermits.htm for more details.

DRIVING DIRECTIONS: From the Tioga Road–Big Oak Flat Road junction in Crane Flat, drive northeast 14.5 miles east along Tioga Road (CA 120) to the White Wolf Lodge turn-off. Follow White Wolf Road 1.1 miles to the trailhead parking area, located on the right, just before the entrance to White Wolf Campground. If you are traveling from the east, take Tioga Road 24.8 miles west from the Tuolumne Meadows Store to the White Wolf Road junction. In early summer, White Wolf Road is often closed, adding 1.1 miles to your hike; there is limited parking at the junction alongside Tioga Road.

trip 40 **Grand Canyon of the Tuolumne**

see map on p. 198

> **Trip Data:** 37.93424°N, 119.50032°W (Cathedral Creek confluence); 30.1 miles; 4/0 days
>
> **Topos:** *Tamarack Flat, Hetch Hetchy Reservoir, Ten Lakes, Falls Ridge, Tioga Pass*

HIGHLIGHTS: In taking this trip, you'll experience firsthand what the mighty Tuolumne River and its Pleistocene glacier have created over tens of millions of years—and the water continues to create today. If you have only a couple of days, an out-and-back trip based on Day 1 of this trip, as far as Morrison Creek, makes an easy weekender with a fine view of the Tuolumne River Canyon.

HEADS UP! *If the preceding winter was a heavy one, this trip may be hazardous in early season because of high water and hazardous at any time if needed bridges have been swept away by high runoff—a remarkably regular occurrence along this route.*

HEADS UP! *YARTS provides daily shuttle services between White Wolf and the Tuolumne Meadows Store. Although not required it is best to make reservations in advance. And certainly check the time table to time your exit —or best of all, see if it works to leave a car where you finish the walk and take the shuttle to the trailhead the morning of your trip, eliminating the need to precisely time your exit.*

SHUTTLE DIRECTIONS: Your trip ends at the Lembert Dome parking area in Tuolumne Meadows, 25.1 miles east along Tioga Road (CA 120) from the White Wolf Road. You can shuttle a car or use the local transit system, YARTS, to return to your car at White Wolf Lodge.

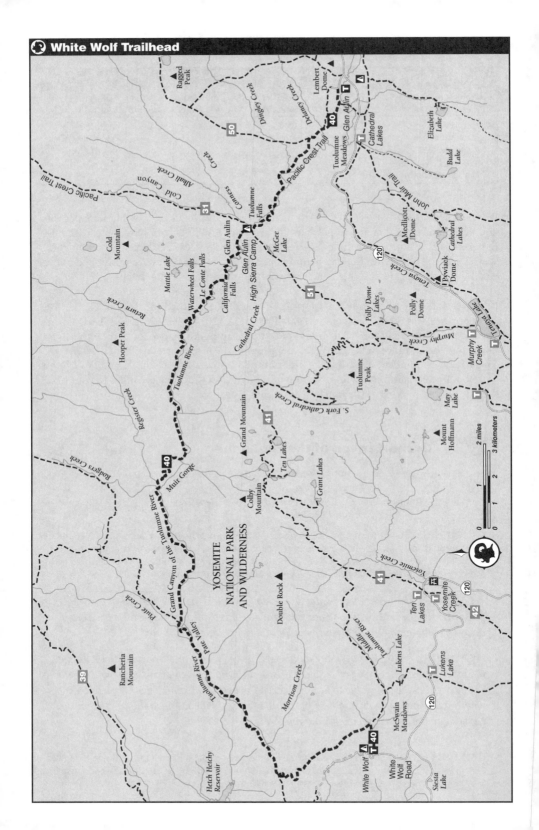

DAY 1 (White Wolf Trailhead to Pate Valley, 10.1 miles): The described trailhead is approximately opposite White Wolf Lodge and just south of the White Wolf Campground entrance road, not along the service road, although you could follow the service road and link back to the described route beyond Harden Lake. The trail begins by skirting the south side of the campground through a flat, lush lodgepole pine forest, continuing much the same to the seasonal Middle Tuolumne River. At full flow it is crossed via a log or sandy-bottomed wade. A few steps farther lead to a signed junction, where you turn left (northwest) toward Pate Valley, while right (south) leads to Lukens Lake. The trail strikes north across rolling uplands to cross a nearly imperceptible ridge. Then descending, the trail follows a lovely creek to a beautiful, forest-fringed meadow dense with flowers until midsummer. Beyond, the route climbs gently for an easy mile to a more open, distinctive ridgetop. Here, you stand on the crest of a moraine that was deposited by a glacier that once flowed down the Grand Canyon of the Tuolumne—and therefore impressively marks the height to which ice filled the valley.

Two long switchbacks take you down to a sandy flat with an easily missed, abandoned and unsigned lateral left (west) to Harden Lake, while you continue ahead (right; north-northeast). At first you cannot see the Tuolumne River Canyon, as the trail crosses several more lateral-moraine crests, but after the grade steepens and you descend on switchbacks sparser forest cover permits your first views across the canyon. Just under a mile of switchbacks leads to another junction, 4.3 miles from the trailhead, where left (west) leads again to Harden Lake and you turn right (east) to Pate Valley. Since your descent followed a bedrock rib, you may not have noticed the verdant slopes left and right of you, rich with flowers and thickets of quaking aspen due to abundant moisture. Water collects in the moraine sediments each winter and spring, slowly oozing out during the summer months and irrigating the hillside.

The trail takes you northeast, winding across slabs and seeps, through pocket meadows, and stepping across many small rivulets draining the slopes above. As you cross one particularly densely forested bench, you can suddenly hear Morrison Creek to the right and cross a tributary on a plank bridge. A little beyond, the forest cover opens, and just south of the trail, on a bedrock granite ridge is a choice break spot (and possible campsite) to enjoy the view

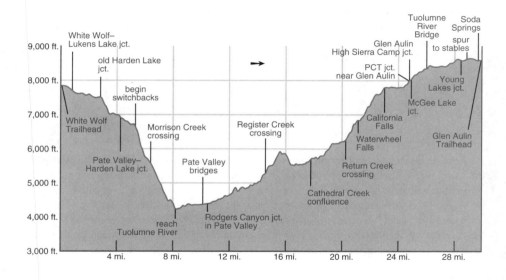

north across the canyon to broad Rancheria Mountain. The trail now begins the final plunge to the bottom of the Grand Canyon of the Tuolumne, still more than 2,000 feet below.

At first, the trail descends steeply on tight, gorgeously constructed switchbacks through the narrow gully that holds Morrison Creek; white fir, incense cedar, sugar pine, and dogwood provide shade. After dropping about 700 feet, the trail leaves the sheltered draw for open slab and views open up dramatically as you traverse north, then east. You cross a bench where you should stop for breathtaking views of this phenomenal canyon, including Hetch Hetchy Reservoir and Rancheria Mountain. There are splendid campsites here as long as Morrison Creek flows (usually through midsummer, but note the flatter stretch of stream near the bench dries out before the steeper sections of creek just 0.1 mile upstream or downstream). Passing another stretch of slab with more camping, you cross Morrison Creek, now shaded by incense cedars, black oaks, and canyon live oaks.

The last 1,200 feet to Pate Valley are mostly across exposed slopes on a steep, in part, cobblestoned trail. Along this magnificent descent you can see and hear the Tuolumne River far below. At an elevation of 5,000 feet, the trail crosses an unmapped seasonal creek channel, doubling as an avalanche chute in the winter. Four hundred feet lower, you cross another mapped seasonal creek. Both of these creeks can be dangerous torrents when runoff is high. At 4,400 feet, the grade levels briefly, and you pass a moraine-dammed seasonal pond before entering tall forest again. Another 200-foot descent brings you to the canyon floor at the western end of Pate Valley.

Here you first encounter campsites on a bench high above the river, under incense cedar shade. If you'd like to camp in grander forest, continue upcanyon; the walking is easy. For the first mile, you are crossing a steep slope without campsites, but thereafter traverse a broad bench. The popular Pate Valley campsites are at the eastern end of this valley, just before the first bridge over the river in a cathedral forest of tall incense cedars, white firs, and ponderosa pines (4,395'; 37.93111°N, 119.59435°W). There are additional campsites on the north side of the river, downstream of the crossing.

DAY 2 (Pate Valley to Cathedral Creek confluence, 7.8 miles): Today's journey takes you through the narrowest and deepest part of the Grand Canyon of the Tuolumne. The trail crosses a pair of bridges, the first over an overflow channel that dries late season, and the second across the main river channel. Once north of the river, you enter a broad flat valley with a densely vegetated wet understory and abundant downed logs from a collection of fires. Surrounded by wildflowers and miniature wild strawberries you come to a junction with the trail that leads left (north) to Pleasant Valley and Rodgers Canyon, while you turn right (east), toward Glen Aulin, passing through a narrow marshy corridor.

WHY THE MARSH?
Perhaps bedrock, acting like an underground dam, has forced groundwater near the surface here to produce a lush, muddy area. Though it's too wet for trees, many species of water-loving flowers and shrubs thrive here, including cow parsnip and rushes.

Beyond, you cross a sandy flat, then where a granite bluff extends right to the river's edge and the trail is just inches from the flow, you cross a short section of cobblestones set in cement to withstand flooding. If there is water over the trail and you find it unsafe, turn back.

A gentle ascent brings you to another burned area, this one dating to 1985, where the lack of tall trees tells you the fire was quite hot. Just beyond this area you leave the flat river terrace you've been following and come to some fantastically large and deep pools in the bedrock—a fine swimming and fishing spot in late summer. Now 1.4 miles beyond the last junction, the canyon narrows, and the trail stays close to the river. Over the next 1.3 miles there are both spots where you may have to wade during high water and locations where the trail is routed high above the riverbank to avoid the flow.

Next you enter a wider, sunnier valley—another river terrace, composed of sediment deposited in long-ago floods. Be advised: The Grand Canyon of the Tuolumne has a well-earned reputation for having a large population of reptiles, including the ubiquitous blue-bellied western fence lizards, alligator lizards, and quite a few rattlesnakes. Look carefully before stepping over logs or taking a break on a sunny rock. Soon the landscape again pinches closed and you walk gradually along narrower terraces and across slab, passing occasional small campsites and enticing swimming holes.

The canyon closes in further as you approach Muir Gorge. Named after John Muir, a man who eagerly sought out inaccessible places, Muir Gorge is the only part of the canyon whose walls are too steep for a trail, so you're obliged to climb around it. Beyond two live oak–shaded campsites, the trail turns north and begins climbing away from the river; at one point you can look straight up the dark chasm of Muir Gorge.

In an alcove, the trail crosses Rodgers Canyon's creek on a bridge, then wades adjacent Register Creek, difficult at high flows. You have now covered 4.6 miles for the day—this terrain is not for fast walking! Tight, shaded switchbacks ascend the side canyon of Register Creek before the trail trends southeast across a sandy passageway between slabs. After a short descent, you switchback up another 500 feet to top a granite spur overlooking the river—it is well worth a short detour south for a better peek into mysterious Muir Gorge.

Cutting across granite slabs and through forested draws, the trail descends back to the river above Muir Gorge where the canyon again widens. In another quarter mile, you come to a seasonal stream channel in white gravel. Between the trail and the river there's an excellent campsite—the first of many good choices over the next gentle 1.2 miles. Soon Cathedral Creek, spilling down the canyon's southern wall will catch your attention. The river jogs a little south at the confluence and here, on a knob overlooking the Tuolumne River and staring straight at Cathedral Creek are some more good campsites (5,654'; 37.93424°N, 119.50032°W).

DAY 3 (Cathedral Creek confluence to Glen Aulin High Sierra Camp, 6.8 miles): You begin today with a steady 1.6-mile ascent, soon entering landscape burned in the 2009 Wildcat Fire, making most of the previously popular campsites below the Return Creek confluence less appealing. At 2.5 miles into your day, a bridge takes you across Return Creek, and now the real climbing—and falls—begin.

Tuolumne River   Photo by Elizabeth Wenk

Waterwheel Falls looms above, and, at peak runoff in June, is thunderous and spectacular as protrusions in the granite throw wheeling sprays of water far out into the air. Don't be in a hurry because these falls are best viewed from below, and on a hot day, you'll appreciate their cooling spray as you begin to climb 600 feet up steep, exposed switchbacks north of the falls.

The trail returns to the river just above the brink of the falls, but the ascent pauses just briefly, soon climbing up an open, juniper-dotted slope, then passing close to the river at Le Conte Falls. These are my favorite of the cascades for a long break, for you can share the granite slabs with the tumbling water, giving you a good vantage point of some smaller waterwheels.

Leaving behind the last incense cedars and sugar pines, the trail becomes increasingly steep and sunny until you pass close beneath the massive south buttress of Wildcat Point. The grade eases just before you reach California Falls, and a relatively short climb then brings you to the top of these, the last of the three major falls below Glen Aulin High Sierra Camp. Glen Aulin itself, the valley through which you soon pass, was extensively burned in 1987 and much of the ground is covered with crisscrossing trunks, with the only campsites tiny nooks near the valley's northern walls about halfway along the glen. At the western end of the glen, you cross the outlet creek from Mattie Lake, which at times disperses to cover 300 feet of trail. Indeed, long stretches of trail through Glen Aulin are wet during June—if you've come when the waterfalls are at their peak, it is wise to accept wet shoes and just wade through here.

CYCLES OF NATURE

This walk takes you through landscape bearing a mosaic of fire scars, the most recent around White Wolf, from 2010, 2014, and 2020. Following fire, species that can resprout, including aspens in Glen Aulin and black oaks at lower elevations, are the first to "bounce back," providing a splash of green within a year. If a fire is sufficiently hot, the conifers die and take decades to reestablish. Glen Aulin was burned more than 30 years ago, but the lodgepole pines have only recently started producing cones, and later germinants, like firs, will take many more years to become mature trees.

After more than a mile of level ground, you leave Glen Aulin and briefly climb slabs to a junction with the Pacific Crest Trail (PCT). Turn right (south) on the PCT and almost immediately meet a spur trail left (east) that crosses Conness Creek on a bridge to Glen Aulin High Sierra Camp. There is a backpackers' campground with pit toilets, piped water, and bear boxes at the back of the camp. This is the last legal camping before Tuolumne Meadows, so you must either stay here (7,930'; 37.91051°N, 119.41699°W) or complete the entire distance described under Day 4.

DAY 4 (Glen Aulin High Sierra Camp to Tuolumne Meadows, 5.4 miles): Follow Trip 31, Day 8 to the Glen Aulin Trailhead.

If you need to take a YARTS shuttle bus back to White Wolf, from Lembert Dome, walk west along the shoulder of CA 120 to the Tuolumne Meadows store.

Ten Lakes Trailhead				7,493'; 37.85231°N, 119.57598°W	
Destination/ GPS Coordinates	Trip Type	Best Season	Pace & Hiking/ Layover Days	Total Mileage	Permit Required
41 Ten Lakes Traverse 37.90218°N 119.51414°W (Ten Lake 6)	Shuttle	Mid to late	Moderate 3/0	20.5	Ten Lakes (Murphy Creek if reversed)

INFORMATION AND PERMITS: This trip is in Yosemite National Park: wilderness permits and bear canisters are required; pets and firearms are prohibited. Quotas apply, with 60% of permits reservable online up to 24 weeks in advance and 40% available first-come, first-served starting at 11 a.m. the day before your trip's start date. Fires are prohibited above 9,600 feet. See nps.gov/yose/planyourvisit/wildpermits.htm for more details.

DRIVING DIRECTIONS: The Ten Lakes Trailhead lies on Tioga Road (CA 120) exactly halfway between Crane Flat and the Tuolumne Meadows Campground—you have a 19.7-mile drive from either location. The trailhead is immediately across the street from the larger pullout signposted for the Yosemite Creek Trailhead; you may park on either side of the road. These pullouts are immediately west of the highway bridges signed YOSEMITE CREEK. YARTS, the transit system servicing Tioga Road, will drop you at this trailhead.

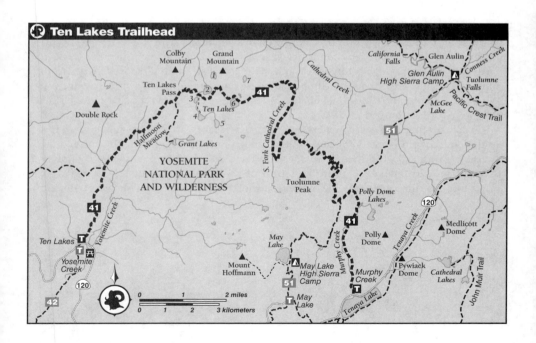

see map on p. 203

trip 41 Ten Lakes Traverse

Trip Data: 37.90218°N, 119.51414°W (Ten Lakes 6);
20.5 miles; 3/0 days

Topos: Yosemite Falls, Ten Lakes, Falls Ridge, Tenaya Lake

HIGHLIGHTS: The Ten Lakes Basin is a popular destination, with seven lakes to choose from, with personalities to fit everyone's preferences. This walk then leads you to a spectacular shelf north of Tuolumne Peak with expansive views across northern Yosemite.

HEADS UP! *YARTS provides daily shuttle services along the CA 120 corridor. Although not required it is best to make reservations in advance. And certainly check the time table to time your exit—or best of all, see if it works to leave a car where you finish the walk and take the shuttle to the trailhead the morning of your trip, eliminating the need to precisely time your exit.*

SHUTTLE DIRECTIONS: Your trip ends at the Murphy Creek Trailhead at Tenaya Lake, 11.75 miles east along Tioga Road (CA 120) from the Ten Lakes Trailhead. You can shuttle a car or use the local transit system, YARTS, to return to your car.

YARTS provides daily bus services along Tioga Road. They will stop at any pullout where it is safe to do so, including the Ten Lakes/Yosemite Creek Trailhead parking area. Since they will not pick you up from unscheduled locations, such as the Murphy Creek Trailhead, from this endpoint, take the Tuolumne Meadows shuttle to the Tuolumne Meadows store and continue onto Yosemite Creek with YARTS.

DAY 1 (Ten Lakes Trailhead to Ten Lake 6, 7.4 miles): From the west end of the northside parking lot, a spur trail goes 0.1 mile northwest to a junction, where you turn right (north) to hike upcanyon, while left (south) leads across CA 120 to follow Yosemite Creek to Yosemite Valley. Tramping through a lodgepole pine flat, the trail soon diverges from unseen Yosemite Creek and you climb moderately onto drier granitic slopes that give you views of the Yosemite Creek Canyon and Mount Hoffmann. (*Note:* the first miles of this trip were partially burned in 2020.)

Eventually the trail levels, enters a forest, and reaches a creekside junction with a trail that leads left (west) to White Wolf, a campground and lodge lying 5.5 miles to the west. You turn right (northeast), boulder-hop the creek, and begin a moderate climb of a well-forested moraine left from the retreat of a large glacier about 15,000 years ago. Your forested climb ends atop the moraine, behind which lies crescent-shaped Halfmoon

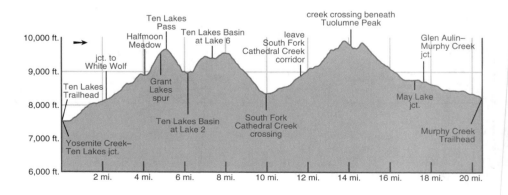

Ten Lake 2   Photo by Elizabeth Wenk

Meadow. The trail cuts across the meadow's relatively dry north edge (with a campsite in the forest at the meadow's northeastern end) and embarks on roughly three dozen short, steep switchbacks that guide you above the meadow. In sections they are dry with sagebrush, but elsewhere a delightful tangle of dense flowers thrives in the seasonal moisture.

Almost reaching the Tuolumne–Merced Rivers drainage divide, you trend right, still in the Merced drainage, and parallel the ridge to a junction with the trail to the Grant Lakes (right; south). There are campsites at both lakes. From the trail junction, the trail to Ten Lakes (the left-hand, northeast-bearing option) climbs gently across a gravelly slope that can be covered in midsummer with large, deliciously scented lupines. These taper off just before you cross the county line crest, Ten Lakes Pass, so strikingly flat that there are view-rich, mosquito-sparse campsites atop it (as long as nearby seeps provide water). A sea of summits lies to the north and east, with three beauties on Yosemite's boundary stealing the show. Due north Tower Peak dominates the view, to the northeast it is the sharp-peaked Sawtooth Range, crowned by Matterhorn Peak, and yet farther east it is the vertical face of Mount Conness that grabs your attention.

As you start your descent, a panorama of steep-sided, glaciated Ten Lakes Basin opens all around you, the three western lakes clearly evident. The view east improves with descent, especially of Mount Dana and Mount Gibbs, gigantic red mountains, while that to the north slowly dwindles. The descent is not particularly fast walking. In places it is sandy, but elsewhere it is rocky underfoot, so take your time and enjoy the view.

The descent ends at a creek that flows from Lake 3 (south of the trail) to Lake 2 (north of the trail). Just across the creek is a use trail that leads 0.1 mile southwest to good camping along Lake 3. Continuing straight (southeast), you approach the southwestern tip of Lake 2 and are soon just 40 feet above it. Here you encounter a maze of use trails descending toward the shore and it is difficult to discern which is the actual trail that continues east—worry not, the network of routes coalesces in a wet meadow at the lake's head where a large sign and helpful arrow proclaim TRAIL. There are camping options all around Lake 2, with the biggest sites at its northern end. Leaving the lakeshore, the main trail reappears and then climbs about 500 feet in elevation to a divide south of Grand Mountain. It next drops southeast, traversing broken slabs with scattered trees, including majestic junipers. The gradient then nearly flattens to zero and enters denser tree cover as you reach Lake 6's shore, 1.25 miles from Lake 2. Its northwest shore has enough flat land to accommodate quite a few groups (9,405'; 37.90218°N, 119.51414°W), with smaller private campsites along its western shores.

TEN LAKES BASIN LAYOVER

It is well worth planning a layover day in the Ten Lakes Basin, for there are seven major lakes to visit—each remarkably unique, some best visited for the views, some for early-morning fishing, and others for swimming. The warmer lakes are those north of the trail, on the bench overlooking the Grand Canyon of the Tuolumne, while the best fishing is to be had in the deep lakes to the south, sitting at the base of the escarpment. In clockwise sequence: Lake 2 sees the most use, being the first lake reached on the trail. It is a relatively warm swimming lake with open views. Lake 1 sites in an open bowl beneath Grand Mountain. It is shallower and probably the best swimming lake. Lake 7 is a small, quite shallow lake ringed by dense lodgepole pine forest and some splendid exfoliating cliffs. It, too, is warm for swimming but far out of the way and with relatively few unvegetated campsites. Crossing to the south side of the trail, Lake 6 is popular and beautiful, up again a steep wall, but with open, flat shores inviting campers and anglers. Lake 5 has a rugged, near-alpine feel to it, but such unexpectedly rugged shorelines make camping near impossible; it would be a good lake for fishing. Notably deep, Lake 4 sits in an enclosed basin, set directly beneath an escarpment. Steep slopes drop straight to the lake on all sides with the only camping to the northeast of the outlet. Fishing is again good. Lake 3 is meadow and forest ringed, with ample campsites, especially near its outlet. It is a splendid camping location, with gentle lakeside terrain and steep ridges rising to the southwest. Decent use trails lead from Lake 2 to Lake 1 and from Lake 2 to Lake 3 and onto Lake 4, but if you're traveling farther afield, it's all cross-country.

DAY 2 (Ten Lakes to Tuolumne Peak Ridge, 7.3 miles): From the eastern end of the Ten Lakes Basin, you climb briefly up a dry slope. Where the slope eases, the trail cuts into a moist drainage and follows it across a very shallow pass. You now descend quite gradually, the trail following a fracture-delineated corridor while hugging the base of low, blocky bluffs; staring up you see its crest is dotted by twisted windswept junipers, but you need to take a 5-minute detour to enjoy the view from atop. The trail itself continues through lush lodgepole forest.

Quite suddenly, the gradient increases, and you are on a dry slope, again with junipers and the occasional Jeffrey pine, switchbacking diligently into the South Fork Cathedral Creek drainage. Impressively steep walls ring the drainage's head and you are glad your route isn't seeking passage through them. A seasonally wet ford takes you to the river's east bank, which you ascend south for 2 miles, passing numerous small campsites along the way; the best are near the top of the creekside climb. (In late season it is wise to camp here for the night, as the water sources along the bench you will follow next can dry up.)

Switchbacks take you east out of the South Fork drainage, alternately climbing across open slabby slopes and through forest pockets, until you cross onto continuous granite slabs for the final zigzags. Rolling over the lip out of the South Fork drainage, the north side of Tuolumne Peak fans out broadly, and the trail follows a series of broken benches across it. It is a beautiful landscape, with repeated granite spurs proffering exquisite views across Yosemite's northern lands and beyond to Emigrant Wilderness. You drop again and again to small tarns and rivulets lasting most of the summer, edged by dense clusters of hemlocks. There are many hidden camping options along here if you collect water from the little creeks and trend north to camp in the sandy flats on a knob. Indeed, starting where the trail first levels out near a seasonal tarn, there are places to stop on every major knob for 1.4 miles east; the waypoint given is near the midpoint (9,895'; 37.88657°N, 119.48295°W; no campfires).

DAY 3 (Tuolumne Peak Ridge to Murphy Creek Trailhead, 5.8 miles): The trail continues along the bench, passing the largest drainage off Tuolumne Peak about 0.4 mile beyond the suggested camp—this is the easiest place to ascend the peak to enjoy its 360-degree view. Another 0.4 mile brings you to a pair of seasonal tarns, with some more superb campsites. The next few switchbacks take you to the top of a spur, beyond which the trail turns to the south and begins a long descent down the northeast side of Tuolumne Peak. The walking is generally pleasant and sandy, with various flower displays breaking the monotony, since views aren't striking compared to those you enjoyed before.

After descending about 750 feet, the trail begins a long, downward traverse to the south, crossing a slope covered with avalanche debris, then lower down, a second. These are immediately identifiable by the sudden lack of tree cover paired with scrubby aspens and an abundance of tree trunks all facing downslope. Soon after the second of the avalanche slopes, the trail hooks to the northeast and reaches a junction, where left (east) is your route to Murphy Creek, while right (south) leads to May Lake (Trip 51).

The next trail segment is just 0.45 mile long, crossing through a lush forest just south of a rather boggy (and buggy) meadow. It leads to another junction, where you turn right (south) to Murphy Creek, while left (northeast) leads to McGee Lake and Glen Aulin (Trip 51). Crossing a landscape of low-angle, polished granite slabs interspersed with lodgepole forest, you spot one tarn after another along the trail's periphery—these are some of the Polly Dome Lakes, the larger and more aesthetic of which lie more than a third of a mile east of the trail (with campsites at the largest). Murphy Creek is their outlet, and you first follow its western bank, eventually stepping across to its eastern side.

Much of your walk down early-drying Murphy Creek is through unassuming lodgepole pine forest and your views are restricted to the ridges on either side of the drainage. There are, however, some wonderful stretches where you are walking down bare, smooth slabs right on the river's banks, perfect for a last snack or lunch break before you reach the trailhead. Back under forest cover, the gradient increases just a little as you traipse the final stretch to the Murphy Creek Trailhead (8,185'; 37.83431°N, 119.46321°W).

Climbing out of the South Fork Cathedral Creek   Photo by Elizabeth Wenk

Yosemite Creek Trailhead   7,406'; 37.85193°N, 119.57672°W

Destination/ GPS Coordinates	Trip Type	Best Season	Pace & Hiking/ Layover Days	Total Mileage	Permit Required
42 Yosemite Creek to Yosemite Valley 37.78156°N 119.61205°W (Bluejay Creek crossing)	Shuttle	Early to late	Leisurely 2/0	12.1	Yosemite Creek (*Yosemite Falls if reversed*)

INFORMATION AND PERMITS: This trip is in Yosemite National Park: wilderness permits and bear canisters are required; pets and firearms are prohibited. Quotas apply, with 60% of permits reservable online up to 24 weeks in advance and 40% available first-come, first-served starting at 11 a.m. the day before your trip's start date. Fires are prohibited above 9,600 feet. See nps.gov/yose/planyourvisit/wildpermits.htm for more details.

DRIVING DIRECTIONS: The trailhead for Yosemite Creek lies on Tioga Road (CA 120) exactly halfway between Crane Flat and the Tuolumne Meadows Campground—you have a 19.7-mile drive from either location. The trailhead is immediately across the street

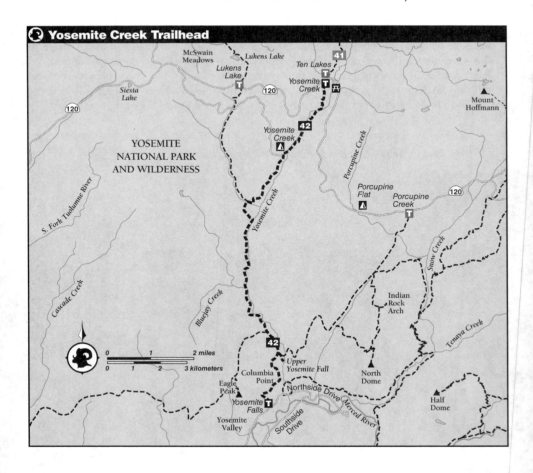

from the smaller Ten Lakes Trailhead; you may park on either side of the road. These pullouts are immediately west of the highway bridges signed YOSEMITE CREEK. YARTS, the transit system servicing Tioga Road and continuing onto Yosemite Valley, will drop you at this trailhead.

trip 42 ## Yosemite Creek to Yosemite Valley

Trip Data: 37.78156°N, 119.61205°W (Bluejay Creek crossing); 12.1 miles; 2/0 days
Topos: *Yosemite Falls, Half Dome*

HIGHLIGHTS: This is perhaps the best hike along which to observe the differences between two distinct landforms: steep-walled Yosemite Valley and the rolling uplands of Yosemite Creek. This route detours to the dramatic viewpoint at the brink of Upper Yosemite Fall before leading you to the Yosemite Valley floor.

HEADS UP! *YARTS provides daily bus services along Tioga Road and to Yosemite Valley, making this shuttle hike feasible if you have a single vehicle. YARTS offers multiple daily services along this route. In Yosemite Valley it stops at the Yosemite Valley Visitor Center, shuttle stops 5 and 9, and then continues along CA 120 to Tuolumne Meadows, passing the Yosemite Creek Trailhead en route. Check their website for schedule details.*

SHUTTLE DIRECTIONS: Your trip ends in Yosemite Valley at the Yosemite Falls Trailhead, located in Camp 4, a campground. Just across Northside Drive is Yosemite Valley Shuttle stop 7 and the Yosemite Falls day-use parking lot. From this location, you can take the Yosemite Valley Shuttle to a YARTS stop (shuttle stops 5 and 9 in Yosemite Village) or pick up a car you shuttled before your hike. In Yosemite Valley, backpackers must leave their car in one of the designated overnight lots, either the Curry Village parking lot (shuttle stops 14 and 20) or the hiker parking area, located along the road to Happy Isles (closest to shuttle stop 15).

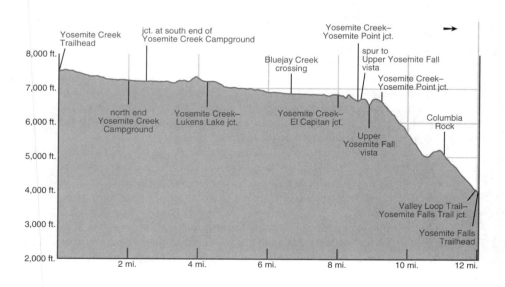

Upper Yosemite Fall   Photo by Elizabeth Wenk

DAY 1 (**Yosemite Creek Trailhead to Bluejay Creek, 6.5 miles**): Departing from the western corner of the parking pullout, the trail soon bends south, following a lush gully at the base of granite bluffs. Jeffrey pines and fibrous-barked junipers cling to the shallow soils of slabs you cross, while lodgepole pines and red fir thrive in deeper soil pockets. After 0.9 mile of following the rambling trail well west of the river, you reach and ford wide Yosemite Creek—potentially quite dangerous from late May through June, if no convenient trees span the channel. The next 1.1 miles follow the creek's east bank, alternating between flower-filled forest and sandy flats and eventually leading to the north end of Yosemite Creek Campground. (If you know it is a high-water year, an alternative start to this hike would be either to walk the campground road or to begin at the "Lukens Lake to Yosemite Creek Trailhead" farther west along CA 120 and follow that trail 3.3 miles south, merging with this hike's description in paragraph 4 and avoiding the ford.)

Walking south along the campground's eastern spur road, you first pass a junction with the old Tioga Road (too overgrown to follow; left, east), and after 0.5 mile recross Yosemite Creek on a bridge. Turning west, you pass a pit toilet and cross a smaller tributary, reaching the western side of the campground. Just beyond the tributary, the trail resumes, departing left (south) of the road.

The hike continues south along a sparsely forested shelf a short way west of the creek with views of the water tumbling down the granite-lined channel. The flower display can be showy, especially in late June when the magenta mountain pride penstemon lives up to its name. About a mile beyond the campground, the shelf peters out and you'll climb up a ridge away from the creek. The route is across barren bedrock (and lightly burned in 2020) but is adequately marked. Large boulders resting atop polished slabs constitute evidence of the glaciers that descended from Mount Hoffmann to the northeast. From the ridge, you can look across the canyon and see a low dome that is exfoliating—shedding slabs of granite as a giant onion might peel its layers.

Short switchbacks guide you down from the ridge, then the trail heads west to three closely spaced creeks of a tributary canyon. Between the first and second is a junction with a lightly used trail, which heads 3.3 miles north to Tioga Road at the Lukens Lake parking area (the alternative, high water starting point). The flat you have just entered was partially burned by the Dark Hole Fire in 2014. You'll note charred patches and adjacent intact conifer stands—this is an example of how a fire *should* burn, clearing some vegetation, but leaving many of the mature trees fairly unscathed. Lucky for hikers as well, the large camping area between the trail and creek is still shaded by live trees.

Descending steeply down a small gully, the trail again reaches the creek's bank 0.5 mile beyond the junction. Small pools soon appear in the creekbed and farther downstream, the pools are interspersed with water-polished slabs. None of the pools is large enough for a swim, though many are suitable for a refreshing dip until the creek dries up in August. There are no good campsites along this stretch, but it is certainly delightful walking. A little over a mile later the gradient eases and the pervasive granite outcrops yield to larger forest patches. For the next mile, such as near (but not at) where Bluejay Creek flows into Yosemite Creek (6,842'; 37.78156°N, 119.61205°W), there are a selection of small campsites; if crossing Yosemite Creek is safe, there are other choices in forested flats on the east side of the creek.

DAY 2 (Bluejay Creek to Yosemite Valley, 5.6 miles): The next day, regain the trail, continuing downstream (south) toward Yosemite Valley. Beyond Bluejay Creek, the trail temporarily veers away from the river channel to skirt around a large gravel bar, then winds southeast to cross seasonal Eagle Peak Creek. A moderate-size campsite lies between it and Yosemite Creek, the last legal camping option along the route. You reach the junction 0.25 mile later with the trail traversing Yosemite Valley's northern rim west to the Tamarack Flat Campground, visiting Eagle Peak and El Capitan. Your trail continues left (south), separated from Yosemite Creek by a series of knobs and climbs in and out of a succession of gullies, all in a straight line, undoubtedly indicative of a major fracture in the bedrock.

The final gully begins to drop more steeply and soon reaches a junction, where left (east) leads to the Upper Yosemite Fall vista and straight ahead (right; southwest) to Yosemite Valley. Not wanting to miss the superb vista from the rim, you turn left and make a brief climb to an adjacent broad crest with another junction, where right (south) leads to the Upper Yosemite Fall vista. Turn right and follow the spur trail south, almost reaching the valley's rim, before you veer east (left) at a juniper and descend steps to a fenced-in viewpoint. Positioned beside the lip of Upper Yosemite Fall you see and hear it plunge all the way down its 1,430-foot drop to the rocks below

After returning up the crest you can briefly take a trail east to a bridge over Yosemite Creek and obtain water. However, be careful! Occasionally people wading in the creek's icy water slip on the glass-smooth creek bottom and are swiftly carried over the fall's brink—this has even occurred at low water flows. From the creek's bridge you could also continue eastward an additional 1 mile up the trail to Yosemite Point, a highly scenic goal.

But, continuing the described route, from the brink of Upper Yosemite Fall, retrace your steps back to the main trail and begin your descent to Yosemite Valley. There are about 135 switchbacks along this trail, and the rocks jutting out of them are too often gravelly and slippery, so take it slow and watch your step, especially since you are wearing a backpack. The first stretch is down a brushy gully, out of sight of the falls, but eventually you trend left into a stand of oaks, bay trees, and Douglas-firs, all receiving some windblown moisture from Upper Yosemite Fall's spray.

You switchback on down beneath forest cover and around here your first views of the fall—from below—appear. Exiting the forest cover again you traverse nearly due south at the base of tall, vertical cliffs, passing a winter closure gate, and immediately completing a single upward switchback.

With 1.4 miles to go to trail's end, you make a mostly shady traverse 0.35 mile to Columbia Rock. From the railing at Columbia Rock, at 5,031 feet elevation, you have a panoramic view of most of Yosemite Valley, from Half Dome and the Quarter Domes in the east to the Cathedral Spires in the west. This is the Goldilocks elevation for viewing Yosemite Valley—high enough that you appreciate its depth, but low enough that the rim and surrounding peaks still tower overhead. Embarking on a series of short, steep, switchbacks down an unstable, gravelly slope, you duck back into forest cover and traverse farther west before beginning the last leg of the trip, a mostly viewless descent zigzagging down under the shade of canyon live oaks and being annoyed by pesky gnats. The endless giant talus blocks are the result of past rockfalls; these fell long ago and are lichen and moss covered, but rockfalls occur annually in Yosemite, continually changing the landscape. The switchbacking ends at the intersection of the Valley Loop Trail, and, on it, you turn left (northeast) and walk the final 400 feet to the trailhead, located near the Camp 4 Walk-In Campground kiosk. If you have a car waiting for you somewhere in Yosemite Valley, the closest shuttle stop is 0.1 mile to the south, across Northside Drive, at the east end of the Yosemite Falls day-use parking area. The YARTS shuttle, with trips back up to the Yosemite Creek Trailhead, stops at the Yosemite Valley Visitor Center, reached by taking the Valley Shuttle to stop 9.

View from near Columbia Point to Yosemite Valley and Half Dome   Photo by Elizabeth Wenk

May Lake Trailhead
8,856'; 37.83280°N, 119.49109°W

Destination/ GPS Coordinates	Trip Type	Best Season	Pace & Hiking/ Layover Days	Total Mileage	Permit Required
51 High Sierra Camp Loop, northwest section (in reverse of description; alternate start point; see page 245)	Shuttle	Mid to late	Moderate 3/0	16.8	May Lake (Glen Aulin as described)

INFORMATION AND PERMITS: This trip is in Yosemite National Park: wilderness permits and bear canisters are required; pets and firearms are prohibited. Quotas apply, with 60% of permits reservable online up to 24 weeks in advance and 40% available first-come, first-served starting at 11 a.m. the day before your trip's start date. Fires are prohibited above 9,600 feet. See nps.gov/yose/planyourvisit/wildpermits.htm for more details.

DRIVING DIRECTIONS: From the Tioga Road–Big Oak Flat Road junction in Crane Flat, drive northeast 27 miles up Tioga Road (CA 120) to May Lake Road, a segment of old CA 120. (This turn is 3.2 miles east of the Porcupine Flat Campground.) If you are driving from the east, the turn is 12.6 miles west of the Tuolumne Meadows Campground or 2.3 miles west of the Olmsted Point vista pullout. Follow May Lake Road 1.8 miles to its end; the trailhead is on the left near the toilets. Note the May Lake Road may be closed for several weeks after Tioga Road opens for the summer, adding 1.8 miles to your hike.

Sunrise Lakes Trailhead
8,166'; 37.82573°N, 119.46996°W

Destination/ GPS Coordinates	Trip Type	Best Season	Pace & Hiking/ Layover Days	Total Mileage	Permit Required
43 Sunrise Lakes and Sunrise High Sierra Camp 37.79404°N 119.43412°W	Out-and-back	Mid to late	Moderate 2/1	10.4	Sunrise Lakes
44 Clouds Rest Traverse to Yosemite Valley 37.76784°N 119.48923°W (Clouds Rest)	Shuttle	Mid to late	Moderate 2/1	16.3	Sunrise Lakes (Happy Isles to Sunrise Pass Thru if reversed)
47 Cathedral Lakes, Echo Creek, and Sunrise Lakes (in reverse of description; see page 230)	Shuttle	Mid to late	Moderate 4/1	23.0	Sunrise Lakes (Cathedral Lakes as described)
51 High Sierra Camp Loop, northwest section (in reverse of description; see page 245)	Shuttle	Mid to late	Moderate 3/0	16.8	May Lake (Glen Aulin as described)

INFORMATION AND PERMITS: These trips are in Yosemite National Park: wilderness permits and bear canisters are required; pets and firearms are prohibited. Quotas apply, with

60% of permits reservable online up to 24 weeks in advance and 40% available first-come, first-served starting at 11 a.m. the day before your trip's start date. Fires are prohibited above 9,600 feet. See nps.gov/yose/planyourvisit/wildpermits.htm for more details.

DRIVING DIRECTIONS: The Sunrise Lakes Trailhead is along Tioga Road (CA 120) at a large pullout at a highway bend near Tenaya Lake's southwest shore. It is located 30.7 miles northeast of Crane Flat and 8.7 miles southwest of the Tuolumne Meadows Campground. There are pit toilets at the trailhead.

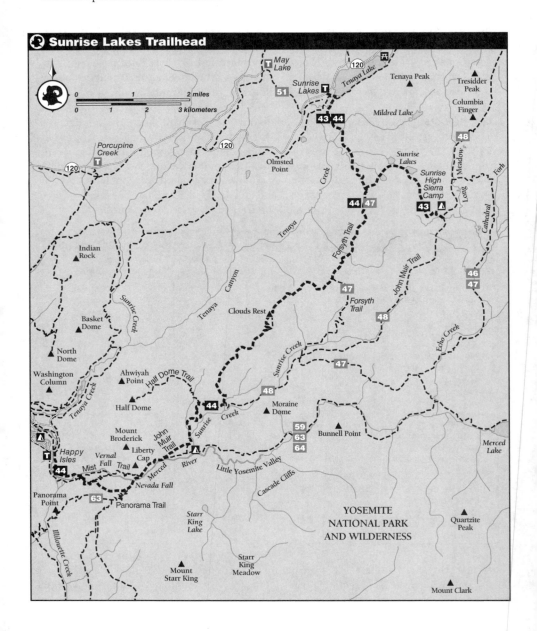

trip 43   ## Sunrise Lakes and Sunrise High Sierra Camp

   Trip Data: 37.79404°N, 119.43412°W; 10.4 miles; 2/1 days
   Topos: *Tenaya Lake*

HIGHLIGHTS: This trip follows very popular trails, but the breathtaking scenery you enjoy along the route more than makes up for the lack of solitude. The terrain passed on this quite short hike is varied and scenic, with two superb camping possibilities, the upper Sunrise Lake and Sunrise High Sierra Camp. The former offers sheltered camping beside a scenic subalpine lake, while those at the latter are rewarded with a beautiful sunrise.

DAY 1 (Sunrise Lakes Trailhead to Sunrise High Sierra Camp, 5.2 miles): From the trailhead parking area, follow the eastbound trail, after a few steps passing a small spur trail that departs to the right (south) toward May Lake and Olmsted Point, then crossing the usually flowing outlet of Tenaya Lake on large rock blocks (an early-season wade). Just beyond this crossing you reach a trail junction, where left (northeast) leads to Tenaya Lake's southeastern shore, while you go right (south-southwest) toward Sunrise High Sierra Camp. Three hundred feet later is a second junction, where left (north) also leads to Tenaya Lake's southeastern shore, while you go right (south). The trail briefly parallels Tenaya Creek before veering a little left, gently crossing a minor rise and dropping to a ford of Mildred Lake's outlet. Beyond, you continue an undulating traverse south in sparse forest. You pass pocket meadows and cross several seasonal tributaries, the Sunrise Lakes outlets, before embarking on a notably steep collection of switchbacks—few Sierra trails ascend 1,000 feet in just 1.1 miles. The trail is also, in places, annoyingly rocky, reflecting the many half-buried boulders and partially submerged slabs with which the trail construction crew had to contend. At least these switchbacks are, for the most part, mercifully shaded, and where they become steepest, they give back with the beauty of astounding views of the surrounding granite landscape as well as a fine wildflower display underfoot. Soon after the hemlock-and-red-fir forest becomes denser, the switchbacks end, and the trail levels out as it arrives at a junction on a shallow, forested saddle, 2.5 miles from the trailhead. Here you turn left (east), while the Forsyth Trail heads right (south) in the direction of Clouds Rest.

ABOUT THE SCENERY

To the south, notice the long, granite slope falling from Clouds Rest into Tenaya Canyon. This slope is a 4,500-foot drop, one of the largest continuous rock slopes in the world.

The Indian name for Tenaya Creek, *Py-wi-ack* ("Stream of the Shining Rocks"), is apt, for this canyon exhibits the largest exposed granite area in Yosemite, and its shining surfaces are barren except for sporadic clumps of hardy conifers that have found root in broken talus pockets.

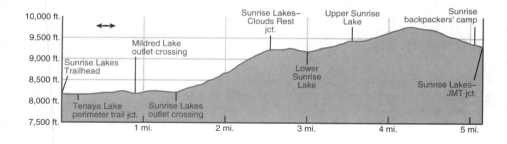

You now stroll on a nearly level path under a sparse forest cover of pine and fir until the trail dips to lower Sunrise Lake, passing a few campsites. After rambling around the west side of the lake on a trail fringed with red mountain heather, you cross the outlet and ascend gradually northeast. Crossing a fairly flat saddle, the middle Sunrise Lake comes into view on the left, but you veer east and climb away from it, paralleling its inlet as you ascend to the upper Sunrise Lake. Attractive campsites hide in the forest to the north of the upper lake's outlet.

With few trees to block the views of the surrounding granite slopes, the trail skirts the edge of the flower-filled meadow fringing the upper lake and, crossing one of the lake's inlet rivulets, begins a gradual ascent up a trough. This leads southeast into and up a second shallow, gravelly gully that you follow nearly due south to a sparsely forested broad gap with magnificent views of the Clark Range piercing the southern sky. Beyond, you drop south into denser cover, veer east, then north, to make a steep descent to the Sunrise backpackers' camp (9,365'; 37.79404°N, 119.43412°W), which is situated on a bench overlooking spacious Long Meadow (may be dry late in the year). There are ample, if crowded, sites here, together with a pit toilet, water faucet, and bear boxes. A few lucky people are able to reserve a meal at the nearby High Sierra Camp—you have to make reservations months in advance. Just a few steps beyond the backpackers' camp you intersect the John Muir Trail (JMT) at the edge of Long Meadow.

On a layover day you may want to follow the JMT north, exploring the Long Meadow environs. Alternatively, you could drop to the headwaters of Echo Creek by following Long Meadow 0.8 mile north, then turning right (east) onto the Echo Creek Trail and following it 1.4 miles until you reach Echo Creek's polished granite slabs.

DAY 2 (Sunrise High Sierra Camp to Tenaya Lake Trailhead, 5.2 miles): Retrace your steps.

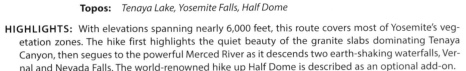

trip 44   Clouds Rest Traverse to Yosemite Valley

see map on p. 214

Trip Data: 37.76784°N, 119.48923°W (Clouds Rest); 16.3 miles; 2/1 days

Topos: *Tenaya Lake, Yosemite Falls, Half Dome*

HIGHLIGHTS: With elevations spanning nearly 6,000 feet, this route covers most of Yosemite's vegetation zones. The hike first highlights the quiet beauty of the granite slabs dominating Tenaya Canyon, then segues to the powerful Merced River as it descends two earth-shaking waterfalls, Vernal and Nevada Falls. The world-renowned hike up Half Dome is described as an optional add-on.

SHUTTLE DIRECTIONS: The endpoint is located at Happy Isles, Yosemite Valley shuttle stop 16, along Happy Isles Loop Road, a location only accessible by shuttle bus or on foot. Overnight hikers should park their cars at the hiker parking area, located along Happy Isles Loop Road about halfway between Curry Village and Happy Isles (a 0.4-mile walk to Happy Isles) or in the Curry Village parking lot (a short shuttle ride to Happy Isles). These parking areas are in the far eastern part of Yosemite Valley: follow Southside Drive, the road all Yosemite Valley access roads funnel into, to its end, continuing straight ahead at every junction until you reach Curry Village. Then either turn right (south) into the Curry Village parking area or continue straight an extra 0.2 mile until a junction where you turn right, ignoring the BUSES ONLY sign, and continue to the hiker parking lot, on the right in 0.25 mile.

    If your group has a single car, YARTS, the transit system serving Yosemite, has several bus services daily between Yosemite Valley (stopping in Yosemite Village at the Yosemite Valley Visitor Center) and Tuolumne Meadows and will drop off (but not necessarily pick up) people at the Sunrise Lakes Trailhead.

DAY 1 (Sunrise Lakes Trailhead to Sunrise Creek, 9.7 miles): From the trailhead parking area, follow the eastbound trail. After a few steps you pass a small spur trail that departs to the right (south) toward May Lake and Olmsted Point, then cross the usually flowing outlet of Tenaya Lake on large rock blocks (an early-season wade). Just beyond this crossing you reach a trail junction, where left (northeast) leads to Tenaya Lake's southeastern shore, while you go right (south-southwest) toward Sunrise High Sierra Camp. Three hundred feet later is a second junction, where left (north) also leads to Tenaya Lake's southeastern shore, while you go right (south). The trail briefly parallels Tenaya Creek before veering a little left, gently crossing a minor rise and dropping to a ford of Mildred Lake's outlet. Beyond, you continue an undulating traverse south in sparse forest. You pass pocket meadows and cross several seasonal tributaries, the Sunrise Lakes outlets, before embarking on a notably steep collection of switchbacks—few Sierra trails ascend 1,000 feet in just 1.1 miles. The trail is also, in places, annoyingly rocky, reflecting the many half-buried boulders and partially submerged slabs with which the trail construction crew had to contend. At least these switchbacks are, for the most part, mercifully shaded, and where they become steepest, they give back with the beauty of astounding views of the surrounding granite landscape as well as a fine wildflower display underfoot. Soon after the hemlock-and-red-fir forest becomes denser, the switchbacks end, and the trail levels out as it arrives at a junction on a shallow, forested saddle, 2.5 miles from the trailhead. This junction was once known as Forsyth Pass, although the name has long since vanished from maps. Right (south) is your route to Clouds Rest, while left (east) leads to the Sunrise Lakes and Sunrise High Sierra Camp (Trip 43).

Continuing straight ahead on the Forsyth Trail, you begin a generally southward, 320-foot, switchbacking descent. At the bottom of the descent, the trail rises over a talus-swollen little ridge and drops beside a pleasant-looking lakelet (small campsites nearby). Continuing

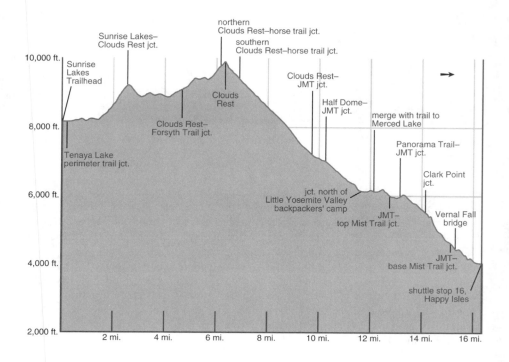

Looking northeast from Clouds Rest's summit to Tenaya Lake and endless granite domes and peaks
Photo by Elizabeth Wenk

south, the trail ascends a lightly forested hillside, crosses an unnamed stream (with small campsites nearby), or in times of high runoff a trio of creeklets. This slope is boggy until midsummer, and the plentiful groundwater nourishes rank gardens of wildflowers throughout the summer. You have the choice to camp in this vicinity or just over 5 miles farther along where you next encounter flat ground and water together.

A 200-foot ascent beyond the streams leads to a junction, where the Forsyth Trail turns left (south), descending a slope decimated by the 2014 Meadow Fire, while you stay right (west) toward Clouds Rest. Trending west, then northwest, you attain a gravelly crest. Onward, you traipse southwest for about a mile, crossing a minor saddle and soon ogling the dramatic granite slabs defining Tenaya Canyon to your north. Ascending more steeply, you reach a junction with a horse trail that bypasses Clouds Rest's actual summit.

ALTERNATE ROUTES UP CLOUDS REST

If you struggle with exposure, at the Clouds Rest–horse trail junction you may wish to consider one of three alternatives. You could bypass the summit, simply trending left (south) on the horse trail, cutting 0.2 mile from the hiking distance, but will miss the view from the summit. You could leave your overnight pack at this junction (securing your food in your bear canister first), and hike to the summit without the cumbersome weight on your back, then return to this junction and take the horse trail bypass, adding a little under 0.2 mile to your distance. Or third, you could for now follow the horse trail 0.55 mile to a second junction where you meet the main Clouds Rest Trail ascending from Yosemite Valley. Here you would leave your pack and turn right (north) to follow this trail 0.6 mile to summit Clouds Rest via its less-exposed western side. This adds nearly a mile to your day, but without your pack. The junction west of the Clouds Rest summit is where all hikers reunite to follow a common route.

The trail essentially dies out beyond the horse trail junction, and the route to the summit of Clouds Rest follows a bedrock rib southwest. You scramble a few feet up to the narrow crest that leads to the summit; although there are drop-offs to either side, following the center of the rib limits your exposure, ensuring you can't fall far. Focus on your footing until you reach the broader summit, then sit and enjoy the view. The panorama from Clouds Rest is among the most spectacular in the Sierra, including a 4,500-foot continuous granite slope stretching all the way down to Tenaya Creek and rising on the other side—the largest exposed granite area in Yosemite. The views are equally stunning in all directions: west to Half Dome and Yosemite Valley, south to the Clark Range, or east to the Sierra Crest.

Continuing on to Yosemite Valley, you negotiate short switchbacks down through a dense growth of chinquapin bushes. Beyond the rocky summit, descend longer switchbacks past western white pines and scattered Jeffrey pines to a junction with the western terminus of the aforementioned horse trail. Staying right (west), the trail descends past the back sides of the two Clouds Rest "pinnacles," both broken with an abundance of horizontal fractures. The trail traverses in front of the pinnacles on a sandy tread decorated with shaggy-barked western junipers and nearly touches the rim of Tenaya Canyon, before initiating a steep switchbacking descent down an open slope. Reentering forest cover, your previously plentiful views of towering Half Dome instantly vanish, and you pass a trickling spring (good drinking water). Your moderate-to-steep descent soon leaves the last red firs behind, and, through a forest of white fir and Jeffrey pine, you drop eventually to a junction with the John Muir Trail (JMT). Here, close to a tributary of Sunrise Creek, you'll find many campsites (7,159'; 37.74396°N, 119.50374°W).

MORAINE DOME

François Matthes, in an interesting "detective story" written in the form of a geological essay, discusses Moraine Dome extensively. He deduced, using three examples, that the moraines around the dome were the product of at least two glacial ages—a notion contrary to the thinking of the time. The morainal till of the last glacial age comprises the underfooting of the descent into Little Yosemite Valley.

DAY 2 (Sunrise Creek to Happy Isles Trailhead in Yosemite Valley, 6.6 miles): You continue descending along the JMT, reaching a junction with the Half Dome Trail after 0.55 mile. If—and only if—you procured a Half Dome permit when you applied for your Wilderness Permit, you may choose to take the approximately 4-mile round-trip detour to the summit of Half Dome from this point.

HALF DOME

If you obtained a permit to summit Half Dome—requested with your wilderness permit—turn right (north). After a 0.6-mile ascent through unassuming forest, the trail bends west and soon reaches a saddle offering filtered views north across Tenaya Canyon. Half Dome's northeast face comes into view just before the trail tops a crest, and beyond you also have views backward to Clouds Rest and its satellites, the Quarter Domes. After a few more switchbacks you achieve a broad ridge, and traverse west. This flat, relaxing interruption in the climb ends all too soon at the base of Half Dome's abruptly ascending shoulder. Beyond here a permit is required for all people, and rangers indeed patrol throughout the day. This is also where you must stop—for your safety—if thunderstorms threaten or the rock is wet. Nearly every fatality on Half Dome's cables has occurred when the rock is wet! Almost two dozen very short switchbacks guide you up the view-blessed ridge of the dome's shoulder.

Topping the shoulder, you are confronted with the dome's intimidating pair of cables, which definitely cause some hikers to retreat. If you stare up the cables and decide this is not for you, feel comfortable in your decision and spend a delightful hour basking in the sun on the shoulder, watching the antlike line of people work their way up and down the cables and decide, quite accurately, that you have already reached an excellent viewpoint.

The ascent starts out gently enough, but it too quickly steepens almost to a 45-degree angle. On this stretch, first timers often slow to a snail's pace, clenching both cables with sweaty hands—hands hopefully ensconced in gloves with a good grip. Most people are surprised by how much they use their arms on the ascent, especially for the middle third of the climb. Most frightening to me is the continual jockeying of people trying to pass or overtake each other, necessitating holding on to just one of the cables. Passing opposing traffic is best done courteously and where boards are laid between the cables in front of periodic posts.

Eventually an easing gradient provides new incentive, and soon you are scrambling up to the broad summit of Half Dome, an area about the size of 17 football fields. From the broad summit of this monolith, you have a 360-degree panorama. You can look down Yosemite Valley to the bald brow of El Capitan and back up Tenaya Canyon past Clouds Rest to Cathedral Peak, the Sierra Crest, and Mount Hoffmann. Mount Starr King—a dome that rises only 250 feet above you—dominates the Illilouette Creek basin to the south, while the Clark Range cuts the sky to the southeast. Looking due east across Moraine Dome's summit, you see Mount Florence, whose broad triangular form hides the park's highest peak, Mount Lyell, behind it. In this direction you will also see the forest charred in the 2014 Meadow Fire.

Meanwhile, the JMT turns left (south) and continues switchbacking down through a changing forest cover—incense cedar and sugar pines become more common along this stretch, providing dense shade, while the higher elevation conifers vanish. A final collection of tight zigzags drops you into the northwestern corner of Little Yosemite Valley, where you turn right (west). The left (south) branch would take you to the large Little Yosemite Valley backpackers' camp, with toilet and bear boxes. If you've climbed Half Dome, you may have chosen to take an extra day for your trip and could spend the night here, the last legal camping before Yosemite Valley. A summer ranger is often stationed at a nearby cabin.

The fork you've taken angles across Little Yosemite Valley and after about 0.5 mile converges with the trail to Merced Lake along the quiet banks of the Merced River. At this junction, you turn right (west), shortly ascend out of Little Yosemite Valley, then descend a dry rocky slope to a junction, with pit toilets, where the JMT meets the famous Mist Trail at the top of a gully. Both descend toward Yosemite Valley, but this trip stays on the

JMT by going left (south, then southwest) from this junction, and climbing briefly to reach the banks of the Merced River at the top of Nevada Fall. Along the river, slabs and pools beckon, but stay out of the rushing water, for people have been swept over 594-foot Nevada Fall. A cryptic lookout on the river's north side offers close-ups of the fall: when you are still about 100 feet north of the bridge, walk toward the rim and you'll find some roughly built steps that lead to a hidden shelf, from which you turn left to reach a railing.

> **MIST TRAIL**
> The Mist Trail drops very steeply on tight, slippery switchbacks to the foot of Nevada Fall, flattens out briefly, descends another bit, crosses the Merced River on a footbridge, passes a junction with the lower end of a connector descending from Clark Point, passes the Emerald Pool, and crosses slab to a vista at the brink of Vernal Fall. The trail then descends down a gully south of Vernal Fall. Partway down the trail sidles closer to the river and is usually soaked by spray from Vernal Fall—as are the hikers descending the tall, wet, slippery steps. After the Mist Trail levels out below Vernal Fall, it rejoins the JMT. We don't recommend the Mist Trail for backpackers until water levels drop in late July, but it's a day hikers' challenge and delight.

Continuing the journey, the JMT crosses the Merced River on a footbridge, climbs briefly beneath conifer cover, and presently meets a couple of junctions with the Panorama Trail, which started at Glacier Point and ends here. At both junctions, trend right (west) on the JMT to begin a high traverse along a trail blasted into the rock. A stout rock wall protects you from the possibility of a slide, so you can instead imbibe the ever-changing panorama of domelike Liberty Cap and broad-topped Mount Broderick—both once over-ridden by glaciers. As you progress west, Half Dome becomes prominent. All the while, Nevada Fall decorates the foreground, its water dancing and churning down through the air. Eventually you descend to Clark Point, where the JMT continues left (west), making a long descent down a gully on quite shaded, cobbled switchbacks. It levels out, meets a signed HORSE TRAIL coming in from the left (west), and presently reaches a junction where the Mist Trail rejoins from the right (east). Turning left (west), the JMT follows the Merced River downstream, curving north to cross the river on a footbridge that offers a superb view of 317-foot Vernal Fall. On the south side of the river, before you cross the bridge, there are restrooms on the left and a drinking fountain on the right.

Once across the bridge, the trail climbs a few steps before beginning a long, reasonably steep descent down a mostly paved trail. Just where the trail makes a prominent bend to the right, looking south, you may glimpse Illilouette Fall high in Illilouette Gorge. Looking west yields views of the steep wall beneath Glacier Point, the scar from a massive rockslide in July 1996 still obvious. The deposit of boulders lies close to the cliff wall, and beyond is a ring of trees, toppled by the air blast that accompanied the slide. Looking north you just catch a glimpse of Yosemite Falls. Continuing down past a small spring, the JMT presently passes above the Happy Isles (named for two rocky islets in the Merced), then a gauging station and the remains of a bridge to the Happy Isles, washed out in 1997 floods. Beyond, the now broad trail intersects the Happy Isles Loop Road, and you turn left and cross a bridge to reach the shuttle stop (4,025'; 37.73242°N, 119.55965°W).

From here, you can walk or take the Valley Shuttle bus to your car (see shuttle directions), the backpackers' campground (at the back of North Pine Campground, across a bridge near site 335) where you're allowed to spend a night, or Yosemite Village where you may be meeting the YARTS bus back to Tenaya Lake.

Murphy Creek Trailhead   8,187'; 37.83431°N, 119.46321°W

Destination/ GPS Coordinates	Trip Type	Best Season	Pace & Hiking/ Layover Days	Total Mileage	Permit Required
41 Ten Lakes Traverse *(in reverse of description; see page 204)*	Shuttle	Mid to late	Moderate 3/0	20.5	Murphy Creek

INFORMATION AND PERMITS: This trip is in Yosemite National Park: wilderness permits and bear canisters are required; pets and firearms are prohibited. Quotas apply, with 60% of permits reservable online up to 24 weeks in advance and 40% available first-come, first-served starting at 11 a.m. the day before your trip's start date. Fires are prohibited above 9,600 feet. See nps.gov/yose/planyourvisit/wildpermits.htm for more details.

DRIVING DIRECTIONS: The trailhead is along Tioga Road (CA 120) opposite a picnic and parking area along the shores of Tenaya Lake, at approximately the lake's midpoint. It is located 31.5 miles northeast of Crane Flat and 8.0 miles southwest of the Tuolumne Meadows Campground. There are pit toilets at the trailhead.

Cathedral Lakes Trailhead   8,574'; 37.87337°N, 119.38251°W

Destination/ GPS Coordinates	Trip Type	Best Season	Pace & Hiking/ Layover Days	Total Mileage	Permit Required
45 Upper Cathedral Lake 37.84108°N 119.41318°W	Out-and-back	Mid to late	Leisurely 2/0	7.6	Cathedral Lakes
46 Cathedral Range Circuit 37.74049°N 119.40718°W (Merced Lake High Sierra Camp)	Shuttle (or Loop)	Mid to late	Moderate 5/1	31.4	Cathedral Lakes *(Rafferty Creek to Vogelsang if reversed)*
47 Cathedral Lakes, Echo Creek, and Sunrise Creek 37.76457°N 119.42043°W (Upper Echo Creek bridge)	Shuttle	Mid to late	Moderate 4/1	23.0	Cathedral Lakes *(Sunrise Lakes if reversed)*
48 John Muir Trail to Yosemite Valley 37.79404°N 119.43412°W (Sunrise High Sierra Camp)	Shuttle	Mid to late	Leisurely 3/0	20.8	Cathedral Lakes *(Happy Isles to Sunrise Pass Thru if reversed)*

INFORMATION AND PERMITS: These trips are in Yosemite National Park: wilderness permits and bear canisters are required; pets and firearms are prohibited. Quotas apply, with 60% of permits reservable online up to 24 weeks in advance and 40% available first-come, first-served starting at 11 a.m. the day before your trip's start date. Fires are prohibited above 9,600 feet. See nps.gov/yose/planyourvisit/wildpermits.htm for more details.

DRIVING DIRECTIONS: The trailhead is along Tioga Road (CA 120) toward the west end of Tuolumne Meadows. It is located 1.5 miles west of the Tuolumne Meadows Campground

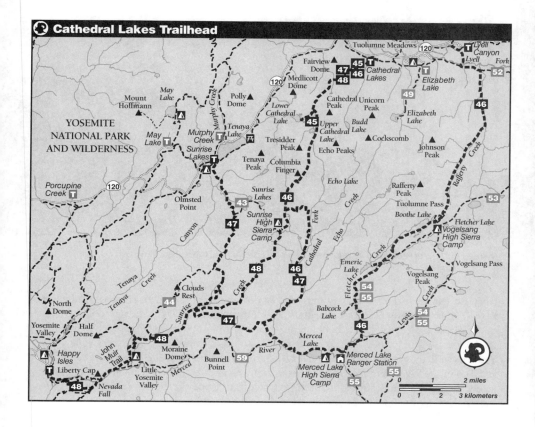

(or 0.4 mile west of the Tuolumne Meadows Visitor Center) and 0.75 mile east of the Pothole Dome parking area, the westernmost trailhead in Tuolumne Meadows. The "parking lot" is the dirt shoulder on either side of CA 120, and on most summer days, vehicles are parked along quite a lengthy stretch of Tioga Road. There are portable toilets at the trailhead.

trip 45 Upper Cathedral Lake

Trip Data: 37.84108°N, 119.41318°W; 7.6 miles; 2/0 days
Topos: *Tenaya Lake*

HIGHLIGHTS: The Cathedral Lakes' scenery is classic Yosemite: a basin of gray-white glacial-polished granite holding an azure lake whose serene waters reflect the unmistakable, elegant spire of Cathedral Peak. With such a short hike into these two spectacular lakes, this trip is ideal for beginners and families. It's also a fine day hike.

DAY 1 (Cathedral Lakes Trailhead to Upper Cathedral Lake, 3.8 miles): Head generally southwest, directly away from the road across a sandy expanse that coalesces into an exceptionally well-used trail. After 0.1 mile, the John Muir Trail (JMT) joins your route at a four-way junction. Continuing straight (south) at the junction, you climb moderately on a stretch that can, at times, be objectionably dusty as thousands of humans and equines churn up the forest floor humus and abundant glacial deposits. After 0.75 mile of ascent under a welcome forest cover, the trail levels off and descends slightly to a small meadow that is boggy in early season. Farther along, meadows, cleared of trees by past avalanches, afford a view north to

Vista of Cathedral Peak from near Upper Cathedral Lake   Photo by Elizabeth Wenk

Fairview Dome, while the craggy outcrops to the south are the north ridge of Cathedral Peak. You step across nascent Cathedral Creek on rocks and switchback up cool, forested slopes, passing a robust spring bubbling to your left. After 300 feet of climbing, your trail's gradient eases and Cathedral Peak, towering 1,400 feet above you, slowly enters your view. You cross a flat, dry, sandy expanse that is the unlikely drainage divide between the Merced and Tuolumne Rivers and make a brief descent through wetter lodgepole forest to a junction, where the JMT continues straight ahead (left; south) to Upper Cathedral Lake, while a spur trail to the Lower Cathedral Lake departs to the right (southwest).

TO LOWER CATHEDRAL LAKE

The spur trail soon crosses the Lower Cathedral Lake inlet stream and descends through lodgepole pines, emerging in a large meadow—or perhaps a shallow lake—which is best encircled on its south side. Across the meadow you reach the bedrock slabs lining the east shore of Lower Cathedral Lake, 0.5 mile from the JMT. It is an additional 0.5 mile to the lake's outlet, reached by following the lakeshore in a counterclockwise direction. You cross back over the inlet creek just above the lakeshore and follow the lake's perimeter west. Campsites exist on both the north (9,288'; 37.84824°N, 119.41478°W; no campfires) and south shores, the northern ones being roomier.

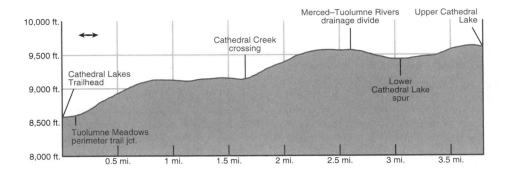

Continue ahead for another 0.75 mile toward Upper Cathedral Lake on an easy climb, then dip slightly into the shallow bowl that holds the lake as you near your goal. Just as you approach the lake, the JMT's tread bends left (southeast), having been rerouted to arc above the lake basin and protect the lake's fragile shores. At the bend, you'll spy a use trail that leads to good slab-and-soil campsites before you reach the lake (9,615'; 37.84108°N, 119.41318°W; no campfires). Rugged Tresidder Peak lies southwest of the lake, while the delicate steeples of Cathedral Peak rise to the northeast.

TO BE OR NOT TO BE GLACIATED

The rounded, polished tops of the domes seen earlier indicate the domes were completely covered by ice, while the jagged summits of Cathedral and Tresidder Peaks prove that they stood a few hundred feet above the grinding ice and hence were not rounded and smoothed by it.

DAY 2 (Upper Cathedral Lake to Cathedral Lakes Trailhead, 3.8 miles): Retrace your steps.

trip 46   **Cathedral Range Circuit**

see map on p. 223

> **Trip Data:**   37.74049°N, 119.40718°W (Merced Lake High Sierra Camp); 31.4 miles (shuttle) or 33.8 miles (loop); 5/1 days
>
> **Topos:**   *Tenaya Lake, Merced Peak, Vogelsang Peak*

HIGHLIGHTS: This looping trip samples everything the Cathedral Range has to offer, from sweeping vistas atop 10,000-foot passes to the deeply glaciated Merced River Canyon to forested side streams with secluded campsites. There's plenty of good fishing, too!

HEADS UP! *You can easily make a loop of this trip. That option is described at the end of the description, adding about 2.4 miles to your last day.*

SHUTTLE DIRECTIONS: If you do this trip as a shuttle, the ending is at the large Dog Lake parking lot on the north side the Tuolumne Meadows Lodge Road. The Dog Lake parking area is the best parking area for hikers departing up Lyell Canyon on the Pacific Crest Trail (PCT) or John Muir Trail (JMT). To reach this lot from Tuolumne Meadows Campground (the only campground in the area), drive 0.6 mile northeast on the Tioga Road, turning right on the Tuolumne Lodge spur road. If you are descending from Tioga Pass, drive 6.4 miles southwest to the only road that branches left before you reach Tuolumne Meadows. Along the spur road, pass the Tuolumne Wilderness Center parking area (another parking option) and a collection of employee houses before reaching the parking lot. The closest water and toilets are at the Tuolumne Wilderness Center. Also, ask at the wilderness center if the Tuolumne Meadows shuttle is running between these trailheads.

DAY 1 (Cathedral Lakes Trailhead to Upper Cathedral Lake, 3.8 miles): Follow Trip 45, Day 1 to Upper Cathedral Lake (9,615'; 37.84108°N, 119.41318°W; no campfires).

DAY 2 (Upper Cathedral Lake to Echo Creek Crossing, 7.6 miles): Continue south along the JMT up to Cathedral Pass, where the excellent views include Cathedral Peak, Tresidder Peak, the Echo Peaks, and Matthes Crest. Beyond the pass is a long, beautiful swale, the headwaters of Echo Creek, where the midseason flower show is alone worth the trip, when the entire slope is covered with shaggy lupine.

The JMT climbs gradually along Tresidder Peak's east flank to the actual high point, a marvelous viewpoint overlooking southern Yosemite National Park. The inspiring panorama includes the peaks around Vogelsang High Sierra Camp to the southeast, the entire Clark Range to the south, and on the southeastern and southern horizons the peaks on the park border.

Beyond this point, the trail switchbacks ruggedly down to the head of the upper lobe of Long Meadow, levels off, and leads down a gradually sloping valley dotted with young lodgepole pine to the head of the second, lower lobe of l-o-n-g Long Meadow (creek may be dry by late season). Soon you reach a junction, exactly 3 miles from Upper Cathedral Lake, where straight ahead (right; south) leads to Sunrise High Sierra Camp (Trip 48), while you turn left (east) on a trail leading to Echo Creek. Within steps you cross Long Meadow's stream and the trail then quickly switchbacks to the top of the ridge before descending through dense hemlock-and-lodgepole forest toward the Cathedral Fork Echo Creek. Where the route approaches this stream, you have fine views of the creek's water gliding down a series of granite slabs. There are small campsites nearby. Then the trail veers away from the creek and descends gently above it for more than a mile. Even in late season, this shady hillside is well watered and abloom. On this downgrade, your route meets and again fords the Long Meadow stream, which has flowed out of that meadow through a gap between the two large domes high above you.

The route now levels out in a mile-long flat, in part burned, section of this valley, where the wet ground yields an abundance of both wildflowers and mosquitoes through mid-July. Beyond this flat "park" the trail descends more open slopes, and eventually you can see, across the valley, the steep course of the main fork of Echo Creek plunging down to its rendezvous with its western Cathedral Fork. Just beyond the confluence, your trail levels off and passes good campsites immediately before you take a metal bridge over Echo Creek (8,137'; 37.76457°N, 119.42043°W). Note that the largest campsites are some distance south of the trail and not visible from the trail. Rainbow and golden trout are present in the creek.

DAY 3 (Echo Creek Crossing to Merced Lake, 4.4 miles): After crossing the bridge over Echo Creek, the trail leads down the forested valley and easily fords a tributary stream, staying well above the main creek. This pleasant, shaded descent soon trends south, diverging from the creek to cross an open slope decorated with fibrous-barked juniper trees and butterscotch-scented Jeffrey pines. The trail now drops to another bridge, beyond which the creek again drops precipitously, while the trail turns west and diagonals more gradually

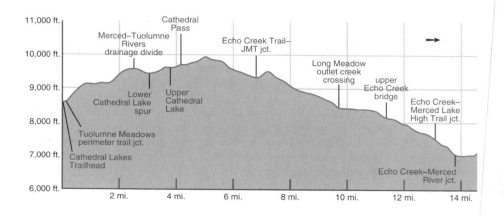

down a decidedly brushy slope. From here the views are excellent of Echo Valley, a flat interruption in the otherwise descending Merced River Canyon. On this slope you arrive at a T-junction, where right (west) is the so-called Merced Lake High Trail, which leads back to the JMT corridor, while your route turns to the left (south). You immediately drop into a lush forest draw, replete with beautiful, big red firs decorated with vibrant chartreuse lichen. A short while later, you return to dry, brushy slopes and complete the descent to Echo Valley and the Merced River, 450 feet below the last junction.

Here you meet and turn left (east) on the trail ascending the Merced River Canyon; right (west) leads toward Yosemite Valley. After crossing several forks of Echo Creek on wooden bridges, strike southeast through boggy Echo Valley, a dense tangle of approximately 15-foot-tall lodgepole pines, regenerating from a series of fires. A 1966 fire killed most of the mature trees, followed by blazes in 1988 and 1993 that would have reset the successional clock twice more. Meadow fringes along the trail are carpeted with flowers, including blue lupine and white yarrow and yampah. Leaving Echo Valley, the trail leads up granite slabs to lovely benches; heading left (north) here leads to some sandy campsites set among slabs. The next ascent offers travelers the sights and sounds of this dramatic part of the river: a long series of chutes, cascades, falls, cataracts, and pools that were all formed by the glacier that roughened the bed of the Merced River.

Above this turbulent stretch, the trail levels off beside the suddenly quiet river and arrives at the outlet of Merced Lake. Follow the trail around the lake's north side to the Merced Lake backpackers' campground (7,242'; 37.74049°N, 119.40718°W), the only legal campsites around the lake, where there is a pit toilet and bear boxes. Another 0.15 mile along the trail leads to the Merced Lake High Sierra Camp at the lake's east end, where you can buy a few snacks at the small store and use a water faucet when the camp is open.

DAY 4 (Merced Lake to Emeric Lake, 5.9 miles): Beyond the High Sierra Camp, the trail loops south around a shallow ridge and proceeds a mile east on an almost level, wide, sandy path under forest canopy, noteworthy for a beautiful grove of Jeffrey pines. You cross the roaring Lewis Creek on a trio of bridges and arrive at a junction with the trail up Lewis Creek. The Merced Lake Ranger Station, sometimes with emergency services in summer, is just south of the junction.

At the junction you turn left (northeast) onto the Lewis Creek Trail, while right (southeast) leads to Washburn Lake. Your cobblestoned trail quickly becomes steep, and it remains so for a panting mile. The predominate trees, Sierra juniper and Jeffrey pine, cast

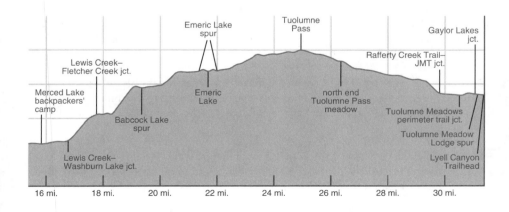

shade only early in the morning, but the lack of a closed canopy provides open views west to Merced Lake and beyond to Half Dome. The 850-foot climb leads to a junction where you turn left (northeast) onto the trail up Fletcher Creek, while right (east) is the continuing route up Lewis Creek to Vogelsang Pass (Trip 54).

Several switchbacks descend to a wooden bridge over Lewis Creek. In a flat to the northeast are a few pretty tent sites, although fallen trees have vanquished most real estate in this previously popular camping area. From here, the trail begins a moderate-to-steep ascent up the unevenly cobblestoned, exposed trail—a grunt on a hot day. The path is bordered by prickly shrubs, in particular featuring whitethorn and huckleberry oak. Just past a tributary a half mile from Lewis Creek, stepping west of the trail provides views of some fine cataracts and waterfalls along Fletcher Creek. Climbing onward, granite slabs open to your left, providing splendid vistas of Fletcher Creek chuting and cascading down the bare bedrock. The trail keeps ascending, steeply at times and mostly some distance east of the creek, often on the now-familiar cobblestones. A detour onto the middle of the slabs is called for, to feel the smooth glacial-polished rock away from the water flow and the water-polished rock within it. The few solitary pine trees clinging to the nearby slabs and the dome overhead testify to nature's extraordinary tenacity.

The trail climbs up to a notch, then levels off, and soon passes a side trail left (west and south) to small Babcock Lake (acceptable campsites). Onward, you walk for 0.6 mile through flat, lush forest, passing springs and small meadow patches brightly colored with flowers. Turning a little west, the trail breaks back into the open and rises more steeply via rocky switchbacks. From these, looking north, one can see the outlet stream of Emeric Lake—though not the lake itself, hidden behind the dome to the right of the outlet's notch.

SHORTCUT TO EMERIC LAKE

For an adventurous shortcut to Emeric Lake, follow the visible outlet up to the lake. First, leave the trail and wade across granite-bottomed Fletcher Creek as best you can—there is no natural place to do so and it is only safe to take this route at low flows. Then follow up Emeric Lake's outlet and stroll along the northwest shore of Emeric Lake to campsites.

On the standard route to Emeric Lake, the switchbacks parallel the dashing creek until the trail tops out in a long, skinny meadow, constrained by domes to either side and overshadowed by Vogelsang Peak to the east. The trail follows the meandering Fletcher Creek northeast to a ford and just beyond reaches a scissor junction, where a sharp left (west-southwest) is the spur trail to Emeric Lake.

Sidling over and around a shallow granite knoll, slabs lead to Emeric Lake (9,338'; 37.77825°N, 119.38150°W; mileage to here). From the eastern corner follow anglers' trails to the excellent campsites midway along its northwest shore. During early summer, this requires a circuitous route to the north end of the meadow to avoid damaging the saturated soils. Fishing is often good for rainbow trout.

DAY 5 (Emeric Lake to Lyell Canyon Trailhead, 9.7 miles for shuttle or 12.1 miles for loop): This is the longest hiking day on this trip, but the ascent to Tuolumne Pass, on the crest of the Cathedral Range, is moderate and occurs at the beginning. Thereafter, the rest is downhill.

Once again, circle the head of Emeric Lake, cross its inlet stream, and follow the spur trail 0.3 mile east-northeast back to the scissor junction along Fletcher Creek. You trend left (northeast) toward Boothe Lake, while straight ahead (east-northeast) leads to Vogelsang High Sierra Camp.

Emeric Lake is a highlight of this trip.   Photo by Elizabeth Wenk

Your route climbs away from Fletcher Creek, passing northwest of a bald prominence that divides the headwaters of Fletcher and Emeric Creeks. Diverging slightly from Emeric Creek, the trail climbs to a bench cradling a series of lovely ponds that are interconnected in early season. You soon stare down at the south end of Boothe Lake (9,845') and its campsites, but these should be reached by continuing north on the meadowy-hillside trail to the signed Boothe Lake spur trail. Beyond, staying right (north), another 0.3 mile takes you to Tuolumne Pass (9,992') and a junction with a trail that goes sharply right (south) to Vogelsang High Sierra Camp. Enjoy the wonderful view ahead before continuing left (north) and down. To the north is the Sierra Crest between Tioga Pass and Mount Conness, while views south take in cliff-bound, dark-banded Fletcher Peak and Vogelsang Peak cradling the Vogelsang area.

You now begin a gradual descent north along Rafferty Creek's headwaters, which begin in this high, boulder-strewn meadow. The year-round creek is east of the trail, sometimes near and sometimes far, on this long, beautiful descent through sparse-to-moderate lodgepole forest. As the trail and the creek make their final drop into Lyell Canyon, you negotiate steeper switchbacks to more rapidly lose about 400 feet.

You meet the combined routes of the John Muir Trail (JMT) and Pacific Crest Trail (PCT) on the flat valley floor, the Lyell Fork Tuolumne River hidden to the north. Turn left (west) and follow the JMT/PCT 0.7 mile to another junction. If you've shuttled your car to the ending trailhead (or plan to use the Tuolumne Meadows shuttle), turn right (north) and the trip's end is 0.9 mile ahead; those deciding to loop back to the Cathedral Lakes Trailhead stay left (west), following a trail around the southern perimeter of Tuolumne Meadows, described below. For the shuttle trip, the trail soon crosses the Lyell Fork on a double footbridge that offers excellent views upcanyon to Mount Dana and Mount Gibbs; a photo is almost mandatory.

Now on the river's north bank, the sandy trail ascends a slight rise, then descends to a junction where you head left (west), while right (east) is signposted for the Gaylor Lakes. The JMT/PCT now crosses the Dana Fork Tuolumne River on a stout footbridge and turns left (northwest), avoiding a spur trail right (northeast) to Tuolumne Meadows Lodge. Your route roughly parallels the Dana Fork for 0.2 mile before curving west to meet a short, wide path on your right (north) that quickly leads to the Tuolumne Meadows Lodge Road and large Dog Lake parking area (8,686'; 37.87779°N, 119.33852°W). There is a shuttle stop at the parking area entrance.

LOOP OPTION

At the junction just before (south of) the double footbridge over the Lyell Fork Tuolumne River, if you wish to complete the loop to the Cathedral Lakes Trailhead, turn left (west-northwest) on the shady Tuolumne Meadows perimeter trail. Initially paralleling the Tuolumne River downstream, you reach a minor junction. The right-trending (northwest) spur trail follows the river to the southeast corner of huge Tuolumne Meadows Campground, while you stay left (southwest) on the main tread, next reaching a four-way junction, where the Elizabeth Lake Trail crosses your path. Continuing straight ahead (west) and eventually leaving the sprawling campground behind, you reach a junction with a right-hand spur (north) to Tioga Road and the Tuolumne Meadows Visitors Center, and again you continue ahead (left; west). Just beyond the bridge across Budd Creek, you meet the trail to Cathedral Lakes you ascended some days ago. Here, you turn right (northeast) and cross the bare area to the trailhead, Tioga Road, and your car.

trip 47 **Cathedral Lakes, Echo Creek, and Sunrise Creek**

see map on p. 223

Trip Data: 37.76457°N, 119.42043°W
(Upper Echo Creek bridge); 23.0 miles; 4/1 days
Topos: *Tenaya Lake, Merced Lake* (for 0.1 mile)

HIGHLIGHTS: Although much of this trip is along favorite, well-used trails, they are popular for a reason: they highlight Yosemite's spectacular glaciated highlands. Views of the immense domes and deep-cut canyons will leave lifetime memories. Note that the Meadow Fire in 2014 charred a 4-mile section of the route, eradicating shade and enhancing views.

SHUTTLE DIRECTIONS: You complete your hike at the Sunrise Lakes Trailhead, at the southwest corner of Tenaya Lake, located along Tioga Road (CA 120) 7.1 miles southwest of the Cathedral Lakes Trailhead. You can shuttle a car to this location or use the Tuolumne Meadows shuttle to return to your car. The shuttles run every 30 minutes during the summer. They charge a fee, so be sure to carry cash.

DAY 1 (Cathedral Lakes Trailhead to Upper Cathedral Lake, 3.8 miles): Follow Trip 45, Day 1 to Upper Cathedral Lake (9,615'; 37.84108°N, 119.41318°W; no campfires).

DAY 2 (Upper Cathedral Lake to Echo Creek Crossing, 7.6 miles): Follow Trip 46, Day 2 to the first bridge across Echo Creek (8,137'; 37.76457°N, 119.42043°W). The largest campsites are some distance south of the trail and not visible from the trail.

DAY 3 (Echo Creek Crossing to Sunrise Creek, 4.7 miles): After crossing the bridge over Echo Creek, the trail leads down the forested valley and easily fords a tributary stream, staying well above the main creek. This pleasant, shaded descent soon trends south, diverging from the creek to cross an open slope decorated with fibrous-barked juniper trees and butterscotch-scented Jeffrey pines. The trail now drops to another bridge, beyond which the creek again drops precipitously, while the trail turns west and diagonals more gradually down a decidedly brushy slope. From here the views are excellent of Echo Valley, a flat interruption in the otherwise descending Merced River Canyon. On this slope you arrive at a T-junction, where you turn right (west) onto the so-called Merced Lake High Trail, while left (south) leads to the Merced River.

> **WAY BACK WHEN . . .**
> This trail segment was part of the route from Yosemite Valley to Merced Lake until a path up the Merced River Canyon was constructed in 1911. Before that, the steep canyon walls coming right down to the river near Bunnell Point, the great dome to the southwest, had made passage impossible. Finally, a trail was built that bypasses the narrowest part of the canyon by climbing high on the south wall, and the trail you are now on fell into relative disuse.

The trail climbs several hundred rocky feet before leveling off above the immense Merced River Canyon. With fine views of obelisk-like Mount Clark in the south, you descend gradually for a half mile over open granite in a setting that is sure to give you a feeling of being above almost everything. Then the trail passes a stagnant lakelet and ascends to even better viewpoints of the immense, glaciated, granitic wonder that nature has spread out before you: Mount Clark, Clouds Rest, Half Dome, Mount Starr King, Bunnell Point, and the great dome across the canyon west of it, colloquially Sugarloaf Dome. The view seeker will find small, sandy campsites near here, but there is no permanent water.

The ascending trail then rounds a ridge and enters terrain mostly charred in the 2014 Meadow Fire—indeed most of your route for the next day lies in the charred zone. A stand of handsome Jeffrey pines remains, but where the trail levels off you'll forego shade for exhilarating views and the vivid green ferns and bright wildflowers that have rapidly colonized this well-irrigated burn zone. Indeed, this slope was burned first in the 1999 Echo Fire, with most of the remaining trees removed in 2014. Eventually, you descend slightly to meet the John Muir Trail (JMT), descending from Sunrise High Sierra Camp (HSC). To end this day, you go right (north) on the JMT (toward Sunrise HSC) climbing for 0.1 mile to a second junction, where you turn left (north) onto the Forsyth Trail and in another 0.2 mile reach a ford across Sunrise Creek (8,031'; 37.75946°N, 119.47727°W)—don't ford just now; instead continue up the south side of Sunrise Creek for about 0.1 mile to some campsites.

DAY 4 (Sunrise Creek to Tenaya Lake, 6.9 miles): Return to the trail and now ford Sunrise Creek and continue up the Forsyth Trail. The 2.4 miles from here to the next junction are

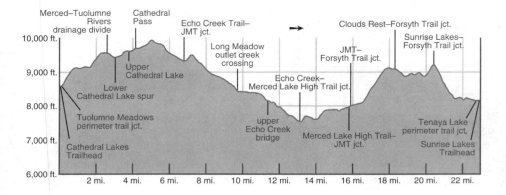

almost entirely burnt—an early start is advised. The trail curves east, then northeast to climb steeply and ford a tributary of Sunrise Creek. Beyond this ford, the mostly shadeless trail continues diligently, reaching gentler terrain at about 8,880 feet. Soon after, the now-sandy tread begins a northward then westward curve to a junction with the trail to Clouds Rest.

Go right (northeast) here, while left (west) leads to Clouds Rest (although its summit is well worth the 3.3-mile round-trip detour if you have spare energy; see Trip 44 page 216 for a description), and stay on the Forsyth Trail as it descends a forested draw to a trio of unnamed streams, passes a lakelet (small campsites nearby), rises and falls over a bouldery ridge with stands of aspen, and reaches a lush pocket of forest with abundant wildflower color. This segues to a switchbacking, 320-foot climb northward to a saddle. At this saddle, once called Forsyth Pass, is a junction with the trail that goes right (east) to Sunrise Lakes and Sunrise High Sierra Camp (Trip 43).

Continuing straight ahead (left; north), your route begins a steep, rocky switchbacking descent, losing 1,000 feet in just 1.1 miles. The views are tremendous: steep, smooth granite slabs that decorate the lands to the north and west of you. Meanwhile, there is a fine wildflower display underfoot. At the bottom of this descent, bear north to cross a couple of streams (the Sunrise Lakes outlet streams, which may be dry by late season), then follow the undulating trail northwest over the multi-stranded outlet of Mildred Lake, into a bouldery wash, and up to a minor ridge.

Dropping north-northwest, you reach the banks of Tenaya Creek and briefly parallel its sandy channel upstream toward Tenaya Lake, reaching a pair of junctions with a trail that heads right (northeast) to circle around the east side of Tenaya Lake. Turning left (north) at each, you cross Tenaya Lake's usually flowing outlet on large rock blocks, pass a small spur trail that departs to the left (south) toward May Lake and Olmsted Point, and just steps farther reach the Sunrise Lakes Trailhead (8,166'; 37.82573°N, 119.46996°W). From here, you will either have a car waiting for you or can take the Tuolumne Meadows shuttle back to the Cathedral Lakes Trailhead.

Looking into the Merced River canyon from the traverse high above it   Photo by Elizabeth Wenk

see map on p. 223

trip 48 **John Muir Trail to Yosemite Valley**

Trip Data: 37.79404°N, 119.43412°W (Sunrise High Sierra Camp); 20.8 miles; 3/0 days

Topos: *Tenaya Lake, Merced Peak* (just barely), *Half Dome*

HIGHLIGHTS: This hike follows the famous John Muir Trail (JMT) from Tuolumne Meadows to Yosemite Valley. It's one of Yosemite's most famous and most used backpack routes, not just because of its famous name tag, but because it truly surveys some of Yosemite's best-known landmarks, taking in delightful views, geologic highlights, and, of course, wildflowers. This is a fine trip for beginner backpackers. On your final day you pass within 2 miles of Half Dome's summit, a fantastic addition to this walk; just note, you must apply for a permit to summit as part of your backpacking permit.

SHUTTLE DIRECTIONS: The endpoint is located at Happy Isles in eastern Yosemite Valley. Happy Isles, Yosemite Valley shuttle stop 16, along Happy Isles Loop Road, is only accessible by shuttle bus or on foot. Overnight hikers should park their cars at the hiker parking area, located along Happy Isles Loop Road about halfway between Curry Village and Happy Isles (a 0.4-mile walk to Happy Isles) or in the Curry Village parking lot (a short shuttle ride to Happy Isles). These parking areas are in the far eastern part of Yosemite Valley: follow Southside Drive, the road all Yosemite Valley access roads funnel into, to its end, continuing straight ahead at every junction until you reach Curry Village. Then either turn right into the Curry Village parking area or continue straight an extra 0.2 mile to a junction where you turn right, ignoring the BUSES ONLY sign, and continue to the hiker parking lot, on the right in 0.25 mile.

If your group has a single car, YARTS, the transit system serving Yosemite, has several bus services daily between Yosemite Valley (stopping in Yosemite Village at Yosemite Valley Visitor Center) and Tuolumne Meadows and will stop at the Tuolumne Meadows Visitor Center, just a short distance past the Cathedral Lakes Trailhead.

DAY 1 (Cathedral Lakes Trailhead to Sunrise High Sierra Camp, 7.6 miles): Head generally southwest, directly away from the road across a sandy expanse that coalesces into an exceptionally well-used trail. After 0.1 mile, the JMT joins your route at a four-way junction. Continuing straight (south) at the junction, you climb moderately on a stretch that can, at times, be objectionably dusty as thousands of humans and equines churn up the forest floor humus and abundant glacial deposits. After 0.75 mile of ascent under a welcome forest cover, the trail levels off and descends to a small meadow that is boggy in early season. Farther along, meadows, cleared of trees by past avalanches, afford a view north to Fairview Dome, while the craggy outcrops to the south are the north ridge of Cathedral Peak. You step across nascent Cathedral Creek on rocks and switchback up cool, forested slopes, passing a robust spring bubbling to your left. After 300 feet of climbing, your trail's gradient eases, and Cathedral Peak, towering 1,400 feet above you, slowly enters your view. You cross a flat, dry, sandy expanse that is the unlikely drainage divide between the Merced and Tuolumne Rivers and make a brief descent through wetter lodgepole forest to a junction, where the JMT continues straight ahead (left; south) to Upper Cathedral Lake, while a spur trail to the Lower Cathedral Lake departs to the right (southwest).

Continue ahead for another 0.75 mile toward Upper Cathedral Lake on an easy climb, then dip slightly into the shallow bowl that holds the lake; the sandy trail stays a little above and east of the lake, having been rerouted to stay away from the lake's fragile shores. Just as you approach the lake, the trail now arcs left (east). Here you'll spy a use trail, the old trail route leading closer to the lakeshore—although this is not an appropriate route to take *around* the lake, it does lead to good campsites before you reach the lake.

Continue south along the JMT up to Cathedral Pass, where the excellent views include Cathedral Peak's delicate steeples, rugged Tresidder Peak, the cluster of pinnacled Echo Peaks, and the sawtooth ridgeline that is Matthes Crest. Beyond the pass is a long, beautiful swale, the headwaters of Echo Creek, where the midseason flower show is alone worth the trip, when the entire slope is covered with shaggy lupine.

The JMT continues climbing gradually along Tresidder Peak's east flank to the actual high point of this segment, a marvelous viewpoint overlooking southern Yosemite National Park. The inspiring panorama includes the peaks around Vogelsang High Sierra Camp in the southeast, the whole Clark Range in the south, and on the southeastern and southern horizons the peaks on the park border.

Beyond this point, the trail switchbacks quickly down to the head of the upper lobe of Long Meadow, levels off, and leads down a gradually sloping valley dotted with young lodgepole pines to the head of the second, lower lobe of *l-o-n-g* Long Meadow (creek may be dry by late season). Soon you reach a junction, exactly 3 miles from Upper Cathedral Lake, where you continue straight ahead (right; south) toward Sunrise High Sierra Camp, while the left (east) branch is a trail leading to Echo Creek (Trips 46 and 47). Another 0.8 mile of walking along Long Meadow leads you past the High Sierra Camp itself to the far southwestern corner of the meadow and a junction with the trail leading to Sunrise Lakes (9,365'; 37.79404°N, 119.43412°W; Trip 43). Turn right (west) onto this trail and almost immediately you reach the Sunrise backpackers' camp, your recommended home for the night. The views here are excellent, especially toward Mount Florence in the southeast. A pit toilet, water tap, and food-storage box are available here.

DAY 2 (Sunrise High Sierra Camp to Sunrise Creek, 6.6 miles): Return the few steps down to the JMT and turn right (south), continuing toward Yosemite Valley. Your day begins with a long, traversing climb of Sunrise Mountain's east slope. About a mile from Long Meadow, you reach a sandy saddle with outstanding views to the south and east. The JMT now descends slightly to skirt an often-dry meadow, then, via tight, steep switchbacks,

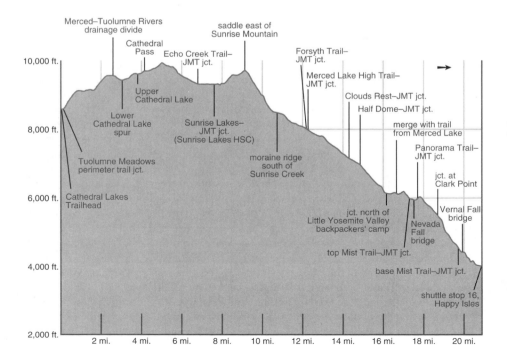

Mount Florence is visible from Sunrise High Sierra Camp.   Photo by Elizabeth Wenk

drops down a rocky moraine roughly paralleling Sunrise Creek's headwaters. At the foot of the descent, the trail enters a rich stand of mature red fir (with lovely campsites), crosses Sunrise Creek, and ascends to the top of a shallow sandy ridge, a large moraine left by the Merced River. The trail then descends the moraine crest.

> **ABOUT THIS MORAINE**
>
> This moraine is the largest of a series of ridgelike glacial deposits in this area, and the gigantic granite boulders along the moraine's sides testify to the power of the *mer de glace* (sea of ice) that once filled Little Yosemite Valley and its tributaries. One such erratic (a boulder that has been transported by a glacier from one place and deposited at another), about the size of a compact car, was found poised on the side of Moraine Dome to the southwest, and geologists have determined that it came from the slopes of the peaks at the northwest end of the Cathedral Range.

Along this moraine you encounter terrain charred by the 2014 Meadow Fire, a destructive, but naturally ignited, fire that burned much of the Sunrise Creek drainage. Descend the ridge westward for 1.4 miles to meet the Forsyth Trail from Tenaya Lake (right; northeast; Trip 47). Turning left (south) to continue on the JMT, in 0.1 mile you encounter a second junction, where the Merced Lake High Trail merges from the left (east; Trip 47), and you continue right (southwest) along the JMT. Continuing down through burned terrain, you eventually descend right to the banks of Sunrise Creek and wind down the drainage to the north of Moraine Dome, crossing the creek about halfway along. Farther along you abruptly reenter intact forest and, starting here, could search for view-rich campsites on occasional knobs north of the trail. Shortly after rounding a ridge, you ford a tributary and meet the trail coming down from Clouds Rest (Trip 44) at a T-junction. Here are a collection of popular campsites—there are choices on the sandy ridge west of the junction and under forest cover south of the junction (7,159'; 37.74396°N, 119.50374°W).

DAY 3 (Sunrise Creek to Happy Isles Trailhead in Yosemite Valley, 6.6 miles): Follow Trip 44, Day 2 to the Happy Isles Trailhead in Yosemite Valley (4,025'; 37.73242°N, 119.55965°W).

Elizabeth Lake Trailhead   8,652'; 37.87077°N, 119.35599°W

Destination/ GPS Coordinates	Trip Type	Best Season	Pace & Hiking/ Layover Days	Total Mileage	Permit Required
49 Nelson Lake 37.80914°N 119.37978°W	Out-and-back	Mid to late	Moderate 2/1	11.0	Nelson Lake

INFORMATION AND PERMITS: This trip is in Yosemite National Park: wilderness permits and bear canisters are required; pets and firearms are prohibited. Quotas apply, with 60% of permits reservable online up to 24 weeks in advance and 40% available first-come, first-served starting at 11 a.m. the day before your trip's start date. Fires are prohibited above 9,600 feet. See nps.gov/yose/planyourvisit/wildpermits.htm for more details.

DRIVING DIRECTIONS: The trailhead is at the back of the Tuolumne Meadows Campground, just past site B49. Once in the campground, follow road signs to the group-campground loop. Follow the spur to a gate just before the signed HORSE CAMP; the trailhead is here. The campground entrance is located along Tioga Road (CA 120), 7.1 west of Tioga Pass (the Yosemite boundary) and 39.5 miles east of Crane Flat. There are toilets and water at the trailhead.

trip 49 Nelson Lake

>   **Trip Data:** 37.80914°N, 119.37978°W; 11.0 miles; 2/1 days
>   **Topos:** *Vogelsang Peak, Tenaya Lake*

HIGHLIGHTS: Nelson Lake is tucked in a little-visited valley in the Cathedral Range, well off-trail along an unnamed tributary of Echo Creek. This interesting and varied route first visits the scenic Elizabeth Lake basin and continues south over the serrated Cathedral Range on a use trail. It makes a good first off-trail journey into Yosemite's backcountry, for a decent use trail exists along much of the distance. Nonetheless, only embark on this trip if you have good navigation skills and a paper topographic map.

HEADS UP! *Between the Elizabeth Lake basin and Nelson Lake, there's a beaten path that fades out at times, leaving you to walk cross-country. You need good navigation skills to find your way. Camping is prohibited within 4 miles of CA 120 and throughout the Elizabeth Lake basin.*

DAY 1 (Elizabeth Lake Trailhead to Nelson Lake, 5.5 miles, part cross-country): From the campground trailhead, the signed Elizabeth Lake Trail goes south and, after just 200 steps, crosses the well-used Tuolumne Meadows perimeter trail; the perimeter trail heads east to Lyell Canyon and west to Tenaya Lake. You continue straight ahead on a steady southward ascent. Along this lodgepole pine–shaded climb, the trail crosses several seasonal runnels and slowly trends more southwesterly as it sidles over a small rise to reach the banks of Unicorn Creek.

After a 700-foot climb, the gradient lessens, and you cut across sandy flats with increasingly stunted lodgepoles. The younger trees tell a story of trying winters, for they are mostly bent and contorted from the weight of the winter snowpack. Only as they grow taller, and the treetops finally extend above the heavy snowpack, do they have a chance to grow upright. A short time later, you emerge at the foot of a long meadow and are faced with a tangle of use trails, 1.9 miles from the trailhead. All lead right (west) to the

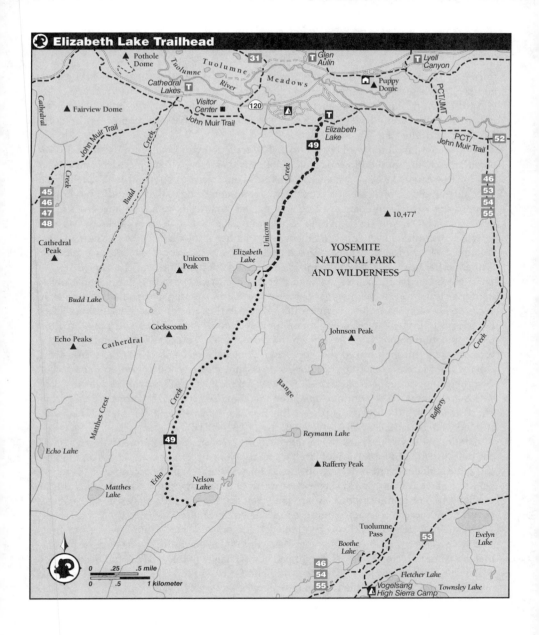

Pothole Dome

Tuolumne River

Glen Aulin

Lyell Canyon

31

Cathedral Lakes T

Tuolumne Meadows

Puppy Dome

PCT/JMT

Fairview Dome

Visitor Center

120

John Muir Trail

Elizabeth Lake

T

49

PCT/
John Muir Trail

52

John Muir Trail

Budd Creek

Cathedral Creek

45
46
47
48

Cathedral Peak

Unicorn Peak

Elizabeth Lake

Unicorn Creek

10,477'

46
53
54
55

YOSEMITE
NATIONAL PARK
AND WILDERNESS

Budd Lake

Cockscomb

Johnson Peak

Echo Peaks

Catherdral

Creek

Range

Rafferty Creek

Matthes Crest

Reymann Lake

49

Rafferty Peak

Echo Lake

Echo Creek

Nelson Lake

Matthes Lake

Tuolumne Pass

Evelyn Lake

53

Boothe Lake

46
54
55

Fletcher Lake

Townsley Lake

Vogelsang
High Sierra Camp

0   .25   .5 mile
0   .5   1 kilometer

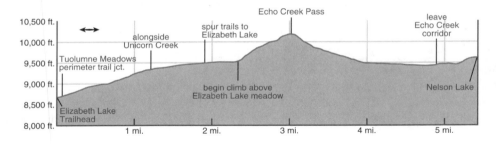

10,500 ft.

10,000 ft.

9,500 ft.

9,000 ft.

8,500 ft.

8,000 ft.

Echo Creek Pass

leave
Echo Creek
corridor

spur trails to
Elizabeth Lake

alongside
Unicorn Creek

Tuolumne Meadows
perimeter trail jct.

begin climb above
Elizabeth Lake meadow

Nelson Lake

Elizabeth Lake
Trailhead

1 mi.   2 mi.   3 mi.   4 mi.   5 mi.

northeastern shores of Elizabeth Lake. Staying left (south), after another 0.1 mile you pass another cluster of right-trending spurs—these lead to the lake's southeastern shores. The view of Unicorn Peak from Elizabeth Lake is not to be missed—walking to the lakeshore is a worthwhile 5-minute detour, despite the sometimes cumbersome hop across Unicorn Creek to reach the lake.

Now on an unmaintained but easy-to-follow trail, you continue south up the meadow corridor, enjoying the wildflowers; pink shooting stars give way to purple asters and yellow monkeyflowers as the season matures. This is a good place to stop and look carefully at your surroundings to ensure you pick the correct route: straight ahead (south) is an open gravelly slope with some late-lasting snow patches that leads to an obvious arc-shaped pass. This is NOT your route. Instead, swivel yourself about 30 degrees clockwise to spy a forested, shallower, lower, less prominent pass that lies immediately east of Knob 10,294, colloquially known as Echo Creek Pass. It leads you across an easy, if unobvious, gap in the Cathedral Range that drops you to the headwaters of the main fork of Echo Creek.

To reach this pass, the use trail soon diverges right (west), trading flat meadow walking for a steady forested climb. It is fairly easy to follow, although, as with all use trails, it occasionally vanishes, only to reappear fully etched in the forest floor a short distance later; the trick is to immediately know you are no longer on a worn pad, so you can search for its continuation before straying far from the correct route. You continue ascending steeply to moderately through mixed lodgepole-and-hemlock forest until 10,000 feet. You then emerge from forest cover onto a shallow, coarse sandy expanse and are led up a channel of decomposing granite between two short but steep rocky ribs. This channel can hold late snow, but is not steep, so continue up it, trending right (west) when outcrops appear ahead. Shortly, you reach the broad, flat pass, sitting between a pair of steep bluffs and dotted with stunted whitebark pines (10,192'; 37.83435°N, 119.37308°W).

Continuing across the pass, the terrain becomes steeper, you are funneled down a gravelly gully. At about the 10,000-foot level, where the slope becomes more vegetated, the trail can quite suddenly vanish. Here, you should turn to the west and descend straight to the banks of nascent Echo Creek, staying just north of a notably wetter slope that is a riot of wildflower color in midsummer. At around 9,900 feet the moisture coalesces into a single channel, and here you resume a more gently angled descent to the valley floor.

Once along Echo Creek, you continue south along the now-again-obvious use trail. The steep glaciated walls loom overhead as you saunter down the shallow valley, passing marmots sunning atop boulders, bright patches of shaggy lupine, and an endless tangle of avalanche-downed trunks. As you descend Echo Creek's valley, take advantage of the fine over-the-shoulder view of the Cockscomb atop the west valley wall.

THE COCKSCOMB

Aptly named by François Matthes, this slender crest bears clear marks of the highest level reached by the ice of the last glacial episode. Its lower shoulders reveal the rounded, well-polished surfaces that betray glacial action, while its jagged, sharply etched crest shows no such markings. Further evidence of glacial action may be clearly seen on the steep descent into the head of long, typically U-shaped Echo Creek valley. The shearing and polishing action of the ice mass that shaped this rounded valley is evident on the cliffs on the west side.

As you approach the end of the second large meadow in this valley, the trail abruptly curves left (east) and leaves Echo Creek (9,436'; 37.81236°N, 119.38509°W; this is about 1.5 miles beyond where you first reach the creek bottom). The track now veers up to a low, rocky ridge, undulates through sparse forest a little below the ridgetop, then vanishes. Now your route—no longer any trail or possibly even cairns to guide you—cuts up and over the shallow bedrock ridgetop, trending just south of due east. Just as you (maybe) pick up a faint pad again, you reach a forested flat with a dense, unappealing tangle of downed logs, dead bleached lodgepoles, and rapidly growing young trees. Ghost forests, as these stands are coined, are the outcome of lodgepole needle-miner damage. This native moth caterpillar moves cyclically through Yosemite's forests, defoliating and often killing the majority of trees.

Of more immediately practical relevance, you are unlikely to successfully follow the use trail through the ghost forest, for the young lodgepoles grow preferentially right in the old trail's depression, forming an impenetrable thicket. Walking where practical, continue your just-south-of-due-east trajectory and you will shortly reach another slab rib, a tad steeper than the previous one. As you climb up it, you may refind the use trail, but it matters little, for you easily surmount it by any number of routes. From atop, turn west to ogle at Matthes Crest, an impressively steep fin of rock lying two drainages to the west, then drop east to reach Nelson Lake's outlet creek. A very brief ascent along the drainage leads to Nelson Lake. Here you'll find some delightful tent sites along its southwestern and southeastern shores. It is a remarkably warm lake for swimming and has perfect shoreline for sitting and admiring the truly stunning view. Anglers will find the lake's waters good fishing for brook trout and wildflower seekers will enjoy the colorful meadows. Peak 11,357, informally named Choo-Choo Ridge, looms to the east, while Rafferty Peak is visible farther northeast (9,629'; 37.80914°N, 119.37978°W).

DAY 2 (Nelson Lake to Elizabeth Lake Trailhead, 5.5 miles, part cross-country): Retrace your steps.

Look back for views of the Mount Conness area as you climb to Echo Pass.   Photo by Elizabeth Wenk

Glen Aulin Trailhead
8,591'; 37.87889°N, 119.35854°W

Destination/ GPS Coordinates	Trip Type	Best Season	Pace & Hiking/ Layover Days	Total Mileage	Permit Required
50 Young Lakes 37.93783°N 119.33566°W (upper Young Lake)	Semiloop	Mid to late	Moderate 2/1	14.1	Young Lakes via Glen Aulin (*Young Lakes via Dog Lake if reversed*)
51 High Sierra Camp Loop, Northwest Section 37.91051°N 119.41699°W (Glen Aulin High Sierra Camp)	Shuttle	Mid to late	Moderate 3/0	16.8	Glen Aulin (*May Lake if reversed*)
31 Pacific Crest Trail to Tuolumne Meadows (*in reverse of description; see page 148*)	Shuttle	Mid to late	Strenuous 8/1	73.9	Glen Aulin
40 Grand Canyon of the Tuolumne (*in reverse of description; see page 197*)	Shuttle	Mid to late	Moderate 4/0	30.1	Glen Aulin
58 Twenty Lakes Basin to Tuolumne Meadows via McCabe Lakes (*in reverse of description; see page 278*)	Shuttle	Mid to late	Strenuous, part cross-country 3/1	21.7	Glen Aulin

INFORMATION AND PERMITS: These trips are in Yosemite National Park: wilderness permits and bear canisters are required; pets and firearms are prohibited. Quotas apply, with 60% of permits reservable online up to 24 weeks in advance and 40% available first-come, first-served starting at 11 a.m. the day before your trip's start date. Fires are prohibited above 9,600 feet. See nps.gov/yose/planyourvisit/wildpermits.htm for more details.

DRIVING DIRECTIONS: The trailhead is just off Tioga Road (CA 120) in Tuolumne Meadows, along the Tuolumne Meadows Stables Road at the base of Lembert Dome. The junction is located just 0.2 mile east of the Tuolumne Meadows Campground entrance, right after you cross the Tuolumne River, or 6.9 miles west of Tioga Pass. The "parking lot" is the dirt shoulder along the Tuolumne Meadows Stables Road with overflow parking available at the stables.

trip 50 Young Lakes

see map on p. 243

Trip Data: 37.93783°N, 119.33566°W (upper Young Lake); 14.1 miles; 2/1 days

Topos: *Tioga Pass, Falls Ridge*

HIGHLIGHTS: The three Young Lakes, cupped under soaring Ragged Peak, are some of the most accessible lakes from Tuolumne Meadows that allow camping. Although busy, they are less crowded than the popular destinations south of Tioga Road. The cluster of lakes offers a large selection of campsites, some in heavy woods and others at timberline. These camps provide a base for exciting excursions into the headwaters of Conness Creek and for climbing Mount Conness itself.

DAY 1 (Glen Aulin Trailhead to Upper Young Lake, 7.3 miles): Go around the locked gate where the road to the stables trends right (north) and continue west on the service road along the lodgepole-dotted flank of Tuolumne Meadows, enjoying fine views south toward the Cathedral Range. After 0.25 mile you meet a smaller trail heading right (northeast) to the horse stables and soon thereafter the main trail splits. Here, the left (southwest) branch heads to a bridge across the nearby Tuolumne River, while your route, the Pacific Crest Trail (PCT), veers right (west), slightly uphill, still on an old road, and quickly encounters a spur trail to the bubbling natural Soda Springs.

> **SODA SPRINGS CAMPGROUND**
> This former campground was once the private holding of John Lembert, namesake of Lembert Dome. His brothers, who survived him, sold it to the Sierra Club in 1912, and for 60 years club members enjoyed a private campground in the marvelous subalpine meadow just northeast of Soda Springs. But in 1972 the club deeded the property to the National Park Service so that everyone could use it.

Above Soda Springs the road forks, and you go right (northwest), still on the PCT. (To take a peek at the nearby buildings—McCauley Cabin and Parsons Memorial Lodge—briefly go left [southwest], then return after having satisfied your curiosity.) Your westbound trail passes a reed-filled lake, then traverses open sandy flats interspersed with lodgepole pine patches. Another spur trail from the stables merges from the right (southwest) and just beyond you descend to cross Delaney Creek, a potentially treacherous crossing in late May and June if no log is availale to balance across. In late season, this is your only water source until the Young Lakes.

Continuing not far from the northern edge of Tuolumne Meadows you soon reach a junction, where you go right (north) to Young Lakes, while the PCT continues left (west) to Glen Aulin High Sierra Camp (Trips 31 and 51). From the junction, you ascend gradually across a broad expanse of boulder-strewn sheets of granite. An open spot affords a look south across broad Tuolumne Meadows to the line of peaks from steep, rounded Fairview Dome to the steeplelike spires of the Cathedral Range. After a little under a mile, the trail dips to first parallel and then cross Dingley Creek (may be dry by late season).

The trail continues winding gently upward in shady pine forest carpeted with a fine flower display even into late season. Through early July, enjoy the delicate, creamy-white flowers of mariposa lilies, with one rich brown spot in the throat of each petal; *mariposa*

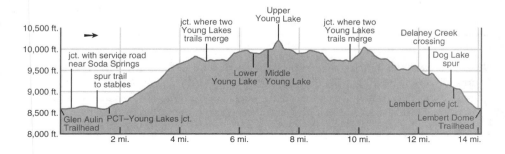

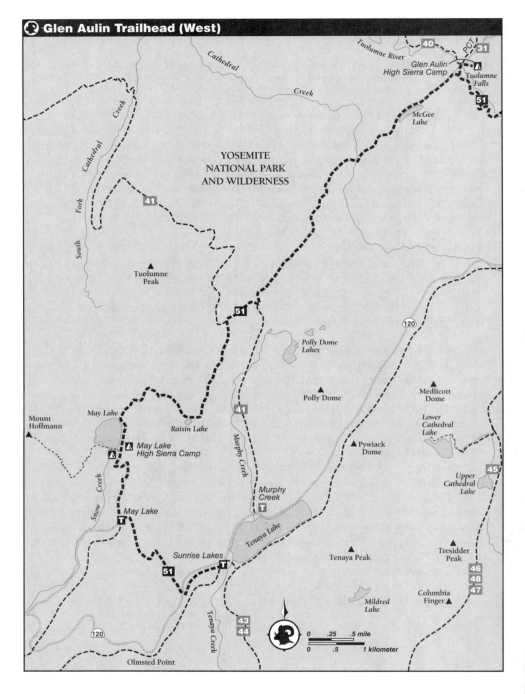

means butterfly in Spanish, for the petals resemble a butterfly's wings. The trail remains just south of the ridge, denying the hiker spectacular northward vistas, so be sure to take a few steps north and enjoy the panoply of peaks: majestic Tower Peak, Doghead and Quarry Peaks, the Finger Peaks, Matterhorn Peak, Sheep Peak, Mount Conness, and the Shepherd Crest. From this viewpoint a moderate descent leads to a step-across crossing of a Conness

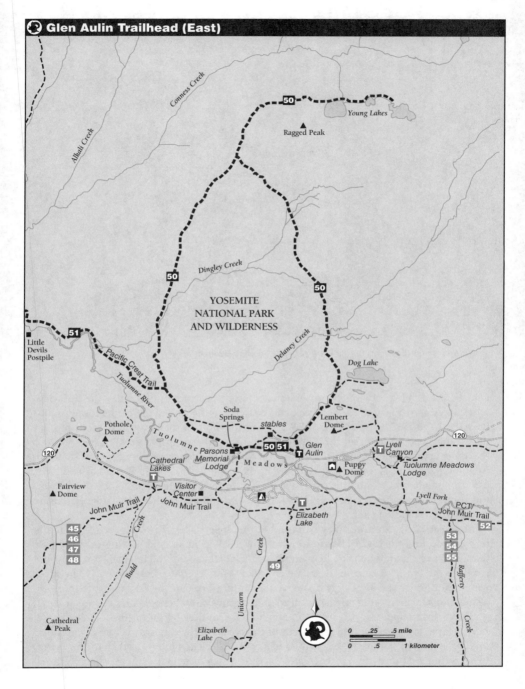

Creek tributary and, just beyond, a junction with a southeast-climbing trail, the other Young Lakes Trail, your return route.

Turn left (generally north) and start a roller-coaster traverse through a cool forest of mountain hemlocks, lodgepoles, and western white pines, crossing seasonal rivulets. Turning east you climb up to a plateau, en route passing a meadow that was the fourth Young

Bog laurel is plentiful near middle Young Lake.   Photo by Elizabeth Wenk

Lake before it filled in with stream sediments. From your high point enjoy the fine view of the steep north face of Ragged Peak and descend to the west shore of the lower Young Lake (9,910'; 37.93718°N, 119.34860°W). The north shore of the lowest lake easily has the most campsites of the three lakes—and indeed most hikers camp here, though I've listed the upper lake as the official destination, as I recommend that everyone visit it as a side trip. At about 9,900 feet, lower Young Lake lies in the subalpine realm, so it still has sufficient trees for shade and to diminish the sometimes strong late-afternoon winds. Fishing on the Young Lakes is fair to good for brook trout. (Stopping here shaves 1.7 miles from the round-trip distance given.)

More secluded campsites may be found at the upper lakes. To reach them, follow the trail east around the lower lake, fording the lower lake's outlet, and picking up a use trail that climbs to the middle lake. Remaining on the north side of the inlet stream, the route parallels the creek east up to the relatively small Middle Young Lake (9,995'). The most used campsites are on a rocky ridge above the middle lake's northwest shore, but there are also options farther to the northeast, nestled in a grove of lodgepole pines.

To reach the uppermost lake, after encircling the middle lake's north shore clockwise, most people follow a use trail just north of the creek, but it is narrow, eroded, and often muddy. A better, if sometimes cryptic, use trail stays just slightly farther to the north, meandering eastward up to benchlands across which you make an easy, nearly level, open, scenic traverse southeast emerging on the slabs ringing this stunning alpine lake. There are a few small campsites along Upper Young Lake's north and west shores (10,210'; 37.93783°N, 119.33566°W). These are small sandy patches among slabs and stunted white-bark pines that offer outstanding views, but little protection from the elements, so many people choose to visit this lake for a view after establishing camp at a lower elevation. From here, relatively easy cross-country travel leads to the giant plateau leading to Mount Conness's summit, although note that the final stretch to the summit is a little exposed.

DAY 2 (Upper Young Lake to Glen Aulin Trailhead, 6.8 miles): After exploring the Young Lakes area, retrace your steps to the junction where the two Young Lakes trails merge. Turning left (south), you will now take the trail that passes close to Dog Lake. First climb the southwest spur of Ragged Peak, a sandy, boulder-scattered slope with moderate lodge-pole-and-hemlock cover. Views from atop are outstanding, with Yosemite's tallest peak, Mount Lyell, crowning the skyline, easily identified by its monumental snowfield. From here, the trail descends through a very large, gently sloping meadow dotted with small lodgepoles. This broad expanse is a wildflower garden in season, laced with meandering brooks, but it may be almost dry late in a low-water year. Expanses of paintbrush and lupine in the fore-ground set off the views of the entire Cathedral Range, strung out on the southern horizon.

Near the lower edge of the meadow, you cross the headwaters of Dingley Creek. Beyond, you descend, steeply at times, past exfoliating Peak 10,410 to reach a seasonal creek in a mixed forest of lodgepole and hemlock. The trail then levels off and veers east on a rolling course through more lodgepole forest, where the sandy soil sprouts thousands of prostrate little lupine plants. After another seasonal creek is crossed, you make a short but noticeable climb to the crest of a large, bouldery ridge. Down its gravelly slopes (that is, slower walk-ing), you descend to a very large, level meadow where the reddish peaks of Mount Dana and Mount Gibbs loom in the east and Delaney Creek meanders lazily through the grass. You cross on a collection of logs because the channel is too wide to leap across and would be a deep (but easy) wade.

After climbing briefly over the crest of a second bouldery ridge, your route begins its final descent into Tuolumne Meadows. Lembert Dome can be glimpsed through the trees along this stretch of trail. The trail levels slightly before it fords Dog Lake's outlet and soon meets the signed lateral that leads 0.1 mile left (northeast) to Dog Lake (worth the brief detour); you continue right (south). After another 0.1 mile, you reach a junction with a trail that leads left (east) along the north side of Lembert Dome and you again stay right (southwest). You parallel the outlet creek from Dog Lake, switchbacking quite steeply down a rocky, dusty trail, dropping approximately 500 feet. As the gradient lessens, there are two spur trails right (west) to the stables, while you continue left (south) on beautiful white polished slabs extending from the western base of Lembert Dome. Passing through a few lodgepole pines, you reach the Lembert Dome parking area; turn right along the road to find your car.

---

trip 51   # High Sierra Camp Loop, Northwest Section

see maps on p. 242–243

Trip Data: 37.91051°N, 119.41699°W (Glen Aulin High Sierra Camp); 16.8 miles; 3/0 days

Topos: *Falls Ridge, Tenaya Lake, Tioga Pass*

HIGHLIGHTS: This three-day section of the Tuolumne area's High Sierra Camp Loop is a beautiful beginner's hike, taking in a selection of the region's stunning scenery, from waterfalls to lakes, with-out any terribly arduous climbs or long mileage days.

HEADS UP! *This trip could end at the May Lake Trailhead at Snow Flat, shaving 2 miles off the distance. Sunrise Lakes Trailhead is given as the ending point for two reasons. First, the Tuolumne Meadows shuttle serves the Sunrise Lakes Trailhead, but not the May Lake Trailhead, meaning you don't need to shuttle cars. Second, the May Lake Road is often closed into July, and this is a great early-summer hike in the Tuolumne Meadows area.*

SHUTTLE DIRECTIONS: You complete your hike at the Sunrise Lakes Trailhead, at the southwest corner of Tenaya Lake, located along Tioga Road (CA 120) 8.9 miles west of the Glen Aulin Trailhead. You can shuttle a car to this location or use the Toulumne Meadows shuttle to return to your car. The shuttles run every 30 minutes during the summer. They charge a fee, so be sure to carry cash.

DAY 1 (Glen Aulin Trailhead to Glen Aulin High Sierra Camp, 5.4 miles): From a locked gate you walk along an old road that skirts the northern edge of Tuolumne Meadows, following the route of the Pacific Crest Trail (PCT). On it you are treated to fine views south toward the Cathedral Range. After 0.25 mile you meet a smaller trail heading northeast to the horse stables and soon thereafter the main trail splits. Here, the left (southwest) branch heads to a bridge across the nearby Tuolumne River, while your route, still on an old road, veers right (west, then north), slightly uphill, and quickly encounters a spur trail to the bubbling natural Soda Springs.

Above the effervescent Soda Springs and nearby historical Parsons Memorial Lodge, your westbound trail passes a reed-filled lake, then traverses open sandy flats interspersed with lodgepole pine patches. Another spur trail from the stables merges from the right (southwest) and just beyond you descend to cross Delaney Creek, a potentially difficult early-season crossing if there isn't a good log to balance across the main flow. Walking not far from the northern edge of Tuolumne Meadows you soon reach a junction with a trail to Young Lakes (Trip 50), where the PCT, your route, veers left (northwest), winding through scattered lodgepoles, then descending some bare granite slabs and entering a flat-floored forest. A glimpse at a satellite photo would show that your route is carefully chosen: your rambling traverse across the granite slabs picks a route that follows a series of shallow, forested depressions, making for pleasant walking. A mile brings you to the west end of a huge meadow near the bank of the Tuolumne River, and beyond to three branches of seasonal Dingley Creek.

From here, the nearly level trail often runs along the river, and in these stretches by the stream there are numerous glacier-smoothed granite slabs on which to take a break—or dip, if the river's current is slow. After a mile-long winding traverse, the trail leaves the last slabs to climb briefly on a granite outcrop to get around the river's gorge. You can leave the trail and walk toward a brink, from where you'll see, on the south side of the gorge below you, Little Devils Postpile, a small outcrop of columnar basalt.

Beyond, the trail winds down, soon reaching a sturdy Tuolumne River bridge. Here, the river flows rapidly down a series of sparkling rapids separated by large pools and wide sheets of water. The trail alongside this beautiful stretch of river also descends more steeply; you will find the walking rockier, slower, and most certainly harder on the knees. As you descend, give yourself time to gaze at Tuolumne Falls in particular. The trail trends away from the creek to a moister glen, turns back to the riverbank for a length, then enters a second glade where

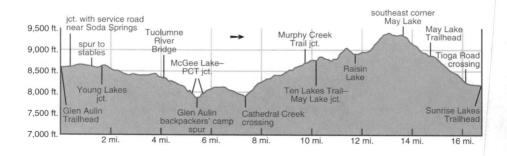

Tuolumne Falls   Photo by Elizabeth Wenk

you reach a junction with the trail left (southwest) to McGee Lake and May Lake; you will head along this route tomorrow morning, but for now, stay right (north) toward Glen Aulin.

Below you, watch White Cascade tumbling into a circular pool and cross another bridge high above the churning Tuolumne River. During high runoff, you may have to wade just to reach this bridge—the expanse of rounded river cobble and boulders strewn across the trail are evidence that this is sometimes a streambed. From here, it is only a few minutes' walk to the junction to Glen Aulin High Sierra Camp, the latter reached on a spur trail by crossing a bridge over Conness Creek. From the camp a short trail leads north past the High Sierra Camp's canvas tents to the heavily used Glen Aulin backpackers' camp (7,930'; 37.91051°N, 119.41699°W), complete with bear-proof food-storage boxes, pit toilets, and, when the Sierra Camp is open, a potable water faucet. If you will be camping at Glen Aulin and have spare hours before nightfall or a layover day, you could detour down the Tuolumne River to see California Falls, Le Conte Falls, and/or Waterwheel Falls, described on page 202 as part of Trip 40.

DAY 2 (Glen Aulin High Sierra Camp to May Lake, 8.3 miles): You retrace your steps for 0.2 mile, to the junction to McGee Lake and May Lake. Heading right (generally southwest), you briefly curve northwest through a notch. Your duff trail then ascends gently southwest, leveling off at long, narrow McGee Lake (limited campsites). In late summer, the lake, perched on a saddle and receiving no incoming water, may dwindle to a stale pond and is not too attractive, while at peak flows it has a pair of outlets. Beyond, your trail descends along the lake's southwest-flowing ephemeral outlet for 0.75 mile, then crosses it. Passing a collection of seasonal tarns and meadow patches thick with corn lilies, you soon have a view northwest through the shallow Cathedral Creek canyon to hulking Falls Ridge.

After several minutes you reach Cathedral Creek, a wade in early summer, transitioning to a boulder hop later. Starting a moderate ascent beyond the creek, you soon reach a stand of tall, healthy red firs set between two granite ribs. Seeing the contrast between these sturdy-trunked, dispersed trees and the straggly overcrowded lodgepoles below is inescapable. You mount a few brief switchbacks to the top of an open bluff, and suddenly the panorama emerges to the northeast, most welcome after several miles of forest walking. In the distant northeast stand Sheep Peak, North Peak, and Mount Conness, the trio encircling the Roosevelt Lake basin. The trail continues up a moderate slope on gravel and granite shelves, through a forest cover of hemlock, red fir, and lodgepole. Stepping across an ephemeral branch of Cathedral Creek, you have one more stretch of uphill hiking under dense hemlock cover to reach a trail junction; on an early-season hike, this final slope may still be snow covered.

From here, you turn right (southwest), while the Murphy Creek Trail departs left (south), descending to Tenaya Lake (Trip 41). Skirting to the south of lush forest and seasonally boggy meadows, the nearly flat trail soon reaches a junction with the Ten Lakes Trail. This route trends right (northwest; Trip 41), while you branch left (south) and ascend briefly to a long, narrow, shallow, forested saddle, beyond which large Tenaya Lake is visible to the south. After traversing somewhat open slopes of sagebrush, huckleberry oak, and lupine, you pass a spring and embark on a series of switchbacks and rock steps. A profusion of wildflowers decorates these slopes, fed by subterranean (and aboveground) moisture. You also enjoy striking views of Mount Conness, Mount Dana, and the other peaks on the Sierra Crest. The trail then passes through a little saddle just north of a glacier-smoothed slab peak.

From here you descend gradually over fairly open granite to a forested flat and bend west above the north shore of Raisin Lake, a notably warm swimming locale, but with limited, albeit lovely, campsites. Skirting the lakeshore, the trail continues beside a seasonal creek under a sparse forest cover of mountain hemlock and western white and lodgepole

Consider camping near beautiful Raisin Lake.　Photo by Elizabeth Wenk

pines, then swings west across three more seasonal trickles. Finally the trail makes a 0.5-mile-long steep ascent, across a conifer-dotted slope. Views improve constantly, and presently you have again earned the panorama of peaks on the Sierra Crest.

At the top of this climb is a gentle upland where several small meadows are strung along the trail. Corn lilies grow at an almost perceptible rate in early summer, while aromatic lupine commands your attention later. In the west, Mount Hoffmann dominates. Now you swing south, descend gently, and reach the northeast corner of May Lake and parallel its east shore to reach first the May Lake High Sierra Camp and then, at the southeast corner of the lake (9,335'; 37.84405°N, 119.49112°W), a water faucet, toilet, and bear boxes; the backpackers' camp is strung west from here, set back a little from May Lake's southern shore. Note that swimming is prohibited at May Lake. Also at May Lake's southeast corner is a junction with a trail striking west—this is the trail to Mount Hoffmann, a worthwhile ascent if you have spare hours.

MOUNT HOFFMANN

Mount Hoffmann lies close to Yosemite's geographic center and from its summit you can see every major peak within the park. To reach Mount Hoffmann strike west along May Lake's southern shore and then, from the lake's southwest corner, begin a gradual climb across metasedimentary rocks cropping out above the lake's southwest shore. You follow the trail southwest, first to a rocky flat atop a small knob and then up through a steeper, boulder-strewn wildflower garden, resplendent with bright colors. The wildflower gully leads to a small, linear meadow occupying a broad saddle. Encircling the meadow along its southeastern edge, the trail continues 300 feet past the meadow's southwestern end and then climbs northwest, switchbacking up a dry, sandy slope dotted with whitebark pines. You climb persistently, absorbing the expanding views and mercifully distracted by colorful flowers, until you reach the lower end of the broad, sloping summit area. A well-trod use trail takes you across this summit plateau to a saddle at its northern end. Mount Hoffmann boasts numerous summits, of which the western summit is the highest, at 10,850 feet, and, turning left (west), you have a relatively easy scramble to its top.

DAY 3 (May Lake to Sunrise Lakes Trailhead, 3.1 miles): You begin the third day's hike by taking the trail south from the junction at the southeast corner of May Lake to the trailhead at Snow Flat. This trail winds briefly down broken slabs, then reenters open forest cover as it follows a passageway nearly due south between two shallow rock ribs. The tree cover shifts between sparse and sparser, reflecting the shallowness of the soils. Passing a shallow, often-buggy tarn you reach the May Lake Trailhead at Snow Flat. You could end your trip here—see "Heads Up!" on page 245 for why the description continues.

Your forward route is at the far back of the parking area (northeast end), behind a locked gate. You will now follow this closed road, old Tioga Road, down to a crossing of the current CA 120, Tioga Road. The walking is fast and uneventful, with broken views of the surrounding scenery. Quite soon you reach Tioga Road and cross it, then turn left (north) to follow the trail that parallels the road downhill, toward Tenaya Lake. At a junction with a wooden sign simply declaring TRAIL JUNCTION, remain to the left (northeast), adjacent to Tioga Road, and cross a small creek. Flat, sandy walking through open lodgepole forest quickly leads to a T-junction with a more prominent trail. Turn left (west) and you are almost immediately at the Sunrise Lakes Trailhead. The Tuolumne Meadows–bound shuttle bus will pull into the parking area just in front of the toilets. This shuttle currently charges a fee, so be sure to bring some cash with you for the ride to your car.

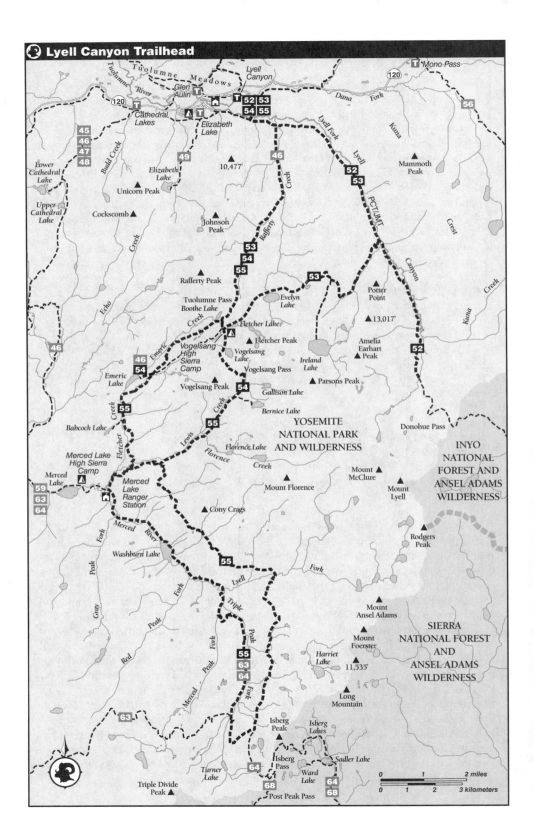

Lyell Canyon Trailhead

Lyell Canyon Trailhead — 8,686'; 37.87779°N, 119.33852°W

Destination/ GPS Coordinates	Trip Type	Best Season	Pace & Hiking/ Layover Days	Total Mileage	Permit Required
52 Lyell Canyon 37.77765°N 119.26211°W (Upper Lyell Fork bridge)	Out-and-back	Mid to late	Leisurely 2/1	20.2	Lyell Canyon
53 Vogelsang High Sierra Camp and Lyell Canyon 37.79622°N 119.34422°W (Vogelsang camping)	Semiloop	Mid to late	Moderate 3/1	19.3	Rafferty Creek to Vogelsang (Lyell Canyon if reversed)
54 Lewis Creek and Emeric Lake 37.77825°N 119.38150°W (Emeric Lake)	Semiloop	Mid to late	Moderate 4/0	27.5	Rafferty Creek to Vogelsang
55 Triple Peak Fork Merced River 37.65847°N 119.34456°W (Triple Peak Fork junction)	Semiloop	Mid to late	Moderate 6/2	47.8	Rafferty Creek to Vogelsang
46 Cathedral Range Circuit (in reverse of description; see page 225)	Shuttle (or Loop)	Mid to late	Moderate 5/1	31.4	Rafferty Creek to Vogelsang

INFORMATION AND PERMITS: These trips are in Yosemite National Park: wilderness permits and bear canisters are required; pets and firearms are prohibited. Quotas apply, with 60% of permits reservable online up to 24 weeks in advance and 40% available first-come, first-served starting at 11 a.m. the day before your trip's start date. Fires are prohibited above 9,600 feet. See nps.gov/yose/planyourvisit/wildpermits.htm for more details.

DRIVING DIRECTIONS: To reach this trailhead, from Tuolumne Meadows Campground (the only campground in the area) drive 0.6 mile northeast on Tioga Road (CA 120), turning right onto Tuolumne Meadows Lodge Road. If you are descending from Tioga Pass, drive 6.4 miles southwest to the only road that branches left before you reach Tuolumne Meadows; you pass it just beyond a pedestrian crossing and reduced speed limit signs. Drive 0.4 mile along Tuolumne Meadows Lodge Road, past the Tuolumne Meadows Wilderness Center parking area (alternate location to park your car) and a collection of employee houses, to reach the Dog Lake parking area, on your left (north). The Lyell Canyon Trailhead is directly across from the parking area, on the south side of the Tuolumne Meadows Lodge Road. The closest water and toilets are at the Tuolumne Meadows Wilderness Center.

Lyell Canyon   Photo by Elizabeth Wenk

trip 52   Lyell Canyon

see map on p. 250

Trip Data: 37.77765°N, 119.26211°W (Upper Lyell Fork bridge);
20.2 miles; 2/1 days
Topos: *Vogelsang Peak, Tioga Pass*

HIGHLIGHTS: The subalpine meadows of Lyell Canyon are the stuff of which favorite backpacking memories are made. Idyllic from beginning to end, this long, gentle grassland with its meandering river is a delight to travel. The first 8.8 miles are nearly flat—you climb only 300 feet, while the final mile is a steady ascent. The described route continues to the uppermost sheltered campsites, but it is strongly recommended that you schedule a layover day to continue an additional 1.5 miles to the upper, alpine part of Lyell Canyon.

DAY 1 (Lyell Canyon Trailhead to Upper Lyell Bridge, 10.1 miles): Walking south, you promptly reach the trail shared by the Pacific Crest Trail (PCT) and the John Muir Trail (JMT) and turn left (east) onto it, following the Dana Fork of the Tuolumne River upstream. You quickly reach a junction with a spur trail that goes left to the west end of the Tuolumne Meadows Lodge's parking lot. You, however, turn right (south) to cross the Dana Fork on a bridge and after a brief walk upstream reach a junction with a trail signposted to the Gaylor Lakes (left; east); you stay right (south) on the JMT/PCT.

Veering south, away from the Dana Fork, your trail leads over a slight rise and descends to the Lyell Fork Tuolumne River, where two substantial bridges span the churning river as it exits a long lobe of Tuolumne Meadows, tumbling down polished, potholed granite. At the southwestern corner of the meadow, you meet a trail that heads right (west), along Tuolumne Meadow's southern perimeter, toward the Tuolumne Meadows Campground. Your route, the JMT/PCT, turns left (east), following the Lyell Fork, although you are sufficiently south of the river corridor that you barely glimpse the water.

REROUTING TRAILS

Many decades ago the National Park Service (NPS) had the foresight to protect part of the Lyell Fork's fragile banks by rerouting the trail. Along the east-to-west-trending length of river closer to Tuolumne Meadows, the trail once followed the meadow corridor, but was rerouted into the fringing lodgepole pines to limit compaction of meadow soils and eliminate the creation of multiple parallel trail treads. More recently, starting in 2012, the NPS turned its attention to the trail segment along Lyell Canyon closer to the Evelyn Lake junction and has now completed rerouting additional sections of trail to less fragile terrain. We must applaud the NPS and their partner organizations the Yosemite Conservancy and John Muir Trail Wilderness Conservancy for their farsighted policies.

The trail, alternately on slab and in lush lodgepole forest, leads to a junction on the west bank of Rafferty Creek, from where the Rafferty Creek Trail to Vogelsang High Sierra Camp departs to the right (south), while the JMT/PCT continues left (east). Crossing Rafferty Creek on a stout footbridge, the trail traverses both wet meadow and forested sections, then veers southward, weaving between two resistant granite outcrops. As you turn south and enter Lyell Canyon, you reunite with the Lyell Fork. Fields of diminutive wildflowers color the grasslands from early to late season, with different species stealing the limelight with each passing week of the brief mountain summer. From the more open parts of the trail, you have excellent views of the Kuna Crest to the southeast. During your walk upriver, take a break at one of the divine riverside slabs you pass and admire the beautiful aqua color in the broad, deep meandering channel. The trail stays to the west of the meadow corridor, part of a just-completed trail reconstruction along much of Lyell Canyon. The human impact on the fragile riparian vegetation was too great and the trail has been rerouted onto slabs and through lodgepole pine stands away from the meadow corridor. Once you are 4 trail miles beyond Tuolumne Meadows, a distance approximately demarcated by a distinct avalanche scar on the slopes to the east, you are permitted to camp, although legal, environmentally acceptable options are sparse. Eventually the trail turns a little more to the right (west) and you quickly reach a large, often-crowded campsite and just beyond a junction. Here the JMT/PCT continues left (south), while right (southwest) leads to Ireland and Evelyn Lakes (Trip 53).

Your route remains well west of the river corridor as it crosses Ireland Creek (a log crossing or wet feet in early summer) and loops back toward the meadow's edge. Still with negligible elevation gain, the JMT/PCT continues up Lyell Canyon, beneath imposing Potter Point. At several locations where the trail diverges slightly from the river, there are a few small campsites to the west of the trail in forest or on slab. Elsewhere the expansive

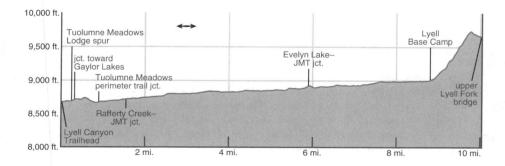

meadows fill the entire valley. Along this stretch you begin to enjoy glimpses of Mount Lyell, Yosemite's highest peak, which quickly dominates the upcanyon view. Then quite suddenly, right where Kuna Creek cascades down from the east, the flat meadowed section of Lyell Canyon ends. This location has long been known as Lyell Base Camp and was where Sierra Club groups would spend their first night on knapsack trips up Lyell Canyon, but it offers only fair campsites, unless you ford the Lyell Fork.

From Lyell Base Camp, you quickly leave lodgepole shade and make an ascending traverse across a well-irrigated slope littered with avalanche debris. Many decades back this massive slide left barely a tree standing and not until 9,575 feet do you cross back to undamaged forest. Now the trail completes a series of tight switchbacks up a hemlock-clad gully to reach a forested bench with campsites—and views north if you detour a little north of the trail. (Note that campfires are prohibited here, even if you find a location just below 9,600 feet!) The trail then crosses the Lyell Fork on a footbridge and just beyond are two spur trails leading east to additional camping (9,653'; 37.77765°N, 119.26211°W; no campfires). There are additional idyllic treeline campsites another 0.9 mile up the trail.

UPPER LYELL CANYON

From the upper Lyell Bridge, a day hike toward Donohue Pass is called for. Continuing an additional 1.5 trail miles south leads to a narrow valley where you could continue south, off-trail to the true headwaters of the Lyell Fork. This wonderland of polished slab and alpine meadows leads to the permanent snowfield (once a glacier) at the base of Mount Lyell. Alternately, continuing yet an additional 1.1 miles along the JMT/PCT leads across flower-speckled broken slab to Donohue Pass. If you climb just 200 feet to the north of Donohue Pass you have wide-ranging views toward the Ritter Range. There are a few good campsites beneath whitebark pines 0.9 mile above the upper Lyell Bridge, but not many trailside options once you are higher.

DAY 2 (Upper Lyell Bridge to Lyell Canyon Trailhead, 10.1 miles): Retrace your steps.

---

trip 53 **Vogelsang High Sierra Camp and Lyell Canyon**

see map on p. 250

Trip Data: 37.79622°N, 119.34422°W; 19.3 miles; 3/1 days
Topos: *Vogelsang Peak*

HIGHLIGHTS: Vogelsang Camp has the most dramatic setting of the famous High Sierra Camps. Located right under the somber north face of Fletcher Peak, it offers views of valleys, granite domes, and lakes. Many nearby lakes offer exciting side trips for anglers, swimmers, and view seekers, and Fletcher Peak, a Class 2 scramble, invites peak baggers. Continuing to Lyell Canyon, an option chosen by many hikers who have three days, takes you along the broad view-rich shelf holding Evelyn Lake and into beloved Lyell Canyon where the Lyell Fork Tuolumne forms deep, turquoise meanders.

DAY 1 (Lyell Canyon Trailhead to Vogelsang High Sierra Camp, 7.3 miles): Walking south through a small meadow, you promptly reach the trail shared by the Pacific Crest Trail (PCT) and the John Muir Trail (JMT) and turn left (east) onto it, following the Dana Fork of the Tuolumne River upstream. You quickly reach a junction with a spur trail that goes left to the west end of the Tuolumne Meadows Lodge's parking lot. You, however, turn right (south) to cross the Dana Fork on a bridge, turn upstream, and quickly reach a junction with a trail signposted to the Gaylor Lakes (left; east); you stay right (south) on the JMT/

PCT. Veering south, away from the Dana Fork, the trail leads over a slight rise and descends to the Lyell Fork Tuolumne River, where two substantial bridges span the river as it churns down polished granite at the west end of a long meadow. At the southwestern corner of the meadow, you reach a junction; the right (westbound) trail follows the Lyell Fork toward the Tuolumne Meadows Campground. The JMT/PCT, your route, turns left (east), traveling upstream parallel to the Lyell Fork, although you are sufficiently south of the river corridor that you barely glimpse the water.

Your route alternates between slab and lush lodgepole forest, leading to a junction on the west bank of Rafferty Creek. Here the JMT/PCT continues left (east), the route on which you will return if you complete the full loop, while today's route, the Rafferty Creek Trail, turns right (south) and immediately begins an often-warm climb at moderate grade through scattered lodgepole pines. The climb eases after half a mile, with the trail assuming a gentler grade to match a change in topography.

Paralleling Rafferty Creek upward, you walk across slabs interspersed with sandy patches. These host colorful blooms for only a few weeks after snowmelt, then dry to a monotonous gray-beige. You cross a few seasonal tributaries that have rocks to balance on at high flows and note the occasional western white pine in the predominately lodgepole forest, for there are suddenly larger cones strewn across the ground. In places the landscape is open and offers good views eastward to reddish-brown Mount Dana and Mount Gibbs as well as gray-white Mammoth Peak, rising northeast of Lyell Canyon. At 3.4 miles the trail changes course slightly and you more closely parallel the now rather diminutive Rafferty Creek upward. Exiting forest cover, you skirt the western side of a meadow, harboring a few mediocre campsites in the surrounding forest, then reenter the thinning lodgepole forest.

Crossing additional seasonal creeks, you exit a stand of trees to find yourself staring up a much larger meadow. Through this you ascend easily upcanyon, having backward views north to the Sierra Crest between Tioga Pass and Mount Conness, and views ahead to cliff-bound, dark-banded Fletcher Peak and Vogelsang Peak to the right of it. This boulder-strewn, marmot-rich meadow leads remarkably gradually to Tuolumne Pass, a major gap in the Cathedral Range, and a junction.

At the pass, a signed trail junction indicates that the left fork (south-southwest), your route, heads south to Vogelsang High Sierra Camp, while the right fork (southwest) goes to Boothe, Emeric, Babcock, and Merced Lakes. The trail traverses gradually upward across a moderately steep slope above Boothe Lake. As it then bends slightly south the tents of Vogelsang High Sierra Camp are immediately in view, spread out at the foot of Fletcher Peak's rock glacier. The camp's buildings are situated just behind a signed four-way junction. At the camp a few snacks may be bought, or dinner or breakfast if you have made a reservation well in advance.

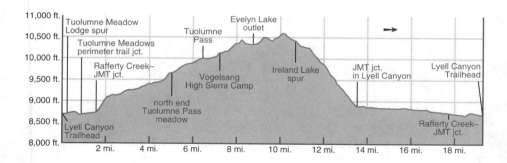

At the junction, turn left (east), signposted for Ireland Lake. Camping on the shores of Fletcher Lake is not allowed. Rather, use a designated camping area just to the northwest of Fletcher Lake (10,135'; 37.79622°N, 119.34422°W; no campfires), complete with animal-proof food-storage boxes; note there is no longer a pit toilet or potable water for backpackers at Vogelsang. Additional, starker camping options are available among slabs at Vogelsang Lake, 0.6 mile along the trail to Vogelsang Pass (often with fewer early-season mosquitoes), in the direction of Evelyn Lake, described under Day 2, or a short distance down the trail that leads southwest to Emeric Lake. Many people will choose to explore the Vogelsang environs for a day and retrace their steps the 7.3 miles to Tuolumne Meadows, but this description suggests a 3-day loop that exits via Lyell Canyon.

VOGELSANG LAYOVER DAY

With so many lakes within 3 miles of Vogelsang—and each remarkably unique in character—it is well worth scheduling a layover day here and visiting some collection of Vogelsang, Emeric, Boothe, Fletcher, and Townsley Lakes before continuing. Those hooked on summits, consider an excursion to Fletcher Peak: take the southbound trail to Vogelsang Lake's outlet, then turn east (left), and ascend the obvious steep, sandy chute breaking the headwall in front of you. This leads to a sandy flat, from which lower-angle sandy slopes rise east to the summit.

DAY 2 (Vogelsang High Sierra Camp to Lyell Canyon, 6.1 miles): Onward, follow the northern shore of Fletcher Lake across sparse gravelly meadows, climbing gently to the northeast once you reach the lake's east end. The landscape remains open, with large expanses of meadow, interspersed with polished slab ribs, grassy benches, and scattered stands of crooked pines. In early summer moisture trickles across the trail, irrigating bright flushes of wildflowers. At the top of the rise, you walk along a meadowy channel, then turn east as you enter the spacious meadow filling the shelf north of Evelyn Lake. Some lovely campsites exist in the sandy patches among slabs both to the west and east of the lake. The

Evelyn Lake   Photo by Elizabeth Wenk

views from here are outstanding—in addition to the open views to the north, the Kuna Crest and Koip Peak are now visible to the east, and Fletcher and Parsons Peaks remain dominant to the southwest. Perhaps the choice campsites appear as you continue eastward, climbing gently toward the next saddle. Here you will stumble across multiple picturesque sites partially sheltered by whitebark pines, all with memorable views. Descending, you pass additional campsites and a smaller unnamed lake that you skirt well to the north to avoid its marshy shores.

Ahead, you ascend to the next ridge through steeper terrain, enjoying views to the east from the high point. Down the east side, the trail zigzags between rock benches—the going is slower—leading to the first continuous forest cover in many miles and the junction to Ireland Lake. A 1.5-mile track leads to Ireland Lake, a big, deep lake at the rear of an enormous moist meadow and backdropped by steep walls. Absolutely worth a detour for the views, but hunting for camping near the lake itself is fruitless, as it is all grass! Instead, there are a few options about halfway there, on sandy knobs near a small stream.

The trail now descends ever more steeply, leading to Lyell Canyon through a dense lodgepole forest just north of Ireland Creek. It is, in places, a surprisingly steep, narrow track—surprising, given the popularity of this route. This is the dampest forest you have walked through on this hike, and the understory is notably dense, with a collection of heath species creating near continuous ground cover. The forest starts to thin during the final mile into Lyell Canyon—first because stretches of forest have suffered recent blowdowns, identifiable by the tangle of trees lying about the forest floor, and later because the slabs are close to the surface, so the soils are thin and fewer trees establish.

Continuing along, you quite suddenly reach a large camping area and a junction with the JMT/PCT corridor (8,930'; 37.82554°N, 119.27966°W). You will almost always share this campsite with other hikers, but there is plenty of room—and not many other options nearby.

DAY 3 (Lyell Canyon to Lyell Canyon Trailhead, 5.9 miles): Turning left (north), you begin a quicker-paced walk along the easy trail through Lyell Canyon. Take a break at one of the divine riverside slabs you pass during the first mile along the river. In early summer, listen to the tumbling water and later splay yourself out on the warm rocks for a quick nap—or take a chilly swim. The trail stays to the west of the meadow corridor, part of a just-completed trail reconstruction along all of Lyell Canyon. The human impact on the fragile riparian vegetation has been too great and the trail is now rerouted onto slabs and through lodgepole pine stands to let the meadow recover. Once you are back within a 4-trail-mile radius of Tuolumne Meadows, camping is prohibited—this is approximately opposite a large avalanche scar. You continue your trot along the river corridor, admiring the beautiful aqua color in the broad, deep meandering channel to your east. Where strips of trees approach the water's edge, detour closer for a riverside break.

Eventually the trail turns completely away from the river's edge, passes through a notch in some small bluffs, then turns decisively to the west. Passing through a meadow pocket that is infamously marshy in early summer, step carefully or accept wet shoes, but take care not to walk off the trail and damage the surrounding vegetation. Then turning back into dry lodgepole forest, you soon reach a sturdy bridge spanning Rafferty Creek. Just beyond is the junction with the trail ascending Rafferty Creek, completing the loop portion of this walk. Now trending right (west), retrace your steps to the trailhead.

see map on p. 250

trip 54 Lewis Creek and Emeric Lake

Trip Data: 37.77825°N, 119.38150°W (Emeric Lake);
27.5 miles; 4/0 days
Topos: *Vogelsang Peak, Mount Lyell, Merced Peak, Tenaya Lake*

HIGHLIGHTS: After a delightful ascent to Tuolumne Pass in the Vogelsang High Sierra Camp environs, this trip "lassos" Vogelsang Peak by dashing down the valley of Lewis Creek and traipsing more slowly back up the valley of Fletcher Creek. The views are spectacular, the flowers delightful, and the fishing on creeks and lakes is good.

DAY 1 (Lyell Canyon Trailhead to Vogelsang High Sierra Camp, 7.3 miles): Walking south through a small meadow, you promptly reach the trail shared by the Pacific Crest Trail (PCT) and the John Muir Trail (JMT) and turn left (east) onto it, following the Dana Fork of the Tuolumne River upstream. You quickly reach a junction with a spur trail that goes left to the west end of the Tuolumne Meadows Lodge's parking lot. You, however, turn right (south) to cross the Dana Fork on a bridge, turn upstream and quickly reach a junction with a trail signposted to the Gaylor Lakes (left; east); you stay right (south) on the JMT/PCT. Veering south, away from the Dana Fork, the trail leads over a slight rise and descends to the Lyell Fork Tuolumne River, where two substantial bridges span the river as it churns down polished granite at the west end of a long meadow. At the southwestern corner of the meadow, you reach a junction; the right (westbound) trail follows the Lyell Fork toward the Tuolumne Meadows Campground. The JMT/PCT, your route, turns left (east), traveling upstream parallel to the Lyell Fork, although you are sufficiently south of the river corridor that you barely glimpse the water.

Your route alternates between slab and lush lodgepole forest, leading to a junction on the west bank of Rafferty Creek. Here the JMT/PCT continues left (east; Trip 52), while your route, the Rafferty Creek Trail, turns right (south) and immediately begins an often-warm climb at moderate grade through scattered lodgepole pines. The climb eases after half a mile, with the trail assuming a gentler grade to match a change in topography.

Paralleling Rafferty Creek upward, you walk across slabs interspersed with sandy patches. These host colorful blooms for only a few weeks after snowmelt, then dry to a monotonous gray-beige. You cross a few seasonal tributaries that have rocks to balance on at high flows and note the occasional western white pine in the predominately lodgepole forest, for there are suddenly larger cones strewn across the ground. In places the landscape is open and offers good views eastward to reddish-brown Mount Dana and Mount Gibbs as

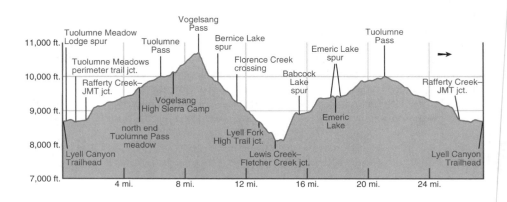

well as gray-white Mammoth Peak, rising northeast of Lyell Canyon. At 3.4 miles the trail changes course slightly and you more closely parallel the now rather diminutive Rafferty Creek upward. Exiting forest cover, you skirt the western side of a meadow, harboring a few mediocre campsites in the surrounding forest, then reenter the thinning lodgepole forest.

Crossing additional seasonal creeks, you exit a stand of trees to find yourself staring up a much larger meadow. Through this you ascend easily upcanyon, having backward views north to the Sierra Crest between Tioga Pass and Mount Conness, and views ahead to cliff-bound, dark-banded Fletcher Peak and Vogelsang Peak to the right of it. This boulder-strewn, marmot-rich meadow leads remarkably gradually to Tuolumne Pass, a major gap in the Cathedral Range, and a junction.

At the pass, a signed trail junction indicates that the left fork (south-southwest), your route, heads south to Vogelsang High Sierra Camp, while the right fork (southwest), your return route, goes to Boothe, Emeric, Babcock, and Merced Lakes. The trail traverses gradually upward across a moderately steep slope above Boothe Lake. As it then bends slightly south, the tents of Vogelsang High Sierra Camp are immediately in view, spread out at the foot of Fletcher Peak's rock glacier. The camp's buildings are situated just behind a signed four-way junction. At the camp a few snacks may be bought, or dinner or breakfast if you have made a reservation in advance.

Camping on the shores of Fletcher Lake is not allowed. Rather, at the junction, turn left (east), signposted for Ireland Lake, to reach a designated camping area on the northwest side of the trail just before you reach Fletcher Lake (10,135'; 37.79622°N, 119.34422°W; no campfires). Here you'll find animal-proof food-storage boxes, but note there is no longer a pit toilet or potable water for backpackers at Vogelsang. Additional, starker camping options are available among slabs at Vogelsang Lake, 0.6 mile along the trail to Vogelsang Pass (often with fewer early-season mosquitoes; part of Day 2's description), and a short distance down the trail southwest to Emeric Lake.

DAY 2 (Vogelsang High Sierra Camp to Florence Creek, 4.2 miles): Return to the trail junction next to the High Sierra Camp and take the trail left (south) to Vogelsang Lake and Pass. The track drops a little along Fletcher Creek, fords it, and begins an ascending traverse across broken granite slabs toward Vogelsang Lake's outlet. En route, enjoy ever-expanding views, with Fletcher Peak rising grandly on the left and Clouds Rest and Half Dome making an appearance to the west-southwest.

Stepping across the outlet of Vogelsang Lake (10,324') on big rock blocks, the trail skirts a selection of small tent sites nestled in sandy patches beside stunted whitebark pines. Initially continuing the climb southwest above the lakeshore, you slowly swing southeast toward the pass, all the while walking across delightful glacially polished granite slabs and admiring an abundance of colorful alpine wildflowers—monkeyflowers where wetter, buckwheats and alpine paintbrush in the sandy patches.

The pass itself, at 10,680 feet, sits in a shallow trough, with the steeper ridges of Vogelsang Peak (to the west) and Fletcher Peak (to the east) blocking most of the view. A few steps beyond the pass, the trail bends to the east and suddenly you have expansive views to the south: From left to right are Parsons Peak, Simmons Peak, Mount Maclure, the tip of Mount Lyell behind Maclure, giant Mount Florence, and, in the south, the entire Clark Range from Triple Divide Peak on the left to Mount Clark on the right. Below and to the southeast sit Gallison and Bernice Lakes in broad subalpine basins—visiting either (or both) is a fantastic way to flesh out this relatively short day; just make sure your food is secured in your bear canister and not in your pack before heading off.

The trail now follows steep, rocky switchbacks through sparse lodgepole forest to the meadowed valley through which nascent Lewis Creek meanders. Here there is ample moisture for thousands of ravenous early-summer mosquitoes and giant, blue-blossomed lupines later on; the perimeter of the meadow harbors some excellent campsites. Note that many lodgepole pines over the ensuing 5 miles have been killed by native lodgepole needle-miners, creating a ghost forest where campsites that aren't overhung by aptly named "widow-makers" (dead trees ready to fall) are surprisingly scarce. These caterpillars cyclically defoliate—and often kill—vast swatches of lodgepoles and are especially prevalent in the Merced River drainage. However, they in turn allow the regeneration of a younger forest; hopefully when you pass through more of the dead trees will have fallen, and there will again be attractive, safe campsites. In this little valley, you ford Lewis Creek, drop another 100 feet, and ford the braided Bernice Lake outlet creek.

In a few minutes, you pass the spur trail left (southeast) that climbs steeply 0.5 mile to Bernice Lake, where there are some splendid treeline campsites; the described route continues ahead (right; southwest). The forested trail winds gently down above the creek's southeast bank under a mixed canopy of lodgepole and hemlock; the hemlock aren't killed by the leaf miners, and now stand out as green patches among the dead lodgepoles.

Crossing additional tributaries, many seasonal and unmarked on maps, you reach a flatter bench with some good campsites beside Florence Creek (9,220'; 37.75556°N, 119.35549°W). Again, leaf-miner kills limit your options a little, but these are your best choices along the Lewis Creek corridor. It is an especially attractive location to camp because Florence Creek cascades dramatically down steep granite sheets into a rock-lined, flower-ringed pool. Fishing in Florence and Lewis Creeks is good for rainbow trout.

DAY 3 (Florence Creek to Emeric Lake, 6.3 miles): Leaving Florence Creek, the trail descends a series of (mostly dead) lodgepole-dotted granite slabs above Lewis Creek, which rumbles through bare granite chutes to your right.

PEELING GRANITE?
Where the creek's channel narrows, you find on the left a lesson in exfoliation: granite layers peeling like an onion. This kind of peeling is typically seen on Yosemite's domes, but this fine example is located on a canyon slope. These fractures likely occur because of the region-wide compressive forces acting on the exposed, curved rock surface. Another school of thought suggests they occur due to depressurization caused by the removal of the weight of the last major glacier, which had pressed upon it for thousands of years.

The trail steepens and eases in tandem with the bed of Lewis Creek. Soon after the trail climbs away from the creek to a shaded alcove, it meets a left-bearing (south) junction with the so-called High Trail to Isberg Pass (Trip 55). You continue ahead (right; generally west-southwest) under a sparse cover of red fir, juniper, lodgepole, and western white pine and switchback down, alternating between steeper sections of broken slab and more forested flats. Exactly 1 mile below the previous junction, you reach another junction on open slabs, where straight ahead (left; west) leads to Merced Lake, while you turn right (north) onto the trail that ascends Fletcher Creek, here signposted to Babcock and Emeric Lakes.

Several switchbacks descend to a wooden bridge over Lewis Creek. In a flat to the northeast are a few attractive tent sites, although fallen trees have vanquished most real estate in this previously popular camping area. From here, the trail begins a moderate-to-steep ascent over unevenly cobblestoned, exposed trail—a grunt on a hot day. The path is bordered by prickly shrubs, in particular featuring whitethorn and huckleberry oak. Just past

Crossing Fletcher Creek near Vogelsang High Sierra Camp Photo by Elizabeth Wenk

a tributary a half mile from Lewis Creek, stepping west of the trail provides views of some fine cataracts and waterfalls along Fletcher Creek. Climbing onward, granite slabs open to your left, providing splendid vistas of Fletcher Creek chuting and cascading down the bare bedrock. The trail keeps ascending, steeply at times and mostly some distance east of the creek, often on the now-familiar cobblestones. A detour onto the middle of the slabs is called for, to feel the smooth glacial-polished rock away from the water flow and the water-polished rock within it. The few solitary pine trees clinging to the nearby slabs and the dome overhead testify to nature's extraordinary tenacity.

The trail climbs up to a notch, then levels off, and soon passes a side trail left (west and south) to small Babcock Lake (acceptable campsites). Onward, you walk for 0.6 mile through flat, marshy forest, passing springs and small meadow patches brightly colored with flowers. Turning a little west, the trail breaks into the open and rises more steeply via rocky switchbacks. From these, looking north, one can see the outlet stream of Emeric Lake—though not the lake itself, hidden behind the dome to the right of the outlet's notch.

The switchbacks parallel dashing Fletcher Creek until it tops out in a long, skinny meadow, constrained by domes to either side. The trail follows the meandering Fletcher Creek northeast to a ford and just beyond reaches a scissor junction, where a sharp left (west south west) is the spur trail to Emeric Lake.

Sidling over and around a shallow granite knoll, slabs lead to Emeric Lake (9,338'; 37.77825°N, 119.38150°W; mileage to here). From the eastern corner follow anglers' trails to the excellent campsites midway along the lake's northwest shore, often a circuitous route to the north end of the meadow to avoid damaging the saturated soils. Fishing is often good for rainbow trout.

DAY 4 (Emeric Lake to Lyell Canyon Trailhead, 9.7 miles): This is the longest hiking day on this trip, but the ascent to Tuolumne Pass is moderate and comes at the beginning. Thereafter, the rest is downhill through familiar terrain.

Once again, circle the head of Emeric Lake, crossing its inlet stream and following the spur trail 0.3 mile east-northeast back to the scissor junction along Fletcher Creek. You trend left (northeast) toward Boothe Lake, while straight ahead (east-northeast) leads to Vogelsang High Sierra Camp.

Your route climbs away from Fletcher Creek, passing northwest of a bald prominence that divides the headwaters of Fletcher and Emeric Creeks. Diverging slightly from Emeric Creek, the trail climbs to a bench cradling a series of lovely ponds that are interconnected in early season. You soon stare down at the south end of Boothe Lake (9,845') and its campsites, reached by continuing north on the meadowy hillside trail to the Boothe Lake spur trail. Beyond, another 0.3 mile takes you to Tuolumne Pass and the junction where you headed toward Vogelsang High Sierra Camp on Day 1. From here retrace Day 1's route to the trailhead.

trip 55   Triple Peak Fork Merced River

see map on p. 250

Trip Data: 37.65847°N, 119.34456°W
(Triple Peak Fork junction); 47.8 miles; 6/2 days
Topos: *Vogelsang Peak, Mount Lyell, Merced Peak, Tenaya Lake*

HIGHLIGHTS: The trails in the far southeastern corner of Yosemite—those visited on this trip—are the park's most remote, so this is a perfect walk for people wanting to escape the crowds. The views are astounding and varied, and there are countless options for sidetrips to hidden valleys and lakes. *Note:* the days are longer than on many other hikes in this book.

DAY 1 (Lyell Canyon Trailhead to Lewis Creek, 9.7 miles): Follow Trip 54, Day 1 for 7.3 miles to the Vogelsang High Sierra Camp and then continue an additional 2.4 miles, as described on the following page. If you wish to have a shorter day than described, there is a designated camping area just to the northwest of Fletcher Lake (10,135'; 37.79622°N, 119.34422°W; no campfires), complete with animal-proof food-storage boxes; note there is no longer a pit toilet or potable water for backpackers at Vogelsang.

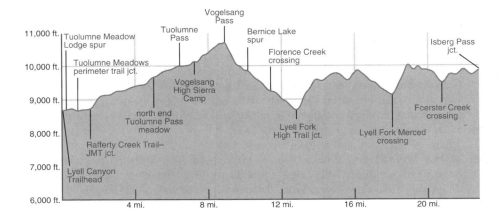

From the four-way trail junction, continue straight ahead (south) to Vogelsang Lake and Pass. The track drops a little along Fletcher Creek, fords it, and begins an ascending traverse across broken granite slabs toward the lake's outlet. En route, enjoy ever-expanding views, with Fletcher Peak rising grandly on the left and Clouds Rest and Half Dome making an appearance to the west-southwest.

Stepping across the outlet of Vogelsang Lake (10,324') on big rock blocks, the trail skirts a selection of small tent sites nestled in sandy patches beside stunted whitebark pines. Initially continuing the climb southwest above the lakeshore, you slowly swing southeast toward the pass, all the while walking across delightful glacially polished granite slabs and admiring an abundance of colorful alpine wildflowers—monkeyflowers where wetter, buckwheats and alpine paintbrush in the sandy patches.

The pass itself, at 10,680 feet, sits in a shallow trough, with the steeper ridges of Vogelsang Peak (to the west) and Fletcher Peak (to the east) blocking most of the view. A few steps beyond the pass, the trail bends to the east and suddenly you have expansive views to the south: From left to right are Parsons Peak, Simmons Peak, Mount Maclure, the tip of Mount Lyell behind Maclure, giant Mount Florence, and, in the south, the entire Clark Range from Triple Divide Peak on the left to Mount Clark on the right. Below and to the southeast sit Gallison and Bernice Lakes in broad subalpine basins.

The trail now follows steep, rocky switchbacks through sparse lodgepole forest to the meadowed valley through which nascent Lewis Creek meanders. Here there is ample moisture for thousands of ravenous early-summer mosquitoes and giant, blue-blossomed lupines later on; the perimeter of the meadow harbors some excellent campsites (9,990'; 37.77342°N, 119.33854°W; no campfires). Note that many lodgepole pines over the ensuing 5 miles have been killed by native lodgepole needle-miners, creating a ghost forest where campsites that aren't overhung by aptly named "widow makers" (dead trees ready to fall) are surprisingly scarce. These caterpillars cyclically defoliate—and often kill—vast swatches of lodgepoles and are especially prevalent in the Merced River drainage. However, they in turn allow the regeneration of a younger forest; hopefully when you pass through more of the dead trees will have fallen, and there will be a greater selection of attractive, safe campsites.

Other campsite options for the night include Bernice Lake (0.5 miles downstream along the trail plus a 0.5-mile/400-foot uphill that isn't included in the trip mileage; 37.76745°N, 119.33385°W; no campfires) and Lewis Creek at the Florence Creek confluence (1.75 miles downstream described as part of Day 2's route; 37.75556°N, 119.35549°W). If you have the

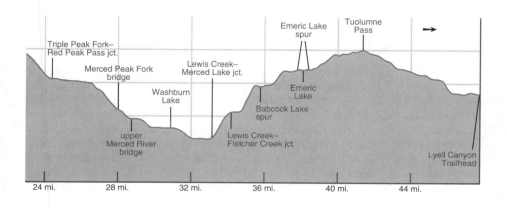

energy for an extraneous 400-foot climb and like a timberline campsite among whitebark pines, then you should head to Bernice Lake for the night.

DAY 2 (Lewis Creek to Lyell Fork Merced River, 8.4 miles): Continuing along Lewis Creek, you drop another 100 feet and ford the braided Bernice Lake outlet creek. Soon, you pass the spur trail left (southeast) that climbs steeply to Bernice Lake and continue straight ahead (right; southwest). The forested trail winds gently down above the creek's southeast bank under a mixed canopy of lodgepole and hemlock; the hemlock aren't killed by the leaf miners and now stand out as green patches among the dead lodgepoles.

Crossing additional tributaries, many seasonal and unmarked on maps, you reach a flatter bench, with some good campsites beside Florence Creek. This is also a beautiful location for a break, gazing at Florence Creek cascading dramatically over steep granite sheets into a beautiful slab-rimmed pool. Leaving the hemlock glade beyond the falls, the trail descends a series of (mostly dead) lodgepole-dotted granite slabs above Lewis Creek, which rumbles through bare granite chutes to your right.

The trail steepens and eases in tandem with the bed of Lewis Creek, and as you drop below 9,000 feet you reach the zone of red firs. Soon after, the trail climbs away from the creek to a shaded alcove, where it meets a trail variously known as the High Trail, Lyell Fork Trail, or Isberg Trail.

Turning left (south) onto this trail, you begin by making a steep 700-foot ascent in 0.75 mile. Initially on an open slope, higher you have the privilege of walking in mottled shade thanks to a canopy of red fir, western white pine, and lodgepole pine.

Above the initial ascent, the trail assumes a more southeasterly bearing and climbs more gradually across a bench on a broad slope, the western side of massive Mount Florence— indeed you cross it for the next 3 miles! Bighorn sheep were released on these slopes in 2015—sheep hadn't scampered up these slopes for most of a century, and this herd will hopefully thrive in the coming years, repopulating this piece of Yosemite.

The beginning of the undulating traverse is memorable for the views west and north to Half Dome, Clouds Rest, the Cockscomb, and Unicorn Peak. Later it is the continuously stunning views of the Clark Range—one of the highlights of this route—that you will stare at. Most of the traverse is across rubbly, rocky terrain and sand, passing through some of Yosemite's most spectacular stands of large western white pines. Soon into your traverse you cross one creek with nearby campsites. The trail climbs repeatedly up and down short slopes, a seemingly superfluous energy expenditure, but one that is required to keep the trail on the bench and off the steeper slopes below.

Halfway along you ford a second, larger stream (may be difficult in early season) that flows into Washburn Lake below. After ascending one more knob the trail slowly turns to the east. Just before the descent to the Lyell Fork Merced River begins there is a spectacular viewpoint for studying the headwaters of the Lyell Fork (in the east) and the Merced Peak Fork (in the south) of the Merced River.

The trail now follows a narrow shelf, a passable route across otherwise steep granite slabs. You ford a third all-year stream, then continue down, quite steeply at times, to the cascading, chuting Lyell Fork Merced River (9,115'; 37.70654°N, 119.32527°W). The last segment of trail before the stream, over granite slabs, is a little hard to follow, but the route leads directly to the creek. The campsites at the ford are poor, but good ones lie 0.1 mile downstream, where chutes and rapids flow over the sculpted granite bedrock. There are also good campsites a half mile upstream, at the edge of a beautiful meadow, a good base if you have scheduled a recommended layover day to explore the endless lakes at the headwaters of the Lyell Fork. Fishing in the Lyell Fork is good for brook trout.

DAY 3 (Lyell Fork Merced River to Triple Peak Fork Meadow, 6.3 miles): This day's hike starts off strenuously, climbing up switchbacks on the south wall of the Lyell Fork Merced River's canyon. Increasingly magnificent views reward your struggle upward. In the northeast, on the Sierra Crest, are Mount Maclure and Mount Lyell, the highest point in Yosemite. After Lyell passes from view, Rodgers Peak, a nearly 13,000-foot summit, appears as a dark triangle south of Lyell. Once close to the lip of the Merced River's canyon, you again have views southwest to the Clark Range.

Beyond the top of the ascent, the route winds among large boulders on *grus*—granite sand—that is the result of the breakup of just such boulders by the fierce erosion forces at work in these alpine climates. The trail undulates, dropping to a seasonal drainage, rising to a broad ridge, and, just where the trail turns west, you could veer left (east) up a use trail, heading 0.2 mile to unofficially named Foerster Lake (about 9,900'). This unsigned trail is indicated by parallel rock borders and occasional blazes on trees. Secluded Foerster Lake has no fish, but swimming and camping there are excellent. You could also explore farther southeast to the spectacular headwaters of Foerster Creek—another excellent choice for a layover day.

Continuing its descent, the main trail soon reaches and parallels first Foerster Lake's outlet creek, then Foerster Creek proper, to a ford of Foerster Creek. The well-shaded trail now climbs beside another tributary to a shallow saddle. Heading west from the trail leads to a tarn and splendid campsites overlooking the valley below. The trail rises and falls twice more as it passes around some steep-fronted spurs and crosses the drainages between. On the second ascent you reach a junction where straight ahead (left; south) leads to Isberg and Post Peak Passes (Trip 64), while right (west) descends to the Triple Peak Fork, your destination. If you have spare time it is absolutely worth a detour along the trail to Isberg Pass either to Lake 10,005, 0.3 mile to the northeast (with good campsites to the north), or to a ridge north of Post Peak Pass (4.4 miles round-trip; see sidebar). Given tomorrow is a shorter day—and without such enticing extras—you could contentedly stop at Lake 10,005 for the night, spending the late afternoon on the excursion toward Post Peak Pass.

SIDE TRIP TO POST PEAK PASS

This 4.4-mile excursion is, perhaps, the best of the many side trips you could add onto today's mileage. Leaving the described route, the trail to Isberg and Post Peak Passes first climbs moderately for 0.25 mile up a beautiful hillside covered with whitish broken granite with alpine wildflowers growing up from within the cracks. Looking west and north from this slope, you can see all the peaks of the Clark Range and most of the peaks of the Cathedral Range. At the top of this little climb, a truly marvelous sight comes into view, for here you enter a large, high, nearly flat bowl encircled by great peaks. The bowl contains an enormous meadow and two sparkling lakes—and there are some beautiful campsites to the northwest of Lake 10,005.

The trail strikes straight across the magnificent meadow, peppered with colorful flowers in June and July, and on the far side begins to rise toward the crest through a gravelly landscape. You soon come to a junction where the right (southeast) fork leads 0.75 mile east to a ridge north of Post Peak Pass and the left (northeast) fork to Isberg Pass, 0.6 mile away. Both have astounding views, but although longer, the walk toward Post Peak Pass is slightly easier. Steep, lushly vegetated switchbacks lead to the crest, the Yosemite boundary, after just 0.4 mile. The trail then continues south along the ridge, which broadens and flattens above the Ward Lakes. You are staring at most of the San Joaquin watershed—due east are the imposing, sharp-tipped summits of the Ritter Range, while the view southwest extends to Goddard Peak, a large dark pyramid 50 miles away on the southern boundary of the San Joaquin River drainage. After reveling in this surreal location, retrace your steps to the junction.

Your route now turns west (left if you're returning from Post Peak Pass; right otherwise) and starts straight downhill. It then veers southwest, traversing into deep hemlock forest before turning north for the last 0.75 mile to the river. Once across the placid Triple Peak Fork of the Merced River you reach a junction (9,105'; 37.65847°N, 119.34456°W), where left (west) is the trail to Red Peak Pass (Trip 63); you stay right (north). There are good forested campsites nearby or ones on open slab if you detour upstream or downstream about 5 minutes. Fishing is good for brook and rainbow trout.

DAY 4 (Triple Peak Fork Meadow to Washburn Lake, 5.9 miles): Stroll north-northeast in passageways between broken slabs, reaching Triple Peak Fork Meadow after 0.5 mile. For the next 0.5 mile you saunter just at the edge of the verdant meadow, admiring the deep meandering channel. Partway along, the river channel and adjacent meadows are briefly constricted by granite outcrops, before again spreading across the valley. However, for the coming mile's walk, the river channel is well east of the trail, and you are walking through drier terrain. There are camping options throughout if you search among slabs west of the trail.

You now begin an 800-foot descent, initially gradual but steepening together with the topography, and eventually begin zigzagging down out of the hanging valley through which you've been traveling. Tree cover thins, then all but disappears, and the flowing water gathers speed, ultimately tumbling down Triple Peak Fork Waterfall. Soon the trail trends southwest, traversing beautiful rock slabs, before switchbacking north again to cross the Merced Peak Fork of the Merced River on a footbridge.

Descending northward on the river's west side through red fir and juniper, the trail soon passes the confluence of the Merced Peak Fork and the Triple Peak Fork. Continuing down, the Lyell Fork merges into the flow near another footbridge; enjoy the view down to the deep, calm, crystal-clear water of what is now simply "the" Merced River, the major forks having merged. Tangles of downed trees (the aftermath of a windstorm) limit camping options but are an impressive sight.

Washburn Lake   Photo by Elizabeth Wenk

Now the trail arcs northwest and west, descending gradually through an idyllic setting. By a lovely waterfall, the trail begins to descend a dry slope and soon reaches Washburn Lake. Significant treefall has also impacted campsites here, but you will still find some choices near the head of Washburn Lake (7,640'; 37.71130°N, 119.36661°W).

DAY 5 (Washburn Lake to Emeric Lake, 7.8 miles): The mostly open, sandy trail continues right along the east side of Washburn Lake. Being deep in a canyon is such a different feel to what you had traversing the bench high above a few days back. Beyond, the trail continues its moderate descent along the river through open forest and across slabs, fording a small stream every quarter mile or so. Where the canyon floor begins to widen, the trail diverges east from the river, hugging the cliff walls as it skirts a big previously burned flat, now dense with scrub and downed trees (but harboring a few campsites in the direction of the river). The trail proceeds levelly to the Merced Lake Ranger Station (emergency services available in summer) and a junction with the Lewis Creek Trail, almost 3 miles from your campsite. Left (west) leads to Merced Lake, while you turn right (northeast), back onto the Lewis Creek Trail.

Your cobblestoned trail quickly becomes steep, and it remains so for a panting mile. The predominate trees, junipers and Jeffrey pines, cast shade only early in the morning, but the lack of a closed canopy provides open views west to Merced Lake and beyond to Half Dome. The 850-foot climb leads to a junction with the trail up Fletcher Creek, signposted for Emeric Lake, where you turn left (northeast), while right (east) is the continuing route up Lewis Creek.

Several switchbacks descend to a wooden bridge over Lewis Creek. In a flat to the northeast are a few attractive tent sites, although fallen trees have also vanquished most real estate in this previously popular camping area. From here, the trail begins a moderate-to-steep ascent over unevenly cobblestoned, exposed trail—a grunt on a hot day. Just past a tributary a half mile from Lewis Creek, stepping west of the trail provides views of some fine cataracts and waterfalls along Fletcher Creek. Climbing onward, granite slabs open to your left, providing splendid vistas of Fletcher Creek cascading down the bare bedrock. The trail keeps ascending, steeply at times and mostly some distance east of the creek, often on cobblestones. A detour onto the middle of the slabs is called for, to feel the smooth glacial-polished rock away from the water flow and the water-polished rock within it. The few solitary pine trees clinging to the nearby slabs and the dome overhead testify to nature's extraordinary tenacity.

The trail climbs to a notch, then levels off, and soon passes a side trail left (west and south) to small Babcock Lake (acceptable campsites). Onward, you walk for 0.6 mile through flat, marshy forest, passing springs and small meadow patches brightly colored with flowers. Turning a little west, the trail breaks into the open and rises more steeply via rocky switchbacks. From these, looking north, you can see the outlet stream of Emeric Lake—though not the lake itself, hidden behind the dome to the right of the outlet's notch.

Switchbacks parallel dashing Fletcher Creek until it tops out in a long, skinny meadow, constrained by domes to either side. The trail follows the meandering Fletcher Creek northeast to a ford and just beyond reaches a scissor junction, where a sharp left (west-southwest) is the spur trail to Emeric Lake.

Sidling over and around a shallow granite knoll, slabs lead to Emeric Lake (9,338'; 37.77825°N, 119.38150°W; mileage to here). From the eastern corner follow anglers' trails to the excellent campsites midway along the lake's northwest shore, often a circuitous route to the north end of the meadow to avoid damaging the saturated soils. Fishing is often good for rainbow trout.

Day 6 (Emeric Lake to Lyell Canyon Trailhead, 9.7 miles): Follow Trip 54, Day 4 to the Lyell Canyon Trailhead.

Mono Pass Trailhead
9,690'; 37.89096°N, 119.26262°W

Destination/ GPS Coordinates	Trip Type	Best Season	Pace & Hiking/ Layover Days	Total Mileage	Permit Required
56 Alger Lakes 37.79347°N 119.17266°W	Shuttle	Mid to late	Moderate 3/1	20.1	Mono Pass (or Rush Creek from Inyo National Forest in reverse)

INFORMATION AND PERMITS: This trip begins in Yosemite National Park: wilderness permits and bear canisters are required; pets and firearms are prohibited. Quotas apply, with 60% of permits reservable online up to 24 weeks in advance and 40% available first-come, first-served starting at 11 a.m. the day before your trip's start date. Fires are prohibited above 10,000 feet in Ansel Adams Wilderness. See nps.gov/yose/planyourvisit /wildpermits.htm for more details. The in-reverse trailhead, Rush Creek Trailhead in Inyo National Forest, is not listed in this book as it falls within the area covered by *Sierra South*. Permits can be reserved up to six months in advance at recreation.gov (search for "Inyo National Forest Wilderness Permits") or requested in person, first-come first-served, a day in advance. Permits can be picked up at one of the Inyo National Forest ranger stations, located in Lone Pine (Eastern Sierra Interagency Visitor Center), Bishop, Mammoth Lakes, and Lee Vining (the Mono Basin Scenic Area Visitor Center).

DRIVING DIRECTIONS: The trailhead is along Tioga Road (CA 120) between Tuolumne Meadows and Tioga Pass. It is located 1.5 miles west of Tioga Pass and 5.7 miles east of the Tuolumne Meadows Campground, on the south side of the road. There are pit toilets at the trailhead.

trip 56 Alger Lakes

Trip Data: 37.79347°N, 119.17266°W; 20.1 miles; 3/1 days
Topos: *Tioga Pass, Mount Dana, Koip Peak*

HIGHLIGHTS: This trip offers a superb combination of views, alpine landscapes, and peaceful forests. Koip Peak Pass is the only major obstacle, and it's easier than you think.

HEADS UP! *Yosemite National Park does not permit camping in the drainage of Dana Fork Tuolumne River, which includes all the lakes and streams on the Yosemite side of Parker and Mono Passes. You must be on the Ansel Adams Wilderness side of Parker Pass before you camp.*

SHUTTLE DIRECTIONS: To reach the endpoint, the Rush Creek Trailhead near Silver Lake, head to the intersection of US 395 and CA 120 in Lee Vining. Turn right and drive 4.4 miles south on US 395. Then turn right (west) onto CA 158, the June Lake Loop. Continue 8.7 miles west and south, turning right into the Rush Creek Trailhead parking area.

DAY 1 (Mono Pass Trailhead to Parker Creek, 6.4 miles): Starting under a dense canopy of lodgepole pines, you leave the trailhead, initially descending on a trail that once was part of a Paiute Indian route across this region of the Sierra, the Mono Trail. About a half mile from the trailhead, you cross the creeks draining Dana Meadows and the Dana Fork

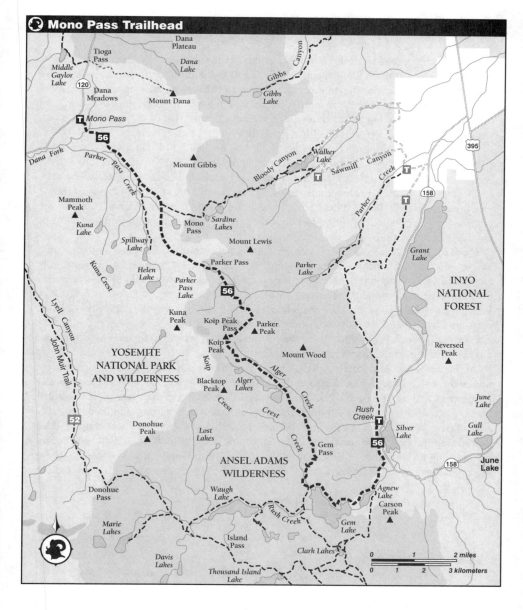

Tuolumne River just above their confluence. There are usually a collection of narrow logs to balance across, although sometimes these are wet-shoe fords. Beyond these two crossings, your trail climbs to the crest of a low moraine, crosses two more moraines, then, near Parker Pass Creek, comes to the ruins of a pioneer log cabin. Sagebrush intermingles with lodgepoles as you pass creekside meadows.

After 2.3 miles, you come to a junction, where you trend left (southeast), while right (south) is the Spillway Lake Trail. Take care to anticipate this junction, for the lesser-traveled trail to Spillway Lake is actually the more obvious at this junction, and if you don't realize you've reached a junction you could easily ascend the wrong path. Up until this junction, your trail has been easy, but now it climbs a steeper 700 feet, up through the lodgepole pine forests covering the western flank of massive Mount Gibbs. Soon after passing the ruins of a second pioneer cabin, the forest cover transitions to multitrunked whitebark pine clusters, and before long you reach another junction, where straight ahead (left; east) leads to Mono Pass and Bloody Canyon, the continuing Paiute trail, while you turn right (south), sign-posted for Parker Pass. (*Note:* Just south of Mono Pass, 0.6 mile from this junction, are a trio of visit-worthy cabins, constructed from local whitebark pines, that once housed workers on the nearby Golden Crown and Ella Bloss gold mines.)

Dropping ever so slightly as you cross a swale, you begin a gentle climb up to the crest of a broad moraine that here and there has rusty exposures of Triassic-period metavolcanics (metamorphosed volcanic rocks), some of the oldest rocks in the Yosemite area. The scattered whitebark pines here are reduced to shrub height, and so you get largely unobstructed views that include shallow Spillway Lake, lying at the base of the Kuna Crest. Note how the granitic upper slopes of this crest differ not only in color but also in shape and texture from the lower metamorphic ones.

Onward, you see the shallow Parker Pass sitting between steep slopes more than a mile before you attain it. Yellow-blossomed bush cinquefoils yield to mats of alpine willow and, finally, to coarse gravel. The metamorphic rocks weather to small cobble-size rocks, forming a near continuous pavement in places. In due course, you reach 11,110-foot Parker Pass, where you have the most amazing broad views across the expansive uplands surrounding Parker Pass and the Mono Pass vicinity. To the north you can see Mount Conness and North Peak, while to the west is the Kuna Crest and to the east Mount Lewis, a rewarding and straightforward climb from here.

At Parker Pass, you enter Ansel Adams Wilderness. Descending on Paleozoic-era metasediments—ones even older than those to the north—you first step across an outlet creek from two nearby ponds, the headwaters of Parker Creek, then recross it at a third pond. You traipse southeast alongside a chain of interconnected, vibrantly colored tarns; different tarns are different colors reflecting the chemicals and silt composition of the trickles descending through disparate bands of metamorphic rock. Initially, the landscape appears unappealing for camping, with steep metamorphic cliff bands and endless cobble, but there are small benches to either side of the drainage that fit a tent. About 0.75 mile beyond the

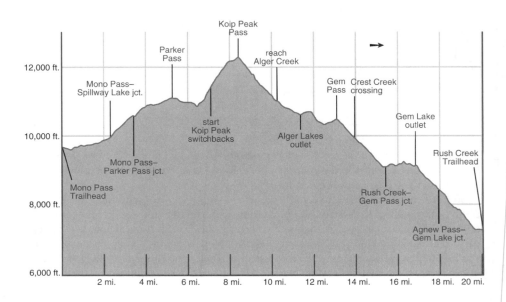

pass, you cross a seasonally churning tributary that gets its vigor from a permanent snow-field lodged high on the slopes between Kuna and Koip Peaks.

After another half mile, you reach an alpine tarn, from which point you can gaze straight down the enormous Parker Creek cleft. Near a tarn with beautiful rock pavings is the low point between Parker and Koip Peak Passes. Near here are some larger campsites, tucked into sandy flats, often adjacent to stunted whitebark pines (10,862'; 37.82808°N, 119.19198°W; no campfires).

DAY 2 (Parker Creek to Alger Lakes, 5.0 miles): Ahead you stare at the series of ominous-looking switchbacks that climb the northwest slope of Parker Peak toward Koip Peak Pass and appreciate how gentle Parker Pass was. Your climb begins by crossing a second snowfield-fed Parker Creek tributary, a broad cobbly crossing where the low-gradient water fans out into a braided network—take care not to slip on the algae here.

While the switchbacks ahead are relentless, the tread is well constructed and the gradient moderate, allowing you to walk upward as rapidly as the rarefied air permits. As you stop for inevitable breathers, you can scan the ever-improving panorama. You now see most of large, alkaline Mono Lake and the summits of Mount Gibbs and Mount Conness, the latter rising behind Parker Pass. During July, you may see the unmistakable sky pilot, a blue-petaled polemonium that thrives in the rockiest alpine environments, rarely growing below 11,000 feet. The basin to the southwest is a favorite site for bighorn sheep to forage—notice the green tinge of vegetation that is superimposed on the rock. The tight switchbacks lead up a northeastern-facing ridge emanating off Parker Peak and the trail then begins a final traverse west to the pass. Before early August, even in average snow years, snowfields may cover parts of the trail to the pass, and they could present a problem, since you have 600 feet of steep slopes below you. Sometimes it is safest to climb above the trail, higher up Parker Peak, to avoid the snow channels, eventually descending to Koip Peak Pass.

The gradually easing ascent southwest finally leads to shallow Koip Peak Pass, which at 12,270 feet is one of the Sierra's highest trail passes. Indeed it is less than a 1,000-foot climb from the pass to the peaks to either side; Parker Peak to the west and Koip Peak to the east are both easily attainable summits if you have surplus energy. Leaving the pass, you exchange views of Mount Conness, Mount Gibbs, Mount Dana, and Mount Lewis to the north for ones of the Alger Lakes basin, the June Lake ski area, volcanic Mammoth Mountain, far away Lake Crowley, and the distant central Sierra Nevada crest to the south, although the Alger Lakes themselves are hidden at first.

While the steep snowfields and bluffs on the north side of Koip Peak Pass required a carefully positioned trail, the drop into the Alger Lakes basin is delightfully easy—you descend a not-too-steep easy talus slope with just the occasional switchback. The metavolcanic rock here is notably different than the older metasedimentary on the north side of the pass—paler, and forming more rounded talus. As the trail's gradient eases, you cross Alger Creek in a thicket of arnicas, and then, with a low, fresh-looking moraine on your right, parallel the creek downstream just at the base of the moraine. To your left are expansive boggy meadows and looking east to Parker Peak and Mount Wood you'll spy countless trickles beginning at springs high on the slope and descending to irrigate the meadow. Other springs appear at the meadows edge, where the slope suddenly breaks and the water table rises to the surface. There are campsites all along the moraine crest, in sandy patches between whitebark pines.

Slowly the trail leads away from Alger Creek to cross the multicrested moraine, the trail becoming indistinct near the summit. You are now looking down upon the two fairly large Alger Lakes. On the descent to their shore it is quite likely you'll lose the trail at some point in the sandy, vegetated moraine soils. Simply aim for the outlet of the southern lake and shortly you'll see a large post; the trail becomes apparent again at this point. Only 150 feet and a 2-foot drop separate the two treeline Alger Lakes. You can set up camp among the windblown whitebark pines on the bedrock landmass that separates them, or immediately across the lower Alger Lake's outlet is a left-trending (east) spur that leads to a larger collection of campsites (10,612'; 37.79347°N, 119.17266°W; no campfires).

DAY 3 (Alger Lakes to Silver Lake, 8.7 miles): From the outlet, you climb up another moraine's low crest, glancing back across the open terrain of this glaciated, somber-toned rock basin. Metasediments compose the northeast canyon wall and metavolcanics the southwest one. You continue following the generally open moraine crest south past a nearby lakelet (with nice campsites), then descend steeply about 300 feet to a second, then third one, these latter lakes offering only quite small camping options. The small islands in the second lakelet are large boulders that have tumbled down from the unstable slope above, a spur extending southeast from Blacktop.

Just a few minutes later, you enter your first stand of lodgepoles, then climb a very gradual 130 feet of elevation to Gem Pass. Meanwhile Alger Creek, now hundreds of feet below you, drops out of sight; you will next see it just steps from your car, where it spills into Silver Lake. It is delightful how easily the trail contours around the valley's head, while the cleft below is impassably rugged. Note that as you begin sidling the final, quite steep slope to Gem Pass, the trail forks. The left branch descends, only to climb again 0.1 mile later. If you're hiking in August or September you'll be understandably confused, for the right-trending (more western) upper trail, the main route, is level and well built; however, in early July, when hard, icy snow is piled deep on the steep slope you traverse, you'll appreciate the alternative low, less exposed route.

From 10,500-foot Gem Pass, you have your first views of the famous Ritter Range, dominated by Mount Ritter and Banner Peak. Now under a continual canopy of protective forest, you descend first through whitebark pines, then lodgepoles. In contrast to the wonderfully green, irrigated slopes you've been on so far, the ground here is mostly sandy, dusty, and parched. You continue down, skirting beneath a corn lily meadow, but mostly just kicking up clouds of dust on other members of your group. After you cross Crest Creek, the trail switchbacks down alongside it, slowly transitioning to a pure lodgepole pine forest, often with red mountain heather or mat manzanita as ground cover. As you descend, views of the Ritter Range are gradually replaced by filtered glimpses southeast to Carson Peak. Your 1,400-foot drop ends above Gem Lake, where you'll meet the Rush Creek Trail near a cluster of well-used campsites. Additional campsites can be found on a peninsula extending south into the lake. Here you turn left (east) to Agnew Lake and the Rush Creek Trailhead, while right (south, then west) leads to Waugh Lake.

You must now cross Crest Creek again, a log balance or rock hop. Here, aspens—brilliant in early fall—join ranks with lodgepoles. Continuing east, the Rush Creek Trail generally stays high above Gem Lake's steep shoreline and the terrain is inhospitable to camping. The aspens have given way to sagebrush, junipers, Jeffrey pines, and even to an occasional whitebark pine. As you stare across Gem Lake you'll notice that a major geologic contact zone cuts across the Rush Creek drainage. This ridge and the bedrock to the north are composed mostly of Paleozoic-age metamorphic rock. These ancient rocks are roughly a hundred times older than the volcanic rocks you see above Gem Lake's forested south slopes and at the base of Carson Peak.

Onward, the trail climbs over a ridge and passes through a corridor delineated by vertically tipped shale beds, channeling you between two rock ribs. Enjoying your view to the Sierra Crest just south of Donohue Pass, a pleasant sandy trail takes you back toward lake level, only to reverse course and force you back upward as you ease your way between bluffs near the dam's outlet. A few spots would offer good camping, but they're high above the lake, and the descent to water is long and steep.

Leaving Gem Lake behind and, for a spell, Ansel Adams Wilderness, you descend above Agnew Lake's northern shore. Mountain mahogany dominates the dry, south-facing slopes, contrasting with the forested, north-facing ones across the lake below Agnew Pass. You pass some small calcitic outcrops and a nearby seep. Farther down grow giant blazing stars, whose oversize glossy yellow flowers will be blooming for late-season hikers. The flowers provide a distraction from the increasingly cobbly trail that can be tough on the feet. Finally you reach the Agnew Lake dam and a junction with the trail leading right (south) to Clark Lakes and Agnew Pass.

Beyond the dam, switchbacks carry you north down alongside a tramway, which you cross twice, before it plummets straight to the valley and you embark on a long descending traverse toward Silver Lake. At first, these slopes have mountain mahogany, juniper, and even pinyon pine, but not far beyond a small waterfall, they are gradually replaced with waist-high brush. You look longingly down to the road far below, but still have several miles to walk.

Near Silver Lake's west corner, your trail almost touches the June Lake Loop Road, then in just over 0.3 mile, it arcs behind Silver Lake Resort and crosses several branches of Alger Creek on small bridges. It finally traverses behind Silver Lake Trailer Court to end at the Rush Creek Trailhead (7,240'; 37.78332°N, 119.12813°W).

Alger Lakes   Photo by Elizabeth Wenk

Saddlebag Lake Trailhead
10,115'; 37.96570°N, 119.27187°W

Destination/ GPS Coordinates	Trip Type	Best Season	Pace & Hiking/ Layover Days	Total Mileage	Permit Required
57 Twenty Lakes Basin Loop 37.99156°N 119.30575°W (Cascade Lake)	Semiloop	Mid to late	Leisurely 2/0	8.6	Saddlebag Lake
58 Twenty Lakes Basin to Tuolumne Meadows via McCabe Lakes 37.99515°N 119.34975°W (Lower McCabe Lake)	Shuttle	Mid to late	Moderate, part cross-country 3/1	21.7	Saddlebag Lake *(Glen Aulin if reversed)*
80 Virginia Lakes to Twenty Lakes Basin via McCabe Lakes *(in reverse of description; see page 379)*	Shuttle	Mid to late	Moderate, part cross-country 3/1	21.0	Saddlebag Lake *(Virginia Lakes as described)*

INFORMATION AND PERMITS: Twenty Lakes Basin lies within Inyo National Forest. Wilderness permits are required, but there is no quota. Pick up your permit at the Mono Lake Scenic Area Visitor Center in Lee Vining or at the Tuolumne Meadows Wilderness Center

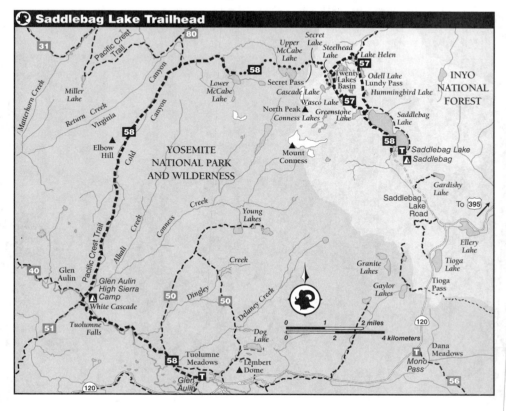

(but not other Yosemite permit-issuing centers). If your trip crosses into Yosemite National Park, all Yosemite rules and regulations apply (for example, bear canisters required; pets and firearms prohibited). Campfires are prohibited throughout the Twenty Lakes Basin and above 9,600 feet in Yosemite.

DRIVING DIRECTIONS: From Tioga Pass drive 2.1 miles east on Tioga Road (CA 120) down to the Saddlebag Lake junction, located a short distance beyond Tioga Pass Resort. Or, from US 395 just south of Lee Vining, drive 9.8 miles west on Tioga Road up to the junction. From the junction, drive 2.4 miles northwest up to Saddlebag Lake on a well-maintained but partially gravel road. Those on a day hike may park in the lot adjacent to the store (and restaurant), but backpackers need to use the lot in the group campground, reached by making a sharp right just as you pass the dam. There are toilets and water faucets near the backpacker parking area and at the parking lot closer to the store (and water taxi wharf).

trip 57   Twenty Lakes Basin Loop

    Trip Data: 37.99156°N, 119.30575°W
                    (Cascade Lake); 8.6 miles; 2/0 days
       Topos: *Tioga Pass, Dunderberg Peak*

HIGHLIGHTS: A short jaunt brings backpackers to a scenic granite subbasin for an overnight in the shadow of beautiful peaks. This is the perfect first backpacking trip for young children, with lakes to splash in, granite slabs to play on, and stunning views for the parents. Sturdy day hikers will have no trouble taking this trip in a single day, with or without the ferry's help.

HEADS UP! *Much of Twenty Lakes Basin, which is "carpeted" by shards of the metamorphic rock out of which most of the basin is carved, offers virtually no camping. The granitic subbasin holding Cascade Lake is an exception, although there are also a few campsites around Lake Helen.*

HEADS UP! *Saddlebag Lake Resort, located at the road's end, sells fishing licenses if you don't have one. The resort also offers water taxi service to the lake's far end, running nonstop all day and shaving 1.5 miles off the hike, each direction; if you wish to use this on the return, book a ticket for a prearranged time before you leave.*

DAY 1 (Saddlebag Lake Trailhead to Cascade Lake, 3.3 miles): To get to the 10,064-foot-high lake's far end, from the trailhead parking entrance, descend to the east end of the dam and cross on the dam wall. Head across to the trail—a blocky tread cutting across open, equally blocky talus slopes. This metamorphic rock talus may be uncomfortable to walk on, but it creates soils superior to those derived from granitic talus, and hence there is a more luxuriant growth of alpine plants.

About 0.5 mile north of the dam, your trail bends northwest, and Mount Dana, in the southeast, disappears from view. Shepherd Crest, straight ahead across Saddlebag Lake, now captivates your attention. Continuing on and on along the red talus slopes, you reach flatter terrain once you round the end of the ridge. Among willows and a seasonally fiery field of Pierson's paintbrush, you pass an unsigned spur trail that leads left to the nearby south shore of 10,143-foot-high Greenstone Lake and beyond to the Conness Lakes. Continuing straight ahead (right; north) you soon reach the north end of Saddlebag Lake and quickly meet a closed mining road; those who chose to take the ferry across, join the route at this point, merging from the right (east).

Turning left (northwest) onto the old road, you climb gently, staring southwest across Greenstone Lake to the granite wall sweeping up to a crest at Mount Conness and sharp-tipped North Peak. The northwest shore of Greenstone Lake sports many camping options, but camping is prohibited on the lake's southern shore as well as upstream toward the Conness Lakes. Your tread climbs northwest, then, nearly imperceptibly, crosses a drainage divide. You are now in the drainage of northeast-flowing Mill Creek—that was probably the easiest pass you have ever ascended! The trail then descends slightly to relatively warm Wasco Lake and a string of tarns often filled with western tree frog tadpoles.

Just past the second tarn a use trail drops into the small entrenched drainage to your left (west) and follows it toward Steelhead Lake's southern tip. It then skirts Steelhead Lake's western shore just long enough to cross an inlet creek and pass the first small lake, colloquially Potter Lake. Then you head briefly west between Potter Lake and Towser Lake (the northern of the unnamed lakes between Cascade and Steelhead Lakes), toward Cascade Lake. From here, trend west and north and pick a campsite that suits you in the Cascade Lake environs—there are many sandy patches among the never-ending slabs in this treeless basin (10,335'; 37.99156°N, 119.30575°W; no campfires). A layover day offers fine off-trail exploring and fishing for golden trout.

DAY 2 (Cascade Lake to Saddlebag Lake Trailhead, 5.3 miles): The remaining loop is much harder going than simply retracing your steps, but assuming you are completing the loop, return to the main trail near Steelhead Lake and follow the former road north alongside the deep lake to its outlet. Diverse and colorful flowers—several species of penstemon, straggly yellow arnicas, and burgundy-colored roseroot—decorate the sandy slopes on either side of the trail. Just before reaching the outlet stream, the old road turns sharply left (west), crossing the creek west of your route, then continuing northwest above the lake's north shore to the Hess Mine. This mine, like others nearby, lies near the contact between rock types, for that is where ore is most likely to be found. Looking at the panorama of peaks you immediately see the distinction in landscape between the sharp-pointed granitic peaks to the west and the more rounded metamorphic summits to the east. You continue straight ahead, north.

As you cross Steelhead Lake's outlet, Mill Creek, you are embarking on a route that follows a narrow use trail that is generally very obvious, but there are a few places where it becomes faint or steep. You head downstream, scramble over a low knoll, and quickly descend to the west shore of tiny Excelsior Lake, unnamed on most maps. At the north end of Excelsior Lake, you go through a notch just west of a low metamorphic rock knoll that is

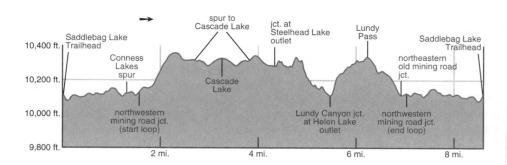

North Peak rises above Greenstone Lake.   Photo by Elizabeth Wenk

strewn with granitic glacial erratics, boulders dropped by melting glaciers. A long, narrow pond comes quickly into view. Your trail skirts its west shore, then swings east to the west shore of adjacent, many-armed Shamrock Lake.

Your ducked (marked with cairns) route—more cross-country than trail along this section—crosses an easily navigated talus fan along Shamrock Lake's northern shore, continues northeast over a low ridge, then descends steep slabs and bluffs to reunite with Mill Creek on flatter terrain. You traipse past two ponds and reach the west shore of Lake Helen, sporting some small campsites beneath whitebark pines. Encircling the lake's north shore on a good trail through dark talus, you loop down to cross Mill Creek on a log or rocks. A step beyond the crossing is a junction: your route is to the right (south) toward Lundy Pass and Odell Lake, while the left branch (northeast) is a rough trail descending to Lundy Canyon.

Heading south, the trail becomes better again, as you skirt the eastern shore of Lake Helen on red scree, then follow an inlet stream upward through a straight, narrow gully that transforms into a wildflower garden as soon as the late-lasting snow melts; the columbines are particularly showy here. The trail continues alongside the remarkably straight channel until you climb above the creek's western bank and soon approach Odell Lake. Climbing gently above the lake's west shore, you parallel it southward. You then continue the most gradual of climbs to reach Lundy Pass, which drops you back into the Lee Vining Creek drainage and on toward Hummingbird Lake, boasting terrific lakeshore for an afternoon break. Beyond, the trail reaches a four-way junction where you again intersect the old mining road. Turn right (west) to retrace your steps around Saddlebag Lake's western shore or head straight ahead (south) to the water taxi dock. You can also turn left to follow the old road around Saddlebag's eastern shore, a slightly longer choice.

trip 58 Twenty Lakes Basin to Tuolumne Meadows via McCabe Lakes

see map on p. 274

Trip Data: 37.99515°N, 119.34975°W (Lower McCabe Lake);
21.7 miles; 3/1 days

Topos: *Tioga Pass, Dunderberg Peak* (barely), *Falls Ridge*

HIGHLIGHTS: This adventurous cross-country trek climbs out of Twenty Lakes Basin and into Yosemite near the lightly visited McCabe Lakes. Breathtaking views and alpine scenery await you. Beyond Lower McCabe Lake, the route merges with the Pacific Crest Trail (PCT) and heads for Tuolumne Meadows via Glen Aulin High Sierra Camp.

HEADS UP! *This trip is only for those experienced in cross-country travel and navigation.*

SHUTTLE DIRECTIONS: Your endpoint is in Tuolumne Meadows, just off Tioga Road (CA 120), along a dirt road extending from the Lembert Dome parking area to the Tuolumne Meadows Stables. From here, regain Tioga Road and drive 9.1 miles northeast along Tioga Road, crossing Tioga Pass and descending to the Saddlebag Lake turnoff.

DAY 1 (Saddlebag Lake Trailhead to Lower McCabe Lake, 6.9 miles, part cross-country): To get to the 10,064-foot-high lake's far end, from the trailhead parking entrance, descend to the east end of the dam and cross on the dam wall. Head across to the trail—a blocky tread cutting across open, equally blocky talus slopes. This metamorphic rock talus may be uncomfortable to walk on, but it creates soils superior to those derived from granitic talus, and hence there is a more luxuriant growth of alpine plants.

About 0.5 mile north of the dam, your trail bends northwest, and Mount Dana, in the southeast, disappears from view. Shepherd Crest, straight ahead across Saddlebag Lake, now captivates your attention. Continuing on and on along the red talus slopes, you reach flatter terrain once you round the end of the ridge. Among willows and a seasonally fiery field of Pierson's paintbrush, you pass an unsigned spur trail that leads left to the nearby south shore of 10,143-foot-high Greenstone Lake and beyond to the Conness Lakes. Continuing straight ahead (right; north) you soon reach the north end of Saddlebag Lake and quickly meet a closed mining road; those who chose to take the ferry across join the route at this point, merging from the right (east).

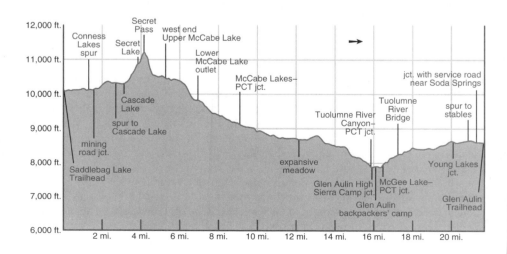

Campsite on a perch near Upper McCabe Lake   Photo by Elizabeth Wenk

Turning left (northwest) onto the old road, you climb gently, staring southwest across Greenstone Lake to the granite wall sweeping up to a crest at Mount Conness and sharp-tipped North Peak. The northwest shore of Greenstone Lake sports many camping options, but camping is prohibited on the lake's southern shore as well as upstream toward the Conness Lakes. Your tread climbs northwest, then, nearly imperceptibly, crosses a drainage divide. You are now in the drainage of northeast-flowing Mill Creek—that was probably the easiest pass you have ever ascended! The trail then descends slightly to relatively warm Wasco Lake and a string of tarns often filled with western tree frog tadpoles.

Just past the second tarn a use trail drops into the small entrenched drainage to your left (west) and follows it toward Steelhead Lake's southern tip. It then skirts Steelhead Lake's western shore just long enough to cross an inlet creek and pass the first small lake, collo-quially Potter Lake. Then you head briefly west between Potter Lake and Towser Lake (the northern of the unnamed lakes between Cascade and Steelhead Lakes), toward Cascade Lake. At this point the well-established use trail fades and the cross-country route begins. There are minor use trails for much of the distance between here and Lower McCabe Lake, but don't depend upon finding them for navigation.

As you approach Cascade Lake, begin heading in a north-northeasterly direction toward the low point in the steep headwall separating North Peak and Shepherd Crest. Your first goal is to get to a small lake perched just below where the wall becomes steepest, unofficially called Secret Lake. Near a tiny, unmapped, flower-lined inlet to Cascade Lake (10,355'; 37.99210°N, 119.30604°W) you should find a good use trail to Secret Lake; locating this trail from the start will save you time and effort on the ascent—and it is the environmentally conscious choice, for otherwise you incessantly trample delicate alpine vegetation.

Pause at Secret Lake to study your choices for the next section of the route and pick the one that best suits you; we offer two suggestions in the sidebar "Two Ways Up Secret Pass" on page 280. Whichever route you take—and that depends on your skillset and the amount of snow present—your next goal is to get to Secret Pass (11,218'), the low point on the ridge.

TWO WAYS UP SECRET PASS
Here are two suggestions for getting to Secret Pass, the low point atop Shepherd Crest:

1. Most people choose this way, especially on the way up: From the south side of Secret Lake, walk directly up the increasingly steep wall until, about halfway up, at just over 11,000 feet, you come to a long ledge that slopes slightly up to the south. Follow this ledge for about 250 feet south, then leave it to zigzag almost directly up steep slabs, ending up near the ridge's low point, Secret Pass (11,218').

2. Hikers who want to put out some extra effort to achieve certainty and avoid steep exposure can pick their way up the blue-gray scree-laden stripe on the wall north of Secret Lake to the lip of what looks like a lake basin, but is simply a giant talus field. From there, traverse slightly upward to the right (northeast), diagonalling up to the crest in a loose scree gully. You reach the main ridge of Shepherd Crest near the uppermost whitebark pines, almost 250 feet above Secret Pass and head south back to the pass. Note this route lacks exposure but holds snow later into the summer.

Once you're on Secret Pass (11,218'; 37.99967°N, 119.31125°W), you need to make your way down to Upper McCabe Lake. You initially stick to broken slabs on the south side of the broad drainage, trending into a narrow vegetated gully just under 11,000 feet. While this upper section has stretches of use trail, you are unlikely to follow it continually—just make tight switchbacks as you pick your way down sandy ramps between short, steep outcrops.

By 10,700 feet you are below the slabs on a sandy slope—now the use trail should be obvious again and you follow it to flatter ground, skirting the east side of a marshy meadow until you approach Upper McCabe Lake. Follow the lake's north shore, passing some tiny campsites nestled among whitebark pines with astonishing views of the surrounding ridges. At Upper McCabe Lake's northwest corner cross nascent McCabe Creek, then strike out for the low saddle due west of the outlet and about 0.3 mile away; do not follow McCabe Creek downward. Cairns may be present to guide you, but expect to have to navigate by map and compass (or GPS).

Beyond this saddle (10,411'; 38.00071°N, 119.33633°W), the best route heads generally west-southwest, remaining north of and well above Middle McCabe Lake. It then drops past snowmelt tarns (and beautiful open campsites) not shown on the topo map and winds down through forest cover to the east shore of Lower McCabe Lake. The biggest campsites (9,820'; 37.99515°N, 119.34975°W; no campfires) are just before you cross Lower McCabe Lake's outlet creek. Fishing for brook trout is excellent.

DAY 2 (Lower McCabe Lake to Glen Aulin High Sierra Camp, 9.4 miles): In late season or during a drier summer, be sure to get water at Lower McCabe Lake or its outlet stream, as this may be your last chance before Glen Aulin—the creek down Cold Canyon can dry up. Crossing Lower McCabe Lake's outlet creek, you pick up a true trail and follow it northwest, then west, mostly beside the creek. For long stretches it is a beautiful, lush forest, at first dense with diminutive hemlocks, then a fairyland of twisted lodgepoles, with a carpet of colorful flowers underfoot. A little farther along you enter a more open forest of lodgepole, hemlocks, western white pine, and occasional red fir. Veering away from the creek, the trail crosses more open terrain, then back in forest, drops more steeply to a junction with the Pacific Crest Trail (PCT), where you turn left (south), toward Glen Aulin, while right (north) is the PCT's route toward Sonora Pass (Trip 31).

Now begins a long, gentle descent down Cold Canyon—you drop just 400 feet over the next 3.5 miles. In patches of moderate to dense forest enjoy the abounding birdlife (chickadees, juncos, warblers, woodpeckers, robins, evening grosbeaks). Elsewhere are meadows, where bluebirds and flycatchers flit about, and occasional drier stretches with broken slabs. When there's water, you may also be able to camp in the occasional dry, forested patch or at a meadow edge, but the streams can be dry by the middle of summer. You enter a particularly beautiful meadow after 3 miles, with some giant boulders along its western edge that is slowly being encroached upon by young lodgepoles.

At the meadow's southern tip, you climb just briefly, drop a bit more steeply back to the river corridor, and continue onward, still mostly through lush lodgepole forest. Wandering fleabane spreads across the forest floor, joined by larkspurs, dwarf bilberry, and one-sided wintergreen. The trail trundles along—this is about as easy as walking gets in Yosemite, with a soft forest floor, gentle grade, and well-maintained trail. About 1.5 miles north of Glen Aulin you emerge from forest cover, crossing more open expanses and descending a bit more steeply. Here are a few possible campsites if there is water in the creek. On the final, rocky downhill to the river, you catch glimpses of Tuolumne Falls and the White Cascade, and their roar carries all the way across the canyon.

Within sight of Glen Aulin High Sierra Camp, you reach a junction with the trail that descends the Grand Canyon of the Tuolumne (right; west; Trip 40) and continuing straight ahead (left; northeast), after 50 feet, come to a spur trail that goes left (east) to Glen Aulin High Sierra Camp, crossing Conness Creek on a footbridge. To reach the backpackers' campground, loop north through the camp, passing the tiny store with its meager supplies, and continue to an open area with many tent sites (7,930'; 37.91051°N, 119.41699°W); there is potable water (when the camp is open), a pit toilet, and animal-proof food-storage boxes. This is the last legal camping before Tuolumne Meadows, so you must camp here or complete the entire Day 3 hike description.

DAY 3 (Glen Aulin High Sierra Camp to Tuolumne Meadows, 5.4 miles): Follow Trip 31, Day 8 to the Glen Aulin Trailhead (8,590'; 37.87889°N, 119.35854°W).

Tarns near Upper McCabe Lake   Photo by Elizabeth Wenk

WESTERN YOSEMITE TRIPS

The trailheads in this section are south of CA 120 within the western part of Yosemite National Park: Yosemite Valley's Happy Isles Trailhead and, two trailheads from Glacier Point Road, Bridalveil Creek and Glacier Point. The Yosemite Falls and Wawona Tunnel Trailheads in Yosemite Valley are also included, as described trails end at these. There's another Yosemite waiting for you in the park's southern backcountry, and these trailheads are your gateways to it.

The Happy Isles Trailhead is probably the prettiest in Yosemite Valley, situated as it is near the cascading Merced River and near the Happy Isles—be sure to visit this pair of islets if time permits.

Beyond the Bridalveil Creek Trailhead, you'll find not only the creekside meadows and abundant wildflowers for which the Bridalveil Creek area is rightly famous but also remote, peaceful lakes and high, rugged peaks.

Yosemite's Glacier Point is justly famed for its incomparable views of Yosemite Valley and of the great waterfalls on the Merced River. And it's a popular starting point for day hikes down into the valley. But had you thought of it as a trailhead for backpacks? If not, prepare to be surprised at the wonderful overnighters possible from Glacier Point, departing along the Pohono Trail, Panorama Trail, or up Illilouette Creek. But whatever you do, don't leave this trailhead without enjoying the world-renowned views from Glacier Point proper.

Trailheads: Wawona Tunnel

Yosemite Falls

Happy Isles

Bridalveil Creek

Glacier Point

Wawona Tunnel Trailhead 3,993'; 37.71510°N, 119.67678°W

Destination/ GPS Coordinates	Trip Type	Best Season	Pace & Hiking/ Layover Days	Total Mileage	Permit Required
62 Pohono Trail (in reverse of description; see page 299)	Shuttle	Early-late	Leisurely 2/0	13.9	Pohono Trail (Wawona Tunnel); (Pohono Trail [Glacier Point] as described)

INFORMATION AND PERMITS: This trip is in Yosemite National Park: wilderness permits and bear canisters are required; pets and firearms are prohibited. Quotas apply, with 60% of permits reservable online up to 24 weeks in advance and 40% available first-come, first-served starting at 11 a.m. the day before your trip's start date. Fires are prohibited above 9,600 feet. See nps.gov/yose/planyourvisit/wildpermits.htm for more details.

DRIVING DIRECTIONS: The endpoint is variously called the Tunnel View Trailhead, the Pohono Trailhead, and the Wawona Tunnel Trailhead. It is located at Discovery View (aka Tunnel View), at the east end of Wawona Tunnel. This is on the Wawona Road (CA 41), 1.5 miles west of where CA 41 merges with Southside Drive in Yosemite Valley—or 7.75 miles north of the Chinquapin junction where the Glacier Point Road begins. The trailhead is on the south side of the road at the back of the smaller, subsidiary parking lot.

Yosemite Falls Trailhead 3,993'; 37.74242°N, 119.60205°W

Destination/ GPS Coordinates	Trip Type	Best Season	Pace & Hiking/ Layover Days	Total Mileage	Permit Required
42 Yosemite Creek to Yosemite Valley (in reverse of description; see page 209)	Shuttle	Early to late	Leisurely 2/0	12.1	Yosemite Falls (Yosemite Creek as described)

INFORMATION AND PERMITS: This trip is in Yosemite National Park: wilderness permits and bear canisters are required; pets and firearms are prohibited. Quotas apply, with 60% of permits reservable online up to 24 weeks in advance and 40% available first-come, first-served starting at 11 a.m. the day before your trip's start date. Fires are prohibited above 9,600 feet. See nps.gov/yose/planyourvisit/wildpermits.htm for more details.

DRIVING DIRECTIONS: This trailhead is in Yosemite Valley at the entrance to Camp 4, a campground, and is located approximately across Northside Drive from the Yosemite Valley Lodge. Overnight hikers must park in the hiker parking lot, located along the road to Happy Isles, or in the large Curry Village parking area. To reach the hiker lot you continue briefly past the NO ACCESS signs at the start of the Happy Isles Loop Road and then turn to your right at the trailhead parking signs. From here, you must retrace your steps to Curry Village to catch the shuttle bus. Take the bus to stop 7, Camp 4. There are toilets and water faucets in the campground.

Happy Isles Trailhead

4,025'; 37.73242°N, 119.55965°W

Destination/ GPS Coordinates	Trip Type	Best Season	Pace & Hiking/ Layover Days	Total Mileage	Permit Required
59 Merced Lake 37.74049°N 119.40718°W	Out-and-back	Early or late	Moderate 4/1	26.8	Happy Isles
44 Clouds Rest Traverse to Yosemite Valley *(in reverse of description; see page 216)*	Shuttle	Mid to late	Moderate 2/1	16.3	Happy Isles to Sunrise Pass Thru *(Sunrise Lakes as described)*
48 John Muir Trail to Yosemite Valley *(in reverse of description; see page 233)*	Shuttle	Mid to late	Leisurely 3/0	20.8	Happy Isles to Sunrise Pass Thru *(Cathedral Lakes as described)*

INFORMATION AND PERMITS: These trips are in Yosemite National Park: wilderness permits and bear canisters are required; pets and firearms are prohibited. Quotas apply, with 60% of permits reservable online up to 24 weeks in advance and 40% available first-come, first-served starting at 11 a.m. the day before your trip's start date. Fires are prohibited above 9,600 feet. See nps.gov/yose/planyourvisit/wildpermits.htm for more details.

DRIVING DIRECTIONS: The trailhead is located at Happy Isles, Yosemite Valley shuttle stop 16, along Happy Isles Loop Road. Because this road is closed to vehicular traffic, except the shuttle buses, use the shuttle bus or walk to reach the trailhead. Overnight hikers should park their cars at the hiker parking area, located along Happy Isles Loop Road about halfway between Curry Village and Happy Isles or in the large Curry Village parking lot. The Happy Isles shuttle stop is a 0.4-mile walk from the hiker parking area—from here it is more efficient to walk than to take the shuttle bus, while those in the main Curry Village lot should take the shuttle to the trailhead. There are water faucets and toilets at the shuttle stop.

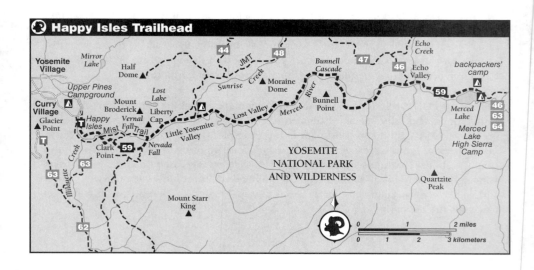

View up the Merced River Canyon toward Mount Florence   Photo by Elizabeth Wenk

trip 59   **Merced Lake**

Trip Data: 37.74049°N, 119.40718°W; 26.8 miles; 4/1 days
Topos: *Half Dome, Merced Peak*

HIGHLIGHTS: A good early-season trip (low altitude, early snowmelt), this route displays Yosemite's scenic grandeur at its best, but it is never too crowded once past Little Yosemite Valley. As you follow the Merced River for more than 10 river miles you admire landscape shaped by glaciers and streams, the pale gray granite always dominating your thoughts.

HEADS UP! *Though this trip is graded moderate, the first hiking day is rigorous, with more than 2,000 feet of hot, steady climbing.*

HEADS UP! *Permits for this trail are very hard to get, so consider two alternative starts. You can request a Happy Isles to Merced Lake Pass Thru permit, necessitating you hike an extra 2-plus miles on Day 1. Alternatively, you can begin at Glacier Point and follow the Panorama Trail until it intersects the John Muir Trail near the top of Nevada Fall, lengthening the first day by 2.4 miles but reducing the elevation gain. Note as well that if you obtain a standard Happy Isles to Little Yosemite Valley permit you must spend your first night in Little Yosemite Valley.*

DAY 1 (Happy Isles to Little Yosemite Valley, 4.7 miles): From the Happy Isles shuttle stop you walk briefly east along the road across a bridge, then turn right (south) onto a trail and soon reach a sign proclaiming the start of the famous John Muir Trail (JMT). Winding past large boulders through a forest of oaks, California laurel, and conifers, your paved path takes you past a small spring-fed cistern, beyond which the climb steepens. At a distinct left bend in the trail, look west at the decimated forest at the base of Glacier Point Apron, the aftermath of a massive rockslide in July 1996. The deposit of boulders lies close to the cliff wall, and beyond is a ring of trees, toppled by the air blast that accompanied the slide—the giant, largely intact rock slabs were tumbling at an astonishing 270 miles per hour by the time they reached the valley floor. Entering forest shade once more, you ascend a steep stretch of trail before making a quick drop to the Vernal Fall bridge. From it you see Vernal Fall, a broad curtain of water plunging 320 feet over a vertical cliff before cascading toward you. Looming above the fall are two glacier-resistant masses, Mount Broderick (left) and Liberty Cap (right). Just beyond the bridge are a drinking fountain and water faucet, with a toilet a few steps farther along.

Now you continue up to the start of the Mist Trail. The 0.8-mile-shorter Mist Trail leads to the brink of Vernal Fall, past Emerald Pool, and across the Silver Apron. It is certainly worth taking, but the stairs ascending the steep stretch to the top of Vernal Fall are no fun with an overnight pack, especially if you are trying to race upward to avoid drenching yourself and all your gear, a spring and early summer scenario. Instead you turn right (southwest), continuing along the JMT corridor, a route yielding different rewards. One is that the miles to Clark Point are along shady, moderately graded switchbacks. Above Clark Point you have spectacular views across the canyon to Half Dome, Mount Broderick, and Liberty Cap, rising to the left of downward-leaping Nevada Fall. Where a stretch of trail has been blasted out of the steep granite slab, a tall wall provides safe passage.

Beyond this section you intersect the end of the Panorama Trail, which started at Glacier Point. Stay left (northeast) at a pair of spurs and descend to the bridge over Nevada Fall. About 100 feet north of the bridge, a cryptic spur trail drops northwest to a viewpoint beside the fall's brink. Back on the main trail, you descend briefly and reach the top of the Mist Trail, where hikers opting for this shorter, steeper trail will rejoin this route description.

From the junction and its adjacent outhouses, you begin the final climb to Little Yosemite Valley, first by ascending a brushy, rocky slope and then briefly descending and reaching both forest shade and the Merced River. Beneath pines, firs, and incense cedars, you continue northeast along the river's azalea-lined bank, soon reaching a trail fork. Bound for Merced Lake, you keep right (east) on the main, riverside trail and continue just out of sight of the river's edge, to reach a junction at the southern edge of the Little Yosemite

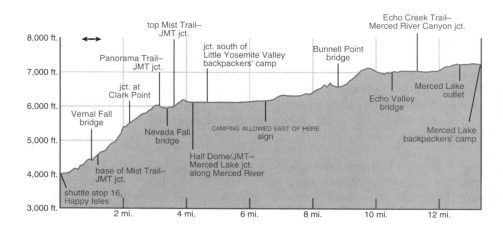

Valley backpackers' camp (6,120'; 37.73196°N, 119.51536°W). Turn left (north) and within steps you'll see the tent city to the right where you will spend your first night. There are toilets and food-storage boxes; a usually-staffed ranger station is hidden to the northeast of the camping area.

DAY 2 (Little Yosemite Valley to Merced Lake, 8.7 miles): Return to the junction south of the backpackers' campground and turn left (east). With the majority of hikers heading toward Half Dome or along the JMT, the trail leading north out of Little Yosemite Valley, your route is now much quieter—and wonderfully flat.

Most of the forest in eastern Little Yosemite Valley and Lost Valley (the next valley east) was burned in the Meadow Fire in September 2014. Previously much of this section had been a dense forest, with abundant dead material on the ground, providing ample fuel for the fire to spread; this is a natural process and was caused by a natural lightning-strike fire, but the lack of shade and loss of beautiful canopy trees is nonetheless unwelcome on a hot day. Trying to be optimistic, you now have a better view of the canyon's walls and can admire the blackened tree trunks as artistic totems. A thick accumulation of glacial sediments covers most of the valley floor, which, like beach sand, makes for harder walking even though the trail is level.

Most of Little Yosemite Valley is a designated day-use area and only once you're beyond a sign in the eastern stretches of the valley may you camp. The valley's east end is graced by the presence of a beautiful pool—the receptacle of a Merced River cascade; this has always been a popular camping area but is now badly charred, although it's still in use as a campsite. Climbing slabs past the cascade, you round the base of a glacier-smoothed dome, unofficially called Sugarloaf Dome, and enter Lost Valley, the next flat valley. This valley has also been scorched by the Meadow Fire, with barely a tree still standing. At the valley's east end, where Bunnell Point and an unnamed dome to the north pinch the valley closed, switchback up past Bunnell Cascade on bare slabs straight above the churning river.

GEOLOGY LESSON

As an indication of how deep glaciers were here, look up at Moraine Dome to the east: ice filled the valley almost to its summit 750,000 years ago. Since then, glaciers have repeatedly entered this valley, but none have been that thick.

Just past the gorge, the canyon floor widens a bit, and, just before a pair of bridges cross the Merced, if you trend east (left) from the trail, you will find a small, beautiful camping area atop some slabs. The trail follows the south bank briefly upstream, but it soon diverges from the water's edge and climbs more than a dozen switchbacks that carry you 400 feet above the river. Your climb reaches its zenith amid a spring-fed wildflower garden bordered by aspens; in midsummer enjoy the colorful array underfoot and in fall the brilliant yellow and orange leaves overhead.

Beyond this glade, you cross a highly polished bedrock surface, then descend back into a grove of white-trunked aspens and cross several creeklets before emerging on a bedrock bench above the river's inner gorge. From the bench, you can study an immense arch on the broad, hulking granitic mass opposite you and watch the water churning below. Traversing the narrow trail, you soon come to a bridge that crosses the Merced just above the brink of these cascades. Strolling east leads to spacious Echo Valley. You pass a few sandy knobs harboring campsites, then reach a junction with a trail ascending Echo Creek (left; north); bear right (east) here, heading toward Merced Lake.

You immediately cross Echo Creek's braided river channels on three bridges, then strike southeast through the boggy eastern half of Echo Valley, a dense tangle of approximately 15-foot-tall lodgepole pines, regenerating after fires in 1988 and 1993; the combination of downed logs and thickets of young trees make camping implausible. After mounting a shelf at the east end of Echo Valley, you again reach the river's edge. There are some small campsites north of the trail here, some in sandy flats among slabs and others in small lodgepole pine stands. Continuing on slabs beside the foaming river, you reach Merced Lake's outlet, at which there are no suitable campsites, and continue around Merced Lake's northern shore to the designated backpackers' camping area (7,242'; 37.74049°N, 119.40718°W), just a little northeast of the lake. This is the only legal camping option along the shores of Merced Lake. Pit toilets and food-storage boxes are an added bonus. Eighty-foot-deep Merced Lake supports three species of trout: brook, brown, and rainbow. The Merced Lake High Sierra Camp is another 0.15 mile east along the trail, if you'd like to take a look or fill your water bottles at their faucet.

DAYS 3–4 (Merced Lake to Happy Isles Trailhead, 13.4 miles): Retrace your steps.

The Merced River's bedrock base, just downstream of Merced Lake   Photo by Elizabeth Wenk

Bridalveil Creek Trailhead 6,958'; 37.66196°N, 119.61925°W

Destination/ GPS Coordinates	Trip Type	Best Season	Pace & Hiking/ Layover Days	Total Mileage	Permit Required
60 Royal Arch, Buena Vista, and Chilnualna Lakes 37.57699°N 119.50415°W (Royal Arch Lake)	Semiloop	Early or mid	Leisurely 4/0	29.2	Bridalveil Creek
61 Glacier Point via Buena Vista Pass 37.60147°N 119.51850°W (Buena Vista Lake)	Shuttle	Early or mid	Moderate 4/1	29.8	Bridalveil Creek *(Glacier Point to Illilouette if reversed)*

INFORMATION AND PERMITS: These trips are in Yosemite National Park: wilderness permits and bear canisters are required; pets and firearms are prohibited. Quotas apply, with 60% of permits reservable online up to 24 weeks in advance and 40% available first-come, first-served starting at 11 a.m. the day before your trip's start date. Fires are prohibited above 9,600 feet. See nps.gov/yose/planyourvisit/wildpermits.htm for more details.

DRIVING DIRECTIONS: From a signed junction (Chinquapin Junction) along Wawona Road (CA 41), drive 7.8 miles on Glacier Point Road to the entrance road to Bridalveil Creek Campground; this is 7.9 miles before Glacier Point. Turn right onto Bridalveil Creek Campground Road and follow it past the camping loops. The trailhead is on your right at a tiny lot with room for perhaps three cars, just before the road crosses Bridalveil Creek.

trip 60 Royal Arch, Buena Vista, and Chilnualna Lakes

see map on p. 290

Trip Data: 37.57699°N, 119.50415°W (Royal Arch Lake); 29.2 miles; 4/1 days

Topos: *Half Dome, Mariposa Grove*

HIGHLIGHTS: In early season, this route is lush with wildflowers of every variety (and unfortunately mosquitoes); the fishing at Royal Arch Lake is excellent. The generally gentle grades make this a fine early-summer choice as you're getting in shape for the summer.

HEADS UP! *The mileage includes the distance along short spur trails to reach Grouse, Crescent, and Johnson Lakes—a grand total of 0.9 mile extra over skipping the lakes. It is strongly recommended you visit these lakes because you barely notice them from the trail.*

DAY 1 (Bridalveil Creek Trailhead to Turner Meadow, 5.9 miles): From the trailhead at the far southeastern corner of the Bridalveil Creek Campground (and just before the road fords Bridalveil Creek to the stock camp), the unmarked and little-used trail begins winding along meandering Bridalveil Creek's western bank. It is a lush streamside walk through dense lodgepole forest that periodically opens into intimate meadows filled with shooting stars. The grade is delightfully gentle—you climb just 100 feet in the 1.6 miles to a junction

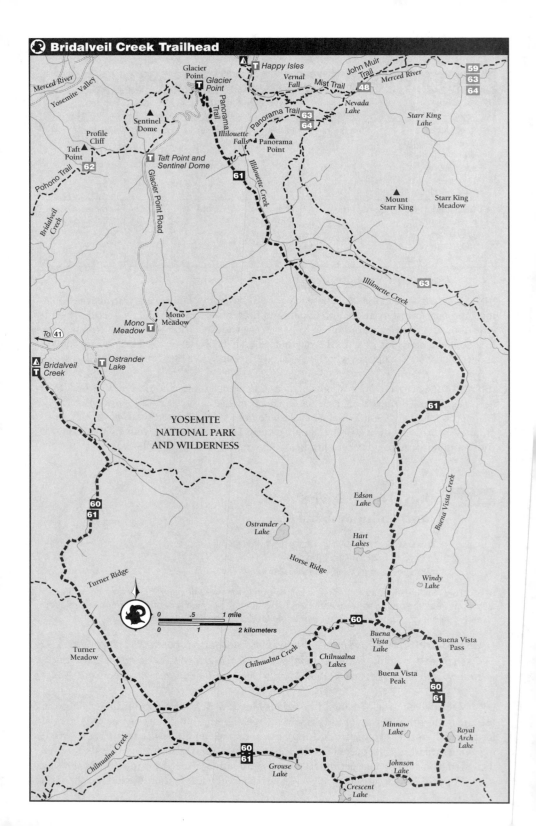

Merced River

Yosemite Valley

Glacier Point

Glacier Point

Panorama Trail

Happy Isles

Vernal Fall

Mist Trail

John Muir Trail

Merced River

59
63
64

Sentinel Dome

Illilouette Falls

Panorama Trail

Panorama Point

Nevada Lake

63
64

Starr King Lake

Profile Cliff

Taft Point

Pohono Trail

62

Taft Point and Sentinel Dome

Illilouette Creek

61

48

Starr King Lake

Mount Starr King

Starr King Meadow

Bridalveil Creek

Glacier Point Road

Illilouette Creek

63

To 41

Mono Meadow

Mono Meadow

Bridalveil Creek

Ostrander Lake

YOSEMITE NATIONAL PARK AND WILDERNESS

61

60
61

Edson Lake

Buena Vista Creek

Ostrander Lake

Hart Lakes

Horse Ridge

Windy Lake

Turner Ridge

0   .5   1 mile
0   1   2 kilometers

Turner Meadow

Chilnualna Creek

Chilnualna Lakes

60

Buena Vista Lake

Buena Vista Pass

Buena Vista Peak

60
61

Chilnualna Creek

Minnow Lake

Royal Arch Lake

60
61

Grouse Lake

Johnson Lake

Crescent Lake

with a spur that hooks sharply left (north) to cross Bridalveil Creek and shortly meet the Ostrander Lake Trail; you stay right (south).

Beyond, the trail veers south beside one of the larger tributaries of Bridalveil Creek. It crosses this tributary on a log and immediately meets a lateral left (northeast) to the Ostrander Lake Trail; again, you trend right (west). The verdant banks are thick with wildflowers, with the lavender shooting stars, elephant's head, and giant red paintbrush among the most evocative. The gradual climb along the creek corridor continues through the burned remnants of a red fir and lodgepole pine forest, the damage caused by the 2017 Empire Fire. Sections of forest are decimated, while elsewhere stands of trees have survived, likely because the expansive meadows and bald sandy areas in the drainage helped curtail the fires' spread. After another mile, you cross the now smaller (and seasonal) tributary, where there are (somewhat burned) campsites when there is water.

The second ford marks the beginning of an easy, 400-foot climb over the unglaciated ridge that separates the Bridalveil Creek and Alder Creek watersheds—and indeed the main Merced and South Fork Merced drainages. The Empire Fire did not spread south here and ahead the canopy is again green. From the top of this ridge, where you can glance east toward Mount Starr King, the trail drops south-southeast to meet the trail that leads right (west) to Deer Camp and Empire Meadows. Continuing straight ahead (left; southeast), climb just briefly, then cross a small creek, and follow a shelf that overlooks Turner Meadow. In early season, you'll ford many little rills, all with abundant corn lilies, as you descend to Turner Meadow. Wildflowers are abundant in early season—and so are mosquitoes.

Just before the ford of a sizable tributary (7,475'; 37.59605°N, 119.59705°W), there's a large packer campsite on your right (southwest) in the trees fringing the meadow. Farther ahead is another site in a slender, open, sandy flat. Make some time to sit quietly by the meadow, especially in the early morning, to see wildlife.

DAY 2 (Turner Meadow to Royal Arch Lake, 8.2 miles): Resume your descent down the long, gently sloping Turner Meadow and soon meet a trail coming across from Chilnualna Falls and Wawona. At the junction, you go left (southeast), continuing through moist lodgepole forest, and in 0.9 mile reach a junction (and an alternative creekside campsite for your first night). Left (east) leads to the Chilnualna (chill-NWAHL-nah) Lakes, your return route, while you turn right (south) and immediately ford swirling Chilnualna Creek on a

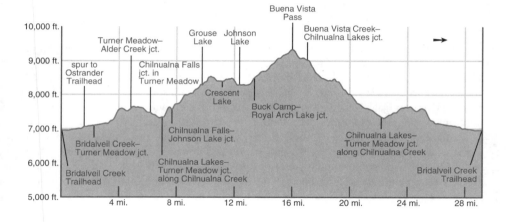

Climbing Buena Vista Pass   Photo by Elizabeth Wenk

cobbled base (can be difficult in early season). From the ford, climb southeast on switch-backs over an eastward-rising ridge and down to a junction; here a second lateral trail leads right (west) to Wawona, while you turn left (eastward), signposted for Buck Camp.

You are paralleling a small tributary of Chilnualna Creek east. Initially your route follows a gully north of the creek corridor, passing a flat that was scarred but not decimated by the 2017 South Fork Fire, then you are channeled up a second shaded gully before finally dropping to the unnamed creek. Quickly exiting the burn zone, you continue upstream for about a mile to a junction with a hard-to-spot spur trail leading 300 feet right (south) to little Grouse Lake and campsites; this junction is located where the main trail turns sharply left.

Back on the main trail, a slightly steeper ascent leads to drier terrain atop a small rise, from which the trail drops southward, then briefly eastward, to ford the inlet of shallow Crescent Lake, just out of sight to the south. Just past the crossing, a minor trail heads south 0.15 mile to the lakeshore and campsites. This spur, like those to the other nearby lakes, is included in the daily mileage, to ensure you've budgeted the time to visit them, for just out of sight of the trail they are easy to forgetfully bypass—and yet aren't they part of the reason for taking this walk? Grouse, Crescent, and Johnson Lakes all sit on a relatively flat bench high above the South Fork Merced River. Each is drained by a separate creek flowing into the South Fork Merced—those exiting Crescent Lake and Johnson Lake drop steeply to the west. At Crescent Lake, you might visit or camp near the lake's south end, for, from its outlet, you can peer into the 2,800-foot-deep South Fork Merced River Canyon.

Eastbound again, another 0.9 mile of level walking through often mosquito-infested forest with superb wildflower patches, brings you to a junction with a spur leading south to Johnson Lake's west shore and more campsites. For the September hiker there is an extra treat—western blueberries. Johnson Lake and its perimeter were one of the last acquisitions of private property within the park's boundaries, and two crumbling cabins remain to remind you of the homesteading era.

The next 0.8 mile is a 170-foot ascent up a lodgepole-covered slope alongside Johnson Lake's inlet stream, the ground sporting expanses of corn lilies and shooting stars in June and July. At a junction you turn left (north) toward Royal Arch Lake, while right (east) leads to Buck Camp, a summer ranger station.

ROYAL ARCH?

This lake probably got its name from the arching pattern of exfoliation on the granite dome on the lake's east side, which strongly resembles that of the famous Royal Arches—also exfoliation features—in Yosemite Valley.

The dense forest almost immediately gives way to more open, drier walking as the trail trends along benches on an open hillside. The landscape flattens as you approach dramatic, small, deep Royal Arch Lake. The best campsites are in the forest fringe on the lake's south shore (8,695'; 37.57699°N, 119.50415°W). Fishing is good for rainbow and brook.

DAY 3 (Royal Arch Lake to Lowest Chilnualna Lake, 5.1 miles): From Royal Arch Lake, resume your northward climb, traversing an idyllic meadow and fording its creek just below Buena Vista Pass on Buena Vista Peak's northeast ridge. Along the creek corridor are additional campsites as long as water is flowing.

CLIMBING BUENA VISTA PEAK

From the pass (9,340'), it is an easy 0.75-mile climb to the top of aptly named Buena Vista Peak (9,709'). As the highest point for miles around, this peak offers some of the most expansive views in this part of the Sierra. Since this day is the trip's shortest, you should have ample time for this detour, simply following the ridgeline southeast to the peak. Sandy walking transitions to broken slab and then to talus for a short distance before the summit.

From the very gentle pass, the trail descends more steeply, crossing through a stream-side pocket meadow and presently reaching deep, rugged Buena Vista Lake—dramatically situated beneath its namesake peak and offering several very scenic campsites in sandy patches between stunted lodgepole pines. The temptation to cut the day short and stay here is almost irresistible.

Resisting, you skirt the lake's north shore and descend to a junction with views extending to Half Dome and Mount Hoffmann to the north and the Clark Range to the east. The right fork descends generally north into the drainage of Buena Vista Creek, on its way to Glacier Point (Trip 61), while you take the left fork westward. It drops just over 400 feet across broken slabs, dotted with clusters of lodgepole pines and solitary junipers, to reach the northernmost of the Chilnualna Lakes. Lying at the headwaters of Chilnualna Creek, each of these little lakes is forested and meadow edged, and each has a good campsite. Fishing is good for brook and rainbow except at the lowest lake. The trail skims the shores of this northernmost lake and, later on, the lowest lake. The other two Chilnualna Lakes are off-trail and, especially the southernmost one, offer better and more secluded camping if you're up to the cross-country leg to get to them.

In denser, damp forest now, trace the northernmost lake's outlet for a short distance before stepping over it and curving south, then west, and finally south again on a pleasant ramble that's mostly a gentle descent. It's not long before you step over the off-trail middle lake's outlet (following it is a possible route to that lake). Going west then south from here, you skirt a small meadow, and climb over a low bouldery morainal ridge to reach the lowest lake with good campsites on its north side (8,380'; 37.59320°N, 119.54127°W). This little lake is quite shallow and is one of this trip's warmest lakes for a dip.

DAY 4 (Lowest Chilnualna Lake to Bridalveil Creek Trailhead, 10.0 miles): From the lowest Chilnualna Lake, resume your gentle, forested descent just out of sight of its outlet creek. After 0.4 mile, where the trail curves west, you step across the outlet creek and traverse out of the lush riparian corridor onto a drier slope, a bouldery ridge that is a recessional moraine. You follow it for 1.4 miles toward the confluence of your outlet creek and Chilnualna Creek proper (the outlet creek of the northernmost lake). Cross Chilnualna Creek on rocks, another tributary on a log, and continue down the drainage, alternating between lush red fir and lodgepole forest and open stretches full of slabs. The moist areas have spectacular wildflowers in late June and early July—alpine lilies, crimson columbine, violets, shooting stars, and larkspur to name just a few. Trending more westerly, away from the creek, exactly 3 miles below lower Chilnualna Lake, you reach the junction where you began the loop part of this trip on Day 2. Turn right (northwest) toward Turner Meadow and retrace your steps of Day 1 and part of Day 2 to the trailhead.

trip 61 Glacier Point via Buena Vista Pass

see map on p. 290

Trip Data: 37.60147°N, 119.51850°W (Buena Vista Lake);
29.8 miles; 4/1 days

Topos: *Half Dome, Mariposa Grove, Merced Peak* (just barely)

HIGHLIGHTS: On this trip, early- and midseason travelers will find splendid forests, lush meadows, delightful wildflower displays, beautiful creeks, and excellent angling, all topped off with vistas of Yosemite's famous scenery. It also makes a beautiful late summer or fall trip, but water sources will be more limited, so plan to camp by a major creek or lake.

SHUTTLE DIRECTIONS: The endpoint is Glacier Point, located at the terminus of the Glacier Point Road. To reach it, from the starting trailhead, drive back out of the Bridalveil Creek Campground to the Glacier Point Road and continue an additional 7.9 miles east and north along it to a large parking area. The Panorama Trail, on which you finish, enters the maze of trails at the far southeastern corner of the Glacier Point environs, near the amphitheater.

HEADS UP! *The mileage includes the distance along short spur trails to reach Grouse, Crescent, and Johnson Lakes—a grand total of 0.9 mile extra over skipping the lakes. It is strongly recommended you visit these lakes, because you barely notice them from the trail.*

DAY 1 (Bridalveil Creek Trailhead to Chilnualna Creek, 7.0 miles): Follow Trip 60, Day 1, which leads you 5.9 miles to Turner Meadow (7,475'; 37.59605°N, 119.59705°W). Then continue an additional 1.1 miles, described here.

Just before the ford of a sizable tributary, there's a large packer campsite on your right (southwest) in the trees fringing the meadow. Farther ahead is another site in a slender, open, sandy flat. Continuing your descent down the long, gently sloping meadow, you soon meet a trail coming across from Chilnualna Falls and Wawona. At the junction, you continue left (southeast), onward through moist lodgepole forest and in 0.9 mile reach

Chilnualna Creek and a beautiful creekside campsite (7,345'; 37.58448°N, 119.58477°W) near a junction.

DAY 2 (Chilnualna Creek to Buena Vista Lake, 9.8 miles): Back at the nearby junction, left (east) leads to the Chilnualna Lakes and would be an alternative, much shorter route to Buena Vista Lake, while you turn right (southeast) and immediately ford swirling Chilnualna Creek on a cobbled base (crossing can be difficult in the early season). From the ford, climb southeast on switchbacks over an eastward-rising ridge and down to a junction; here a second lateral trail leads right (west) to Wawona, while you turn left (eastward), signposted for Buck Camp.

You are paralleling a small tributary of Chilnualna Creek east. Initially your route follows a gully north of the creek corridor, passing a flat that was scarred but not decimated by the 2017 South Fork Fire, then you are channeled up a second shaded gully before finally dropping to the unnamed creek. Quickly exiting the burn zone, you continue upstream for about a mile to a junction with a hard-to-spot spur trail leading 300 feet right (south) to little Grouse Lake and campsites; this junction is located where the main trail turns sharply left.

Back on the main trail, a slightly steeper ascent leads to drier terrain atop a small rise, from which the trail drops southward, then briefly eastward, to ford the inlet of shallow Crescent Lake, just out of sight to the south. Just past the crossing, a minor trail heads south 0.15 mile to the lakeshore and campsites. This spur, like those to the other nearby lakes, is included in the daily mileage, to ensure you've budgeted the time to visit them, for just out of sight of the trail they are easy to forgetfully bypass—and yet aren't they part of the reason for taking this walk? Grouse, Crescent, and Johnson Lakes all sit on a relatively flat bench high above the South Fork Merced River. Each is drained by a separate creek flowing into the South Fork Merced—those exiting Crescent Lake and Johnson Lake drop steeply to the west. At Crescent Lake, you might visit or camp near the lake's south end, for, from its outlet, you can peer into the 2,800-foot-deep South Fork Merced River Canyon. Indeed, if you have time to make this a 5-day trip, a night at Crescent Lake or Johnson Lake is recommended as soon as the mosquito population moderates.

Eastbound again, another 0.9 mile of level walking through often mosquito-infested forest with superb wildflower patches, brings you to a junction with a spur leading south to Johnson Lake's west shore and more campsites. For the September hiker there is an extra treat—western blueberries. Johnson Lake and its perimeter were one of the last acquisitions

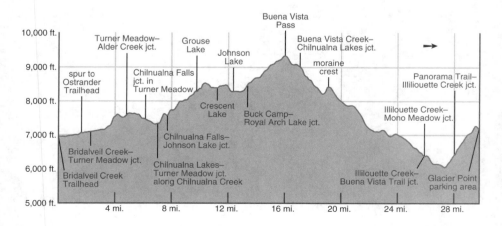

of private property within the park's boundaries, and two crumbling cabins remain to remind you of the homesteading era.

The next 0.8 mile is a 170-foot ascent up a lodgepole-covered slope alongside Johnson Lake's inlet stream, the ground sporting expanses of corn lilies and shooting stars in June and July. At a junction you turn left (north) toward Royal Arch Lake, while right (east) leads to Buck Camp, a summer ranger station.

The dense forest almost immediately gives way to more open, drier walking as the trail trends along benches on an open hillside. The landscape flattens as you approach dramatic, small, deep Royal Arch Lake. The best campsites are in the forest fringe on the lake's south shore. Fishing is good for rainbow and brook.

From Royal Arch Lake, resume your northward climb, traversing an idyllic meadow and fording its creek just below Buena Vista Pass on Buena Vista Peak's northeast ridge. Along the creek corridor are additional campsites as long as water is flowing. From the very gentle pass, the trail descends more steeply, crossing through a streamside pocket meadow and presently reaching deep, rugged Buena Vista Lake—dramatically situated beneath its namesake peak and offering several very scenic campsites in sandy patches between stunted lodgepole pines to either side of the trail (9,903'; 37.60147°N, 119.51850°W; no campfires).

DAY 3 (Buena Vista Lake to Illilouette Creek, 9.1 miles): In the morning, skirt the lake's north shore and descend to a junction where left (west) leads back to Turner Meadow via the Chilnualna Lakes (Trip 60), while the right (north) fork, your route, descends generally north into the drainage of Buena Vista Creek. From the junction the view extends to Half Dome and Mount Hoffmann to the north and the Clark Range to the east—a vista you'll be enjoying repeatedly on today's walk.

View east to Half Dome, Vernal and Nevada Falls, and up the Merced River drainage from the Panorama Trail   Photo by Elizabeth Wenk

Turn right and descend steeply down a short headwall to two ponds (possible campsites) and into the Buena Vista Creek canyon. After crossing Buena Vista Creek several times, the trail trends north away from the drainage, crosses a shallow saddle (with a possible campsite) and descends into the valley draining Hart Lake's outlet creek. Crossing this creek, the trail now climbs dry, scrubby slopes up the eastern face of a large moraine, the ascent boasting outstanding views of the Clark Range. West of the moraine crest, the trail begins a gentle descent down sandy slopes and through scattered red fir stands, until, 1.25 miles north of the moraine crest, you suddenly enter burned forest—a flat of logs and regenerating trees, the result of the 2001 Hoover Fire. A little beyond, you cross the seasonal outlet from Edson Lake between two wet meadows (there are good campsites at the lake).

Turning northeast, the grade soon steepens, and the trail descends over indistinct glacial moraines, all the while walking through a mostly burned landscape—indeed for the next 5 miles the trail passes continually through landscape burned in at least one blaze in the past four decades. The 1980 Fat Head and 1981 Buena Vista Fires were the first to burn some proportion of the trees here, while the area was, in part, retorched in 2001, 2004, and 2017. Until you are close to Illilouette Creek, stretches of intact forest are rare, with the landscape, in many places, crisscrossed by downed logs and carpeted in dense shrubs or thickets of young trees.

As the trail nears the sometimes seasonal Buena Vista Creek, stare down the remarkably steep escarpment to the creek below. Notice the giant boulders at the channel's edge and the cobble bars, all evidence of long-ago floods. The trail then turns westward and climbs gently as it passes through a lovely stand of dispersed, stately Jeffrey pines, then crosses a broad flowery meadow at the head of a seasonal tributary; there are some splendid campsites northeast of the trail near the first creek crossing where some stands of trees remain. The bald dome rising across the drainage is Mount Starr King.

FIRE AND TREES

Fire is a natural part of the ecology of the Sierra's midelevation coniferous forests, with the fires generally ignited by lightning strikes. Historically, fires were frequent and mostly burnt at low intensity, preventing a large buildup of dead wood, which in turn prevented subsequent fires from reaching severe intensity and killing the canopy trees. Unfortunately, a century of fire suppression (putting out every fire that ignited) led to dense understory growth and the accumulation of dead wood, such that when fires have ignited in the past 30–40 years, they have been increasingly catastrophic for the plant community. Along this stretch of trail there are only a few patches of intact forest that escaped the flames, and the conifer forest will take at least a century to reestablish. However, the fires have created an elegant mosaic of trees' ages, openings filled with spring wildflower displays, and have spared enough mature trees that there is still a local seed source.

Following fires, lodgepole pines are the first to appear, germinating quickly and profusely and producing cones after about 20 years. The trail passes through one dense thicket of lodgepoles that are just starting to reproduce—as long as another fire doesn't again reset the successional clock before you walk the trail. In time, this thicket will thin and later-germinating conifers, such as fir and Jeffrey pine, will begin to mature.

Climbing gently, the trail passes through a thicket of young lodgepole pines and drops into the drainage of another Illilouette Creek tributary, descending along its margins. Most of the landscape here has been well charred, and dense shrubs, especially whitethorn, encroach rapidly on the trail between trimmings. There are a few places to camp, but better sites await along Illilouette Creek. As you approach this trail junction you

Leichtlin's mariposa lily grows in dry, sandy areas. Photo by Elizabeth Wenk

walk past a beautiful forest with several giant sugar pines, survivors of many fires over the centuries. At the trail junction, turning right (east) leads to some beautiful, albeit well-used, campsites to either side of the trail just before a ford of Illilouette Creek (6,396'; 37.68641°N, 119.54685°W).

DAY 4 (Illilouette Creek to Glacier Point, 3.9 miles): Returning to the junction with the Buena Vista Trail, head right (north), signposted for Glacier Point. After just 100 feet, you reach a second junction, where left (west) leads to Mono Meadow (an alternate ending point), while you turn right (north-northwest), soon descending more steeply down a mostly open slope back toward Illilouette Creek. At 0.6 mile from the last junction, just as you approach Illilouette Creek's banks, you ford the creek descending from Mono Meadow.

For nearly a mile you now descend parallel to Illilouette Creek as it winds through a gorge, a most spectacular experience. There are cascades; big, deep pools; mill holes in rocks created by the churning water; and smooth, giant boulders. Pink and yellow azalea flowers grace the banks. Although you pass some attractive riverside benches, camping is not permitted here. Leaving the river corridor, the trail begins to ascend a steep sandy slope through firs, manzanita, and spiny chinquapin, leading to a junction with the Panorama Trail.

From here you have 1.75 miles remaining to the Glacier Point parking area and another 800 feet of ascent. If you have time and energy and water flows are still decent, a detour to the top of Illilouette Fall is highly recommended—although be forewarned the viewpoint does require an extra 400-foot descent and ascent.

ILLILOUETTE FALL VISTA
To reach the Illilouette Fall vista, from the junction where you meet the Panorama Trail, head down (right; northeast) five switchbacks (counted as the number of straights); the fifth switchback is the longest, and as you reach its northern end, follow a use trail carefully to an unfenced overlook of the fall. You are staring at Illilouette Fall head-on, and it is beautifully backdropped by Half Dome.

At the junction with the Panorama Trail, turn left (north-northwest) and begin the exposed and hot, but scenic, ascent to Glacier Point. The shade vanished and the views improved following a 1986 fire. Unfortunately, the shade is still absent, but with each passing year, the wall of scrub is higher and only occasionally are the views east still unfettered. The panorama extends northeast to Half Dome, east to Vernal and Nevada Falls, up the Merced River Canyon, and southeast across Illilouette Creek to naked Mount Starr King and sharp-tipped Mount Clark. A few switchbacks climb the final distance to Glacier Point. Once you reach the tangle of trails signaling your imminent arrival at the trailhead, continue first north to the east-facing amphitheater and then make your way west to the parking area (7,185'; 37.72757°N, 119.57439°W). If you've never visited Glacier Point, certainly do so now. The short trail to it is on your right (northeast) and the main vista point offers incredible views down into Yosemite Valley.

Glacier Point Trailheads					7,185'; 37.72757°N, 119.57439°W
Destination/ GPS Coordinates	Trip Type	Best Season	Pace & Hiking/ Layover Days	Total Mileage	Permit Required
62 Pohono Trail 37.70448°N 119.65016°W (Dewey Point)	Shuttle	Early–late	Leisurely 2/0	13.9	Pohono Trail (Glacier Point) *(or Pohono Trail [Wawona Tun- nel] in reverse)*
63 Clark Range Circuit 37.65056°N 119.40444°W (Red Peak Pass)	Loop	Mid to late	Strenuous 6/1	50.1	Glacier Point to Illilouette Creek *(or Glacier Point to Little Yosemite Valley in reverse)*
64 Merced River Drainage to Isberg Trailhead 37.64430°N 119.32642°W (Isberg Pass)	Shuttle	Mid to late	Moderate 5/1	41.0	Glacier Point to Little Yosemite Valley *(or Isberg Trail issued by Sierra National Forest in reverse)*
61 Glacier Point via Buena Vista Pass *(in reverse of descrip- tion; see page 294)*	Shuttle	Early or mid	Moderate 4/1	29.8	Glacier Point to Illilouette *(Bridalveil Creek as described)*

INFORMATION AND PERMITS: These trips begin in Yosemite National Park: wilderness permits and bear canisters are required; pets and firearms are prohibited. Quotas apply, with 60% of permits reservable online up to 24 weeks in advance and 40% available first-come, first-served starting at 11 a.m. the day before your trip's start date. Fires are prohibited above 9,600 feet. See nps.gov/yose/planyourvisit/wildpermits.htm for more details.

DRIVING DIRECTIONS: From a signed junction (Chinquapin Junction) along Wawona Road (CA 41), drive 15.7 miles on Glacier Point Road to its end; the hikes start from the road-end parking area.

see
map on
p. 300–
301

trip 62   Pohono Trail

Trip Data: 37.70448°N, 119.65016°W (Dewey Point);
13.9 miles; 2/0 days

Topos: *Half Dome, El Capitan*

HIGHLIGHTS: The Pohono Trail follows Yosemite Valley's southern rim, visiting five major viewpoints as it traverses west from Glacier Point. Along this hike you will encounter mostly day hikers, and indeed the trip can be quite easily completed in a day. However, it is well worth making it an overnight trip, for it is a route with endless opportunities for sitting and absorbing the views, especially during the evening and morning hours.

SHUTTLE DIRECTIONS: The endpoint is variously called Tunnel View Trailhead, Pohono Trailhead, and Wawona Tunnel Trailhead. It is located at Discovery View (aka Tunnel View), at the east end of the Wawona Tunnel. This is on Wawona Road (CA 41), 1.5 miles west of where CA 41 merges with Southside Drive in Yosemite Valley—or 7.75 miles north of the Chinquapin junction where the Glacier Point Road begins. The trailhead is on the south side of the road at the back of the smaller, subsidiary parking lot.

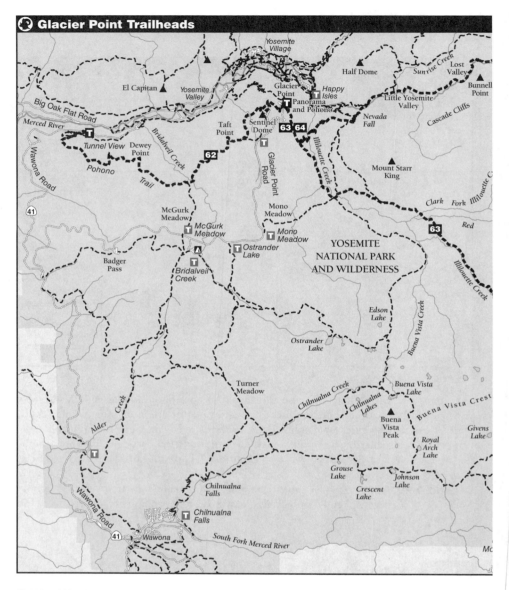

DAY 1 (Glacier Point to Bridalveil Creek, 6.5 miles): The shortest way to the correct trail is to make your way east from the parking area to the Glacier Point amphitheater, but if you have never been to Glacier Point itself, you should first detour to the main vista point overlooking Yosemite Valley.

You pick up a trail at the southern edge of the amphitheater and follow it, quickly reaching a fork where the Panorama Trail veers left (southeast), but you trend right (southwest), on the Pohono Trail. The Pohono Trail soon crosses the Glacier Point Road and completes a pair of switchbacks up through an open red fir forest, before the trail begins a long northwesterly traverse around a ridge. The trail turns south to continue circumventing the ridge, and soon you reach a junction in a cool gully where the Pohono Trail continues right (southwest), while left (northeast) is a spur leading to Sentinel Dome. Your eventual route is along the Pohono Trail, but first take the detour to Sentinel Dome, Yosemite Valley rim's second highest viewpoint—only Half Dome is taller.

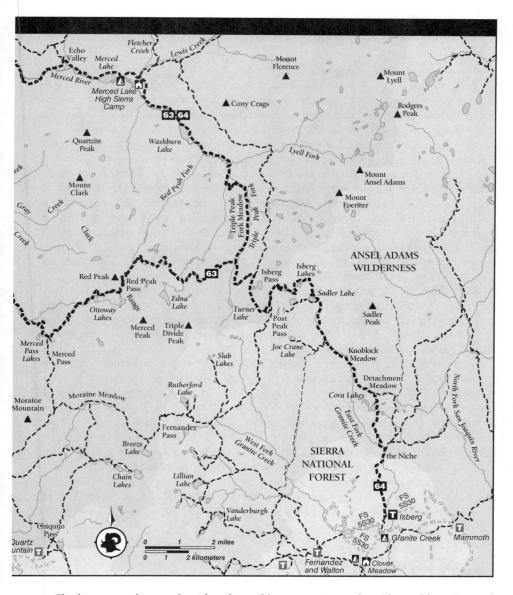

Climbing onto, then up the ridge, the trail keeps crossing paths with an old service road leading to a radio facility; stick to the steep trail. At a signed trail junction you meet the route standardly used to access Sentinel Dome and turn right (southwest) to ascend the final slope to the summit. As you ascend the bedrock slopes, watch your footing, for although there is nowhere far to fall, it is remarkably easy to slip on the gravel and sand lying atop slabs of rock.

Sentinel Dome was formed by the exfoliation of rock layers, rather than by glaciation and the rock exposed here—like everywhere on this walk—has been weathering for hundreds of thousands of years. Exfoliation is the shedding of thin layers of granite slab from the surface of the dome, and if you stare closely at the steep sides of Sentinel Dome, you can, without too much imagination, see it as a giant onion slowly being peeled apart. But the view is likely what most captures your attention, especially the panopoly of summits to the east that will be hidden for the remainder of your walk. Meanwhile, El Capitan, Yosemite Falls, and Half Dome stand out as the three most prominent valley landmarks.

Northwest of Half Dome are two bald features, North and Basket Domes. On the skyline above North Dome stands blocky Mount Hoffmann, the park's geographic center, while to the east, above Mount Starr King, an impressive unglaciated dome, stands the rugged crest of the Clark Range. A disc atop the summit identifies these landmarks and many others. Now return to the junction with the Pohono Trail, and turn left, continuing west.

Over the coming 0.8 mile, the trail descends gently but steadily, dropping 400 feet as it skirts around the steep northwestern slopes of Sentinel Dome toward seasonal Sentinel Creek. Approaching the crossing, you drop from drier, shrub-dominated slopes into a dense red fir forest, step across the creek, and soon exit the closed forest canopy again to ascend a drier ridge of broken slabs dotted with Jeffrey pines. In spring, detour along Sentinel Creek's eastern bank toward the valley rim for an exposed view of ephemeral Sentinel Falls and a little-visited view to Yosemite Falls. Onward, the grade slowly increases, leading to a junction, where left (east) leads back to a Glacier Point Road parking area, the trailhead commonly used to hike to Sentinel Dome and Taft Point, while the Pohono Trail continues right (west) toward Taft Point.

Around the first corner you enjoy a seeping creeklet that drains through a small field of corn lilies, bracken fern, and a rainbow of other tall flowers that thrive in this moist, shaded glade. Leaving this colorful distraction behind, the trail continues descending toward the Yosemite Valley rim, now across drier slopes of broken slabs, which are covered with shrubs and drought-tolerant wildflowers.

Soon you arrive at The Fissures—five vertical, parallel fractures that cut through overhanging Profile Cliff just beneath your feet. Because this area, like your entire route, is unglaciated, there is much loose rock and gravel; take care, for a misstep could be dangerous in this area. A short unsigned spur trail leads to fantastic views down the slots.

Just beyond The Fissures, where the Pohono Trail makes a near U-turn, you turn right (north) and walk briefly up a spur trail to "Taft Point," where a small railing, offering remarkably little protection, marks the viewpoint at the brink of overhanging Profile Cliff. From this viewpoint, and true Taft Point, off to your left (northwest) and completely unprotected, your sight line of the valley's monuments is unobstructed. It includes the Cathedral Spires, Cathedral Rocks, El Capitan, the Three Brothers, Yosemite Falls, and Sentinel Rock. But it is the view northwest to the prow of El Capitan that Taft Point showcases better than

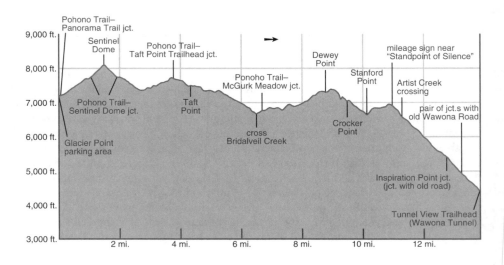

Vista of Yosemite Valley from Stanford Point   Photo by Elizabeth Wenk

any other Yosemite rim vista—how the gentle rolling upland is abruptly truncated with the 3,000-foot-tall granite wall is truly awe inspiring.

Most day hikers turn back at Taft Point and the next miles of trail are much less walked. You traverse open stretches, where slabs lie close to the surface and vegetation is sparse, step across small trickles whose banks are densely decorated with colorful wildflowers, and walk through beautiful dense fir forests, first red fir, then as you drop in elevation, white fir. The fir forest here is wonderful—this is one of the rare bits of Yosemite to not yet suffer the consequences of a catastrophic forest fire, and it is well worth enjoying the deep shade that the lichen-laden firs provide. This wonderful, relaxing, downhill walking continues until you cross Bridalveil Creek on a bridge. This is the only permanent water source along the route and is therefore the best place to spend the night; there are various small campsites just northwest of the bridge (6,680'; 37.69399°N, 119.62195°W). If you want to make a dry camp (that is, carry water from here), there are also flat sandy sites closer to Dewey Point.

DAY 2 (Bridalveil Creek to Discovery View at Wawona Tunnel, 7.4 miles): Continuing along the Pohono Trail, you soon reach a junction with the lateral to Glacier Point Road that passes through McGurk Meadow. Still continuing westward (right) along the Pohono Trail, you pass through a series of sandy flats, then cross a broad, low divide. As with yesterday's walk, you are repeatedly treated to beautiful rich fir forests, the chartreuse lichen on their trunks marking the winter snow level. Traipsing along you cross three seasonal Bridalveil Creek tributaries, the first two larger, the third smaller, then start up a fourth that drains a curving gully. To your right (north) are some small campsites, if there is still water. On the gully's upper slopes, Jeffrey pine, huckleberry oak, and greenleaf manzanita replace the fir cover.

In a few minutes you reach highly scenic 7,385-foot Dewey Point, located at the end of a short spur trail. If you have a head for heights, you can look straight down the massive face that supports Leaning Tower. Just to the right are the steep Cathedral Rocks rising on the other side of Bridalveil Creek. Looking across Yosemite Valley, the broad, smooth face of El Capitan rises high above the valley floor. Also intriguing is the back side of Middle Cathedral Rock, with an iron-rich, rust-stained surface.

Returning to the Pohono Trail again, you continue west. The remaining 5.1 miles are almost entirely downhill, and you descend 0.75 mile to Crocker Point, the vista point again located at the end of a spur trail on the brink of an overhanging cliff that provides a heart-pounding view similar to the last one. Thereafter, a 0.65-mile descent, mostly well south of the rim, takes you down to Stanford Point, also at the end of a short spur trail. Its views are similar to those from Crocker Point, although more of Yosemite Valley's walls are hidden behind nearby features.

From that point, you climb 250 feet south up the ridge rising above Stanford Point, leading away from the valley rim, passing a welcome spring, and soon dropping slightly to Meadow Brook. If any water remains along this trail through midsummer, it will be found here. Thickets of tasty thimbleberries, azaleas, and scrubby red-stemmed American dogwood lap up the moisture. Among red firs, you make an undulating traverse, shortly reaching a puzzling metal mileage sign that is neither at a junction nor an obvious vista (6,920'; 37.70284°N, 119.67270°W). Just 100 feet (in elevation) downslope of here is the location of one of many old vista points along the next section of trail, this one once dubbed the "Standpoint of Silence."

> **OLD INSPIRATION POINT**
>
> About 0.15 mile past the mileage sign, turning right (north) *off the trail* leads to the valley rim at the location still marked "Old Inspiration Point" on the topo maps; however, few people will find the brushy 200-foot off-trail descent worth the detour. Before construction of the old Wawona Road, the stock trail built by the Mann brothers in 1856 offered access to it, for it would have been the first major Yosemite Valley vista on their route from Wawona to Yosemite Valley.

Continuing, the Pohono Trail now completes a 300-foot descent into the Artist Creek drainage. Crossing Artist Creek, the trail continues down, the first 400 feet steeply as the north-trending trail traverses from the drainage onto a ridge. Where the trail bends west, there is another brushy opportunity to descend 200 feet off-trail to the northeast to another rocky vista point, this one labeled Mount Beatitude on old maps—although it is unlikely more blessed than the other vista points you've enjoyed. The trail descends slightly more gradually for the following 600 feet. The forest here is increasingly open and the temperatures warmer.

At 5,600 feet the trail turns more northeasterly again and continues down to a junction with an old road which leads left (west) to the *next* "Inspiration Point," a commanding viewpoint passed by travelers on the stage road built to replace the Mann Brothers' trail, but now somewhat overgrown. You stay right (northeast), on the trail, and descend another 500 feet via short switchbacks, now having oaks and conifers shade you, but also hiding most of the scenery. After 0.5 mile, you intersect the old Wawona Road itself and jog just 30 feet left (west) along it, then turn right (northeast) to continue your downward route. The final 0.6 mile is again steep and scrubby, with only broken views, taking you to the Pohono Trail's end at the southside parking lot of tourist populated Discovery View at the eastern entrance to the Wawona Tunnel. This is the inspiring first viewpoint to Yosemite Valley that is enjoyed by throngs of today's travelers on the modern road from Wawona (4,398'; 37.71510°N, 119.67678°W)!

trip 63   Clark Range Circuit

Trip Data: 37.65056°N, 119.40444°W (Red Peak Pass);
50.1 miles; 6/1 days

Topos: *Half Dome, Merced Peak, Mount Lyell,*

HIGHLIGHTS: The Clark Range is the rugged crest bisecting southern Yosemite; it is striking from any vista point in the southern half of the park. This remote loop encircles the range, providing endless views and leading you along two beautiful river drainages, the lesser visited corridor harboring Illilouette Creek and the deep, rugged canyons through which the mighty Merced River flows, as well as over alpine Red Peak Pass.

HEADS UP! *This hike can also be started at the Mono Meadow Trailhead, in which case you will join the trail at the Illilouette Creek–Mono Meadow junction, 3.9 miles into the hike. If you are unable to secure a permit leaving Glacier Point, this is a good alternative. It is actually 1 mile shorter but requires a (short) car shuttle.*

DAY 1 (Glacier Point parking area to Clark Fork Illilouette Creek, 6.9 miles): The shortest way to the correct trail is to make your way east from the parking area to the Glacier Point amphitheater, but if you have never been to Glacier Point itself, you should first detour to the main vista point overlooking Yosemite Valley.

You pick up a trail at the southern edge of the amphitheater and follow it south, quickly reaching a fork, where you trend left (southeast) on the Panorama Trail, while the Pohono Trail veers right (southwest; Trip 62). You climb a bit more before starting a moderate descent, initially with grand views to the east. A 1986 natural fire blackened most of the forest from near the trailhead to just beyond the upcoming Buena Vista Trail junction, with only patches of trees surviving. In the open areas, black oaks are thriving, and shrubs have regenerated with a vengeance, but in open patches there are still great views of Half Dome, Mount Broderick, Liberty Cap, Nevada Fall, and Mount Starr King between blackened trunks. Views become more restricted as you descend, and eventually you meet the Buena Vista Trail.

Lower Ottoway Lake   Photo by Elizabeth Wenk

Turning right (south) to follow the Buena Vista Trail, you now descend a steep sandy slope through firs, manzanita, and spiny chinquapin leading to the banks of Illilouette Creek. Then, for nearly a mile you climb along the creek corridor as it winds through a gorge, a most spectacular experience. There are cascades; big, deep pools; giant, smooth boulders; and mill holes in rocks created by the churning water. Pink and yellow azalea flowers grace the banks.

Fording a creek descending from Mono Meadow, you leave Illilouette Creek's banks and climb a mostly open slope to a junction where right (west) leads to Mono Meadow, while you continue left (east). Just 100 feet later you reach a second junction, where right (north) is the Buena Vista Trail (Trip 61), while you turn left (east) to continue ascending the Illilouette Creek drainage. Passing campsites to either side of the trail, you immediately drop to a ford. Notoriously dangerous at high flows and still a knee-height wade in midsummer, contemplate the large rounded cobble on the riverbed—such large rocks indicate how tumultuous the water here can be. (*Note:* If, when picking up your wilderness permit you are warned this crossing is hazardous, there is an alternative route that is 2.4 miles longer and requires more climbing, but it crosses Illilouette Creek on a footbridge. At the junction 1.7 miles from the trailhead, stay on the Panorama Trail for an additional 2.9 miles, then turn right (south), staying right (south) at a second junction and rejoining the described route at the 5.7-mile mark, at the Illilouette Creek eastern cut-off junction shown on the elevation profile.) Climbing up the far riverbank, you come to yet another junction, this one on a sandy flat. Here, you head right (east), up the Illilouette Creek drainage, while left (north) leads back toward the Panorama Trail.

Following the bare slope eastward, you gently ascend a ridge while enjoying views ahead to Mount Starr King, a striking, bald dome. Even the forest stands you pass through are sparse, for only shallow soils lay atop the bedrock here. Gradually the trail trends southeasterly and sidles up into an Illilouette Creek tributary that you follow to the next junction, where those taking the "hazardous crossing" detour rejoin the route.

Turning right (southeast), your southeasterly-trending route continues on a bench well above Illilouette Creek through a dry open forest dominated by Jeffrey pines and red fir. Some giant fractured boulders undoubtedly catch your eye; these fell from a dome north

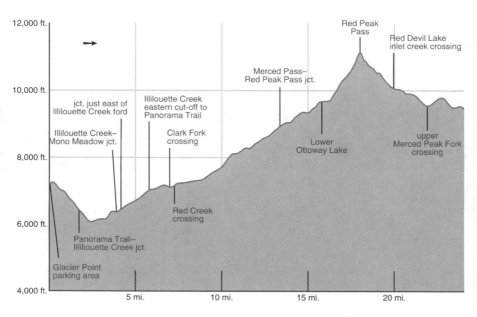

of here hundreds of years ago. Some tree bases bear fire scars from low-intensity burns in decades past. Traipsing onto a more open slope, Grey Peak and Red Peak become visible through the trees to the southeast, their bedrock hues matching their names. Ahead you come to a pair of creek crossings, the Clark Fork Illilouette Creek and Red Creek, both currently crossed via logs at high flow. Below the trail, the Clark Fork cascades impressively down slabs as it drops to unite with Illilouette Creek. There are a number of good campsites on knobs and in sandy flats near the first crossing—a good place to spend your first night (7,111'; 37.67938°N, 119.50118°W).

DAY 2 (Clark Fork Illilouette Creek to Lower Ottoway Lake, 8.9 miles): The trail continues its southerly bearing, initially still high above Illilouette Creek, crossing the crests of a series of low moraines. The ground cover here is lush, even grass covered in patches, for the soil is, in part, derived from the metamorphic rocks comprising Grey and Red Peaks. Metamorphic soils are more nutrient rich and hold water better than the surrounding granitic sands, supporting more luxuriant plant growth. It also makes for pleasant, soft walking underfoot.

Beneath a moraine, 1.4 miles from the Clark Fork, you reach the banks of Illilouette Creek and begin a delightful, albeit exposed, journey upstream along its eastern bank. The forest is mostly open and granite slabs extend right to the water's edge, allowing you to continually enjoy the beautiful bubbling, cascading creek. Near the start of this section, water seeps from the base of the moraine, irrigating small wildflower gardens, while cracks in the slabs are filled with magenta mountain pride penstemon. Aspen groves fill many of the flatter pockets, contrasting with the familiar conifer forests. The distractions are welcome, for you are walking uphill across slabs, stepping over rocks, and ascending uneven steps—this is not a fast stretch of trail. Along the way, you can find several, mostly small, places to camp along the creek's east bank.

At 3.3 miles after reaching Illilouette Creek's banks, you step across a tributary, then Illilouette Creek itself in rapid succession (campsites nearby); both crossings currently have handy logs. The trail now winds upward among outcrops and boulders, leveling out to weave through a small glade before ascending another narrow corridor between steeper

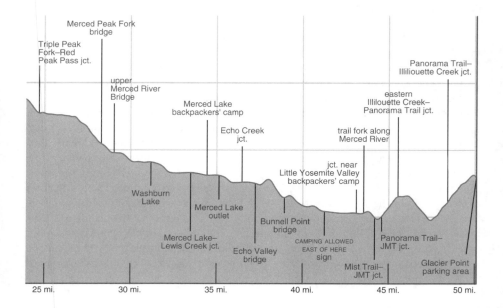

slabs. Crossing Illilouette Creek again, now often barely flowing in late summer, the trail soon passes close to Lower Merced Pass Lake, a forest-rimmed lake with bright white slabs descending to its western shore; there are ample campsites near here. Beyond, one more upward step in the landscape brings you to a junction, where you turn left (east) toward Lower Ottoway Lake and Red Peak Pass, while right (south) leads to Merced Pass. Upper Merced Pass Lake, just out of sight to the southeast, has lovely campsites along its western shore; from the main trail junction, you'll notice a blocked off but well-worn use trail heading to it. If you're short on water, take the short detour to the lake, for most of the unnamed creeklets nearby are dry by midsummer.

Striking out in a generally northeasterly direction, the trail to Lower Ottoway Lake rises and falls over a series of ridges emanating from a spur west of Merced Peak, as it slowly traverses toward Ottoway Creek. The landscape shifts in tandem, dropping into moist red fir communities in the draws, then climbing back to drier slab environments. After 1.7 miles you cross Ottoway Creek (currently on a log), near a small campsite, and begin a more diligent upward trajectory. With increasing elevation, fewer forested glades interrupt the rocky switchbacks up slabs, and after another 0.75 mile you reach the shores of Lower Ottoway Lake. There are campsites both on a flat knob northwest of the lake (9,678'; 37.64324°N, 119.42044°W; no campfires) and in forest stands to its east. Anglers can dangle lines for tasty rainbow trout.

DAY 3 (Lower Ottoway Lake to Triple Peak Fork Merced River, 8.9 miles): Red Peak Pass, your immediate goal, lies just 2.25 miles beyond Lower Ottoway Lake's outlet, but with a nearly 1,500-foot climb, it takes a little time. After a pleasant 0.4 mile dawdle to the eastern side of the lake, the steep climb begins, oscillating between metamorphic and granite rock. The upcoming mile is a delight for wildflower enthusiasts—bright bursts of color decorate the ground on both the dry, slabby stretches of trail and beside the numerous trickles of water you step across. What better distraction from the arduous climb? After just over a mile and 800 feet of ascent, there is a brief interlude in the slope. If you were to cut south from here across broken, reddish-hued slabs you would pass a small lake, then reach Upper Ottoway Lake, offering imposing views of Merced and Ottoway Peaks' headwalls and the deep cirque beneath them that once held Merced Peak's Little Ice Age glacier, but virtually no campsites.

On the trail, you now trend north, briefly along a grassy meadow, then onto the final 28 switchbacks to the pass, zigzagging up a generally dry, sandy slope to the summit of 11,143-foot Red Peak Pass. From the pass, you have views as far as Matterhorn Peak along the park's north rim. Closer, Mount Lyell crowns the upper Merced River basin and is flanked on the northwest by Mount Maclure and on the southeast by Rodgers Peak. Pyramid-shaded Mount Florence breaks the horizon west of this trio, while east of all of them, the dark, sawtooth Ritter Range pokes above the horizon. Below the peaks lies a broad upland surface that is cleft by the 2,000-foot-deep Merced River Canyon, at whose headwaters you will finish your day.

After a well-earned break, you begin the 6.6-mile descent to the Triple Peak Fork Merced River. The initial headwall is descended via tight switchbacks down a steep talus slope; fortunately the trail is in good shape, having been reworked and rerouted to minimize summer snow cover and rockfall damage. The trail next leads into a drainage where a cluster of tarns marks the headwaters of the Red Peak Fork, then cuts northeast down a rocky rib. Past the first stunted whitebark pines, the trail turns south to reach a shelf cradling a shallow tarn. On a map, this looks like tempting camping terrain, but keep your expectations in check, for you may enjoy beautiful flower displays on metamorphic substrates, but you will be less enamored by how it generally decomposes to form a pavement of sharp-tipped cobble and boulders—not ideal for a tent.

Absorbing the exquisite views of the Cathedral Range, you continue past another cluster of ponds, turn north to descend a rib, and quite suddenly find yourself back in granite. Indeed, at the next lake you pass, at 9,900 feet, there are amazing treeline campsites in sandy patches among the granite slabs northeast of the lake.

Continuing your descent, note that the cliffs overhead are all grayish metamorphic rock, while you are on the other side of the geologic contact, walking among the most beautifully polished granite slabs, with trees growing only in strips of deeper soil between the ribs of rocks. You cross the Merced Peak Fork where it meanders through a beautiful meadow ringed by hemlock trees (limited campsites) and climb north, then east across a shallow rib to a small saddle cradling two tarns.

The final 1.9 miles to the Triple Peak Fork are mostly under forest cover, a mix of hemlock, western white pine, and, of course, lodgepoles, some of them magnificently large specimens. The trail's location is well placed, winding down forested ramps. Near the bottom, broken rock and small bluffs further constrain the trail's route, restricting it to the sinuous passageways between them. Then quite suddenly you reach the bright white slabs of the river corridor and a junction (9,105'; 37.65847°N, 119.34456°W). There are good forested campsites near the junction or ones on open slab a few minutes upstream or downstream. Fishing is good for brook and rainbow trout.

DAY 4 (Triple Peak Fork Merced River to Merced Lake, 9.7 miles): Follow Trip 55, Day 4 for the 5.9 miles to Washburn Lake (7,640'; 37.71130°N, 119.36661°W). Today's description then continues another 3.8 miles downriver.

Continuing, the mostly open, sandy trail continues right along the east side of Washburn Lake. Beyond the lake, the trail continues its moderate descent along the river through open forest and across slabs, fording a small stream every quarter mile or so. Where the canyon floor begins to widen, the trail diverges east from the river, hugging the cliff walls as it skirts a big previously burned flat, now dense with scrub and downed trees (but harboring a few campsites in the direction of the river). The trail proceeds levelly to the Merced Lake Ranger Station (emergency services available in summer) and a junction where you turn left (west) toward Merced Lake, while right (north) leads up Lewis Creek (Trip 55).

Crossing multistranded Lewis Creek on a series of footbridges, the nearly flat trail soon leads past some campsites and through a peaceful Jeffrey pine forest—this is one of the few places in the park where such a forest exists, with well-spaced trees and a beautiful forest floor of large cones and long, shiny needles. If you'd like a private campsite for this night, search in the direction of the Merced River along this length. Trending north, west, and then south the trail skirts around a rocky rib and descends briefly into the Merced Lake basin. Turning north again, you pass the Merced Lake High Sierra Camp, with its meager store and drinking water faucet, and continuing along the trail, soon reach the Merced Lake backpackers' camp (7,242'; 37.74049°N, 119.40718°W) to the north of the trail (and before reaching Merced Lake itself). The only legal camping along Merced Lake, it offers a pit toilet and bear boxes. The relatively warm lake is ideal for swimming, and fishing is also fair.

DAY 5 (Merced Lake to Little Yosemite Valley, 8.7 miles): West of the backpackers' camp, the trail skirts Merced Lake's quiet northern shore. At its outlet, the steep granite slabs comprising the canyon walls pinch together and the river chutes downstream, foaming and churning as its races down slabs—you enjoy this spectacle just feet from the river's edge. Where the trail turns away from the river are some small campsites north of the trail, some on sand, others in lodgepole glades. Descending again, you reach the east end of boggy Echo Valley, a dense tangle of approximately 15-foot-tall lodgepole pines, regenerating after fires in 1988 and 1993. In the middle of the thicket you cross Echo Creek's braided river channels on three bridges and come to a junction with a trail ascending right (north) up Echo Creek (Trip 46), while you continue straight ahead (west) down the Merced River corridor. The western end of spacious Echo Valley was less impacted by fire, and a few campsites exist atop sandy knobs.

At the valley's western end, you cross the river on a sturdy bridge and skirt across a steep slab slope on a narrow trail. From the bench you can study an immense arch on the broad, hulking granitic mass opposite you and watch the water churning below. Continuing alternately across bedrock and through small glades, your climb reaches its zenith amid a spring-fed wildflower garden bordered by aspens.

The trail then descends more than a dozen switchbacks down an open, rocky slope for 400 feet back to the river's banks. You follow the south bank briefly downstream and then cross the Merced River on a pair of bridges. Just after the crossing there are small campsites atop slabs right (east) of the trail. Within minutes, the trail and creek are together forced into the center of a narrow gorge, as Bunnell Point to the south and a steep unnamed dome to the north constrict the river corridor. The river tumbles down bare granite slabs, culminating in Bunnell Cascade, while the trail switchbacks to its side. You drop into Lost Valley, badly charred in the 2014 Meadow Fire. Previously much of this section had been a dense forest with abundant dead material on the ground, providing ample fuel for the fire to spread; this is a natural process and was caused by a lightning-strike fire, but the lack of shade and loss of beautiful dense forest stands are nonetheless unwelcome to a backpacker.

At its end, the Merced's flow is again pinched, this time by unofficially named Sugarloaf Dome to the north, and again chutes down bare slabs. It lands in a beautiful pool, a superb swimming hole—and a popular campsite until the Meadow Fire blackened the environs. The next 0.3 mile is the last legal camping before Little Yosemite Valley's backpackers' campground 2.2 miles to the west. Trying to be optimistic about the fire-scorched landscape, admire the blackened tree trunks as artistic totems and note that the lack of trees improves the views of the canyon's walls. A thick accumulation of glacial sediments covers most of the valley floor, which, like beach sand, makes you work even though the trail is level. Soon after you enter standing forest, you cross Sunrise Creek and reach a junction at the southern edge of Little Yosemite Valley's backpackers' camp (6,120'; 37.73196°N, 119.51536°W), the last campsite before the trailhead. Turning right (north) you'll quickly reach the large camping area, with toilets, food-storage boxes, and (usually) a ranger stationed just to the northeast.

Day 6 (Little Yosemite Valley to Glacier Point, 7.0 miles): Returning to the junction just south of the camping area, turn right (west) and proceed just out of sight of the Merced River's edge to a junction where your trail merges with a second Little Yosemite Valley route. You continue straight ahead (left; west), first along the river's azalea-lined bank and then over a small saddle. On its far side, the trail descends a brushy, rocky slope to reach a junction (and pit toilets) where the John Muir Trail (JMT), the route you've been following since the campsite, trends left (south), while the infamously steep Mist Trail descends the steep gully to the right (west), en route to Yosemite Valley.

Staying on the JMT, you climb briefly to slabs lining a picturesque stretch of river—but do not swim here, for you are just steps from the brink of Nevada Fall. For an aerial vista, about 100 feet before the bridge, strike northwest (right) to find a short spur trail that drops to a shelf with a fenced viewpoint beside the fall's brink. Returning to the trail, cross the bridge, climb briefly through a glade of tall firs, and soon reach a junction with the Panorama Trail, where you turn southwest (left) toward Glacier Point, while the JMT stays right (west), bound for Yosemite Valley destinations.

Climbing diligently for the first time in many miles, you pass slabs with a low rock wall, once built to divert runoff away from the JMT, located at the base of the cliff face. You then disappear under forest cover and switchback up a pleasantly cool slope with soft conifer duff underfoot. A 600-foot ascent brings you to a junction, where the Panorama Trail, your route, stays right (west), while left (south) leads back up the Illilouette Creek drainage.

The trail now makes a broad, arcing contour around the top of Panorama Cliff. The name is fitting, for your senses are soon dominated by the vista to the east: Half Dome, Mount Broderick, Liberty Cap, Clouds Rest, and Nevada Fall. Stay a few steps back from the cliff edge—a former viewpoint near Panorama Point, a little farther west, was under-mined, in part, by a monstrous rockfall that occurred in spring 1977 and left the vista's railing hanging in midair. After imbibing the views, the route begins to descend, first on two long switchbacks, then on a long traverse to the southwest, and finally via a series of tighter switchbacks that drop you to the banks of Illilouette Creek. The trail briefly traces the creek upstream before crossing it on a bridge.

While the broad views and creek have been beautiful, you are still waiting for a glimpse of Illilouette Fall itself. This comes 0.3 mile past the bridge, on your first long switchback north. Just as you are about to turn south again, note an indistinct spur trail that goes a few steps below the trail to a viewpoint. Here, from atop an overhanging cliff, you have an unobstructed view of 370-foot-high Illilouette Fall, which splashes just 600 feet away over a low point on the rim of massive Panorama Cliff. Behind it Half Dome rises boldly, while above Illilouette Creek, Mount Starr King rises even higher. Returning to the trail, five more switchbacks lead up to the trail junction, where on the first day you headed south up Illilouette Creek. Now, turn right (north) and retrace your steps to Glacier Point.

trip 64 Merced River Drainage to Isberg Trailhead

see map on p. 300–301

Trip Data: 37.64430°N, 119.32642°W (Isberg Pass); 41.0 miles; 5/1 days

Topos: *Half Dome, Merced Peak, Mount Lyell, Timber Knob*

HIGHLIGHTS: This route traverses the very heart of southeastern Yosemite, following the Merced River to its headwaters. You then climb to Isberg Pass, boasting one of Yosemite's premier views, before descending into the San Joaquin River watershed and passing a sequence of beautiful lakes. Remoteness and panoramic vistas invite you to take this trip. Only the notably long car shuttle might dissuade you—if you are able to take additional days, you could loop back to Glacier Point via Fernandez Pass, Merced Pass, and the trail down Illilouette Creek.

SHUTTLE DIRECTIONS: The Isberg Trailhead near Clover Meadow is the most remote trailhead in this book—and a long car shuttle from Glacier Point. From Yosemite Forks on CA 41 (3.4 miles north of Oakhurst and about 12 miles south of Yosemite National Park's Wawona entrance station) follow Road 222, signposted for Bass Lake, 3.5 miles east. Here the road becomes Malum Ridge Road (Road 274). Continue straight ahead (east) 2.4 more miles to a junction with FS 7 (5S07), where you turn left (north) onto Beasore Road.

Now reset your odometer to zero. Paved but windy Beasore Road climbs north, passing Chilkoot Campground at 4 miles, followed by a series of dirt roads departing westward. At 11.6 miles, you reach a four-way intersection at Cold Spring Summit, with Sky Ranch Road (FS 6S10X) to the left and a parking area with toilets is on the right. Continuing straight ahead on Beasore Road (FS 5S07), you wind past Beasore Meadows, Jones Store, Mugler Meadow, and Long Meadow. At 20.2 miles, you reach Globe Rock (on your right; toilets) and FS 5S04 (on your left).

Beyond Globe Rock the road surface can be speckled with potholes, although it is being resurfaced during the summer of 2020. Ahead you pass a spur to Upper Chiquito Campground (21.3 miles), the impressive granite domes named the Balls (24.2 miles), the Jackass Lakes Trailhead (26.8 miles), and the Bowler Campground (27.1 miles). Soon thereafter two prominent spur roads bear left, first one to the Norris Trailhead (FS 5S86; 27.5 miles) and just beyond one to the Fernandez and Walton Trailheads (FS 5S05; 27.6 miles).

Continuing on Beasore Road, you pass FS 5S88 (branches south 0.4 mile to Minarets Pack Station; 29.6 miles) and quickly meet the end of paved Minarets Road (FS 4S81; 29.8 miles), which has ascended 52 paved miles north from the community of North Fork. At this junction, stay left (northeast), turning onto FS 5S30, and drive 1.8 miles to a junction at Clover Meadow Ranger Station. The entrance to Clover Meadow Campground is just beyond it, a pleasant campground with piped water, vault toilets, and—amazingly—cell reception!

You still have a short distance to reach your trailhead. Remaining on FS 5S30, you bear left at a junction with FS 4S60 (bound for primitive Granite Creek Campground), descend to cross the West Fork of Granite Creek, then immediately turn right and parallel the creek east, now on a truly unpaved road. At a Y-junction, bear left (right descends back to Granite Creek Campground), briefly climb a steep hill (yes, it is two-wheel drive), level out, and almost immediately turn right into the quite large Isberg Trailhead parking area, 3.1 miles past the Clover Meadow Ranger Station.

DAY 1 (Glacier Point parking area to Little Yosemite Valley, 7.0 miles): The shortest way to the correct trail is to make your way east from the parking area to the Glacier Point amphitheater, but if you have never been to Glacier Point itself, you should first detour to the main vista point overlooking Yosemite Valley.

You pick up a trail at the southern edge of the amphitheater and follow it south, quickly reaching a fork, where you trend left (southeast) on the Panorama Trail, while the Pohono Trail veers right (southwest). You climb a bit more before starting a moderate descent, initially with grand views to the east. A 1986 natural fire blackened most of the forest from near the trailhead to just beyond the upcoming Buena Vista Trail junction, with only patches of trees surviving. In the open areas, black oaks are thriving, and shrubs have regenerated with a vengeance, but in open patches there are still great views of Half Dome, Mount Broderick, Liberty Cap, Nevada Fall, and Mount Starr King between blackened

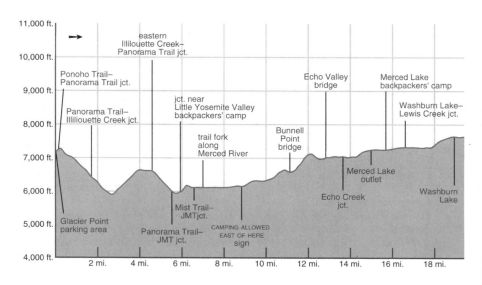

trunks. Views become more restricted as you descend, and eventually you meet the Buena Vista Trail (Trips 61 and 63).

You turn left (north) here and switchback down toward seasonally raging Illilouette Creek. At the northern end of the fifth (one-way) switchback, an indistinct spur trail goes a few steps below the trail to a viewpoint. Here, from atop an overhanging cliff, you have an unobstructed view of 370-foot-high Illilouette Fall, Half Dome rising boldly behind it. This is not a vista point to be missed, for Illilouette Fall, nestled in a narrow alcove, mostly hides itself from view. The trail makes one final switchback and then crosses the creek on a wide bridge.

Now begins an 800-foot ascent to the top of Panorama Cliff. The trail first climbs briefly along the rim, then switchbacks away from the cliff edge, before once again returning to the rim as you round Panorama Point. After another moderate climb of 200 feet, you descend gently to the rim for more views, now dominated by the monuments to the east: Half Dome, Mount Broderick, Liberty Cap, Clouds Rest, and Nevada Fall. Your contour ends at a junction with a trail up Illilouette Creek.

Here, you go left (east) to stay on the Panorama Trail, which now descends 800 feet toward Nevada Fall via a long series of switchbacks, mostly through a dense forest of tall, water-loving Douglas-firs and incense cedars. When you reach a junction with the John Muir Trail (JMT), turn right (east) onto the JMT and descend to the bridge over the Merced River at Nevada Fall. About 100 feet due north of the bridge, strike northwest (left) to find a short spur trail that drops to a shelf that leads south to a fenced viewpoint beside the fall's brink. Back on the main trail, you descend briefly and reach the top of the Mist Trail, which has ascended steeply beside the Merced River from Yosemite Valley.

From the junction and its adjacent outhouses, you begin the final climb to Little Yosemite Valley, first by ascending a brushy, rocky slope and then quickly descending and reaching both forest shade and the Merced River. Beneath pine, white fir, and incense cedar, you continue northeast along the river's azalea-lined bank, soon reaching a trail fork. You keep right (east) on the main, riverside trail and continue just out of sight of the river's edge, to reach a junction at the southern edge of the Little Yosemite Valley backpackers' camp (6,120'; 37.73196°N, 119.51536°W). Turn left (north) and within steps you'll see the tent city to the right where you will spend your first night. There are toilets and food-storage boxes; a usually staffed ranger station is hidden to the northeast of the camping area.

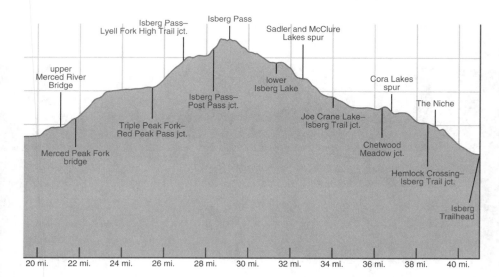

DAY 2 (Little Yosemite Valley to Merced Lake, 8.7 miles): Follow Trip 59, Day 2 from Little Yosemite Valley to the backpackers' campground at Merced Lake (7,242'; 37.74049°N, 119.40718°W).

DAY 3 (Merced Lake to Triple Peak Fork Meadow, 9.7 miles): Beyond the High Sierra Camp, the trail loops south around a shallow ridge and proceeds a mile east on an almost level, wide, sandy path under forest canopy, noteworthy for the beautiful grove of Jeffrey pines; there are possible campsites here. You cross roaring Lewis Creek on a pair of bridges and arrive at a junction with the trail up Lewis Creek (Trip 46). The Merced Lake Ranger Station, with emergency services in summer, is just south of the junction.

You turn right (south), toward Washburn Lake. For the next 0.6 mile you continue through a broad, flat valley. The trail stays well northeast of the river as it hugs the cliff walls, skirting a previously burned flat dense with scrub and downed trees. Beyond, the valley narrows, but the route is nearly flat for another 0.7 mile, before beginning a moderate ascent alongside the river through open forest and across slabs, fording a small stream about every quarter mile.

The gradient flattens after about a mile and you soon reach Washburn Lake's outlet, a nice spot for your first break of the day, with the still water mirroring the soaring granite cliffs across the lake on a typically calm morning. Skirting the northeast shore of the lake on a mostly open, sandy trail, you reach an expansive flat near the inlet, with a few campsites interspersed with some downed trees. Continuing to traverse dry slopes above the forested flats, you pass a lovely waterfall and climb to the next broad, flat, valley, where the trail arcs southeast and then south, ascending gradually through an idyllic setting.

You bridge the Merced River just near the confluence of its Lyell and Triple Peak forks. Tangles of downed trees here, the aftermath of a windstorm, limit camping options, but are an impressive sight. After meandering for a third of a mile through valley-bottom forest, the river splits again, with the Triple Peak Fork trending east, while you climb along the Merced Peak Fork; the mighty river has quickly divided into a collection of tributaries emanating from individual cirque basins at the cachement headwaters. For the next 0.7 mile, you continue southward up the river's west bank through red fir and juniper, the gradient now sufficiently steep to necessitate an occasional switchback. You'll undoubtedly sense

Looking down on the upper Isberg Lake basin   Photo by Elizabeth Wenk

that steep walls are suddenly encroaching upon you, and indeed after crossing the Merced Peak Fork on a bridge, the trail begins switchbacking up the exfoliating slab wall east of the river. In places, beautiful rock walls support the trail and elsewhere it follows natural passageways. At the end of a long switchback to the northeast you are treated to views of Triple Peak Falls along the Triple Peak Fork and then turn to the southeast to follow the drainage upward.

About a mile above the bridge the gradient starts to ease and forest cover returns, becoming denser as you pass a stock drift fence and turn due south. You are now in a lovely, long-hanging valley that the trail follows creekside for more than 2 miles. In places there are slabs right up to the banks, but mostly the Triple Peak Fork fills a deep, lazy channel that meanders down the middle of the verdant Triple Peak Fork Meadow. At the southwestern tip of the meadow are a number of good campsites, some among slabs west of the meadow and others in lodgepole forest near a junction with the westbound trail to Red Peak Pass (9,105'; 37.65847°N, 119.34456°W). Fishing is good for brook and rainbow trout.

DAY 4 (Triple Peak Fork Meadow to Sadler Lake, 7.2 miles): At the aforementioned junction, right (west) leads up to Red Peak Pass (Trip 63), while you turn left (east) and cross the creek on a convenient log—hopefully still present. Leaving behind the wonderful landscape of polished slabs, you ascend southward through dry lodgepole forest. The trail turns north after 0.7 mile and soon big hemlock trees garner your attention. The forested climb continues to a junction, where you are greeted by all-consuming views of the Clark Range and beyond. At this junction, you turn right (south) toward Isberg Pass, while left (north) leads to the headwaters of the Lyell Fork Merced along a route often referred to as the High Trail (Trip 55).

Your route skirts the side of steep granite bluffs and within steps a magical landscape emerges ahead—a strikingly flat, long shelf perched high on the mountain side. At the north end of this basin lies long, oval-shaped Lake 10,005 and a smaller companion. There is camping at the north end of the larger lake, set back from its sandy northern beach in the lodgepole forest. The trail itself skirts well west of the lakes, traversing straight across the expansive flower-dotted meadow—staring down you'll see endless colorful dots, including diminutive lupines, cinquefoil, and daisies. This delightful stroll leads you back to steeper terrain, as you cross two small creeks, the first seasonal, the second spring fed and permanent, and begin climbing coarse decomposing granite.

A beautiful, lush slope of fell-field species leads to a junction, where you turn left (northeast) toward Isberg Pass, while right (southeast) leads to Post Peak Pass (Trip 68). It is only 0.6 mile from here to Isberg Pass and with only 250 feet of elevation gain, but it is the slowest stretch of trail on your route: at first you ascend a steep, loose trail across a steeper, looser slope and then begin winding between slabs and broken blocks. It is cumbersome walking, as on many occasions you climb a few steps downward to bypass a small obstacle. Finally you reach Isberg Pass (10,510'), dropping your pack atop beautiful polished slabs while gawking at the view—most immediately striking is the sawtoothed Ritter Range to the east, but much of southern Yosemite is laid out to the north and west, while to the southeast you are staring across the expansive San Joaquin River drainage.

The pass marks the boundary between Yosemite National Park and the Ansel Adams Wilderness. Leaving the park, you descend easier terrain to the northeast. The rock here is colorful—admire the red-and-gray-striped summit of Isberg Peak—because you are near the contact between granitic and metamorphic rock, and many of the granitic rocks on this slope were partially altered during long-ago geologic skirmishes. A long traverse leads to 26 tight but relatively gentle switchbacks down a south-facing rib. Soon the narrow, winding, often incised trail skirts upper Isberg Lake and passes two small tarns. The views are tremendous and the rocks engaging, dotted with inclusions, blobs of older, darker rocks engulfed in the lighter-colored granite. Verdant slopes are irrigated by endless trickles and wildflowers abound as you loop down a 300-foot slope to lower Isberg Lake. Fishing in these lakes is fair to good for brook and rainbow trout. The campsites around lower Isberg Lake are mostly tiny, with space for only a single tent in each sandy patch, for most of the ground is covered by sedge meadows and expanses of dwarf bilberry and red mountain heather.

The trail crosses a shallow rib and descends 500 feet down a steep slope sparsely covered with lodgepole pines. The landscape flattens abruptly where you reach the marshy north shore of Sadler Lake and the trail skirts east around the lake. Camping is only legal along the south and west sides of the lake; to reach them continue south until you come to a junction, located just where you feel you're leaving the lake behind. Here a spur trail strikes west (right; 9,377'; 37.64194°N, 119.30058°W; no campfires), signposted for McClure Lake, after passing ample camping around Sadler Lake's shores.

DAY 5 (Sadler Lake to Isberg Trailhead, 8.4 miles): Returning to the main Isberg Trail, turn right (south) and continue down. Leaving Sadler Lake's shelf behind, the trail descends again, the lodgepole pine cover now denser, to a ford of East Fork Granite Creek. Its gradient easing, the trail follows the orange bedrock channel for a half mile before veering away from the creek and passing a junction where you continue left (southeast) down the main trail, while right (northwest) is a spur to Joe Crane Lake (Trip 67). The trail continues to descend, crossing several small creeks before it levels off in Knoblock Meadow.

Cross East Fork Granite Creek again, a ford at high flows, and skirt the meadow's eastern edge, where you pass a few small campsites. Abundant tarns and marshy meadows make the ensuing miles a mosquito factory in June and July, but this stretch is correspondingly resplendent with water-loving wildflowers. The trail then swings south-southeast away from the creek to cross a low bedrock ridge and 1.2 miles past the ford reaches a junction with a little-used lateral left (east) toward Chetwood Creek. Staying right (southeast), it is an easy half mile over a low moraine down to an unmarked spur junction at the northeast corner of Middle Cora Lake, leading to campsites along the southwest shore (8,386'; 37.59755°N, 119.26961°W; Trip 67). Camping is prohibited, however, within 400 feet of the lake's eastern shore, the corridor through which the trail passes. *Note:* from here to the trailhead, much of the landscape was burned in the 2020 Creek Fire, the flames still active as this book goes to press.

Onward, ford Middle Cora Lake's outlet, and sidle around the east side of a small dome on slabs. Beyond, you drop more steeply into a lush tributary that you descend to its confluence with East Fork Granite Creek. Here you ford East Fork Granite Creek for the last time (wet feet in early season) and follow its bank downstream. Ignore a succession of old, unmarked trail treads that depart to the right, staying along the creek's western bank. You reach a junction with the Stevenson Trail that leads east (left), back across the creek, bound for the Hemlock Crossing along the North Fork San Joaquin River (Trip 69).

Continuing downstream, sometimes through moist forest, other times along the creek's riparian corridor, you reach a wonderful passageway, the Niche. Here the ridges to the east and west converge on the creek, whose channel narrows as it passes through this slot and then drops steeply on its journey south. With just over 2 miles remaining, the trail swings west to leave Ansel Adams Wilderness and descends a brushy slope before again turning south. Continue onward, following a seasonal tributary as you head down the increasingly dusty trail, which ends at a dirt road. Here you turn left (east) and walk just a few steps to a parking area on the south side of the road. Note this road, Forest Service Road 5S30, is not shown on USGS topo maps, making it difficult to visualize where you've just landed. The Isberg Trailhead is, however, correctly plotted on U.S. Forest Service maps (7,100'; 37.54710°N; 119.26610°W).

CA 41 TO SOUTH OF YOSEMITE TRIPS

This region includes trips departing from a trio of trailheads just south of Yosemite's border. From west to east, they are the Quartz Mountain Trailhead, Fernandez and Walton Trailheads, and Isberg Trailhead. These trailheads all sit within the mighty San Joaquin River drainage, a region mostly included in the companion guide *Sierra South*. However, the trails departing from these trailheads either mostly lead quickly into Yosemite or visit the peak-ringed cirque basins just south of the park boundary and are better paired with Yosemite's hikes. Only Trip 69, leading from the Isberg Trailhead to Hemlock Crossing on the North Fork San Joaquin River visits the river.

From Quartz Mountain Trailhead you quickly cross into Yosemite at Chiquito Pass and then journey to the Chain Lakes, the justifiably popular lake basin in southeastern Yosemite.

The Fernandez Trailhead leads into the far northwestern corner of Ansel Adams Wilderness, where a plethora of lake basins await. Far less crowded than similarly accessible areas off Tioga Road (CA 120; Tuolumne Meadows area), the scenery is every bit as enticing. The Lillian Lakes Loop is written up here, but it's only the first of several spurs you could take. *Note:* the Walton Trail departs along a second trail from the same parking lot.

Third is the popular Isberg Trailhead, offering access to a succession of lakes within Ansel Adams Wilderness and onward into Yosemite via Isberg Pass. It is also the starting point to travel to the North Fork San Joaquin River, one of the Sierra's hidden gems; you get to experience it for a length downstream from Hemlock Crossing to Sheep Crossing.

Trailheads: Quartz Mountain

Fernandez and Walton

Isberg

Quartz Mountain Trailhead				8,251'; 37.53076°N, 119.44716°W	
Destination/ GPS Coordinates	Trip Type	Best Season	Pace & Hiking/ Layover Days	Total Mileage	Permit Required
65 Chain Lakes 37.56822°N 119.39838°W (Upper Chain Lake)	Out-and-back	Mid to late	Leisurely 2/0	11.2	Quartz Mountain

INFORMATION AND PERMITS: This trip begins in Sierra National Forest and wilderness permits are required. Once you enter Yosemite National Park, its regulations apply: bear canisters are required, pets and firearms are prohibited, and no fires are allowed above 9,600 feet. Quotas apply from May to October, with 60% of permits reservable online starting in January each year and 40% available first-come, first-served starting the day before your

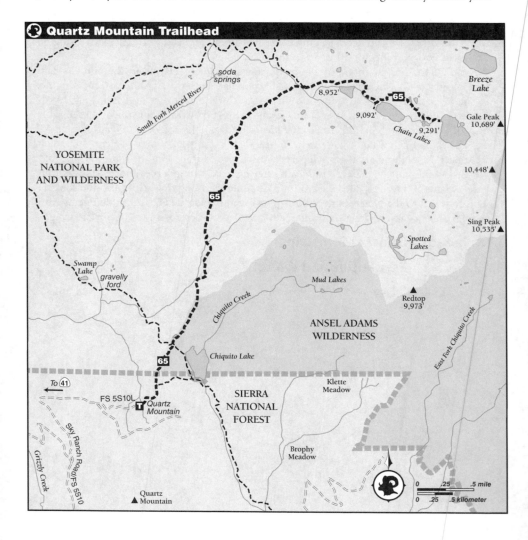

trip's start date. See tinyurl.com/sierranfwildernesspermits for more details. Monday–Friday, permits can be picked up at the Bass Lake Ranger District at 57003 Forest Service Road 225, North Fork (559-877-2218), and seven days a week in summer at the Yosemite Sierra Visitors Bureau, located in downtown Oakhurst at 40343 CA 41 (559-658-7588). If you plan to use a stove or have a campfire, you also require a California Campfire Permit, available from a U.S. Forest Service office or online at readyforwildfire.org/permits/campfire-permit.

DRIVING DIRECTIONS: This is a quite remote trailhead just south of the Yosemite boundary. First, drive to the start of Sky Ranch Road, located on CA 41 a little north of Yosemite Forks (11.7 miles south of Yosemite National Park's Wawona entrance station and 4.1 miles north of Oakhurst).

Turn onto Sky Ranch Road (Forest Service Road 5S10) and follow it east for 26.25 miles. Some waypoints are the junction to Soquel Campground (8.25 miles from CA 41), junction with FS 5S06 (14.5 miles from CA 41), Fresno Dome Trailhead (15.75 miles from CA 41), and Grizzly Lakes Trailhead (18.0 miles from CA 41). At the 26.25-mile mark, turn left onto FS 5S10L and follow it 0.4 mile to the Quartz Mountain Trailhead.

trip 65   Chain Lakes

> **Trip Data:**   37.56822°N, 119.39838°W (Upper Chain Lake); 11.2 miles; 2/0 days
> **Topos:**   *Sing Peak*

HIGHLIGHTS: Chain Lakes is the most popular destination in southeastern Yosemite, a string of three subalpine lakes in a narrow, steep-walled granite valley. The greatest challenge getting there is driving to the trailhead, more than an hour up dirt roads from the Oakhurst environs. The walking is pleasant and the destination is stunning lakes.

DAY 1 (Quartz Mountain Trailhead to Upper Chain Lake, 5.6 miles): The trail departs east from the Quartz Mountain Trailhead parking area, dropping steeply down a shaded slope to a lush flat where you step across consecutive trickles. Turning north, you pass a little-used spur trail descending right (east) to Chiquito Lake and continue straight (left; north) through gorgeous red fir stands before emerging on a dry, rubbly slope you follow to the Yosemite National Park boundary fence, and just beyond, Chiquito Pass.

Here you find a diffuse four-way junction, a little difficult to interpret due to a maze of tracks in the sand. Continue straight (northeast), following the route signposted to Chain

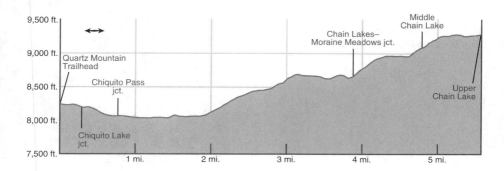

Lakes and Moraine Meadow; left (northwest) leads to Gravelly Ford and a hard right (south-southeast) to Chiquito Lake. You soon pass by a stagnant pond trapped between the crests of two bouldery, brushy moraines. The moraine to the left remains to your side for a full half mile before you cross it and make a slight descent to a flat-floored forest. In early summer, several creeks and creeklets are flowing, and, during those times, the traverse can be a muddy one that hikers hurry through to evade a marauding horde of mosquitoes.

The creek descending from the Spotted Lakes is the widest, and the only one plotted on maps. Beyond it, you have a 1.3-mile-long ascent, broken at about 8,400 feet elevation by a small, moraine-dammed meadow. As you climb, the trail alternates between drier slabs and lush flower-filled forest pockets. Here there are predominately red firs, with some lodgepole and western white pines in the mix. The climb leads to a low point on a glacier-polished ridge, which you cross and then make a rolling 0.75-mile traverse northeast to a junction on the north bank of the boulder-choked Chain Lakes outlet creek.

Turn right (east), upstream, and hike along a moderate-to-steep trail up to shallow, moraine-rimmed Lower Chain Lake (8,950'). Camps here are inferior to those by the deeper middle lake. From the lower lake's outlet, your trail skirts the northern shore of the lake and then passes a boggy meadow, from where you could head south to some possible campsites. Next, you make a short, fairly steep ascent up along the creek to picturesque, island-dotted Middle Chain Lake. The warm bedrock islands are easily reached, particularly from the excellent large camp along the lake's southwest shore (9,085';37.57038°N, 119.40884°W). To reach that camp, cross the lake's two outlet creeks, and then follow a primitive path along the west shore. Twenty feet deep, this is a classic subalpine lake, rimmed with lodgepole pines, western white pines, and mountain hemlocks and understoried with Labrador tea, red heather, western blueberry, and dwarf bilberry. The backdrop to the east, Gale Peak, is perfectly centered over the water. Sitting on slabs on the lake's western shore, just 4.8 miles from the trailhead, you can understand why this location is so popular.

Beyond the middle lake, the trail is less traveled. It climbs steeply to the bouldery crest of a moraine, winds over to a stagnant pond, and drops south to a photogenic lakelet. Near this lakelet, the trail may divide and reunite, and then it briefly climbs to deep Upper Chain Lake (9,291'; 37.56822°N, 119.39838°W). Cold, windswept, and rock rimmed, it offers only tiny single-tent exposed campsites, but it is a good staging area for adventurers planning to climb Gale Peak, along the park's southeast boundary crest. Anglers may have a better chance up here than down at heavily fished Middle Chain Lake.

DAY 2 (Upper Chain Lake to Quartz Mountain Trailhead, 5.6 miles): Retrace your steps.

Alpine lilies   Photo by Elizabeth Wenk

Fernandez and Walton Trailheads				7,538'; 37.53140°N, 119.30070°W	
Destination/ GPS Coordinates	Trip Type	Best Season	Pace & Hiking/ Layover Days	Total Mileage	Permit Required
66 Lillian Lake Loop 37.56303°N 119.36065°W (Lillian Lake outlet)	Loop	Mid to late	Moderate 3/0	12.2	Fernandez Trailhead (*Walton Trailhead in reverse*)

INFORMATION AND PERMITS: This trip begins in Sierra National Forest and wilderness permits are required. Quotas apply from May to October, with 60% of permits reservable online starting in January each year and 40% available first-come, first-served starting the day before your trip's start date. See tinyurl.com/sierranfwildernesspermits for more details. Monday–Friday, permits can be picked up at the Bass Lake Ranger District at 57003 Forest Service Road 225, North Fork (559-877-2218), and seven days a week in summer at the Yosemite Sierra Visitors Bureau, located in downtown Oakhurst at 40343 CA 41 (559-658-7588), *or* the Clover Meadow Ranger Station (559-877-2218, ext. 3136). If you plan to use a stove or have a campfire, you also need a California Campfire Permit, available from a U.S. Forest Service office or online at readyforwildfire.org/permits/campfire-permit.

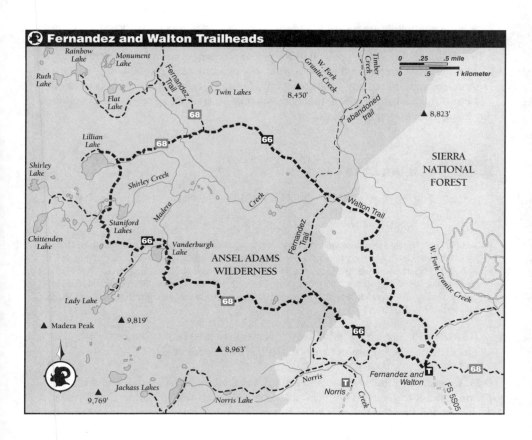

DRIVING DIRECTIONS: From the CA 49 junction in Oakhurst, drive north on CA 41 for 3.4 miles to a junction with Forest Service Road 222, signposted for Bass Lake. Follow FS 222 east 3.5 miles. Beyond, continue straight for an additional 2.4 miles, but your road is now called Malum Ridge Road (FS 274). Then turn left (north) onto Beasore Road (FS 5S07) and reset your trip odometer to zero. Paved but windy Beasore Road climbs north, passing Chilkoot Campground at 4 miles, followed by a series of dirt roads departing westward. At an odometer reading of 11.6 miles, you reach a four-way intersection at Cold Spring Summit, where Sky Ranch Road (FS 6S10X) departs to the left and a parking area with toilets is on the right. Continuing straight ahead on Beasore Road (FS 5S07), you wind past Beasore Meadows, Jones Store, Mugler Meadow, and Long Meadow. At 20.2 miles, you reach Globe Rock (on your right; toilets) and FS 5S04 which leads left (north) to the Upper Chiquito Lake Trailhead.

Beyond Globe Rock the road surface can be speckled with potholes, although parts are being resurfaced during the summer of 2020. You pass a spur to Upper Chiquito Campground (21.3 miles), the impressive granite domes named the Balls (24.2 miles), the Jackass Lakes Trailhead (26.8 miles), and the Bowler Campground (27.1 miles). Soon thereafter two prominent spur roads bear left, first one to the Norris Trailhead (FS 5S86; 27.5 miles) and just beyond one to the Fernandez and Walton Trailheads (FS 5S05; 27.6 miles). You follow FS 5S05 2.3 miles to its terminus in a large parking area.

If you do not yet have your wilderness permit or need to camp for a night before starting, instead of turning onto FS 5S05, continue along Beasore Road. You pass FS 5S88 (branches south 0.4 mile to Minarets Pack Station; 29.6 miles) and quickly meet the end of paved Minarets Road (FS 4S81; 29.8 miles), which has ascended 52 paved miles north from the community of North Fork. At this junction, you stay left (northeast), turning onto FS 5S30, and drive 1.8 miles to a junction at the Clover Meadow Ranger Station. Here is the small building where you will pick up your wilderness permit. The entrance to the Clover Meadow Campground is just beyond it, a pleasant campground with piped water, vault toilets, and—amazingly—cell reception! There are also vault toilets at the trailhead.

Note: If you are traveling from the south, you may wish to access the trailhead via Minarets Road; use a map app for directions.

trip 66   Lillian Lake Loop

see map on p. 321

Trip Data: 37.56303°N, 119.36065°W (Lillian Lake outlet);
12.2 miles; 3 days

Topos: *Timber Knob*

HIGHLIGHTS: Nestled beneath Madera, Gale, and Sing Peaks, just southwest of Yosemite National Park, the many lakes and easy mileage on this trip provide ample opportunity for exploring, fishing, and dayhiking in Ansel Adams Wilderness. The lakes along this loop rival the diversity offered in any Sierran lake basin around the 9,000-foot mark. The 12.2-mile distance includes only the main loop, but budget in hiking an additional 2–5 miles for detours to Lady Lake or Chittenden Lake or to more fully explore Lillian Lake.

HEADS UP! *The first and last miles of this hike have been partially burned by the 2020 Creek Fire, but the lake basins remain untouched as this book goes to press.*

DAY 1 (Fernandez Trailhead to Vanderburgh Lake, 4.3 miles): Two trails depart from the parking area at the end of Forest Service Road 5S05, the Walton Trail and the Fernandez Trail. You will be departing along the Fernandez Trail, located along the western side of the parking area, and returning along the Walton Trail, located at the northern tip of the parking area. Both are signposted with their respective names.

Departing west along the Fernandez Trail, you pass through a typical midelevation Sierran forest: white fir, Jeffrey pine, and lodgepole pine in the flats and draws and scrubby huckleberry oak on open sandy slopes where slabs lie near the surface. A gentle ascent across morainal slopes leads to the lower end of a small meadow, where you reach a junction with an easily missed and little-used trail that branches left (southwest) and meanders 1.2 miles to the Norris Trailhead; here your route bends to the right (northwest). Beyond the junction your trail's gradient becomes a moderate one and red fir quickly begin to replace white fir. The forest then temporarily yields to brush as you struggle up short, steep gravelly switchbacks below a small, exfoliating dome. The slope becomes steeper yet near where you enter Ansel Adams Wilderness. Merging from the left is a steep trail that also leads to the Norris Trailhead. Again staying right (west), you continue your steady pull up the Fernandez Trail for a few more minutes to a near-crest junction.

Here, find a signed junction with the Lillian Lake Loop: The right (east) fork, the continuing Fernandez Trail, would be the most direct route to Lillian Lake itself, while left (west) leads there via Vanderburgh Lake, the Staniford Lakes, and the many other lakes in the Madera Creek drainage. Your turn left onto the Lillian Lake Loop and enjoy a generally easy 2-mile tread. Conifers shade your way first past a waist-deep pond, on your right, then later past two often-wet, moraine-dammed, flower-filled meadows. Beyond, the trail climbs to a bedrock notch in a granitic crest. Turning around, you enjoy your first views of the San Joaquin drainage, including dark-colored, pyramidal-shaped Mount Goddard, nearly 50 miles southeast in Kings Canyon National Park. On the crest you arc around a stagnant pond and then make a short descent to Madera Creek.

Note that there is much confusion—and probably sloppiness—in the spelling of Vanderburgh Lake in both official and unofficial sources. For years the name was spelled *Vandeberg* on maps, but the most recent (online) USGS topo maps are using *Vanderburgh,* matching the spelling of its namesake, Chester M. Vanderburgh, a Fresno-area physician who enjoyed stock trips to the area. From Madera Creek, the trail curves west past good-to-excellent campsites along the lake's north shore (8,656'; 37.55039°N, 119.35162°W; no campfires), where steep, granitic Peak 9,852, on Madera Peak's northeast ridge, is reflected in the lake's placid early-morning waters as you cast for brook or rainbow trout. If you are trying to decide which of the many nearby lakes to camp near, this is the lowest elevation and most forested of the choices, making it more or less appealing based on your predilection.

DAY 2 (Vanderburgh Lake to Lillian Lake, 1.9 miles): This short-but-sweet hiking day gives you a chance to admire the views, discover the lakes, fish, and maybe even bag a peak.

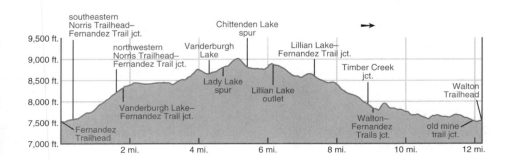

Gale Peak reflected in Lillian Lake's waters   Photo by Elizabeth Wenk

At the west end of Vanderburgh Lake, climb bedrock to the edge of a lodgepole flat that has a junction with a trail to Lady Lake, well worth the easy detour (see sidebar on the facing page). Beyond, the trail crosses a lodgepole flat and then climbs a few hundred feet on fairly open granitic slabs to a ridge. Here you can stop and appreciate the skyline panorama from the Minarets south to the Mount Goddard area. Descending northwest on a moderate-to-steep gradient, you reach an easily missed junction, where a small sign indicates that a left (northwest) turn leads to Chittenden Lake. The junction is soon after the gradient has lessened and where the main trail bends a little to the right (northeast).

Just 0.1 mile past the Chittenden Lake Trail junction, you see a Staniford lake. A waist-deep, grass-lined lakelet, this water body is *not* the Staniford Lake that attracts attention. Instead, continue a few more steps until you come to a trailside pond atop a broad granitic crest. In this vicinity you can leave the trail and descend southeast briefly cross-country on low-angle slabs to the largest of the Staniford Lakes, lying at 8,708 feet. This large, mostly shallow lake is wonderful for swimming, sometimes warming up to the low 70s in early August. The great bulk of the lake is less than 5 feet deep, with its only deep spot being at a diving area along the west shore. Among the slabs you can find sandy camp spots.

More ponds, still part of the Staniford Lakes cluster, are seen along the northbound Lillian Lake Loop Trail before it dips into a usually dry gully. It then traverses diagonally up along a ridge of glacier-polished slabs with truly outstanding views to the Ritter Range and the entire San Joaquin drainage—your best views yet. You cross the nose of the ridge and then quickly descend to Lillian Lake's outlet creek. Just beyond is a junction with the spur trail around Lillian Lake's eastern and northern shores (8,870'; 37.56303°N, 119.36065°W).

Myriad use trails dive into the beautiful, dense hemlock forest ringing Lillian Lake's northeastern shore. Camping is prohibited within 400 feet of the northeastern shoreline, but if you continue about 0.25 mile to the north, you will encounter a series of well-used-but-splendid sites set sufficiently back from the lake. As the largest and deepest lake you'll pass along this hike, Lillian Lake is also the coldest, and its large brook and rainbow trout population is attractive to anglers; the rugged crest rising from the lake's southwestern shore provides an elegant backdrop.

OTHER NEARBY LAKES

Lady Lake: A spur trail takes off south (left) and climbs gently to moderately 0.6 mile to Lady Lake. As you walk along the outlet creek, about halfway to the lake, you will note an unsigned trail departing from the creek. From here, right leads to a large campsite above the north shore of the lake, while left leads to the east-shore moraine that juts into the lake, with an even better campsite. If you miss this cryptic junction, don't worry because you will most certainly realize when you've reached the shore of granite-rimmed, 8,908-foot-high Lady Lake and can follow the shore between the two trail ends. Both campsites are ideal for large groups—this is one of the few subalpine lakes that can accommodate many tents without environmental concerns.

Chittenden Lake: 9,182-foot-high Chittenden Lake, the highest of the lakes in the vicinity, is reached by a 1-mile spur trail. The trail leads west then northwest from the shelf holding the Staniford Lakes. After climbing open slabs, the trail sidles up to the eastern bank of Shirley Creek. Stepping across the creek, the trail turns sharply left (south), continues briefly under forest cover, and then traverses open slabs. Across here there is no indication of a trail—just continue due south, and before long the lake comes into view. If there are more than two backpackers in your group, don't plan to camp at this lake because flat space is really at a premium. The best site is on the ridge east of the lake, boasting absolutely stunning views. Peakbaggers may choose to continue from Chittenden Lake southwest to the crest—and Yosemite boundary—then follow Sing Peak's southeastern ridge to its panoramic summit.

DAY 3 (Lillian Lake to Walton Trailhead, 6.0 miles): Lillian Lake is the last of the lakes along this loop, and from its outlet the trail descends a forested mile east to a two-branched creek with easy fords. After a short, stiff climb over a gravelly knoll, the trail descends to a junction on a fairly open slope. Here the Lillian Lake Loop Trail ends and you rejoin the Fernandez Trail, on which you turn right (east, later south); left (northwest) leads to additional lake basins and onward to Fernandez and Post Peak Passes (Trip 68). The forest cover quickly thickens, and the trail enters a dense forest glade situated in a shallow trough. You are next routed back onto a ridgeline, an old moraine. Drier and sandier again, the trail follows the moraine crest to its end before switchbacking to the drainage below. Soon you then reach a junction with the trail up Timber Creek. Though the junction itself is signposted and obvious, the unmaintained trail rapidly deteriorates, helped on its path to oblivion by abundant uncleared tree falls. Staying right (southeast), you continue down beneath forest cover, quickly reaching a junction in a sandy flat, where the Fernandez Trail forks right (southwest) and the Walton Trail leads left (southeast). Given that these two trails lead to the same parking area and both are 3.2 miles in length, it is up to you which you take, though the Walton Trail requires less elevation gain, has more open views, and takes you through all new terrain—hence it is the route described here. Turning left and walking through the open flat, along which there are many camping options, you soon cross Madera Creek. A possible wade under the highest of flows, this crossing becomes a rock hop by midsummer and can dry out in late summer. To your left (north) is an interesting geological feature, a dark plug of olivine basalt, which was once part of the throat of a cinder cone. This dark monument is most obvious if you look north after you climb the few short, steep switchbacks up the open slope to the south.

Enjoy the open views as you cross this slabby slope, with a slightly different vista north to the Yosemite boundary near Post Peak Pass and south to the Silver Divide in the South Fork San Joaquin drainage. Dropping off the bare slabs into open lodgepole forest, the trail trends south, continuing its descending traverse. Stretches of dry lodgepole pine forest are interspersed with wetter glades where red fir dominates and drier rocky knobs where manzanita and huckleberry oak replace the trees. Turning right (southwest), where an old road once led left (east) to the Strawberry Mine, you promptly reach the trailhead.

Isberg Trailhead
7,100'; 37.54710°N, 119.26610°W

Destination/ GPS Coordinates	Trip Type	Best Season	Pace & Hiking/ Layover Days	Total Mileage	Permit Required
67 Cora and Joe Crane Lakes 37.62428°N 119.31295°W (Joe Crane Lake)	Semiloop	Mid to late	Leisurely 3/1	17.1	Isberg Trailhead
68 Sadler Lake, Isberg Lakes, and Post Peak Pass 37.63076°N 119.32839°W (Post Peak Pass)	Loop	Mid to late	Moderate 4/2	31.6	Isberg Trailhead *(Fernandez Trail- head in reverse)*
69 Hemlock Crossing 37.63872°N 119.22407°W	Loop	Mid to late	Moderate 3/1	23.5	Isberg Trailhead *(Mammoth Trail- head in reverse)*
64 Merced River Drainage to Isberg Trailhead *(in reverse of descrip- tion; see page 311)*	Shuttle	Mid to late	Moderate 5/1	41.0	Isberg Trailhead *(Glacier Point to Little Yosem- ite Valley as described)*

INFORMATION AND PERMITS: This trip begins in Sierra National Forest and wilderness permits are required. If you enter Yosemite National Park, its regulations apply: bear canisters are required, and pets and firearms are prohibited. Quotas apply from May to October, with 60% of permits reservable online starting in January each year and 40% available first-come, first-served starting the day before your trip's start date. See tinyurl.com/sierranf wildernesspermits for more details. Monday–Friday, permits can be picked up at the Bass Lake Ranger District at 57003 Forest Service Road 225, North Fork (559-877-2218), and seven days a week in summer at the Yosemite Sierra Visitors Bureau, located in downtown Oakhurst at 40343 CA 41 (559-658-7588), *or* the Clover Meadow Ranger Station, located near the Walton, Fernandez, and Isberg Trailheads (559-877-2218, ext. 3136). If you plan to use a stove or have a campfire, you also need a California Campfire Permit, available from a U.S. Forest Service office or online at readyforwildfire.org/permits/campfire-permit.

DRIVING DIRECTIONS: From the CA 49 junction in Oakhurst, drive north on CA 41 for 3.4 miles to a junction with Forest Service Road 222, signposted for Bass Lake. Follow FS 222 east 3.5 miles. Beyond, continue straight ahead for an additional 2.4 miles, but your road is now called Malum Ridge Road (FS 274). Then turn left (north) onto Beasore Road (FS 5S07) and reset your trip odometer to zero. Paved but windy Beasore Road climbs north, passing Chilkoot Campground at 4 miles, followed by a series of dirt roads departing westward. At an odometer reading of 11.6 miles, you reach a four-way intersection at Cold Spring Summit, where Sky Ranch Road (FS 6S10X) departs to the left and a parking area with toilets is on the right. Continuing straight ahead on Beasore Road (FS 5S07), you wind past Beasore Meadows, Jones Store, Mugler Meadow, and Long Meadow. At 20.2 miles from the start of Beasore Road, you reach Globe Rock (on your right; toilets) and FS 5S04, which leads left (north) to the Upper Chiquito Lake Trailhead.

Beyond Globe Rock the road surface can be speckled with potholes, although parts were resurfaced in 2020. Ahead you pass a spur to Upper Chiquito Campground (21.3 miles), the impressive granite domes named the Balls (24.2 miles), the Jackass Lakes Trailhead (26.8 miles), and the Bowler Campground (27.1 miles). Soon thereafter two prominent spur roads bear left, first one to the Norris Trailhead (FS 5S86; 27.5 miles) and just beyond one to the Fernandez and Walton Trailheads (FS 5S05; 27.6 miles).

Continuing on Beasore Road, you pass FS 5S88 (branches south 0.4 mile to Minarets Pack Station; 29.6 miles) and quickly meet the end of paved Minarets Road (FS 4S81; 29.8 miles), which has ascended 52 paved miles north from the community of North Fork. Stay left (northeast), turning onto FS 5S30, and drive 1.8 miles to a junction at the Clover Meadow Ranger Station. Here is the small building where you will pick up your wilderness permit. The entrance to the Clover Meadow Campground is just beyond it, a pleasant campground with piped water, vault toilets, and—amazingly—cell reception!

You still have a short distance to reach your trailhead, however. Staying on FS 5S30, you stay left at a junction with right-trending FS 4S60 (bound for primitive Granite Creek Campground), descend to cross the West Fork of Granite Creek on a bridge, then immediately turn right and parallel the creek east, now on a truly unpaved road. At a Y-junction, bear left (right descends back to the Granite Creek Campground), briefly drive up a steep hill (yes, it is two-wheel drive), level out, and almost immediately turn right into the quite large Isberg Trailhead parking area, 3.1 miles past the Clover Meadow Ranger Station. The only facilities at the trailhead are food-storage boxes.

trip 67   **Cora and Joe Crane Lakes**

see maps on p. 328–329

Trip Data: 37.62428°N, 119.31295°W (Joe Crane Lake); 17.1 miles; 3/1
Topos: *Timber Knob*

HIGHLIGHTS: The lakes along the East Fork Granite Creek drainage make perfect summer destinations, especially since permits are not as hard to come by as at most Sierran trailheads. The Cora Lakes are a lovely cluster of montane forest-ringed lakes, ideal for an easy overnight trip or day hike, while adding a second night at Joe Crane Lake offers a longer trip to a stunning subalpine lake.

HEADS UP! *The terrain between the trailhead and just before the Cora Lakes was burned in the 2020 Creek Fire, but the described campsites were not touched.*

DAY 1 (Isberg Trailhead to Middle Cora Lake, 4.2 miles): After the long drive to the Isberg Trailhead, walking, even with a full pack on, probably feels good. The trailhead is on the north side of the road, about 300 feet west of the parking lot. The trail takes you north, roughly paralleling the mostly unseen East Fork Granite Creek. During past glaciations, only the metavolcanic summit of Timber Knob, high above Cora Lakes, rose above the sea of ice in the broad Granite Creek basin. You plod upward along the rather dusty trail under red fir and lodgepole pine cover. The first miles of this trail receive heavy horse traffic, hence the dust, but the walking is pleasant and the trail mostly in good shape. Reaching the head of the draw you've been following, the trail slowly begins an ascending traverse across a brushy slope, affording the first views to the south and southeast, including pyramidal Squaw Dome, 6 miles to the south, and broad, gentle Kaiser Ridge, on the far horizon behind it. First north facing and then trending more northeasterly, you make your way toward a passageway known as the Niche, a narrow slot through which the East Fork Granite Creek flows, before dropping steeply on its journey south.

continued on page 330

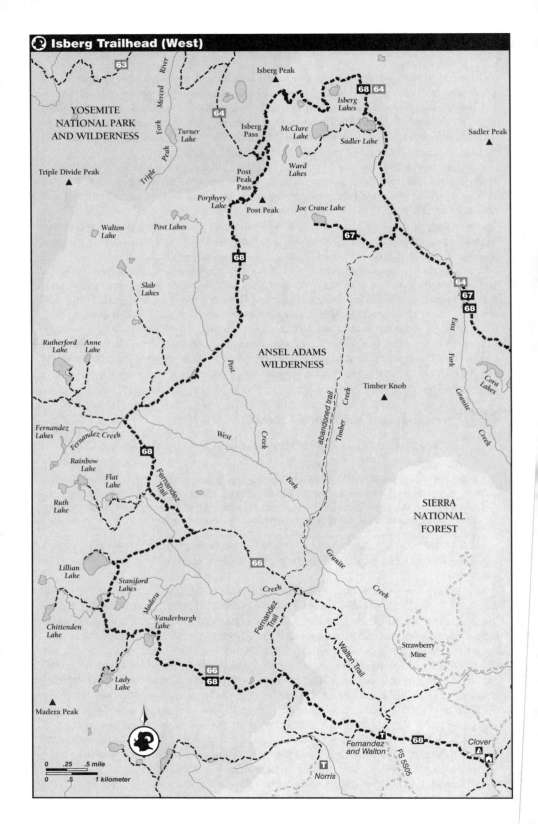

YOSEMITE NATIONAL PARK AND WILDERNESS

63

Isberg Peak ▲

68 64

Isberg Lakes

64

Turner Lake

Isberg Pass

McClure Lake

Sadler Lake

Sadler Peak ▲

Triple Divide Peak ▲

Post Peak Pass

Ward Lakes

Porphyry Lake

Post Peak ▲

Joe Crane Lake

67

Walton Lake

Post Lakes

64
67
68

68

Slab Lakes

ANSEL ADAMS WILDERNESS

East Fork

Cora Lakes

Rutherford Lake

Anne Lake

Post

Timber Knob ▲

Granite

Fernandez Lakes

Fernandez Creek

West

Creek

abandoned trail

Timber Creek

Rainbow Lake

68

Fernandez Trail

Fork

SIERRA NATIONAL FOREST

Flat Lake

Ruth Lake

Lillian Lake

Staniford Lakes

66

Granite

Chittenden Lake

Madera

Vanderburgh Lake

Creek

Creek

Fernandez Trail

Walton Trail

Strawberry Mine

Lady Lake

66
68

Madera Peak ▲

Fernandez and Walton

FS 5S05

68

Clover

T

Norris

| 0 | .25 | .5 mile |
| 0 | .5 | 1 kilometer |

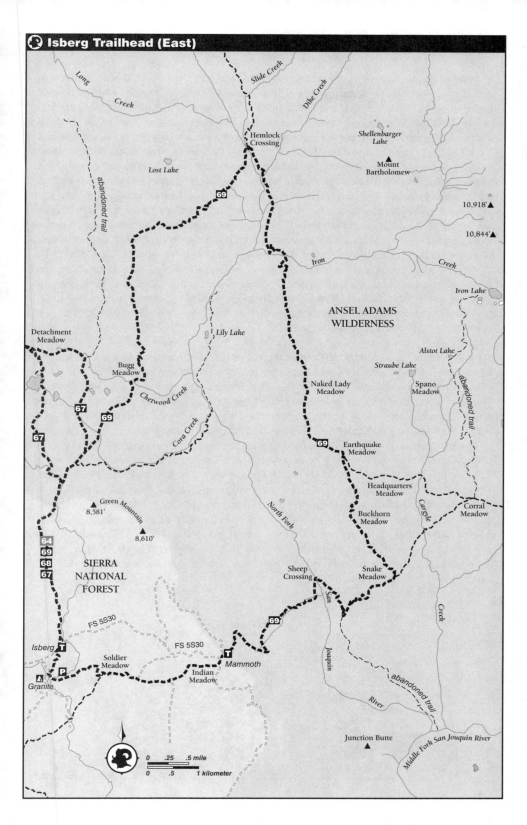

Long Creek

Slide Creek

Dike Creek

Hemlock Crossing

Shellenbarger Lake

Lost Lake

Mount Bartholomew

69

10,918'▲

10,844'▲

Iron Creek

Iron Lake

ANSEL ADAMS WILDERNESS

Detachment Meadow

Lily Lake

Alstot Lake

Bugg Meadow

Straube Lake

Spano Meadow

abandoned trail

67

69

Chetwood Creek

Naked Lady Meadow

67

Cora Creek

69 Earthquake Meadow

Green Mountain 8,581'

Headquarters Meadow

Corral Meadow

8,610'

North Fork

Buckhorn Meadow

Cargyle

64

69

68

67

Sheep Crossing

Snake Meadow

SIERRA NATIONAL FOREST

San

Creek

FS 5S30

69

Isberg 🅣

FS 5S30

🅣

Joaquin

Soldier Meadow

Mammoth

🅿

Indian Meadow

abandoned trail

🅐

Granite

River

Middle Fork San Jouquin River

Junction Butte ▲

0   .25   .5 mile
0   .5   1 kilometer

Now in a quite flat lodgepole pine forest beside the creek, the vegetation is lusher with abundant color in early summer. At full flow the creek tumbles rapidly, with its base of rounded cobble and boulders revealed as flows are reduced. At a signed junction, the Stevenson Trail heads right (northeast) toward Hemlock Crossing (Trip 69), while you stay left (north), continuing along the creek's western bank for a few more steps. Soon your trail fords the East Fork Granite Creek, a broad crossing that means wet feet in early summer and a rock hop later on. The trail diverges east of the main river channel and you follow a smaller tributary upward through mostly lush forest. Climbing more steeply, the trail then sidles around the east side of a small dome, crossing slabs and entering barren forest.

Beyond a shallow saddle, a brief descent leads into the Cora Creek drainage and to the triplet of Cora Lakes, though only the center one, Lake 8,348 (also known as Middle Cora), is visible from the trail. This grassy-shored lake offers ample camping opportunities, with use trails departing west along both its south and north shores (8,432'; 37.59653°N, 119.27319°W). Camping is prohibited, however, within 400 feet of its eastern shore, the corridor through which the trail passes. The lake is sufficiently shallow, to be warm and excellent for swimming, yet deep enough to support rainbow trout. Upper Cora Lake, though depicted as large on maps, is a very shallow lake, with only about one-fourth of its surface still covered by water by September.

DAY 2 (Middle Cora Lake to Joe Crane Lake, 4.1 miles): Return to the trail east of Middle Cora Lake, and climb briefly over a small knob, where you may note some volcanic rocks mixed in with the dominant granite; these are 3.5-million-year-old basalt flows. Ahead, you reach a junction with the little-used trail that leads right (east) to Detachment Meadow and Chetwood Creek, the described return route, while now you stay straight ahead (left; north) and descend back into the East Fork Granite Creek drainage.

For a stretch, the trail hugs the base of a volcanic plateau, keeping just above wet meadows. Abundant tarns and marshy meadows make the ensuing miles a mosquito factory in July, but this stretch is also resplendent with water-loving wildflowers. Reaching Knoblock Meadow, you skirt its eastern edge, pass a few small campsites, and cross East Fork Granite Creek, again a wet ford at high flows. The gradient increases as you continue beside the creek, admiring the flowers and crossing a series of often-dry side channels. Just beyond some small springs, noteworthy mainly for the tiny, red-streaked channels that develop in the soil downslope of them, you reach a junction with the left-trending (west) spur trail to Joe Crane Lake; the Isberg Trail continues right (north) toward Sadler and Isberg Lakes and on to Yosemite (Trips 64 and 68).

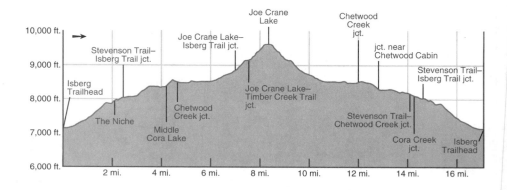

Turning left, you ascend south through a lush forest of hemlocks, lodgepoles, and western white pine, a small trickle to your side and alpine prickly currant crawling along the ground. As the trail then turns to the northwest, the forest cover thins, and looping back to the south again you emerge on broken slabs above the Joe Crane Lake outlet creek. Here is a junction, denoted by a decomposing wooden sign declaring MADERA CREEK and a rock cairn (9,158'; 37.62003°N, 119.30190°W), where right (northwest) leads to Joe Crane Lake and left (southwest, then south) is the abandoned Timber Creek Trail cutting across to the Fernandez Trail.

Staying right, the infrequently traveled trail to Joe Crane Lake initially skirts the northern edge of the boggy meadow and then slowly ascends up a drier slope. If you lose the trail on the slabs, note that it stays well below (and west of) the ridge dropping southeast from Joe Crane Lake. At 9,400 feet, your route sidles up to—and then crosses—the Joe Crane Lake outlet creek and continues up through dry lodgepole forest, fording the creek twice more. As you approach Joe Crane Lake the gradient eases and you traverse a forested flat to the outlet (9,626'; 37.62428°N, 119.31295°W). Little-visited Joe Crane Lake sits in a broad bowl beneath steep cliffs descending off Post Peak and offers some lovely campsites along its southern shore and a healthy population of rainbow trout. A dead-end location on a rarely traveled trail means you're likely to have the lake to yourself. If you're keen to explore, it is possible to walk cross-country up to Post Peak Pass or across to the Ward Lakes and down to McClure and Sadler Lakes.

DAY 3 (Joe Crane Lake to Isberg Trailhead, 8.8 miles): Your return to the trailhead can, of course, be split over two days, with another night at Knoblock Meadow or the Cora Lakes, but it is nearly all downhill and you shouldn't have any difficulty completing it in a single day. If you retrace your steps exactly, the distance is 8.3 miles, but the description includes a minor loop to see some new terrain and a historic cabin, hopefully spared by the fires.

You begin by retracing your steps to the junction leading to Chetwood Creek that lies a little north of the Cora Lakes (8,507'; 37.60223°N, 119.27322°W). Turning left (east) off the Isberg Trail, toward Chetwood Creek, you pass some obvious volcanic outcrops—again the same basalt as near Knoblock Meadow—and then traipse through quite moist red fir and lodgepole forest just south of willow-filled Detachment Meadow. Chetwood Creek materializes at the meadow's eastern edge, and you now accompany the tiny drainage downward. The little-used trail leads to the caved-in Chetwood Cabin that was first built by cattlemen and then used as a hunting lodge through the 1950s. From here, maps still show a junction with a trail leading north toward Sadler Peak. This, too, was once popular with hunting parties, and parts of this trail are still plausible to follow, but here vegetation has obliterated it.

Your route now bends right (south), skirting the western edge of a flower-filled wet meadow through which Chetwood Creek flows. Corn lilies, cow parsnip, dusky horkelia, and yampah are among the many flowers coloring the trail verges. Diverging from Chetwood Creek and just barely ascending to cross a shallow rib, you descend to cross Cora Creek. Another minuscule rise, still through moist forest, and you reach a flat with a junction; a sharp left (northeast) is the Stevenson Trail to Hemlock Crossing (Trip 69), while right (southwest) is your route back to the Isberg Trailhead. A short downhill leads to a second junction, where left (east) is a pleasant-but-little-used trail down Cora Creek to the North Fork San Joaquin River, while you again stay right (southwest). The trail sidles across a broad saddle, gaining effectively no elevation, to drop into the East Fork Granite Creek drainage and pass through a once-upon-a-time meadow that is being rapidly invaded by young trees. Here the trail reaches the banks of the East Fork Granite Creek, requiring a wade through large rounded cobble at peak flows and later transitioning to an easy rock hop. Just across the creek, you again meet the Isberg Trail and turn left (south) to retrace your steps.

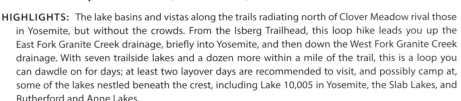

trip 68 **Sadler Lake, Isberg Lakes, and Post Peak Pass**

see maps on p. 328–329

Trip Data: 37.63076°N, 119.32839°W (Post Peak Pass); 4/2; 31.6 miles
Topos: Timber Knob, Cattle Mountain, Mount Ritter

HIGHLIGHTS: The lake basins and vistas along the trails radiating north of Clover Meadow rival those in Yosemite, but without the crowds. From the Isberg Trailhead, this loop hike leads you up the East Fork Granite Creek drainage, briefly into Yosemite, and then down the West Fork Granite Creek drainage. With seven trailside lakes and a dozen more within a mile of the trail, this is a loop you can dawdle on for days; at least two layover days are recommended to visit, and possibly camp at, some of the lakes nestled beneath the crest, including Lake 10,005 in Yosemite, the Slab Lakes, and Rutherford and Anne Lakes.

HEADS UP! *To avoid the final 3.5 miles of this hike, in part along dirt roads, shuttle a car to the Fernandez Trailhead, at the end of Forest Service Road 5S05. You could begin and end your loop hike at the Clover Meadow Ranger Station, hiking the final 2 miles at the start of the hike. This reduces your driving time and has no effect on your hiking distance; the hike is described from the starting trailhead, the Isberg Trailhead, simply because it is the declared starting point per your Wilderness permit.*

HEADS UP! *The first and last 4 miles of this loop are burning in the 2020 Creek Fire as this book goes to press. However, the upper lake basins all remain untouched by the flames.*

DAY 1 (Isberg Trailhead to Sadler Lake, 8.4 miles): Follow Trip 67, Day 1 for 4.2 miles to Middle Cora Lake. Then continue an additional 4.2 miles, described on the following page.

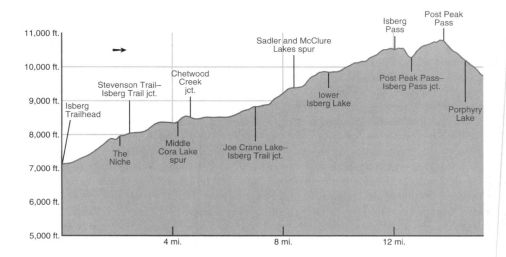

Beyond Middle Cora Lake, the trail climbs briefly over a small knob, where you may note some volcanic rocks mixed in with the dominant granite; these are 3.5-million-year-old basalt flows. Ahead, you reach a junction with the little-used trail that leads right (east) to Detachment Meadow and Chetwood Creek; stay straight ahead (left; north) and descend back into the East Fork Granite Creek drainage.

For a stretch, the trail hugs the base of a volcanic plateau, keeping just above wet meadows. Abundant tarns and marshy meadows make the ensuing miles a mosquito factory in July, but this stretch is also resplendent with water-loving wildflowers. Reaching Knoblock Meadow, you skirt its eastern edge, pass a few small campsites, and recross East Fork Granite Creek, again a wet ford at high flows. The gradient increases as you continue beside the creek, admiring the flowers and crossing a series of often-dry side channels. Just beyond some small springs, noteworthy mainly for the tiny, red-streaked channels that develop in the soil downslope of them, you reach a junction with the left-trending (west) trail to Joe Crane Lake (Trip 67); you stay right (north) on the Isberg Trail, toward Sadler and Isberg Lakes and the Yosemite boundary.

Continuing along the creek's bank, you note that, with increasing elevation, the forest is slowly thinning and the red fir have all but disappeared, replaced by a mixture of hemlocks and lodgepole pine, as you slowly transition from the upper montane to subalpine zones. Crossing the East Fork Granite Creek a final time at a location with grand clumps of clasping arnica, water flows are now lower and you can rock-hop across under all but the highest runoff. Switchbacks up a dry lodgepole slope lead to a shelf holding Sadler Lake. With the lake still out of view, you reach a small junction signposted for McClure Lake (9,377'; 37.64194°N, 119.30058°W). This lateral leads to fine campsites around the southern and western shores of Sadler Lake (no campfires). In particular, seek out the flat, sandy locales nestled between the similarly flat slabs that ring its southern shore. However, camping is prohibited within 400 feet of the north shore of Sadler Lake, a seasonally marshy area.

DAY 2 (Sadler Lake to Post Creek, 7.2 miles): Back on the main trail, look up at the near-vertical walls to your north—it is atop these that the Isberg Lakes are perched. To reach this clutch of alpine gems, you climb due north up a slope under sparse lodgepole pine cover, turn west and cross a shallow rib, then descend to the bedrock-lined lower

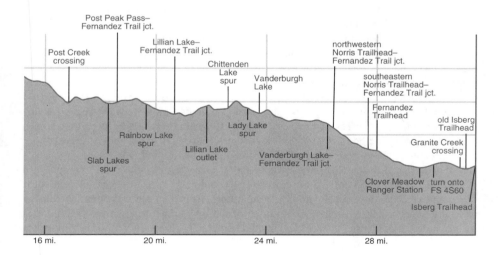

Isberg Lake. At this alpine retreat you'll find a few single-tent sites between stunted pine trees, but the shelf offers little protection against wind or a storm; take care to camp on bare ground, not the pervasive heath cover.

Onward, the trail traipses across the remarkably vegetated landscape—sedge meadows surround the lake and expanses of dwarf bilberry and red mountain heather creep along the edge of protruding boulders. A 300-foot slope separates the lower—and largest— Isberg Lake from the higher cluster, and to reach them you wind up slabs, strips of sand, and verdant slopes irrigated by endless trickles. The views are tremendous, for you are standing just 150 feet north of the 400-foot cliff overtopping McClure Lake. Ahead, the trail is much slower walking: narrow, in places incised and, because it is following little strips of vegetation between the rocks or winding between fractured slabs, it is almost never straight. Gazing up toward the pass, you see that the rock on the slope above has fractured into big smooth platters. It is also colorful—admire the red-and-gray-striped summit of Isberg Peak—because you are near the contact between the newer granitic and older metamorphic rocks, and many of the rocks were partially altered during geologic skirmishes as the granite formed. Skirting high around the upper Isberg Lake and its satellite tarn, the trail makes 26 tight, but relatively gentle, switchbacks up a south-facing rib—the trail located where the snow melts earliest—and then cuts southwest beneath Isberg Peak to Isberg Pass (10,512').

Reaching Isberg Pass, position yourself atop one of the pleasantly flat boulders adorning the ridge between prostrate whitebark pine and enjoy the view east to the crest between Sadler Peak and Long Mountain with the Ritter Range peeking out behind, southeast across the expansive San Joaquin River drainage, and west and northwest into Yosemite. Procrastinating on top, you pull yourself away and begin a surprisingly slow descent of the west side of the pass. It is slow because steep slabs and broken blocks cover the slope directly below you, forcing the trail to traverse south to avoid the steepest terrain. But the ridge is also comprised of broken rock making for cumbersome walking, as on many occasions you climb a few steps upward to bypass a small obstacle. Where the trail's gradient increases, you descend a steep, loose trail, eventually reaching a junction where you turn left (south) toward Post Peak Pass, while right (west) drops into the Merced River drainage. If you want a shorter day, you could continue 1.2 miles into Yosemite to the northern end of Lake 10,050, the giant oval lake you spy to the north, where there are some excellent campsites.

Your route now switchbacks steadily back to the crest, climbing a tad under 400 feet up a lushly vegetated slope. At the crest begins a sublime traverse south—the trail makes a skyline traverse with views west to the Clark Range and east to the Ritter Range as you walk along sandy benches. To the south, you look out over much of the enormous San Joaquin River basin. Slowly the trail trends a little east of the ridge, eventually resolving into switchbacks to ascend the final talus slopes to Post Peak Pass (10,769'). Nestled between Post Peak and its northern satellite, the view from Post Peak Pass is inferior to that you garnered earlier.

The initial descent from Post Peak Pass is steep, tedious, and slow. It is a rocky trail, in stretches riprap (angular rock chunks) filled and elsewhere there are big steps to descend. After dropping more than 550 feet, you skirt across bedrock benches above the east shore of tiny Porphyry Lake. Your eyes will almost certainly be drawn to slabs and large boulders sporting gigantic, dark-colored spots in a light-colored matrix. In places the spots are perfectly rounded, like a collection of beach balls, and elsewhere more reminiscent of an exotic animal hide; these are again the aftermath of past geologic altercations. The darker rocks are older and were broken apart and engulfed by younger magma (molten granite) that intruded. Usually the older rock is melted completely (or nearly so), and it is rare for so many large pieces to survive.

View to the Minarets from the traverse to Post Peak Pass   Photo by Elizabeth Wenk

Although Porphyry Lake is a beautiful location for a break, camp space here is nearly nonexistent; you'll only find spots to pitch single, small tents. Most groups will choose to continue another mile to forested terrain. After following a slab rib south from Porphyry Lake, the trail drops steeply into a gully, crosses a small creek, and reaches the gentler landscape at the headwaters of a Post Creek tributary. The trail traverses south through wet meadows, before angling onto some higher ground, the snout of a giant, broad lateral moraine that you descend. For the coming 0.5 mile, among the lodgepole pine or at the meadow's edge are some campsites, with water in creeks to the west or southeast (9,612'; 37.61653°N, 119.33223°W).

DAY 3 (Post Creek to Lillian Lake, 6.3 miles): At the end of the shelf, the trail drops steeply down a lodgepole pine–shaded slope and then descends southwest to Post Creek. On the west bank of Post Creek, you'll find another adequate campsite. The route then climbs southwest, cutting through a low divide on rolling slabs and then descending toward a reedy lake with clusters of pond lilies and abundant dragonflies. Your trail skirts along the southeast shore of the small lake and then climbs to a second tarn, this one lacking the interesting aquatic plants, and then across a low divide that makes a decent campsite. From here you descend past (and sometimes through) other early-drying ponds. Entering a drier landscape, the forest changes to a wonderful assemblage of red fir, lodgepole pine, and towering western white pine. Soon you reach a little step-across creekbed and then the junction with the Slab Lakes Trail.

SLAB LAKES

It is 1.5 miles to the lower Slab Lake and an additional 0.7 mile to the upper lakes (those marked "Slab Lakes" on the USGS 7.5' topos). There are campsites at both lakes; those at the lower lake offer more space and are sheltered by lodgepoles, while at the upper lake there are spots in small sandy patches among the pervasive slabs that proffer stupendous views and a readily visible route to climb Triple Divide Peak. The trail is easy to follow as far as the lower lake, while only a cairn-marked route continues to the upper lakes.

Just 150 feet west of the trail junction, you cross the main Slab Lakes creek—one of three parallel washes—then momentarily enter a small meadow where you cross Fernandez Creek. Camps can be found among lodgepoles near the confluence of the Slab Lakes creek and Fernandez Creek, as well as along both banks of Fernandez Creek. Although old maps show trails paralleling each bank of Fernandez Creek here, only the southern one still exists; you cross Fernandez Creek in the meadow corridor and then walk briefly through the forest to reach the junction with the Fernandez Trail.

RUTHERFORD AND ANNE LAKES

Rutherford and Anne Lakes lie 1.7 miles to the north, reached by following the Fernandez Trail north (and up) for 1.1 miles and then turning right onto a spur trail that leads to the lakes. Rutherford Lake is slab encrusted and offers multiple camping options along its southern and eastern shores. Anne Lake lies on a lower shelf farther east and is ringed by lodgepole forest and grassy shores, with forested campsites near its southeastern edge.

You continue your descent, the next stretch mostly open and sandy with slabs not far beneath the surface, only entering stands of trees where joints in the bedrock have resulted in the accumulation of deeper soils. The trail makes a distinct bend to continue following one such forested bench downward, leading across a minor drainage divide to, beside a tarn, a righthand (southwest) junction with the trail to Rainbow, Ruth, and Flat Lakes. Rainbow and Ruth are spectacular lakes, but the flat terrain near their shores is all within a camping exclusion zone, so they are best visited for a lunch break.

The Fernandez Trail, the left branch, now turns to the southeast again, trending back onto a rocky rib and descending through an open landscape of dark-colored rock and intermittent trees, always with broken views to the south and east. At the next junction, the right option leads 1.2 miles to lovely Lillian Lake, where you should spend your final night. If you are in a hurry to reach the car, left (east) leads to the Fernandez Trailhead in 4.9 miles, versus 7.4 on the described route, but passes no more lake basins. Turn right (west) onto the Lillian Loop Trail and climb a fairly open slope to a gravelly knoll, then descend west to a two-branched creek with easy fords, and thereafter climb briefly but steadily alongside the Lillian Lake outlet creek.

Soon you reach the lake's outlet (8,870'; 37.56303°N, 119.36065°W) and turn right (north), diving into the beautiful, dense hemlock forest ringing Lillian Lake's northeastern shore. Camping is prohibited within 400 feet of the northeastern shoreline, but if you continue about 0.25 mile to the north, you will encounter a series of well-used, but splendid, sites set a little back from the lake. Lillian Lake has a large brook and rainbow trout population that is attractive to anglers and is backdropped by a spectacularly steep crest.

DAY 4 (Lillian Lake to Isberg Trailhead, 9.7 miles): From Lillian Lake, you can either continue south along the Lillian Loop Trail or retrace your steps to the Fernandez Trail. The former is just 0.1 mile longer and takes you past additional lakes, so the described route leads in that direction. From Lillian Lake, you skirt around a rib and emerge onto glacier-polished slabs with a stupendous panorama of the San Joaquin drainage from the Minarets south to the Mount Goddard area. Descending, you reach the first ponds of the Staniford Lakes cluster. The selection of waist-deep, grass-lined lakelets that are alongside the trail are missable, but the largest Staniford Lake, lying at 8,708 feet a short distance below and east of the trail, is worth a detour. This large, mostly shallow lake is wonderful for swimming, sometimes warming up to the low 70s in early August. Among the slabs on its western shore you can find sandy camp spots.

Passing a junction that leads right (northwest) to the Chittenden Lakes—another worthwhile detour described in a sidebar in Trip 66—staying left, your trail makes a moderate ascent south to a saddle, from which you are again treated to memorable views. Beyond, the trail turns east and descends a couple of hundred feet on fairly open granitic slabs to another junction; right (south) leads to Lady Lake, another gorgeous lake with excellent camping (Trip 66 sidebar, page 325), while the Lillian Lake Loop continues straight ahead (left; east). Another rocky drop leads to the basin harboring Vanderburgh Lake (spelled *Vandeburg* on most maps). On its north shore are more good campsites, where steep, granitic Peak 9,852, on Madera Peak's northeast ridge, is reflected in the lake's placid early-morning waters.

Continuing around the north side of Vanderburgh Lake, you cross Madera Creek and arc south to climb to a bedrock notch in a granitic crest. Enjoying the expansive views south a final time, the trail descends steeply and then turns east for easier walking, passing two often-wet, moraine-dammed, flower-filled meadows and then a waist-deep pond. Ahead, right on a ridge, is a junction where you again intersect the Fernandez Trail. Right (southeast) is your route to the trailhead, while left (north) leads back toward Post Peak Pass.

The trail now descends quite steeply down a trough in the sandy ridge, reaching a junction after just 0.2 mile, where you continue left (southeast), while right (southwest) leads steeply to the Norris Trailhead. Exiting Ansel Adams Wilderness, you drop down steep gravelly switchbacks below a small, exfoliating dome. Slowly the brushy slopes yield to a pleasant red fir forest and then the gradient decreases. Skirting a crescent meadow edged by a thicket of young trees, you reach another junction, where right (southwest) is another little-used spur to the Norris Trailhead, while you again stay left (east). Just a short distance through a typical midelevation Sierran forest of white fir, Jeffrey pine, and lodgepole pine leads to the Fernandez Trailhead and a large parking area, located at the end of Forest Service Road 5S05.

If your group has two cars, you can shuttle a car to this location and save the final 3.6 miles of walking. Otherwise, walk to the northern end of the parking lot. Here you'll find two trails—the bigger Walton Trail that leads back upcanyon and, to its right (east), a small trail signposted to Clover Meadow; you head toward Clover Meadow. This trail leads a pleasant 1.5 miles to the Clover Meadow Ranger Station, passing through beautiful mature fir forests, across open sandy flats, and eventually skirting the edge of the Clover Meadow Campground. From the ranger station, the most direct way to your car is to follow FS 5S30 (the road on which you drove to the trailhead on the first day) 0.5 mile east, then turn onto FS 4S60, signposted for the Granite Creek Campground. This road leads 1.1 miles to the campground. You cross Granite Creek, sometimes a wade, and turn left (north). After 150 feet, along the eastern side of the road, is an old Isberg Trailhead marker; follow a short trail segment back uphill to the newer parking lot, a final 0.4 mile.

<hr>

trip 69   **Hemlock Crossing**

see maps on p. 328–329

> **Trip Data:** 37.63872°N, 119.22407°W (Hemlock Crossing);
> 3/1; 23.5 miles
>
> **Topos:** *Timber Knob, Cattle Mountain, Mount Ritter*

HIGHLIGHTS: This trip starts in the forested Granite Creek basin and leads to the spectacular metavolcanic North Fork San Joaquin drainage. On the way back, take the historic Mammoth Trail, first an important American Indian route and then a toll route between Oakhurst and Mammoth mining district in the 1870s and '80s. The first and second days of this trip are relatively long because there are stretches without reliable water and several spur trails that are in poor condition are avoided. Being at fairly low elevations, mostly on pleasant trails and without enormous elevation gain, hikers shouldn't experience too much trouble completing these legs, but don't head on this hike in August and expect to find halfway campsites. Some hikers will choose to instead complete an out-and-back hike to Hemlock Crossing and then explore the headwaters of the North Fork San Joaquin.

HEADS UP! *To avoid the final 3 miles of this hike, in part along dirt roads, shuttle a car to the Mammoth Trailhead, at the extreme east end of Forest Service Road 5S30.*

HEADS UP! *Many of the trails described for this trip burned in the 2020 Creek Fire. The burn is likely patchy in places, but expect more limited shade than what is described in the text.*

DAY 1 (Isberg Trailhead to Hemlock Crossing, 8.9 miles): After the long drive to the Isberg Trailhead, walking, even with a full pack on, probably feels good. The trailhead is on the north side of the road, about 300 feet west of the parking lot. The trail takes you north, roughly paralleling the mostly unseen East Fork Granite Creek. During past glaciations, only the metavolcanic summit of Timber Knob, high above Cora Lakes, rose above the sea of ice in the broad Granite Creek basin. You plod upward along the rather dusty trail under red fir and lodgepole pine cover. The first miles of this trail receive heavy horse traffic, hence the dust, but the walking is pleasant and the trail mostly in good shape. Reaching the head of the draw you've been following, the trail slowly begins an ascending traverse across a brushy slope, affording the first views to the south and southeast, including pyramidal Squaw Dome, 6 miles to the south, and broad, gentle Kaiser Ridge, on the far horizon behind it. First north facing and then trending more northeasterly, you make your way toward a passageway known as the Niche, a narrow slot through which the East Fork Granite Creek flows, before dropping steeply on its journey south.

Now in a quite flat lodgepole pine forest beside the creek, the vegetation is more lush with abundant color in early summer. At full flow the creek tumbles rapidly, with its base of rounded cobble and boulders revealed as flows are reduced. At 0.35 mile north of the Niche you reach a signed junction with the Stevenson Trail to Hemlock Crossing and turn right (east) onto it, while the Isberg Trail continues left (north; Trips 64, 67, and 68). You almost immediately ford East Fork Granite Creek, requiring a wade through large rounded cobble at peak flows and later transitioning to an easy rock hop. In late season, this may be your last water until Hemlock Crossing—fill your water bottles. Cutting across a lush meadow, its perimeters overgrown by lodgepole pine and red fir, the trail climbs a tad to a junction

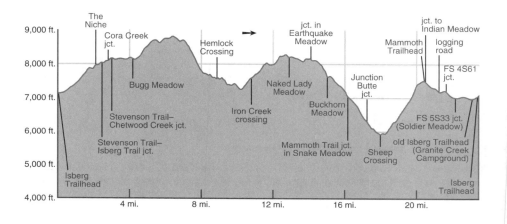

The water slide at Hemlock Crossing   Photo by Elizabeth Wenk

atop an imperceptible saddle, where right (east) leads down Cora Creek to the North Fork San Joaquin River on a pleasant but little-used trail, while you stay left (northeast). Climbing gently through lodgepole pine and red fir you reach a second junction after 0.2 mile where left (north) leads toward the Chetwood Cabin (Trip 67), while you stay right (still northeast) on the Stevenson Trail, bound for Hemlock Crossing.

The forest floor is lush with near continuous vegetation cover, as the trail wiggles across a slope and drops to step-across, seasonal Cora Creek. Rising and falling across a minor spur, the trail continues through a sequence of brightly colored meadows and stands of trees. Flowers are abundant, nourished by local volcanic soils and irrigated by groundwater. You drop to cross Chetwood Creek in one lobe of overgrown Bugg Meadow, where corn lily, meadow rue, dusky horkelia, and twinberry all vie for your attention. Beyond the northern lobe of Bugg Meadow, an aspen glade, the trail climbs rockily to the crest of a ridge. Still in volcanic rock, you are now on a dry shelf with scattered juniper and Jeffrey pine; most notably, there are expansive views east to the Minarets. The next 2 miles mostly follow this shelf high above the North Fork San Joaquin. Near the beginning, the trail meanders just at the valley's lip, and it is easy (and essential) to detour onto rocky knobs to enjoy the panoramas. Farther north, the trail follows forested flats—sometimes populated by red fir, elsewhere by hemlock or lodgepole pine—or skirts flower-speckled meadows. Eventually it turns east and drops to cross an unnamed creek. As long as there is water (there usually is), there are a few small campsites beneath diminutive hemlock cover near the step-across ford.

You have now reached the end of the shelf and must negotiate a 1,100-foot descent to Hemlock Crossing. Briefly in lush hemlock forest, the grade quickly steepens and the trail descends just north of a rocky ridge of metamorphosed volcanic rock. In places it follows forested slopes and elsewhere detours onto the mat manzanita–cloaked ridge, offering views across to the Ritter Range and down into the deep, steep North Fork San Joaquin Canyon. After losing 800 feet over a particularly grueling 0.8 mile, the gradient eases, and you traverse lodgepole pine flats and pass seasonal tarns surrounded by thickets of

Labrador tea and bracken fern. Between each flat is a brief rocky descent to another sheltered shelf, and then you complete a final descending traverse through glacial-polished dark-colored metavolcanic slab ribs to the North Fork San Joaquin at Hemlock Crossing (7,595'; 37.63872°N, 119.22407°W). The largest campsites are southwest of the bridge—those closest to the trail have been disturbed by blowdowns, but continuing a few more steps south leads to good choices. Just upstream of the bridge the river pours over a granite lip into two large, inviting, chilly pools—delightful late-summer swimming holes. The small cascade is a popular water slide when water flows are low. If the main sites are occupied, cross the bridge and turn right (south), going a short distance to a campsite at a large waterfall on the river, or backtrack slightly uphill to some small sites nested among the slabs.

HEADWATERS OF THE NORTH FORK SAN JOAQUIN

From Hemlock Crossing, spend a layover day fishing or exploring the headwaters of the North Fork San Joaquin by taking the left (north) fork after crossing the bridge. This trail gradually rises up and away from the river, following a secondary drainage to elongate, lush Stevenson Meadow. Approximately 2.2 miles beyond Hemlock Crossing, the trail is indistinct as it crosses an open slope of avalanche debris, but it reappears as soon as it turns west to round a rocky promontory and reunite with the North Fork San Joaquin near the mouth of Bench Canyon. Onward, the trail continues beside the river, climbing more steadily past a series of delightful cascades and eventually emerging from forest cover in broad subalpine meadows ringed by slabs and overshadowed by impressive peaks. About 5 miles upstream of Hemlock Crossing, where there is a prominent waterfall to the right (spilling from Catherine Lake and the Ritter Lakes), the obvious trail ends. However, cross-country travel to the sought-after Twin Island Lakes is straightforward: head up one drainage east of their outlet stream drainage and then drop to the northeastern shore of the northern (lower) lake, where you will find abundant sandy campsites. The Ritter Lakes and Catherine Lake are also beguiling; off-trail enthusiasts, including your author, find this landscape some of the Sierra's most enticing.

DAY 2 (Hemlock Crossing to Sheep Crossing, 9.1 miles): On the east side of the Hemlock Crossing bridge, turn right (south), and climb briefly to a bench on the river's eastern bank. Following the shelf to its end, the trail winds quickly down to ford Dike Creek near a few tent sites. The waterfalls along both the North Fork San Joaquin and Dike Creek are worth admiring, for the metavolcanic rocks erode readily into the deepset slots and blocky gorges, such different geometries than you will see in granitic landscapes. After following another forested flat, the trail begins a traversing ascent south, first through a thicket of bracken ferns and willows (and flowers!) and then up a scrubbier slope, soon far above the tumbling river. As you approach a giant slope of gray-green metamorphic talus, your eyes are drawn south to Iron Creek, which tumbles dramatically down a slot in the canyon wall. A few long switchbacks carry you closer to the channel, but you'll have to leave the trail for a satisfactory view—or better yet, detour down the south side, as described below. Entering conifer cover you round a final corner and meet cascading Iron Creek; there are some mediocre campsites in the surrounding forest and fantastic ones if you're willing to detour a half mile up Iron Creek.

IRON CREEK CASCADES

An essential detour is to drop your pack and walk down the south bank of Iron Creek beside the falls and cascades. From this side of the gorge, you can look into its deep pools and stand not far from the water's edge as it splashes down the dark, fractured rock all the way to the North Fork San Joaquin. If you have spare time, it is worth walking most of the way to this confluence.

Beyond Iron Creek, the trail leaves the canyon's edge and begins a gradual, forested ascent to Naked Lady Meadow, a marshy aspen grove that got its name from the bawdy images that lonely shepherds carved into tree trunks long before the area's 1964 wilderness designation. Over the subsequent 1.2 miles, the trail traverses a hillside, wandering in and out of forest stands and across shrubby slopes, ultimately skirting across the top of slanted, spring-fed Earthquake Meadow, a sea of corn lilies and coneflowers that is ringed by drier slopes of sagebrush and mountain whitethorn. The springs in the middle of the meadow should always provide water, but the area is too sloping to be an appealing campsite.

At a junction in Earthquake Meadow, you face a dilemma. The "main route" has always been the left (southeast) fork that leads 2 miles to Corral Meadow (originally known as 77 Corral after a drought in 1877 forced shepherds to seek higher, wilder grazing lands), but the trail is in awful condition, barely maintained since a 2003 fire decimated the forest. Along the eastern mile, there are vast whitethorn thickets, waist-high flowers, and the "trail" is only identified by the occasional long-ago-cut log lying beneath the vegetation. The area was, in part, reburned in 2018, but the shrubs will quickly regrow again. It is not that arduous to push your way through, but given the Corral Meadow creeklet can run dry, the trip description now directs you south. The main reason to continue to Corral Meadow is if you want to detour north toward Alstot Lake or Iron Lake (effectively a cross-country route for the first mile, where the old Iron Lake Trail has completely vanished in the burn area, but the upper stretches are in good condition and lead to spectacular country) or continue onto Mammoth Lakes in the eastern Sierra.

Following the description, continue right (due south) at the Earthquake Meadow junction on a very sparingly used trail, soon entering landscape lightly burned in the 2010 Buckhorn Fire—in most places at least some of the mature conifers are still alive. In places this trail is faint from disuse; when in doubt stop and make sure you're on route before continuing. The initially gradual traverse becomes steeper as the trail winds down the north side of elongate Buckhorn Meadow. This, too, is a spring-fed meadow, and if there is good water flow, you may want to check out a large old campsite just south of the meadow strip. The partially burned landscape finally yields to intact forest about 0.3 mile before the Snake Meadow junction, and the trail then continues its steady descent beneath incense cedar, white fir, and ponderosa pine cover.

At Snake Meadow, a small dry opening in a conifer forest, you intersect the much more prominent Mammoth Trail that leads 10.9 easy miles east (left) to Devils Postpile. Initially an American Indian route, the historic Mammoth Trail was a toll route that brought supplies from Fresno Flats (Oakhurst) to the eastside mining camps around Mammoth Lakes back in the 1870s and 1880s.

This trip, however, turns right; briefly continues through flat, lush lower montane conifer forest; and then begins a switchbacking descent to the North Fork San Joaquin. At a right-bending switchback a sign declares JUNCTION BUTTE, marking the start of a long-abandoned trail that drops to the confluence of the Middle Fork and North Fork San Joaquin. Thereafter the Mammoth Trail begins a final long northward switchback to the river, the terrain ever more broken by rocky bluffs and the trail more cobbly underfoot. You reach the river at Sheep Crossing, where you cross the North Fork San Joaquin on a large wood-and-metal bridge (5,923'; 37.56031°N, 119.20851°W). Once across you quickly reach campsites on a broad, open shelf above the river's western bank. It is a dramatic setting, with steep bluffs rising upward and giant river boulders indicating the force of the river in flood.

DAY 3 (Sheep Crossing to Isberg Trailhead, 5.5 miles): On the west side of the river, the trail turns south, following a shelf above the riverbank for a pleasant 0.25 mile. The trail then curves west to ascend a lovely shaded drainage, where black oak, incense cedar, and white fir provide thick shade. Shade-loving species carpet the forest floor—trail plant, thimbleberry (with tasty raspberrylike berries in late summer), and western azalea. Leaving the sheltered draw at about 7,000 feet, the trail turns northwest, ascending into drier scrubbier terrain, then switchbacking back south and southwest to reach the ridgetop Mammoth Trailhead.

If you do not have a car shuttled here, you have 2.4 miles remaining via Forest Service Road 5S30 or 3.0 miles via a collection of trails. Once you exit the parking area, turning right leads directly to the Isberg Trailhead along FS 5S30, while left, the Mammoth Trail, is the route described here. So, turn left (south), and after just 100 feet turn right (west) down a small trail, the continuing Mammoth Trail that is possibly still signposted for Indian Meadow; the trail is marked as a road on the USGS 7.5' topo maps, but it is just a trail. Following a narrow creeklet downward, you reach a dirt road after 0.75 mile (7,191'; 37.54154°N, 119.24109°W). Turn right and continue due west on this logging road (FS 4S61). After 0.4 mile the road bends north (right) and you continue straight ahead (left; west) (7,214'; 37.54190°N, 119.24797°W), now back on a trail. The Mammoth Trail loops around the southern side of Soldier Meadow, a fence separating the meadow from the lush forest through which you are traveling. At the western end of Soldier Meadow, the Mammoth Trail departs left (southwest), bound for the Clover Meadow Ranger Station, while you turn right (north and then west) onto FS 5S33 (7,010'; 37.54311°N, 119.25566°W). After 0.9 mile you arrive

The bridge at Sheep Crossing   Photo by Elizabeth Wenk

at the primitive Granite Creek Campground along Granite Creek. Turning upstream, you'll almost immediately reach an inconspicuous trailhead on the right, the old Isberg Trailhead (or Granite Creek Campground Trailhead; 6,976'; 37.54308°N, 119.26783°W). Follow it 0.35 mile north (uphill) to reach FS 5S30 almost exactly across the road from the Isberg Trailhead. Turn right (northeast), and you'll quickly reach your car.

SHUTTLE OPTION

Forest Service Road 5S30 continues east from the Isberg Trailhead for an additional 2.4 miles to the Mammoth Trailhead. If your group has two cars, you will most certainly want to shuttle a car to the endpoint. If you have only a single car, you can walk the road, or take the described 3-mile route that follows less-used logging roads and actual trails back to the trailhead; the latter is the route described.

TRANS-SIERRA HIKE

For an easy 10.9-mile trans-Sierra hike, from Snake Meadow, go left on the eastbound Mammoth Trail over Cargyle Creek to Corral Meadow. Continue across East Fork Cargyle Creek and a tributary and then through beautiful Cargyle Meadow (once a popular meeting and trading place for American Indian tribes from the east and west sides of the Sierra). Climb to Stairway Meadow and the Granite Stairway (neither granite nor a stairway, oddly) to enter Inyo National Forest. Pass Summit Meadow (not a meadow, and not at a summit) as the trail descends into Snow Canyon. At a junction with the trail to Fern and Beck Lakes (good camping at Fern Lake), go right (northeast) to begin a pumiceous, rocky descent with great views over the Middle Fork San Joaquin River drainage.

At the bottom of the descent, ford King Creek (campsite) and curve northeast around a low ridge to reach an X-junction with the north–south John Muir Trail (JMT)/Pacific Crest Trail. Cross the JMT, continue northeast, and soon reach a junction on the riverbank. Turn right (briefly south and then east) over the river on a footbridge toward the Devils Postpile Trailhead. Across the river, find another junction: go left (north) a quarter mile to the trailhead or right (south) to see the Postpile itself in just a few yards. (Why not?)

The most difficult part of this journey—returning to your car—begins once you are at Devils Postpile. Getting back to your car at Isberg Trailhead will possibly take you longer than reversing your walk, the only downside to this very pleasant forested route. You begin by taking the mandatory shuttle bus to the main lodge of Mammoth Mountain Ski Area; only in early summer and in fall are most people allowed to drive into the Reds Meadow/Devils Postpile area.

From the Mammoth Mount Ski Area, continue 4.2 miles down Minaret Road (also CA 203) into the town of Mammoth Lakes (optional buses run along this route as well). Now at a prominent intersection, CA 203 turns left (east) and continues 3.7 miles through town to the US 395 and CA 203 (the Mammoth) junction. From here, consult a map app for the various routes back to the western Sierra.

US 395 TRIPS

Whether you come from the north or the south, US 395 is a scenic delight. Better yet, it offers easy access to trailheads from which you can explore the wonder and beauty of, for this book, Carson-Iceberg and Hoover Wildernesses and northern Yosemite National Park. We invite you to enjoy Sierra adventures from four major trailheads: Corral Valley, Robinson Creek, Green Creek, and Virginia Lakes. The Buckeye Creek Trailhead is also included, for Trips 36 and 73 end here.

At the Corral Valley Trailhead, diverse topography awaits backpackers embarking from the east side of the 160,000-acre Carson-Iceberg Wilderness, where fellow travelers are few and far between.

Few trailheads that aren't already in Yosemite National Park offer such fine access to the spectacular backcountry of northern Yosemite as does the Robinson Creek Trailhead out of Twin Lakes, west of Bridgeport. This trailhead offers six irresistible trips in Hoover Wilderness and Yosemite's northern backcountry.

The Green Creek and Virginia Lakes drainages are eastside gems, less crowded than the more popular trailheads out of Twin Lakes to the north and Tuolumne Meadows to the south. The trips out of these trailheads showcase the surrounding peaks and wildflower gardens, plus they offer easy access to the northern Yosemite backcountry.

Trailheads: Corral Valley

Buckeye Creek

Robinson Creek

Green Creek

Virginia Lakes

Corral Valley Trailhead					8,199'; 38.51691°N, 119.55665°W	
Destination/ GPS Coordinates	Trip Type	Best Season	Pace & Hiking/ Layover Days	Total Mileage	Permit Required
70 Lower Fish Valley 38.47283°N 119.61453°W	Semiloop	Mid to late	Leisurely 2/1	14.0	Carson-Iceberg Wilderness
71 Poison Lake 38.48208°N 119.65449°W	Out-and-back	Mid	Moderate 2/1	14.0	Carson-Iceberg Wilderness

INFORMATION AND PERMITS: Responsibility for Carson-Iceberg Wilderness is split between Stanislaus and Humboldt-Toiyabe National Forests. For trips from the Corral Valley Trailhead out of Rodriguez Flat, get information from Humboldt-Toiyabe National Forest's (HTNF's) Carson Ranger District: 1536 S. Carson St., Carson City, NV 89701; 775-882-7766, fs.usda.gov/htnf. Wilderness permits are required, but there are no quotas, and permits can be self-issued at the information bulletin boards near the trailhead or procured at HTNF ranger stations. Note that for trail information, the USDA/USFS Carson-Iceberg Wilderness Map is generally more accurate than the topos.

DRIVING DIRECTIONS: From the junction of US 395 and CA 89, travel 5.5 miles south on US 395 to Coleville and continue another 2.2 miles to Mill Canyon Road heading west, signed MILL CANYON ROAD (for northbound motorists, this junction is 15.5 miles north of the US 395/CA 108 junction, about 2.5 miles north of Walker). Follow the road west and, following signs for Little Antelope Pack Station, proceed up the dirt road 0.3 mile to a fork and veer right. Continue another 5.7 miles to a mountain-crest road junction at broad, open Rodriguez Flat. Turn left (south), following signed directions for the Corral Valley Trailhead, and drive a narrow, rocky 0.4 mile to the end and the signed trailhead.

trip 70   **Lower Fish Valley**

see map on p. 346

Trip Data: 38.47283°N, 119.61453°W; 14.0 miles; 2/1 days
Topos: *Coleville, Lost Cannon Peak*

HIGHLIGHTS: A fine weekend selection, this two-day trip visits five subalpine valleys. The country contains some of the largest Sierra junipers to be found anywhere. In addition, more than a half dozen side trips can be made from the Silver Creek Trail.

HEADS UP! *The 2020 Slink Fire is burning near the Corral Valley Trailhead as this book goes to press and will likely impact the initial stretch of trail.*

DAY 1 (Corral Valley Trailhead to Lower Fish Valley, 7.5 miles): On the Corral Valley Trail, make a moderate climb southwest, shortly reaching a trail on the right from the Little Antelope Pack Station and almost immediately entering signed Carson-Iceberg Wilderness. Continue ahead (southwest) through a cover of white firs, western white pines, and lodgepole pines on a stiff, 0.3-mile climb. Break out of the trees into an extensive area of sagebrush scrub, where the old, metamorphosed sediments of Rodriguez Flat give way to much younger volcanic rocks. The view here is quite spectacular on clear days, with desert ranges visible in the northeast well beyond Rodriguez Flat.

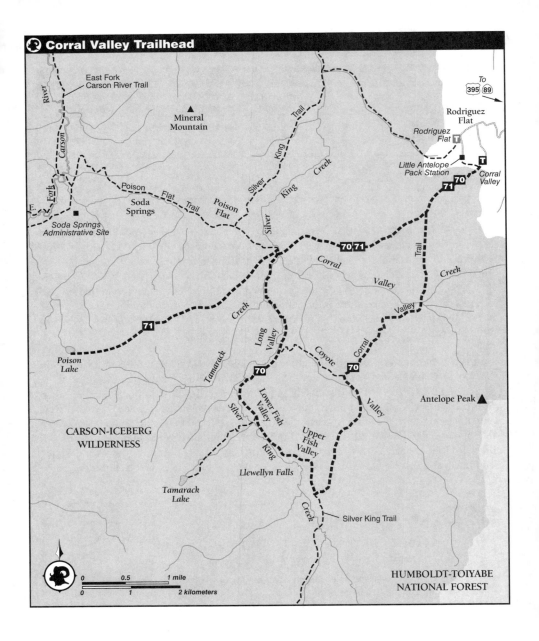

Corral Valley Trailhead

East Fork
Carson River Trail

Carson River

Mineral
Mountain

Silver King Trail

Rodriguez
Flat

To
395 89

Rodriguez
Flat

Little Antelope
Pack Station

Corral
Valley

71 70

E. Fork Carson

Poison Flat Trail

Soda
Springs

Poison
Flat

Soda Springs
Administrative Site

Silver King

70 71

Corral

Valley

Valley

Creek

Trail

71

Poison
Lake

Tamarack Creek

Long
Valley

Coyote

70

Corral

70

Valley

Antelope Peak

CARSON-ICEBERG
WILDERNESS

Silver

Lower Fish
Valley

Upper
Fish
Valley

King

Tamarack
Lake

Llewellyn Falls

Creek

Silver King Trail

0   0.5   1 mile
0   1   2 kilometers

HUMBOLDT-TOIYABE
NATIONAL FOREST

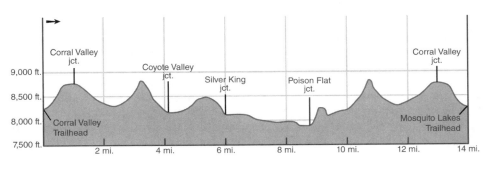

9,000 ft.

Corral Valley
jct.

Coyote Valley
jct.

Silver King
jct.

Poison Flat
jct.

Corral Valley
jct.

8,500 ft.

8,000 ft.

Corral Valley
Trailhead

Mosquito Lakes
Trailhead

7,500 ft.

2 mi.   4 mi.   6 mi.   8 mi.   10 mi.   12 mi.   14 mi.

The short, open ascent soon arcs around the base of a volcanic hill to provide new views of Slinkard Valley in the north and the Sierra Crest in the northwest. A traverse south-southwest across broad, gentle, sagebrush-covered slopes leads to a signed junction, where the trail to Long Valley forks right (southwest; tomorrow's return route).

Veer left (south) at the junction, remaining on the Corral Valley Trail, and descend moderately through sagebrush and bitterbrush to the well-used grazing lands of Corral Valley Creek. On the valley floor, the trail crosses two branches of Corral Valley Creek. Paiute trout, an endangered and protected species, live in Corral Valley Creek, as well as in Silver King Creek and Coyote Valley Creek, so there's no fishing!

Beyond Corral Valley Creek, the southbound trail heads into the forest, curves west, parallels the valley for a short distance, and then climbs an ever-increasing slope to a dry saddle. From here, the descent into Coyote Valley is steep, made slightly easier by the cushioning effect of the deep gravel. Near the bottom of a gully, the trail crosses a seasonal creek and continues a short distance southwest before encountering an enormous, twin-trunked juniper. Beyond, the trail winds south down toward Coyote Valley, reaching the sagebrush-covered floor beside a large, 5-foot-diameter lodgepole pine (a key landmark for northbound hikers).

Hike a level quarter mile across the valley floor to an easy ford of Coyote Valley Creek. Beyond the ford, the trail veers away from the creek and gradually climbs south. Near the crest above Upper Fish Valley, the forest becomes denser and dominated by aspens. Pass through a fence gate at the crest's broad saddle and descend steeply to Upper Fish Valley. On the floor of the valley, near an orange snow-depth marker, reach a signed junction with a lateral left (southwest) to Whitecliff Lake. Go right (north) about 300 yards past the junction to a meeting of three fences, each with a gate. Go through the north gate and follow the path that parallels the west side of the north-northeast–trending fence. The trail soon curves northwest, climbs over a low moraine, and then comes to within earshot of unseen Llewellyn Falls, just a short distance southwest. A short walk leads to the significant 20-foot cascade of Llewellyn Falls.

WHAT'S FISHY ABOUT LLEWELLYN FALLS

Biologists speculate that as a giant glacier slowly retreated up Silver King Canyon, perhaps 50,000 years ago, cutthroat trout followed its path. The fish were able to swim into Upper Fish Valley and beyond before Silver King Creek eroded away bedrock to form Llewellyn Falls. Once isolated, the trout evolved into a subspecies known as Paiute cutthroat trout (*Salmo clarki seleniris*), or simply Paiute trout. Ironically, these fish became endangered not because of overfishing but rather through the introduction of Lahontan cutthroats and rainbows, which bred with the Paiutes to produce hybrids. Once this miscegenation was discovered, Department of Fish and Game workers removed the purebreds and, in 1964, treated Silver King Creek with rotenone to kill the hybrids. After the purebreds were reintroduced to the stream above the falls, their numbers grew from approximately 150 in the late 1960s to about 600 in the early 1970s. By 1975, the population stabilized, but fishing is strictly prohibited, as the Paiute could easily be fished out of existence.

From Llewellyn Falls gorge, the trail descends briefly northeast into Lower Fish Valley. The trail approaches Silver King Creek several times before crossing the stream at the north end of this grassland. Although tree-shaded campsites are nearby (7,937'; 38.47283°N, 119.61453°W), they may be less than desirable if people and cattle have left too much of a mess. Fishing along Silver King Creek below Llewellyn Falls may yield rainbow, Paiute, or rainbow–Paiute hybrids. But beware: Taking Paiute purebreds is prohibited.

The Sierra Crest is the backdrop for this equestrian on the Corral Valley Trail.   Photo by Mike White

DAY 2 (Lower Fish Valley to Corral Valley Trailhead, 6.5 miles): Continuing downstream, walk northwest toward a low ridge that hides the forested, little-visited valley of Tamarack Creek. The path leaves Lower Fish Valley, turns northeast, and climbs over a low granitic saddle before entering the south end of Long Valley. To avoid springs and boggy meadows, follow the trail that circles around the east side of the valley. Partway down the flat valley, the trails rejoin and then approach Silver King Creek, which meanders lazily through the glacial sediments that buried the canyon's bedrock floor long ago. The trail approaches several of these meanders before exiting the valley at the north end.

Following Silver King Creek, the trail passes the confluence of Tamarack Creek and, after an easy half mile of shaded descent, leads to a ford of the stream where granite outcrops force the path to the west bank. Anticipate a wet ford in early season. About 200 yards downstream is a junction with multiple trails: your route goes right (northeast) across the creek; to the left (north), the trail you've been on for a while climbs a sandy slope to meet the trail to Poison Lake.

Heading right, now on the Long Valley Trail, make another wet ford of the creek (last water late in the season) and begin ascending a largely unshaded slope above the creek on long, gentle-to-moderate switchbacks through chaparral. When the switchbacks end, the dusty trail bears generally east and then northeast across the sunstruck hillside on a gentle, occasionally moderate, grade. As you approach the next junction, you'll see an unusual monument, an *arri mutillak,* on your left.

ARRI MUTILLAK

An *arri mutillak* is a large stone cairn—this one is said to be 7 feet high—built to pass the time by lonely Basque sheepherders who once tended flocks in this area. You can make your way through the chaparral to take a closer look, but don't alter the *arri mutillak,* which means "stone boy" in Basque.

Shortly beyond the *arri mutillak,* you reach the junction with the Corral Valley Trail, onto which you turned on Day 1. Here, 2.5 hot, dusty miles from your last crossing of Silver King Creek, you close the loop and turn left (north-northeast) to retrace your steps.

see map on p. 346

trip 71 **Poison Lake**

Trip Data: 38.48208°N, 119.65449°W; 14.0 miles, 2 days
Topos: *Coleville, Lost Cannon Peak, Disaster Peak*

HIGHLIGHTS: Solitude usually abounds on this overnight trip into a beautiful lake in the Carson-Iceberg Wilderness, where good swimming and fishing await. Despite the name, Poison Lake is not poisonous at all. Along the way, you'll experience sweeping views of canyons and mountains.

HEADS UP! *The 2020 Slink Fire is burning near the Corral Valley Trailhead as this book goes to press and will likely impact the initial stretch of trail.*

DAY 1 (Corral Valley Trailhead to Poison Lake, 7.0 miles): On the Corral Valley Trail, make a moderate climb southwest, shortly reaching a trail on the right from the Little Antelope Pack Station immediately prior to the signed Carson-Iceberg Wilderness boundary. Continue ahead (southwest) through a forest cover of white firs, western white pines, and lodgepole pines on a stiff, 0.3-mile climb. Break out of the trees into an extensive area of sagebrush scrub, where the old, metamorphosed sediments of Rodriguez Flat give way to much younger volcanic rocks. The view here is quite spectacular on clear days, with desert ranges visible in the northeast well beyond Rodriguez Flat.

The short, open ascent soon arcs around the base of a volcanic hill to provide new views of Slinkard Valley in the north and the peaks along the Sierra Crest in the northwest. A traverse south-southwest across broad, gentle sagebrush scrub–covered slopes leads to a marked junction, where the Corral Valley Trail veers left (south) and your route forks to the right.

Gently graded tread leads away from the junction through acres of sagebrush scrub, sprinkled with wildflowers in early season, including mule ears, phlox, lupine, common dandelion, and others. Fine views of the Sierra Crest are your constant companion along the protracted descent. Eventually the trail descends more steeply toward Silver King Creek, culminating in a series of switchbacks amid widely scattered junipers on the way to a ford. While the water is not deep here, it's deep enough for the use of an extra pair of water shoes or bare feet for the crossing. Once on the far bank, turn right (north) onto the Silver King Creek Trail (21017) for about 100 yards to a junction with the trail to Poison Lake.

Turn left (southwest) and climb steeply for a while before the grade eases on the way to the top of a ridgecrest, and then follow the trail along the top of the ridge for the next mile. At the end of the ridge, near the base of a steep slope, climb stiffly southwest to a minor ridge, which provides a sweeping view of the ragged Sierra Crest to the southwest. From the ridge, the trail continues to ascend through thick brush. Soon, short, very steep switchbacks lead up into forest shade once more, as the grade becomes more pleasant.

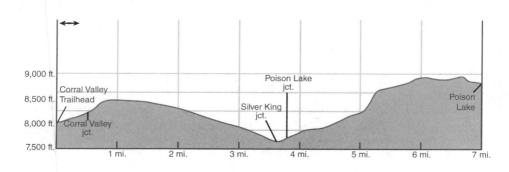

More climbing leads to a small, rocky flat densely covered with sagebrush and bitter-brush. At the south end of the flat is a good view up the canyon into Lower Fish Valley, Upper Fish Valley, and Fourmile Canyon. Beyond the flat, the path makes an undulating traverse west toward a small canyon, passing just above its head. From there, the trail turns briefly northwest and then resumes the southwest journey, passing several meadows before leveling off on a broad ridge above Poison Lake. A short, steep descent down this ridge leads to the lake's willow-lined south shore (9,152′; 38.48208°N, 119.65449°W). Good lodgepole-pine-and-hemlock-shaded campsites may be found on the northwest shore. Fishing can be good for brook trout.

DAY 2 (Poison Lake to Corral Valley Trailhead, 7.0 miles): Retrace your steps.

A spring near Poison Lake   Photo by Mike White

Buckeye Creek Trailhead 7,216'; 38.23458°N, 119.35158°W

Destination/ GPS Coordinates	Trip Type	Best Season	Pace & Hiking/ Layover Days	Total Mileage	Permit Required
36 Kirkwood Pass and Buckeye Forks (in reverse of description; see page 177)	Shuttle	Early to late	Moderate 4/1	31.1	Buckeye Creek (Leavitt Meadows as described)
73 Buckeye Pass and Buckeye Forks (in reverse of description; see page 356)	Shuttle	Mid to late	Moderate 3/0	22.7	Buckeye Creek (Robinson Creek as described)

INFORMATION AND PERMITS: This trailhead is in Humboldt-Toiyabe National Forest, accessing Hoover Wilderness. Wilderness permits are required for overnight stays and quotas apply from the last Friday in June through September 15. Fifty percent of permits can be reserved in advance through recreation.gov (search for "Humboldt-Toiyabe National Forest Wilderness Permits"), and 50% are available on a first-come, first-served basis at the Bridgeport Ranger District office beginning at 1 p.m. the day before your trip starts. Both reserved and first-come, first-served permits are picked up at the Bridgeport Ranger Station, located at 75694 US 395 at the south end of Bridgeport. If you want the ranger station to leave a reserved permit in their dropbox for you to pick up outside of office hours, call 760-932-7070. Bear canisters are required. Visit tinyurl.com/hooverwildernesspermits for more information on reserving permits.

DRIVING DIRECTIONS: From US 395 near the northwest side of Bridgeport, take paved Twin Lakes Road southwest 7.2 miles to a junction signed BUCKEYE CAMPGROUND. Turn left (north) onto dirt Buckeye Road and immediately pass Doc and Al's Resort. Continue 2.8 miles to a T-junction with Forest Service Road 017, just beyond Buckeye Creek. Turn left (west) here and go 1.3 miles, passing through a U.S. Forest Service campground, to a parking lot on the left (south) just before the end of the road.

Robinson Creek Trailhead 7,108'; 38.14751°N, 119.37825°W

Destination/ GPS Coordinates	Trip Type	Best Season	Pace & Hiking/ Layover Days	Total Mileage	Permit Required
72 Barney and Peeler Lakes 38.12367°N 119.47048°W (Peeler Lake)	Out-and-back	Mid to late	Moderate 2/1	16.2	Robinson Creek
73 Buckeye Pass and Buckeye Forks 38.17283°N 119.47316°W	Shuttle	Mid to late	Moderate 3/0	22.7	Robinson Creek (or Buckeye Creek in reverse)
74 Upper Piute Creek 38.09632°N 119.40734°W	Out-and-back	Mid to late	Moderate 4/1	27.0	Robinson Creek

(table continued on next page)

Robinson Creek Trailhead (continued)   7,108'; 38.14751°N, 119.37825°W

Destination/ GPS Coordinates	Trip Type	Best Season	Pace & Hiking/ Layover Days	Total Mileage	Permit Required
75 Rock Island Pass– Kerrick Meadow– Peeler Lake Loop 38.09885°N 119.46395°W (Rock Island Pass)	Semiloop	Mid to late	Moderate 3/0	22.6	Robinson Creek
76 Benson Lake 38.01894°N 119.52328°W	Out-and-back	Mid to late	Moderate 5/1	39.2	Robinson Creek
77 Benson Lake– Smedberg Lake– Matterhorn Canyon– Mule Pass Loop 38.01270°N 119.48802°W (Smedberg Lake)	Semiloop	Mid to late	Strenuous 6/1	51.0	Robinson Creek

INFORMATION AND PERMITS: This trailhead is in Humboldt-Toiyabe National Forest, accessing Hoover Wilderness. Wilderness permits are required for overnight stays and quotas apply from the last Friday in June through September 15. 50% of permits can be reserved in advance through recreation.gov (search for "Humboldt-Toiyabe National Forest Wilderness Permits") and 50% are available on a first-come, first-served basis at the Bridgeport Ranger District office beginning at 1 p.m. the day before your trip starts. Both reserved and first-come, first-served permits are picked up at the Bridgeport Ranger Station, located at 75694 US 395 at the south end of Bridgeport. If you want the ranger station to leave a reserved permit in their dropbox for you to pick up outside of office hours, call 760-932-7070. Bear canisters are required. Visit tinyurl.com/hooverwildernesspermits for more information on reserving permits

Campfires are prohibited within a quarter mile of Barney and Peeler Lakes, and camping is prohibited within a quarter mile of Barney Lake for consecutive nights. All trips except Trip 72 enter Yosemite National Park, where pets and firearms are prohibited and campfires are prohibited above 9,600 feet.

DRIVING DIRECTIONS: From US 395 near the northwest side of Bridgeport, take paved Twin Lakes Road southwest 13.6 miles to the entrance of Mono Village at the west end of the upper Twin Lake. The trailhead is at road's end in Mono Village, a private resort and campground. Overnight users must pay to park their cars here—drive about 0.1 mile past the day-use parking area where you first turn into the Mono Village complex to the overnight parking lot, located farther south along the lake's shore. Then visit the obvious campground entrance kiosk and pay $10 per trip, regardless if it is one night's parking or many. Water and toilets are present throughout the campground.

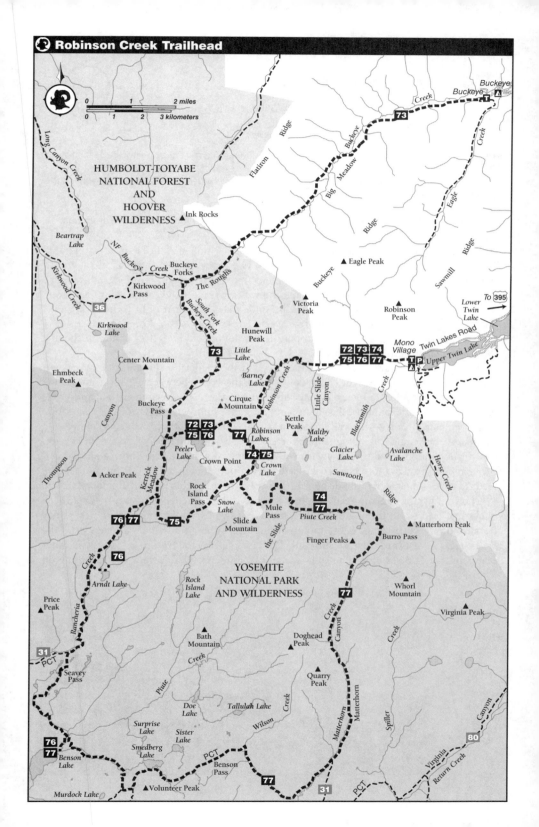

HUMBOLDT-TOIYABE
NATIONAL FOREST
AND
HOOVER
WILDERNESS

Ink Rocks

Long Canyon Creek

Beartrap
Lake

Kirkwood Creek

NF Buckeye Creek

Buckeye
Forks

The Roughs

Kirkwood
Pass

South Fork Buckeye Creek

36

Kirkwood
Lake

73

Center Mountain

Ehmbeck
Peak

Buckeye
Pass

Little
Lake

Hunewill
Peak

Barney
Lake

Cirque
Mountain

Robinson Creek

Flatiron Ridge

Big Meadow

Buckeye Ridge

73

Buckeye Creek

Buckeye

Victoria
Peak

Eagle Peak

Robinson
Peak

Sawmill Ridge

Eagle Creek

Buckeye
Buckeye

1

To 395

Lower
Twin
Lake

Mono
Village

Twin Lakes Road

72 73 74
75 76 77

Upper Twin Lake

Little Slide Canyon

Kettle
Peak

Maltby
Lake

Blacksmith Creek

Glacier
Lake

Avalanche
Lake

Horse Creek

72 73
75 76

77

Robinson
Lakes

74 75

Crown
Lake

Peeler
Lake

Crown Point

Acker Peak

Kerrick Meadow

Rock
Island
Pass

Snow
Lake

Slide
Mountain

Mule
Pass

the Slide

Piute Creek

74
77

Sawtooth Ridge

Matterhorn Peak

Finger Peaks

Burro Pass

76 77

75

76

Rancheria Creek

Arndt Lake

Price
Peak

Rock
Island
Lake

YOSEMITE
NATIONAL PARK
AND WILDERNESS

77

Whorl
Mountain

Virginia Peak

31

PCT

Seavey
Pass

Bath
Mountain

Piute Creek

Doe
Lake

Tallulah Lake

Surprise
Lake

Sister
Lake

Smedberg
Lake

76
77

Benson
Lake

Murdock Lake

Volunteer Peak

Doghead
Peak

Quarry
Peak

Wilson Creek

Matterhorn Canyon

Matterhorn

Spiller Creek

Virginia Canyon

80

PCT

Benson
Pass

77

Benson
Lake

31

PCT

Virginia Return Creek

see
map on
p. 353

trip 72   Barney and Peeler Lakes

Trip Data: 38.12367°N, 119.47048°W (Peeler Lake);
16.2 miles; 2/1 days
Topos: *Buckeye Ridge, Matterhorn Peak*

HIGHLIGHTS: Beautiful Peeler Lake is a delightful and unique Sierra destination: You camp literally on the Sierra Crest, for this lake pours its waters down both sides of the Sierra. It's an excellent destination for a long weekend. Those in search of an easier trip will be delighted to spend the night on the northern side of Barney Lake.

HEADS UP! *Get an early start: This trip requires a stiff, 2,500-foot climb to its destination.*

DAY 1 (Mono Village parking area to Peeler Lake, 8.1 miles): You begin at Mono Village's campground entrance booth, from which two main roads depart east through the campground—either works, but the right-hand (more northerly) option is slightly more direct, and after about 0.2 mile you reach the western end of the campground and continue upcanyon on a closed road. At the 0.5-mile mark you turn right (northwest) onto the Robinson Creek Trail, while the road veers left (south) across Robinson Creek on a bridge. The first part of your hike is open forest, dominated by Jeffrey pines on the dry slopes and aspens on wetter soils.

At the 1.2-mile mark, a short distance beyond the wilderness boundary marker, you reach a persistent stream, chortling down from the basin between Victoria and Eagle Peaks. Afterward, the trail winds gently up through more open terrain with sparse conifers, sagebrush, and bitterbrush, giving you your first unbroken views of the beautifully U-shaped glacial valley—the valley bottom is nearly flat, abruptly truncated to either side by steep valley walls, cascading watercourses, and sharp-tipped peaks. At 7,600 feet you pass through a grove of aspens, ablaze with yellow leaves in late September and October, then saunter through more sagebrush, scattered junipers, and boulders. The pleasant amble leads to a welcome patch of shade beneath white fir cover beside tumbling Robinson Creek.

The trail up the canyon headwall then ascends a dozen well-graded but rocky switchbacks that lead north through head-high jungles of shrubs, stifling on a hot summer's day because the tall brush blocks the mountain breezes. Where the switchbacks end and the trail begins a westward traverse alongside Robinson Creek, the track is often wet, as water from springs dribbles along the trail, sustaining abundant wildflowers. You continue up

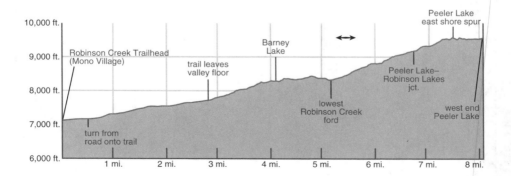

Barney Lake features expansive wetlands at its inlet.   Photo by Elizabeth Wenk

the gradual incline, often only a few steps from the bubbling creek's edge, and soon find yourself in a stunningly dense aspen forest.

Just after you step across a tributary, you reach the north end of a large flat that extends to the shore of Barney Lake. The lodgepole forest here is littered with campsites, with an additional selection of sites to the southeast of the creek on a flat behind a granitic mass at the lake's northeast corner; you cross the creek on a large logjam just downstream of the lake's outlet. (Campfires are prohibited within a quarter mile of the lake.) Barney Lake's north shore has a sandy beach, a fine spot for a lunch break and perfect after a swim.

Your trail follows the western shoreline, a dry talus slope mixed with glacial debris. In sections the walking is fast, while elsewhere protruding rocks break your stride. Once past Barney Lake, your gaze is drawn to the domain of industrious beavers, the marshy meadow upstream of the lake. This was once a lake itself and is slowly filling with sediment. Eventually you descend several short switchbacks, wind through broken rock, past avalanche-twisted aspens, and step over two freshets draining Cirque Mountain before descending back to creek level. Beyond a small campsite to the right (southwest) of the path, the trail fords Robinson Creek. This crossing can be reasonably deep in spring and early summer, becoming a rock hop by midsummer.

From the far bank, you climb easily south above the riverbank through a mix of red fir and lodgepole pine. The trail soon leads back to the west bank of Robinson Creek, which you cross on rocks or (currently) a downed log; this crossing can be a wade and occasionally is quite dangerous. Next the trail crosses the much smaller cascading stream from Peeler Lake. By late season or in a dry year, this is your last chance to easily refill your water bottles until you reach the lake. Ahead lies a dry glacial till–covered slope, which you ascend via a long series of notably gentle switchbacks. Beyond, you level off for a quick breather before darting north to a steeper ascent. Adjacent to the trail are impressive rock fins, some nearly overhung, reflecting the jointed rock that is pervasive throughout this region.

Eventually you reach a small saddle at 9,185 feet and a trail junction. You turn right (northwest) toward Peeler Lake, while the left (southerly) fork is a trail bound for the Robinson Lakes (Trips 74 and 75). You climb moderately for 0.25 mile to a small flat where the trail crosses Peeler Lake's east outlet twice, before switchbacking south up a narrow gully. The final stretch to Peeler Lake is along a magical little shelf above the Peeler Lake outlet creek, replete with a collection of picturesque mountain hemlocks. Just as you sense the lakeshore is imminent, a spur trail leads left (south) to a collection of nice campsites on the lake's eastern shore.

Continuing on the main trail, the often-windswept waters of 9,489-foot Peeler Lake suddenly come into view. A short descent leads you to—then through—car-size granodiorite blocks that dam the lake's east-flowing outlet and beyond to the dynamited trail tread on the north shore of Peeler Lake. The trail now undulates along the lakeshore, climbing and descending repeatedly to bypass small bluffs. The lake's largest campsite is located in a forest pocket along the north shore. Alternatively, continue to the Yosemite National Park boundary at the lake's northwestern corner (9,540'; 38.12367°N, 119.47048°W; no campfires). Areas near the trail are closed to camping, but exploring south along the lake's western shore will undoubtedly yield some private campsites among the extensive slabs. Fishing for rainbow and brook trout can be good.

DAY 2 (Peeler Lake to Mono Village parking area, 8.1 miles): Retrace your steps.

---

trip 73　**Buckeye Pass and Buckeye Forks**

see map on p. 353

Trip Data:　38.17283°N, 119.47316°W; 22.7 miles; 3/0 days
Topos:　Buckeye Ridge, Matterhorn Peak, Twin Lakes

HIGHLIGHTS: This trip around Buckeye Ridge visits a surprising range of Sierran environments, from the sagebrush scrub of the east side, to spectacular Peeler Lake, subalpine Kerrick Meadow, and past water-loving clumps of quaking aspen.

HEADS UP! *Be sure to get an early start: This trip requires a stiff, 2,500-foot climb to Day 1's destination.*

SHUTTLE DIRECTIONS: To access the endpoint, Buckeye Trailhead (just past Buckeye Campground), from Mono Village, the trailhead, drive 6.2 miles back along Twin Lakes Road toward Bridgeport to a junction signed BUCKEYE CAMPGROUND. (This junction is 7.2 miles from the start of Twin Lakes Road in Bridgeport.) Turn right (north) onto dirt Buckeye Road and immediately pass Doc and Al's Resort. Continue 2.8 miles to a T-junction with Forest Service Road 017, just beyond Buckeye Creek. Turn left (west) here and go 1.3 miles, passing through a USFS campground, to a parking lot on the left (south) just before the end of the road. Turning right at this intersection would lead to the famous Buckeye Hotsprings, a free, undeveloped collection of pools that would be a fantastic end to your trip.

DAY 1 (Mono Village parking area to Peeler Lake, 8.1 miles): Follow Trip 72, Day 1 to Peeler Lake (9,540'; 38.12367°N, 119.47048°W; no campfires).

DAY 2 (Peeler Lake to Buckeye Forks, 5.5 miles): From the western side of Peeler Lake, continue into Yosemite National Park, descending along the lake's western outlet. The 0.7-mile walk to Kerrick Meadow is delightful, strolling in and out of lodgepole stands, across short stretches with slabs, and past fingers of meadow. Slowly, your grade lessens, the lodgepole forest retreats to the north, and the meadow pockets coalesce into a verdant cover of grass and dwarf bilberry as you enter Kerrick Meadow. Head north of the trail to find campsites on forested shelves and among small patches of slab. You soon reach a junction where you turn right (north) toward Buckeye Pass, while left leads south through Kerrick Meadow (Trips 75–77).

The next 0.7 mile to Buckeye Pass is a gentle 200-foot climb first up a dry, gravelly granite slope, then through hemlocks and crowded lodgepoles alongside the margin of a meadow. Until late summer there is water and flat camping just to the west, near the pass. Crossing Buckeye Pass (9,572'), you exit Yosemite again and, descending a duff trail, soon step across infant South Fork Buckeye Creek. For the next mile, until the next ford, the gentle descent through lodgepole pine forest skirts a series of charmingly meadowed and richly flowered steps on the northwest side of the creek; there are a number of campsites along the way. Soon after refording the now-wider creek, the trail bends more northward. Here, the avalanche-riddled slopes descending from Hunewill Peak drop steeply right to the trail corridor. The vegetation on the slopes alternates between dry scrub and moist stripes where you step across a series of spring-fed rivulets. Excepting the occasional sandy flat, the trail descends diligently, mimicking the creek's gradient, sometimes in the open and elsewhere under lodgepole-and-hemlock cover. Along the final mile to the valley bottom there are a few campsites on shelves overlooking the creek—good alternatives if mosquitoes are vicious. The trail continues its steady descent right to where it fords South Fork Buckeye Creek a final time; a slimy log currently bridges the flow. Crossing marshy flats, chest high with colorful flowers, you next cross the smaller North Fork Buckeye Creek and reach a junction. Just east of the junction is a dilapidated cabin, a Snow Survey Cabin dating to 1928 and no longer in use. There are good campsites near it, a little east along the river (for example, 8,445'; 38.17291°N, 119.47140°W), or a few hundred feet to the northwest, alongside the trail ascending the North Fork Buckeye Creek (8,460'; 38.17283°N, 119.47316°W). Fishing for rainbow and brook trout is good.

DAY 3 (Buckeye Forks to Buckeye Creek Trailhead, 9.1 miles): Follow Trip 36, Day 4 to the Buckeye Creek Trailhead (7,215'; 38.23458°N, 119.35158°W).

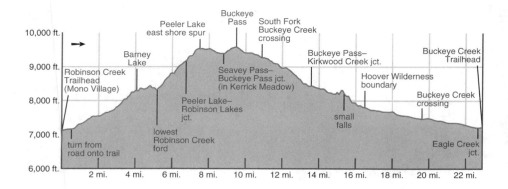

see map on p. 353

trip 74   Upper Piute Creek

Trip Data: 38.09632°N, 119.40734°W; 27.0 miles; 4/1 days
Topos: *Buckeye Ridge, Matterhorn Peak*

HIGHLIGHTS: Following Robinson Creek nearly to the crest of the Sierra, this route circles the west end of the Sawtooth Ridge, ending in the scenic upper reaches of Piute Creek. Those who appreciate spectacularly rugged alpine scenery should consider this trip a must. While all the trails described here are also part of the longer loop described in Trip 77, this is listed separately as a shorter route, encouraging more off-trail exploration once in the Piute Creek drainage.

HEADS UP! *Get an early start: This trip requires a stiff climb to Day 1's destination.*

DAY 1 (Mono Village parking area to Crown Lake, 8.2 miles): Follow Trip 72, Day 1 for 6.75 miles to a small saddle at 9,185 feet and a trail junction. Then continue an additional 1.45 miles, described below.

At the junction, you turn left (south) toward the Robinson Lakes and Crown Lake, while the right (initially northwesterly) fork is the trail bound for Peeler Lake (Trips 72, 73, 76, and 77). The trail ascends a hemlock-clad slope to a flat and then winds through some giant boulders, the terminal moraine of the Crown Point cirque glacier. The blocks comprise part of the shoreline of a tarn whose water is a brilliant translucent blue-green. You loop around to the upper Robinson Lake and at its southeastern end find a legal campsite atop a knob. For the coming mile you will find occasional sandy sites for a single tent, but the narrow canyon, steep granite bluffs, and talus mean the selection is rather limited. A rocky isthmus divides the two main Robinson Lakes, and walking its length you reach the larger (and lower) of these rockbound lakes.

Encircling it, you ford Robinson Creek and snake up a series of narrow forested corridors between granite outcrops; deep in a hemlock glade, tiny campsites beckon. The gradient eases as you approach Crown Lake (9,483'; 38.11418°N, 119.44461°W; no campfires), but the trail continues tracing a sinuous line through narrow sandy passageways. Meadow-ringed Crown Lake is beautifully situated, boasting excellent views to Kettle Peak and Crown Point, and is a desirable destination. However, with the once-popular sites to either side of the Crown Lake outlet recognized to be damaging to the lakeside riparian zone (and hence closed to camping), there are only small sandy sites within view of the trail. Be prepared to spend some time searching for a campsite, either looking well northeast of the lake or continuing farther toward Mule Pass.

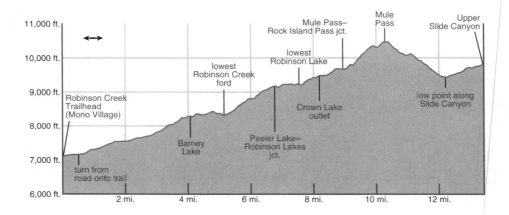

DAY 2 (Crown Lake to Upper Piute Creek, 5.3 miles): From Crown Lake's outlet, the trail loops around its western shore at the base of fractured near-vertical walls. Passing its boggy inlet meadow, you embark on a steep switchbacking climb up a sandy corridor between fins of rock and adorned with some truly magnificent hemlocks. Atop is another meadowed shelf holding tannin-rich tarns—offering some small campsites along their sandy margins—and a junction, where you turn left (south-southeast) to Mule Pass, while right (southwest) leads up to Snow Lake and Rock Island Pass (Trip 75).

You soon begin zigzagging steeply up a talus and scree pile, a moraine, leveling briefly at another meadow, before ascending tight switchbacks to the east of a large rockslide. Massive, angular blocks fill the sheltered passageway you ascend and snow remains here long into the summer. The next shelf holds a small whitebark pine–encircled lake; following the labyrinth of sandy passageways between the stunted trees leads to some small campsites along its north and northeastern sides. Continuing around the lake you step into a beautiful alpine meadow, daintily decorated in diminutive flowers and surrounded by steep, fractured walls. Look back north at Crown Point, whose many points exist due to erosion along these same joints in the rock. Turning east, another brief climb leads up a sandy slope to a broad dry flat, in the middle of which is Mule Pass, the Hoover Wilderness–Yosemite National Park boundary: water on the western half of the flat drains into Robinson Creek and that on the eastern half flows down Piute Creek and eventually into the Tuolumne River.

Another brief climb leads to the actual high point that you probably expected to be Mule Pass. This is a beautiful viewpoint: pinnacled Kettle Peak, Sawtooth Ridge, and Matterhorn Peak ring the horizon, with the Finger Peaks in the foreground. The east side of Mule Pass is a collection of steep granite bluffs and polished slabs, interrupted repeatedly by flat grassy benches, creating a mysterious landscape—even staring at the map you keep wondering just where the trail will jog next. With pockets holding snow well into July—or beyond—the small streams bisecting the meadows flow through most of the summer, providing water should you wish to camp in one of the many sandy patches among slabs east

Mule Pass   Photo by Elizabeth Wenk

of the trail. Indeed, if you are partial to an alpine camp, you may well wish to leave your overnight gear here and explore upper Piute Creek without much weight on your back.

Shortly the trail dives due south down a narrow, incised gulch and then turns east, emerging on a lovely shelf, again with possible campsites. A cross-country route to Ice and Maltby Lakes strikes north from here—another possible direction for exploration, with excellent fishing for eastern brook in these two lakes and lovely alpine surroundings— while the trail steps across a small creek and disappears beneath lodgepole pine cover as it descends 400 feet to Piute Creek.

Six switchbacks later you approach the creek, and the trail resumes its upward trajectory. Here is another possible cross-country detour—you could instead follow Piute Creek about a mile downstream to stare at the Slide.

THE SLIDE

The Slide is an impressive rockslide in upper Slide Canyon, formed when an estimated 2.5 million cubic yards of rock detached from the eastern side of Slide Mountain and fell 1,400 feet, forming a 40-foot-tall dam on the valley floor. Dating trees pinned beneath the slide, researchers estimate it occurred in 1739 or 1740, although the bright white, angular granite blocks look like they could have fallen yesterday.

The trail winds up through the forested valley, initially through sections with abundant tree fall, the aftermath of a November 2011 windstorm. Soon the forest cover is broken by patches of slabs, and you will begin to find possible campsites, either in sandy spots or under lodgepole cover. With a few exceptions, the trail's gradient is a continuously moderate ascent. Around 9,700 feet you begin to have filtered views of Sawtooth Ridge, now directly north of you. If you prefer a tree-sheltered campsite, your last choice is at about 9,840' (38.09632°N, 119.40734°W; no campfires; the listed mileage is to this point), while those seeking view-rich tundra sites will choose to continue yet higher. The views of Sawtooth Ridge are phenomenal. After a few moments of staring at the odd-shaped protrusions and pinnacles on the skyline, one immediately comprehends the inventive names assigned to these features: the Dragtooth, the Doodad, Three Teeth, and Cleaver Peak. One of the showiest (and most exposed) campsite choices can be reached by heading to a bench south of the trail cradling a pair of tarns, adding 1 mile each way to your distance.

HISTORICAL NOTE

The lodgepoles and hemlocks that line the trail are marked with the historic T-blaze typical of the older trails in Yosemite National Park. These signs were emblazoned on these trails by the US Cavalry in the early part of the 20th century when it was their responsibility to patrol the park, ridding the remote northern Yosemite lands of illegal sheep and shepherds.

Days 3–4 (Upper Piute Creek to Mono Village parking area, 13.5 miles): Retrace your steps, but consider selecting a different one of the described campsites for your third night to reduce the impact at Crown Lake.

trip 75   Rock Island Pass–Kerrick Meadow–Peeler Lake Loop

see map on p. 353

Trip Data: 38.09885°N, 119.46395°W (Rock Island Pass); 22.6 miles; 3/0 days

Topos: *Buckeye Ridge, Matterhorn Peak*

HIGHLIGHTS: This hike circumnavigates towering Crown Point and in the process delivers an astounding diversity of subalpine scenery over just three days, including Crown, Snow, and Peeler Lakes and the idyllic beauty of Kerrick Meadow.

HEADS UP! *Get an early start: This trip requires a stiff climb to Day 1's destination.*

DAY 1 (Mono Village parking area to Crown Lake, 8.2 miles): Follow Trip 74, Day 1 to Crown Lake (9,483'; 38.11418°N, 119.44461°W; no campfires).

DAY 2 (Crown Lake to Peeler Lake's eastern shore, 6.9 miles): From Crown Lake's outlet, the trail loops around its western shore at the base of fractured, near-vertical walls. Passing its boggy inlet meadow, you embark on a steep switchbacking climb up a sandy corridor between fins of rock and adorned with some truly magnificent hemlocks. Atop is another meadowed shelf holding tannin-rich tarns—offering some small campsites along their sandy margins—and a junction, where you turn right (west) to Snow Lake and Rock Island Pass, while left (south-southeast) leads up to Mule Pass (Trip 74).

Ascending from the sandy flat, tight switchbacks channeled between steep outcrops and a rock rib transition to a long, steadily traversing climb. This traverse again gives way to zigzags as you climb up another narrow corridor, this time beside a bubbling streamlet. The rock here is strikingly jointed along parallel fracture planes, creating the endless near-vertical walls that hem in your ascent—not to mention that pinnacled visage of Crown Point. Looking back from the top of this climb, you have fine views to the east of the many-tipped summit of Kettle Peak and the west end of the Sawtooth Ridge (informally Blacksmith Peak). When your ascent next eases, you cross a meadowed flat and descend briefly toward Snow Lake's basin (good fishing for golden trout). The trail stays well above the lakeshore, winding over sandy knobs with multistemmed whitebark pines (and occasional campsites) and across tiny rivulets. You reach Snow Lake's shore at its southwestern corner amid delicate meadow fringes that touch the lake. The trail

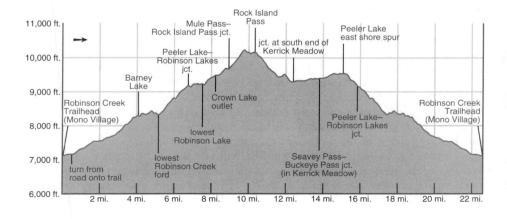

Kerrick Meadow   Photo by Elizabeth Wenk

follows the gentle sandy slopes past some gigantic picturesque boulders (and interspersed campsites) toward Rock Island Pass (10,165').

At Rock Island Pass, you step out of Hoover Wilderness and into Yosemite National Park. The 2-mile trail from here to Kerrick Meadow is lightly used and not as highly constructed as most of Yosemite's trails—it is in perfectly good condition, but less graded and narrower. You begin by descending an elongate meadow that dries early, then you switchback briefly through a cool moist forest, a mixture of hemlock and lodgepole pine. Continuing west around a Crown Point spur, the trail winds through slots and past odd-shaded granite outcrops—stacks and boulders with notches—that have formed as the coarse-grained rock has been weathered by wind and rain. You stay high above a meadowed valley, whose stream dries out in late summer, and then turn north for the final descent to the southern tip of Kerrick Meadow. A brief jaunt into the meadow leads to a leap-across crossing of nascent Rancheria Creek and just beyond you reach a junction, where you turn right (north) to walk the length of Kerrick Meadow, while left (south) leads to Seavey Pass (Trips 76 and 77).

Though limited in camping opportunities to a few small sandy spots atop knobs, Kerrick Meadow is a stunning location. Both tarns and small rocky outcrops add dimension to the meadow; the slightly elevated meadow patches turn yellow in late summer, while the depressions remain a bright green. Rancheria Creek meanders through these grasslands, leaving behind large accumulations of sand when it changes channels. The meadow bottlenecks briefly where the creek tumbles over a silver cascade and then opens into a beautiful, open, wetter section near the headwaters. Here you reach a junction, where straight ahead (left; north) continues to Buckeye Pass (Trip 73), while you turn right (east) to Peeler Lake.

Just beyond the junction, you can head northeast of the trail to find campsites on forested shelves and between slabs. You briefly follow Kerrick Meadow's northern boundary and then begin strolling in and out of lodgepole stands, across short stretches with slabs, and past fingers of meadow. After 0.7 mile, at a sign, you step out of Yosemite and back into Hoover Wilderness. At this boundary, camping is prohibited near the trail, but you could search farther south for campsites. The trail next begins a traverse of large, deep Peeler Lake's north shore. Camping is limited, but you will find one large site in a forested pocket about halfway along the north shore. The trail continues undulating along the lakeshore, climbing and descending repeatedly to bypass small bluffs. You then descend to cross Peeler Lake's outlet creek among the car-size granodiorite blocks that dam the lake's east-flowing outlet. Climbing briefly above a sandy bench overlooking the lake, you reach an unsigned spur trail at a switchback (9,556'; 38.12248°N, 119.46395°W). This short track leads 0.15 mile (not included in the trip mileage) to Peeler Lake's eastern shore and additional campsites (no campfires), providing views of Crown Point from a different angle than last night!

DAY 3 (Peeler Lake's east shore to Mono Village parking area, 7.5 miles): Regaining the main trail, you traverse a magical little shelf above the Peeler Lake outlet creek, replete with a collection of picturesque mountain hemlocks. Beyond, the trail makes a steep descent down a draw to a lush, forested flat where you ford Peeler Lake's outlet creek twice. Descending again down a passageway between broken slabs, you soon reach a familiar junction, where right (southwest, then southeast) is the trail you took to Crown Lake, while you turn left (east) to descend back to Twin Lakes, reversing the first 6.75 miles of this trip.

see map on p. 353

trip 76	**Benson Lake**

Trip Data: 38.01894°N, 119.52328°W; 39.2 miles; 5/1 days
Topos: *Buckeye Ridge, Matterhorn Peak, Piute Mountain*

HIGHLIGHTS: This trip leads to the heart of northern Yosemite, reaching Benson Lake with its "Benson Riviera"—a long, wide, sandy beach at the lake's northeast end. This is one of the more remote lakes to which every Yosemite lover makes a pilgrimage, so you'll likely have company. The brief cross-country leg to Arndt Lake is very easy and can be skipped if you want to stick to maintained trails.

HEADS UP! *Get an early start: This trip requires a stiff climb to Day 1's destination.*

DAY 1 (Mono Village parking area to Peeler Lake's east shore, 7.5 miles): Follow Trip 72, Day 1 to Peeler Lake. Just as you sense the lakeshore is imminent, a spur trail (9,556'; 38.12248°N, 119.46395°W) leads left (south) 0.15 mile to a collection of nice campsites on the lake's still unseen eastern shore (no campfires). Fishing can be good for rainbow and brook trout.

DAY 2 (Peeler Lake to Arndt Lake, 5.3 miles, part cross-country): Continuing on the main trail, the often-windswept waters of 9,489-foot Peeler Lake suddenly come into view. A short descent leads you to—and then through—car-size granodiorite blocks that dam the lake's east-flowing outlet and beyond to the dynamited trail tread on the north shore of Peeler Lake. The trail now undulates along the lakeshore, climbing and descending repeatedly to bypass small bluffs. The lake's largest campsite is located in a forest pocket along the north shore. Emerging back onto broken slabs, continue to the lake's northwestern corner, where you cross into Yosemite National Park. Areas near the trail are closed to camping, but exploring south along the lake's western shore will undoubtedly yield some private campsites among the extensive slabs.

The trail descends along the lake's west outlet—for yes, sitting atop the ridge, Peeler Lake has two outlets at high flow. The 0.7-mile walk to Kerrick Meadow is delightful, strolling in and out of lodgepole stands, across short stretches with slabs, and past fingers of meadow. Slowly, your grade lessens, the lodgepole forest retreats to the north, and the meadow pockets coalesce into a verdant cover of grass and dwarf bilberry as you enter Kerrick Meadow.

There are campsites on forested shelves north of the trail. You soon reach a junction where right (north) leads to Buckeye Pass (Trip 73), while you turn left (south) to walk the length of Kerrick Meadow.

Though limited in camping opportunities to a few small sandy spots atop knobs, Kerrick Meadow is a stunning location. Both tarns and small rocky outcrops add dimension to the meadow; the slightly elevated meadow patches turn yellow in late summer, while the depressions remain a bright green. Rancheria Creek meanders through these grasslands, leaving behind large accumulations of sand when it changes channels. The meadow bottlenecks briefly where the creek tumbles over a silver cascade and then opens into another beautiful expanse of grass, which leads to a junction, where you stay right (south), bound for Seavey Pass, while left (east) leads to Rock Island Pass (Trip 75).

Beyond the junction the meadow narrows and the gradient steepens as you drop down through open lodgepole forest to reach a second, even longer meadow with Rancheria Creek meandering down its middle and flanked to the southwest by Price Peak. The landscape here is drier than Kerrick Meadow, and you note some possible sandy campsites at the meadow's edge. Sandpipers, always seeming out of place in a subalpine setting, ply the riverside sandbanks for a meal. Your views now extend south to dark-colored Piute Mountain, around whose eastern base the trail will pass.

After more than 30 minutes of walking, where the meadow pinches closed (9,176'; 38.08345°N, 119.50692°W), you'll spy a side tributary descending from the left (east) to Rancheria Creek—this is the outlet creek from Arndt Lake, whose slab-encrusted shores offer some good campsites. Your short, very easy, cross-country segment fords Rancheria Creek and then strikes first southeastward and then southward as it ascends the swale beside the tundra-lined outlet of Arndt Lake. A good route to the north shore campsites (9,236'; 38.07734°N, 119.50359°W) of hidden Arndt Lake is via a forested saddle in the granite that lies a little north of where the outlet leaves the lake—cut northeast away from the outlet shortly before it hooks east toward the lake.

DAY 3 (Arndt Lake to Benson Lake, 7.5 miles, part cross-country): From Arndt Lake, retrace your steps cross-country to the trail down Rancheria Creek. Continuing south, Rancheria Creek soon follows a broken gorge, the trail paralling its flow from gravelly benches, until the pair strikes another sandy meadow, this one with a flanking cluster of steep glacial-polished domes, some with black water stains and a striking red weathering patina. Through here, the landscape feels not that different from the striking domes ringing Tenaya Lake, except that here you also experience solitude. Dropping again you reach yet another expanse of meadow, in the middle of which you cross Rancheria Creek, a broad

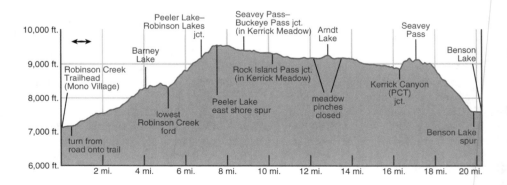

sandy wade in all but the driest conditions. Presently a master joint in the bedrock directs Rancheria Creek briefly east, and you follow its splashing course down over broken, bedrock slabs adorned with large crystals, then back west on another master joint along shaded slopes to a junction with the Pacific Crest Trail (PCT). Your route heads left (southwest), toward Seavey Pass and Benson Lake, while right (west) leads down Kerrick Canyon toward Wilma Lake (Trip 31).

Heading uphill for the first time in many miles, you switchback up a steep slope bedecked with mountain hemlocks to a little passageway nestled between two domes. The trail bends slightly left to reach a cluster of small tarns, while straight ahead lays a lake with some camping options on its western side. Winding along past small wildflower patches, between slabs, and through two beautiful gaps that aren't yet Seavey Pass, you finally cross the unsigned pass to a third gap; Seavey Pass is one of the few geographic points in the Sierra named a "pass" that doesn't correspond with a drainage divide, but it's instead just a passageway through the landscape. Your descent is gradual at first, continuing along a high shelf cradling additional lakes, all with slabs extending to their shores and some with possible campsites. Scooting past the last in the series of lakes, the trail begins to descend more seriously, with short switchbacks down a steep, sheltered draw with lodgepoles and hemlocks.

The grade abruptly ends at a meadow at the imposing eastern base of Piute Mountain as the trail bends south to follow a tributary toward Piute Creek. Excepting brief forested glades, the trail diligently descends a dry slope where pinemat manzanita and huckleberry oak grow atop a mixture of light-colored granite and darker metamorphic rocks. This is a tough, slow descent, for the track is steep, often gravelly, and you're forever stepping over embedded rocks, continually breaking your stride. Rounding a corner, you see Benson Lake ahead. Your trail eventually reaches the valley bottom, and after a short, flat stretch through lush forest, you reach a junction with a spur trail that leads right (southwest) to the lake's shore.

Although it's not on the trail, the west side of Benson Lake affords beautiful views.
Photo by Elizabeth Wenk

The 0.4-mile spur trail leads through nearly flat forest of white fir, lodgepole pine, and the occasional aspen. To your side is Piute Creek, a gushing torrent in early summer, transforming to a lazy trickle with big sandbars by early fall. Just beyond, you reach the famous Benson Lake beach (7,591'; 38.01894°N, 119.52328°W), an alluvial fan of granite sand that was once deposited by Piute Creek and has been reshaped into a beach. The entire northeast shore is an open sandy bank, growing even wider as the lake's water level drops in late summer. At relatively low elevation, Benson Lake is remarkably warm for swimming, or you can simply bury your feet in the warm sand while staring across the expanse of water and the dark cliffs descending from Piute Mountain. You will find campsites at the back of the beach or in the forest at the far northeastern tip of the lake (7,591'; 38.02028°N, 119.52428°W). Fishing is good for rainbow and eastern brook trout.

Days 4–5 (Benson Lake to Twin Lakes Trailhead, 18.9 miles): Retrace your steps, but skip the extra 1.3-mile side trip to Arndt Lake, instead breaking your trip in half with a night along the Rancheria Creek or Kerrick Meadow corridor.

> **OPTIONAL SEMILOOP**
> You could easily add a little loop to this trip on your way back: At the south end of Kerrick Meadow, at the Kerrick Meadow-Rock Island Pass junction, turn right (east, then south) toward Rock Island Pass, Snow Lake, and Crown Lake and reverse Trip 75, Days 2 and 1. Beyond the Robinson Lakes you will reach the junction you passed on Day 1, where you continued west to Peeler Lake. From there, reverse the rest of Day 1 of this trip. This choice adds only 2.5 miles to your total hiking distance.

trip 77   Benson Lake–Smedberg Lake–Matterhorn Canyon–Mule Pass Loop

see map on p. 353

Trip Data: 38.01270°N, 119.48802°W (Smedberg Lake); 51.0 miles; 6/1 days

Topos: *Buckeye Ridge, Matterhorn Peak, Piute Mountain*

HIGHLIGHTS: Making a grand semiloop through northern Yosemite, this trip traces three major watersheds, visits six spectacular lakes, and views the finest scenery in the region. There are plenty of opportunities for rewarding side trips on layover days.

HEADS UP! *Get an early start: This trip requires a stiff climb to Day 1's destination.*

DAY 1 (Mono Village parking area to Peeler Lake's east shore, 7.5 miles): Follow Trip 72, Day 1 to Peeler Lake. Just as you sense the lakeshore is imminent, a spur trail (9,556'; 38.12248°N, 119.46395°W; no campfires) leads left (south) 0.15 mile to a collection of campsites on the lake's still unseen eastern shore. Fishing for rainbow and brook trout can be good.

DAY 2 (Peeler Lake to Benson Lake, 11.4 miles): Follow Trip 76, Days 2 and 3 to Benson Lake, skipping the detour to Arndt Lake. At Benson Lake, you will find campsites at the back of the beach or in the forest at the far northeastern tip of the lake (7,591'; 38.02028°N, 119.52428°W). Fishing is good.

NORTHERN YOSEMITE'S WASHBOARD

At higher elevations—that is, where you just were along upper Rancheria Creek—are the long, linear valleys for which northern Yosemite is so celebrated. For the coming miles you will be cutting across the grain of Yosemite topography, as you drop into and climb out of the bottom stretches of one long canyon after another. Instead of being frustrated, accept that the continuous ups and downs for the coming miles will reduce your walking speed. Not only is the terrain never flat, but you are also winding between domes, descending gravelly slopes, and stepping over embedded rocks as you cross from Rancheria Creek to Piute Creek (flowing into Benson Lake) to Matterhorn Creek. You will again be treated to long, gradual, flatter-bottomed valleys as you ascend Matterhorn Canyon and descend Slide Canyon.

DAY 3 (Benson Lake to Smedberg Lake, 4.6 miles): From Benson Lake, return to the Pacific Crest Trail (PCT) and turn right (southeast). In just a few steps, you must ford Piute Creek just where a substantial tributary merges; you cross both creeks independently, hopefully finding fallen logs. Should these logs be missing, this is a dangerous crossing in early summer. Beyond, ascend a rocky knob and descend to the banks of the Smedberg Lake outlet creek—more of a raging stream in early summer when it is also a difficult ford.

Now begins an 1,800-foot climb along the creek as you head up a dry slope, again a mixture of granite and metamorphic rocks. You note occasional junipers decorating exposed knobs and small clusters of lodgepoles or hemlock growing on flatter creekside benches as you keep climbing up slabs and through gravelly corridors. Crossing the creek again, you briefly enter a wet glade with possible campsites, and then revert to dry, rocky terrain beside the cascading river. Passing a small tarn, you spy a headwall ahead, down which tumbles a small waterfall. Here you must again cross the creek, almost always a wade and a difficult one at high flow; head a little upstream of the trail for the best options.

The trail's gradient now increases and you quite rapidly climb 700 feet via steep, tight switchbacks; thankfully the walking is on soft forest floor beneath cool hemlock cover. Soon after the ascent eases you reach your first trail junction in nearly 3 miles, where you turn left (east), staying on the PCT toward Smedberg Lake, while right (southwest) leads past Murdock Lake (campsites) and down Rodgers Canyon toward Pate Valley. Your route continues along a lovely lodgepole pine and hemlock shelf, dwarf bilberry carpeting the forest floor, and quite soon reaches another junction, where your route, the PCT, continues left (north) to Smedberg Lake, while a right (south) turn heads over a pass to Rodgers Lake.

Continuing toward Smedberg Lake, you wind along forested shelves and between narrow passageways in the pervading slabs and bluffs, all the while circumnavigating the base of near-vertical Volunteer Peak. Though vertical fractures adorn its face, the minimal talus at the peak's base attests to the rocks' integrity. Climbing again, admire the views west to massive Piute Mountain, Benson Lake visible at its foot. Soon you crest a small ridge and begin your final descent to Smedberg Lake. Small single-tent sites present themselves in sandy patches among the slabs as you descend, or as soon as you reach the lake, turn left to find abundant, and justifiably popular, campsites along the lake's western edge. Note that this lake—like others nearby—is a mosquito haven until late July (9,230'; 38.01270°N, 119.48802°W).

DAY 4 (Smedberg Lake to upper Matterhorn Canyon, 9.7 miles): Beyond the oasis of Smedberg Lake, you climb gradually alongside meadows and then more steeply as you trend toward Benson Pass and mount a series of sand-and-slab benches. Some of the outcropping granite here contains giant rectangular feldspar crystals and in general decomposes to a coarse-grained sand that creates a decidedly slippery walking surface atop underlying slabs. The gradient eases as you pass through a broad meadow that dries early and is covered with lupines in late summer. It segues to a narrow, sandy gully that you ascend. Though unmarked on maps, this channel has water in it late into the summer. At its head the trail sidles south across a steep, gravelly, heavily eroded slope, leading to the flat summit of Benson Pass (10,125'). The pass boasts excellent views to the northeast.

Continuing east, the trail descends through more slippery decomposing granite and then skirts north above a broad, often-dry meadow landscape. A few camping options present themselves at the meadow's edge if water remains. The topography again steepens, and while the trail descends steep switchbacks, the creek pours down a narrow slot in rocks. Below you reach a small meadow opening ringed by lodgepole pines (with campsites) and then the shores of Wilson Creek, marking the halfway point in your loop.

After crossing Wilson Creek atop logs or rocks, the trail turns southeast to begin a 2-mile descent to Matterhorn Canyon. There are massive avalanche scars down both canyon walls, a testament to the tremendous slides that sporadically tear down these slopes. The trees lay flattened, all pointing away from the flow of snow, meaning uphill directed trees were knocked down by slides that crossed the creek and flowed up the other side. Only beneath steep cliffs where deep snow never accumulates do mature forests persist. The beautiful slabs lining the creek also demand your attention, especially if your feet need a soak in one of the small pools as you bask on the smooth, sunny rocks for lunch. On this descent, camping is limited to a few small forested shelves overlooking the stream. Toward the bottom of the straightaway, topography dictates that the trail twice crosses the creek. Soon beyond the second crossing, the trail sidles away from Wilson Creek, leading you onto steep bluffs, where gnarled juniper trees clasp at small soil pockets, and your rocky route switchbacks steeply down among them. You are now staring at the lower reaches of Matterhorn Canyon and soon reach the relative flat of the canyon floor.

Here Matterhorn Creek is a meandering stream flowing alternately beside willowed meadows and stands of mixed lodgepole and western white pine. You are initially traipsing well west of the creek, slowly trending closer to the riparian corridor as you continue north. You will find an acceptable tent site just about anywhere you wish along the first mile, up to where the trail strikes east into the meadow and fords the creek. Fishing for eastern brook and rainbow trout is good. The crossing of Matterhorn Creek is a wade over rounded boulders in all but the lowest of flows and requiring caution at peak runoff. Just beyond the ford, you reach a junction where you part ways with the PCT; it continues right (south) toward Miller Lake and Spiller Canyon (Trip 31).

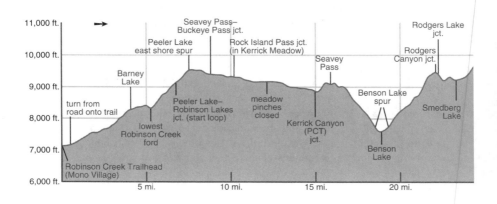

Turning left (north) and walking up along the stream's eastern bank, your route is mostly within lodgepole pine forest, occasionally trending into small meadow patches. The vegetation is mostly quite lush—grass grows beneath the lodgepole pine forests and the meadows are thick with color. Crossing to the west bank of the creek, on rocks or wading at high flows, you traipse briefly along a narrower shelf above the drainage and then drop back to the creek to ford it again in the middle of a meadow. This time you cross on a series of rocks that only emerge at low water and otherwise you have a long, broad wade.

Back on the stream's eastern bank, the forest starts to thin as you approach the 9,000-foot mark. Your eyes are drawn upward to the steep eastern wall of Quarry Peak and the bright white talus blocks that lie at its base. This stretch of Matterhorn Canyon is undeniably U-shaped, but while scoured clean, deepened and steepened by the glaciers, its orientation was achieved long before the ice fields covered the landscape, the result of landscape-wide joints. The sandy flats along this stretch of trail are the last guaranteed campsites for a large group as you head upward; from here until you cross Burro Pass, there are only a few sites with space for more than two tents. The upper stretches of Matterhorn Canyon are very wet, as endless seeps ooze water where the steep walls flatten and only small, flat, generally tree-covered knobs offer tent sites. The creek still bubbling by your side, you continue up and eventually cross Matterhorn Creek for a fourth time.

About now you leave forest cover for good, marching up along a meadow corridor. Evidence of endless avalanches partially explains the lack of forest stands. The abundant moisture contributes as well—conifer species do not establish in locations where their roots are wet most of the summer growing season. This combination of factors gives the landscape a decidedly alpine feel, even though you are just above 9,000 feet, barely higher than lodgepole-clad Tuolumne Meadows. Rounding one corner, the sharp-tipped Finger Peaks come into view, and around the next bend, Sawtooth Ridge and Burro Pass are visible to the north. About 0.7 mile above the last crossing is a lovely campsite for about three tents in a small stand of lodgepole pines with excellent upcanyon views (9,151'; 38.05556°N, 119.41376°W).

DAY 5 (upper Matterhorn Canyon to Crown Lake, 9.6 miles): With continued uphill walking, the surrounding peaks become ever more dramatic, especially Whorl Peak, soon due east of the trail. Excepting a few particularly marshy areas, the walking is quite easy, with few rocks to break your stride. Belding's ground squirrels stand at attention throughout the meadows. Almost imperceptibly the trail's grade increases, until it is suddenly noticeably steep, first continuing its due-north trajectory and then bending more eastward. Climbing through meadows and past little seeps, you soon begin an ascending traverse across the base

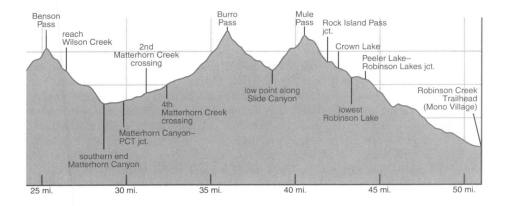

Matterhorn Canyon   Photo by Elizabeth Wenk

of the Finger Peaks toward Burro Pass. The plants dwindle in height, while polished slabs and large boulders become more prominent. You soon find yourself climbing the first switchbacks since you entered Matterhorn Canyon. They lead purposefully to the summit of Burro Pass (10,660'), where you will undoubtedly take a well-earned break. The view from here is stunning, especially north to Sawtooth Ridge. A few moments of staring at the odd-shaped protrusions and pinnacles on the skyline, and one immediately comprehends the inventive names assigned to these features: the Dragtooth, the Doodad, Three Teeth, and Cleaver Peak.

> **HISTORICAL NOTE**
> The first recorded crossing of this pass was made by Lt. N. F. McClure in 1894. Today's travelers can compare their observations of the pass and its surroundings with those of McClure, who said, "The route now led for 5 miles through little meadows on each side of the stream, until a comparatively low saddle was seen to the left of you and near the head of the canyon. Investigating this, I found it was a natural pass. The scenery here was truly sublime. I doubt if any part of the main chain of the Sierra presents a greater ruggedness."

The north side of Burro Pass holds snow long into the summer season, so take care as you descend the uppermost switchbacks. Soon on flatter terrain, you begin your descent of upper Slide Canyon, walking through flower-filled wet meadow environments and across slabs, Sawtooth Ridge always looming over your right shoulder. White mountain heather with bell-shaped flowers, light purple alpine shooting stars, and orange-red-colored Peirson's paintbrush are three of the most ubiquitous companions underfoot. Two small tarns lie on a shelf southwest of the trail, providing beautiful alpine campsites (albeit poor swimming choices), reached with a short detour off the trail. The trail is steep, rocky, and incised, dictating a slow pace as you pick your steps carefully. Continuing down, you pass occasional small campsites, eventually crossing nascent Piute Creek. You skirt a large, often marshy meadow and depart into continuous lodgepole pine forest for the first time in many miles.

The going is pleasant as you continue downstream. Though still mostly a narrow trail, it is less eroded once under forest cover. Beautifully glacial-polished slabs glisten beside the trail, several with sandy flats at their centers that make enticing campsites, and elsewhere there are forested openings. As you're walking down, look regularly ahead and to the left, where Slide Canyon bends southward, trying to glean glimpses of a monumental rockslide that scarred the side of Slide Mountain more than 200 years ago, burying Slide Canyon under 2.5 million cubic yards of rocks. This stretch of trail is also noteworthy for the tangles of downed logs, the aftermath of a 2011 windstorm.

Soon you reach the trail's low point in Slide Canyon and begin a steady climb through dry, open lodgepole pine forest. Finally, six switchbacks lead toward a creek, which you follow upward, emerging into a finger of meadow before stepping across the creek. How quickly you find yourself back in an alpine environment always astonishes me—and in a lovely patch of meadow surrounded by flat slabs and sandy patches; camping options exist with a little snooping away from the trail and meadow corridor. From here, heading north off-trail leads to Ice and Maltby Lakes.

The trail cuts west across a grassy shelf with scattered trees, then up through a narrow slot, positioned between two steep, polished granite outcrops, that leads to another sandy flat. The entire east side of Mule Pass is a collection of steep bluffs and polished slabs, interrupted repeatedly by these flat benches. With the surrounding slopes holding snow well into July—or beyond—the small streams bisecting the meadows flow through most of the summer, providing water should you wish to camp in one of the many sandy patches east of the trail. The view of pinnacled Kettle Peak, Sawtooth Ridge, and Matterhorn Peak ringing the horizon is truly stunning in the evening light. Steep, rough switchbacks climb the final slope to the high point. Facing forward, you are probably surprised to realize Mule Pass, the drainage divide and administrative boundary, lies in the middle of the sandy flat to your west, so descending briefly you leave Yosemite National Park and reenter Hoover Wilderness.

Another brief set of switchbacks leads to a wet meadow, resplendent with diminutive meadow wildflowers, including yellow primrose monkeyflower, pink mountain laurel, and purple Lemmon's paintbrush. At the northern end of the meadow lies a small whitebark pine–encircled lake, offering some campsites along its north and northeastern shores reached by picking your way through the labyrinth of trees. Beyond, tight switchbacks descend to the east of a large rockslide and down a gully that holds snow late into the year. Ahead is Crown Point, whose pinnacled visage exists due to joints in the rock, causing it to fracture along perfectly straight planes. Leveling out briefly, you descend again, down a gravelly, sandy slope, a moraine, before crossing the Snow Lake outlet creek and reaching a junction where you trend right (northeast) toward the Robinson Lakes, while left (southwest) leads to Snow Lake and Rock Island Pass (Trip 75).

After briefly walking along a sandy slope above a series of tannin-rich tarns (with some nearby campsites), you resume a switchbacking descent between fins of rock. The trail soon reaches the next flat, this one cradling Crown Lake. Camping is prohibited near the outlet of this well-used lake, but there are possible campsites if you head about 0.1 mile east of the outlet or a little downstream (9,483'; 38.11418°N, 119.44461°W; no campfires).

DAY 6 (Crown Lake to Mono Village parking area, 8.2 miles): Granite bluffs border the trail almost continually as you wind your way ever lower. Robinson Creek bubbles to the side, comical dippers (water ouzels) bobbing endlessly on midstream boulders. Dense glades of hemlock provide shade as you drop toward the larger—and lower elevation—of the Robinson Lakes. Like at Crown Lake, the cliff bands and boulder fields limit camping options around most of the perimeter; the best site is on a knob at the northwestern corner of the lake. Climbing gently, you promptly reach the second Robinson Lake, at which camping is prohibited. Skirting the edge of the lake you reach a tarn, its waters a brilliant translucent blue-green. Giant rock blocks, the terminal moraine of the Crown Point cirque glacier, comprise part of its shoreline, and the trail winds through these, soon reaching a flat hemlock glade and then descending to reach a junction you will recognize from several days ago; left (northwest) leads back to Peeler Lake, while you now turn right (northeast) toward the trailhead, reversing the first 6.75 miles of Day 1 of this trip.

Green Creek Trailhead

8,011'; 38.11221°N, 119.27541°W

Destination/ GPS Coordinates	Trip Type	Best Season	Pace & Hiking/ Layover Days	Total Mileage	Permit Required
78 Green Lake and East Lake 38.07670°N 119.30130°W	Out-and-back	Mid to late	Leisurely 2/0	8.8	Green Creek
79 Virginia Lakes and the Green Creek Lakes (in reverse of description; see page 376)	Shuttle	Mid to late	Leisurely 2/1	11.8	Green Creek (Virginia Lakes, as described)

INFORMATION AND PERMITS: This trailhead is in Humboldt-Toiyabe National Forest, accessing Hoover Wilderness. Wilderness permits are required for overnight stays and quotas apply from the last Friday in June through September 15. Fifty percent of permits can be reserved in advance through recreation.gov (search for "Humboldt-Toiyabe National Forest Wilderness Permits"), and 50% are available on a first-come, first-served basis at the Bridgeport Ranger District office beginning at 1 p.m. the day before your trip starts. Both reserved and first-come, first-served permits are picked up at the Bridgeport Ranger Station, located at 75694 US 395 at the south end of Bridgeport. If you want the ranger station to leave a reserved permit in their dropbox for you to pick up outside of office hours, call 760-932-7070. Visit tinyurl.com/hooverwildernesspermits for more information on reserving permits. Bear canisters are required. Campfires are prohibited above 9,000 feet in the Virginia Lakes and Green Creek basins.

DRIVING DIRECTIONS: From Bridgeport, drive south on US 395 through the town to the Bridgeport Ranger Station, near its south edge. Continue 3.8 miles south on US 395 to a junction with Green Creek Road, Forest Service Road 142. If you're traveling north on US 395, you'll meet this junction about 8.1 miles north of US 395's Conway Summit. Turn west and take FS 142 about 3.5 miles to a T. At the T you branch right, still on FS 142, and go 5.1 miles to an obvious trailhead parking area on the right. There is an outhouse and a water spigot. (Just 300 feet past this is the Green Creek Campground. You first pass the group sites, on the left, and 0.25 mile farther you enter the campground proper.)

trip 78 Green Lake and East Lake

> **Trip Data:** 38.07670°N, 119.30130°W; 8.8 miles; 2/0 days
> **Topos:** *Dunderberg Peak*

HIGHLIGHTS: This is a fine beginner's weekend hike. East Lake's scenery includes three colorful peaks, Gabbro, Page, and Epidote, each of which are composed of rocks varying in hue from vermilion reds to ochre and set in metavolcanic blacks for contrast. Nearby Nutter, Gilman, and Hoover Lakes offer good fishing to supplement the angling in East Lake, and the wide-ranging scenery along the way rivals any found on longer backpacking trips.

DAY 1 (Green Creek Trailhead to East Lake, 4.4 miles): From the back of the trailhead parking area, the trail diverges north from the road to encircle the Green Creek Campground through a moist aspen glade. The trail winds and undulates upcanyon before

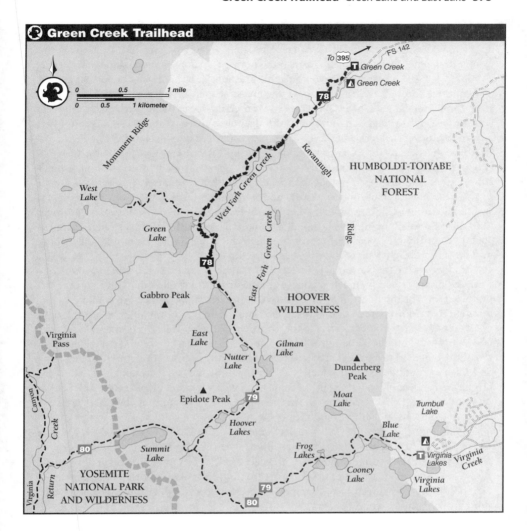

Green Creek Trailhead

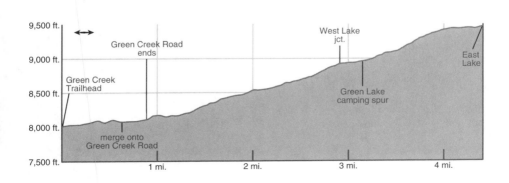

reintersecting Green Creek Road. The trail now temporarily ends and you must continue up the road 0.3 mile to its end at a small private cabin and a step-across trickle. Leaving the giant Jeffrey pines that grace the roadsides, the proper trail now begins its multistep ascent.

With a few steep switchbacks you quickly surmount a dry, juniper-dotted rocky knob and continue through open forest above the creek, the terrain alternating between brief, steep climbs and flatter benches. Whereas you started up slopes dominated by Jeffrey pines, you now ascend through a damp forest of lodgepole pines and aspens. At 1.3 miles you cross into Hoover Wilderness and climb a dozen short, rocky switchbacks.

Above the switchbacks, you pass beside a marshy flat, the confluence of Green Creek's two forks, and above encounter a stretch of lushly vegetated trail, irrigated by both a small tributary descending the steep slope to the right and Green Creek itself. Just muddy enough to be a possible nuisance for some early- and midsummer hikers, the trail cuts through a swath of luxuriant wildflowers that dazzle the eye with their myriad colors: orange alpine lilies, lilac fireweed, purple monkshood, and violet larkspur. In fall this stretch of trail is equally colorful; the aspens are not much taller than a person, so you are literally in the middle of their bright yellow and orange canopies.

For a stretch the trail's meanders match those of the unseen creek, but then you diverge from the drainage and complete a couple of switchbacks to reach a dry ridge dotted with juniper trees. For the first time you now have unbroken views of the surrounding mountains and back down Green Creek. Just ahead you'll arrive at a trail junction. To the right (west) is a trail that provides access to the northwest shore of Green Lake and to West Lake and its western outliers, while you will turn left (south) and make a brief jaunt 0.2 mile to a crossing of Green Lake's outlet creek. In spring and early summer this creek can be raging and hikers should cross it on a logjam downstream of the stock crossing. Just after this creek, you can head west to the lake to some good campsites and picnic spots. At an elevation of 8,940 feet, Green Lake can be on the nippy side for swimming, but there are slabs for drying out and sunbathing, and the cool waters support a good-size trout population.

Continuing on the main trail, you have another 1.3 miles to East Lake, a moderate ascent through a relatively dense conifer forest. Partway up you'll cross the lake's outlet creek, which in early summer can be swift—take care not to slip into its cascading course. Above, you recross it, a broad ford negotiated on big rock blocks. After about a 500-foot elevation gain (from Green Lake) the grade becomes more leisurely and you soon reach a third crossing. Just beyond is East Lake (9,476'; 38.07670°N, 119.30130°W; no campfires; the mileage is measured to here). This is a large subalpine lake, fully 0.75 mile long, and the trail parallels its east side for most of its length. From the outlet south to the southeast shore, there are scattered, usually small campsites on granite benches shaded mostly by whitebark pines. Fishing for rainbow trout on this 75-acre lake is good. This lake makes a fine basecamp for forays to nearby Nutter, Gilman, and Hoover Lakes.

DAY 2 (East Lake to Green Creek Trailhead, **4.4 miles):** Retrace your steps.

Green Lake Photo by Elizabeth Wenk

Virginia Lakes Trailhead			9,849'; 38.04793°N, 119.26331°W		
Destination/ GPS Coordinates	Trip Type	Best Season	Pace & Hiking/ Layover Days	Total Mileage	Permit Required
79 Virginia Lakes and the Green Creek Lakes 38.07670°N 119.30130°W (East Lake)	Shuttle	Mid to late	Leisurely 2/1	11.8	Virginia Lakes
80 Virginia Lakes to Twenty Lakes Basin via McCabe Lakes 37.99515°N 119.34975°W (Lower McCabe Lake)	Shuttle	Mid to late	Moderate, part cross-country 3/1	21.0	Virginia Lakes

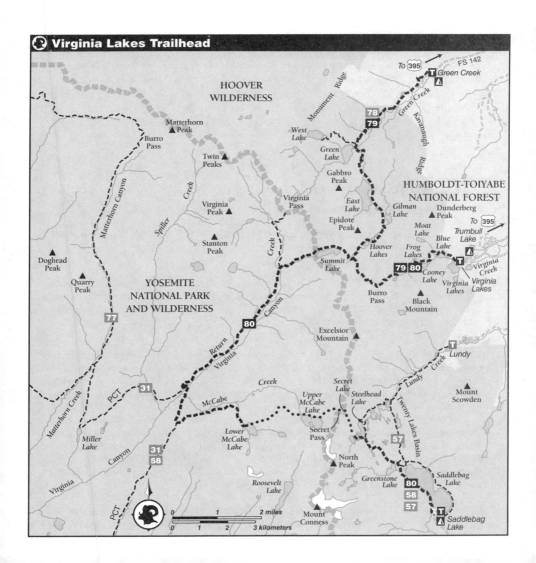

INFORMATION AND PERMITS: Wilderness permits are required for overnight stays and quotas apply from the last Friday in June through September 15. Fifty percent of permits can be reserved in advance through recreation.gov (search for "Humboldt-Toiyabe National Forest Wilderness Permits"), and 50% are available on a first-come, first-served basis at the Bridgeport Ranger District office beginning at 1 p.m. the day before your trip starts. Both reserved and first-come, first-served permits are picked up at the Bridgeport Ranger Station, located at 75694 US 395 at the south end of Bridgeport. If you want the ranger station to leave a reserved permit in their dropbox for you to pick up outside of office hours, call 760-932-7070. Visit tinyurl.com/hooverwildernesspermits.com for more information on reserving permits. Bear canisters are required. Campfires are prohibited above 9,000 feet in the Virginia Lakes and Green Creek basins and above 9,600 feet in Yosemite. Trip 80 enters Yosemite National Park, where pets and firearms are prohibited.

DRIVING DIRECTIONS: From Bridgeport, drive south on US 395 through the town to the Bridgeport Ranger Station, near its south edge. Continue 12.1 miles south on US 395 to Conway Summit and the Virginia Lakes Road (Forest Service Road 21) junction. If you're traveling from the south, Conway Summit lies 12.8 miles north of the CA 120 junction in Lee Vining. Turn west onto Virginia Lakes Road, and follow it 5.1 miles to its terminus, a large dirt parking area with pit toilets. En route you'll have passed the Virginia Lakes Pack Station on the right, a tract of vacation homes, the Virginia Lakes Resort (with café) on the left, and finally the Trumbull Lake Campground on the right. Just past the campground, the road reverts to gravel. Trumbull Lake Campground has a water faucet, and there are pit toilets at the trailhead.

---

trip 79

Virginia Lakes and the Green Creek Lakes

see map on p. 375

Trip Data: 38.07670°N, 119.30130°W (East Lake); 11.8 miles; 2/1 days
Topos: Dunderberg Peak

HIGHLIGHTS: This U-shaped trip circles around Kavanaugh Ridge and Dunderberg Peak, touching the shores of 14 lakes. Scenery along this route is subalpine and alpine, providing a fine sampling of the majestic Sierra Crest. This trip is an excellent choice for a weekend excursion, especially by wildflower enthusiasts and anglers.

SHUTTLE DIRECTIONS: There are two routes between the Virginia Lakes Trailhead and the Green Creek Trailhead, the latter trailhead located along Forest Service Road 142. You can return to US 395 and drive 8.4 miles north to the start of Green Creek Road/FS 142. Take FS 142 3.4 miles to a T-junction with the Dunderberg Meadow Road (FS 20), branch right (north), still on FS 142, and go 5.1 miles to an obvious trailhead parking area, on the right. The second route is to cut between the Virginia Lakes and Green Creek drainages on the Dunderberg Meadow Road: from the Virginia Lakes Trailhead, retrace your steps 1.55 miles down the Virginia Lakes Road, then turn left onto the Dunderberg Meadow Road (FS 20). This dirt road winds 8.5 miles north across the eastern base of Kavanaugh Ridge to the previously noted T-junction with Green Creek Road (FS 142); turn left here and follow the Green Creek Road the final 5.1 miles to the trailhead. Dunderberg Meadow Road is in good condition and much more direct, but both routes take a similar amount of time.

DAY 1 (Virginia Lakes Trailhead to East Lake, 7.0 miles): The trail departs behind the information signs. Numerous use trails around Big Virginia Lake can make it difficult to discern the correct route—once behind the trailhead placard turn right (northwest) and continue not far from the water's edge until the shoreline bends west. The trail now briefly jogs north, enters a stand of aspens, and curves left again where a horse trail merges from the right (east). Under sparse subalpine shade, your trail quickly passes a tarn and then reaches the Hoover Wilderness boundary. Blue Lake comes into view soon afterward, cupped in steep slopes of ruddy-brown hornfels—a metamorphic rock that doesn't have layers. In early summer an astonishing diversity of colorful wildflowers emerges from the scant soil covering the rock. You climb gently to moderately across a talus field above the north shore of Blue Lake, while Dunderberg Peak looms to the north.

At Blue Lake's western headwall, your way climbs steeply, the ascent pausing briefly along the verdant banks of Moat Lake's merrily descending outlet stream. Now your trail switchbacks more gradually up a forested hillside to reach a small miner's cabin in a clearing. After another short climb among steep bluffs, you arrive at the outlet of Cooney Lake. As you leave the lake, views open to your trip's barren high point, Burro Pass (a local name; the pass is unnamed on maps but is also sometimes called Summit Pass or Virginia Lakes Pass), saddling the western horizon.

Beyond Cooney Lake you ascend dry slopes leading to a shelf harboring a clutch of small lakelets—the Frog Lakes—named for once-numerous mountain yellow-legged frogs that have disappeared due to nonnative trout and disease. You cross infant Virginia Creek on rocks and logs, requiring a keen sense of balance (or wet feet) during high flows, and swing south around the meadowy, lowest Frog Lake. Continuing upward on lush alpine turf, you step across the river again and reach the highest lake, where good camps are found among scattered whitebark pines.

You now leave the meadows and lakes behind and diverge north from the creek corridor to climb steadily through a rocky landscape dotted by whitebark pines. Finally, the trail resolves into switchbacks, then leaves the last whitebark pines behind for an alpine ascent along the west wall of a cirque. The relatively warm, mineral-rich, moist metavolcanic soil here supports an abundance of alpine wildflowers rarely seen along a trail. Views across the Virginia Lakes basin continue to improve, then after a burst of short switchbacks—often snow covered through much of July—you gain broad 11,130-foot-high Burro Pass. By walking north just a minute from the trail's high point, you can also view the Hoover Lakes, at the base of Epidote Peak, and, in the northwest, Summit Lake, at the base of Camiaca Peak.

From the barren, windswept crest, you make an initial descent south, then momentarily switchback northwest. Colorful wildflowers continue to emerge beneath every boulder. Your

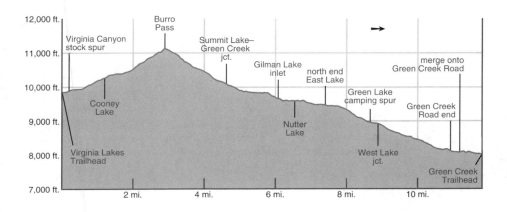

trail switchbacks northwest down through a small, stark side canyon to a sloping subalpine bench, with small campsites tucked north of the trail. After another set of switchbacks, you arrive at a junction on a small shelf just above East Fork Green Creek, where you turn right (northeast) to head down Green Creek, while left (northwest) leads to Summit Lake (Trip 80).

From the junction, your trail descends northeast past a tarn to an excellent overlook downcanyon to the windswept, largely desolate Hoover Lakes. Beyond, light-colored granitic Kavanaugh Ridge peeks over the massive red shoulder of Dunderberg Peak. Heading north, you descend the bench you've been following to the drainage, step across East Fork Green Creek, and cross talus above the west shore of upper Hoover Lake before traversing its north shore. At the northeast corner of upper Hoover Lake, you cross its wide, rocky outlet stream. The trail next follows the east shore of the lower Hoover Lake across a talus slope and then drops easily over willowed benches before crossing the East Fork Green Creek again, this time in a stand of hemlocks and whitebark pines. Less-visited Gilman Lake lies far below at first, the trail eventually coming close to its western shore after passing some small tarns.

Beyond, your route rises gently to cross an expanse of bare rocks, still mostly red metamorphic rock. But you also pass outcrops of conglomerate rocks, easily recognized as a collection of pebbles, cobbles, and boulders cemented together. The trail then follows a shallow trench that leads shortly to small, green Nutter Lake. A short northwest climb from Nutter Lake on a pinemat manzanita–patched slope next presents East Lake, the largest of the Green Creek lakes, spread 100 feet below you under the iron-stained talus skirts of crumbly Epidote Peak, Page Peaks, and Gabbro Peak. The trail parallels the east side of East Lake for most of its 0.75-mile length, passing scattered, usually small campsites to either side of the trail; there are more camping options along the northern half of the shore, where you transition onto granite, offering sandier camping options. The trail soon reaches the north end of East Lake (9,476'; 38.07670°N, 119.30130°W; no campfires). There were once popular campsites here, but most are either too close to water or covered by downed trees; those along the eastern shore are better choices.

Virginia Peak rises steeply in the distance as you descend toward the East Fork of Green Creek.
Photo by Elizabeth Wenk

DAY 2 (East Lake to Green Creek Trailhead, 4.8 miles): Just past East Lake, your trail makes the first of three outlet creek crossings, then traipses through flat forest for 0.3-mile (with possible camping to the east), before beginning a 500-foot drop through hemlock-and-lodgepole forest. Soon you reach the second crossing, broad and negotiated on big rock blocks. A short distance later, a third crossing requires much care; there are also rock blocks to step upon, but steep cascades just downstream. After another set of tight switchbacks, the trail levels off. Here you'll note a spur trail departing left (west) toward Green Lake and its excellent campsites (8,940'). The lake's relatively large volume and chilly temperatures make it ideal for a good-size trout population, although less appealing for swimming.

Next the trail fords Green Lake's outlet creek, for hikers best executed on a logjam downstream of the stock crossing. A brief jaunt leads to a junction, where left (west, then northwest) is a trail climbing steeply 1.6 miles up to West Lake, situated in a basin of barren rock. You turn right (northeast) to descend the Green Creek canyon, soon pausing at a rocky knob that provides an unbroken view of the canyon. Next, the trail descends through a swath of luxuriant wildflowers that dazzle the eyes with myriad colors. By early August, the display is diminished, but so is the water flowing down the trail. In fall this stretch of trail is equally showy, as the leaves on the scrubby aspen trees turn a brilliant yellow.

Beyond, you reenter a taller forest dominated by lodgepole pines and aspens; soon descend a dozen short, rocky switchbacks; cross out of Hoover Wilderness; and then traverse along a rocky bench. Below you, tall, stately Jeffrey pines dominate the forest, and you complete your descent with a brief drop to a step-across creek crossing beyond which you reach the dirt Green Creek Road. You follow the road for about 5 minutes before taking a trail branching left (north), which winds and undulates downcanyon, passing above the campground and reaching the parking area at the Green Creek Trailhead. (Note that you could follow the road all the way to the trailhead, and indeed this is the slightly quicker route, but the trail is a much more scenic way to end your excursion.)

see map on p. 375

trip 80 Virginia Lakes to Twenty Lakes Basin via McCabe Lakes

Trip Data: 37.99515°N, 119.34975°W
(Lower McCabe Lake); 21.0 miles; 3/1 days
Topos: *Dunderberg Peak, Tioga Pass*

HIGHLIGHTS: Much of this scenic route travels through relatively remote sections of northeastern Yosemite National Park that see few visitors. Upper Virginia Canyon and the McCabe Lakes both offer solitude and stunning scenery. This makes a good first off-trail trip, with straightforward navigation and sections with use trails.

HEADS UP! *This trip spends both nights in Yosemite National Park. All Yosemite rules and regulations (for example, bear canisters required; pets and firearms prohibited) apply once you cross the park boundary.*

SHUTTLE DIRECTIONS: To reach the Saddlebag Trailhead, the trip's endpoint, from the CA 120–US 395 junction just south of Lee Vining, drive 9.8 miles west on Tioga Road up to the junction with the Saddlebag Lake Road. Turn right (north) and drive 2.4 miles northwest up to Saddlebag Lake on a well-maintained but partially gravel road. Backpackers need to use the lot adjacent to the group campground, reached by making a sharp right just as you pass the dam. There are toilets and water faucets near the backpacker parking area and at the day-use parking lot closer to the water taxi wharf.

DAY 1 (Virginia Lakes Trailhead to Virginia Canyon, 6.8 miles): The trail departs behind the information signs. Numerous use trails around Big Virginia Lake can make it difficult to discern the correct route—once behind the trailhead placard turn right (northwest) and continue not far from the water's edge until the shoreline bends west. The trail now briefly jogs north, enters a stand of aspens, and curves left (west) again where a horse trail merges from the right (east). Under sparse subalpine shade, your trail quickly passes a tarn and then reaches the Hoover Wilderness boundary. Blue Lake comes into view soon afterward, cupped in steep slopes of ruddy-brown hornfels—a metamorphic rock that doesn't have layers. In early summer an astonishing diversity of colorful wildflowers emerges from the scant soil covering the rock. You climb gently to moderately across a talus field above the north shore of Blue Lake, while Dunderberg Peak looms to the north.

At Blue Lake's western headwall, your way climbs steeply, the ascent pausing briefly along the verdant banks of Moat Lake's merrily descending outlet stream. Now your trail switchbacks more gradually up a forested hillside to reach a small miner's cabin in a clearing. After another short climb among steep bluffs, you arrive at the outlet of Cooney Lake. As you leave the lake, views open to your trip's barren high point, Burro Pass (a local name, the pass is unnamed on maps; also sometimes called Summit Pass or Virginia Lakes Pass), saddling the western horizon.

Beyond Cooney Lake you ascend dry slopes leading to a shelf harboring a clutch of small lakelets—the Frog Lakes—named for once-numerous mountain yellow-legged frogs that have disappeared due to disease and nonnative, but tasty, trout. You cross infant Virginia Creek on rocks and logs, requiring a keen sense of balance (or wet feet) during high flows, and swing south around the meadowy, lowest Frog Lake. Continuing upward on lush alpine turf, you step across the river again and reach the highest lake, where good camps are found among scattered whitebark pines.

You now leave the meadows and lakes behind and diverge north from the creek corridor to climb steadily through a rocky landscape dotted by whitebark pines. Finally, the trail resolves into switchbacks, then leaves the last whitebark pines behind for an alpine ascent along the west wall of a cirque. The relatively warm, mineral-rich, moist metavolcanic soil here supports an abundance of alpine wildflowers rarely seen along a trail. Views across the Virginia Lakes basin continue to improve, then after a burst of short switchbacks—often snow covered through much of July—you gain broad 11,130-foot-high Burro Pass. By walking north just a minute from the trail's high point, you can also view the Hoover Lakes, at the base of Epidote Peak, and, in the northwest, Summit Lake, at the base of Camiaca Peak.

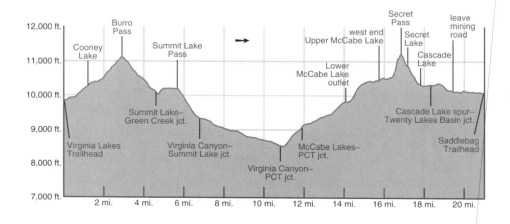

From the barren, windswept crest, you make an initial descent south, then momentarily switchback northwest. Colorful wildflowers continue to emerge beneath every boulder. Your trail switchbacks northwest down through a small, stark side canyon to a sloping subalpine bench, with small campsites tucked north of the trail. After another set of switchbacks, you arrive at a junction on a small shelf just above East Fork Green Creek, where you turn left (northwest), toward Summit Lake, while right (northeast) leads down Green Creek (Trip 79).

From the junction you turn southwest and drop into a seasonally verdant—indeed downright marshy—meadow and cross three broad, shallow, cobble-paved freshets. Just beyond the valley bottom you step across the faster-flowing outlet stream from Summit Lake and begin a short but steep and cobbly ascent, paralleling the outlet stream. Where the climb moderates, you traverse dry sedge flats and benches past some good—but small—hemlock-bower campsites, and soon level off and begin curving west along the north shore of Summit Lake. In midsummer the moist flats you pass through deliver an astonishing burst of color, with dense fields of arnicas and lupines providing foreground for your mountain photos. At the west end of the lake, you reach the Yosemite National Park boundary, barely rising above the 10,195-foot-high lake. Standing at the pass, you are gazing down into remote, lush Virginia Canyon. Staring at the skyline, you can readily identify Virginia Peak, a sharp-pointed metamorphic summit that rises above and north of the summits of Stanton Peak and Gray Butte. A few exposed campsites with spectacular sunset views can be found among clusters of whitebark pines near the pass.

You now drop a rapid 850 feet over the 1.1 miles to the bottom of Virginia Canyon, descending a slope of mixed lodgepole and whitebark pine and enjoying the views up and down Virginia Canyon. The slope is well irrigated and still underlain by metamorphic soils and is correspondingly densely vegetated and colorful. The trail levels out in an equally verdant meadow environment—although a stunning location, the only legal campsites are in trees a short way onward, for almost everywhere is vegetated. You pass a signed junction with a faint trail that turns right (north), climbing up Virginia Canyon (a worthwhile detour for a layover day), and ford Return Creek, the stream draining Virginia Canyon. Just beyond the crossing is a campsite under lodgepole pine cover (9,327'; 38.04670°N, 119.33748°W).

DAY 2 (Virginia Canyon to Lower McCabe Lake, 7.3 miles): The first 4 miles today are a gentle descent down Virginia Canyon, in and out of lodgepole cover. Like most of northern Yosemite's long, linear, U-shaped canyons, water is abundant on the valley floor, leading to a riot of color well into August. Corn lilies, larkspur, wandering fleabane, primrose monkeyflower, arnicas, violets, and mariposa lilies—to name just a few—all vie for your attention. You regularly step over tributaries draining the slope to the west. One of the most striking aspects of this walk is the many-avalanche-decimated slopes. The canyon walls are steep, granite slabs, just shallow enough to accumulate deep snow that then detaches and flows to the valley floor, taking out the forest en route. Some locations are subjected to such frequent avalanches that only shrubs and scrubby aspen grow, while elsewhere avalanches occur only rarely and mature forests establish—only to be obliterated following a tremendous blizzard. As you continue downward, you pass a selection of small campsites and eventually reach a junction with the Pacific Crest Trail (PCT).

You now turn left (east, then south), signposted for Glen Aulin, while right (west) leads to Benson Pass and Smedberg Lake (Trip 31). Within steps you must ford Return Creek, a broad, cobble- and boulder-bottomed channel that requires extreme caution in early season and may be difficult throughout the summer. If the ford is too intimidating, backtrack about a quarter mile upstream to find a wider but easier ford—where campsites are nearby in the rocks above—and follow a use trail back downstream to the trail. Once across Return

Creek, there are some good campsites upstream along its southeastern bank. The trail now hooks south and fords smaller McCabe Creek, a possibly frightening wade itself, for cascades churn just below the crossing.

Once across, the trail begins a steady 600-foot climb up a cool, predominately hemlock-clad slope. The ground is uncharacteristically vegetated, with abundant flowers and even some moss cover. The forest thins near the top of the climb, where slabs again break to the surface and lodgepole pines dominate. A few switchbacks lead to a junction, where you turn left (east), toward the McCabe Lakes, while the PCT continues right (south) down Cold Canyon to Glen Aulin (Trip 31).

Your route continues upward, passing between draws harboring hemlocks and slabbier sections with lodgepoles, western white pines, and the occasional red fir. An ascending traverse takes you into McCabe Creek's drainage, although the trail remains well south of the creek bank. Your route through here is delightful; a fairyland of twisted lodgepoles and then dense hemlocks with a carpet of colorful flowers underfoot. The grade increases where the trail turns south, following a tributary of McCabe Creek to the lower McCabe Lake. The pleasant streamside walk leads right to the lake's outlet. Stepping across the creek on logs, the biggest campsite is located east of the outlet under a lovely canopy of lodgepole, hemlock, and even a few whitebark pines (9,820'; 37.99515°N, 119.34975°W; no campfires).

DAY 3 (Lower McCabe Lake to Saddlebag Lake Trailhead, 6.9 miles): Today's walk begins with 4 off-trail miles, sections of which have decent use trails and elsewhere travelers spread out too much to erode a single route, but only for a short stretch over Secret Pass is the terrain difficult.

Your immediate goal is the upper McCabe Lake, located just over a mile to the east—although you can expect your walking distance to be nearly twice this. From the northeastern corner of Lower McCabe Lake, strike east-northeast up through the forest, aiming for the least steep terrain and staying well north of the inlet creek from the middle McCabe Lake; there is not a use trail for this section. A nearly 600-foot ascent leads to a spectacular high-elevation flat, tarn dotted in all but the driest years—if there are no thunderstorms forecast, this is a delightful, view-rich camp. (You are heading for the northwestern of the two such flats obvious on the USGS 7.5' topo maps; 10,373'; 37.99896°N, 119.33804°W.)

From the flat, continue north, hooking left (north) over a shallow lateral moraine and around a steeper ridge before turning southeast on a gentle sandy slope with boulders. Alpine tundra species, including alpine paintbrush and white mountain heather, continually cheer you onward. A 0.5-mile walk along this slope leads to the upper McCabe Lake outlet. Here a trail suddenly materializes, for everyone follows the same narrow corridor along the lake's northern shore—you spend the walk staring at the deep, clear, dark-blue waters of this large lake backdropped by steep cliffs to the south. Tiny campsites beneath whitebark pines beckon the true alpinists, until you reach the lake's northeastern corner and a broad meadow.

Trend northeast across the meadow, taking care to avoid the boggiest bits while aiming for a sand-and-slab slope ahead. At the north end of the meadow, swivel to face due east, pointing just left (north) of steeper rocks. A selection of use trails switchbacks steeply upward, coalescing in a single narrow vegetated chute between steeper bluffs before trending in a more due-easterly direction around 11,000 feet. Here the gradient eases, and you cross sandy alpine tundra toward the ridge's low point, locally called Secret Pass (11,218'; 37.99967°N, 119.31125°W).

Walking through flower-filled fields around Summit Lake   Photo by Elizabeth Wenk

Peering over into Twenty Lakes Basin, you can see tiny Secret Lake (unnamed on maps) just 300 feet below you and large Steelhead Lake in the basin, where you will pick up the main trail. There are two commonly used descent routes—if you are comfortable descending some moderately steep slab, starting from Secret Pass, zigzagging straight down and then a little north from the pass is the most direct route to Secret Lake. Others will choose to climb 200 feet up the ridge to the north, toward Shepherd Crest to bypass the steepest terrain, and descend northeast into the open bowl with mine tailing—but note this option can hold late snow in the descent gully. All routes reunite at Secret Lake, where you can pick up a decent use trail near its outlet. (See also the sidebar "Two Ways Up Secret Pass" on page 280.)

This use trail leads down densely vegetated slopes, crisscrossed by endless rivulets until late in the summer, with flowers absolutely everywhere. Continuing more or less south-southeast, you reach broad, polished slabs between Cascade Lake and the two smaller lakes to the east, so-called Towser Lake to the north and Potter Lake to the south. Passing between Towser and Potter Lakes you then wind down toward Steelhead Lake's western shore. Follow the shoreline south, cross Potter Lake's outlet, drop into an incised gulch, and climb briefly to reach the old mining road through Twenty Lakes Basin. Here you turn right (southeast) to complete the final 2.7 miles of your trip, while left (north) continues through Twenty Lakes Basin to Helen Lake (Trip 58).

The road leads southeast, passing a collection of tarns and long, skinny Wasco Lake, before cutting east out of the Mill Creek drainage; the "pass" is almost imperceptible. Dropping again, now in the Lee Vining Creek catchment, you gaze down upon Greenstone Lake and giant Saddlebag Lake. At a junction as you approach Saddlebag Lake you have an option—a water taxi allows a more rapid trip to Saddlebag Lake's southern end (and the trailhead), but it is often booked out on summer afternoons by day trippers; this is the lefthand (east) branch that continues along the mining road. The trail—now no longer an old road—branches right (south) and continues around the western shore of Saddlebag Lake, first through lush meadows, then across a slope of angular, red talus, leading to the lake's dam. Recent work has made it safe to cross the dam, and you quickly find yourself walking the last steps up to the Saddlebag Lake Road and Trailhead (10,115'; 37.9657°N, 119.27187°W).

Useful Books

BACKPACKING AND MOUNTAINEERING

Aksamit, Inga. *The Hungry Spork: A Long Distance Hiker's Guide to Meal Planning.* Pacific Adventures Press, 2017.

Aksamit, Inga, Kenny Meyer, and Leslie Rozier. *An Unofficial Acclimatization Guideline: Your High-Altitude Guideline for the John Muir Trail, 2020.*

Beck, Steve. *Yosemite Trout Fishing Guide.* Portland, OR: Frank Amato Publications, 1996.

Beffort, Brian. *Joy of Backpacking: Your Complete Guide to Attaining Pure Happiness in the Outdoors.* Berkeley, CA: Wilderness Press, 2007.

Berger, Karen. *Hiking Light Handbook: Carry Less, Enjoy More.* Seattle, WA: Mountaineers Books, 2004.

Clelland, Mike. *Ultralight Backpackin' Tips: 153 Amazing & Inexpensive Tips for Extremely Lightweight Camping.* Lanham, MD: Rowman & Littlefield, 2011.

Forgey, M. D. William W. *Wilderness Medicine: Beyond First Aid.* 7th ed. Guilford, CT: Falcon Guides, 2017.

Ghiglieri, Michael Patrick, and Charles R. Farabee. *Off the Wall: Death in Yosemite : Gripping Accounts of All Known Fatal Mishaps in America's First Protected Land of Scenic Wonders.* Flagstaff, AZ: Puma Press, 2007.

Ladigin, Don. *Lighten Up!: A Complete Handbook for Light and Ultralight Backpacking.* Lanham, MD: Rowman & Littlefield, 2005.

Wilkerson, James A. *Medicine for Mountaineering & Other Wilderness Activities.* 6th ed. Seattle, WA: The Mountaineers Books, 2010.

GUIDEBOOKS

Medley, Steven P. *The Complete Guidebook to Yosemite National Park.* El Portal, CA: Yosemite Association, 2002.

Schaffer, Jeffrey P. *Yosemite National Park: A Complete Hikers Guide.* Berkeley, CA: Wilderness Press, 2006. [to be updated in 2020]

Wenk, Elizabeth. *50 Best Short Hikes: Yosemite National Park and Vicinity.* Birmingham, AL: Wilderness Press, 2012.

Wenk, Elizabeth, and Jeffrey P. Schaffer.*Top Trails: Yosemite: 45 Must-Do Hikes for Everyone.* 2nd ed. Birmingham, AL: Wilderness Press, 2018.

Roper, Steve. *The Sierra High Route: Traversing Timberline Country.* Seattle, WA: The Mountaineers Books, 1997.

Secor, R. J. *The High Sierra: Peaks, Passes, Trails.* Seattle, WA: The Mountaineers Books, 2009.

Wenk, Elizabeth. *John Muir Trail: The Essential Guide to Hiking America's Most Famous Trail.* 5th ed. Birmingham, AL: Wilderness Press, 2014

White, Mike. *Top Trails: Lake Tahoe: 50 Must-Do Hikes for Everyone.* 3rd ed. Birmingham, AL: Wilderness Press, 2015.

HISTORY AND LITERATURE

Aksamit, Inga. *Highs and Lows on the John Muir Trail.* San Bernardino, CA: Pacific Adventures Press, 2015.

Alsup, William. *Missing in the Minarets: The Search for Walter A. Starr, Jr. Illustrated Edition.* El Portal, CA: Yosemite Conservancy, 2005.

Arnold, Daniel. *Early Days in the Range of Light: Encounters with Legendary Mountaineers.* Berkeley, CA: Counterpoint Press, 2011.

Blehm, Eric. *The Last Season.* New York: HarperCollins, 2009.

Brewer, William H. *Up and Down California in 1860–1864: The Journal of William H. Brewer.* Berkeley, CA: University of California Press, 2003.

Brewer, William Henry, William H. Alsup, and Yosemite Association. *Such a Landscape!: A Narrative of the 1864 California Geological Survey Exploration of Yosemite, Sequoia & Kings Canyon from the Diary, Field Notes, Letters & Reports of William Henry Brewer.* El Portal, CA: Yosemite Association, 1999.

Browning, Peter. *Sierra Nevada Place Names.* 3rd ed. Lafayette, CA: Great West Books, 2011.

———. *Splendid Mountains.* Lafayette, CA: Great West Books, 2007.

———. *Yosemite Place Names: The Historic Background of Geographic Names in Yosemite National Park.* Lafayette, CA: Great West Books, 2005.

Bunnell, Lafayette H. *Discovery of the Yosemite in 1851.* El Portal, CA: Yosemite Association, 1880 (1990).

Farquhar, Francis Peloubet. *History of the Sierra Nevada.* Berkeley, CA: University of California Press, 2007.

Jackson, Louise A. *The Sierra Nevada Before History: Ancient Landscapes, Early Peoples.* Mountain Press Publishing Company, Incorporated, 2010.

Johnson, Shelton. *Gloryland: A Novel.* Berkeley, CA: Counterpoint Press, 2010.

Johnston, Hank. *The Yosemite Grant, 1864–1906: A Pictorial History.* El Portal, CA: Yosemite Association, 1995.

King, Clarence. *Mountaineering in the Sierra Nevada.* Lincoln, NE: University of Nebraska Press, 1997.

Le Conte, Joseph N. "The High Mountain Route Between Yosemite and the King's River Canon." Sierra Club Bulletin 7, no. 1 (1909): 1–22.

Muir, John. *The Mountains of California.* Berkeley, CA: Ten Speed Press, 1894 (1977).

———. *My First Summer in the Sierra.* San Francisco, CA: Sierra Club, 1911 (1990).

Rose, Gene. *Yosemite's Tioga Country: A History and Appreciation.* El Portal, CA: Yosemite Association, 2006.

Russell, Carl Parcher. *One Hundred Years in Yosemite: The Story of a Great Park and Its Friends.* El Portal, CA: Yosemite Association, 1968 (1992).

Sanborn, Margaret. *Yosemite: Its Discovery, Its Wonders and Its People.* El Portal, CA: Yosemite Association, 1989.

Sargent, Shirley. *Solomons of the Sierra: The Pioneer of the John Muir Trail.* Flying Spur Press, 1989.

GEOLOGY

Glazner, Allen F., and Greg M. Stock. *Geology Underfoot in Yosemite National Park.* Missoula, MT: Mountain Press, 2010.

Guyton, Bill. *Glaciers of California: Modern Glaciers, Ice Age Glaciers, Origin of Yosemite Valley, and a Glacier Tour in the Sierra Nevada.* Berkeley, CA: University of California Press, 2001.

Huber, N. King, and Wymond W. Eckhardt. *Devils Postpile Story.* Three Rivers, CA: Sequoia Natural History Association, 2001.

Huber, N. King. *The Geologic Story of Yosemite National Park.* US Geological Survey Bulletin 1595, 1987.

Huber, Norman King. *Geological Ramblings in Yosemite.* Berkeley, CA: Heyday, 2007.

Matthes, François E. *Geologic History of the Yosemite Valley.* US Geological Survey Professional Paper 160, 1930.

———. *The Incomparable Valley: A Geologic Interpretation of the Yosemite.* Berkeley, CA: University of California Press, 1950.

BIOLOGY

Anderson, M. Kat. *Tending the Wild: Native American Knowledge and the Management of California's Natural Resources.* Berkeley, CA: University of California Press, 2013.

Beedy, Edward C., and Edward R. Pandolfino. *Birds of the Sierra Nevada: Their Natural History, Status, and Distribution.* Berkeley, CA: University of California Press, 2013.

Gaines, David. *Birds of Yosemite and the East Slope.* Lee Vining, CA: Artemisia Press, 1992.

Laws, John Muir. *The Laws Field Guide to the Sierra Nevada.* Berkeley, CA: Heyday, 2007.

Johnston, V. R. *Sierra Nevada: The Naturalist's Companion.* Berkeley, CA: University of California Press, 2000.

Sibley, David. *The Sibley Field Guide to Birds of Western North America.* New York: Knopf, 2003.

Storer, Tracy I., Robert L. Usinger, and David Lukas. *Sierra Nevada Natural History.* Berkeley, CA: University of California Press, 2004.

Weeden, Norman F. *A Sierra Nevada Flora.* Berkeley, CA: Wilderness Press, 1996.

Wiese, Karen. *Sierra Nevada Wildflowers.* 2nd ed. Lanham, MD: Rowman & Littlefield, 2013.

Wenk, Elizabeth. *Wildflowers of the High Sierra and John Muir Trail.* Birmingham, AL: Wilderness Press, 2015.

Willard, Dwight. *A Guide to the Sequoia Groves of California.* El Portal, CA: Yosemite Association, 2000.

Guides to the Sierra Nevada from Wilderness Press

AFOOT & AFIELD: TAHOE-RENO   *by Mike White*
The completely updated second edition of this comprehensive guide features more than 175 trips in a diverse range of terrain around Lake Tahoe and the communities of Reno, Sparks, Carson City, and Minden-Gardnerville. These trips are tailored for every type of hiker, and many are suited for mountain bikers.

JOHN MUIR TRAIL: THE ESSENTIAL GUIDE TO HIKING AMERICA'S MOST FAMOUS TRAIL
by Elizabeth Wenk
This is the best guide to the legendary trail that runs from Yosemite Valley to Mt. Whitney. Written for both northbound and southbound hikers, it includes updated two-color maps.

SEQUOIA & KINGS CANYON NATIONAL PARKS   *by Mike White*
This information-packed guide to the peaks and gorges of the majestic apex of the Sierra Nevada includes detailed maps, comprehensive trail descriptions, and enlightening background chapters.

SIERRA SOUTH   *by Elizabeth Wenk and Mike White*
This completely revised and updated classic—the companion to *Sierra North*—showcases new trips and old favorites. With trips organized around major highway sections, using this guide is easier than ever.

TOP TRAILS: LAKE TAHOE   *by Mike White*
This indispensable guide features the 50 best hikes in the Tahoe area, including the north side's splendid backcountry; the lake's sedate western side; the picturesque and popular areas south of the lake, including Desolation Wilderness and D. L. Bliss and Emerald Bay State Parks; and the relatively undeveloped eastern side.

TOP TRAILS: SEQUOIA AND KINGS CANYON NATIONAL PARKS   *by Mike White*
The southern High Sierra, including Sequoia and Kings Canyon National Parks and the surrounding John Muir, Jennie Lakes, and Monarch Wildernesses, is one of the most magnificent natural areas in the world. This guide presents the best curated selection of trips suitable for varied skill levels to explore this wonderland.

TOP TRAILS: YOSEMITE   *by Elizabeth Wenk and Jeffrey P. Schaffer*
Now in full color, the second edition of *Top Trails Yosemite* helps you sort through the amazing number of choice hiking destinations in Yosemite National Park. Whether you're looking for a scenic stroll, a full-day adventure, or a spectacular backpacking trip, you'll find it here.

YOSEMITE NATIONAL PARK   *by Elizabeth Wenk and Jeffrey P. Schaffer*
Called the Cadillac of Yosemite books by the National Park Service, the completely revised sixth edition of this guide details more than 90 trips, from day hikes to extended backpacks, and now includes a map specific to each trip.

Index

About the Authors

Elizabeth Wenk has hiked and climbed in the Sierra Nevada since childhood and continues the tradition with her husband, Douglas Bock, and daughters, Eleanor and Sophia. As she obtained a PhD in Sierran alpine plant ecology from the University of California, Berkeley, her love of the mountain range morphed into a profession. Writing guidebooks has become her way to share her love and knowledge of the Sierra Nevada with others. Lizzy continues to obsessively explore every bit of the Sierra, spending summers hiking on- and off-trail throughout the range, but she currently lives in Sydney, Australia, during the "off-season." Other Wilderness Press titles she has authored include *John Muir Trail, Top Trails Yosemite, One Best Hike: Mount Whitney, One Best Hike: Grand Canyon, Backpacking California, Sierra South, 50 Best Short Hikes: Yosemite,* and *Wildflowers of the High Sierra and John Muir Trail,* the latter a perfect companion book for all naturalists. Lizzy is also a board member of the John Muir Trail Wilderness Conservancy, a foundation dedicated to the preservation of the JMT corridor and surrounding High Sierra lands.

Photo by Douglas Bock

Mike White was born and raised in Portland, Oregon. He learned to hike, backpack, and climb in the Cascade Mountains, and he honed his outdoor skills further while obtaining a bachelor's degree from Seattle Pacific University. After college, Mike and his wife, Robin, relocated to the Nevada desert, where he was drawn to the majesty of the High Sierra. In the early 1990s, Mike began writing about the outdoors, expanding the third edition of Luther Linkhart's *The Trinity Alps* for Wilderness Press. His first solo title was *Nevada Wilderness Areas and Great Basin National Park.* Many more books for Wilderness followed, including the Snowshoe Trails series; books about Sequoia, Kings Canyon, and Lassen Volcanic National Parks; *Backpacking Nevada; Top Trails: Northern California's Redwood Coast; Best Backpacking Trips in California and Nevada; Best Backpacking Trips in Utah, Arizona, and New Mexico; 50 of the Best Strolls, Walks, and Hikes Around Reno;* and *Afoot & Afield: Tahoe-Reno.* Mike has also contributed to the Wilderness classic, *Backpacking California.* Two of his books, *Top Trails: Lake Tahoe* and *50 Classic Hikes in Nevada,* have won national awards.

Photo by Ari Nordgren/Amen Photography

A former community college instructor, Mike is a featured speaker for outdoor groups. He and Robin live in Reno; his two sons, David and Stephen, live in the area as well.